T0328927

Late Republican Rome, 88-31 BC

Second Edition

LACTOR Sourcebooks in Ancient History

For more than half a century, *LACTOR Sourcebooks in Ancient History* have been providing for the needs of students at schools and universities who are studying ancient history in English translation. Each volume focuses on a particular period or topic and offers a generous and judicious selection of primary texts in new translations. The texts selected include not only extracts from important literary sources but also numerous inscriptions, coin legends and extracts from legal and other texts, which are not otherwise easy for students to access. Many volumes include annotation as well as a glossary, maps and other relevant illustrations, and sometimes a short Introduction. The volumes are written and reviewed by experienced teachers of ancient history at both schools and universities. The series is now being published in print and digital form by Cambridge University Press, with plans for both new editions and completely new volumes.

Osborne	*The Athenian Empire*
Osborne	*The Old Oligarch*
Cooley	*Cicero's Consulship Campaign*
Grocock	*Inscriptions of Roman Britain*
Osborne	*Athenian Democracy*
Santangelo	*Late Republican Rome, 88-31 BC*
Warmington/Miller	*Inscriptions of the Roman Empire, AD 14-117*
Treggiari	*Cicero's Cilician Letters*
Rathbone/Rathbone	*Literary Sources for Roman Britain*
Sabben-Clare/Warman	*The Culture of Athens*
Stockton	*From the Gracchi to Sulla*
Edmondson	*Dio: the Julio-Claudians*
Brosius	*The Persian Empire from Cyrus II to Artaxerxes I*
Cooley/Wilson	*The Age of Augustus*
Levick	*The High Tide of Empire*
Cooley	*Tiberius to Nero*
Cooley	*The Flavians*
Cooley	*Sparta*

Late Republican Rome, 88-31 BC

Second Edition

Edited by
FEDERICO SANTANGELO
University of Newcastle upon Tyne

Translated by
JOHN MURRELL AND FEDERICO
SANTANGELO

Major contributions by
M. G. L. COOLEY AND MICHAEL H. CRAWFORD

 CAMBRIDGE
UNIVERSITY PRESS

Shaftesbury Road, Cambridge CB2 8EA, United Kingdom

One Liberty Plaza, 20th Floor, New York, NY 10006, USA

477 Williamstown Road, Port Melbourne, VIC 3207, Australia

314–321, 3rd Floor, Plot 3, Splendor Forum, Jasola District Centre, New Delhi – 110025, India

103 Penang Road, #05–06/07, Visioncrest Commercial, Singapore 238467

Cambridge University Press is part of Cambridge University Press & Assessment, a department of the University of Cambridge.

We share the University's mission to contribute to society through the pursuit of education, learning and research at the highest international levels of excellence.

www.cambridge.org
Information on this title: www.cambridge.org/9781009383356
DOI: 10.1017/9781009383349

First edition © The London Association of Classical Teachers 2017.

Second edition published by Cambridge University Press and Assessment, © The London Association of Classical Teachers 2023.

First published 2023

A catalogue record for this publication is available from the British Library.

A Cataloging-in-Publication data record for this book is available from the Library of Congress.

ISBN 978-1-009-38335-6 Paperback

Cambridge University Press & Assessment has no responsibility for the persistence or accuracy of URLs for external or third-party internet websites referred to in this publication and does not guarantee that any content on such websites is, or will remain, accurate or appropriate.

PREFACE

This book replaces *Roman Politics 80–44 BC* as the seventh instalment of the LACTOR series. Its title, *Late Republican Rome 88–31 BC*, summarizes the two key differences with that earlier work, now out of print: a broader chronological range, which reflects that of the current OCR Ancient History A2 unit, and the choice not to take Roman politics as its only focus. The ambition is to offer a broader picture of the historical developments of the late Republican period, and do some justice to economic, social, and cultural developments.

LACTOR 7 has been out of print since 1994. Students of late Republican Rome have since been able to find valuable guidance on specific texts and problems in several LACTOR volumes (no. 3, *A Short Guide to Electioneering*; no. 6, *Sallust. Fragments of the Histories and pseudo-Sallust: Letters to Caesar*, now out of print; no. 10, *Cicero's Cilician Letters*; no. 14, *Plutarch. Cato the Younger*; and, to some extent, no. 17, *The Age of Augustus*). However, it was widely felt that a full, and indeed expanded, collection of evidence for the late Republic was a necessary addition to the series.

A considerable amount of work on a new LACTOR sourcebook on the late Republic was carried out in the 1990s by Michael Crawford and John Murrell, who devised a structure and selected hundreds of sources for inclusion. Their work was supported by grants from the Society for the Promotion of Roman Studies and from the Joint Association of Classical Teachers. Murrell also took care of the translations, and his version of some of those passages was included in the 2009 edition of LACTOR 3.

I am very grateful to the LACTOR Publications Sub-Committee for inviting me to bring the project to completion and for giving me access the material produced by Crawford and Murrell. I have comprehensively revisited the structure of the volume, not least in light of the need to extend its chronological focus, selected and translated a host of new sources, and provided a set of annotations. Like those produced by Murrell, the translations are intended to provide the student with a close rendering of the original in modern English: readable, but not necessarily as accessible and elegant as would be required in the Penguin or Oxford World Classics series, which are designed for a different readership.

It is a pleasure to record a number of debts I have incurred in working on this volume. Melvin Cooley has been the most knowledgeable, dedicated, and good-humoured editor I could have possibly wished to meet: his expert advice and unstinting encouragement have improved this book in countless ways, from its inception to the finishing touches. John Murrell kindly read through the first full version of the typescript and provided valuable feedback on matters large and small. Michael Crawford has generously offered advice on the selection of the numismatic material included in this volume. Few scholars can claim to have forged a stronger bond between their research and their teaching, and to have shown greater dedication to their students than he has. I hope that at least a small measure of my debt to his example of how to think and talk about history will be apparent from what follows.

I greatly benefited from a conversation on the scope of this volume with the audience of an INSET day organized at Basingstoke by the Classical Association Teaching Board in November 2016; Peter Liddel was a most genial and supportive host. The selection and framing of the source material has been greatly aided by extensive discussion with the Newcastle third year students that took my *Fall of the Roman Republic* module in Autumn 2016. At Newcastle a group of research students – Sara Borrello, Luigi Di Iorio, Lauren Emslie, Chris Mowat, and Emilio Zucchetti – have also offered invaluable comments on an advanced version of the typescript. My thanks to them all.

I am very grateful to the Ancient World Mapping Centre for allowing us to reproduce their maps of Roman Italy, the city of Rome, the Roman Empire, and the campaigns of Caesar, Crassus and Pompey: a wonderful study resource that is also freely accessible on the web (http://awmc.unc.edu/wordpress/free-maps/).

This book is intended for the classroom, and feedback from teachers and students would be extremely welcome. Feel free to email any questions, suggestions, and corrections to federico.santangelo@ncl.ac.uk. Thank you very much.

Federico Santangelo
Newcastle University, May 2017

TABLE OF CONTENTS

6

NOTES ON SOURCES

Appian: an Alexandrian Greek of the second century AD, he wrote a history of Rome in 24 books, about half of which survive, including those on the civil wars, for which he is the main surviving source. He reproduced earlier history, but with the distinct slant of an unusual interest in ethnography, and a considerable amount of information on economic and social matters. He admired Rome and the monarchical system, held Roman citizenship, and had a distinguished career in the imperial administration.

Asconius (Q. Asconius Pedianus) wrote commentaries on Cicero's speeches between AD 54 and 57, ostensibly to give his sons the benefit of his first-hand experience of senatorial procedure, albeit under the Principate. He had access to works of Cicero that no longer survive, as well as to other historical accounts.

Gaius Asinius Pollio (76 BC – AD 4) was a prominent politician and historian of the late Republic. His history, which does not survive, except through quotations in other writers, was an important source for Plutarch, Appian and Cassius Dio.

Aulus Gellius published his 'Attic Nights' around AD 180, gathering material on a great variety of topics, which he read during the long nights in Athens (Attica).

Caesar (C. Julius Caesar 100 – 44 BC). An important writer and orator as well as a major political figure. His accounts (*commentarii*) of the Gallic Wars and the Civil War were written with the stated aim of providing raw material for history, and to ensure that history would be kind to him: they are in fact sophisticated literary works in their own right.

Cassius Dio was born *c.* AD 163/5 into one of the most prominent Greek families in Bithynia (NW Turkey). A distinguished political career over 40 years included two consulships (*c.* AD 222 and 229. His *Roman History* was written in Greek in 80 books, covering the entire period from Rome's foundation to his own day. Its greatest value is in providing an extant and detailed chronological account from 69 BC onwards (the account of 146 – 69 BC is completely lost). But caution is needed too – he often writes anachronistically, viewing the political struggles of the late Republic as if they were equivalent to the 'Year of the Four Emperors' or 'Year of the Five Emperors' (AD 193, which Dio lived through). His history can be shown to include distortions, omissions, and mistakes (there is no mention of the conference of Luca, for example).

Cicero: Marcus Tullius Cicero, 106 to 43 BC. He was born at Arpinum in southern Latium, and quickly rose to prominence in Rome as an advocate. His skill as an orator and the connections he forged through the cases he took up enabled him to embark on a successful political career: he was quaestor in 75 BC, aedile in 69, praetor in 66, and consul in 63. He was the first member of his family to become a senator. His body of work is of unrivalled importance to the understanding of the history of late Republican Rome. – His surviving speeches are mostly defence speeches, although he also undertook the high-profile prosecution of Verres, a governor of Sicily who was accused of corruption. Even the speeches which are most closely focused on the legal merit of the case are crucial to the understanding of specific historical problems (e.g. the *pro Roscio Amerino* on the Sullan proscriptions; the *pro Flacco* on the government of Asia Minor; the *pro Fonteio* on the impact of Rome in Southern Gaul). A number of speeches deal with major political issues of the time: the speech of 66 on the grant of the command of the Mithridatic command to Pompey; those of his consular year on the agrarian bill of the tribune Servilius, and on Catiline's conspiracy; the speeches against Clodius in the aftermath of his return from the exile, in 57 and 56; and the series of interventions against Mark Antony between 44 and 43, which played a decisive role in determining his inclusion on the proscription list and his assassination, at Formiae, in December 43.

The intensity and importance of Cicero's political activity is further shown by a unique category of evidence: his correspondence. Hundreds of letters survive. They are grouped into two main collections, both in sixteen books: those to his friend T. Pomponius Atticus (*ad Atticum*), and those to his relatives, friends, and political counterparts (*ad familiares*); the latter collection also includes a considerable number of letters addressed *to* Cicero. Shorter collections of letters to his brother Quintus and to M. Junius Brutus also survive. The corpora are extensive, but far from comprehensive. The circumstances that led to the compilation of the collections are elusive, as well as the selection criteria, and must at least in part be explained with the political situation following Cicero's death. They only date from the last two decades of his life. The importance of these letters to the understanding of the intricacies of Roman politics is unrivalled; they also offer unique insights into Cicero's intellectual interests, and indeed on his character.

Cicero also produced an impressive series of works on major intellectual problems. He wrote five treatises of rhetorical theory, in which his own practice as a prominent orator in judiciary and political settings plays a major role. He also developed, especially in the last fifteen years of his life, a strong interest in philosophy, and across a wide range of topics: political thought (*On the* res publica, *On laws*), moral philosophy (*On the ends of good and evil, Tusculan Disputations, On old age, On friendship, On duties*), and theological problems (*On the nature of the gods, On divination, On fate*). His ambition to produce philosophical work in Latin by critically developing the lesson of Greek philosophy was unprecedented. Far from being a politically neutral intellectual pursuit for its own sake, Cicero's philosophical work was closely integrated with his engagement in the *res publica*. – Cicero also wrote some poetry, including a poem on his consulship, which survives only in fragments. He did not write an historical work, although he did entertain the prospect of producing one, and late in his life circulated an account of his time in office, which does not survive.

Diodoros: (active 60–30 BC). A native of Sicily, Diodoros wrote a *Library of History* in 40 books, in Greek, which attempts to provide a universal history of mankind, setting events in Greece alongside those in Rome, and concluding in 60 BC. His work is difficult to use: it exists only in fragments for our period.

Florus: probably 2nd century, under the emperor Hadrian. He wrote a 'pious and ecstatic' (R. Syme) account of Rome's triumphs in 1,200 years of war until Augustus brought peace to the world, mainly, it seems, based on Livy.

Gaius: A famous Roman jurist of the latter half of the second century AD, whose *nomen* and *cognomen* are unknown. He wrote several commentaries on legal topics, and his best-known work, the *Institutes*, a highly influential introductory handbook for law students, was the basis for the imperial *Institutiones* published in the reign of Justinian.

Hirtius: Aulus Hirtius was an officer of Julius Caesar from *c.* 54 BC; he wrote the eighth book of Caesar's *Gallic Wars* and an account of Caesar's operations in Alexandria. He was elected consul for 43 BC, and was killed at Mutina.

Horace (Quintus Horatius Flaccus, 65 – 8 BC): Roman poet. Born to a wealthy freedman, fighting at Philippi on the side of the Liberators, loss of property in the confiscations, and eventual close friendship to Maecenas and Augustus gave him a unique range of experience. However, his poems vary so much in tone and *persona* that historical information is hard to deduce.

Livy: the foremost historian of Republican Rome. His very lengthy *History from the Founding of the City* is lost for all of our period except for very brief 'Summaries' created in the fourth century, which turn each 'book' (modern equivalent *c.* 50 pages) into a single short paragraph. His account of Cicero's death (**C4a**) survives through being quoted by the Elder Seneca.

Nepos (Cornelius Nepos) *c.* 110-24 BC, from Cisalpine Gaul, lived in Rome from the 60s. Amongst various works, some of his biographies of famous men survive, including, from a group of biographies of Roman historians, one of Atticus (110–32 BC). Nepos published his biography before Atticus' death and then a second version afterwards, claiming close familiarity with Atticus.

Pliny the Elder (Gaius Plinius Secundus) AD 23/4 to 79. Prominent equestrian in command of the Roman fleet at Misenum at the eruption of Vesuvius. His 37-book *Natural History*, in his words, 'tells the story of nature, that is to say, life.' It includes, according to his reckoning, 20,000 important facts derived from 2,000 books.

Plutarch: (before AD 50 – after AD 120, from Chaironeia in Boiotia, Central Greece), author of biographical and philosophical writings. Plutarch was a very prolific writer and diligent researcher, and he often preserves information that is otherwise lost. But on his own insistence, his *Parallel Lives* of Greeks and Romans were not history – his main aim was to draw characters which could be instructive as moral examples.

Pomponius: Roman lawyer of mid-second century AD, who wrote an *Introduction to Roman Law* giving an historical account of Roman law and lawyers.

Quintilian (Marcus Fabius Quintilianus) was born *c.* AD 35 in Spain and became the best known teacher of rhetoric in Rome. *The Orator's Education* (*Institutio Oratoria*) gives lengthy and detailed advice on writing speeches, including his judgement on Roman authors.

Sallust (Gaius Sallustius Crispus), *c.* 86-35 BC, tribune of the plebs in 52 BC and commander of a legion for Caesar in 49 BC, he turned to history after he was charged with malpractice as governor of Africa in 46 BC. He wrote two monographs on *Catiline's War* and *The Jugurthine War,* and *Histories* covering 78 to after 67 BC, which now survives only in fragments and in the set-piece speeches and letters he composed, following the model of the Greek historian, Thucydides. A major theme of his works is of Rome's political and moral decline.

Seneca the Elder (Lucius Annaeus Seneca), *c.* 50 BC – *c.* AD 40, was born in Corduba in Spain, but seems to have spent much time in Rome. His *Controversiae* and *Suasoriae*, a collection of high points from rhetoricians he had heard, were addressed to his three sons (one of whom was the great philosopher and writer Seneca the Younger).

Strabo, *c.* 64 BC–AD 21 or later, was born into a well-connected family in Amasia in Pontus. His 17-book *Geography*, which was compiled during the reigns of Augustus and Tiberius, provides an account of the entire world known to the Romans, albeit one largely compiled from earlier literary sources.

Suetonius (Gaius Suetonius Tranquillus) *c.* AD 70–130. Author of *The Lives of the Caesars* (biographies of Julius Caesar and the emperors from Augustus to Domitian). He held important posts in imperial administration under Trajan and Hadrian. His biographies concentrate on personality and characteristics, often conveyed by anecdotes and with only a loose chronological framework. The first few chapters of his biography of Caesar are lost.

Tacitus (born *c.* AD 56): the great historian of the early Principate with his *Histories* (AD 69–96) and then *Annals* (AD 14–68). His insight, sense of perspective, and literary style make occasional digressions into Republican period interesting and important.

Valerius Maximus compiled his book of 'memorable deeds and sayings from the City of Rome and foreign nations' in the reign of Tiberius (AD 14–37). He makes no claim to originality, compiling a convenient selection of exemplary, morally instructive stories from famous authors.

Varro (Marcus Terentius Varro) 116–27 BC, great polymath of the period (see **L25–L30**): of his very many works including historical information, only a tiny proportion survives, in the shape of occasional quotations and a work on agriculture.

Velleius Paterculus: Velleius (20/19 BC – *c.* AD 31) served and wrote under Tiberius, whom he regards (with reason) as a superb general and (with less reason) as a superb emperor. His *History of Rome* in just two books is extremely summary to begin with, becoming highly detailed on Tiberius' achievements as commander under Augustus and then as emperor. His praise extends to Tiberius' adoptive father, Augustus and *his* adoptive father, Julius Caesar. Velleius' forebears won citizenship in the Social War and his grandfather served with Pompey and Brutus.

Virgil (Publius Vergilius Maro, 70 – 19 BC): Rome's greatest poet, from Mantua in Northern Italy; his family suffered in the Triumviral confiscations. After his move to Rome, he became part of the circle of Maecenas and Augustus, writing the great national epic, *The Aeneid*.

GLOSSARY

aedile: a junior magistrate in Rome, mainly in charge of buildings and games.

ambitus: this word, originally meaning simply 'going around', comes to be used as the term for unlawful canvassing for office, usually by bribery. A standing court of law (*quaestio perpetua*) investigated cases.

as (pl. *asses*): the base-unit of Roman currency, a small value coin.

auctoritas: authority rather than actual power (*potestas*), hence the ability to obtain a result by one's personal standing rather than magisterial office.

augur: a priest, especially responsible for interpreting the will of the gods based on flights of birds.

aureus: the highest value coin, made of gold, worth 100 sesterces.

boni – good men or good citizens (male gender is shown by the ending). Used in politics (esp. in Cicero's writing) it essentially means men of sound views, i.e. those in support of the speaker/writer!

censor: traditionally one of two senior senators, elected for eighteen months every five years, responsible for carrying out a comprehensive assessment of the wealth and circumstances of the citizens, chiefly for military purposes, and for revising the roll of the Senate, according to financial and moral standards.

client: a citizen who voluntarily paid his respects to a richer, more powerful patron, in return for his protection.

cognomen: the last of a Roman's names, sometimes a type of 'nickname', often distinguishing not just an individual, but a branch of a large family.

collegia: private associations of a political, professional or religious kind (see **L10b**).

colony: a settlement of Roman citizens (often, esp. in the late Republic, army veterans) with its own local constitution.

centuria, pl. *centuriae*: these were voting-groups at an assembly of the people, the *comitia centuriata*, which elected consuls and praetors. Membership and voting-order depended on property-qualifications.

Comitium and *comitia*: the Comitium was the main area for political assemblies, situated at the North of the Forum, at the foot of the Capitoline Hill. A meeting of the people there or elsewhere, summoned by a magistrate, to vote on a specific proposal was called *comitia* (technically plural in Latin).

curia: a senate-house, usually that in the forum, the *curia Hostilia*, later replaced by the *curia Julia*. But the Senate also met elsewhere, albeit always within a consecrated precinct (*templum*).

confiscations: in the late Republic, the terms usually refers to the seizure of land or wealth in Italy to pay off veterans upon discharge.

consul: the highest political office in the Republic. Two consuls were elected each year to serve for one year.

consular: (Latin '*consularis*') (1) adjective from 'consul'; (2) as noun, it refers to someone who has previously been consul.

contio: originally '*conventio*' – a coming together, designating a meeting or assembly called by a magistrate or priest. Hence the term also comes to mean a speech given as such an assembly. (see **B51a** for both uses and **B105**).

decuriones: councillors in a self-governing town.

denarius: small silver coin worth 4 sesterces.

dictator: magistrate appointed in time of emergency in the Roman Republic, with sweeping powers. The word is connected with Latin *dico,* 'I say', i.e. a dictator's word was enough (the usual legislative process was not necessary).

dignitas: 'dignity', 'worthiness', but especially the holding of high office that reinforced the social status of a member of Rome's upper classes.

dominatio: this Latin word is closely connected to *dominus* – a master, in the original sense of someone who has conquered; in everyday Latin, *dominus* meant 'slave-master' (with absolute power over his slaves). Hence in political discourse, *dominatio* almost always means unrestricted power – closest in our language to 'despotism', with all its negative connotations.

Divus: 'God', especially of those officially deified, like Julius Caesar (see **C19**).

eques (*pl. equites*) or equestrian(s): a member of a class in Rome below that of the senatorial class, based on property qualification of 400,000 sesterces. Equestrians were not usually involved in Roman politics.

factio: 'faction' – used to describe a group of political opponents, usually with the implication that this group is aiming to take power for themselves as an oligarchy.

fasces: bundles of rods and an axe carried by the attendants of a magistrate as symbols of his authority, including to inflict corporal or even capital punishment.

fasti: publicly inscribed lists of various sorts: dates, consuls, notable events.

fathers: the term used within the Roman Senate of its members, *patres conscripti* = 'conscript (because their names were written on a list) fathers'.

flamen: a senior priest.

freedman: a slave formally set free by his master, automatically becoming a Roman citizen (and the client of his former master).

gratia: favour or kindness, perhaps incurring an obligation (for which one would say '*gratias* (*ago*)' – 'thanks').

honor: this term covers both the abstract English 'honour', but also the idea of holding public office.

hostis: 'enemy', but since Latin has a separate word, '*inimicus*' (= 'not-friend') to describe a personal enemy, *hostes* (plural) usually describes foreign foes in battle, and the singular, *hostis* means a 'public enemy'.

imagines – wax portrait-busts of distinguished ancestors displayed in aristocratic houses and at funerals.

imperator: originally a title given by Roman troops to their general after a major victory, such as would merit a triumph, it becomes effectively a title, used permanently by Julius Caesar and usurped as a *praenomen* by Octavian (from 38 BC).

imperium: the power to command invested in a magistrate (*e.g.* consul, praetor or governor); hence the power of Rome to rule others; hence 'the empire'.

improbi: 'wicked men' or 'trouble-makers' in political discourse, the opposite of *boni*, i.e. a term used to impugn the morals and motives of the other side.

interregnum: literally a period between reigns, hence in Latin as English, a gap when no one is holding (consular) office, meant to be filled by ex-consuls acting as *interreges* to supervise elections.

iustitium: cessation of legal business (see **L18**).

laurel crown: worn by a general in his triumph, but adopted as a symbol of military distinction.

legate: anyone to whom authority is delegated, *e.g.* a military officer, or an ambassador.

magistrate: an official elected for a year at Rome or in local government.

maiestas: originally '*crimen maiestatis*' – an offence against the 'majesty' or 'greatness' of the Roman people. 'The crime of *maiestas,* because he dared to overthrow and carry off monuments of the glory of our rule and of our achievements' (Cicero, *Verrines* 2.4.41). A standing court of law (*quaestio perpetua*) dealt with those cases.

manumission: the formal freeing of a slave, resulting in his attaining citizenship.

municeps: inhabitant of a *municipium*, see **D3**.

municipium (pl. *municipia*): town, usually in Italy, whose inhabitants possessed Roman citizenship and also the rights to make their own local laws, and elect their own local magistrates.

nobiles: 'nobles', with the technical sense of someone whose direct ancestor had held a senior magistracy in Rome (as aedile, praetor, but, especially, consul)

novus homo: literally 'new man', the term could apply to someone in politics, none of whose direct ancestors had been a senator; or to someone, none of whose direct ancestors had been a consul (but had still reached the Senate); or, especially, to someone like Cicero, who reached the consulship despite having no senatorial ancestors.

optimates (Latin plural): connected with *optimus* – 'best', in politics it refers to those who broadly wished to preserve the *status quo,* as against more radical, democratic policies (see *popularis*). This was certainly no organized political party.

otium: 'leisure', 'free-time'. A rather complex term with meanings ranging from idleness (**B33**) through to peace (**B115**). It could also refer, for example, to Cicero having the time away from the *negotium* (literally – non-*otium*) of his involvement in law-courts/politics to devote to literature.

patrician: the Roman nobility, a status attainable only by birth into one of the original noble families of the early Republic or even the period of kings.

patron: a wealthy and influential citizen who looked after the interests of poorer clients in return for their support and public deference.

plebs: the proper term for the ordinary citizen body of Rome, defining all the citizens who do not belong to a patrician family.

pontifex maximus: the most senior priest in the college of the pontiffs.

popularis (pl. *populares*): adjective referring to a politician or policy espousing the support of the *populus* ('people'), and thus through popular assemblies rather than the Senate.

praetor: one of eight annually elected magistrates, ranking between consul and quaestor. Ex-praetors usually governed the less important provinces. They had *imperium*, but their main functions were mainly judicial, and included presiding over courts.

prefect: someone 'put in charge of' something.

princeps: the word, meaning 'leader' of 'chief' was the one chosen by Augustus to designate his position, hence the term 'Principate' to describe the period of his rule.

privilegium: literally a 'special law' – *privus-lex*, in other words one that was aimed at a particular case or individual, see **B132**.

proconsul: a former consul, retaining his former official power, usually as governor of a major province.

propraetor: someone granted the power of a praetor, usually as governor of a minor province.

proscription: 'legalized murder' (Syme). The procedure by which Sulla and later the triumvirs outlawed their enemies, making their lives and property forfeit.

publicani: 'tax-collectors'. They were of equestrian standing, and formed companies that typically bid to collect the taxes from a particular province on behalf of the Roman government. This formed a binding contract: if they could not collect this amount, it was their loss, but any excess formed their profit, see **B93b**.

quaestiones perpetuae: standing courts of enquiry, dealing with particular offences (*repetundae, ambitus, maiestas, vis* (see those entries). A magistrate presided, but there was no appeal against the majority verdict of the juries (75 or 51), which from 70–46 BC comprised equal numbers of senators, equestrians, and treasury tribunes.

quaestor: one of twenty men elected annually to serve in various capacities, including two in charge of the treasury, and others as assistants to provincial governors. They gained entry to the Senate.

repetundae: extortion, usually of money, by a provincial governor. A standing court of law (*quaestio perpetua*) investigated cases.

Republic(an): modern usage to refer to the period when Rome was governed by elected magistrates (rather than emperors), roughly from 510/9 BC to Caesar's dictatorship.

res publica: literally 'the public thing', i.e. the state, the commonwealth.

rostra: a speaker's platform, especially that near the *Comitium*. The name reflects its decoration of prows of ships captured in a naval battle of 338 BC.

senatus consultum: decree of the senate. Technically this gave advice on an issue to the magistrates, but, unless vetoed by a tribune, had force of law (see **L26**).

sesterces: the units of currency in Rome.

suffect: replacement magistrate, especially a consul, appointed after the death of the incumbent.

toga picta: an embroidered toga worn by a victor in his triumph (see **B38**).

tribe: all citizens were formally a member of one of 35 tribes (voting districts), and voted in these tribes.

tribuni aerarii: literally 'tribunes of the treasury'; their role was as one of the three panels from which jurymen were drawn for the *quaestiones perpetuae* (see above). Their precise status and property qualification are disputed, though perhaps similar to those of the equestrians.

tribunus (pl. – *tribuni*) *plebis*: the *tribuni plebis*, tribunes of the plebs (often just 'tribunes'), were ten annually elected officers armed with negative or obstructive powers designed to protect the plebeians from victimization by magistrates. A tribune could intercede on behalf of an individual, arrest any magistrate, and veto assemblies and any decision of the Senate. Tribunes were the main proposers of legislation in the later Republic.

triumvirate (board of three men): the formal set of powers given to Antony, Lepidus, and Octavian under the *lex Titia* of 43 BC (properly 'triumvirs for settling the *res publica*' and see **C1** and **C2**).

vis: 'force' or, as a criminal offence, any sort of 'violence', ranging from an attack on a house to arson and murder (**B132**). A standing court of law (*quaestio perpetua*) investigated cases.

Map 1: Map of Roman Italy

16

© The Ancient World Mapping Center

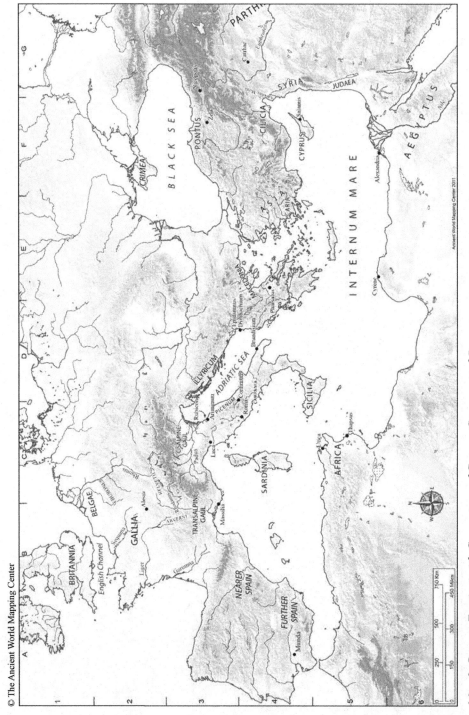

Map 2: Roman Empire, with Campaigns of Caesar, Crassus, and Pompey

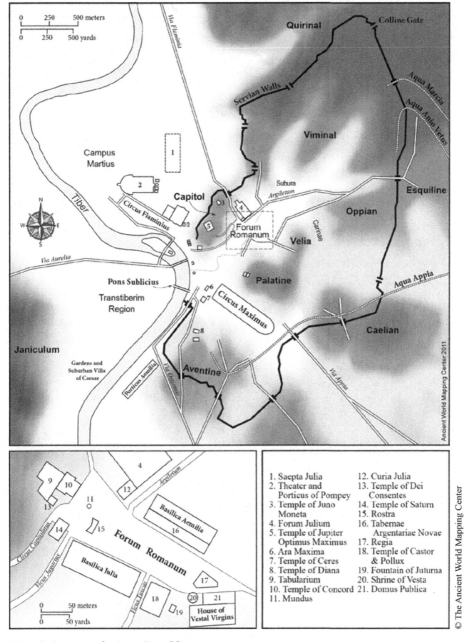

Map 3: *Rome in the Late Republic*

0 250 500 meters
0 250 500 yards

Via Flaminia

Quirinal
Colline Gate
Aqua Marcia
Aqua Anio Vetus

Servian Walls

Campus Martius

1

2

Capitol

Circus Flaminius

Tiber

Via Aurelia

Viminal

Subura
Argiletum

3
4

5

Forum Romanum

Esquiline

Oppian

Carinae

Velia

Aqua Appia

Pons Sublicius

Transtiberim Region

6
7

Circus Maximus

Palatine

Caelian

8

Janiculum

Gardens and Suburban Villa of Caesar

Porticus Aemilia

Via Ostiensis

Aventine

Via Appia

Ancient World Mapping Center 2011

9
10
11
13
14

12

4

Argiletum

Basilica Aemilia

16

15

Forum Romanum

Clivus Capitolinus

Vicus Jugarius

Basilica Julia

Vicus Tuscus

17

18

20
19
21

House of Vestal Virgins

0 50 meters
0 50 yards

1. Saepta Julia
2. Theater and Porticus of Pompey
3. Temple of Juno Moneta
4. Forum Julium
5. Temple of Jupiter Optimus Maximus
6. Ara Maxima
7. Temple of Ceres
8. Temple of Diana
9. Tabularium
10. Temple of Concord
11. Mundus
12. Curia Julia
13. Temple of Dei Consentes
14. Temple of Saturn
15. Rostra
16. Tabernae Argentariae Novae
17. Regia
18. Temple of Castor & Pollux
19. Fountain of Juturna
20. Shrine of Vesta
21. Domus Publica

© The Ancient World Mapping Center

PART I: NARRATIVE

A. A PROLOGUE: LAND AND POLITICS IN
ROMAN ITALY, 133–88 BC

This book focuses on the period between 88 and 31 BC: roughly, between Sulla's march on Rome and Octavian's victory at Actium. These two military developments had major political consequences, and serve as useful chronological reference points to the study of the late Roman Republic. They are not, by any means, the only watershed dates that one could choose to frame such a discussion, and it seems useful to introduce the overview of the evidence for the main developments of the late Republic with a brief set of sources that shed light on what was arguably the defining problem of the half century that preceded the age of Marius and Sulla: the political and economic setup of Roman Italy, in which the problem of the division and exploitation of agricultural land was closely related to the need to define a new legal settlement for the Italian allies, providing for their inclusion in the Roman citizen body and enabling them to have a share in the empire that they had crucially contributed to building.

A1   Public land (*ager publicus*) and its history

[7] As the Romans subdued Italy bit by bit in war, they used to seize part of the land. They would establish towns or choose settlers from their own people for towns that already existed. They devised these practices in place of garrisons. Of the land, which became theirs on each occasion by right of war, they would at once distribute the part that had been worked to settlers or sell or lease it. But the part that then lay idle as a result of war, which was indeed the greatest part, they did not have spare time to allocate; so they proclaimed that in the meantime those who wished could work it for a payment of the annual crops, one tenth for what had been sown and one fifth for fruits. Payments were also set for those who were grazing larger and smaller animals. They did these things to increase the numbers (*poluandría*) of the people of Italy so that they might have their kin as allies, for these seemed to the Romans most tolerant of hard toil. But the net result was the exact opposite for them. For the rich took over most of the undistributed land and through lapse of time grew confident that no one would ever take it back from them. They took over land adjoining their own or any other smallholdings of poor men, buying some by persuasion and seizing some by force. They came to work great estates instead of single farms. They employed slaves as farm workers and shepherds on these estates to avoid having free men dragged off from farming to service in the army. This form of ownership brought them great profit too, since the slaves had many children and their numbers increased without risk, because they were not liable to service in the army. For these reasons the powerful were becoming extremely rich and the slave population throughout the country was increasing in number. On the other hand, declining numbers and manpower (*dusandría*) were overtaking the people of Italy, since they were being worn down by poverty, taxes and expeditions. And if they had any respite from these misfortunes, they passed their time in idleness because the land was possessed by the rich and they used slaves as farm workers instead of free men.

Appian, Civil Wars 1.7

Appian of Alexandria (c. AD 95–c. 165) starts his account of the late Republican civil wars with the tribunates of the Gracchi (133 and 123/121 BC) and the major political controversy prompted by their agrarian reform plans. In setting the scene for that, he sketches an account of the economic and social predicament of Italy in the mid-second century BC that is utterly unique within what survives of ancient historiography. Much of this picture has been questioned or invalidated by the archaeological evidence that has emerged over the last half a century or so, but the link between the making of the empire, wealth distribution, and new political and social tensions should be retained as valid. – The meaning of the term *dusandría* in this context has been much debated: the translation chosen here emphasizes the demographic problem, but the word is likely to reflect a wider concern over the economic and social welfare of the people of Italy.

A2   Land and citizenship

[21] Even so those who were in possession of the land were postponing the distribution on various pretexts for a very long time. And some proposed enrolling as Roman citizens all those allies who were making the most opposition about the land, so that because of the greater favour they would not quarrel about the land. The Italians gladly accepted this, preferring the citizenship to estates. Fulvius Flaccus, who was both consul and [a member of the board] in charge of land distributions, worked with them for this purpose more than anyone else; but the Senate was annoyed at their subjects being made citizens with equal political rights. This attempt was thus abandoned and the people, who had been for so long in the hope of land, were despondent.

Appian, *Civil Wars* 1.21

The land proposal of Tiberius Gracchus found widespread opposition among the Italian Allies, who were set to be severely affected by the assignments proposed. In 125 BC the consul M. Fulvius Flaccus, an ally of the Gracchi, sought to allay the opposition of the Italians by offering them the Roman citizenship; his proposal met with much hostility in Rome and was soon abandoned. The enfranchisement of the Allies and their entitlement to take a share in the rewards of the empire, however, remained a major, unsolved issue for many decades to come.

A3   Measures of Gaius Gracchus, tribune of the plebs, 123–121 BC

[23] Gracchus also constructed long roads throughout Italy, having a great number of contractors and workmen under him, ready for whatever he ordered. He proposed many colonies. He summoned the Latins to seek all the rights of the Romans, on the grounds that the Senate could not decently refuse them to their kinsmen. In the case of those other allies, who were not allowed to cast a vote in the Roman assemblies, he was proposing to give them the right to vote in future so as to have them too working along with him in the legislative assemblies. The Senate was very much alarmed at this, and instructed the consuls to issue a proclamation that no one who did not have the right to vote was to stay in the city or to approach within five miles of the city during the period when voting on these laws was to take place. And it persuaded Livius Drusus, another of the tribunes, to veto the laws of Gracchus, but not to tell the people his reasons: for a tribune interposing his veto was not required to give his reasons. The senators also authorized Drusus to conciliate the people with twelve colonies. The people were so very much delighted with this that they looked with scorn on the laws of Gracchus.

Appian, *Civil Wars* 1.23

In 123 and 122 BC the tribune Gaius Gracchus embarked on an ambitious reform programme, in which the revival of colonial foundations and the extension of the Roman franchise to the communities of Latin status played a prominent role. The Latin right consisted of a set of legal rights that fell short of the Roman citizenship, but entailed some privileges, notably that of marrying a Roman citizen and doing trade on equal terms with Roman citizens, with access to the same form of contracts. It therefore enabled a non-Roman citizen to have his rights protected by Roman law and by the Roman courts. – Appian's reference to road networks is noteworthy: highways were important economic infrastructures and could serve as valuable tools for the control of the territory. – The Senate came to the conclusion that the best reaction to Gracchus' plan was to devise a set of demagogic proposals that would overshadow Gracchus', and found a tribune who was willing to act as mouthpiece for those (see Plutarch, *Gaius Gracchus* 9). The gamble proved effective. – Cf. Wars 1.27, where Appian discusses the end of the land reform after the death of Gaius Gracchus, and contends that it led to a further spiral of destitution and demographic decline.

A4   Background to the Social War, 91 BC

[34] Such was their state of affairs when the so-called Social War broke out, involving many peoples throughout Italy. It began unexpectedly, rapidly grew to major proportions and its threat extinguished factional strife (Gk: *stasis*) in Rome for some time. But when it ceased, it led to other factional strife and to more powerful faction leaders, who operated against one another, only this was now with whole armies, not just by introducing laws, or by bribery. And because of this I have included it in this history, since it began from the factional strife in Rome and it resulted in another conflict, similar but much worse. It began as follows.

It was Fulvius Flaccus who, when consul [125 BC], was the first most forcefully to rouse the Italians in a very open way to desire the Roman citizenship, so that they would be partners in the position of dominance instead of subjects. He introduced the proposal and persisted in it resolutely. He was sent off by the Senate on some military campaign for this reason. In the course of this his consulship expired. Later he was elected also to be tribune [122 BC] and contrived to be tribune together with the younger Gracchus, introducing other such measures on behalf of Italy together with him. And when both of them were done away with ... Italy was still further aroused; for they did not think it right either to be treated as subjects instead of partners, or for Flaccus and Gracchus to have suffered such a fate when they were campaigning on their behalf.

[35] After them another tribune, Livius Drusus [91 BC], a man of a most distinguished family, at the request of the Italians promised to re-introduce a law concerning the citizenship; for it was this that they wanted most of all, on the grounds that they would immediately become in this one act leaders instead of subjects. He won over the plebs to this proposal in advance and led them on with many colonies in Italy and Sicily, which had been voted some time before but not yet established. ... [36] The Italians, on whose particular behalf Drusus was contriving these proposals, were afraid about the law for colonies on the grounds that the public land of the Romans they were farming, some by force, others clandestinely, which was still undistributed, would be taken from them at once, and that they would face many troubles even over their private land. The Etruscans and the Umbrians had the same fears as the Italians and were brought into the city, so it appeared, by the consuls, ostensibly to speak against the law, but in reality to do away with Drusus. They were openly shouting down the law and waiting for the day of the assembly for voting.

Appian, *Civil Wars* 1.34–36, with omissions

Appian's contention that the war between Rome and the Italian Allies (91–88 BC) is rooted in Roman factional strife and belongs within the account of the Civil Wars should not be taken at face value. The aims, hopes, and frustrations of the communities that took on Rome played a crucial role, and should receive due recognition (the account of Diodorus of Sicily, *Library of History* 37.1–2 sets out to do just that). On the other hand, as Appian duly recognizes, the status of the Italians had been a major political issue in Rome for at least three decades. M. Livius Drusus, the tribune of 91 BC who put forward an abortive bill for their enfranchisement, was the son of the rival of Gaius Gracchus: his story stands as an example that the same political views and allegiances should not be assumed in the same family over different generations. – Note the opposition of the Etruscans and Umbrians to the bill: their élites were mindful of the possible link between extension of the Roman franchise and land assignments.

A5   Brief overview of the Social War, 91–89 BC

[15.1] The death of Drusus caused the Italian war that had long been coming to a head to break out. For 120 years ago, in the consulship of L. Caesar and P. Rutilius [91 BC], all Italy took up arms against the Romans. This trouble began with the people of Asculum, who had killed the praetor Servilius and his deputy Fonteius; it was then taken up by the Marsi, and from them it made its way into all the districts of Italy. [2] The situation of the Italians was as frightful as their cause was most just; for they were seeking the citizenship of a state whose empire (*imperium*) they were defending by their arms; in all years and in all wars they were serving with a double number of infantry and cavalry, and yet were not admitted to the rights of citizenship in the state which had, through them, reached the highest position from which it could look down with scorn upon men of the same race and blood as foreigners and aliens. [3] This war carried off more than 300,000 of the youth of Italy. The most illustrious Roman commanders in this war were Cn. Pompeius, the father of Pompey the Great, C. Marius ... L. Sulla, who had been praetor in the previous year, Q. Metellus, the son of Numidicus ...

[16.3] The most celebrated commanders of the Italians were Silo Popaedius, Herius Asinius, Insteius Cato, C. Pontidius, Telesinus Pontius, Marius Egnatius, and Papius Mutilus ... [4] So frightful and changeable were the fortunes of the Italian war, that in two successive years two Roman consuls, Rutilius and then Cato Porcius, were slain by the enemy; the armies of the Roman people were routed in many places; and the Romans had to put on military dress and to remain for a long time in that habit. The Italians chose Corfinium as the capital of their state (*imperium*), and named it *Italica*. Then little by little the strength of the Romans was restored by admitting to the citizenship those who had either not taken up arms or had been more quick to lay them down, with Pompey, Sulla, and Marius restoring the drooping and tottering Roman commonwealth (*res publica*).

Velleius Paterculus, Histories 2.15–16, with omissions

Velleius (c. 19 BC–c. AD 31) brings a distinctive viewpoint to our understanding of the Social War. He lived under the emperor Tiberius and the political integration of Italy was an irreversible reality to him; yet, his family hailed from Hirpinia, a region of Southern Italy, and he was very aware of the motives of those who joined the war against Rome, of how the conflict had unfolded, and who the main figures were; elsewhere he stresses that his great-grandfather, Minatus Magius from Aeclanum, had taken Rome's side (2.16.2). However, he is sympathetic with the grievances of the Allies, and identifies the appetite for Roman citizenship as *the* explanation for the outbreak of the war. When Rome gave in on that crucial point, the conflict came to a resolution. The decision of the Italians to set up a state with its own capital remains unexplained. – The Italian chief Herius Asinius was an ancestor of C. Asinius Pollio, whom we shall encounter by Caesar's side at the crossing of the Rubicon in 49 BC (cf. **B143**) and who went on to play a major role in the Triumviral period (see Index of persons).

A6   The Italian Allies

Beyond the Picentine territory are the Vestini, the Marsi, the Paeligni, the Marrucini and the Frentani, a Samnite tribe. They occupy the mountain country, their territory touching upon the sea in a few places. These communities are very small, but they are very brave and have often displayed this quality to the Romans: first, when they went to war with them: secondly, when they fought alongside them; and thirdly, when they sought freedom and citizenship, and not obtaining them, revolted. They kindled the war that is called Marsic and they proclaimed Corfinium, the metropolis of the Paeligni, the common city for all the Italic peoples, instead of Rome, making it their base of operations for the war and changing its name to Italica. It was there that they mustered all their followers and elected consuls and praetors. And they persisted together in the war for two years until they achieved the partnership for which they were fighting the war. They called it the Marsic War after those who began the revolt, and in particular Pompaedius.

Strabo, *Geography* 5.4.2

Strabo (from Amasia, in Asia Minor, 64/63 BC–AD 24) frequently discusses the major political developments that occurred in the regions covered by in his great geographical work. The account of the Apennine regions in Central Italy is inextricably linked to the Social War and to the role that the local communities played in it. Some more information is offered on the federal structure created by the Allies, and the role of the Marsi is especially singled out: as we know from a number of other sources, in the first century BC the war was most commonly known in Rome as the 'Marsic War' – a label that also conveniently overshadowed the involvement of communities that had until recently been allies of Rome.

A7   Corfinium – the capital *Italica*, 91 BC

[4] There were fighting against the Romans, the Samnites, the people of Asculum, the Lucanians, the Picentines, the people of Nola and other towns and tribes. Among them the largest and most notable city was Corfinium, which had recently been established as the common city for all the Italians. In it they had provided everything necessary to strengthen a great city and empire: a forum of good size and a senate-house, and all the necessities for war in abundance, a large amount of money and a copious abundance of food. [5] They also set up a common senate of five hundred members there, from which those worthy to rule the state and those able to deliberate for the common safety would be promoted. To these they entrusted the conduct of the war policy, having given the senators full powers. The senators ordained that two consuls and twelve praetors should be chosen annually.

Diodorus, *Library of History* 37.2.4–5

Diodorus of Agyrion in Sicily (hence often known as Diodorus Siculus) lived *c.* 90– *c.* 30 BC and is the author of a work of 'universal history', with a very broad geographical and chronological remit, in which the Social War is singled out as a military and political event of unparalleled importance. The interests and aims of the Italians receive close attention. On the one hand, Diodorus stresses that the coalition that clashed with Rome was an ethnically diverse compact of independent communities and peoples; on the other, he sketches a complex federal structure, with a capital city, a treasury (from which a substantial output of coinage was produced, see **A8**), and a set of institutions, which closely mirror those of the Roman Republic (note esp. the yearly elected consular pair). The existence of this framework strongly questions the thesis that by 91 BC the main aim of the insurgents was merely inclusion in the Roman citizen body.

A8   Silver *denarius* showing Italia and soldiers swearing an oath

Ghey, Leins & Crawford 2010, 553.415.7 = BM 2002,0102.4921

Obv: Head of Italia, laureate, left; behind, inscription. ITALIA
Rev: Oath-taking scene of eight warriors, four on each side of pig held by
         attendant; behind, standard; in exergue, control-mark (V.)

The military and financial might of the Italian coalition is shown by the considerable coinage output it
produced in order to fund its war effort. This silver *denarius* shows the close similarities between Roman
and Italian institutions, both in the structure of the coin issue (a personification of a goddess on the obverse
and a scene on the reverse) and in the nature of the military oath that is depicted (a similar ritual, involving
the killing of a piglet, is also attested in Rome). At the same time, it is a sign of clear hostility towards
Rome, and a powerful political statement: the Allies define themselves as a political entity called 'Italy':
on this coin issue they refer to it in Latin, while elsewhere they refer to it with its Oscan equivalent, *víteliú*.
What is depicted here is the earliest known personification of Italy.

A9   The Romans grant citizenship to the Italians, 90 BC
[49] When they learned of these operations on the Adriatic side of Italy, the peoples
on the other side of Rome, the people of Etruria and Umbria and some other tribes
neighbouring them, were all incited to revolt. The Senate was afraid that the war
would encircle it and that it would be unprotected and therefore garrisoned the coast
from Cumae to Rome with freedmen, then for the first time conscripted into the army
because of the shortage of men, and voted that the Italians who were still remaining
in the alliance should be citizens, which was the one thing they all desired most of all.
They made known this decision among the people of Etruria, who gladly took on the
citizenship. By this favour the Senate made the loyal more loyal, strengthened those
who were in doubt, and made those they were fighting less hostile through a hope of
similar treatment.

Appian, *Civil Wars* 1.49

Appian places the turning point of the conflict at the end of the first year of campaigning. The Italians made
significant inroads, and the communities that had not supported them (the Etruscans and the Umbrians)
start considering joining their coalition. Faced with that potentially fatal threat, Rome decides to offer
citizenship to them and those who had stayed loyal: that political concession, which was triggered by
pressing military concerns, ends up changing the whole balance of the war, and prepares the ground for its
eventual conclusion – but it should not be read as the outcome intended by those who had taken on Rome
in 91 BC.

A10   End of the Social War: incorporation of the allies in the citizen body
a) Lucius Calpurnius Piso ... in accordance with a decree of the Senate ... two new tribes ...

    Sisenna, *History* fragment 38 = Nonius 484 Mercier = 777 Lindsay = *FRH* 26 F 38

L. Cornelius Sisenna (*c.* 119–67 BC) was a contemporary historian, whose history of the period between the Social War and the death of Sulla survives in meagre quotations by later authors, usually to illustrate points of language and vocabulary. His work is saluted as a significant achievement by Sallust (*Jugurthine War* 95.3), who at the same time denounces his political bias: Sisenna was close to Sulla, and held the praetorship in 78 BC.

b) But the Romans did not then enrol these new citizens in the thirty-five voting tribes, which they had at that time, so that they should not, being more numerous than the old citizens, have the advantage in voting, *but making ten sections, created other tribes* in which they voted last. Their vote was often useless, since the thirty-five were called first and formed more than half. This either escaped notice at first, or else the Italians were content even with just this; when it was observed later, it began another civil conflict.

    Appian, *Civil Wars* 1.49

The translation, the text of which is in *italics,* is conjectural and the source of much scholarly argument. Clearly the *Lex Julia* of 90 BC restricted the voting power of the new citizens in the *comitia tributa* in some way. Velleius reports that the new citizens were distributed in eight tribes for the same reason that Appian gives (2.20.2).

c) And these were the events around Italy during the Social War, which raged with very great violence until this point when all Italy joined the Roman state, except, for the time being, the Lucanians and the Samnites; and they too, I think, gained what they desired at a later date. They were each enrolled in the tribes in the same way as those who had obtained citizenship earlier, so as not by being mixed in with the old citizens to have the advantage in the voting, being more numerous.

    Appian, *Civil Wars* 1.53

Accepting the principle that the Italian Allies should be included in the Roman citizen body was not the end of what had already been a highly divisive matter. The main outstanding issue was how their votes would be counted within the tribal system, in which the Roman citizens were enrolled into thirty-five voting districts: as Appian makes clear in source b), the arrangement that was devised was intended to reduce the impact of their votes by listing them in a few tribes, and preventing from swaying the vote of a high number of voting districts. Their impact on the *comitia tributa* (assemblies voting by tribes), which had important legislative powers and elected a number of junior magistrates, was therefore strongly curtailed. Moreover, the timing of their enfranchisement was uneven: those who fought on were enfranchised some time later than those who agreed to disarm, and the specifics of the legal process that was applied to them are unclear.

B. NARRATIVE, 88–44 BC

THE EIGHTIES

B1   The disaster of the eighties

[7] And then in the first year after he had held all the higher offices, as the path to the highest authority was opened to him, with everyone's approval, death overturned all his hopes and life plans. [8] This was grievous to those who were dear to him, bitter to the fatherland, and a heavy blow to all good men. However, such disaster befell the commonwealth that I am persuaded that Lucius Crassus' life was not snatched from him by the immortal gods, but that death was gifted to him. He did not see Italy blazing with war, nor the Senate burning with factional strife, nor leading statesmen on trial for a hideous crime, nor the grief of his daughter, nor the exile of his son-in-law, nor the most bitter flight of Gaius Marius, nor that slaughter after his return, the cruellest of all, nor in short the city being disfigured in every respect – the city in which he had stood out among all others in glory, when it used to be very prosperous.

Cicero, *On the Good Orator* 3.7–8

L. Licinius Crassus (140-91 BC) was one of the greatest orators of his age, and Cicero cast him as one of the characters of a fictional dialogue on the qualities and skills that make up a good orator. He was consul in 95 BC. In introducing the section of the dialogue in which Crassus takes centre stage, he recalls his death, which occurred shortly before the outbreak of the Social War. It was a great loss to the city, but spared him the catastrophic developments of the following decade, which are concisely summarized: interestingly, the massacre that followed Marius' return to Rome in 87 is regarded as the most traumatic event; no mention is made of the consequences of Sulla's victory. The overall judgment on the decade following the Social War as an age of political and social upheaval is especially significant.

B2   The tribune Sulpicius, 88 BC

[306] In the following year [88 BC], in which Sulla and Pompey were consuls, since Sulpicius addressed public gatherings (*contiones*) almost every day during his tribunate, I acquainted myself thoroughly with his manner of speaking.

Cicero, *Brutus* 306

In 88 BC a capable and formidably active tribune, P. Sulpicius, set the political agenda along bold and radical lines, putting forward an ambitious legislative programme. Cicero who was then a young man, describes Sulpicius' ability earlier in his rhetorical treatise (= **G37**). Cicero's view on Sulpicius' oratory does not carry a political judgment: his ability to speak powerfully and persuasively is matched by a willingness to engage with the citizens in a considerable number of public meetings, in which his rhetorical ability and his radical politics play a crucial role in mobilizing support.

B3   Roman commanders and ambassadors begin war on their own initiative, 89 BC

[17] Having said this, the Roman commanders and the ambassadors did not wait for the Senate or the people to become informed of this great war, but gathered forces from Bithynia, Cappadocia, Paphlagonia and the Galatians in Asia. When his own army, which Lucius Cassius, the governor of Asia, had with him, was ready and all their allies had come together, they divided the forces and began the campaign: Cassius was between Bithynia and Galatia, Manius where Mithridates would cross into Bithynia, while Oppius the other commander was on the mountains of Cappadocia. Each of them

had cavalry and infantry of about forty thousand men. They also had a naval force, which Minucius Rufus and Gaius Popilius commanded around Byzantium, guarding the mouth of the Black Sea. Nicomedes was also present with them, commanding another fifty thousand infantry and six thousand cavalry.

[*The forces and allies of Mithridates are then detailed. A major battle takes place between the army of Nicomedes and Mithridatic forces, resulting in a severe defeat for Nicomedes: his camp, his money and many prisoners are captured.*]

[19] This was the first action of the Mithridatic war and the Roman commanders were greatly disturbed because they had started so great a war not with good sense but precipitately, and without a decree of the people. For a small force had defeated much larger numbers, not through any good fortune in their position, nor enemy error, but through the quality of their commanders and the courage of the soldiery.

Appian, *Mithridatic Wars* 17–19, with omissions

In spite of the detailed provisions of the law on the praetorian provinces (**E4**), there were circumstances in which swift action had to be taken by a provincial governor, without seeking prior approval from the Senate and the people. The attack of Mithridates Eupator of Pontus on the province of Asia in 89 BC required immediate intervention, and Appian gives a brief overview of the forces at the disposal of L. Cassius. Shortly after the outbreak of the conflict it becomes apparent that, quite apart from any legal or political concerns, the Roman contingents are not in a position to effectively tackle the offensive of the King.

B4   Rome and Mithridates, 89–66 BC
[8] The fact is that until recently our commanders have campaigned against that king in such a way that they have brought back the outward trappings of victory, not victory itself. L. Sulla triumphed, L. Murena triumphed over Mithridates, two very brave men and very great commanders, but they triumphed in such a way that that man, beaten and defeated, remained king. Nevertheless praise must be accorded to those commanders for what they achieved, indulgence granted for what they left because the *res publica* called Sulla back from that war to Italy, Sulla called Murena back.

[9] Mithridates, however, devoted all the time thereafter not to forgetting about the previous war, but to preparing for a new one. When he had built and equipped very large fleets and raised huge armies from whatever nations he could and was pretending that he was waging war on the people of the Bosporus, his neighbours, he then sent envoys and a letter as far as Spain to those leaders with whom we were then waging war so that in two places, completely separate and utterly different, war might be waged by land and sea by two enemy forces with one plan, with the result that you were fighting for your empire (*imperium*) distracted by campaigns in two places. [10] But the danger on the one front, that involving Sertorius and Spain, which was much more substantial and potent, was removed by the inspired strategy and outstanding courage of Pompey; while on the other front things were so organized by L. Lucullus, a very great man, that it seems those great and glorious beginnings to his achievements ought to be attributed not to good luck but to his courage, while the final events, which have happened recently, should be attributed not to his fault, but to bad luck.

Cicero, *On the Manilian Law / On Pompey's Command* 8–10

As he makes the case for the passing of law that will grant Pompey a special command against Mithridates (66 BC), Cicero reflects on more than two decades of hostility between Rome and the king. The difference between actual victory and the celebration of a triumph is worth stressing: for different reasons, both Sulla and Murena did not bring to completion their campaigns against Mithridates, although they were both granted a triumph, and Lucullus' action – in spite of Cicero's broadly positive comments (cf. also ch. 25 of the same speech) – had been inadequate. Mithridates is depicted as an implacable and effective enemy, minded to rekindle his enmity with Rome even in the interludes of peace. The hostile portrait is compounded by the reference to his talks with Sertorius: had it taken shape, the alliance between the external enemy and a runaway Roman commander would have presented a fatal threat. Pompey's victory against Sertorius removed it, and that recent success makes him the obvious contender for the command against Mithridates.

B5   Sulla's march on Rome, July/August 88

[56] Sulla annulled the suspension of legal business (*iustitium*), and hurried off to Capua, where the army was, in order to move it from Capua across to Asia to fight the war against Mithridates: he did not have any sense of what being prepared against him. Since the suspension had been annulled and Sulla had left the city, Sulpicius had the law [i.e. *on the distribution of the new citizens into the tribes*] passed, and through a vote he immediately arranged for the command of the war against Mithridates to be assigned to Marius (for whose sake that whole string of developments had happened) instead of Sulla.

[57] When Sulla was informed of this, he decided to resolve the matter by war, and summoned the army to an assembly. They were eager to go on campaign against Mithridates, because they expected it to be profitable, and thought that Marius would enrol other soldiers for it instead of them. Sulla, having denounced the insult made to him by Sulpicius and Marius, and without explicitly adding anything else (he did not dare to speak of a war of that sort) he urged them to be ready to follow orders. They understood what he meant and feared being excluded from the campaign, and revealed the hidden thought of Sulla by urging him to lead them to Rome without hesitation. Sulla was delighted, and took the lead of six legions. However, the senior officers of the army, except for one quaestor, abandoned him and fled to Rome, as they could not bear leading the army against the fatherland. Some envoys met him on the road and asked him why he was moving in arms against the fatherland. He replied: to free it from those who are ruling it tyrannically.

                                                                    Appian, *Civil Wars* 1.56–57

The defining event of 88 BC was the march led by Sulla on Rome: an unprecedented development, which was to mark a sea change in Roman political practice and culture for decades to come. The decision to lead an army into the city, and within its sacred boundary (*pomerium*), where it was unlawful to carry weapons, was in many respects subversive, indeed revolutionary: Sulla, however, justified it on the basis of a legal claim to his entitlement to the command against Mithridates, and coated it in a rhetoric of liberty, and as a reaction against the threat of a tyrannical power. – The reaction of the officers who surrounded Sulla, who mostly refused to follow him, is telling of the many political and moral problems presented by his choice.

B6   Opposition to Sulla in Rome, 88 BC

I would place no one ahead of him [Q. Caecilius Metellus Numidicus], but I would deservedly compare Q. Scaevola the Augur to him. Having scattered and struck down the faction (*partes*) of his enemies, and having occupied Rome, Sulla under arms summoned the Senate. He proposed, with a very keen desire, that C. Marius be declared a public enemy (*hostis*) as quickly as possible. None dared oppose his will, except only Scaevola, who, when the question was put to him, refused to give an opinion. Moreover, when Sulla truculently urged him to give an answer, he said: 'You may show me your troops of soldiers, with which you have surrounded the senate-house, you may threaten me with death, but you will never get me, for the sake of a small amount of aged blood, to judge Marius, by whom Rome and Italy were saved, a public enemy (*hostis*).'

Valerius Maximus, *Memorable Deeds and Sayings* 3.8.5

Shortly after the march on Rome, Sulla promoted an unprecedented legal act, under which twelve exponents of the faction that had supported the grant of the Mithridatic command to Marius were declared 'public enemies': Marius and Sulpicius were of course on top of the list. The issue was debated in the Senate, and the firm opposition of an elder statesman, Quintus Mucius Scaevola the Augur (*c.* 159-88 BC), a leading authority on Roman law, who died shortly afterwards, is recorded. Marius' victories against the Teutones and the Cimbrians (105-102 BC) are singled out as an achievement that puts the city in lasting debt towards Marius. – Scaevola's pointed reference to the presence of the army in the vicinity of the Senate is telling of the role that coercion and intimidation played in that fraught political context.

B7   Atticus and young Marius, 88/87 BC

Atticus' father died early. As a young man, because of his family connection with P. Sulpicus, who was killed during his tribunate, Atticus had a share in that danger. Anicia, a cousin of Pomponius [Atticus] on his mother's side, had married Servius, Sulpicius' brother. [2] When Sulpicius was killed, Atticus saw that the city had been thrown into turmoil by the disorder caused by Cinna, and that he was not afforded any chance to live in keeping with his standing (*dignitas*) without causing offence to one side or the other, since the minds of the citizens were divided, with some favouring the side of Sulla, and others that of Cinna. He therefore thought that it was the right time for him to pursue his own studies, and moved to Athens. Nonetheless, he helped young Marius, who had been declared a public enemy (*hostis*), and he supported his escape with financial help. [3] And so that his time overseas should do his estate no harm, he moved across a large part of his assets. He lived in such a way that he deservedly became very dear to all the Athenians.

Cornelius Nepos, *Life of Atticus* 2.1–3

T. Pomponius Atticus, a wealthy and influential member of the equestrian order, is best known because of his extensive correspondence with Cicero: in the early part of his life he also formed a connection with another young man whose family hailed from Arpinum: the son of Gaius Marius. His financial support to young Marius' escape from Rome does not translate into a straightforward political allegiance. In fact, Atticus' long-term choice not to get directly involved with politics and to pursue his financial interests and his studies dates back to the eighties. The reference to the movement of a considerable part of his assets to Greece is revealing of the potential and scope for establishing financial and economic connections between different regions of the Mediterranean world.

B8   The victory of Marius and Cinna, 87 BC

[71] Cinna and Marius entered the city and everybody received them with fear. They immediately began to plunder without restraint everything that belonged to those whom they regarded to be opposed to them ... Now the victors sent out spies to search for their enemies of senatorial and equestrian rank. When an *eques* was killed, no further attention was paid to him, but all the heads of senators were put on display before the rostra. Neither the fear of the gods, nor the blame of men, nor the fear of hostility for their acts had any significance in these circumstances. On the contrary,

after committing savage deeds they turned to impious sights. They killed without pity and severed the necks of men already dead, and they displayed these horrific sights before the public eye, either to inspire fear and terror, or for the sake of an impious spectacle ... [73] It was not permitted to give burial to any of the slain, but the bodies of such distinguished men were torn in pieces by birds and dogs. Moreover, there were many private and unjustified assassinations committed by the members of the factions (Gk: *stasis*) upon each other; there were banishments of others, property was confiscated, men were deposed from public office, and the laws enacted during Sulla's consulship were repealed. All of Sulla's friends were put to death, his house was razed to the ground, his assets confiscated, and he was voted a public enemy. His wife and children were being pursued, but they managed to escape. Altogether nothing was missing in these great and manifold evils.

Appian, Civil Wars 1.71, 73, with omissions

While Sulla was leading his campaign in the East, political developments moved quickly in Rome, where power was seized by a faction that was strongly opposed to him, and soon clashed with the Senate, or at least its majority: hostile sources refer to this period as an age of terror, in which C. Cornelius Cinna, the consul of 87 BC, played a central role. Sulla, who had declared twelve of his opponents 'public enemies' in 88, suffered the same fate. Gaius Marius, on the other hand, returned to Italy, played a leading role in the violent retaliation carried out by Cinna and his opponents, and was elected to the consulship for 86 BC. Cinna was killed in 84 in a mutiny of his soldiers, as he was preparing to cross over to the East and take on Sulla (*Civil Wars* 1.78).

B9   Brothers at war, 87 BC

For in the battle which was fought on the Janiculum against Cinna, a soldier of Pompey killed his brother; then, having discovered what he had done, killed himself, as Sisenna relates.

Tacitus, Histories 3.51.1

L. Cornelius Sisenna wrote an historical work on the period between the Social War and the death of Sulla: it was very influential in antiquity, but no longer survives. Tacitus mentions an episode from Sisenna's account of the clashes between the troops of Cinna and those of Cn. Pompeius Strabo (*Fragments of the Roman Historians* 26 F132), constrasting it with an episode from the civil war of AD 69, when a soldier who had killed his brother asked his commanders for a special reward. – The incident reported by Sisenna served as a most powerful illustration of the nefarious consequences of internal strife. Tacitus uses it to draw a contrast between recent and distant past, but it is a safe guess that others read it as an example of the sea-change that had intervened in Rome in the eighties (see **B1**). It did not fail to make an impression on other authors: Livy related it in vivid terms (*Summaries* 89.2).

B10   Death of Marius, 15 January 86 BC

[9] After having committed many crimes, Marius died on the Ides of January [13 January]. [10] If we consider his flaws along with his virtues, it is not easy to say whether he was better in wartime or more damaging in peacetime. He saved the *res publica* in arms, and he equally upset it as a citizen, first with all sorts of frauds, and finally with the weapons, like an enemy (*hostiliter*).

Livy, Summaries 80.9–10

Most sources explain Marius' sudden death, two weeks into his seventh consulship, as due to natural causes: the compressed summary of Livy's epitomator effectively conveys the unresolved tension of his political life, and indeed of his legacy: on the one hand, he had been a great military leader; on the other, he had been a major destabilizing force in Roman internal politics, since the day of his alliance with Saturninus and Glaucia [100 BC], and he had played a leading, dark role in a grim season of civil war.

B11   Sulla and his supporters, 86/85 BC

[1] Now, since Cinna and Carbo at Rome were inflicting illegal and violent treatment upon the most distinguished men, many of these had fled their tyranny and repaired to Sulla's camp as to a harbour, and in a short time a semblance of a senate took shape around him. [2] Metella, too, who had managed with difficulty to extricate herself and her children, came reporting that his house and his villas had been burned down by his enemies, and begged him to come to the rescue of those who were left home. [3] While he was uncertain on what to do, and could neither accept neglecting his country when it was being harmed, nor persuade himself to go away and leave unfinished such a great task like the war with Mithridates, a merchant of Delos, named Archelaus, came to him, and secretly conveyed to him certain vague hopes and propositions from Archelaus, the commander of the King.

Plutarch, *Life of Sulla* 22.1–3

The flight of a large number of senators to the East and Plutarch's comment on the 'semblance of a senate' reflect the deep divide that is crippling the *res publica* in the mid-eighties, and is quickly leading to the emergence of two alternative states. – In Plutarch's account, Sulla's decision to hasten a peace agreement with Mithridates, without completing a decisive counteroffensive against the king's forces, is directly caused by the urgent need to take on his enemies in Italy. A significant and controversial role in the final part of the campaign was played by Archelaus, the commander that Mithridates had put in charge of the campaign to Greece, who held preliminary talks with Sulla, after suffering two major defeats at Chaeronea and Orchomenus.

B12   Sulla meets Mithridates: the 'Peace of Dardanus', 85 BC

[3] At this time the ambassadors from Mithridates arrived and declared that he accepted the rest of the terms, but reckoned that Paphlagonia should not be taken away from him and that the ships should not be any part of the agreement. Sulla became angry and said: 'What do you say? Mithridates lays claim to Paphlagonia and refuses to give up the ships? I thought he would prostrate himself before me if I were to leave him his right hand, with which he took the lives of so many Romans. [4] He will very quickly utter different words when I have crossed into Asia; now he sits in Pergamum and conducts a war he has not seen.' The ambassadors were frightened and remained silent, but Archelaus entreated Sulla and tried to soothe his anger, grasping his right hand and weeping. Finally he persuaded Sulla that he himself should be sent to Mithridates; he would arrange the peace on the terms Sulla wanted, but if he could not persuade the king, he would kill himself. [5] With these assurances Sulla sent him off ... and received Archelaus at Philippi, bringing news that all was well; but that Mithridates wanted most of all to come to a conference with him. [6] It was Fimbria who was chiefly responsible for this: having killed Flaccus, the consul of the opposing faction (Gk: *stasis*), he had overcome the Mithridatic commanders and was marching against the king himself. Mithridates was afraid of this and chose rather to become a friend of Sulla.

[24.1] Thus they met at Dardanus in the Troad; Mithridates had two hundred oared ships there, twenty thousand infantry troops, six thousand cavalry and a great number of scythed chariots, while Sulla had four cohorts and two hundred cavalry. When Mithridates came to meet him and stretched out his right hand, Sulla asked him if he was going to put a stop to the war on the terms, which Archelaus had agreed. When the king remained silent, Sulla said: 'Surely it is for those who are asking to speak first, while for the victors it is sufficient to be silent.' [2] When Mithridates began a defence of himself and tried partly to turn the war on the gods and partly to blame the Romans themselves, Sulla interrupted, saying that he had long ago heard from others, but now realized himself that Mithridates was a very clever orator since he had not been at a loss for plausible words to justify his wicked and illegal actions. [3] Sulla reproached him bitterly, denounced what had been done by him and asked him again if he would carry out the agreements made through Archelaus. When Mithridates said he would, Sulla then greeted him, embraced him and kissed him. Later he brought in the kings Nicomedes and Ariobarzanes and reconciled them with Mithridates. So Mithridates handed over seventy ships and five hundred archers and sailed away to Pontus.

Plutarch, *Life of Sulla* 23.3–24.3

Plutarch's account shows that the decision of Sulla and Mithridates to hold peace talks in 85 BC was driven by pressing concerns on both sides: Mithridates had suffered heavy defeats in Greece and feared the offensive of the troops of Fimbria in Asia Minor; Sulla was keen to draw the campaign to a close and concentrate on the civil war in Italy. A crucial role in paving the way for their talks was played by Archelaus, a commander of Mithridates, with whom Sulla struck a preliminary agreement. The encounter at Dardanus, near Troy, was also an opportunity for both men to state the case for their involvement in the war (cf. Appian, *Mithridatic Wars* 56–58). As is often the case in the history of Roman diplomacy, the conference is not a negotiation, but a formal occasion in which the counterpart is urged to accept the terms set by Rome. When Mithridates accepts them, a formal reconciliation takes place, which also involves two key allies of Rome in the region, the kings of Bithynia and Cappadocia, with whom Mithridates had long been clashing. – The agreement between the two men, however, was never formally ratified by the Senate, and that in due course contributed to a new deterioration of the relations between Rome and Pontus.

B13   Sulla and Mithridates: unfinished business
[11] The war would have been brought to an end if Sulla had not preferred a speedy triumph over Mithridates rather than a true one. [12] And this was then the state of things in Asia that Sulla had organized: a treaty had been concluded with the people of Pontus, Nicomedes recovered Bithynia from King Mithridates; Ariobarzanes received Cappadocia, Asia was ours again as it had been before; Mithridates had only been driven out. And so this state of affairs did not break the people of Pontus but inflamed them ... [14] ... so Mithridates, with his forces increased to a greater size, indeed with the whole weight of his kingdom, came again afresh to Asia by sea, land and rivers.

Florus, *Summary of Roman History* 1.40.11–14, with omissions

Sulla's decision to end the war with Mithridates without pursuing the full destruction of the king was not received favourably in some quarters (including sectors of his army: cf. Plutarch, *Sulla* 24.4). Florus, a second century AD author who relies heavily on Livy, voices a critical viewpoint, whilst recognizing that Sulla had also carried out a political and administrative resettlement of the region: however, the appeasement of 85 BC is singled out as the factor that enabled the king to regroup and mount a new offensive.

THE CIVIL WAR AND SULLA'S VICTORY, 83–78 BC

B14 An assessment of the effects of the civil war, 80 BC

[136] Those who know me are aware that, when an agreement (which I desired above all), became impossible, I strove most keenly, to the best of my slight and feeble abilities, to ensure the victory of those who have won. For was there anyone who could not see that men of low rank were competing for the highest honours with men of rank (*dignitas*)? In such a contest it would have been the act of a degenerate citizen not to join those by whose safety the dignity (*dignitas*) of the commonwealth at home and its authority (*auctoritas*) overseas are assured. I am glad, judges, and absolutely delighted that this has been accomplished, and that everyone has been granted the degree of office (*honor*) that befits him; I can clearly see that all this has been made possible by the will of the gods, by the favour of the Roman people, and by the wisdom, lawful power, and good fortune of Sulla.

Cicero, *Defence of Roscius of Ameria* 136

In 80 BC the young advocate Marcus Tullius Cicero took on the case of the son of a victim of the Sullan proscriptions, who had been charged with the assassination of his father. In spite of the political ramifications of the case (see A41), he did not fail to express his support to the political settlement brought about by Sulla: in his view, the regime of Cinna and his associates has enabled the rise of a number of individuals of low rank and no distinction. Although Cicero does point out that the prospect of a reconciliation would have been preferable, the choice of which side to embrace was a straightforward one to him. Sulla's role is of course singled out, but the support of more traditional forces – the gods and the people (from whom the power of the magistrates stems) – is also invoked.

B15 The events of 83 BC

[84] This war, then, began when Sulla arrived at Brundisium, in the one hundred and seventy-fourth Olympiad [84–81 BC]; but the length of it, in view of the scale of the operations, with people rushing furiously against one another as if against private enemies, was not long by comparison with such great conflicts. And it was chiefly for this reason that their sufferings, as they pressed hard upon one another in a brief period of time, turned out to be greater and more painful. Nevertheless it went on for three years, at least in Italy, until Sulla assumed power; since in Spain it lasted longer even after Sulla. Many battles, skirmishes, sieges, and all sorts of warfare took place throughout Italy, with commanders engaging both with whole armies and with detachments, and all were noteworthy ...

[86] But since the army of the consuls was all the time increasing from the greater part of Italy, which still stood by them, and from neighbouring Gaul beyond the Po, not even Sulla could neglect action, sending around messengers to all the parts of Italy he could, raising troops by friendship, fear, money, and hopes, until the rest of the summer had been spent by both sides in these activities.

Appian, *Civil Wars* 1.84, 86

Upon his return to Italy from the Mithridatic War Sulla knew that he had to take on the army of his opponents, who still regarded him as an enemy of the state (*hostis*). However, he readily conveyed conciliatory messages towards the Italians and his intention to respect their newly gained citizen rights: he needed, in fact, their support, or at least their acquiescence, as he was getting ready for a clash with his enemies within the Roman political establishment. – Cicero, *Philippics* 12.27, records a meeting between Sulla and one of the consuls of 83, L. Cornelius Scipio Asiagenus, at which constitutional issues – the authority of the Senate, the votes of the people, and the rights of citizenship – were discussed. Those talks had no discernible outcome, and were quickly followed by a battle at Mount Tifata, near Capua, which was Sulla's first major success in the war.

B16   The coinage of Sulla's enemies, *denarius* **83 BC**

Obv: Head of Venus, wearing a diadem.
         C. NORBANVS [Gaius Norbanus]
Rev: Prow-stem, *fasces* with axe, *caduceus* (herald's staff) and corn-ear.

      RRC 357/1a = Ghey, Leins & Crawford 2010, 357.1.1 = BM 1902,0206.67

This coin issue (a silver *denarius*) was struck in 83 BC by Gaius Norbanus, a moneyer who was the son of the serving consul of the same name. The presence of the symbol of legitimate power, the *fasces* (rods of office), along with symbols of plenty and good fortune, is both a claim to constitutional legitimacy and an auspicious message about the conflict that was about to unfold.

B17   Sulla's coinage, 83–82 BC
a) *Aureus*

Obv: Head of Venus, wearing diadem; on the right, Cupid holding a palm-branch
         L. SVLLA. [Lucius Sulla]
Rev: Two trophies; in between, a jug and a *lituus*
         IMPER [*imperator*] ITERVM [twice].

      RRC 359/1 = Ghey, Leins & Crawford 2010, 359.23 = BM 1946,1004.70

Sulla produced this coin issue with part of the proceeds of his victory in the East, as he was making his way back to Italy: its main purpose was to fund the war effort, but it also conveyed powerful messages: the association between Sulla and Venus; the reference to his victories against Mithridates, emphasized by the two trophies; and a claim to the legitimacy of his command through the depiction of tools that the augurs routinely used for ritual purposes (the jug and the curved staff known as *lituus*). The presence of Sulla's name on this coin issue is arguably the most striking aspect, though: he was neither a serving magistrate nor a moneyer. – This coin issue was struck both in gold and in silver (as *aurei* and *denarii* respectively): the silver units were of course meant to be spent as cash usually is, while the gold ones were especially valuable items, which will have been used as lump payment.

b) *Denarius*

RRC 367/3 = Ghey, Leins & Crawford 2010, 367.3.7 = BM 2002,0102.3154

Obv: Helmeted head of *Roma*, right
        PROQ L.MANLI [L. Manlius proquaestor]
Rev: A triumphing commander, crowned by a flying Victory, in a quadriga, right,
        holding reins in left hand and a *caduceus* in right hand
        L.SVLLA.IMP. [L. Sulla, *imperator*]

This issue was struck both as an *aureus* and a *denarius*: it appears to have been struck in Italy, and may be dated after Sulla's return, but before his victory in the war (the *cognomen Felix* is still absent; cf. **B20** The depiction of a triumph is no doubt a reference to the anticipated victory; the caduceus (two snakes winding around a winged staff) is an auspicious sign (see **B16** and **B46b**). The personification of Rome may be viewed as part of Sulla's commitment to restoring the proper constitutional order – an intention he repeatedly stated after his return.

B18   The coinage of a lieutenant of Sulla, *denarius* 81 BC.

Obv: Head of *Pietas* [Piety], wearing diadem; before, stork.
Rev: Elephant, left
        Q.C.M.P.I. [Quintus Caecilius Metellus Pius *imperator*].
        RRC 374/1 = Ghey, Leins & Crawford 2010, 374.1.4 = BM 1867,0101.1149

This issue was struck by Q. Caecilius Metellus, who led Sulla's troops in Northern Italy during the Civil War, and made a significant contribution to the final victory. The reference to a goddess personifying piety is remarkable in the context of a civil war, but far from unparalleled (compare the coinage of Pompey's son, **C16**): Metellus is here stressing the piety he showed towards his father, Q. Caecilius Metellus Numidicus, in securing his return from exile. The *cognomen* Pius is also to be explained in this light. The stork symbolized piety for the Romans (Petronius, *Satyricon* 55). The presence of the elephant on the reverse is a reference to a deed of his ancestor L. Caecilius Metellus, who captured the elephants of the Carthaginian commander Hasdrubal in 251. – On the reverse of another type struck by Metellus (*RRC* 374/2) the reference to the family traditions is replaced by the augural symbols used by Sulla on the reverse of *RRC* 359: that is surely significant.

B19   Sulla's victory monument on *aureus*, 81 BC

RRC 381a = Ghey, Leins & Crawford 2010, 381.1.1 = BM 1848,0819.77

Obv: Helmeted bust of Rome, draped, right
        A. MAN; LI.[A.F.Q.] [Aulus Manlius son of Aulus, quaestor]
Rev: Equestrian statue – horseman wearing laurel-wreath and *sagum* (woollen cloak),
        L.SVLLA.FE; LI.DIC [Lucius Sulla Felix, dictator]

B20   Sulla Felix

Every decision that Sulla had taken as consul or as proconsul was confirmed and fully legalized, and his gilded equestrian statue was erected in front of the *rostra* with the inscription 'Cornelius Sulla, the Fortunate (*Eutuches*)'. For that is how his flatterers named him on account of his success against his enemies – and flattery made the name permanent.

Appian, *Civil Wars* 1.97

The statue mentioned by Appian is the same monument depicted in the coinage of the quaestor A. Manlius in 80 BC (**B19**): the inscription draws attention both to the magistracy that Sulla held after his victory in the civil war, the dictatorship, which enabled him to embark on a programme of political reforms with minimal scrutiny by the people and the Senate, and the name that he added to his *tria nomina, Felix,* which Appian translates into Greek as *Eutuches. Felix,* a Latin adjective that may roughly be translated as 'fortunate', was turned into a name that stressed Sulla's special connection with the gods, and his ability to attract and secure their enduring favour. – Note the profound difference between this name and those that some victorious commanders received after obtaining a major success in a particular place (e.g. Scipio Africanus, Metellus Numidicus).

B21   Sulla's constitutional reforms

As a dictator Sulla, who had almost regal powers, was above the consuls. Twenty-four axes were carried in front of him as dictator, the same number that were carried before the kings of old, and he had around him a large bodyguard. He repealed laws and introduced others. He prevented anyone from holding the praetorship before the quaestorship, and the consulship before the praetorship, and the same magistracy before ten years had elapsed. At the same time, he reduced the power of the tribunes, making it very feeble, and prohibiting by law that a tribune could hold a magistracy afterwards. In this way all the men of distinction or high rank, who would have sought it in the past, avoided it thereafter. ... To the Senate itself, which was reduced in number because of the seditions and the wars, he added about three hundred members, chosen from the best of the equestrian order, giving to the tribes a vote on each one. He added to the people the youngest and most vigorous slaves of the proscribed, more than 10,000 of them: he freed them, established them as Roman citizens, and named them *Cornelii* after himself, so that he could rely on 10,000 men among the commoners, ready to obey his orders. In order to put in place the same sort of protection across Italy he distributed a great deal of land, as I said earlier [1.96], to the twenty-three legions that had fought under him – both land that was unassigned and land that was confiscated by way of a penalty.

Appian, *Civil Wars* 1.100

This passage is not comprehensively detailed or unfailingly accurate on points of public law, but gives a very powerful account of the range, ambition, and impact of Sulla's work after his decision to take up the dictatorship at the end of the civil war. The detail on the number of lictors (attendants) that surrounded him draws attention to the quasi-regal nature of his power, which enabled him to pass legislation on a whole range of controversial issues, and to redesign some crucial aspects of what we call (with a considerable degree of approximation) the 'Roman constitution': the access to magistracies, the powers of the tribunate of the plebs, the size and influence of the Senate. The proscriptions are very much in the background of this major political resettlement, and so is the memory of the civil war: the freed slaves of the proscribed are a sort of reserve force on which Sulla can rely upon to strengthen his control over the city as he is embarking on such a divisive programme, and the soldiers that fought the war with him receive their rewards, at the expense of a number of communities across Italy that have their land confiscated to make room for the new settlers.

B22   Sulla and the freedmen
The freedmen to L. Cornelius Sulla Felix, son of Lucius, dictator.

ILLRP 353 = *ILS* 871 = EDCS-17800203

This dedication from Minturnae , in Latium, records the gratitude of a group of freedmen to Sulla: it is attractive to see a link with the mass enfranchisement of the slaves of the proscribed recorded by Appian above.

B23   Sulla's proscriptions 82/81 BC
a) When he left off [charges] against individuals, Sulla went after the towns and punished them too, demolishing their citadels or pulling down their walls or imposing communal fines, or exhausting them with very heavy levies; in the majority of them he settled the soldiers who had fought with him in order to have garrisons throughout Italy. He transferred their land and houses and divided these out among the latter; this made them all the more loyal to him even after he died. Now, as they would not be secure in their possessions unless all Sulla's arrangements were secure, they were staunch on his behalf even when he had passed on.

Appian, *Civil Wars* 1.96

b) Proscriptions were made not only in Rome, but also in every town in Italy; no temple of a god, no hearth of friendship, and no ancestral home was free from the stain of bloodshed. Husbands were butchered in the arms of their wedded wives and sons in the arms of their mothers. Those who were destroyed because of anger or enmity were as nothing compared with those whose throats were cut because of their property. It even occurred to the executioners to say that his great house killed this man, his gardens that man, his warm waters another.

Plutarch, *Life of Sulla* 31.5

The Civil War of the late eighties ended, as civil wars almost unfailingly do, with a round of retaliations and a huge transfer of resources from the defeated to the victors. Italy was heavily affected, as many prominent members of the anti-Sullan coalition were of municipal background: Appian (a) focuses on confiscations of land and on the heavy military presence that was installed in a number of communities, in breach of their status of self-governing cities; Plutarch (b), who is ever interested in the ethical dimension of the political events he discusses, stresses the moral impact of the confiscations. While these attracted much opposition and resentment, they also played an important role, as Appian makes clear, in consolidating the loyalty of Sulla's supporters to their leader and his political legacy.

B24   Sullan confiscations and settlement of Pompeii, 81–80 BC

a) Marcus Holconius Rufus, duumvir, ... saw to the building of a private wall belonging to the *colonia Veneria Cornelia* ...

ILS 5915 = EDCS-11400871* = Cooley, *Pompeii and Herculaneum* E1

b) Gaius Quinctius Valgus, son of Gaius, Marcus Porcius, son of Marcus, duumvirs, in accordance with a decree of the town councillors, let the contract for the construction of the covered theatre and also approved the work.

CIL 10.844 = *ILLRP* 646 = EDCS-11400928

c) Gaius Quinctius Valgus, son of Gaius, Marcus Porcius, son of Marcus, quinquennial duumvirs, for the colony's honour saw to the construction of the amphitheatre with their own money and gave the space to the colonists in perpetuity.

CIL 10.852 = *ILLRP* 645 = EDCS-11400936

d) And I do not think that I ought to pass over this merit of Publius Sulla either: although this colony was established by him and although the fortune of the *res publica* created a division between the advantages of the colonists and the fortunes of the Pompeians, he is so dear and popular with both parties that he is thought not to have removed the one but to have established both.

Cicero, *Defence of (Publius) Sulla* 62

One of Sulla's priorities after his victory was the foundation of a number of colonies, which were settled on land confiscated from communities that had opposed him in the war and assigned to the veterans of his army. Sulla himself had besieged and captured Pompeii, and his name has even been found written on the walls. Around 81/0 he imposed a settlement of veterans there, led by his nephew P. Sulla. The town became *colonia Veneria Cornelia Pompeianorum*, taking Sulla's family name (Cornelius), and asserting its links to Venus (traditionally important in Pompeii, but also to Sulla). The town, which was already a *municipium* (community of Roman citizens), adopted the constitution of a Roman colony. Public inscriptions (in Latin, which has by now replaced Oscan as the official language) record significant and Roman-style building activity soon after 80 BC by two magistrates, Porcius and Valgus; the latter was probably the father-in-law of Servilius Rullus, the tribune of 63 and certainly had a direct personal connection with Sulla. Political tensions between the indigenous community and veterans, whose names dominate the public records until the time of Augustus, were inevitable and recorded in a speech of Cicero. In defending P. Sulla in a criminal case in 62 BC he claims his client helped alleviate such tensions.

B25 Sullan settlements at Arretium, Faesulae

Meanwhile Catiline was active and happy, accompanied by his band of young men, protected by informers and hit-men, buoyed up with the hope of military forces and also, as he himself used to say, with promises from my colleague, surrounded by an army of colonists from Arretium and Faesulae; a crowd made distinct by men of a very different sort, those ruined by the calamity of the Sullan era.

Cicero, *Defence of Murena* 49 (for context, see **B66**)

Some of Sulla's colonies proved unsuccessful, whether because of the opposition they met locally or because of the inability of the settlers to adjust to the demands of rural life: many colonists settled in Etruria, especially at Arretium and Faesulae, were impoverished by the late sixties, and ended up joining Catiline's conspiracy.

B26 The Samnites in the late Republic: an imperial view

The Samnites previously made expeditions even as far as the country around Ardea in Latium and after that ravaged Campania itself. They had gained great power; for certainly the Campanians had learned to be ruled by other despots and they quickly submitted to the commands of the Samnites. But now the Samnites had been completely worn out by other peoples and last of all by the Romans when Sulla was dictator. And Sulla, when he had put an end to the insurrection of the Italians in many battles and saw that these people almost alone were remaining steadfast together and were as before on their border, ready to march against Rome, joined battle with them before the walls.

Some of them he cut down in the battle – he had given orders not to take prisoners – while the rest, who had thrown down their arms, they say about three or four thousand men, he led down to the Villa Publica in the Campus and imprisoned. Three days later, however, he sent soldiers among them and slaughtered the lot of them. He did not stop making proscriptions until he had either destroyed all the Samnites of note or banished them from Italy; to those who found fault with such excessive anger he said he had come to learn from experience that not even one Roman could ever live in peace as long as Samnites should remain steadfast together by themselves. And in fact their towns have now become just villages, while some have been completely abandoned: Bovianum, Aesernia, Panna, and Telesia close to Venafrum, and others like them, none of which deserves to be regarded as a town.

Strabo, *Geography* 5.4.11

Strabo stresses the warlike nature of the Samnites and their involvement in a number of conflicts against Rome, the final one being the Civil War. They had also been among the last ones to surrender to Rome at the end of the Social War, and the terms of their inclusion into the citizen body are not entirely clear. They joined the coalition of Sulla's enemies, and Sulla is said to have indulged into some anti-Samnite rhetoric: a convenient strategy, which helped to present the civil war as one in which an external enemy played a major role. Strabo's statement on the impact of Sulla on Samnium is not quite borne out by the archaeological evidence from the region for this period. It is worth bearing in mind that Strabo had no direct knowledge of Samnium, and that he relied on literary traditions that were closer to the events in time and space, and are lost to us.

B27   A municipal notable, 81 BC

[15] Sextus Roscius, the father of this man here, was a citizen (*municeps*) of the
free-town (*municipium*) of Ameria. By birth, by rank and by wealth he was easily
the leading person not only of his own *municipium* but also of that neighbourhood.
He was also distinguished by his influence and his social ties with men of the highest
rank. He not only had social ties with the Metelli, the Servilii and the Scipiones, but
also personal relations and intimacy with these families, which I mention by name, as
is right, because of their honour and distinction.

Cicero, *Defence of Roscius of Ameria* 15

The defence of Sextus Roscius from Ameria (a town in Umbria) was the first high-profile case that Cicero
took up in 80 BC. Roscius was charged with having killed his father, whose name was included on Sulla's
proscription list on the initiative of several friends of the Dictator: like many victims of the proscriptions,
he was a very wealthy individual, and in this passage Cicero insists both on the size of his assets and on
the range and quality of his connections with sectors of the Roman political élite. Roscius' predicament
was certainly not unparalled: there was in fact a long history of close personal and political relationships
between families of the Roman nobility and sectors of the local élites across the Italian peninsula.

B28   A municipal delegation visits Sulla, 81 BC

[25] Thus a decree of the town councillors (*decuriones*) was passed immediately, that ten
leading citizens should go to L. Sulla and inform him what sort of a man Sex. Roscius had
been, complain about the crime and the outrages committed by these men and beg him
to be willing to preserve the reputation of the dead father and the fortunes of the innocent
son. I ask you then, listen to the decree. [*The decree of the* decuriones *is read out, but is
not included in the text of the speech.*] The delegation reached the camp. It is understood,
jurors, as I have said earlier, that these crimes and outrages were committed without the
knowledge of L. Sulla. For Chrysogonus at once went to them in person and commissioned
certain noblemen (*nobiles*) to ask them not to approach Sulla and to promise them that
Chrysogonus would do everything they wished. [26] Now Chrysogonus had become so
frightened that he would rather die than that Sulla be informed about these matters.

Cicero, *Defence of Roscius of Ameria* 25–26

Italian cities are self-governing communities, and can take independent initiatives: in the instance described
here, the city council of Ameria responds to the news of Roscius' proscription by seeking an audience with
Sulla, who is still busy besieging the Etruscan city of Volaterrae, the last stronghold of his enemies. The
stated aim of their mission is to secure the rehabilitation of Roscius. However, the ten envoys do not get
access to the dictator. Two details are revealing of the political climate of the period: the notables of Ameria
do not seek an audience with the Senate, but approach the victor of the civil war; however, even getting
access to an individual of Sulla's importance can prove an impossible undertaking for those who lack the
right connections. In this context, the members of the 'inner circles' of major political figures have the
scope to play an increasingly significant role.

B29   Repercussions of civil war at Larinum, 82 BC

[25] After that flight, witness alike to his crime and to his guilty conscience, he [Aulus
Oppianicus] never dared expose himself to the courts, never to the laws, never to his
enemies, unless he was armed: but taking advantage of the victory and the violence under
Sulla, he swooped down upon Larinum with armed men to the utmost fear of all; he
removed the *quattuorviri* (chief magistrates) whom the townspeople had chosen. He said
that he and three others had been appointed by Sulla and that he had been ordered by
him to see to the proscription and execution of that Aulus Aurius who had made clear he

would prosecute him and bring a capital charge, together with another Aulus Aurius, his son Lucius, and Sextus Vibius, whom he was alleged to have used as an intermediary in bribing the informant. Thus they were put to death in a most cruel manner while the rest of the townspeople were terrified by him with no small fear of proscription and death.

Cicero, *Defence of Cluentius* 23–25

The civil war had far-reaching political ramifications across the Italian peninsula, which were not always directly caused by Sulla's personal intervention. In a defence speech delivered in 66 BC, Cicero discusses the aftermath of the war in the town of Larinum, in Southern Italy, where the local notable Oppianicus, who had fought in Sulla's ranks, returned at the helm of an armed contingent and took power in town. The seizing of power is closely linked with the proscription of a political opponent. It is unclear whether his claim that he had a mandate from Sulla had any substance. Cicero's emphasis on the fact that the local magistrates (*quattuorviri*, 'board of four') had been elected is a reminder of the importance of the dimension of local government, as well as an indictment of Oppianicus' conduct.

AFTER SULLA, 78–71 BC

B30   Funeral of Sulla, 78 BC

Many were eager and joined Lepidus to prevent Sulla's body from receiving the accustomed obsequies. Although Pompey found fault with Sulla, for Sulla left him alone of his friends out of his will, nevertheless driving off some by kindness and entreaty, others by threat, he had the body conveyed to Rome and provided security and honour for the burial. [2] And it is said that the women contributed such a huge quantity of spices that, apart from what was carried on two hundred and ten stretchers, a large image of Sulla himself and another of a lictor were moulded from costly frankincense and cinnamon. The day was cloudy in the early morning and they were expecting rain; they finally placed the body on the pyre about the ninth hour. [3] Then a strong wind rushed down on the pyre and roused many a flame. The remains were collected, while the pyre was smouldering and the fire going out, before heavy rain poured forth and continued through the night so that his good fortune seemed to remain with him and to take part in the funeral.

Plutarch, *Life of Sulla* 38.1–3

Sulla died in his villa in Campania, and his funeral turned into a major political event, no doubt carefully planned by the man himself. The procession of the body to Rome witnessed the attendance of large crowds, in which Sulla's veterans had of course a very prominent place. This passage of Plutarch's biography makes reference to the debate in the Senate on whether Sulla should be given a public funeral: Lepidus and others argued that it would be a disruption to public order. Catulus, Pompey, and the majority in the Senate took a different view, which prevailed (see also Plutarch, *Life of Pompey* 15.2-3; Appian, *Civil Wars* 1.105-107). Sulla's body was cremated: a breach from established practice, no doubt prompted by concerns that the body might eventually suffer the same fate as Marius', which was removed from the grave and dispersed into the river Anio by Sulla's supporters in 82 BC (Cicero, *On Laws* 2.56-57).

B31   Consulship of Lepidus and Catulus, 78 BC

a) Sulla died and the honour was decreed to him by the Senate that he should be buried in the Campus Martius. When M. Lepidus tried to rescind the measures of Sulla, he stirred up war. Driven from Italy by his colleague Q. Catulus, he died, vainly plotting war in Sardinia.

Livy, *Summaries* 90

b) [1] In the consulship of Marcus Lepidus and Quintus Catulus [78 BC], civil war was suppressed almost more speedily than it began. Yet the spark of that disturbance, however insignificant, flared up from the funeral pyre of Sulla. [2] Coveting political change, Lepidus was arrogantly preparing to rescind the acts of that great man; and not without justification, if he were able to do it without great disaster to the *res publica*. [3] For since Sulla as dictator, by right of war, had proscribed his enemies, when Lepidus recalled those who survived, for what were they being summoned other than war? And since Sulla assigned the estates of condemned men, and, though wrongfully seized, they were now being held by law, the demand for their restoration undermined the settled condition of the *res publica*. [4] It was expedient, therefore, that the *res publica*, sick and wounded as it was, should enjoy some respite, so that its wounds should not be cut open again in the very act of curing it. [5] When, therefore, Lepidus had terrified the state by his turbulent speeches, like a trumpet-call, he set out for Etruria and from there moved his arms and his army against the city. [6] But Lutatius Catulus and Pompey, leaders and standard-bearers of the Sullan despotism (*dominatio*), had already occupied the Milvian Bridge and the Janiculan hill with another army. Lepidus was at once driven back at his first attack by these commanders and was declared a public enemy (*hostis*) by the Senate. He fled without bloodshed to Etruria and from there withdrew to Sardinia where he died of disease and remorse.

Florus, *Summary of Roman History* 2. 11

Two compressed accounts of the rise and fall of M. Aemilius Lepidus, consul of 78 BC, who ended up joining an uprising in Etruria that he had been sent to repress: his decision to lead an army against Rome led to a robust military reaction on the Senate's part, in which the other consul of 78, Lutatius Catulus, and the young warlord Pompey the Great, then still a private citizen who was not even a member of the Senate, played a leading role. Lepidus' aims are in fact elusive: it is far from certain, for example, that he intended to dismantle the Sullan settlement as soon as he got into office. He was not in favour, of restoring the powers of the tribunes of the plebs (Granius Licinianus p. 33.14–34.4 Flemisch = p. 27.4–27.7 Criniti). – Note Florus' comparison of the *res publica* to a 'sick and wounded' body: the metaphor of the 'body politic' often occurs in the sources on the late Republic, contemporary and later alike.

B32   Social unrest and food shortage in Rome, 70s BC
a) By Hercules, I will honestly say this: I thought at that time that people in Rome were talking about nothing other than my quaestorship. At a time when the price of corn was very high I had dispatched a very large amount.

Cicero, *Defence of Plancius* 64

Cicero is boasting about his quaestorship in Sicily in 75 BC (see **E16**). Mention is also made, in Cicero, *Against Verres*, 2.3.215, of Hortensius making corn available cheaply to the people of Rome when he was aedile in 75 BC.

b) Nor was it counted a fault against M. Seius either that he gave the people corn at one *as* per *modius* at a time when the price was very high; for he freed himself from a considerable and long-standing unpopularity, at a price that was not disgraceful nor very great, since he was aedile at the time.

Cicero, *On Duties* 2.58

Marcus Seius was curule aedile in 74 BC. A *modius* is a Roman measure of capacity for dry goods, corresponding to a sixth of a *medimnus* (i.e. between 8 and 9 litres). In 122 BC Gaius Gracchus had sold corn at six-and-one-third *asses* for each *modius* (Bobbio Scholiast, p. 135 Stangl; Asconius, *Commentaries* p.8C.15-17); Seius' scheme was considerably more generous.

c) Crassus made a great sacrifice to Hercules, feasted the people at ten thousand tables, and made them an allowance of corn for three months.

Plutarch, *Life of Crassus* 12. 2

Plutarch places this intervention during the consulship of Crassus in 70 BC. This episode, along with the previous two, provides fragmentary, but clear evidence for difficulties in the corn supply of the city of Rome, which required extraordinary action from the government or from private individuals, such as the famously wealthy M. Licinius Crassus.

B33   The tribune Macer addresses the Roman people, 73 BC
[1] 'Citizens of Rome, you are perfectly well aware of the difference between the rights bequeathed to you by your ancestors and this state of slavery engineered by Sulla. I need not, therefore, address you at length and inform you of how many times and because of what wrongs the plebs took up arms and seceded from the patricians; nor of how they created the tribunes of the plebs to safeguard all their rights. [2] Now all I have to do is to encourage you and to lead you on the path by which I believe we must get our liberty back. [3] Nor do I overlook the vast resources of the nobility whose despotism (*dominatio*) I seek to overthrow, single-handed and powerless, clad in the empty illusion of magistracy. I know too how much more safely a faction (*factio*) of wicked men operates than upright men standing alone. [4] But apart from the bright hope that I have in you, which has outweighed my fear, I have decided that defeat in the struggle for liberty is better for a brave man than never to have fought at all. …

[9] When Sulla died, who had imposed this criminal slavery upon you, you thought your troubles were at an end: but then came Catulus, far more savage. [10] An uprising interrupted the consulship of Brutus and Mamercus [77 BC]. Then C. Curio exercised despotism (*dominatio*) to the extent of ruining an innocent tribune. [11] Last year you witnessed the ferocity with which Lucullus attacked L. Quintius. Finally, look at the turmoil now being stirred up against me! This action of theirs will certainly turn out to have been futile, if they bring about the end of their own despotism (*dominatio*) before you put an end to your own slavery; especially since in this struggle of citizen with citizen other reasons are alleged, but on both sides the fight is about despotism (*dominatio*) over you. [12] Other matters have flared up from time to time, arising from indiscipline or hatred or greed. One thing only has remained constant, which was coveted by both sides and has been snatched away for the future: the tribunician power, the weapon that our ancestors fashioned in defence of freedom. [13] I advise you, I beg you, to take good heed of this and not, by changing the names of things to suit your own cowardice, to call slavery 'leisure' (*otium*). To enjoy this very leisure (*otium*) now is not some concession gained, if wickedness has overcome truth and honesty: you would still have had it, if you had remained entirely passive. Now they are on their guard, and if you are not victorious, they will oppress you more terribly, since wrongdoing is always more secure the wider it extends. …

[26] Some apathy has gripped you. As a result you are stirred neither by glory nor by outrage. In your present spiritless condition you have changed your view of everything and think you have freedom in abundance, I suppose, because your backs are spared the rod and you are allowed to come and go as you please – the gifts of your rich masters. [27] Now the country people do not have these same privileges, but

are slaughtered amid the quarrels of the powerful and are sent as gifts to magistrates in the provinces. [28] Thus, battle is fought and victory is won for the few; the plebs, whatever happens, are treated as the conquered and this will become truer every day, if they make greater effort to retain their despotism (*dominatio*) than you to regain your freedom.'

Sallust, *Histories* 3.34.1–4, 9–13, 26–28, with omissions, McG = 3.15 R.

Macer, tribune of the plebs in 73 BC (usually identified with the noted Roman annalist C. Licinius Macer), catalogues the woes of the Roman people under the Sullan regime and records attempts to restore their rights to the tribunes. Those rights would be fully restored in 70 BC by a statute sponsored by Crassus and Pompey, with momentous consequences. – As ever in ancient historiography, the correspondence between Sallust's version of this speech and Macer's statements before the people is a matter for conjecture at best. It is also impossible to establish what place this speech had in the wider framework of the third book of Sallust's *Histories,* which does not survive. Moreover, it is important not to lose sight of the highly partisan viewpoint that is put forward here: the victory of Sulla is denounced as the beginning of an age of slavery for the Roman people, made even more unbearable by those who came to prominence after Sulla, and from which Macer is undertaking to set the people free. – We are presented with a disturbing picture of civil discord, which must have had special resonance with Sallust's contemporary readers in the triumviral period: if the plebs have effectively been enslaved by their masters, the only way forward is an effort of liberation, which may conceivably develop into civil strife. The language employed by Macer leaves that possibility open, quite apart from the emphasis on the restoration of the tribunician powers. Macer became praetor in 68 BC, was accused before the praetor Cicero on corruption charges in 66 BC, and committed suicide.

The Sertorian War

B34   Pompey is given a command against Sertorius, 77 BC
[62] What could be so unusual than that when there were two distinguished and brave consuls, a Roman equestrian should be sent to a very serious and formidable war as proconsul? Sent he was. Indeed at that time when someone in the senate said, 'A private citizen ought not to be sent as proconsul', L. Philippus is reported to have said: 'in his opinion he was sending Pompey not as proconsul, but instead of the consuls'. So great was the expectation of a successful outcome placed in him that the function of two consuls was entrusted to the talents of a single young man.

Cicero, *On the Manilian Law / On Pompey's Command* 62

The witticism of Philippus, *non proconsule sed pro consulibus,* became much quoted (see Cicero, *Philippics* 11.18). Pompey's career trajectory had already been most unusual, after his involvement in the civil war, his triumph in 81 BC, and his later participation in the campaign against Lepidus. The decision to deploy him in the campaign against Sertorius was not just driven by his outstanding military record, as Cicero claims in his laudatory speech, but by the unwillingness of some senior figures to take up the task and by the hope of many members of the Senate that Pompey might lose his life in the war. The 'two distinguished and brave consuls' who declined the command against Sertorius were Decimus Junius Brutus and Mamercus Aemilius Lepidus Livianus, who held the magistracy in 77 BC (on their ineptitude and for further discussion of Catulus' comment see Plutarch, *Life of Pompey* 17). – The potential 'monarchic' implications of Cicero's argument must not have been lost on many members of his audience.

B35   Speech of C. Aurelius Cotta to the Roman people, 75 BC
[A] A few days later Cotta having changed into clothes of mourning and very much distressed, because in place of the good will longed for [...corrupt text...], spoke at an assembly (*contio*) of the people in this way:
[1] 'Citizens of Rome, many have been the dangers at home and abroad that I have met, many the adversities; some of them I have endured, some I have repulsed with the help of the gods and by my own courage. In all of them my resolve never fell short of what I had to, nor did my effort fail what I had decided to do; failures and successes altered my resources not my character. [2] But, by contrast, in these present troubles good fortune has deserted me and taken everything with it. Furthermore old age, burdensome in itself, is doubling my anxiety; my life's course now run, it is not possible for me, in my wretched misfortune, to hope even for an honourable death. [3] For if I am your murderer, and if, having been born a second time here, I hold cheap my household gods, my country and the highest command (*imperium*), what torture would be sufficient for me if I were living, what punishment if I were dead? Indeed, with this crime of mine I have surpassed all the famous punishments of the damned.

[4] 'From early manhood I have passed my life before your gaze, as a private citizen and in magistracies; those who wished, have made use of my tongue, my advice and my money; and I have not put my talent for public speaking or my intelligence to evil uses. Most avid for private gratitude (*gratia*), I have incurred grave personal enmities on behalf of the *res publica*; and when I was overcome together with it, and, lacking help from others, was expecting worse misfortunes, you, the citizens of Rome, gave me back again my country and my household gods, together with very great status (*dignitas*). [5] For these favours I would scarcely seem sufficiently grateful even if I were to give my life for each of you. Which I cannot; for life and death are subject to the laws of nature; but to live without disgrace among one's fellow-citizens, with fame and fortune intact, that is a thing which may be given and received as a gift.

[6] 'You have elected us consuls, citizens of Rome, when the *res publica* is hampered by very great difficulties both at home and abroad. Our commanders in Spain are demanding pay, soldiers, weapons and food; and the situation compels this, since with the defection of the allies and the flight of Sertorius over the mountains they can neither engage in battle with the enemy nor obtain what they need. [7] Armies are being maintained in the provinces of Asia and Cilicia because of the excessive strength of Mithridates, Macedonia is full of enemies, and no less the coastal areas of Italy and of the provinces, while in the meantime our revenues, small and unreliable because of the wars, scarcely meet a portion of our expenses: thus we sail with a fleet, smaller than that which previously used to protect our food supplies,. [8] If these troubles have been brought on by our deceit or laziness, go ahead as your anger demands, exact punishment; but if it is our general misfortune that afflicts us more, why do you embark on actions unworthy of yourselves, of us and of the *res publica*?

[9] 'And what is more, I, whose age brings death closer, do not beg to be spared it, if by my death some inconvenience is removed from you; nor, given the nature of my aging body, is there any more honourable way for me to put an end to my life in the near future than for the sake of your well-being. [10] Behold, here I am C. Cotta the consul; I do what our ancestors often did in grim wars; I consecrate and give myself

up for the *res publica.* [11] Look around then for one to whom you may entrust her; for no good man will want such an honour, when he must render account for fortune, for the sea and for war waged by others, or must die in disgrace. [12] Only bear this in mind, that I was not slain because of crime or avarice but that I gave my life willingly as a gift for the greatest benefits. [13] For your own sakes, citizens, and for the glory of your ancestors, endure adversity and take thought for the interests of the *res publica.* [14] The greatest empire involves great anxiety, many huge burdens; in vain do you repudiate them and look for the affluence of peace, when all provinces, kingdoms, lands and seas are hostile or exhausted by wars.'

Sallust, *Histories* 2.44 McG = 43 R.

This speech to the people of C. Aurelius Cotta, consul in 75, is no doubt a free creation of Sallust, who attached great weight to the role of oratory in his historical works, as was also the case with his great model, the Athenian historian Thucydides. Cotta is speaking as the elder statesman who has been entrusted with a burdensome task at a time of great difficulty for the Republic, but is prepared to make the ultimate sacrifice if necessary. No continuous narrative survives for the seventies; much of Sallust's *Histories* is lost. Cotta's speech is highly partisan, and should not be taken as a reliable factual account: however, the emphasis on the instability of the Empire, both in the West and in the East, is corroborated by references to some specific circumstances, and should be taken seriously. The reference to the unstable flow of the revenues generated by the empire is also notable. The overall message of the speech is that the empire presents a number of challenges that have not been fully addressed.

B36   Indigenous resistance to Pompey's campaign in Spain against Sertorius, 75 BC

Whenever the men set off to war or brigandage, their mothers used to remind them of the warlike deeds of their fathers when they sang of their brave achievements. When it was discovered that Pompey was approaching with an army intent on war, the older men counselled peace and that they should carry out his orders. When the women achieved nothing by refusal, they separated from the men and took up arms. Having seized as secure a position as they could near Meo[riga?], they called upon the men to witness that they were destitute of country, of those able give birth and of freedom and that therefore breastfeeding, giving birth and all the other duties of women were left to the men. Roused by these actions the young men [...] the decisions of their elders ...

Sallust, *Histories* 2.75 McG = 79 R.

Sallust's *Histories* devoted much attention to the war against Sertorius: this remarkable anecdote, whose interpretation is much complicated by the fragmentary context in which it is told, portrays the reactions of the Celtiberian allies of Sertorius to the coming of Pompey, and shows the women taking a leading role in spurring their men to resistance, against the advice of the elders. The fragment belongs in the narrative of the operations in Spain in the late months of 75.

B37   Letter of Pompey to the Senate, 75 BC

[1] 'If it had been against you and my country and my household gods that I had undertaken all the toil and dangers which have accompanied the many occasions since my early manhood when under my leadership the most dangerous enemies have been routed and safety secured for you, you could have passed no more severe decree against me in my absence, conscript fathers, than you have been doing up to now. In defiance of the normal age limits I have been thrust out to a most savage war with an army of the most distinguished service. And yet you have done all you could to

destroy us by famine, the most miserable of all deaths. [2] Is this what the Roman people expected when they sent their sons to war? Are these the rewards for wounds and blood so often shed for the *res publica*? Weary of writing and sending deputations, I have used up all my personal wealth and private means of credit, and all the time, over the space of three years, you have barely granted me the expenses of one. [3] By the immortal gods, do you think I am taking the place of the treasury, or can maintain an army without pay and provisions?

[4] 'In truth, I admit that I set out for this war with more enthusiasm than sense, given that receiving a titular command (*imperium*) from you, within forty days I had commissioned an army and driven an enemy, which was already at Italy's throat, from the Alps to Spain. I opened up a route through the Alps, different from Hannibal's but more convenient for us. [5] I recovered Gaul, the Pyrenees, Lacetania and the Indigetes. I withstood the first attack of the victorious Sertorius with raw and much outnumbered forces. I passed the winter in camp surrounded by the fiercest enemies, neither in towns nor by increasing my own popularity. [6] So why should I catalogue the battles, the winter forays, the towns destroyed or recovered, since actions speak louder than words? The capture of the enemy camp at the Sucro and the battle at the river Turia and the destruction of the enemy commander C. Herennius, together with his army, and the city of Valentia are sufficiently well known to you. In exchange for them, grateful fathers, you present me with famine and shortage.

[7] 'Thus the position for my army and the enemy's is the same; for pay is given to neither of them; and either of them, if victorious, can come to Italy. [8] I remind you of this and ask you to take notice of it, and not to compel me to find a way out of my difficulties by abandoning the interests of the state for my own. [9] Nearer Spain, so far as it is not occupied by the enemy, we or Sertorius have laid waste with terrible carnage, except for the coastal cities; it is, what is more, an expense and a burden for us. Last year Gaul provided Metellus' army with pay and provisions; now, because of a bad harvest, it is hardly able to support itself. I have used up not only my own property, but my credit as well. [10] You are my last resort: if you do not help, against my wishes and as I have already warned you, my army will cross over from here to Italy and bring with it the whole Spanish war.'

This letter was read in the senate at the beginning of the following year. But the consuls agreed between themselves the provinces allotted by the Senate: Cotta took Cisalpine Gaul, Octavius Cilicia. Then the next consuls, L. Lucullus and M. Cotta, gravely disturbed by the letter and messages of Pompey, not only because of the favour (*gratia*) to be won in such an important matter, but also because if the army was brought back to Italy they would have neither glory nor status (*dignitas*), exerted all their efforts to provide pay and provisions. The nobility, the majority of whom were then openly expressing their eagerness for war and backing their words with deeds, gave them energetic support.

Sallust, Histories 2.82 McG = 86 R.

This extraordinary text plays a role that is broadly comparable to that of a speech, as it adds a further voice to the narrative presented by Sallust, and furthers the depth of the historical account. In this case, however, it can be assumed with a fair degree of likelihood that a version of this text was archived in the

Senate records. The message serves three purposes: providing an account of the military operations and of Pompey's achievements (in spite of the rhetorical claim that actions speak louder than words); complaining at length about the failure of the Senate to provide Pompey with suitable support; and threatening hostile actions if the request were not heeded. The prospect of a war against the Senate is clearly mooted, and leads to the acceptance of Pompey's request. – The letter draws attention to two issues of wider significance: the serious difficulties in securing adequate supplies to the army in a provincial war, and Pompey's ability to fund the campaign with his own funds, albeit grudgingly. There was a precedent for that: in 82 BC, in the early stages of the civil war, he had raised a private army, which proved the crucial element in establishing his profile on the military and political scene.

B38   Metellus celebrates victory over Sertorius at Segontia, 74 BC

[1] But Metellus, having returned after a year to Farther Spain, was greeted with great honour by all, both men and women, who rushed through streets and buildings from everywhere around to see him. [2] When the quaestor C. Urbinius and others, knowing his wishes, had invited him to dinner, they took care of him in a manner beyond normal Roman practice and indeed that of any human beings. The house was decked with tapestries and decorations, stages were erected for the shows of actors; at the same time the floor was strewn with saffron, and other features characteristic of a famous temple. [3] In addition to that, when he was seated, a statue of Victory, let down by a rope and with mechanically contrived sound of thunder, would place a crown on his head; then when he arrived he was worshipped with incense as if he were a god. [4] The victor's toga (*toga picta*) was generally his dress when he was reclining at table, banquets were extremely elaborate with fare not only from the entire province, but over the sea from Mauretania, with many kinds of birds and wild beasts previously unknown. By these actions Metellus diminished a considerable part of his glory, especially among old-fashioned and pious men who reckoned such actions arrogant, excessive and unworthy of Roman rule (*imperium*).

Sallust, *Histories* 2.59 McG = 3.10 R.

Pompey was not the only Roman commander who fought successfully against Sertorius. In this fragment of the *Histories* Sallust records a success of Q. Caecilius Metellus Pius and the attention he commanded in the province of Farther Spain for his achievements: his main aim, however, is to focus on the lavish honours he received from the quaestor C. Urbinius: an instance of unrestrained extravagance that conveys a wider message about the lack of moral standards of large sectors of Roman society – a topical theme in Sallust's work. Quite apart from the moralizing point, this anecdote provides valuable evidence for the use and display of wealth in a provincial setting, and for the far-reaching political consequences it can have in shaping the behaviour, standing, and aspirations of members of the Roman élite. – On Metellus' celebrations see also Plutarch, *Life of Sertorius* 22.1-3.

B39   An *aureus* celebrating Pompey's triumph on Sertorius, 71 BC

Obv: Head of Africa, wearing an elephant's skin; on the left, a jug with a handle;
        on the right, a *lituus*; Laurel-wreath as border.
        MAGNVS ['Great']
Rev: Pompey in triumphal four-horse chariot, right, holding branch in the right
        hand; above, flying Victory with wreath.
        PROCOS. [proconsul]

> *RRC* 402/1a = Ghey, Leins & Crawford 2010, 402.1.1 = BM 1867,0101.584

In this coin issue Pompey celebrates and depicts his own triumph after the campaign against Sertorius: in doing so, he emphasizes his legal position as proconsul and the lawfulness of his involvement in the war, which is stressed by the presence of augural symbols (see above, **B17**). His gentilician, *Pompeius*, is replaced by *Magnus*, 'Great', a nickname that he received during the Sullan civil war, and readily became a *cognomen*. The presence of the personification of Africa is probably a reference to Pompey's very successful campaign in North Africa during the Civil War, which had led to his first triumph being held in March 81 BC, when he was still a private citizen.

THE SLAVE REVOLT IN SOUTHERN ITALY

B40   Spartacus and his followers

[1] One can put up with the disgrace of a war against slaves; for although by fortune they are liable to everything, yet they are as it were a second class of human beings and are adopted into the benefits of our freedom: I do not know by what name I should called the war stirred up under the leadership of Spartacus; [2] for since slaves were the soldiers, and gladiators gave the orders, the former men of the lowest sort, the latter of the worst, they increased the disaster for the Romans by such insults. [3] Spartacus, Crixus and Oenomaus having broken out of the gladiatorial school of Lentulus with thirty or rather more men of the same condition escaped from Capua. Summoning slaves to their standard, they quickly gathered more than ten thousand men. These men were happy just to have escaped but then they wanted to gain revenge.

[4] They chose as their first base Mount Vesuvius as though they were wild beasts. They were besieged there by Clodius Glaber, but they slid down by means of ropes made of vine twigs through gaps in the hollow of the mountain and got down to its very bottom. They made an unseen exit and seized by a sudden attack the camp of the commander who was not expecting anything of this sort. [5] Then they attacked other camps, that of Varinius, then that of Thorius; they ranged over the whole of Campania. Not content with the devastation of houses and villages they ravaged Nola, Nuceria, Thurii and Metapontum with terrifying slaughter. [6] With forces flocking to them day by day they had by now become a regular army. They fashioned for themselves crude shields with wickerwork and animal pelts and swords and weapons from the melted down iron of slave prisons. [7] So that nothing proper should be missing from their regular army, cavalry was organized by taming herds they came upon and they brought to their leader the rods of office (*fasces*) and insignia captured from praetors. [8] Nor did that man refuse them; he had been a Thracian mercenary, then a soldier; a soldier, then a deserter; after that a highway robber and then, by virtue of his strength, a gladiator. [9] Furthermore, he celebrated the funerals of leaders who had been killed in battle with the funeral rites of Roman commanders and he ordered prisoners to fight with weapons around the pyre as though he would clearly wipe out completely

all past disgrace if, from being a gladiator, he became the giver of games. [10] Next he attacked consular armies too: he defeated the army of Lentulus in the Apennines and he destroyed the camp of Publius Crassus at Mutina. [11] Encouraged by these victories he contemplated invading Rome – a sufficient disgrace for us. [12] Finally the full resources of the empire were gathered against the heavy-armed gladiator and Licinius Crassus reclaimed Roman honour.

Florus, *Summary of Roman History* 2.8.20.1–12

A highly compressed account of the Spartacus war, probably based on the lost narrative of Livy: the focus of the narrative is on the outbreak of the conflict and the early development of Spartacus' offensive, and on its swift impact across Southern Italy; much less so on the reaction of the *res publica*. Spartacus' army is an army of non-citizens, but the remarkable ability of his leader – who had direct military experience before being enslaved – readily gives it the capability and semblance of a regular force, which poses a real, if short-lived existential threat to Rome. – For a powerful, if fragmentary account of an early success of Spartacus cf. Sallust, *Histories* 3.64 McG = 42 R. A full narrative of the war may be found in Plutarch, *Life of Crassus* 8-11.

B41 The Roman surge, 73 BC

[119] When the Romans in the city heard of the siege and thought of the disgrace should their war with the gladiators become prolonged, they appointed Pompey, who had recently arrived from Spain, as an additional commander for the campaign, believing that the task of dealing with Spartacus was now difficult and substantial. [120] As a result of this appointment Crassus, to prevent the glory of the war being Pompey's, pressed on urgently by every means and attacked Spartacus, while Spartacus, deciding to anticipate Pompey, invited Crassus to come to terms. When Crassus paid no attention, Spartacus decided to make a desperate attempt and forced a way through the encircling fortifications with his whole army, including the cavalry which had by now arrived. He then retreated towards Brundisium, with Crassus in pursuit. But when he discovered that Lucullus had returned to Brundisium after his victory over Mithridates, he despaired of everything, and, at the head of a still large force, joined battle with Crassus. The battle was long and grimly contested, since so many tens of thousands had no hope. Spartacus himself was wounded with a spear-thrust in the thigh, but went down on one knee, held his shield in front of him, and fought off his attackers until he and a great number of his followers were encircled and fell. The rest of his army was already in disorder and being cut down in huge numbers; consequently the death toll of the one side was not easy to count, while that of the Romans was around a thousand. Spartacus' body was never found. There was still a very large number in the mountains, fugitives from the battle; Crassus advanced against them. They formed themselves into four groups and kept up their resistance until they were all killed except for six thousand, who were taken prisoner and crucified, all the way along the road from Rome to Capua.

Appian, *Civil Wars* 1.119–120 (continued in **B43a**)

Like Florus, Appian understands Spartacus' campaign as an offensive against Rome. The turning point of the war is the combined effect of Pompey's return to Rome from Spain and of the growing awareness of the extent of the threat presented by the slave army. Pompey's intervention gives further momentum to the campaign that was already being waged by Crassus. Defeating Spartacus' army was not the final act of the campaign: chasing and executing any runaway slave that had joined Spartacus had to be its necessary endpoint, and the gruesome punishment that the fugitives faced stood as a warning against any similar attempt. As Appian notes, those who fought on Spartacus' side were aware that defeat would entail that outcome: fighting an army of men that had nothing to lose was an especially tough challenge.

B42 M. Crassus takes rapid action against Spartacus to anticipate Pompey

a) [21] After this Pompey remained in Spain long enough to quell the greatest disturbances and to settle and to resolve the most explosive situations. He then led his army back to Italy, coming by chance upon the slave war, which was then at its height. That is why Crassus, who was in command, recklessly pressed on with the battle, and was quite successful, killing twelve thousand three hundred of the enemy. But even in this success fortune somehow or other brought in Pompey; for five thousand fugitives from the battle came up against him and he completely annihilated them; he then got in before Crassus with a despatch to the Senate: that, while Crassus had defeated the slaves in pitched battle, he had rooted out the war altogether. But as for Spain and the war against Sertorius no one would have said, even as a joke, that anyone but Pompey had accomplished the whole business.

Plutarch, *Life of Pompey* 21

b) Crassus, therefore, pressed on to start the battle himself, and having encamped near the enemy, began to dig a trench. The slaves leaped into this and began to fight with those who were working there. [6] Since fresh men from both sides kept coming to help their comrades, Spartacus saw what the situation required, and drew up his whole army in order of battle. First, when his horse was brought to him, he drew his sword, and said that if he won the day he would have many fine horses of the enemies, but that if he lost it he would not want any – and he slew his horse. Then, pushing his way towards Crassus himself through many flying weapons and wounded men, he did not manage to reach him, but slew two centurions, who had attacked him together. [7] Finally, while those around him were fleeing, he stood alone, surrounded by a multitude of enemies, he was cut down as he was still defending himself. Although Crassus had been fortunate, had shown excellent military leadership, and had exposed his person to danger, still his success did not fail to enhance the reputation of Pompey. For the fugitives from the battle encountered that commander and were massacred, so he could write to the Senate that in open battle, indeed, Crassus had defeated the fugitives, but that he himself had extirpated the root of the war. [8] Pompey therefore celebrated a splendid triumph for his victories over Sertorius and in Spain, but Crassus, for all his self-approval, did not venture to ask for the great triumph, and it was thought ignoble and mean in him to celebrate even the minor triumph on foot, called the ovation, for a war against slaves.

Plutarch, *Life of Crassus* 11.5–8

The relationship between Crassus and Pompey was a complex, and often difficult, one for the best part of their careers: their involvement in the Spartacus War was arguably the starting point of a string of difficulties, as Pompey's late participation in the conflict overshadowed, to the eyes of some, the importance of Crassus' contribution to the war effort. Effective and quick communication with the Senate may have played a part in shaping the perception that Pompey had made a crucial contribution to the Roman success. The controversy over their respective merits played a significant role in complicating their relationship in 70 BC, when they both held the consulship. – Cf. Plutarch, *Life of Marcellus* 22, for the difference between a triumph and an *ovatio*.

A YEAR OF CHANGES: 70 BC

B43   Consulship of Pompey and Crassus, 70 BC

a) Crassus achieved this in six months, and this immediately gave rise to fierce rivalry with Pompey for honours. Crassus did not dismiss his army, for Pompey did not either. Both announced their candidacy for the consulship, Crassus having been praetor in accordance with the law of Sulla, while Pompey had been neither praetor nor quaestor, being but thirty-four years old; he had promised the tribunes that he would restore many of their powers to their previous state. Having been elected consuls, they did not even then dismiss their armies, which they had near the city, each offering an excuse: Pompey that he was awaiting the return of Metellus for the Spanish triumph, while Crassus said that it was necessary for Pompey to dismiss his army first.

Appian, *Civil Wars* 1. 121 (continued from **B41**)

The consulship of Pompey and Crassus followed their major achievements against Sertorius and Spartacus respectively, and is often depicted as the dysfunctional cooperation of two men that did not like or trust each other: Appian's anecdote plays into this theme, and draws attention to the role that not yet demobilized armies can have in a tense political context. In fact, 70 BC was a year of substantial political and legislative developments, in which both consuls played a significant role: the restoration of the tribunate and the reform of the lawcourts.

b) Pompey was consul designate for the first time with M. Crassus. When Pompey was about to enter that magistracy, since through his lengthy military service he was inexperienced in conducting and consulting the Senate and in city affairs, he asked his close friend M. Varro to write a handbook – *Eisagogikos* is what Varro himself entitles it – so that he could learn from it what he ought to do and say when he was consulting the Senate.

Aulus Gellius, *Attic Nights* 14.7.1–2

The handbook called *Eisagogikos* ('Introductory [text]') does not survive: this anecdote shows the long-standing connection between Pompey and Varro, and gives a useful example of the importance that years of experience in the Senate could have in establishing a satisfactory degree of political and legislative knowledge. Pompey sensibly sought the advice of Varro, who was both a senator (he had been quaestor in 86/85 BC) and one of the most learned men of his generation (see **H25–H30**). The developing genres of antiquarian writing that are widely attested in late Republican Rome are not just evidence for a new aspect of Roman intellectual life; they also provided new or aspiring members of the political élite with valuable opportunities to fill the gap in expertise and awareness that their peers from established senatorial families or with a more solid background in public office could more easily bridge.

c) When the magistracy of Pompey was on the point of expiring, but the disagreement with Crassus was increasing, a certain Gaius Aurelius, an *eques*, who had spent a life without involvement in public affairs, during an assembly (*contio*) went up to the rostra and stepped forward to say that Jupiter had appeared to him in a dream and ordered him to say to the consuls that they should not lay down their office before becoming friends with one another. [2] When these words had been spoken, Pompey stood in silence, but Crassus, taking the initiative, greeted him with his right hand and addressed him. 'I do not think, citizens' he said, 'that I am doing anything ignoble or mean, in giving in first to Pompey, whom you saw fit to call Magnus when his beard had not yet grown, to whom you voted two triumphs when he was not yet a member of the Senate'. At this they were reconciled and laid down their magistracy.

Plutarch, *Life of Pompey* 23.1–2

The public reconciliation between the two consuls of 70 BC did not have lasting consequences; it took the intervention of Julius Caesar, a decade later, to bring about a political partnership between two men who shared many enemies within the Senate. – The use of a dream in which a god is said to have urged the reconciliation between the two men is an especially interesting case of the use of a religious argument in the context of a *contio*. Speculating on the background of that curious episode is unhelpful; what it is clear is it must have had genuine appeal on many members of the audience. – The same story is told in Plutarch, *Life of Crassus* 12.3-4.

B44   Restoration of tribunician powers, 70 BC
a) In fact, when Pompey himself held his first assembly (*contio*) near the city as consul designate, at which he made clear that he would restore the powers of the tribunes, something that appeared to be widely expected, there was a loud noise at this and an approving murmur from the assembly (*contio*).

Cicero, *Against Verres* 1.45

b) The city (*civitas*) tolerated, as long as it had to, that monarchical despotism (*regia dominatio*) of yours in the courts and in the *res publica* as a whole; but on the day on which the tribunes of the plebs were restored to the Roman people, all those things, though you may not yet realize it, were taken and snatched away from you.

Cicero, *Against Verres* 2.5.175

c) For after the power of the tribunes had been restored in the consulship of Pompey and M. Crassus, young men, whose age and temperament made them militant and high-spirited, gained that high office; they began by making accusations against the Senate to stir up the plebs; they then inflamed them further by giving handouts and making promises: they thereby became distinguished and powerful themselves.

Sallust, *Catiline's War* 38.1

These three passages provide glimpses into three different responses to the restoration of the powers of the tribunes in 70 BC. Pompey had not been among those who had advocated it, but endorsed the reform shortly after the beginning of his time in office. Significantly, he chose a *contio* to make that announcement. Cicero acknowledges the major political impact of that reform in the *Verrines*, which he gave a few months later: as he points out to his opponent Hortensius, the whole climate has suddenly shifted, and that change also had a considerable impact on Verres' position, as it further undermined senatorial control over the courts. Sallust makes a disparaging comment on the political effect of the reform: by reviving the tribunate it unleashed a new generation of demagogues, who were prepared to exploit the magistracy to further their career prospects.

B45   *Lex Aurelia* and the jury-courts, 70 BC
[174] Am I able to put before the court a matter more fully judged, to bring before it a defendant more wholly condemned? But condemned by whose judgement! Why, clearly by the judgement of those whom the people, who are wanting stricter courts, think ought to be judging these matters; the people are now clearly demanding such men as jurors; and a statute that we have them as jurors has been promulgated by

a man not of our sort, not coming from an equestrian background, but one of the noblest birth.

Cicero, *Against Verres* 2.2.174

Calls for a reform of the lawcourts are echoed in various parts of Cicero's case against Verres, which was presented before a jury of senators: after the restoration of the tribunate, many are invoking stricter courts, which are not under the exclusive control of the senatorial order (cf. also Cicero, *Against Verres*, 2.3.223 and **G42**). In this passage the law presented by the praetor M. Aurelius Cotta for the reform of the court is briefly alluded to; Cicero stresses that he hails (unlike him) from a distinguished senatorial family. – The law was passed later in the year (see also Velleius Paterculus, *Histories* 2.32.3): it created permanent juries with a mixed membership, consisting of senators, equestrians, and *tribuni aerarii* ('tribunes of the treasury'): the definition of the latter category is uncertain, but it is likely that included individuals whose census was just below that of the equestrian order. In practice, therefore, the courts were no longer under senatorial control.

B46   Census of 70 BC
a) Cn. Lentulus and L. Gellius conducted a severe census, removing sixty-four from the Senate. When they had completed the *lustrum*, 900,000 citizens were enrolled.

Livy, *Summaries* 98

Another manuscript records the figure of 950,000 citizens. On census figures see **G24** and note.

b) In the third year of the 177th Olympiad [70 BC], 910,000 Romans were enrolled at the census.

Phlegon, *Olympiads*, *FGrH* 257 F12

c) I shall not allow this case to be decided at a time when this multitude of people of all Italy, which has gathered here at one time from all over for the purpose of elections, of the games and of the census, has departed from Rome.

Cicero, *Against Verres* 1.54

d) *Denarius*, 70 BC

Obv: Heads of Honos and Virtus, right
        HO; VIRT; KALENI. [Honour; Virtue; of (Q. Fufius) Calenus]
Rev: Italia on left and Roma on right clasping hands; between clasped hands,
        cornucopia (horn of plenty); behind Italia, *caduceus* (winged staff); Roma
        wears diadem, holding *fasces* in the left hand and placing her foot on a globe
        ITA; RO; CORDI. [Italy; Rome; of (Mucius Scaevola) Cordus]

    RRC 403 = Ghey, Leins & Crawford 2010, 403.1.2 = BM 1843,0116.530

70 BC was a crucial year for a number of reasons. The joint consulship of Pompey and Crassus brought about a series of major political and legislative developments; the census that began in the same year marked the completion of the enfranchisement of the allies, who after that enrolment were able to cast their vote in the *comitia centuriata*, the assembly that elected the senior magistrates. It also led to the expulsion from the Senate of 64 members, barely more than a decade after the appointment of 300 new senators by Sulla. It is unclear how many of those new appointees were expelled in 70 BC: only a handful of names are on record for both lists. – This 'severe' census was the last one to be successfully completed before that of 28 BC carried out by Caesar (Octavianus; he was given the name Augustus on 16 January 27 BC) and Marcus Vipsanius Agrippa. The feature to note here is the number of citizens: in the census of 86/85 BC the number of citizens was 463,000 (Jerome, p. 151 Helm). There are a considerable number of imponderables: the necessity for personal presence in Rome (though given the numbers this was surely not a practical possibility), how far, given the political situation, 'new citizens' were enrolled, and the fact that by this time assignment to a property class (*classis*) was of practical significance only to the wealthy. – A *denarius* struck in 70 BC (d) vividly conveys the political and ideological significance of the census: the personifications of Italy and Rome hold hands, in a gesture that some have read as a sign of reconciliation, and others as an indication that concord has been restored under Rome's hegemony. At any rate, the new state of affairs is supposed to bring about prosperity, symbolized by the *cornucopia.*

POLITICAL FRONTS, HOME AND AWAY: 69–64 BC

B47 The aedileship of Marcus Tullius Cicero, 69 BC

Now I am aedile elect. I fully understand the responsibility I have received from the Roman people: in my celebration, therefore, of the holy festival of Ceres, Liber and Libera, I shall be meticulous and ceremonious in the extreme. By holding games, which many will attend in honour of Mother Flora, I shall intercede with her for the people and community of Rome. With the utmost solemn devotion I shall perform the most ancient festival of all, the earliest to be given the name of 'Roman', in honour of Jupiter, Juno and Minerva. The maintenance of our sacred buildings has been entrusted to my care. And so, indeed, has the protection of the whole of our city.

Cicero, *Against Verres* 2.5.36

Cicero delivered the *Verrines* as aedile elect: he was due to take office at the beginning of 69 BC. In this passage he briefly refers to the duties that await him: the organization of some major religious festivals and the upkeep of the temples play a central role. Cicero's emphasis on the protection to the welfare of the city that the effective fulfillment of these tasks can enable is not merely rhetorical. – Cf. Cicero, *Against Verres* 1.18-25, where Verres' attempt to prevent his election by resorting to bribery is recalled in emphatic terms.

B48 The Eastern Front, 60s BC

In 69 BC L. Licinius Lucullus had invaded Armenia, without any specific authority. Having reported earlier to the senate the conquest of Pontus and requested the senatorial commission of ten to organize the country, he was now relieved of the province of Asia and in 68 BC Cilicia was withdrawn from him. Although he had captured the capital of Armenia, Tigranocerta, he was experiencing difficulties with his troops and with his brother-in-law, Publius Clodius, who was fomenting trouble.

[33.4] When the soldiers were in this state of mind, the popular leaders (*demagogoi*) lent them the greatest excuse, in their envy of Lucullus accusing him of dragging out the war through love of power and love of wealth; and of all but controlling on his own Cilicia, Asia, Bithynia, Paphlagonia, Galatia, Pontus, Armenia, and the regions extending to Phasis, and that now he had plundered the royal palaces of Tigranes, as though he had been sent to strip the kings not to campaign against them. [5] For they say that one of the praetors, Lucius Quintus, said this; they were persuaded by him most of all and they voted to send successors to Lucullus in his provinces. They also voted that many who had served under him should be released from military service. ...

[34.3] For this reason they were happy to receive him [Publius Clodius] and they addressed him as the soldiers' friend, since he put on that he was angry on their behalf, if there were to be no limit to their many wars and toils; but while fighting against every nation and roaming over every land they were wearying their lives and winning nothing worthy from such military service but convoying the wagons and camels of Lucullus which were laden with gold goblets and precious stones, [4] while the soldiers of Pompey, now being citizens, were settled somewhere with their wives and children, possessing prosperous land and cities, not having driven Mithridates and Tigranes into uninhabited deserts, nor thrown down the royal palaces of Asia, but having made war on fugitives in Spain and runaway slaves in Italy. 'Why then' he said, 'if we must never stop campaigning, do we not keep the remains of our bodies and our lives for that commander who thinks the wealth of the soldiers campaigning is the most important thing?' [5] For such reasons as these the army of Lucullus was ruined.

Plutarch, *Life of Lucullus* 33.4–5, 34.3–4

This passage sheds light on the process through which Lucullus' authority among his soldiers is swiftly eroded, largely by the action of political agitators in Rome: remarkably, the political conversation in Rome reaches the soldiers quartered in the East, and rumours (not quite substantiated) about the rewards that Pompey's soldiers had earned after their participation in the war against Sertorius, which Lucullus' men regarded as a far less arduous conflict. The campaign soon becomes impossible owing to such vociferous dissent, which might even present a risk of mutiny, and gave further impetus to the process that led to the removal of Lucullus and the assignment of the command to Pompey. The armies quartered across the empire could often be weighty political forces in the late Republican period. – L. Quintus: Lucius Quinctius, tribune of the plebs in 74 BC, whom Lucullus, who was consul in that year, vigorously attacked (Sallust, *Histories* 3.34.11 McG = 15 R.). In 67 BC Lucullus lost his remaining provinces, Bithynia and Pontus, to Glabrio, and in 66 BC Pompey eventually superseded him. They met at a spot in Galatia for an unfriendly conference, from which Lucullus returned to Rome to wait until 63 for his triumph.

B49   Caesar and the legacy of Marius, 65 BC
[1] There were two factions (Gk: *stasis*) in the city, one that had been dominant since Sulla's day, and the Marian one, which was then in an altogether abject state, humiliated and fragmented. Caesar decided to revive this faction and attach it to himself. When the displays of his aedileship were at their peak, he had portraits of Marius secretly made, along with trophy-bearing Victories. He had these carried to the Capitol by night and set up. [2] At dawn they could be seen glittering with gold and exquisitely crafted, bearing inscriptions recording the Cimbrian successes of Marius, and bystanders were amazed at the daring of the man who had set them up. It was evident who had done it. Word spread quickly, and everybody gathered for the sight. [3] Some cried out that Caesar was aiming for tyranny: he was reviving honours that had been buried by laws and decrees, and it was a test of the people, whose feelings towards him he had previously softened, to see whether they had been made submissive by his ambitious displays and would allow him to amuse himself with such innovations. [4] The Marians, however, encouraged one another. They suddenly showed themselves in astonishing numbers, and noisily took over the Capitol. [5] Many of them were even moved to tears of joy when they saw the features

of Marius, and Caesar was praised to skies, and they said he was the one man who was worthy of his kinship with Marius.

Plutarch, *Life of Caesar* 6.1–4

Marius died in office, a couple of weeks into his seventh consulship, in January 86 BC. His associates were comprehensively defeated in the civil war a few years later, and Marius' public memory was effectively wiped out for the following two decades. It was powerfully revived by an ambitious family relation of the late consular, the patrician C. Julius Caesar, who arranged for Marius' portrait to be displayed in public at the funeral of his aunt Julia, Marius' widow (Plutarch, *Life of Caesar* 5.1-5: it had not been seen in public since Sulla's victory). Two years later, he stressed his connection with Marius by putting back on display the monuments in honour of Marius that had been torn down after the civil war. Plutarch's account suggests that the memory of Marius was still cherished by many in Rome, nearly two decades after his death. Speaking of a faction 'of Marius' is perhaps excessive, but it is clear that Caesar felt that he could draw considerable political advantages from his public statements of loyalty to Marius' legacy.

B50   Cicero on Caesar's oratory

[261] Caesar, however, by invoking a rational approach, corrects distorted and corrupt usage with pure and uncorrupted usage. Thus by combining with this careful choice of Latin words – a necessary task for any Roman citizen, whether orator or not – the typical ornaments of oratory, he seems to be placing in a good light some nicely painted pictures. Since he has this special quality along with those shared by others, I do not see anyone who should have the edge over him. He has a splendid way of speaking, without a hint of routine, which, in respect of voice, gesture, and physical presence, has a certain magnificence and noble quality to it.

Cicero, *Brutus* 261

In spite of their deep political differences, Cicero repeatedly acknowledged the great intellectual stature of Caesar: in his overview of the history of Roman oratory, written in 46 BC, he also celebrates Caesar's extraordinary talent as a public speaker. From this cursory assessment we draw the strong impression that Caesar's ability to establish close political and emotional ties with the Roman populace had much to do with his ability to use the spoken word as a powerful means of persuasion.

B51   Tribunate of Cornelius, 67 BC

a) He so conducted himself in that office that he seemed more stubborn than was proper; for this reason he was alienated from the Senate. He proposed that since money was being given to the ambassadors of foreign nations at interest and disgraceful and notorious profits were being made from this, no one should expend money on the ambassadors of foreign nations. The Senate rejected his proposal and decreed that enough attention seemed to have been paid by that decree of the Senate (*senatus consultum*) which had been passed a number of years previously when L. Domitius and C. Caelius had been consuls, since the Senate had decreed a very few years previously in accordance with that same decree of the Senate that no one should lend money to the Cretans. Cornelius, displeased with the Senate in this matter, complained in an assembly-speech (*contio*): "the provinces were being drained by usury for the sole reason that ambassadors should have the resources to pay for favours on the spot"; and he promulgated a law by which he reduced the authority of the Senate: that no one should be released from the laws except by the people. ... The most powerful and the members of the Senate, whose influence was being greatly diminished, had resented the proposal of Cornelius; and then P. Servilius Globulus, tribune of the plebs, was found to resist Cornelius. When the day of voting the law came and the herald, with the scribe prompting him, began to read out the words of the law he did not allow the scribe to prompt nor the herald to announce the proposal publicly. Then Cornelius himself read out the text. When the consul Piso protested that this was improper action and declared that the tribunician veto was being done away with, he was greeted by the people with loud abuse; and when he had given orders that those who were threatening to lay hands upon him be arrested by his lictor, his rods of office (*fasces*) were broken and from the furthest part of the assembly (*contio*) stones were thrown at the consul; Cornelius, much upset at this disorder dismissed the assembly at once. The issue was then discussed in the Senate amid considerable differences of opinion. Then Cornelius began to introduce a modified proposal that no one should be released from the laws in the Senate unless two hundred had been present, and that, when someone had been so released, no one should interpose a veto when the proposal concerning that matter was put before the people. This motion was enacted without disorder. For nobody was able to say that this law was not favourable to the authority of the Senate; even so he enacted it against the wishes of the *optimates*, who were accustomed through small numbers, to use such decrees of the Senate as gifts. Next Cornelius enacted a law, which, although no one dared to oppose it, was yet contrary to the wishes of many: that the praetors should administer justice in accordance with their perpetual edicts; this proposal removed all source of favour from ambitious praetors who had become accustomed to administer justice inconsistently. Cornelius proposed several other laws too, most of which his colleagues vetoed; the whole period of his tribunate was passed amid such dissensions.

Asconius, *Commentary on Cicero's Defence of Cornelius* p. 57C.7–59C.14, with omissions

'A number of years previously' is the reading of the OCT edition. An alternative is 'seven and XX'. – This passage of Asconius records (*aliquot ante annos*) the ambitious political and legislative action of Cornelius, who was tribune in 67 BC: the ability with which he responds to senatorial obstruction show a great deal of ingenuity and determination, and a readiness to find complex technical constitutional arguments in support of his measures, especially when presented with tribunician opposition. At the same time, Cornelius uses the support of the crowd in silencing or intimidating his opponents. The initiative on the embassies from the provinces is especially significant, as it draws a link between the risk of senatorial corruption and the economic position of the inhabitants of the provinces. – On Cornelius' tribunate see also Cassius Dio, *Roman History* 36.38–42. 2.

B52   Cicero addresses the people on the Manilian law, 66 BC

Although the sight of you crowded here, citizens, has always seemed to me much the most pleasing, this place the most important for doing public business, and the most dignified for public speaking, it has not been my choice, however, which has kept me away from this access to fame, which has always been wide open to anyone of excellence, but my plan of life which I have adopted from my earliest youth. For since earlier in my life I did not yet dare to make contact with this prestigious place and since I resolved that nothing ought to be brought here unless perfected by my natural talent and worked out with my diligence, I thought that all my time ought to be given over to the circumstances of my friends. [2] Thus this place was never without people to maintain your cause while my hard work, employed with integrity and disinterest in the perils of private individuals, has borne the greatest fruit as a result of your judgement. For when, owing to the postponement of the elections, I was three times declared praetor at the head of the poll by all the centuries, I realized clearly, citizens, what judgement you were making about me and what you were prescribing for others. Now since I possess as much influence as you wished me to possess by conferring political offices upon me, and as much capacity for public business as an almost daily routine of public speaking has been able to provide for a man who is alert as a result of his forensic experience, I shall certainly make use of such authority as I possess before those who have given it to me and whatever I can achieve in public speaking I shall display above all to those who by their judgement of me have thought that rewards should be granted to this activity too.

Cicero, *On the Manilian Law / On Pompey's Command* 1. 1–2

In 66 BC Cicero made the case to the people for the assignment of the Mithridatic command to Pompey in his capacity as praetor. In opening his speech, he proudly refers to his recent election, and to the close link between his political success and his ability as a public speaker: the crucial factor in his rise to prominence as a 'new man'.

B53   C. Julius Caesar aedile, 65 BC
Further, as aedile he adorned the Comitium and the forum, the basilicas and even the Capitol with porticoes constructed so that the equipment for his shows might be exhibited in them amid a great wealth of material. He put on wild beast shows and games both with his colleague and separately… [2] In addition Caesar put on a gladiatorial show, but with somewhat fewer pairs than he had planned; for he had terrified his enemies by gathering an enormous troop of gladiators from everywhere. Therefore a decree was passed concerning the number of gladiators; no one in Rome was allowed to have a greater number.

Suetonius, *Divus Julius* 10

During his aedileship Julius Caesar made use of the opportunities afforded by his office to raise his profile in the city: on the one hand, he embarked on a programme of refurbishment in the Forum and other public locations; on the other, he organized lavish games. The concern over the number of gladiators he had recruited reflects wider preoccupations over the role of political violence and intimidation across the city, which soon became even more pressing with Catiline's conspiracy and with the rise of Clodius and Milo in the fifties. – Caesar's work as an aedile was of course supported by high levels of expenditure, which were partly funded by his ruthless resorting to debt: cf. Plutarch, *Caesar* 5.9 and the story on the use of silver weapons in gladiatorial games in Pliny, *Natural History* 33.53. – Cf. Cicero's comments on his own aedileship, above **B47a)**

B54   Abortive conspiracy, 65 BC
a) Previously a few people had similarly conspired against the *res publica*, among them Catiline; [2] about this I will speak as precisely as I am able. In the consulship of L. Tullus and M'. Lepidus, P. Autronius and P. Sulla, the consuls designate, had been indicted for electoral malpractice (*ambitus*) and had been punished. [3] Shortly afterwards, Catiline, prosecuted on a charge of extortion (*repetundae*), was prevented from being a candidate for the consulship, because he had been unable to submit his nomination within the legal period of days. [4] There was at the same time, one Cn. Piso, a young man of noble birth, of the utmost recklessness, needy, factious, whose lack of resources and bad character encouraged him to disrupt the *res publica*. [5] Having communicated their plans to him around the Nones of December [5 December], Catiline and Autronius began preparations to kill the consuls L. Cotta and L. Torquatus on the Capitol on 1 January, and having themselves seized the rods of office (*fasces*), to send Piso with an army to take possession of the two Spains.

[6] When their plan was discovered, they had put off the plan for the slaughter to the Nones of February [5 February]. [7] At that time they plotted destruction not only for the consuls, but also for several senators. [8] Had not Catiline been hasty in giving the signal to his associates in front of the senate-house, the most heinous act since the foundation of Rome would have been perpetrated on that day. Because the armed conspirators had not yet assembled in full numbers, his action scotched the plan.

Sallust, *Catiline's War* 18

b) Nonetheless he soon became involved in a more serious plot in the city; for a few days before he entered upon his aedileship, he came under suspicion of having conspired with the consular Marcus Crassus, likewise with Publius Sulla and L. Autronius, who after designation for the consulship had been condemned for electoral malpractice (*ambitus*); that at the beginning of the year they would attack the senate and that, having slaughtered those whom they had decided upon, Crassus would enter upon the dictatorship, that Caesar himself should be declared master of the horse by Crassus, and that when the *res publica* had been organized as they wished, the consulship should be restored to Sulla and Autronius. [2] Tanusius Geminus records this conspiracy in his history, Marcus Bibulus in his edicts, C. Curio, the father, in his speeches. It seems that Cicero is referring to this in a letter to Axius, when he reports that Caesar established in his consulship the kingship (*regnum*) he has thought about as aedile. Tanusius adds that Crassus, either through shame or fear, did not show on the day arranged for the slaughter and that therefore Caesar did not give the signal, which it had been agreed would be given by him; Curio says it had been agreed, that he would let his toga fall down from his shoulder.

Suetonius, *Divus Julius* 9. 1–2

Before starting his account of Catiline's conspiracy, Sallust briefly mentions a plot of which Catiline was allegedly part two years earlier, in 65 BC, which involved the assassination of both consuls and the takeover of the Spanish provinces. Like the conspiracy of 63, this plot was reportedly foiled in time, but why it was not followed by any prosecution is left unexplained. Its historicity has been questioned with plausible arguments by modern scholars. See also Asconius, *Commentaries* p. 92C.15–25 and Cassius Dio, *Roman History* 36.44.3–5. – Suetonius speaks of a different plot, which allegedly took shape in the same year, and points to the same scenario of grave instability: two consuls elect, who had been prevented from taking office because of their convictions on electoral corruption charges, sought to gain power through violent means: their envisaged *coup d'état* involved the participation of Crassus and Caesar, who were also rumoured by some to have had a measure of involvement with Catiline's conspiracy of 63. – Suetonius mentions a number of sources on the conspiracy that no longer survive, including a collection of letters from Cicero to Q. Axius, a wealthy senator: these were known in antiquity, but none survives. – P. Sulla was a nephew of the late Dictator, and was defended by Cicero in 62 BC on a charge of having been a member of Catiline's plot. – Whatever the actual historicity of the events discussed here, they point to a scenario in which a number of ambitious and capable individuals seem prepared to resort to violent means in order to further their position and achieve offices that would not be within their reach if they were to stay within the bounds of traditional political competition.

B55   Cicero on his electoral prospects, 65 BC
a) Cicero to Atticus, greetings.
[1] Regarding my election campaign, which I know is of great interest to you, the situation, as far as one can guess at present, is this: Publius Galba alone is campaigning. He is meeting a plain, unvarnished, old-fashioned, "no". The word on the street is that this premature canvass of his has done my prospects no harm. For people generally are refusing to support him because they say they owe me their support. So I hope

to derive some advantage when it becomes generally known that very many of my friends are coming forward. I was actually thinking of starting my campaign at the same time as Cincius says your slave will set off with this letter, that is on 17 July, at the elections for tribunes in the Campus Martius. My rivals who seem certain to stand are Galba, Antonius and – I think this will make you laugh or cry – Quintus Cornificius. You will scratch your head at the news that some think Caesonius will join the list. Aquilius, I think, is unlikely to: he has stated he will not, has entered a plea of ill-health, and has offered his judicial dominion as an excuse. Catiline will certainly stand if the jury in his case adjudges that it's dark at midday. As for Aufidius and Palicanus, I don't think you are holding your breath for news from me.

[2] On those who are seeking election this time, Caesar is thought a certainty. Thermus and Silanus are thought to be contesting the other place. They are so short of friends or reputation that in my opinion it's not impossible for Turius to overtake them; but no one else seems to agree. It would be greatly to my advantage for Thermus to make it together with Caesar, since none of the current candidates would seem to be as strong a candidate if left over to my year, especially given that he is Curator of the Flaminian Way which will then be finished, no question. I would happily now stick him in with the consul Caesar. This is my current way of thinking of the candidates. I shall apply myself to the best of my ability in fulfilling every requirement of a candidate. Perhaps, since Cisalpine Gaul looks very important in determining the result, when the courts at Rome are in recess, I shall run down in September to assist Piso and return in January. When I have investigated the preferences of the *nobiles* I shall write to you. I hope the rest is going well, at least as regards my rivals in the city. Since you are closer at hand, make sure you answer for the other group, that of our friend, Pompey. Say that I won't mind if he doesn't come for my election.
Rome, shortly before 17 July 65 BC.

Cicero, To Atticus 1.1.1–2 (SB 10)

This long and rather intricate letter is the opening text of the collection of Cicero's letters to his friend T. Pomponius Atticus, and it gives a clear overview of the value that this sort of evidence has to our understanding of late Republican politics: through Cicero's comments and musings we achieve a degree of detail and depth that is otherwise inaccessible to us for any other period. – Cicero, who is planning to stand for the consulship in the not too distant future, is already taking a close look at the field of potential electoral opponents, and talks his friend through the list of those who are likely to put themselves forward in the elections for the consulship of 64, which are due to take place in the summer of 65 BC. Two names stand out in Cicero's quick survey: C. Antonius, who was indeed his colleague in the consulship of 63, and of course Catiline, who indeed put his candidacy forward for the elections of both 64 and 63. (Caesar, however, is not the (later) *dictator*, but L. Julius Caesar, a cousin) – Note the reference to the electoral weight of Cisalpine Gaul (modern Northern Italy), where there were communities of Roman citizens whose vote could be mobilized to good effect, and to the position of the more distinguished families of the senatorial order, the *nobiles*, whose support Cicero hopes to secure in due course.

b) [1] On the day on which Lucius Julius Caesar and Gaius Marcius Figulus were elected consuls, I am blessed with a little boy. Terentia is doing well. I have not heard from you for a long time. I wrote to you in detail earlier about my position. At this moment I am thinking of defending Catiline, my fellow-candidate. We have the jurors we want, with the full agreement of the prosecutor. I hope if he is acquitted, he will be more closely associated with me in the matter for campaigning; if it turns out otherwise, I shall grin and bear it.

[2] I need your early return home. For there is a distinctly widespread feeling among people that your friends, men of noble birth, will oppose my election. I can see that you will be of the greatest benefit to me in winning over their support for me. So do see that you are in Rome at the beginning of January, as arranged.
Rome, shortly after the previous letter.

Cicero, *To Atticus* 1.2 (SB 11)

In a letter written to Atticus shortly after the one quoted above, Cicero asked for his friend's direct support in earning him the support of the nobility. He also mentions a hypothesis he has been entertaining in trying to secure wider support for his candidacy: undertaking to defend Catiline in a corruption case. The prosecutor was P. Clodius Pulcher. Cicero did not pursue that option, but it is remarkable that a mere two years before taking the lead in repressing Catiline's conspiracy he was prepared to join forces with him for reasons of political expediency.

B56   The quaestorship of M. Porcius Cato, 64 BC

[16.2] The office of quaestor now being open to him, he did not stand for it until he had read the rules concerning the quaestorship, found out the details from those who had had experience and gained an outline understanding of the function of the office. [3] As soon, therefore, as he had been elected quaestor he made a great change among the treasury assistants and clerks. These men were regularly handling the treasury accounts and laws and when they had put over them as magistrates young men, who because of their inexperience and ignorance actually needed others to teach and to guide them, they would not give up any of their power to the newcomers, but became the magistrates themselves, [4] until Cato applied himself rigorously to these matters. He had not only the name and rank of a magistrate, but also intelligence, insight and judgement. He thought it right to treat the clerks as assistants, which is what they really were, sometimes proving them wrong when they were doing wrong and putting them right when they were making mistakes through inexperience... [17.1] By thus reducing the power of the clerks and making them subject to authority, and by conducting the business as he himself wished, in a short time he gave the treasury greater prestige than the Senate, so that everyone said and believed that Cato had given to the quaestorship the prestige of the consulship. [2] In the first place, when he found that many people owed longstanding debts to the treasury and that the treasury owed money to many creditors, he simultaneously put an end to the wrongs being done to and by the state, by rigorously demanding payment from debtors and by quickly and promptly paying the creditors. The result was that the people were delighted when they saw men who thought they were going to defraud the state actually paying their debts, and others receiving the payments they had not expected to get. [3] Secondly, many people were improperly depositing title deeds and fraudulent decrees which Cato's predecessors had been accustomed to accept as a favour for the asking. No such action escaped the notice of Cato; [4] indeed, on one occasion, when he was in doubt whether a certain decree was valid and many people gave evidence that it was, he did not accept their evidence and did not register the decree until the consuls had sworn to its validity in his presence. [5] There were many men whom the famous Sulla had rewarded to the extent of twelve thousand drachmas for killing those who had been proscribed. Everyone hated them as being stained with blood and under a curse but no one dared to take action against them. [6] Cato summoned each of them for having public money in his possession without a right to it and made them return the money, at the same time reprimanding them with force and eloquence for their wicked and unjust action.

[18.1] Cato also won over the masses by his ceaseless and untiring attention to his work. For none of his colleagues ever came to the treasury earlier in the day than he or left it later. [2] He never missed a meeting of the assembly or of the Senate, for he feared and kept a careful watch on those who, seeking to win favour, readily voted for cancellation of debts and taxes, or the distribution of gifts to all and sundry. [3] And by displaying the treasury free of informers and inaccessible to them, but full of money, he showed how it was possible for the state to be rich without committing injustice.

Plutarch, Life of Cato the Younger 16.2–18.3, with omissions

This passage shows that public office could be used not merely as a way to further one's position and career, but as a way of enabling good and effective government: Cato the Younger is singled out for having taken a junior magistracy, the quaestorship, very seriously indeed, and having brought about a number of significant changes, which had positive implications on the public treasury. The attention that he paid to the proper organization of public records is in keeping with the care that he devoted to the tasks entailed by his office. The quaestorship was also a turning point in his career, as it enabled him to become a member of the Senate, where he soon emerged as a figure of remarkable ability and authority.

63 BC: A FATEFUL YEAR?

B57 Consular elections, 64 BC

Cicero had six rivals in his campaign for the consulship: two were patricians, P. Sulpicius Galba and L. Sergius Catiline; four were plebeians, two of whom were *nobiles*: C. Antonius, the son of the orator M. Antonius, and L. Cassius Longinus. The other two were almost the first in their families to achieve office: Q. Cornificius, and C. Licinius Sacerdos. Cicero alone of his rivals was of equestrian status by birth; and he lost his father during the election campaign. The rest of his rivals conducted themselves with restraint, and Q. Cornificius and Galba were thought sound and virtuous men, Sacerdos was not known for any lack of principle; Cassius, though at that time he seemed more dull than vicious, was revealed a few months later to be in Catiline's conspiracy and to have been behind its most bloodthirsty proposals. These four, therefore, were all but finished. Catiline and Antonius, however, though their lifestyle was absolutely notorious, were nonetheless very strong candidates. For the two of them had formed an election pact, with the very strong support of Marcus Crassus and Gaius [Julius] Caesar, aimed at preventing Cicero being elected consul. This is why this speech attacks only Catiline and Antonius. The occasion for Cicero making a speech of this sort in the Senate was that blatant electoral malpractice (*ambitus*) was increasing day by day because of the extraordinarily arrogant behaviour of Catiline and Antonius, the Senate had decreed that a law on electoral malpractice (*ambitus*) should be passed with further increased added penalties. The tribune of the people, Q. Mucius Orestinus, had vetoed this. At that point, with the Senate particularly angry at the veto, Cicero rose and launched his attack upon the election pact of Catiline and Antonius a few days before polling day.

Asconius, Commentary on Cicero's Speech as a Candidate p. 82C.4–83C.12

Cicero's *Speech as a Candidate* (*oratio in toga candida*) made to the senate no longer survives, but we get extensive quotations in Asconius' commentary. This gives a clear picture of the field that Cicero faced in the consular election of 64 BC, in which an alliance between Catiline and Antonius would have thwarted his prospects of success. Electoral corruption is here said to have played a part in bolstering the chances of Cicero's opponents, and to have prompted action on the Senate's part. In the speech he gave before the Senate wearing the white toga that candidates traditionally sported, Cicero tapped into that hostile mood and denounced the alliance between his opponents, shifting the mood of the campaign and taking a decisive step towards the election. A translation of this whole commentary can be found in LACTOR 3.

B58   Electoral candidates: problems of a 'new man'

In a candidate it is excellence, honesty and integrity that is generally sought, not a ready tongue, skill, or knowledge. Just as in buying slaves, if we have bought a man, however honest, as a craftsman or plasterer, we are normally annoyed if he does not, so it happens, know the skills which we have been after in their purchase; while if we have bought someone to install as an estate supervisor, to put in charge of the livestock, we are looking for him to show nothing other than restraint, hard work and vigilance, so the Roman people chooses its magistrates as the estate managers of the *res publica*: if in addition they possess some skill, the people readily accept it, but if not, are satisfied with their excellence and integrity.

Cicero, *Defence of Plancius* 62

The appetite for decent and competent magistrates was clearly widespread in a society that was often presented with instances of senatorial corruption: in a speech in defence of Cn. Plancius, a new man from a municipal background like himself, Cicero stressed the importance of these qualities, somewhat downplaying the significance of his intellectual prowess and eloquence, which he emphasized on other occasions.

B59   A critical judgement on Cicero

[4] Cicero wished to lead the state, and was making clear to both the plebs and the *optimates* that whichever side he joined he would make the more powerful. [5] For he was playing a double game, and he would carry out the policy of the former at one moment, at another the policy of the latter, so that he would be eagerly sought by both. For example, saying previously that he preferred the *optimates* and that he therefore intended to be aedile rather than tribune he then changed over to the mob.

Cassius Dio, *Roman History* 36.43.4–5

Dio voices a thought-provoking criticism of Cicero's politics, which should be read in association with what Cicero himself has to say about his approach to the campaign for the consulship: what could be constructed as the shrewd approach of a candidate who is keeping his options open and as the middle-ground politics of a man who has no set loyalty to a section of the Roman society, is here dismissed as duplicitous and manipulative behaviour.

B60   Agrarian proposal of Servilius Rullus, 64/63 BC

[2] The tribunes were introducing statutes with the intention of establishing a ten man commission of men with absolute power, and entrusting to them all Italy, all Syria and all the lands that Pompey had recently added to the empire, and the right to sell public lands, to bring to trial whomsoever they wished, to send people into exile, to found cities, to take moneys from the treasury, to levy and to pay as many soldiers as they wanted. [3] Thus many eminent people were in favour of the proposal and Antonius, the fellow consul of Cicero, most of all because he would be among the ten.

Plutarch, *Life of Cicero* 12.2–3

Cicero's first major act as consul was publicly to oppose an agrarian bill presented by the tribune Rullus: his three speeches on this topic survive. In this brief notice Plutarch stresses that support for the bill was actually quite widespread, as many would have benefited from its implementation.

B61   Trial of Rabirius, 63 BC

[18] I shall now speak about the charge concerning Saturninus and the death of your most distinguished uncle. You declare that L. Saturninus was killed by C. Rabirius. But C. Rabirius has already shown this to be false, based on accounts of many witnesses, and Q. Haterius' lengthy defence speech. If only the case allowed me the opportunity to declare openly that L. Saturninus, the public enemy (*hostis*) of the Roman people, had been killed by the hand of C. Rabirius – that shouting does not move me in the slightest but gives me comfort since it makes clear that there are some ignorant citizens, but not many. ... [19] I admit that C. Rabirius took up arms for the purpose of killing Saturninus. ... [20] A decree of the Senate was passed that C. Marius and L. Valerius, the consuls, should make use of those tribunes of the plebs and praetors, whom they so decided, *to see to it that the empire* (imperium) *and greatness* (maiestas) *of the Roman people should be preserved.* They used all the tribunes apart from Saturninus, [praetors] apart from Glaucia; they ordered such as wanted the *res publica* to be safe to take up arms and follow them. All obeyed. From the temple of Saucus and from the public arsenals arms were given out to the Roman people for distribution by the consul Marius. At this point, I now ask you this question in person: Saturninus was occupying the Capitol with armed force ... in the Forum were the consuls, C. Marius and L. Valerius Flaccus, then the whole Senate ..., then the equestrian order ..., then all men of every order, who thought that their own safety was dependent upon the safety of the state. When all of these people had taken up arms – what then ought C. Rabirius to have done?

Cicero, *Defence of Rabirius Charged with Treason* 18

In 63 BC a criminal case of *perduellio* ('high treason') was brought against the elderly senator C. Rabirius for the role he had played in the events leadings to assassination of Saturninus and Glaucia nearly four decades earlier, in 100 BC. That such controversy was revived is in itself a symptom of deep-seated political tensions in Rome. Cicero took up the defence of Rabirius and based his case on the endorsement that had been given to the attack on Saturninus and Glaucia by a decree of the Senate. A few months later, when Cicero took the lead in the repression of the conspiracy, the role of the *senatus consultum ultimum* became highly relevant again. – For a full overview of the Rabirius affair see also Cassius Dio, *Roman History* 37.26-28.4.

B62   C. Julius Caesar – *pontifex maximus*, 63 BC

On the proposal of Labienus, to whom Caesar gave his support, the plebs restored the priestly elections to the people, contrary to the law of Sulla, but renewing the law of Domitius. For Caesar, when Metellus Pius died, was eager for his priesthood, although he was young and had not yet been praetor. [2] He placed his hope of it on the plebs, because he joined with Labienus in the prosecution of Rabirius and had not voted that Lentulus be put to death. He achieved his aim and was elected *pontifex maximus*, although many others, Catulus in particular, were contending with him for this office.

Cassius Dio, *Roman History* 37.37.1–2

Caesar's election to the highest pontificate took place in a year of major political developments, which also involved access to priestly offices: the principle of popular election was reinstated, after a law passed by Sulla in 81 had introduced the principle of co-optation. However, the lifetime priesthood of *pontifex maximus* had been elective since the third century BC. Caesar reached it at a relatively early age, when he had not yet been elected praetor: he could look forward to retaining a prominent and potentially very influential role in Roman politics and society for a long time to come. The priesthood had attracted distinguished candidates: Q. Servilius Vatia Isauricus, consul 79 in BC, and Q. Lutatius Catulus, consul in 78 BC.

B63   Character of Catiline

[5] L. Catiline was born of a noble family. He had great strength both of mind and body, but an evil and depraved temperament. [2] In his youth he had enjoyed civil wars, murder, robbery and political discord. It was in such activities that he occupied his early manhood. [3] His body was capable of enduring hunger, cold and lack of sleep to an incredible degree. [4] His mind was daring, cunning and untrustworthy, capable of any pretence and dissimulation; he was greedy for other people's possessions, extravagant with his own and enthusiastic in his passions. He was reasonably eloquent, but lacked sound judgement. [5] His mind was boundless and always wanted what was excessive, unbelievable and unattainable. [6] After the despotism (*dominatio*) of Sulla, a tremendous urge had come over him to seize control of the *res publica* and he had no scruple whatsoever as to how he achieved it provided he obtained a kingdom (*regnum*) for himself. [7] Day by day his ferocious ambition was driven on more and more by domestic poverty and the consciousness of his crimes both of which had increased as a result of the activities, which I have mentioned above. [8] The corruption of public morals, which was being continuously harmed by those diverse but highly damaging evils, luxury and greed, was a further incitement.

Sallust, *Catiline's War* 5

Sallust sketches this memorable portrait of Catiline right at the outset of his account of the conspiracy. The plot leader is depicted as a remarkable combination of exceptional talent and deep-seated flaws: a bundle of paradoxes and contradictions that epitomizes some of the main trends in the history of his own time. Indeed, Sallust firmly sets his character within the context of late Republican Rome, and makes clear that Catiline's subversive plans were shaped by recent historical developments, and notably by Sulla's victory in the Civil War: since it had proved possible for an individual to achieve sole domination, it was conceivable for Catiline to covet the same aspiration.

B64   The situation in Italy, 60s BC

a) All of Etruria was roused to revolt and most of Cisalpine Gaul. Rome was absolutely ready for change because of the inequality of wealth; men of the highest reputation and spirit had reduced themselves to beggars on shows, banquets, political ambitions and houses, while riches had poured onto the ignoble and mean, with the result that things needed only a small turn of the scale and it would be within the power of every bold man to overthrow the republic, which was of itself in a sick state.

Plutarch, *Life of Cicero* 10.5

Most ancient sources dealing with the conspiracy of Catiline, including Sallust, stress that it was not just a Roman affair, but had far-reaching ramifications across Italy. Plutarch establishes a link with the inequality in the allocation of land, and with a wider pattern of debt and deprivation. Note the familiar analogy between the *res publica* and an ailing body with which Plutarch ends his summary.

b) [3] For the tribunes gave their help to Antonius, the consul, who was of a character very like themselves; one of them was for bringing the sons of those who had been exiled by Sulla to public office, while another was for making it possible for Publius [Autronius] Paetus and [Publius] Cornelius Sulla, who had been convicted with him, to become members of the Senate and to hold public office. [4] Another brought in a proposal for cancellation of debts, another for allotments of land to be made both in Italy and the provinces.

Cassius Dio, *Roman History* 37.25.3–4

Debt relief and land reform loom large in the political debate of the late sixties, and are closely linked with the fraught competition within the political élite. Dio records some initiatives mooted by the tribunes of 63 BC and the alliances they sought to form with Antonius, Cicero's consular colleague. There is no ideological consistency among the tribunes' proposals: the contrast between the call for rehabilitation of Sulla's nephew, P. Sulla, and the plan to reinstate the sons of the victims of the Sullan proscriptions is a case in point. – The descendants of the proscribed were not allowed to return to Rome until 49.

c) Cicero on Catiline's supporters
[17] I will firstly, citizens, reveal to you the different groups that make up Catiline's forces: then I shall give you, for each particular group, whatever intelligent remedy my speech can suggest.

[18] The first group are those who are steeped in debt, and yet refuse to solve the problem by relinquishing the ample properties they love so much. Outwardly these men seem honourable – for they are wealthy – but their intentions and policy are shameless. You, sir, apparently wealthy and cosseted, with your lands and houses, your silver and property, why do you hesitate to surrender just a little of this to win back your credit? Are you hoping for war? Do you really think that in the universal destruction your property will be sacrosanct? Perhaps you await a list announcing a general cancellation of debts? Those who expect this from Catiline are fools. I myself will publish lists, but they will be lists of property up for auction; for those who have property cannot become solvent except by selling it. If only they had been prepared to do this earlier and had not stupidly decided to try to match the interest on their loans with the income from their estates, we would find them now richer and better citizens. But these fellows, I think, are not greatly to be feared, because one can either deflect them from their point of view or, if they persist, they seem more likely to assail the state with prayers than with arms.

[19] A second group are also debtors, but are men who await despotism (*dominatio*), who wish to seize power, who think that they can obtain positions through civil strife that are closed to them in peace. These fellows must learn – as indeed all the others too – to abandon all hope of achieving this: for in the first place, I am awake and at hand, watching over the state: secondly the decent elements (*boni*) in the state are full of determination, there is a unanimity of feeling among all classes, and we possess numerical superiority in the city and in the armed forces: finally, they must reflect that the gods will, in person, help this invincible people, this famous empire (*imperium*), and this beautiful city to resist these vast criminal forces. Again, suppose these criminal lunatics get what they so lust for, do they really expect, amid the ashes of their city and the blood of their citizens, to rule as consuls or dictators or kings

(*regnum*)? Don't they see that if they got what they wanted the same right would have to be given to runaway slaves and gladiators?

[20] There is a third group, now elderly, but tough through years of training: the scoundrel Manlius, from whom Catiline is now taking over, is one of these. These are the people from the colonies Sulla set up; taken as a whole, they are all, I am sure, full of the best and bravest men, but these particular settlers are men who have, in their sudden and unlooked-for prosperity, flaunted themselves too extravagantly and arrogantly. While they build and amuse themselves with choice estates, large retinues, elaborate banquets, they have fallen into such debt that they are never likely to become solvent again – except by recalling Sulla from the dead. Moreover, they tainted some of the peasants, men of little wealth or prospects, with the same hope of plunder. Both of these groups I class as predators and scavengers; I advise them to pull themselves together and to forget about proscriptions and dictatorships: for so deeply is the grief and pain of those days engraved on the heart of the state that I fancy not even the beasts of the field, never mind the people, would allow them to return.

[21] The fourth group are indeed a motley and seditious crew, men long since overwhelmed by life, who never break through to the surface, men who stagger under old debts, partly by extravagance, men harassed by having to pay bail, by the trial procedure, by the confiscation of their property – thousands in all who are said to have left the city and country to flock to Catiline's standard. These people, I fancy, are not so much eager soldiers as bad debtors. If these men cannot be solvent, let them collapse instantly, but in such a way that neither the state nor even their nearest neighbour may realise it. I do not understand why, if they cannot live honourably, they should want to die in disgrace or why they should believe they will die less painfully in a group than alone.

[22] A fifth group is made up of murderers and cut-throats and criminals of all sorts. These I have no interest in recalling from Catiline. They cannot be torn from him; so let them die like the brigands they are, since our prison is not big enough to hold them.

Finally, there are those who are not only last in place but last in the way they live; they are closest to Catiline, his own choice, his bosom friends; you can recognise them by their combed and gleaming locks, either beardless or luxuriantly bearded, wearing sleeved tunics reaching to their ankles, more like veils than togas. They devote their whole lives and all their waking hours to the vast labour of banqueting all night long. [23] In this herd is found the gambler and adulterer, and all the filth of Rome. These charming and refined lads have learned not only to make love and to suffer it, to dance and sing, but also to murder with dagger or poison. You may be sure that, unless these join Catiline and die, – and even if he himself dies, – they will be a breeding ground for future Catilines. What do these wretches want for themselves? They are surely not going to take their lady friends with them to camp? Yet how could they survive without them, now the nights have turned so cold? How will these hardy soldiers endure the frosts and snows of the Apennines? Unless, of course, they believe they will bear the winter more easily because bare is the way they have learnt to dance at their parties!

Cicero, *Catilinarians* 2.17–23

In this passage Cicero offers a polemical, but invaluable overview of the coalition that supports Catiline: although his main concern is to cast them as people that no longer have a place in the political community, he also provides some informed insights into the backgrounds and motives of those who joined the conspiracy. On the one hand, debt plays a crucial role, at various ends of the social spectrum; on the other hand, the relatively recent memory of the Sullan civil war had led some to think that a political upheaval would lead to a major redistribution of wealth, partly through land confiscations, partly through debt cancellations. Debt is an issue that brings together very different groups: the impoverished veterans that Sulla had settled in his colonies across Italy in the late eighties and the young offspring of senatorial families whose extravagant lifestyle has led them to squander their family fortunes. As he does on many other occasions, Cicero establishes a close connection between the flawed moral conduct of his opponents and their political choices. – Another overview of the camp of Catiline's supporters may be found in Sallust, *Catiline's War* 37, where the historian points out that large sectors of the plebs of Rome were initially sympathetic towards the conspiracy: the memory of the rewards obtained by the victors of the civil war played a major role in mobilizing the interest of the urban poor (whom he depicts as an increasingly large constituency). Sallust also mentions a group that is overlooked by Cicero: the sons of the victims of the Sullan proscriptions regarded the conspiracy as an opportunity to regain the wealth and standing that they had lost.

B65   Triumph of Lucullus, 63 BC

Memmius changed tack and provoked the people against Lucullus, charging that he had appropriated many things and had prolonged the war; he finally persuaded them not to grant him a triumph. [2] When Lucullus began a great struggle over this, the foremost and most influential men mingled with the tribes, and by many requests just about persuaded the people to allow him to celebrate a triumph; not, however, like some, a triumph, startling and unruly from the length of the procession and the multitude of spoils being carried in it. But he decorated the Flaminian Circus with the weapons of the enemy which were very numerous and with the king's engines of war; and this was a great spectacle in itself and not at all contemptible. [3] But in the procession, a few of the *cataphracts* and ten of the scythe-bearing chariots moved along, together with sixty of the king's friends and commanders. A hundred and ten bronze-beaked warships were also carried along, a golden statue of Mithridates himself, six foot in height, a wonderful shield set with precious stones, twenty stretchers with silver vessels, and thirty-two with gold goblets, arms and coined money. [4] Men were carrying all this along; eight mules were carrying couches of gold, fifty-six with silver ingots, and another hundred and seven more bearing silver coin, something less than two million seven hundred thousand pieces. On tablets there were records of the sums of money that had already been paid by Lucullus to Pompey for the war against the pirates and to those in charge of the public treasury, and besides that each of his soldiers had received nine hundred and fifty drachmas. In addition to all this, Lucullus gave a splendid feast to the city and to the surrounding districts, called *vici*.

Plutarch, *Life of Lucullus* 37

The cataphracts were mail-clad horsemen. Lucullus had returned to Rome from the East in 66 BC. His celebration of a triumph was long blocked by the tribune C. Memmius (see also Cicero, *Academica* 2.3), until it was made possible by the mobilization of the friends that Lucullus retained in the senatorial order: the criticism of unlawful appropriation that had been voiced against him were offset by the display of a lavish war booty, which was proof of the extent of Lucullus' success and of the contribution it had made to the public treasury. Written documents recording the handover of resources to Pompey for the continuation of the campaign also played a significant role. The triumph took place shortly before the elections of 63 BC and the arrival of the soldiers of Lucullus to participate in it was a factor, Cicero claimed (*Defence of Murena* 37), in the election success of Murena, who had served with Lucullus. The occasion was not just about celebrating Lucullus' achievements, but was rounded off by a feast in which part of the proceeds of the victory were spread out across the neighbourhoods of the city – a tangible display of the rewards of the empire, and a demonstration of the role that the districts play in the political life of the city.

B66   Consular elections, 63 BC

But, Servius, what sort of an axe-blow do you think you delivered to your election campaign, when you induced so much fear in the Roman people that they worried that Catiline would become consul, while you were preparing a prosecution, having laid aside and abandoned your own election campaign? [49] For people saw you making enquiries, yourself in sad state, your friends in mourning; they were noticing your surveillance, affidavits, your taking aside of witnesses, your private discussions with assistant prosecutors, actions by which the faces of candidates normally become less obvious to people's sight. Meanwhile Catiline was active and happy, accompanied by his band of young men, protected by informers and hit-men, buoyed up with the hope of military forces and also, as he himself used to say, with promises from my colleague, surrounded by an army of colonists from Arretium and Faesulae; a crowd made distinct by men of a very different sort, those ruined by the calamity of the Sullan era. His very face was full of fury, his eyes with crime, his speech with insolence such that he already considered the consulship a certainty and stored in his house. He held Murena in contempt; he reckoned Sulpicius his prosecutor, not his competitor. He threatened him with violence, he was menacing the *res publica*. [50] Do not ask to be reminded by me what fear was inflicted upon the good citizens (*boni*) by all these actions, nor how great the despair of the *res publica*, had he been elected. For you remember, when the words of that wicked gladiator became public knowledge, words which it was said he had spoken in an assembly-speech (*contio*) in his own home; when he had said that a reliable champion of the poor could not be found unless he were one who was poor himself; those who were poor and wounded ought not to trust the promises of the well-off and those untouched by misfortunes; thus those who wished to replace what had been spent, to recover what had been taken away from them should look at what he owed, what he possessed, what risks he was prepared to take; the one who would be the leader and standard-bearer of those who were wretched and unfortunate ought to be a person the least afraid and the most wretched and unfortunate.

Cicero, *Defence of Murena*, 48–50

Catiline stood for election to the consulship in the summer of 63: if Cicero's account is to be believed, he stood on a platform in which the support to the poor and the indebted played a central part. Cicero describes him surrounded by a tight network of enthusiastic and youthful supporters, as well as by a ring of impoverished Sullan veterans. Cicero acknowledges the role of Murena and Servius Sulpicius Rufus as electoral competitors of Catiline, and stresses the impact that Catiline's rhetoric in favour of the poor and the underprivileged made among the *boni*, the 'good people' that Cicero identifies with the traditional core of the senatorial nobility.

B67   Two voting-bowls from elections of 63 BC
a) M. Cato who seeks the tribunate of the plebs.

CIL 6.40904 = *AE* 1979,64 = EDCS-01000016*

b) Cassius Longinus who is voting for Catiline

CIL 6.40897 = *AE* 1979,63 = EDCS-01000009*

The collection of the Museo Nazionale Romano in Rome includes two unique pieces, which are of great significance to anyone interested in Roman politics: two small clay bowls, of very similar size, bearing graffiti advertising the election of Cato the Younger and Catiline also respectively. It is not made clear what office Catiline is standing for, while Cato is mentioned as a candidate for the tribunate: that places the cup in the successful election campaign of the summer of 63 BC; in the same year Catiline failed again to be elected to the consulship. Cassius Longinus was a member of the conspiracy that was foiled a few months later. These cups are otherwise unparalleled (a fact that has led some to question their authenticity), and one can only speculate on their function and purpose: the likeliest explanation is that they contained gifts to be handed out to potential voters, possibly food; the inscribed name would remind the recipient of whom the present had come from.

B68   Confrontation in the Senate, November 63 BC
a) In heaven's name, Catiline, how much longer are you going to exploit our patience? How much longer will that madness of yours make fun of us? To what length will that unbridled effrontery of yours vaunt itself? Have you not been in any way moved by the nocturnal defence on the Palatine, in any way by the night guards in the city, in any way by the fears of the people, in any way by the rallying of all good citizens (*boni*), in any way by this heavily fortified spot for the meeting of the Senate, by the looks and countenances of all around you here? Do you not realize that your plans are known? Do you not see that your conspiracy is held fast through being known by all here? Do you think that any one of us does not know what you did last night or the night before, where you were, whom you met, what plan you made? [2] What times, what habits! The Senate knows these things, the consul sees them; yet this man lives. Lives, do I say? More than that, he even comes into the Senate, takes part in public debate, marks down and designates with his gaze each one of us for slaughter. We, brave souls, seem to satisfy the *res publica* if we avoid his madness and his weapons. You ought long ago, Catiline, to have been led to your death on the order of the consul; upon you should have been directed the destruction which you have long been scheming for all of us ... [3] ... are we consuls going to tolerate Catiline who is wanting to lay waste the world with slaughter and fires? ... Gone, gone is that courage which once existed in this *res publica* so that brave men suppressed a traitorous citizen with sharper punishment than the bitterest enemy. We have a decree of the Senate against you, Catiline, powerful and weighty; it is not the deliberation and authority of this order which is failing the *res publica*; it is we, I say it openly, we, the consuls, who are failing. [4] Once the Senate passed a decree that the consul, Lucius Opimius, should see to it *that the res publica suffer no harm*. Not a single night intervened. Gaius Gracchus, for all the distinction of his father, grandfather and ancestors, was killed on vague suspicions of treason. Marcus Fulvius, a consular, was killed together with his children. A similar decree of the Senate entrusted the *res publica* to the consuls, C. Marius and L. Valerius. Did the tribune of the plebs, L. Saturninus, and the praetor C. Servilius [Glaucia] have to wait a single day for the death penalty of the *res publica*? But we are now in the twentieth day of allowing the sharp edge of the authority (*auctoritas*) of senators here to become blunted. We have a decree of the Senate like theirs but it is locked up in the records, like a sword buried in its sheath. Yet it is a decree by which you, Catiline, ought to have been executed immediately. You still live and as long as you live, you do not cease your acts of recklessness but add to their number. It is my wish, senators, to be merciful, it is my wish amid such great dangers to the *res publica* not to appear easy going, but I now condemn myself for being idle and useless. [5] There is in Italy a camp situated in the passes of Etruria against the

Roman people; the number of the enemies grows day by day. The commander of that camp and the leader of the enemy you see within the walls and, even further, in the senate, plotting from within day by day some destruction for the res publica. If I arrested you, Catiline, if I ordered you to be killed, I shall have to fear not so much that all good citizens (*boni*) say it has been done too late as that someone may say it has been done with too much cruelty. But there is one particular reason why I am not yet led to do what I ought to have done long ago. You shall in the end be killed at a time when no one so evil, so wicked, so like yourself can be found to acknowledge that it has been done illegally. [6] So long as there is anyone to dare to defend you, you will remain alive, and you will live as you now live, beset with my many stout defences so that you cannot move against the *res publica*. What is more, the eyes and ears of many people will be observing you and keeping a close watch on you, though you do not realize it, just as they have been doing until now.

Cicero, *Catilinarians* 1.1–5

b) [5] Finally, either to deceive or to clear himself, as if he were about to be attacked with some insult, he came into the senate. [6] Then M. Tullius, the consul, either fearing his presence or moved by anger, made a speech, brilliant and beneficial for the *res publica*, which he later wrote up and published. [7] When he sat down, Catiline, as he was ready to be wholly deceitful, with downcast head, began to demand of the fathers with the words of a suppliant that they should not believe anything about him without good reason: he was born of such a family, he had organized his life from his youth in such a way that he had all good things to hope for; let them not think that he, a patrician, whose own and whose ancestors' services to the Roman plebs were very many, needed the ruin of the *res publica*, while M. Tullius, an immigrant citizen in the city of Rome, was saving it. [8] When to this he began adding other insults, they all protested loudly, calling him a public enemy (*hostis*) and an assassin. [9] Then, beside himself with rage, 'since I am surrounded by enemies,' he replied 'and driven over the top, I shall put out the fire which threatens me by the ruin of all.' [32] Then he rushed out of the senate-house and went home.

Sallust, *Catiline's War* 31.5–32.1

Cicero opened his first speech against Catiline (a), which was delivered in the Senate on 8 November 63 BC, with a famous attack on Catiline and his plotting against the *res publica*, stressing that he had full knowledge of his plans and gathered all the necessary evidence to take action against him. Catiline was in the senate-house that day, and Cicero's attack on him presupposes, and is made much forceful by, his presence in the room. Explicit analogies are drawn between his conduct and the actions of individuals like C. Gracchus or Saturninus, who were punished under a *senatus consultum ultimum*: the scenario of a drastic repression is therefore clearly conjured up. This speech does not include an explicit call to action, but laments, in a rather ambiguous fashion, the unwillingness of part of the political establishment to take the sort of repressive action that Catiline's threat would warrant. Catiline is warned that the consul is aware of his plans, but further consequences are being mentioned only as a vague threat. – The Catilinarian speeches only give us Cicero's standpoint on the matter, of course, and Catiline's viewpoint is much harder to elicit from the surviving evidence (see below, **B69**). However, Sallust's narrative does record Catiline's reaction to the first speech, albeit in far from sympathetic terms: he did not engage with Cicero's accusations, but stressed the contrast between his patrician origins and the far less distinguished ancestry of his opponent, a new man from a *municipium*. When he saw that this line of attack was not earning him much support in the Senate (where a number of men of municipal origin sat), he stormed out of the Senate, allegedly overcome by anger (cf. Sallust's portrayal in *Catiline's War* 5), and threatening violent actions (demolitions were used in ancient Rome as a method of stopping the spread of a fire from a building to others). He then started to prepare his escape from Rome.

B69 Agenda of Catiline and his supporters, 63 BC

[34.2] But Catiline, on his journey, sent a letter to several consulars and to all *optimates*: he wrote that he had been unjustly convicted on false charges and since he had not been able to resist the faction (*factio*) of his personal enemies, he was yielding to fortune and going off into exile at Massilia, not because of any admission on his part of so heinous a crime but so that the *res publica* could be peaceful and no dissension arise as a result of his quarrel. [3] A very different letter was read in the Senate by Quintus Catulus, who said that it had been sent to him in Catiline's name. A copy of the latter is given below.

[35] 'L. Catiline to Q. Catulus. Your outstanding loyalty to me known from experience, welcome to me in my great dangers, has given confidence to this appeal of mine. [2] I have decided, therefore, not to prepare a defence in this new policy; I have decided to set out an explanation, not through any consciousness of guilt, which, so help me gods, you may know is true. [3] Provoked by wrongs and insults, because deprived of the rewards of my hard work and effort I did not get a position of status (*dignitas*), I undertook, as was my custom, the cause of all the poor not because I was unable to pay from my own estate debts in my name – and the generosity of Orestilla and of her daughter could pay off all the debts in other people's names – but because I saw unworthy men honoured with office and felt that I had been treated as an outcast through false suspicion. [4] It is on these grounds that I have pursued hopes, honourable enough in view of my situation, of preserving what remains of my reputation (*dignitas*). [5] Though I should like to write more, news has come that force is being organized against me. [6] Now I commend Orestilla to you and hand her over to your protection. Protect her from harm, I ask you in the name of your children. Farewell.'

Sallust, Catiline's War 34.2–35

Sallust quotes the text of a letter addressed by Catiline to Q. Lutatius Catulus, who had been consul in 78 BC and was one of the most authoritative members of the senatorial order: there is no basis to deny the authenticity of this text. Similar letters were addressed to other members of the senatorial order, with whom Catiline could claim established ties of friendship. Catulus' choice to divulge the text of the letter was a deliberate political move, in which the old statesman sought to mark a clear distance from a man that had by that point been denounced as the leader of a vast conspiracy against the *res publica*. – The letter is not an admission of guilt, but a firm denunciation of the attacks on Catiline's personal prestige (*dignitas*) and of the obstacles that were placed on his rise to the the consulship. The escape from Rome is described as an attempt to defend himself from the repressive action launched by the consuls; the request to afford protection to his wife Orestilla is both a restatement of a personal bond with Catulus and a statement of Catiline's commitment to piety towards his family.

B70 Crassus and the conspiracy, 63 BC

[2] In the affair of Catiline, which was a serious matter, and almost subverted Rome, some suspicion attached itself to Crassus, and a man publicly named him as one of the conspirators, but no one believed him. [3] However, in one of his speeches Cicero plainly blamed Crassus and Caesar. This speech, it is true, was not published until after both were dead, while in *On his consulship* Cicero says that Crassus came to him by night with a letter that gave details of the plans of Catiline, and he seemed at last to confirm the existence of a conspiracy. [4] Crassus, accordingly, always hated Cicero for that, but was kept from openly harming him by his son. For Publius, being a lover of literature and learning, was attached to Cicero, so much so that he put on mourning

when Cicero did that at the time of his trial, and persuaded the other young men to do the same. Finally he persuaded his father to become a friend of Cicero.

Plutarch, *Life of Crassus* 13.2–4

Catiline was a reasonably high-profile figure, a former praetor who had come close to being elected to the consulship on two occasions. However, speculation on whether he had secret and more powerful backers readily flared up in Rome, and Crassus was rumoured by many to have had a degree of involvement with the conspiracy, at least in its early stages (see also Sallust, *Catiline's War* 17.7, 48.5-9). Plutarch claims that Cicero played a role in feeding this tradition, both in the Greek memoir he wrote about his consulship (see *Fragments of the Roman Historians* no. 39) and in a text that was published only posthumously. Caesar was also accused of connivance with Catiline, and his plea not to execute the five conspirators was regarded by some as suspicious; according to Cassius Dio, *Roman History* 39.10, Cicero denounced his involvement in a posthumous work, in which Crassus also came under attack. – Establishing the value of allegations reportedly contained in lost posthumous works is an almost impossible undertaking. If they were genuine, Cicero's decision not to pursue Crassus and Caesar during his consulship could reasonably be explained with the intention to isolate Catiline without unleashing political opposition that he would have had trouble containing or overcoming.

B71   Historical comparisons, 63 BC

Do strive, conscript fathers, to save the commonwealth, be vigilant against all the storms that hang over you, unless you take measures against them. It is no Tiberius Gracchus, who sought to be elected to the tribunate a second time; no Gaius Gracchus, who tried to incite to violence those who favoured the agrarian reform; no Lucius Saturninus, who killed Gaius Memmius, who are being put to your scrutiny and to your severe judgment. It is men that stayed in Rome to burn the city down, to slaughter you all, to welcome Catiline, who are under our custody; their letters, their seals, their handwritten notes are under our custody. The Allobroges are being courted, the slaves are called out, and Catiline is about to be sent for. Their plan is that no one should survive in the universal slaughter, and that no one should be left to deplore the name of the Roman people and lament the ruin of such a great empire.

Cicero, *Catilinarians* 4.4

In building his cumulative case against Catiline, Cicero does not just rely on the incriminating evidence that he has been gathering, but also draws highly suggestive analogies with other moments in the history of the Republic: in this passage he establishes a comparison between Catiline and several 'seditious' tribunes (the Gracchi and L. Appuleius Saturninus), only to bring home the point that Catiline poses a much greater threat: far from merely coveting radical reforms or being involved in isolated episodes of political violence, he and his associates are posing a fundamental threat to the survival of the *res publica*.

B72   Catiline and Manlius – public enemies, 63 BC

[1] But Catiline himself stayed for a few days with C. Flaminius in the area of Arretium, while he supplied with weapons a district which had previously been stirred up, and hurried to the camp of Manlius with rods of office (*fasces*) and other insignia of authority. [2] When this information became known in Rome, the Senate judged Catiline and Manlius public enemies (*hostes*). It fixed a day for the rest of their number to be able to lay down arms in safety, except for those who had been condemned on capital charges. [3] It further decreed that the consuls should conduct a levy, that Antonius should without delay pursue Catiline with an army, while Cicero should defend the city.

Sallust, *Catiline's War* 36

After his escape from Rome, Catiline started to rally his forces in Etruria, no doubt with a view to launching a counter-attack on the city. The detail that Catiline started to display the symbols of official power is used, both by his opponents and by Sallust, as a symptom of the fact that his plans are indeed subversive, and that his forces are those of a hostile army. The mobilization of his forces is the factor that leads to drastic action on the part of the Senate, to the formal declaration of Catiline and his friend Manlius as public enemies, and the entrusting to the consul Antonius of the military action against Catiline. The endpoint of that campaign was the battle at Pistoriae, in early 62, where Catiline lost his life (see Sallust, *Catiline's War* 61.4 and Dio 37.39 = **B79**).

B73   Trial of Murena for electoral malpractice (*ambitus*), 63 BC

[81] And to these evils, jurors, do you not see what further evil is being added? It is you I am calling by name, you, Cato! You surely see the stormy weather ahead for your year, don't you? For already in an assembly (*contio*) yesterday there thundered a deadly voice of a tribune designate, your colleague; against him, your own decision and all the good citizens (*boni*) who summoned you to stand as a candidate for the tribunate have taken many precautions. All the disruption over this last three years – ever since that time when you know a plan was initiated by L. Catiline and Cn. Piso of slaughtering the Senate – is breaking out in these days, in these months, at this time. [82] What place, jurors, is there, what time, what day, what night when I am not snatched away from their ambushes and escape not only through my own planning but much more so by divine intervention? For it is not as a private individual that these criminals intend that I be done away with, but that a vigilant consul be removed from defence of the *res publica*. And no less would they intend to get rid of you too, Cato, by some means were they able; a thing which, believe me, they are working on and planning. They see what great courage you possess, what ability, what authority, and what a source of protection to the *res publica* you are; but, when they see the power of tribunes deprived of the authority and assistance of the consuls, they then think they will easily overwhelm you unarmed and weakened. For they have no fear that another consul will be elected in place of Murena. They see this will be in the power of your colleagues; they hope that D. Silanus, a distinguished man, can be cast before them without a colleague, you without a consul, the *res publica* without a defence. [83] In such important matters and in such great dangers, it is your duty, M. Cato, you who seem to me to have been born not for yourself but for your country, to see what needs to be done, to keep as helper, as defender and as ally in the *res publica*, a consul who is not ambitious, but a consul – as this time above all demands – disposed by fortune to devote himself to peace (*otium*), by knowledge to wage war, by character and experience to undertake any business you wish.

Cicero, Defence of Murena 81–83

D. Junius Silanus and L. Licinius Murena had been elected consuls in the elections of 63 BC. Murena was prosecuted for electoral malpractice (*ambitus*) by Ser. Sulpicius Rufus, an unsuccessful candidate, and by M. Porcius Cato, the stern upholder of traditional morality and principles and the unbending critic of any irregularity in public and political life. Gifts of money to voters were a traditional feature of Roman elections; legislation to deal with electoral bribery, including a law sponsored by Cicero in 63, reveal how the vast profits of empire were being used to further political careers and to inflate traditional practice beyond what was regarded as tolerable. Murena was defended by Hortensius, Crassus and Cicero, who spoke last. Besides defending Murena, Cicero had personal and political objectives: personal to rebut charges of betraying a friend, because, while he had supported Sulpicius in his canvass, he was now defending his opponent in court; political, in that Cicero was, above all, anxious that there should be two consuls in office on the Kalends of January (1 January) 62 BC to deal with the Catilinarians and, perhaps, to anticipate the return of Pompey from the East, which was a concern to the *principes civitatis*. – The point that Cicero makes here does not address the merit of the case: his emphasis is that the *res publica* cannot bear the absence of a consul at the beginning of a year in which the threat presented by Catiline and his associates is still pressing. Interestingly, the point is developed within a lengthy tirade (polemical and flattering in equal measure) to addressed to Cato, one of the prosecutors, who was about to take up the tribunate of the plebs for the year 62. Cicero claims that, without the support of a wise consul like Murena, even Cato will be isolated and overwhelmed by the other members of the tribunician college during his year in office.

B74   Apprehension of the conspirators, November 63 BC

[45.1] When these arrangements had been completed on the night which it had been agreed that they would set out; Cicero was informed of the all facts through the envoys and ordered the praetors L. Valerius Flaccus and C. Pomptinus to set a trap on the Milvian bridge and to arrest the Allobroges and their company. He revealed to them all the details of why they were being sent and gave them permission to do anything else that needed to be done. [2] They, military men, placed the guards without fuss, as they had been instructed, and covertly occupied the bridge. [3] When the envoys with Volturcius had reached that point and a shout had been raised from each side simultaneously, the Gauls quickly realized what was happening and surrendered to the praetors. [4] Volturcius at first encouraged the rest and fended off the large number with his sword; then, when he was deserted by the envoys, he first earnestly begged Pomptinus, because he was known to him, for his safety, and finally in fear and despair for his life gave himself up to the praetors as though to enemies.

[46.1] When these actions were completed all the details were hastily made known to the consul through messengers. [2] But great anxiety and joy took hold of him at one and the same time. For he was delighted that with the revealing of the conspiracy the state had been rescued from dangers; then he was anxious, not knowing what action should be taken in the case of such important citizens caught in the act of such a heinous crime; he believed that their punishment would be a problem for him, while not punishing them would destroy the *res publica*. [3] Having steeled his resolve, he ordered Lentulus, Cethegus, Gabinius and likewise Caeparius from Tarracina, who was getting ready to set out for Apulia to stir up the slaves, to be summoned before him. [4] The others came without delay; Caeparius, learning of the discovery of the plot, had left his house shortly before and fled from the city. [5] The consul in person led Lentulus, because he was a praetor, by hand into the Senate and ordered the rest to come with guards to the temple of Concordia. [6] He summoned the Senate to meet there; he introduced Volturcius together with the envoys to a crowded meeting of that order; he ordered the praetor Flaccus to bring there too the case with the letters which he had received from the envoys. [47.1] Volturcius, questioned about his journey, about the letters, finally about his plan and the reason for it, at first prevaricated and pretended not to know about the conspiracy; then, when he was ordered to speak on the promise of immunity, revealed all that had taken place and explained that he had been recruited as an ally only a few days previously by Gabinius and Caeparius and knew nothing more than the envoys; he had just heard frequently from Gabinius that P. Autronius, Ser. Sulla, L. Vargunteius, and many other besides were in the conspiracy. [2] The Gauls gave the same evidence; they proved Lentulus guilty, when he was pretending he did not know about it, apart from the letter, by the conversations that he had regularly had with them: from the

Sibylline books, rule at Rome was prophesied for three Cornelii; first were Cinna and Sulla, he was the third for whom it was fated to be master of the city; furthermore it was the twentieth year since the burning of the Capitol, which the soothsayers (*haruspices*) had frequently declared from portents would be stained with blood from civil war. [3] Thus the letters were read out, when they had all first acknowledged their seals; the Senate decreed that Lentulus should resign his magistracy and like the rest be held under house arrest. [4] And so Lentulus was handed over to P. Lentulus Spinther, who was then aedile, Cethegus to Q. Cornificius, Statilius to C. Caesar, Gabinius to M. Crassus, Caeparius – for he had been caught in flight shortly before and brought back – to Cn. Terentius, a senator.

[48.1] Meanwhile the plebs, which at first, eager for revolution (*res novae*), was very much in favour of war, when the conspiracy was revealed, changed its mind, cursed the plans of Catiline and lauded Cicero to the skies; they exuded joy and delight as if they had been rescued from slavery. [2] For some acts of war they thought would be more gain than loss for them, but fire was cruel, a calamity without limit and the greatest for them since all they possessed were their articles of daily use and their clothing.

Sallust, Catiline's War 45–48.2

Sallust provides a condensed and fast-paced summary of the circumstances that lead to the arrest of several associates of Catiline who, unlike the leader of the conspiracy, are still in Rome. Some are apprehended thanks to the cooperation of the Allobroges, who had agreed to help Cicero gather incriminating evidence; others are summoned by the consul, who undertakes to escort P. Cornelius Lentulus (by then a serving praetor) into the Senate, where the allegations agains the conspirators are set out. Lentulus had allegedly made use of a prophecy on the rule of three Cornelii to draw support to the conspiracy. The Senate decrees the arrest of the five conspirators, who are then placed under house arrest: Julius Caesar is among the senators who agree to host them while their fate is being decided. Sallust has a dismissive comment on the swift change of allegiance of the Roman plebs: as soon as it becomes apparent that the conspiracy would lead to major devastation in the city of Rome and that its livelihood would likely be threatened, the mood swung in favour of Cicero and the Senate.

B75 Rome enjoys the protection of the gods, 63 BC

[18] However, all these matters have been managed by me in such a way that they seem to have been done and taken care of with the assent and counsel of the immortal gods. And not only can we infer this because it seems scarcely within human compass that such great matters could have been controlled, but also because at this time the gods have brought us help and aid so promptly that we can almost see them with our own eyes. For not to omit such matters, meteors seen by night in the west and the sky lit up, not to leave aside thunderbolts and earthquakes, not to omit all the many other happenings during my consulship, so that those things which the gods seemed to be prophesying are now happening, this point which I am going to speak about, must not be passed over or left aside. [19] For you undoubtedly remember that during the consulship of Cotta and Torquatus [65 BC] very many things on the Capitol were struck by lightning, when images of the gods were pushed down and statues of men of old were knocked down and the bronze tablets of the laws melted and even that Romulus, who founded our city, was struck; you remember it was on the Capitol, gilded, a little boy sucking, his mouth wide open to the udders of the she-wolf. At the very time when the *haruspices* had gathered from all over Etruria, they said that murders, fires, destruction of the laws, civil war and revolution, the downfall of the city and empire were approaching, had not the

immortal gods, placated by every means, and by their own divine power almost changed the course of fate itself.

Cicero, *Catilinarians* 3.18–19

Preoccupation with the position of the gods towards human affairs tends to become more intense at times of political crisis. Lentulus' use of the Sibylline prophecy on the three Cornelii was not an isolated instance. Cicero here refers to a number of occurrences that were deemed supernatural and were treated as prodigies, both in 63 BC and two years earlier: prodigies were not simply received in awe, but became the focus of official expiation. The prodigies of 65 BC were expiated on the instruction of the Etruscan priests known as haruspices, who regarded them as premonitions of dreadful events to come, which would have befallen upon Rome had proper ritual remedies not been taken. Cicero's wider claim is that the gods have now firmly sided with the *res publica*, and are offering it their benevolent support.

B76   'The great debate', 5 December 63 BC

a) [7] I see that two proposals have been made so far, the first by Decimus Silanus, whose opinion is that the men who have tried to destroy the state should be put to death, the other by Gaius Caesar, who rejects the death penalty but is eager to see all other punishments inflicted in their full rigour. As you can imagine from their rank (*dignitas*) and from the gravity of the situation, each of them is determined on severe measures. Silanus considers that the men who have plotted against the lives not merely of all of us here in the Senate but also of the Roman people as a whole, who have tried to destroy our rule (*imperium*) and blot out the name of Rome, should no longer be permitted to share the air we all breathe and should be executed immediately; he reminds us that this form of punishment has often been employed in this *res publica* against vicious citizens. Caesar is of the opinion that the gods did not establish death as a punishment, but as an inevitable end to our natural life or as a respite from hardship and sorrow. He is supported by the fact that wise men have never been unwilling to face death, while brave men have often advanced to meet it. But imprisonment, and especially life imprisonment, was clearly established as the special punishment for crimes of exceptional wickedness. He proposes that the guilty men should be distributed among the free towns (*municipia*) and kept there in prison. But, if we insist on this measure, the citizens of these towns may think we are acting unjustly, while merely to request it might bring other problems. Nevertheless, senators, if you approve of this proposal, let it be passed.

[8] I shall not shirk the ensuing responsibility and shall hope to find some men among the *municipia* who would consider it beneath their dignity (*dignitas*) to refuse a request you have made in the interest of our general security. Caesar also proposes a heavy penalty for the *municipia* if any prisoner escapes. The criminals are to be kept under severe restrictions, in keeping with the terrifying atrocity of their acts. He proposes a binding decree to make it impossible for anyone to reduce their punishment by action either in the Senate or before the people and thus robs them even of hope, traditionally man's sole comfort in adversity. Moreover he proposes that their possessions be confiscated. Life itself is all he leaves the criminals. Had he taken this too, a single moment of pain would have spared them all the manifold agony of body and soul that is the penalty of their crimes. And so it was to find some means of terrifying criminals here on earth that men of earlier times would have had us believe that similar punishments awaited the guilty after death, for they realised that without some such belief there was no reason to be afraid of death.

[9] Now I see what is in my own interest, senators: if you adopt the proposal of C. Caesar, since in matters of the *res publica,* he follows the line which is regarded as *popularis,* I may in future have less reason to fear attacks by the *populares,* for people will recognize that it was Caesar who thought up the proposal and put it forward. But, if you adopt Silanus' proposal, I may well be letting myself in for further trouble. Nevertheless, I shall not set consideration for my personal safety above the good of the *res publica.* We have in Caesar's proposal a pledge of his lasting goodwill towards the state, as indeed his personal standing (*dignitas*) and the distinction of his ancestors led one to expect. Now we can see the great difference between the fickleness of those who frequent the assemblies (*contiones*), quite without any deeply held convictions, and the man who can justly be called *popularis* because he genuinely seeks the people's welfare. [10] I can see that several of those who would like to be considered *populares* are not present in the Senate today: presumably they wish to avoid having to vote on a charge involving the lives of Roman citizens. Yet only the day before yesterday these very men backed the decree to put Roman citizens in custody and the thanksgiving to myself, while yesterday they supported the move to reward the witnesses generously. They have voted for the arrest of the criminals, for a thanksgiving to the investigator, and for a reward for the witnesses; their general opinion about this case must now be clear to everyone. It is not that Caesar does not know the Sempronian law which protects Roman citizens; he realises, though, that the man who is a public enemy of the state cannot possibly be a citizen and knows that Gaius Gracchus himself, the author of this law, paid the penalty of death to the state, a decision later ratified by the people. Nor does Caesar think that Publius Lentulus – for all his extravagant spending – can still be called a friend of the people, now that he has plotted the ruin of the Roman people and destruction of the city with such utter lack of pity or restraint. So even Caesar – for all his gentleness and humanity – has no scruples about committing Lentulus to the darkness of life imprisonment, and proposes a decree binding for all time to prevent anyone ever being able to claim credit for reducing his punishment and so prove his adherence to the popular cause to the ruin of the Roman people. He also proposes the confiscation of their property, so that on top of all their mental and physical anguish they may not even escape poverty and beggary.

Cicero, *Catilinarians* 4.7–10

b) [20] Now before I ask you to vote, I shall make a few brief remarks about my own position. You see how numerous the conspirators are. I am well aware that I have incurred the enmity of each and every one of them, but I consider them base, weak and insignificant. Yet if ever a time comes when some wicked and depraved man can rouse them and they come to have more power than a general recognition of your prestige (*dignitas*) and of the state's would allow; even then, senators, I shall never feel that I have acted wrongly myself or encouraged you to do so. They may threaten to kill me, but death awaits all men. But no one else has ever won such glory in his lifetime as your decrees have bestowed on me; decrees of public thanksgiving to other men have always been a reward for their services, but I am the only man so honoured for preserving our *res publica* from destruction. [21] No one can deny the glory of Scipio, whose determined strategy forced Hannibal to leave Italy and return to Africa. There can be no question as to the exceptional merit of the second Africanus, who destroyed Carthage and Numantia, two cities which dangerously threatened this empire (*imperium*). We admit the outstanding success of Lucius Aemilius Paulus, whose triumph was adorned by the presence of Perses, once a mighty and famous monarch. Marius twice saved Italy from blockade and freed us from the threat of slavery, and his distinction will never be forgotten. Pompey, who swept in glorious success through all lands under the sun, outshines them all. All these are justly praised, but I feel confident that my own achievement will rank among them – unless, of course, you consider it a greater distinction to extend our empire by opening up new provinces than to ensure that our victorious commanders and soldiers may have some home to which they can return. [22] And yet in one respect success in a war overseas is better than victory in a civil war. Foreign enemies are either crushed and become slaves or are accepted as friends and consider themselves bound by ties of gratitude. With citizens the position is more difficult; a kind of criminal madness possesses them, and, once they have started to work openly against their own country, you may prevent them destroying the state, but you will never be able to crush them by force or win them over by kindness. I realise, therefore, that my war against these criminals will never end. But I rely both on your support and of that of all respectable citizens (*boni*) and upon the fact that the terrible dangers from which the Roman people have been saved will not be forgotten either here in Rome or anywhere else in the world, and am confident that I and my supporters will not come to any harm at their hands. For it is quite certain that no force will ever be found strong enough to shatter your alliance with the *equites* or to destroy the current powerful unanimity of opinion among all decent citizens (*boni*).

Cicero, *Catilinarians* 4.20–22

In his last intervention in the Senate on the Catilinarian crisis Cicero discussed the two available options on the fate of the five conspirators that he had arrested: Decimus Silanus (and others) argued for capital punishment, while Julius Caesar called for life imprisonment, confinement in a *municipium*, and confiscation of their assets. – Cicero makes a correct prediction on the political and personal consequences that the decision to sentence the conspirators to death might have to him, and expresses nonetheless a preference for capital punishment. Caesar nonetheless receives a positive assessment, and an instructive distinction is made between a man like him, who is a true *popularis* that cares for the welfare of the people, and those who habitually frequent the *contiones,* and are in fact driven by personal ambition. Passage a) offers a useful summary of Caesar's proposal and spells out the significance of the law of Gaius Gracchus (Sempronian law) of 122 BC that entitled the Roman citizens who were indicted on capital charges to legal protection. Passage b) does not spell out Cicero's position on the fate of the conspirators, but puts the emphasis on his own predicament: the consul, as the end of his tenure in office is fast approaching, sets up his contribution to the struggle against an internal enemy as an achievement that can rightly be compared to those of commanders who won great overseas wars, and is in fact best understood as a struggle for which no end is in sight. The final point is a political remark of wider import: a restatement of the importance of an effective alliance between senators and equestrians. Whatever decision is made on the day, that is the fundamental principle that should inform any future developments in Roman politics.

c) [3] On the following day, a certain L. Tarquinius, whom they said had been apprehended and brought back as he was on his way to Catiline, was brought before the Senate. [4] When he said that he would give information about the conspiracy if he was given immunity from prosecution, he was ordered by the consul to tell what he knew; he told the Senate virtually the same as Volturcius about the preparations for fires, the slaughter of the good citizens (*boni*), and the march of the enemies of the state; furthermore he said that he had been sent by M. Crassus to tell Catiline that the arrest of Lentulus, Cethegus and the others in the conspiracy should not frighten him but that he should make all the more haste to approach the city to restore the morale of the rest and so that they might the more easily be snatched from danger. [5] But when Tarquinius named Crassus, a man of noble birth, of very great wealth, and enormous power, some thought the statement incredible; to others, though they thought it to be true, it seemed nonetheless better, since there was such a crisis, that a man of such power should be placated rather than stirred up, while very many were under obligation to Crassus as a result of private business; they all shouted out that the information was false and demanded that the matter be put before the Senate. [6] And so on the proposal of Cicero, a full meeting decided that the information of Tarquinius appeared to be false and that he should be held in prison and given no further opportunity unless he gave information about the person at whose instigation he had lied about so serious a matter. [7] There were at that time some who thought that the information had been contrived by P. Autronius so that by naming Crassus and associating him in the danger the power of that man might the more easily protect the rest. [8] Others declared that Tarquinius had been instigated by Cicero to prevent Crassus from taking up the cause of the wicked, as was his custom, and throwing the *res publica* into chaos. [9] I heard Crassus himself assert afterwards that Cicero put this grave insult upon him. [49.1] But at the same time Q. Catulus and C. Piso were unable to persuade Cicero by prayers or by influence or by bribery that C. Caesar be falsely accused through the Allobroges or any other informer. [2] For each of them was involved in deep hostility with him: Piso, having been attacked in a court action for extortion (*repetundae*) on account of an unjust punishment of a Transpadane; Catulus, embittered with hate over the electoral campaign for the priesthood, because at a great age, having held the highest public offices, he had emerged defeated by the young man Caesar. [3] The issue seemed opportune, since Caesar owed an enormous sum of money, in private because of his outstanding generosity, in public because of his magnificent shows.

Sallust, *Catiline's War* 48.3–49.3

Even on the day when the fate of the conspirators was debated in the Senate there was some uncertainty on who the backers of the plot were, and on whether some associates of Catiline were still at large. An informant, L. Tarquinius, accuses Crassus. The allegation is rejected on the spot by the Senate, but rumours keep circulating on the possible involvement of Cicero in inspiring that statement: airing the report of his involvement was sufficient to weaken Crassus' position. Attempts were also made to implicate Caesar, who later that day made the case for relative clemency towards the conspirators: he was also heavily in debt, and that was a predicament he shared with many supporters of Catiline. Cicero, however, is here said to have refused to forge incriminating evidence about him, in spite of pressures from several senators.

d) [53] When Cato sat down, all the consulars and likewise a large part of the Senate praised his view and lauded his courage to the sky, criticizing one another for their timidity. Cato was reckoned great and glorious; a decree of the Senate was passed as he had proposed. ... [55] When, as I have said, the Senate voted the proposal of Cato, the consul thought it best to act and to anticipate the night that was approaching so that no new attempt might be made in the intervening period; he ordered the three magistrates [in charge of prisons and executions] to get ready what the punishment required. [2] He himself, having placed guards at intervals, escorted Lentulus to the prison; the same was done for the others by the praetors. [3] There is in the prison a place, which is called the Tullianum, when you have gone up a little way on the left, about twelve feet deep down in the earth. [4] Walls enclose it on all sides and above it a chamber with a vaulted stone roof. Dirty, dark, smelly, it looks foul and frightening. [5] Into this place Lentulus was let down and the executioners to whom the instructions had been given, broke his neck with a noose. [6] And so that man, a patrician from the most distinguished family of the Cornelii, who had held consular power (*imperium*) at Rome, met an end to his life worthy of his character and his deeds. Cethegus, Statilius, Gabinius and Caeparius were executed in the same way.

Sallust, *Catiline's War* 53, 55, with omissions

The case in favour of capital punishment prevailed after the intervention in the debate of Cato the Younger, whose speech is memorably rewritten by Sallust (*Catiline's War* 52). The Senate passed a decree that entrusted the consul with the executions of the conspirators: Sallust focuses on the fate of Lentulus, the most distinguished of the five prisoners, and of the strident contrast between his social status and his undignified end. – Cicero plays a marginal role in Sallust's account of the debate in the Senate: as a letter to Atticus of March 45 shows (*Atticus* 12.21.1 = SB 260), he would have firmly disagreed with that view, as he regarded his role on the day to have been as important as Cato's.

e) When the conspiracy of Catiline was detected and the whole Senate was deciding upon the extreme penalty for those party to the plot, Caesar, having been elected praetor, alone proposed that they be divided separately among the free-towns (*municipia*) and held in custody, with their goods confiscated. Furthermore, he inspired such fear in those who were recommending harsher measures, picturing at the same time the great hatred the Roman plebs would feel for them for all future time, that Decimus Silanus, consul elect, was not ashamed to put a milder interpretation on his proposal, since it would have been degrading to change it, alleging that it had been taken in a harsher sense than he intended. [2] Caesar would have prevailed, too, for a majority had already gone over to him, among them [Q.] Cicero, the brother of the consul, if the speech of M. Cato had not strengthened the unsteady line. Yet not even then did Caesar cease to raise objections, until a troop of Roman *equites* that was standing on guard about the place threatened him with death as he persisted without sign of restraint. They even menaced him with drawn swords so much so that his friends who were sitting next to him deserted him, while a few with difficulty shielded him in their embrace or with their togas. Then, obviously intimidated, he not only yielded, but also stayed away from the senate-house for the remainder of the year.

Suetonius, *Divus Julius* 14

Suetonius' account concentrates on the role of Caesar in the debate of 5 December 63: preoccupations over the political (and possibly legal) consequences of a decision in favour of capital punishment was not simply Cicero's, but was more widely shared across the senatorial order. A law put forward by Gaius Gracchus in 122 BC, the *lex Sempronia de capite civis*, stated that a Roman citizen had the right to appeal to a citizen assembly before being sentenced to death (Cicero, *Defence of Rabirius Charged with Treason* 12). The argument of those who supported the capital punishment was that the conspirators were no longer citizens, and should be deemed public enemies (*hostes*). – The incident that occurs to Caesar on the way out of the Senate casts the whole debate under a different light to what we read in Sallust: it was not just a disagreement among distinguished gentlemen, but the political context was debased by an ugly atmosphere of intimidation and looming violence.

B77   End of Cicero's consulship, December 63 BC
a) These were the deeds of Catiline and such was his downfall; indeed he gained a reputation more than the value of what he did as a result of the fame of Cicero and the speeches he made against him; Cicero on the other hand came close at that very moment to being tried for the killing of Lentulus and the rest of those who had been imprisoned. [2] This charge, while it was actually brought against him, was really being put together against the Senate; for they faced a mighty outcry among the plebs, above all at the instigation of Metellus Nepos on the grounds that they were not allowed to condemn any citizen to death without the vote of the people. [3] Certainly he did not incur any punishment at the time; for the Senate granted immunity to all who had had a hand in what had been done at that time and, furthermore, gave notice that if anyone should at a later date call any of them to account, he would be considered a personal enemy and an enemy of the state. Nepos was frightened and caused no further trouble.

Cassius Dio, *Roman History* 37.42

b) [7] And yet, as I am sure you have heard, on 31 December he [Metellus Nepos] insulted me, the consul, with an insult such as had never been put upon even the most depraved citizen in any magistracy, although I had saved the *res publica*; and he deprived me of the possibility of making a speech when I was leaving office. However, his insult was a matter of the greatest honour for me; for since he allowed me nothing other than to swear the oath, in a loud voice I swore the truest and most beautiful oath and the people swore too with a loud voice that I had sworn the truth.
Rome, mid-January 62 BC.

Cicero to Metellus Celer, *To his Friends* 5.2.7 (SB 2)

Deep reservations on Cicero's conduct during his consulship were voiced shortly after the end of his term of office: interestingly, one of his most outspoken critics was Q. Metellus Nepos, a member of one of the most distinguished senatorial families, then a tribune of the plebs. Cicero complained about his conduct on the last day of his consulship in a letter to Nepos' brother (b). The oath to which he refers is a customary oath that consuls made at the end of their mandate, swearing that they had nothing against the laws: Cicero managed to turn even that customary formula into a powerful rhetorical and political statement, and into an opportunity to interact with his audience. Although the Senate endorsed Cicero's conduct, the controversy was not going to fade away.

B78   Cicero reflects on his consulship, Summer 55 BC
It is a more splendid matter to relate how we conducted our consulship than how we gained it. [4] I, on 1 January, freed the Senate and all good citizens (*boni*) from fear of an agrarian law and a vast distribution of land. If Campanian land ought not to have been split up, I preserved it; if it should have been, I reserved it for better authorities. In the case of Rabirius being charged with *perduellio*, I upheld and maintained the authority of the senate, established forty years before I was consul. I prevented some young men from having their votes counted: though loyal and brave, they had experienced such circumstances of personal fortune that, if they had obtained magistracies, they seemed likely to overthrow the constitution of the *res publica*. For this I incurred hostily myself, while the Senate suffered no unpopularity. [5] I reconciled my colleague Antonius, who desired a province and

was engaging in a good deal of political intrigue. I set aside in an assembly (*contio*) the province of Gaul that had been provided and furnished with an army and money, although the Roman people protested loudly; I exchanged it with Antonius because I thought the circumstances such as to require it. I ordered L. Catiline to get out of the city since he was plotting the slaughter of the Senate and the destruction of the city not in secret but openly, so that while we were unable to be safe from him through the laws we should be safe with walls. In the final month of my consulship the weapons, which were aimed at the throats of the citizen-body, I wrenched from the nefarious hands of the conspirators. The firebrands that had been lit to fire the city I seized hold of, put on view and put out. [6] It was I whom Q. Catulus, the leading citizen of this order and the instigator of public policy, in a very full meeting of the senate named 'parent of the fatherland' (*parens patriae*). To me, the most distinguished man, L. Gellius, who is sitting next to you, declared in the hearing of these jurors that a civic crown was owed. To me, though a civilian, the Senate opened the temples of the immortal gods in a unique kind of thanksgiving, not as in the case of many for having conducted the affairs of the state well but for having saved it. I, when I was prohibited on leaving office by a tribune of the plebs in an assembly (*contio*) from saying what I had planned and when he merely allowed me to swear the oath, without any hesitation swore that the *res publica* and this city were safe through my sole effort. [7] To me the entire Roman people in that assembly (*contio*) gave thanks, not for one day, but everlasting and eternal, when on oath with one unanimous voice it gave its approval to such and so great an oath of mine. At that very time such was my return home from the Forum that no one appeared to belong to the citizen-body unless he were with me. And that is how the tenure of my consulship was completed so that I did nothing without the advice of the Senate, nothing without the Roman people approving; so that I always defended the Senate on the *rostra*, the people in the Senate, so that I united the masses with their leaders, the equestrian order with the Senate. I have briefly described my consulship.

Cicero, *Against Piso* 3–7

Cicero returned to his consulship and his achievements in office on a number of occasions. This section of a speech he delivered in 55 BC against L. Calpurnius Piso Caesoninus (consul 58 BC) provides a powerful, compact summary of his consulship: it is not just a (heavily partisan) summary of major events, but an illustration of the ideal of civic concord and constitutional balance that Cicero invoked in several moments of his literary and philosophical production. To be sure, self-promotion and self-justification play a major role here, but we should also allow for the considerable weight of ideological convictions, with all their inspiring and deforming power.

AFTER CATILINE, 62–60 BC

B79   End of Catiline, 62 BC

[39.1] Catiline perished at the very beginning of the year in which Junius Silanus and Lucius Licinius held office. Although he had no small force, for a time he kept an eye on the activities of Lentulus and delayed in the hope that if Cicero and those with him should be slaughtered first he would easily carry out his remaining plans. [2] But when he learned that Lentulus had perished and that for this reason considerable numbers of his supporters were deserting, since Antonius and Metellus Celer were besieging Faesulae and were not permitting him to advance in any direction, he was compelled to risk everything. He moved against Antonius (for he and Metellus had separate camps), although he was superior to Metellus in rank and was in possession of a larger force. [3] The reason for this was that he had a hope that Antonius would deliberately allow himself to be beaten as a result of his involvement in the conspiracy. Antonius suspected this and was no longer well disposed towards him because he was weak ... and because he was also afraid that, if Catiline saw them fighting with enthusiasm he might utter some bitter reproach and reveal some of their secrets; he therefore alleged that he was ill and entrusted the battle to Marcus Petreius. [40] Thus the latter met them in battle and cut down Catiline and three thousand others not without bloodshed, for none of them fled but they fell where they stood.

Cassius Dio, *Roman History* 37.39–40.1, with omissions

Cassius Dio endorses the view that Antonius was initially involved with the conspiracy, but argues that he switched sides by the time he launched the campaign against the conspirators (one could draw a contrast with Lepidus, the consul of 78). – This version is absent in Sallust, who ends his work with a memorable portrayal of Catiline as he is drawing his last breath on the battlefield of Pistoriae (*Catiline's War* 61.4).

B80   Cicero buys a house on the Palatine, 62 BC

a) I was moved by your congratulations; you wrote to me some time ago that you wished that my purchase of Crassus' house would turn out well. I bought that selfsame house some time after your congratulations for HS 3,500,000. And so be aware now that I have such debts that I want to join a conspiracy if anyone will admit me.
Rome, mid or late December 62 BC.

Cicero to P. Sestius, *Letters to his Friends*, 5.6.2 (SB 4)

b) What news am I to write to you? Well, the consul Messalla has bought the house of Autronius for HS 13,400,000. 'What's that to do with me?' you say. Just that in view of that purchase I am reckoned to have made a good purchase, and people are beginning to realize that it is permissible to reach a position of some standing (*dignitas*) in purchasing through the resources of one's friends.
Rome, 25 January 61 BC.

Cicero, *Letters to Atticus* 1.13.6 (SB 13)

Shortly after the end of his consulship, Cicero purchased a house at a high-profile location in the city, the Palatine, which enabled him to place himself in a very central position within the urban landscape, not just within the political debate and controversy of his time. He was prepared to run into considerable debt (note his joke on that in (a)), but he clearly felt that the investment would enable him to enhance his political and social standing (*dignitas*). – The previous owner of the house was M. Licinius Crassus, the wealthy former consul of 70 BC. The expense had been considerable, but news of recent purchases of comparable properties led Cicero to think that he had managed to strike an advantageous deal.

B81   Return of Pompey, 62 BC

a) From your official letter, which you sent, I have taken extraordinary pleasure in company with everyone else; for you have held out so great a hope for peace as I, relying on you alone, have always promised everyone. But be aware of this: your former enemies, now your friends, badly shattered and deprived of their high hopes, are despondent. … But be aware that what I have done for the salvation of our country is approved in the judgement and testimony of the world; when you arrive, you will find out what has been done by me with so much resolution and with so much courage that you will readily permit yourself, a far greater man than Africanus was, to be associated in politics and friendship with me, a not much lesser Laelius.
Rome, April 62 BC.

Cicero to Pompey, *To his Friends* 5.7.1–3 (SB 3), with omission

Whatever developments the year 63 BC had brought, it was clear that Pompey's return from the East had the potential to change the political landscape irreversibly. Cicero had been a committed supporter of Pompey in the previous years, and he sought to keep as close a relationship as possible with him during his absence. He had written Pompey an enthusing letter about his achievements as consul in 63 BC, and received a cool response. The passage above is Cicero's reply, in which Pompey is compared to Scipio Aemilianus, the conqueror of Carthage and Numantia. – Pompey's main preoccupation had been to maintain his contacts with the Senate ahead of his arrival: reference is made here to an official dispatch he had recently sent.

b) At the end of the winter Pompey distributed rewards to the army, fifteen hundred Attic drachmas to each soldier and a proportionate sum to the leaders – they say that it was sixteen thousand talents. He himself came down to Ephesus, embarked for Italy and hastened to Rome. He dismissed his soldiers at Brundisium to their homes. He surprised the Romans very much by this democratic action. As he approached the city there came out to meet him in turn, furthermost from the city the young men, then successively each age group according to its ability, and last of all the Senate, amazed at what he had done. For no one had yet defeated so many enemies, added at the same time so many of the greatest nations to the empire, and extended the boundary of the Roman empire to the Euphrates.

Appian, *Mithridatic Wars* 116

Pompey chose the opposite course of action to Sulla's in 83 BC: he disbanded his army shortly after its return to Italy, and returned to Rome as a victorious commander who was prepared to support the return to established and orderly constitutional practice. Before discharging his men, however, he made them considerable donations: both a reward and a token of the lasting bond (personal and political) with them. Their predicament was to remain a major issue on the political agenda for the years to come.

B82   Clodius and the *Bona Dea*, 62/61 BC

[3] I imagine you have heard that when a sacrifice was being conducted at the house of Caesar on behalf of the people, a man in woman's clothes entered the house; that when the Vestals had conducted the sacrifice afresh, mention was made of the matter in the Senate by Q. Cornificius (he was the prime mover in case perhaps you think it was one of us); then the matter was referred, following a decree of the Senate, to the Vestals and the pontiffs and it was decreed by them to be a religious crime; next, in accordance with a decree of the Senate the consuls promulgated a bill (*rogatio*); Caesar sent his wife notice of divorce. In this issue, Piso, influenced by his friendship with Clodius, is working hard so that the bill, which he himself is proposing and proposing

in accordance with a senatorial decree and on a religious matter, be rejected. Messalla is so far taking strong and severe action. Good men (*boni*) are withdrawing from the case as a result of Clodius' intercessions, the gangs are being got ready. I myself, though I was like Lycurgus in the beginning, am becoming calmer day by day. Cato is pursuing eagerly and pressing hard. In brief, I fear that these *actions* by good men (*boni*) and these acts of resistance by troublemakers (*improbi*) may be the cause of great misfortunes to the *res publica*.
Rome, 25 January 61 BC.

Cicero, To Atticus 1.13.3 (SB 13)

This letter provides contemporary evidence for the scandal triggered by the discovery of Clodius in the house of the pontifex maximus Caesar during the festival of Bona Dea, which only women were allowed to attend: the fact that the young man was wearing women's clothes led many to suspect the faithfulness of Caesar's wife, and prompted Caesar's decision to divorce her (see Plutarch, *Caesar* 10 for the saying that Caesar's wife should be above suspicion). A bill for the creation of an extraordinary public enquiry is being discussed, and Cicero is among those who support it (Cato being one of its most vocal advocates). That trial would be the beginning of the enmity between Cicero and Clodius, and would have major political and personal consequences for Cicero: the final sentence has a ring of premonition to it. – '*Actions*' provides a neutral rendering of an unsatisfactory Latin text for which no editor has provided a convincing emendation. It clearly refers to their withdrawal from the case mentioned earlier.

B83   Pompey and the *res publica*, 61 BC

a) [4] As for that friend of yours (you know whom I am talking about? – That person about whom you write to me that he began to praise when he did not dare to criticize), he has the highest regard for me as he demonstrates, he shows esteem for me, he is fond of me, he praises me publicly, but secretly, and in such a way that it is obvious he is envious. There is nothing gracious, nothing straightforward, nothing distinguished in his politics, nothing honourable, nothing brave, nothing candid. But on these matters I shall write to you on another occasion in more detail.
Rome, 25 January 61 BC.

Cicero, To Atticus 1.13.4 (SB 13)

For the best part of the sixties Cicero had expressed admiration for Pompey both in public and in private. Shortly after Pompey's return to Italy it became apparent that he did not regard Cicero as a worthy political partner. In this letter to Atticus Cicero airs his frustration with Pompey's conduct towards him, and expresses a disparaging assessment of his personality. The envy that Pompey harbours towards him is driven, in Cicero's view, by his great achievements in the consulship of 63.

b) [1] I fear that it is tiresome to tell you how busy I am, but in fact I am so distracted with work that I have scarcely time even for this brief note and that has been snatched from most important matters of business. I have already told you what the first assembly-speech (*contio*) of Pompey was like: it was not pleasing to the poor, contained nothing for troublemakers (*improbi*), was not liked by the well-to-do, and lacked substance for the good men (*boni*). Thus it fell flat. Then at the prompting of the consul Piso, a most irresponsible tribune of the plebs brought Pompey forward to speak at an assembly (*contio*). This was taking place in the Flaminian circus and on a market day; there was in that very place a holiday crowd. He asked Pompey whether he thought the jurors should be chosen by the praetor so that the same praetor should use them as a jury. [2] This proposal had been adopted by the Senate in the case of Clodius' sacrilege. Then Pompey spoke in a very aristocratic manner and replied that the authority (*auctoritas*) of the Senate seemed to him and had always seemed to be of the greatest importance – and that at great length.

Later the consul Messalla asked Pompey in the Senate what he felt about the sacrilege and the proposal that had been promulgated. He then spoke in the Senate to the effect that he praised all the decrees of that order in general terms and said to me when he sat down next to me that he thought that he had now given enough answer on these matters. [3] When Crassus saw that he had garnered praise from the fact that people here inferred that my consulship was pleasing to him, he got up and spoke in the most ecstatic terms about my consulship, in such a way as to say that he acknowledged his debt to me that he was a senator, that he was a citizen, that he was free and that he was alive; whenever he saw his wife, his homeland, he then saw a gift from me. In short, he wove together with great dignity this whole subject, which I am accustomed to paint in many varied ways (you know my colouring boxes), about flame, about sword, in my speeches of which you are the Aristarchus. I was sitting next to Pompey. I realized the fellow was put out either that Crassus had gained the thanks which he had let slip or that my achievements are so great as to be praised by so willing a Senate, and by one in particular who owed me that praise all the less because in all my writings he had received unfavourable mention, while Pompey had been praised. [4] This day has brought me very close to Crassus, even though I gladly accepted whatever was given by Pompey openly or obliquely.

Rome, 13 February 61 BC.

Cicero, *To Atticus* 1.14.1–4 (SB 14)

About two weeks after voicing his reservations about Pompey to Atticus, Cicero came back to the topic in at greater length: he gave Atticus a summary of the recent political developments in Rome, and notably of Pompey's conduct. The victor of the Eastern campaign emerges as a far less capable political operator than one could have expected him to be: he seems set on a middle course, which fails to please either the people or the Senate. He also struggles to take a strong line on the most prominent issue of the day, which was also very close to Cicero's heart: Clodius' prosecution after the Bona Dea scandal and the Senate's handling of it. – Cicero contrasts Pompey's position with the emphatic praise he received from Crassus in the same Senate session: an example of the political repositioning that Crassus was engaged with at the time, which must be understood within the same context that led him, a few months later, to forge a partnership with Pompey and Caesar – an arrangement that caught many by surprise.

B84   Trial of Clodius, 61 BC

In 61 BC, Publius Clodius was put on trial for trespassing on the women-only Bona Dea festival held in the house of the *pontifex maximus* (Julius Caesar) the previous December, see **K7b/c**. The case inevitably provoked huge public interest and was the context for Caesar divorcing his wife, Pompeia (**K8b**). Equally inevitably, the case became political. Cicero gave evidence against the alibi claimed by Clodius, thus incurring his hatred. This lengthy letter to Atticus summarizes the trial of Clodius on the Bona Dea case: it is of course a heavily partisan account, in which Cicero voices allegations of jury corruption. The picture of intimidation and disruption that he depicts, however, can hardly be dismissed, and points to a scenario of organized political violence that was bound to have even more impact in the following decade. The letter should be read as a literary text – not just, and indeed not mainly, as personal communication: the account of the trial is constructed according to a familiar literary device, already present in Homer, starting from the end (the *husteron proteron*, 'last coming first').

[1] You ask me what happened in the trial that its result was so contrary to everyone's expectation and you want to know how I battled less than I am accustomed to. I will answer you *husteron proteron* ('the latter placed as former') – Homerically.

For, as long as I had to defend the authority of the Senate, I battled with such energy and vigour that shouting and gatherings took place amid the greatest praise for my actions. If you ever thought me courageous in the *res publica,* you would certainly have admired my performance in this case. For when that man took refuge in public gatherings (*contiones*) and was using my name in them to stir up envy – you immortal gods – what battles I fought, what destruction I wreaked! What attacks I made on Piso, on Curio, on that whole gang! How I harried the fickleness of old men, the vice of youth! Often, may the gods help me, I have missed you not only to support my policies but also to witness my splendid battles. [2] But when Hortensius later had the idea that Fufius, the tribune of the plebs, should propose a law about sacrilege, in which nothing differed from the consular proposal except the composition of the jury (everything depended upon that) and fought that this should be passed, because he had persuaded himself and others that the fellow could not escape conviction with any juror, I shortened my sails when I saw before me the poverty of the jurors and I said nothing in evidence except what was so well known and attested that I could not leave it unsaid.

And so if you ask the reason for the acquittal, to revert now to the *proteron* it was the poverty and the disreputable character of the jurors. That this should happen was brought about by the idea of Hortensius. He was afraid that Fufius would veto the proposal that was being put forward in accordance with the senatorial decree. He did not see the fact that it would have been better that that man be left in disrepute and in suppliant state than be committed to a weak jury. But his hatred led him to rush to bring the issue to court; for he said that the man's throat would even be cut with a sword made of lead.

[3] If you ask what sort of a trial it was, its incredible result means that now, after the event, the idea of Hortensius is being blamed by others, while I blamed it from the very outset. For the challenging of the jury took place amid vociferous shouting; the accuser, like a good censor, was rejecting all the depraved characters, while the accused, like some indulgent trainer of gladiators was setting aside all those of good character. As soon as the jurors took their seats, the good men (*boni*) began to lose all confidence, for there never was a more disgraceful audience in a low grade dance hall; senators stained with disgrace, destitute equestrians, and tribunes more after treasure than of the treasury (*tribune aerarii*), as they are called. There were a few good men (*boni*) among them, whom that man had not been able to eliminate by challenge. They were sitting gloomy and sorrowing among people unlike themselves and were most concerned at the infection of disgrace. [4] As individual matters were brought up to the court for decision during the preliminary application, the court showed an incredible strictness with complete unanimity. The accused did not gain any request, the accuser was given more than he asked for. In brief Hortensius was triumphant that he had had such foresight; there was no one who thought that the accused had not been convicted a thousand times. When I was brought into court as a witness, I believe you heard the shouting of Clodius' supporters, how the jurors all stood up to surround me, how they showed off their bare throats to Clodius in exchange for my life. ... *(Cicero now mentions two episodes from legal history of comparable, but, he thinks, less heroic actions of jurors)* ... [5] And so when I was defended by the shouts of the jurors, just as if I were the salvation of Rome, the accused and all his supporters collapsed. On the following day the same sort of crowd gathered at my house as that by which I was

escorted back home when I laid down my consulship. Our distinguished Areiopagites shouted that they would not come to court unless a bodyguard was provided for them. The matter was referred to the court. There just one voter did not want the bodyguard. The matter was referred to the Senate. A decree was passed in solemn and elaborate words. The jurors were praised and the task was given to the magistrates. No one thought the fellow would reply to the charges.

'Tell me now, Muses …how the first fire fell.' You know Baldhead, the one of the Nanneian lot, that eulogist of mine, of whose flattering speech about me I had written to you. Within two days, through one slave, and that from a gladiatorial establishment, he completed the whole business. He summoned them to his house, made promises, stood surety, and made gifts. On top of that (ye gods, a shocking affair) nights with certain ladies and introductions to noble youths some of the jurors had as a bonus to their pay. Most of the good citizens (*boni*) departed, the forum was full of slaves. Yet twenty-five jurors were courageous enough, though very great danger was put before them: they preferred even to perish than to destroy all. There were thirty-one whose hunger moved them more than their reputation. When Catulus saw one of them, he asked: [6] 'why did you demand a bodyguard of us? Was it because you were afraid your cash would be stolen?' There then, as briefly as I could, you have the sort of trial and the reason for the acquittal.

Cicero, *To Atticus* 1.16.1–6 (SB 16)

C. Scribonius Curio, consul 76 BC defended Clodius. The identification of **Baldhead** has long been controversial. The most credible hypothesis identifies him with C. Licinius Calvus (*calvus* means 'bald' in Latin); '**one of the Nannean lot** (*ex Nanneiani*) remains a hopeless puzzle, unless we see in *Nanneianis* the corruption of the Greek word *neaniais* (young man), and translate the passage as 'that Calvus, so well known among young men'. Cicero often used Greek words, or indeed whole sentences in his correspondence with Atticus.' - This explanation does not account for the reference to a speech of 'Baldhead' in praise of Cicero. Those who identify this character with M. Licinius Crassus invoke a speech in which Crassus did pay tribute to Cicero not long before the Bona Dea trial (*To Atticus* 1.14.3).'

B84b   Aftermath of Clodius' trial, 61 BC
In the second part of the letter Cicero reflects on the political implications of the case, in which Clodius' position and his enmity with Cicero were not the only issues at stake: the outcome of the trial had marked a major blow to the primacy of senatorial authority, and to the credibility of the courts. Cicero made that point in the Senate, shortly after Clodius' acquittal, establishing an explicit analogy between him and Catiline, engaging in an altercation with Clodius himself: he depicts himself as having the upper hand, not least thanks to the support of the audience, which was of course very different to that at Clodius' trial, and likely to be receptive to statements in support of senatorial authority.

You next ask about the present state of affairs and my own. That situation of the *res publica*, which *you* thought had been secured by *my* counsel, and *I* by the counsel of the *gods*, and which appeared to have been fixed and founded upon the unity of all god men *(boni)*, and the influence of my consulship, be aware – unless some god turns back and looks upon us – that it has slipped through our hands as a result of this one trial, if it is a trial when thirty of the most fickle and criminal persons, having received their money, destroy law and religion; and what not only all men but also cattle know to have happened, Talna and Plautus and Spongia and the rest of the garbage of this sort decide has never happened. [7] However, to offer you some consolation concerning the *res publica*: wickedness is not dancing with joy in victory in the way that evildoers had hoped, after inflicting so great a wound upon the *res publica*. For they clearly thought that, when religion, chastity, trust in the courts, and the authority of the Senate had collapsed, wickedness and lust would openly seek the punishment of all the best sort for the pain which the strictness of my consulship had branded upon all the most criminal elements. [8] It was I too (for I do not think it arrogant to boast when I am talking about myself to you, especially in a letter that I do not want to be read by others) I, as I say, who restored the shattered morale of the god men (*boni*), strengthening each one individually and giving them confidence; by harrying and harassing all the venal jurors and the supporters of that victory I took away all of their loud mouthing; I did not even let the consul Piso take up a firm stance on any matter and I deprived the fellow of Syria, which had then been promised to him; I recalled the Senate to its earlier strictness and gave it confidence when it had become reduced to despair; I broke Clodius in person in the Senate, not only with a formal speech full of authority, but also in an altercation along the following lines –you may taste some of its flavour, but the rest cannot have the same vim and sparkle when the excitement of the fight, which you people call the contest, has been removed.

[9] Now when we met in the Senate on the Ides of May [15 May] I was asked my opinion and I spoke at length about high politics; that topic was beautifully introduced by me, that the Senate should not give in, nor weaken because it had suffered a single blow; the wound was of a kind that I thought should not be disguised nor one of which we ought be afraid; Lentulus had twice been acquitted, likewise Catiline, now this fellow, the third, had been let loose against the *res publica* by the jurors. 'You are making a mistake, Clodius. The jurors have not kept you back for the city but for prison. They did not wish to keep you in the state but to deprive you of exile. Therefore, senators, raise your spirits, keep hold of your reputation (*dignitas*). That unity of all good men (*boni*) in the *res publica* remains in being; indignation has come upon them, but their courage has not been diminished. No new loss has occurred; one that was there has been found. In the trial of one single desperate citizen more like him have been discovered.' [10] But what am I doing? I have almost included the speech in my letter. I return to the altercation.

The little beauty boy gets up and charges me with having been at Baiae. Untrue, however I reply, 'Well, isn't this just like your saying I was in a secret place?' 'What's a man from Arpinum,' he says, 'doing with the hot springs?' 'Tell that to your advocate,' I say, 'who was after the springs belonging to a man from Arpinum' (for you are aware of the estate of Marius). 'How much longer shall we put up with this king?' 'You call me a king,' I say, 'when Rex made no mention of you at all.' He has, in his optimism squandered the inheritance of Rex. 'You have bought a house,' he says. 'You would think I was saying,' I said, 'you have bought the jurors.' 'They did not believe you,' he says, 'when you were on oath.' 'Actually,' I say, 'twenty-five jurors did believe me; thirty-one did not give any credence to you since they took their cash first.' Assailed with loud shouts he remained silent and collapsed.
Rome, beginning of Quinctilis [July], 61 BC.

Cicero, *To Atticus* 1.16.6–10 (SB 16)

Lentulus was the leading Catilinarian conspirator in Rome, executed on 5 December 63 BC. **Baiae** was a notorious watering hole on the bay of Naples. Cicero had an estate in the neighbourhood and was not in Baiae itself. C. Scribonius Curio, consul 76 BC, had obtained in the Sullan proscriptions a villa of **Marius** in the area of Baiae. He defended Clodius in his trial in 61. Rex ('king') was a term of political abuse, but also the name of noble family, to which Marcius Rex belonged. Cicero has a play on words. Quintus Marcius Rex, consul 68 BC, had been married to Clodia Tertia, youngest sister of Clodius. He died without leaving Clodius anything in his will. After his consulship in 63 BC, Cicero had purchased a house on the Palatine from M. Crassus for a sum of 3.6 million HS, borrowing money from C. Antonius and P. Sulla (see above, **B80**). The house was next door to Clodius'. According to Cicero, thirty-one of the jurors had been bribed to deliver Clodius' acquittal.

B85   Pompey's third triumph, 61 BC

a) Pompey had inscribed on a tablet his own deeds, which he achieved in Asia, and set it up as a dedication of which the following is a copy: 'Pompey the Great, son of Gnaeus, imperator, having liberated the seacoast of the inhabited world and all islands on this side of the Ocean in the war with the pirates; the one who once rescued from siege the kingdom of Ariobarzanes, Galatia and the lands and eparchies lying beyond it, Asia and Bithynia; who protected Paphlagonia and Pontus, Armenia and Achaia, as well as Iberia, Colchis, Mesopotamia, Sophene and Gordyene; brought into subjection Darius king of the Medes, Artoles king of the Iberians, Aristobulus, king of the Jews, Aretas, king of the Nabataean Arabs, Syria bordering on Cilicia, Judaea, Arabia, the province of Cyrene, the Achaeans, the Iozygi, the Soani, the Heniochi, and the other tribes inhabiting the seacoast between Colchis and the Maeotic sea, with their kings, nine in number, and all the nations that dwell between the Pontic and the Red seas; who extended the frontiers of the empire to the ends of the earth; and secured the revenues of the Roman people and increased some; he confiscated the statues and the images of the gods, and all other valuables of the enemy and dedicated to the goddess twelve thousand and sixty pieces of gold and three hundred and seven talents of silver.'

Diodorus, *Library of History* 40.4

b) [1] His triumph was of such magnitude that, although it was distributed over two days, the time would not suffice, but much of what had been prepared could not find a place in the spectacle, although it would have been enough to dignify and adorn another triumphal procession. Inscriptions carried at the forefront of the procession indicated the peoples over which he triumphed. [2] These were: Pontus, Armenia, Cappadocia, Paphlagonia, Media, Colchis, Iberia, Albania, Syria, Cilicia, Mesopotamia, Phoenicia and Palestine, Judaea, Arabia, and all the organization of the pirates, by sea and land, which had been overthrown. According to the inscriptions, no fewer than a thousand strongholds had been conquered in those parts, and not much under nine hundred cities, besides eight hundred piratical ships, and thirty-nine cities had been founded. [3] Moreover, the inscriptions recorded that, while the public revenues from taxes had amounted to fifty million drachmas, they were receiving eighty-five million from the additions that Pompey had made to the city, and that he was bringing into the public treasury twenty thousand talents in coined money and vessels of gold and silver, without including the money that had been given to his soldiers; the one among them whose share was the smallest had received fifteen hundred drachmas. [4] The captives led in triumph, besides the leaders of the pirates, were the son of Tigranes the Armenian with his wife and daughter, Zosime, a wife of King Tigranes himself, Aristobulus, king of the Jews, a sister and five children of Mithridates, Scythian women, and hostages given by the Iberians, the Albanians, and the king of Commagene; there were also a great number of trophies, equal in number to all the battles in which Pompey had won either in person or through his lieutenants. [5] But that which most enhanced his glory and had never befallen to any Roman before, was that he celebrated his third triumph over the third continent. For others before him had celebrated three triumphs; but he celebrated his first over Libya, his second over Europe, and this, his last, over Asia, so that he seemed in a way to have encompassed the whole world in his three triumphs.

Plutarch, *Life of Pompey* 45

c) The high water mark of his fame, as he himself said in an assembly when talking about his career, was finding Asia Minor the furthest of provinces, and making it the central one.

Pliny, *Natural History* 7.99

Pompey's lavish triumph in September 61 was not just about the celebration of his achievements and of the prowess of his army: it was, first and foremost, about displaying the consequences of the Eastern victory for the empire and the city of Rome. Much of that display involved wealth, of course, whether in the form of precious metal or artworks, but pointing out the political consequences of the victory, and the change it had brought about in the shape and scope of Roman rule. The list recorded by Diodorus made that point very emphatically, and was itself a part of Pompey's triumph, in which written texts had a prominent role. Detailed information was given on the nature and quantity of the revenue that had been extracted from the conquered territories. The overall aim of this operation is to show that a new phase in the history of the empire had begun; the emphasis on the donations that the soldiers of Pompey received in the aftermath of the campaign also suggests that the victory in the East paved the way for new political developments in Rome. See **E9-E11** for more on Pompey's achievements in the East and honours paid him. The statement recorded by Pliny the Elder was a briefer and more striking version of the same message, which had a strong visual power: it is not by chance that Pompey used it in a speech to the people. – Other sources on Pompey's triumph: Livy, *Summaries* 103; Velleius Paterculus, *Histories* 2.40.3-4; Pliny, *Natural History* 7.97-99; Appian, *Mithridatic Wars* 116-117; Cassius Dio, *Roman History* 37.21.

B86   Conflict between Senate and *equites*: Asian taxes, 61 BC
Now another delight from the *equites*, hardly tolerable. I have not only tolerated it, but even supported it with my eloquence. Those who had purchased the tax contract for Asia from the censors complained that through eagerness they had fallen into error and paid much too high a price; they asked that the contract be cancelled. I was the leader among their supporters or actually the second; for Crassus encouraged them to dare to make the request. A disagreeable matter, a disgraceful request and an admission of recklessness. There was the greatest danger that if they had not gained their request, they would be openly alienated from the Senate. In this matter help was brought by me most of all and it was brought about that they might treat with a very full meeting of a most generous Senate. On the Kalends of December and the day following [1–2 December], I spoke at length about the dignity of the orders and about unity. The issue has not yet been resolved but the wishes of the Senate have been made clear. For one person had spoken against it, Metellus, the consul designate; because of the shortness of daylight it did not get as far as that hero of ours, Cato, who was going to speak.
Rome, 5 December 61 BC.

Cicero, *To Atticus* 1.17.9 (SB 17)

Cicero regarded cohesion and cooperation among Senate and equestrian order as a cornerstone of orderly political and constitutional life. This view was as deep-seated as it was dogmatic, and stemmed from abstract and genuinely held political and philosophical principles. In this letter Cicero candidly admits to having expressed a political view that was at odds with his convictions, because he felt that meeting the unfair requests of the tax-farmers in the province of Asia would have benefited the relationship between the Senate and the *equites* at a time of grave political instability. Upholding that key principle was more important than opposing a view that one found undesirable, and indeed unprincipled. – Cato, who is ironically mentioned towards the end of this passage, took a very different view. (On his lengthy intervention cf. the Bobbian Scholiast, *Defence of Plancius*, p. 157 Stangl: 'M. Cato spoke against it with all his vigour and rigour and took up all day with the excessive length of his speech, so that the Senate did not have time to make a decision'.)

B87   Dissent between Cicero and Cato

I have often disagreed even with my friend Cato; he seemed to me to guard the treasury and the revenues too rigidly, to refuse everything to the tax-collectors (*publicani*) and much to the allies, though we ought to have been kind towards the latter and to have been dealing with the former as we were accustomed to deal with our tenants, and that all the more so because that uniting of the orders was directed towards the safety of the *res publica*.

Cicero, *On Duties* 3.88

In a philosophical work written shortly before Cato's death, Cicero reflects on the instances in which he disagreed with his distinguished contemporary, and comes back to their different attitudes towards the equestrian orders and their economic interests: in doing so, he comes back to the problem of the concord and cooperation between the two most prominent orders and its political implications. – The reference to the 'allies' is also noteworthy: the reference is here to the subjects of the empire, towards whom Cato had a less lenient attitude than Cicero did. – For a comparable comment cf. what Cicero wrote about Cato to Atticus in June 60 BC (*To Atticus, 2.1.5-8 (SB 21)*): 'even though he has the best will in the world and the highest integrity, he sometimes does harm to the *res publica*: he gives his views as if he were in the Republic of Plato, not in the cesspit of Romulus'.

B88   Senatorial opposition to Pompey, 61/60 BC

[1] At this time Pompey entered Italy and brought about the election of Lucius Afranius and Metellus Celer as consuls, vainly hoping through them to achieve whatever he wished. [2] For he wanted a number of things, in particular, that land be given to those who had campaigned with him and that all the things done by him be ratified. But he failed of these aims at that time. For the powerful (Gk: *dunatoi*), who were not pleased with him even before, prevented these matters being put to the vote; [3] and of the consuls, Afranius (for he knew better how to dance than to conduct business) gave him no help at all, while Metellus, in anger because Pompey had divorced his sister, although he had children by her, did everything possible to oppose him. [4] And Lucius Lucullus, whom Pompey had once met in Galatia and treated contemptuously, was very hostile to him and ordered him to go through, individually and separately, the things he had done and not to ask for ratification for them all together at the same time. [5] For he said that it was in general not right that everything he had done, which none of them knew anything about, should simply be approved as if they had been brought about by some tyrant. And since Pompey had discarded some of Lucullus' own arrangements, he asked that an examination of the deeds of each of them should take place in the senate in order that they might ratify whichever of them

they approved. [50] Cato, Metellus and those of like mind gave their strong support to him in his campaign.

Thus when a tribune introduced a proposal to distribute land to the adherents of Pompey, then adding to the proposal that some allotments be given to all citizens as well, in order that they might more readily vote for this actual proposal and ratify what had been done by him, Metellus proceeded to oppose him on every point so that he was thrown into prison by the tribune; Metellus then intended to convene the Senate there. [2] When the tribune (his name was Lucius Flavius) placed the tribunes' bench in the actual entrance of the prison and sat on it blocking the way so that no one could enter, Metellus ordered them to cut through the wall of the prison so that the senators could enter through it and prepare spend the night there.

[3] When Pompey learned of this, he was ashamed and at the same time feared that the people might be displeased; he instructed Flavius to leave off. He said this as if Metellus had requested it, but he was not believed for Metellus' pride was obvious to all. [4] Indeed, when the other tribunes wanted to set him free, he refused. Not even later, when Flavius threatened not to allow him to go out to the province that he had been assigned by lot unless he agree that the proposal be carried and be made law, did Metellus yield to him, but he was quite delighted to remain in the city. [5] Thus when Pompey did not achieve anything because of Metellus and because of the others, he said that they were jealous of him and that he would make this plain to the plebs; but fearing that he might fail in that aim too and risk greater shame, he dropped his request. [6] And thus he realized that he was not at all powerful in reality, but that he was known and envied for the power he once had, while he actually gained no benefit from it and he regretted having dismissed his forces first and giving himself up to his enemies.

Cassius Dio, *Roman History* 37.49–50

This condensed account gives a summary of the opposition encountered by Pompey in persuading the Senate to ratify the decisions he had made in the East: his isolation is as political as it is personal, and some of his opponents are said to be driven by personal resentment and jealousy (e.g., for different reasons, Metellus and Lucullus). The involvement of a tribune in Pompey's support is reminiscent of the role that some tribunes played in helping him secure the commands against the pirates and Mithridates: in this case, however, there was a heavy clash between a tribune, a consul, and later also other members of the tribunician college. The action of the tribune Flavius, at any rate, proves ineffective because of Metellus' staunch resistance; Pompey, on the other hand, gives further evidence of his reluctance to take a firm political line – a shortcoming that was also lamented by Cicero in this very period (see **B63**).

A NEW CONTEXT: CAESAR'S CONSULSHIP

B89   Political situation in Rome, 60 BC
[3] The *res publica* has been shattered by a bought and debauched trial. See what
followed thereafter. A consul was imposed upon us of a sort that none apart from us
philosophers could look upon without sighing. How great a wound this was! When
a decree of the Senate was passed about electoral malpractice (*ambitus*), about the
courts, no law was carried; the Senate was harassed, the Roman *equites* were alienated
because of that '*who on account of being a juror*'. So that year has overturned two of
the foundations of the *res publica* established by myself alone: it has thrown away the
authority of the Senate and it has split the concord of the orders. Now this outstanding
year is upon us. Its beginning was of such a sort that the annual rites of the goddess
of Youth were not begun; for Memmius initiated the wife of M. Lucullus in his own
rites. Menelaus took it badly and divorced. Although that shepherd of Mount Ida only
despised Menelaus, this Paris of ours has considered Agamemnon as much a slave as
Menelaus. [4] There is one C. Herennius, a tribune of the plebs, whom you perhaps
do not even know; yet you may know of him, he is one of your tribe and Sextus, his
father, used to distribute money for you. He is transferring Clodius to the plebs and
proposing that the whole people take a vote on the matter of Clodius in the Campus
Martius. I gave him a reception in the Senate, as is my custom, but there is nothing
more slow-witted than this fellow.

[5] Metellus is an outstanding consul and has a high regard for me, but has diminished
his standing, because he has for the sake of appearance issued exactly the same
promulgation concerning Clodius. As for Aulus' son – ye gods – what a lazy fellow,
what a spiritless soldier! How fitting for him to show his face daily for Palicanus' abuse,
which is what he does. [6] An agrarian law has been promulgated by Flavius, quite
insignificant, almost the same as that Plotian law. Meanwhile not one statesman can
be found, not even in a dream. The person who could have been, our friend, (for so
he is, I want you to know this) Pompey, looks in silence upon that embroidered little
toga (*toga picta*) of his. Crassus utters not a word to endanger his popularity. The rest
you know: they are so stupid that they seem to hope that their fish-ponds will be safe,
if the *res publica* is lost [7] The one to care with more determination and integrity than
discernment and intellect, so it seems to me, is Cato; he has for three months now been
harassing the wretched tax-collectors (*publicani*), whom he used to have as his most
devoted supporters and is not allowing any response to be given them in the Senate.
And so we are compelled to make no decision on remaining matters before a response is
given to the tax-collectors (*publicani*). Thus I think the embassies too will be postponed.
Rome, 22 January 60 BC.

                                          Cicero, *To Atticus* 1.18.3–7 (SB 18)

Much of the surviving narrative for this period is provided by Cicero's correspondence. This letter gives a
powerful, if unilateral account of the political situation in the late sixties, where Clodius' acquittal remains
the dominant theme, and the process that will lead to Clodius' adoption into a plebeian family has started
to unfold. Clodius aimed to be adopted into the plebs so that we could be eligible to run for the tribunate
and pursue his political agenda from that influential position: Cicero is trying to oppose that process, partly
on grounds of principle, and partly in the knowledge that Clodius would seek to launch an attack on him
during his tribunate. Neither Pompey nor Crassus (who had recently expressed his admiration for Cicero) are
posing any meaningful resistance. Cato is on Cicero's side of the argument, but their views on the role of the

equestrian order remain strongly different, and make a long-term political cooperation unlikely. – The piece of gossip that Cicero summarizes with an allusion to Paris, Menelaus, and Agamemnon was probably about L. Licinius Lucullus, his brother Marcus, and C. Memmius, tribune of 66 BC, who was rumoured to have seduced the wives of both brothers. Aulus' son is Cicero's scathingly dismissive way of referring to other consul of 60 BC, L. Afranius, whom he describes in his next letter as 'a nothing' – On the Plotian law, see **L27**.

B90   Cicero opposes the agrarian law of Flavius, 60 BC

[4] Affairs in the city are as follows: an agrarian law is being vigorously pushed by Flavius, a tribune of the plebs, at the instigation of Pompey, which has nothing *popularis* about it apart from its *proposer/instigator*. With the agreement of an assembly (*contio*) I removed all those items, which made for the disadvantage of private citizens; I released that land which had been public in the consulship of P. Mucius and L. Calpurnius; I confirmed the possessions of the Sullan settlers; I kept the people of Volaterrae and Arretium, whose properties Sulla had confiscated but not distributed, in possession of their land; one clause I did not reject that land might be purchased with this windfall money, which is being received from the new revenues over the period of five years. The Senate is opposed to this whole scheme of an agrarian law suspecting that some new position of power is being sought for Pompey; Pompey has applied himself vigorously to his wish for the law to be carried. I, with great gratitude from the beneficiaries of the law, am confirming the holdings of all private owners: for that is my army – the men of means, as you know. I am satisfying the people and Pompey (for I wanted that too) by the purchase; when this is carefully settled I think the dregs of the city can be cleared away and the desolation of Italy filled with people. But this whole issue has been interrupted by war and has gone into cold storage.

Cicero, *To Atticus* 1.19.4 (SB 19)

Cicero discusses another important issue of the political history of the year 60 BC: an agrarian law presented by the tribune Flavius, with Pompey's backing. The proposal finds opposition within the Senate, especially because it is seen as benefiting Pompey and his veterans. Cicero focuses on his response, which is one of moderate openness to a plan of land assignments, but is also very preoccupied with the interests of private landowners in Italy – notably in Etruria, where he has personal connections. The new assignments, in his view, must not be carried out on land confiscated from private owners. The prospect of Clodius' adoption into the plebs is still on the table, and Cicero feels the need to broaden his base of political support among the Italian *élites*. – Proposer/instigator: textual variants in the Latin (*actorem* or *auctorem*).

B91   Background to the Caesar/Pompey/Crassus alliance, 60 BC

No ancient source speaks of a 'First Triumvirate', which was a private political partnership, unlike the so-called 'Second Triumvirate' of 43 BC, which was a fully-fledged magistracy, and should in fact be referred as *the* 'Triumvirate', without preceding numerals. Yet, an agreement as significant as that between Pompey, Crassus, and Caesar was not merely a private matter, not just for its political implications: the oath that the three men are said to have pronounced is a solemn declaration of good faith, made before the gods.

a) For Cornelius has been at my house, that's Balbus, I mean, the close friend of Caesar. He assures me that Caesar will use my advice and that of Pompey in everything, and will do his utmost to bring Crassus and Pompey together. These are the consequences: the closest association for me with Pompey, if I want it even with Caesar, a return to favour with my enemies, peace with the masses, security in old age. I do not think I ought to hesitate, except that there always seems to me 'one omen best – to fight for the fatherland'. Rome (?), late December 60 BC.

Cicero, *To Atticus* 2.3.3–4 (SB 23)

Shortly before the beginning of his consulship, Caesar instructs his friend Cornelius Balbus to convey to Cicero his intention to seek advice from him: more broadly, Cicero is offered a role in a political season of renewed political stability; the reference to the 'return to favour' with his enemies is a clear promise to protect him from Clodius' attacks. – Cicero's mild reluctance is conveyed through a quote from Homer (*Iliad* 12.243): literary allusions are very common in his correspondence with Atticus. – Balbus was a prominent citizen of Gades (modern Cadiz), in Spain, who had received the Roman citizenship in the late seventies and had since established a close personal connection with Caesar. His involvement in this affair is noteworthy: he is not a member of the Senate at this stage, but Caesar resorts to him as a trusted political envoy.

b) You [Pollio] deal with the civil disorder beginning in the consulship of Metellus, the causes of the war, the evils and the phases of it and the play of Fortune, the grim friendships of the chief citizens (*principes*) and weapons stained with blood still unexpiated, a work full of danger and risk, and you walk over fires placed beneath treacherous ash.

Horace, *Odes* 2.1.1–8

Horace is here referring to the history of Asinius Pollio, which began in 60 BC: a significant choice of periodization, which seems to place considerable significance on the events of that year to the later developments in the late Republican crisis.

c) Gaius Caesar conquered the Lusitanians; when he was a candidate for the consulship and striving to attack the *res publica,* a conspiracy was formed between three leaders (*principes*) of the state (*civitas*), Pompey, M. Crassus, C. Caesar.

Livy, *Summaries* 103

d) [44] Thus, when Caesar was consul that alliance of power was begun between him and Pompey and M. Crassus, which was deadly for the city and for the world and no less for each of the partners themselves at different times. [2] Pompey's reason for following this policy had been that his arrangements in the overseas provinces, which, as I have said before, many were objecting to, were at last confirmed with Caesar as consul; Caesar, because he realized that by yielding to the fame of Pompey he would increase his own, and that when the odium for their joint power was shifted upon Pompey he would strengthen his own power; Crassus, in that he was unable to attain to the leading position on his own, would get it with the authority of Pompey and the power of Caesar. [3] The close association between Caesar and Pompey was further strengthened by a marriage tie; for Cn. Magnus married the daughter of C. Caesar.

Velleius Paterculus, *Histories* 2.44.1–3

This brief summary outlines the political and personal rewards that the alliance between Pompey, Crassus, and Caesar yielded for the three men. (For a later and lengthier account of the hopes and concerns that led the three men to form their partnership, see Dio 37.54-57.) The association between Pompey and Caesar is strengthened by a marriage alliance, as was often the case in the Roman nobility: Pompey married Julia, Caesar's daughter. It is interesting to see that even an early imperial author like Velleius regards the alliance between Caesar, Pompey, and Crassus as a devastating blow to Rome and her freedom.

e) Meanwhile, Lucullus was disputing with Pompey over the arrangements in Pontus, for each claimed that his own arrangements should be put into effect. Cato stood up for Lucullus, who was obviously wronged; Pompey, being defeated in the Senate and acting as a *popularis*, summoned his soldiers for a distribution of land. [2] But when Cato opposed him in this also and frustrated the proposed law, Pompey attached himself to

Clodius, at this time the boldest of the *populares*, and won Caesar over to his side. Cato in a way caused this situation, [3] for Caesar having returned from his propraetorship in Spain, wanted to stand for the consulship and at the same time was seeking a triumph. [4] But since those who were canvassing for office had by law to be present in Rome, while those who were intending to celebrate a triumph had to remain outside the walls, Caesar asked the Senate for permission to seek office by means of others. [5] Many were in favour of granting this request, but Cato spoke against the proposal. When he saw that others were willing to please Caesar, he used up the whole day in speaking and caused the proposal to be rejected.

Plutarch, *Life of Cato the Younger* 31.1–5

Plutarch frames his discussion of the year 60 BC around the ambitions and frustrations of some key political players, as one would expect of a biographer: Pompey's initiatives are frustrated by the opposition he encounters in the Senate, and he considers joining forces with Clodius and, through him, with Caesar; Cato is the main figurehead of senatorial opposition, and he also stands in the way of Caesar's ambition to celebrate a triumph before putting forward his candidacy to the consulship. Cato's attempt was successful; the picture that Plutarch conjures up, however, is one in which the alliance between Pompey and Caesar, which would have fatal consequences for the authority and standing of the Senate, was brought about by the intransigence and shortsightedness of the senatorial nobility.

f) [18.1] Having pacified his province, he left with equal haste, without having waited for his successor, for a triumph and at the same time for a consulship. [2] But with the elections having already been publicly notified, his official candidacy could not be accepted unless he had entered the city as a private citizen and many people were opposing his canvassing that he be exempted from the laws; he was compelled to leave his triumph so that he would not be excluded from the consulship.

[19.1] Of his two competitors for the consulship, Lucius Lucceius and Marcus Bibulus, Caesar joined in making an agreement that Lucceius since he was weaker in influence but had more money, should publicly promise cash among the centuries in their joint names. When this became known, the *optimates*, who were seized by the fear that there was nothing Caesar would not dare in that magistracy with a like-minded colleague who felt as he did, authorized Bibulus to promise just as much; and many of them contributed money, while not even Cato denied that this bribery was in the interests of the *res publica*. [2] In this way Caesar was elected consul with Bibulus. And for the same reason, great trouble was taken by the *optimates* that provinces of minimal importance, namely the commissionership of public woodlands and cattle paths and pastures, should be assigned to the future consuls. Utterly infuriated by this insult, Caesar gave total support, through acts of friendship, to Pompey, who was at loggerheads with the Senate because, having defeated Mithridates, it was taking too long to ratify his arrangements; and Caesar reconciled Pompey to Marcus Crassus, an inveterate enemy since their consulship, which they had conducted together in complete disagreement on everything. He entered into an alliance with each that nothing should be done in the *res publica*, which did not have the agreement of all three.

Suetonius, *Divus Julius* 18–19

Suetonius places the formation of the alliance with Pompey and Crassus to the year of Caesar's consulship, rather than to the months preceding his election, and identifies an interesting factor of explanation: Caesar wanted to receive a prestigious and remunerative province after his consulship, and had to overcome senatorial opposition to his plan – hence his decision to reach out to two unlikely partners.

B92   Consulship of Caesar and Bibulus, 59 BC

a) [1] At the beginning of his consulship, he first of all established that the proceedings of the Senate and the people should be recorded in writing and published. ... Having promulgated an agrarian law, Caesar drove his colleague from the forum by armed force when he announced unfavourable omens. On the following day Bibulus complained in the Senate, but no one was found to dare to bring a motion before the Senate on such disorder or to censure it in any way, although many such decrees had been passed on less serious disturbances. Bibulus was driven to such desperation that, until he left office, he hid himself at home and did nothing else except issue announcements of unfavourable omen by means of edicts.

[2] From that time on he alone managed all affairs in the *res publica* in accordance with his wishes, so that some city dwellers when they were signing some document as a witness jokingly wrote not 'signed in the consulship of Caesar and Bibulus' but 'signed in the consulship of Julius and Caesar', putting the same person twice with his name and his *cognomen*, so that these verses soon spread among the people:

> *A thing happened recently not when Bibulus was consul but Caesar,*
> *For I do not recall anything when Bibulus was consul.*

Suetonius, *Divus Julius* 20.1–2, with omission

This notice in Suetonius draws attention to two different, but complementary aspects of innovation in Caesar's consulship: on the one hand, his decision to publicize the proceedings of the Senate, which is clear evidence of his wider commitment to the principle that the people had a right to scrutinize the actions of the nobility; on the other, the rather cavalier attitude with which he appeared to react to the extraordinary decision of his colleague, M. Calpurnius Bibulus, to withdraw from public affairs for the rest of his term in office (see **B94**). For more on how Caesar got his agrarian law past the opposition of Bibulus, see **L18**. The ironic comment on the consulship of 'Julius and Caesar' had a pointed ring to it: the tradition on the origins of the Republic portrayed the consulship as a dual office, which retained the set of powers of the kings while splitting them between two men. On a reading of his quip, Caesar could be regarded as having briefly revived the monarchy.

B93   Legislation of Caesar, 59 BC

a) [7] Cato, in particular, already suspecting that the friendship and alliance between Caesar and Pompey had not come about for any just purpose, said that what he was afraid of was not the distribution of land but the reward, which those who were seeking to ensnare the people and win their favour, would demand for this.

[32] By these words he made the Senate of one mind; many men, who were not senators, supported him because they were indignant at Caesar's unusual behaviour; [2] for the policies, which the boldest and most arrogant of the tribunes used to pursue to win the favour of the masses, were the very policies which Caesar was using, with the backing of his consular authority, in a shameful and degrading way insinuating himself into the people's favour. [3] Now, because they were terrified, they had recourse to violence. Firstly, as Bibulus was going down to the forum, he had a bucket of shit thrown over his head; next they assaulted his lictors and broke their rods of office (*fasces*); [4] finally, when missiles were flying and a great many people were being injured, all the other senators ran in flight from the forum, but Cato was the very last to leave at walking pace, all the time turning back and protesting to the citizens. [5] In this way, they not only ratified the distribution of land, but

they also voted that the whole Senate should swear to uphold the law and give its support if anyone should act against it ... [*Cato is reluctant, but finally concedes to the persuasive advice of Cicero.*]

[33] Elated by this, Caesar introduced another law distributing in addition almost all the Campanian land to the poor and needy. [2] No one spoke against the law except Cato. And Caesar had him dragged from the *rostra* to prison. Cato in no way gave up his outspoken criticism but, as he walked along, continued to discuss the proposed law and to advise the people to stop those who proposed such policies. [3] The Senate followed in dejection and the better element among the people followed too in silent anger and indignation, so that Caesar could not fail to notice their annoyance. However, he was obstinate, and was expecting that Cato would appeal and plead with him and continued to lead him away to prison. [4] But when it became obvious that Cato was not intending to do any such thing, Caesar was overcome with shame and disgrace and himself secretly persuaded one of the tribunes to release Cato.

Plutarch, *Life of Cato the Younger* 31.7–33.4, with omission

Cato stands out as one of the most vocal opponents of Caesar during his consulship. His opposition fails to prevent the passing of the agrarian laws, but makes an impact in one important respect: his arrest, carried out with the involvement of a tribune of the plebs, alienates the sympathy of part of the Senate and even of the people from Caesar. – Plutarch often understands, and ultimately misconstrues, Roman politics in essentially Greek terms, through the familiar opposition between the few and the many, the Senate and the people, hence failing to do justice to important aspects of its complexity.

b) [20.3] The plain of Stellas, which had been consecrated by our ancestors, and the Campanian land, which had been left subject to taxation to aid the *res publica*, he divided without ballot among twenty thousand citizens who each had three or more children. When the tax-collectors (*publicani*) sought relief, he freed them from a third part of the sum they were due to pay, and openly warned them that they should not bid too recklessly in contracting for taxes in the future. In other matters, whatever had taken anyone's fancy, he likewise freely granted everything, either without opposition or by frightening off anyone who tried to oppose. [4] He ordered Marcus Cato, who tried to interrupt proceedings, to be dragged from the senate-house by a lictor and taken off to prison. When Lucius Lucullus was putting up rather too resolute resistance, he struck such fear of false charges being brought against him that he spontaneously fell on his knees before him. When Cicero, while pleading in court, deplored the state of the times, Caesar transferred that very same day and at the ninth hour his enemy Publius Clodius, who had been striving vainly for a long time to transfer from the patricians to the plebs. [5] Finally, against all opposition, he bribed an informer to admit that he had been instigated by certain men to attack Pompey and, having been brought forward on to the rostra in accordance with the agreement, to name those responsible. But when the informer had named one or two to no purpose, and not without suspicion of fraud, Caesar, despairing of the outcome of his hasty scheme, is believed to have removed him by poison.

[21] At about the same time he married Calpurnia, the daughter of L. Piso, who was to succeed him in the consulship, and betrothed his own daughter Julia to Pompey, breaking a prior engagement with Servilius Caepio, although he had shortly before

given him conspicuous help in his fight with Bibulus. And after this new marriage alliance he began to call on Pompey first of all to give his opinion in the Senate, although he was accustomed to begin with Crassus and it was the custom that the consul should adhere throughout the year to the order of asking for opinions, which he had established on the Kalends of January [1 January].

Suetonius, *Divus Julius* 20.3–21.1, with omission

Suetonius takes a broader look at Caesar's achievements during his consulship, and discusses his ruthless political work: notably the blend of persuasion and threats with which he got rid of potential opponents, or even of potential threats to his plans. The reference to Caesar's marriage to Calpurnia and to the marriage of Pompey conveys a sense of an increasingly tight and effective control over the political scene, and of the consolidation of a coalition of forces around a successful and ambitious consul. The decision to let Pompey give his opinion first in the Senate is also a break with tradition that some will have found disturbing. - Sulla had abolished the position of *princeps senatus* and the consul who presided the first session of the Senate each year decided the order of speaking, which was then observed for the rest of the year. Cicero had been annoyed in 61 BC not to be asked to speak first. The consuls designate, if in existence, spoke first, then the ex-consuls, as is clearly the case in the 'great debate' in December 63 BC. Aulus Gellius states that prior to his time the order of speaking was varied; sometimes the man first enrolled in the Senate by the censors, sometimes the consuls designate; sometimes according to the personal inclination of the consuls contrary to regular order: 'It is said that C. Caesar, when he was consul with M. Bibulus, called on only four senators out of order. The first of these was M. Crassus, but after Caesar had betrothed his daughter to Pompey, he began to call on Pompey first' (*Attic Nights*, 4.10.5).

c) He brought forward laws winning over the plebs and had all of the acts of Pompey ratified, as he had promised him. The so-called *equites*, who held the middle rank between the plebs and the Senate, were very powerful in all ways because of their wealth and of their contract for the taxes and tribute, which were paid by the provincials. They contracted for their collection and kept a large number of most trustworthy staff for this purpose. They had been asking the Senate for a long time to have relief from a part of their dues. The Senate regularly deferred the matter. As Caesar did not make any request of the Senate, but only dealt with the people, he released them from a third part of their obligations. For this unexpected favour beyond what they deserved the *equites* extolled Caesar as a god and a body more powerful than the plebs was added to Caesar through one political act. He put on shows and hunts of wild animals beyond his means, borrowing money for everything and surpassing all previous shows in lavish provision and display and with wonderful gifts, as a consequence of which they appointed him governor of both Cisalpine and Transalpine Gaul for five years, and gave him an army of four legions for the post.

Appian, *Civil Wars* 2.13

Seeking the favour of the equestrian order had long been a key preoccupation for Cicero; Caesar pursued the same aim very assertively during his consulship by passing a law that exempted the *publicani* from part of their financial obligations towards the treasury: his decision to resort to a vote of the people without seeking the prior endorsement of the Senate proved crucial. At the same time, he made sure to consolidate his following among the people, pursuing a method that he had already adopted during his aedileship.

B94   Bibulus and *obnuntiatio*, 59 BC
Then Clodius declared, both here and in assemblies (*contiones*), that the Julian laws had been passed contrary to the auspices; among those laws was included that law passed by a popular assembly (*lex curiata*), which embraced the whole of his tribunate. This he did not see, blinded by madness as he was. He brought forward that most courageous

man, M. Bibulus; he asked him if he had been watching the heavens all the time while Caesar was passing his laws. He said that he had been watching all the time. Clodius put the question to the augurs whether laws, which had been passed in these circumstances, had been properly passed. They stated that their passing had been flawed.

Cicero, *On the Response of the Haruspices* 48

The argument that Bibulus resorted to in his attempt to block Caesar's agrarian law was one of religious procedure: he claimed that he could see signs of divine hostility in the sky. After he was removed from the Comitium and the law was passed, Bibulus attempted to block Caesar's legislation by remaining at home for most of his year of office and declaring he was looking for propitious omens: see Velleius Paterculus, *Roman History* 2.44.5 and Suetonius, *Divus Julius* 20.1 = **B92b**. Cicero here records an attack launched by Clodius on Caesar's legislation, during his tribunate of 58: far from acting as a mere pawn of Caesar, he sought support even among those who had questioned the legitimacy of Caesar's actions during his consulship, invoking religious arguments, which Cicero readily turns against him: if the acts of the year 59 were invalid, that also applies to the adoption of Clodius into the plebs under a *lex curiata* (passed by the *comitia curiata*), and his entitlement to stand for the tribunate.

B95   Recognition of Ptolemy Auletes, 59 BC

a) [My client] had many business interests; he had many contracts. He had many shares in the firms of tax-collectors (*publicani*); he made loans to communities. His business straddled many provinces; he even gave his services to kings. He had at an earlier time lent a large sum of money to this very king of Alexandria.

Cicero, *Defence of Rabirius Postumus* 4

b) After this there were further disturbances on account of King Ptolemy. He had lavished large sums of money upon some of the Romans, some out of his own purse and some borrowed, so that he might have his rule confirmed and be named friend and ally.

Cassius Dio, *Roman History* 39.12.1

c) He made alliances and kingdoms at a price, for he extorted from Ptolemy alone nearly six thousand talents in his own name and that of Pompey.

Suetonius, *Divus Julius* 54.3

Egypt retained its independence even after the fall of the Seleucid kingdom, and the dynasty of the Ptolemies was the last surviving political force from the age of the Successors of Alexander the Great. It owed its existence, however, to the support and protection of Rome, and at various points in the history of the first century BC the Senate and some prominent individuals took an active interest in the affairs of the kingdom, especially when a succession crisis was looming. There were, at the same time, various attempts on the part of members of the royal house to influence the decisions taken on Egypt in Rome: Ptolemy XII Auletes was especially active in the fifties, and there is evidence for his personal and financial dealings with a number of members of the Roman élite: to some he donated money, clearly with a view of getting a more conciliatory or supportive approach, while from others he borrowed significant sums of money. Suetonius draws attention to another kind of financial interaction: Caesar asked the king to pay him and Pompey a hefty sum in exchange for their patronage.

B96   Clodius becomes a plebeian, 59 BC

Are they to deny that Publius has been made a plebeian? This certainly is tyranny (*regnum*) and cannot by any means be tolerated. … My young friend Curio runs into me on his way from Rome. At that precise moment your boy was there with the letters from you. Curio asked me whether I had heard any news. I said I had not. 'Publius,' he said, 'is a candidate for the tribunate of the plebs.' 'What are you saying?' 'And further, most hostile to Caesar, so that he may repeal all those laws of his.' 'What about Caesar?' I ask. 'He says he had nothing to do with the adoption.' Tres Tabernae, 19 April 59 BC.

Cicero, *To Atticus*, 2.12.1–2 (SB 30), with omission

This letter is the closest contemporary source on the adoption of Clodius: the degree of support that Caesar had lent to that bold political operation was still unclear at the time; Cicero was told that Clodius would soon be pursuing a plan for the repeal of Caesar's recent legislation. – Other sources, however, regard Caesar as a driving force behind Clodius' adoption into the plebs, which took place during his consulship (cf. Suetonius, *Divus Julius* 20.4, above B93b; Cassius Dio, *Roman History* 38.12.1-2).

B97 Cicero's reactions, 59 BC

a) I wholly agree with what you write. Sampsiceramus is stirring up trouble. *He is avowedly preparing tyranny* [Gk: *tyrannis*]. For what does this sudden marriage alliance mean, the Campanian land, the vast spending of money? If these were the end of it, it would be excessively bad; but the nature of the matter is such that these cannot be the end of it. They cannot take delight in these measures of themselves. They would never have come to this point if they were not paving their way for other destructive enterprises.
Formiae, May 59 BC.

Cicero, *To Atticus* 2.17.1 (SB 37)

A few months into the consulship of Caesar, it becomes clear to Cicero that his partnership with Pompey is solid and likely to make a considerable impact: Pompey is now regarded as one who is harbouring tyrannical ambitions. – Sampsiceramus was a Near Eastern dynast: his name is turned into a derogatory nickname for Pompey, whose achievements in the East are turned into an opportunity to denounce his monarchic ambitions (see also 2.23.2 = SB 43).

b) [1] I have received several letters from you, which made me realize the suspense and anxiety with which you longed to know what news there was. We are held tight on all sides and no longer refuse to be slaves. We fear death and banishment as if they were greater evils. They are much less. And this state of affairs, which is universally moaned about in the talk of all, is not relieved by any deed or words from anyone. The <u>object</u> of those who hold power, so I suspect, is to leave no largesse for anyone else. One person speaks out and openly opposes – the young man Curio. He is greatly applauded, receives the most complimentary greetings in the forum, and is given very many signs of goodwill from the good men (*boni*) besides. Fufius they pursue with shouts, abuse and hisses. But this gives rise not to greater hope, but rather anguish, when one sees that the will of the citizen body is free, but its courage is shackled. [2] But to save you asking about individual matters <u>in detail</u>, the whole situation has been brought to the point that there is no hope that either private citizens or even magistrates will ever be free. However, in this oppressive atmosphere conversation is freer than it used to be in social circles, that is, and at dinner parties. Resentment is beginning to conquer fear, but in such a way that there is absolute despair everywhere.
Rome, June 59 BC.

Cicero, *To Atticus* 2.18.1–2 (SB 38)

The sense that the advent of tyranny might be imminent and that regular and lawful political practice may be drawing to an abrupt end is voiced in other letters of Cicero from this period. In this letter to Atticus there is a degree of ambiguity: the fear that Cicero talks about is both about his own position and that of the *res publica*. The comments on the contrast between an increasingly stifled public discourse and the greater freedom of speech in private contexts are especially perceptive, and draw attention to an important level of the political conversation, which takes place beyond public and official contexts.

c) [1] I have many anxieties arising from the grave political situation and from the dangers which threaten me personally. They are countless, but none is more annoying to me than the manumission of Statius: "*That my authority* (imperium)*, no, I let that pass, that my displeasure be not even heeded.*" I do not know what to do and it is not so much what has happened as what is being said. However, I cannot even be angry with those I love dearly. I am simply hurt – and deeply hurt at that.

My other anxieties concern important matters. The threats of Clodius and the campaigns prepared against me disturb me little: for I think I can face them all with dignity (*auctoritas*) or avoid them without personal inconvenience. Perhaps you will say 'Enough of dignity (*auctoritas*). That's out of date. Please, I beg you, take thought for your security.' Oh dear! Why are you not here? I am sure nothing would escape your notice. Perhaps I am blind and too attached to the ideal. [2] You may be certain that nothing has ever been so infamous, so disgraceful, so generally odious to men of all sorts, classes and ages as the present state of affairs; more so, in truth, than I would have wished, let alone imagined. Those *populares* have taught even moderate men to hiss. Bibulus is praised to the skies – why I don't know – just as though

"*One man alone, by delay, restored the state for us.*"

Pompey, my hero, has brought about his own ruin, a fact which causes me great pain. They hold no one by goodwill. I fear they may have resort to terror. But I do not oppose their cause because of my friendship with him. I do not approve it either. That would be to nullify all that I have done previously. I keep to the highway. [3] The feeling of the people has been manifested particularly at the theatre and the shows. For at the gladiatorial show, the master and his guests were overwhelmed with hisses. At the Games of Apollo, the tragic actor Diphilus made a vicious attack on our Pompey:

"*To our sorrow you are great ...*"

It received a thousand encores. He spoke the line

"*A time will come when you will rue that same prowess*"

to shouts from the whole theatre. Other lines received the same response. For the lines are such that you might think that they had been written for the occasion by an enemy of Pompey.

"*If neither laws nor customs compel ...*"

and other lines were spoken amid loud groans and shouts. When Caesar entered, the applause died. Curio's son followed him. He was applauded just as Pompey used to be when the *res publica* was in good health. Caesar was annoyed, and people say a letter is on its way post-haste to Pompey at Capua. They are hated by the equestrians, who stood and applauded Curio. They are public enemies of all. They threaten the Roscian law and even the corn law. Things really are in a pretty mess. For my part, I should have preferred their undertaking to be passed over in silence, but I fear this may not be possible. People are not tolerating what apparently they must. All now speak with one voice, but this unanimity is based only on hatred, not on strength.

[4] Our friend Publius is constantly threatening me; he is hostile. The business is looming up and you will, I am sure, come in haste for it. I think I have the support of the army of good men (*boni*) and moderately good ones too – the support I had when consul. Pompey shows considerable favour towards me; he declares that Clodius will not say one word against me. In this he does not deceive me; he deceived himself. On the death of Cosconius, I was invited to fill his place on the land commission for Campania. That would be stepping into a dead man's shoes! Nothing would have degraded me more in men's eyes, nothing could have been further removed from that security you are always talking about. For the commissioners are unpopular with decent citizens (*boni*), I with the law-breakers (*improbi*); I should have kept my own unpopularity and taken on other people's as well. [5] Caesar wants me to join his staff – a more honourable way out of the danger, certainly, but that is not what I want. Why is that? I prefer to fight. But nothing is decided. I say again: 'If only you were here.' Yet, if it becomes essential, I will send for you. Anything else? Just this, I think. I am certain all is lost. Why mince words any longer? But I write this hurriedly and – believe me – in trembling. In future, I shall write everything plainly to you, if I have a trustworthy messenger, or else, if I write obscurely to you, you will understand all the same. In such letters I will call myself Laelius and you Furius. The rest will be in riddles. Here I am cultivating your uncle Caecilius and playing close attention to you. Our friend Pompey is passionately upset and angry at them.
Rome, mid-July 59.

Cicero, *To Atticus* 2.19 (SB 39)

In this letter Cicero gives Atticus, who is in Epirus, an overview of the political situation of 59 BC, and of the impact that Caesar's consulship is making: the land bill has changed the terms of the political controversy, and the circumstances that led to its passing have raised considerable discontent among those who favour a more consensual approach to politics. Bibulus may be in self-imposed confinement in his home, but many still praise his actions, while Pompey has lost much of his standing both with the people and in the Senate. The atmosphere at some recent theatre shows is invoked as a useful indicator of the shifting loyalties in the city. The young C. Scribonius Curio plays a leading role in mobilizing opposition to the agrarian law; less than a decade later, in 50 BC, he will be one of the two tribunes defending Caesar's position in the Senate (**B137**): a stark reminder that political loyalties are hardly set in stone in Republican Rome.

Caesar has invited Cicero to join the committee that will implementation of the agrarian law, but Cicero is minded to refuse the offer, even though that might have the effect of diffusing the pressure created by Clodius ('our friend Publius'), who has embarked on a political offensive against him. – As is often the case in Cicero's correspondence with Atticus, the letter blends political and private concerns: the opening comments are on the decision of his brother Quintus of manumitting one of his slaves, Staius, whom Cicero strongly disapproved of.

d) [2] Clodius is still threatening me with trouble. Pompey declares there is no danger, he swears it; he even adds he will be killed by Clodius before I am violated ... . [3] On the *res publica* I shall write to you briefly; for I now fear the very paper will betray us. So hereafter, if there are more things I have to write to you, I shall make them obscure by veiled language. But now the state is dying through some strange disease, such that while all disapprove, complain and grieve at what has happened, while there is no disagreement on any matter and they speak out openly and are now groaning clearly, no medicine, however, is being brought forward. For we do not think resistance can be put up without carnage, and we do not see what the end result of giving way will be other than ruin. [4] Bibulus is in seventh heaven, surrounded by admiration and goodwill. His edicts and speeches they copy and read. He has come to a high point of glory in a new kind of way. Nothing is so popular now as hatred of the *populares*. I am afraid of where all this is going to erupt; but if I start to perceive anything, I shall write to you more openly.

Rome, mid-July 59 BC.

Cicero, *To Atticus* 2.20.2–4 (SB 40)

Pompey's pledge to protect Cicero against Clodius' attacks was soon going to prove hollow. Cicero's main comment, however, is of special interest here: he points to a context in which Caesar faced significant opposition among the plebs, and Bibulus was far from isolated. The later developments of the year suggest that this assessment was considerably optimistic. Cicero's comment on the real potential for internal strife on a large scale, however, should be taken seriously, and might be part of the explanation for the ineffectiveness of the opposition to Caesar in 59: taking opposition to its extreme consequences may have seemed undesirable to many.

e) [1] Concerning the *res publica*, no need of great detail: it is completely lost; and, in this respect, in a more wretched state than when you left it. It seemed at that time that a despotism (*dominatio*) had overwhelmed the state, of a sort such as was pleasing to the masses, and while irksome to good men (*boni*) at least not lethal. However, it is now so odious to all that we shudder to think in what direction it is going to erupt. For we have experienced the anger and recklessness of those men, who in their anger at Cato have destroyed everything. They seemed at that time to be using such gentle poisons that we appeared to be able to die without pain; but now with the hisses of the masses, the talk of good men (*boni*) and the murmurings in Italy, I fear they have become inflamed with anger. [2] For my part I hoped, as I often used to say to you, that the wheel of the *res publica* had turned in such a way that we could scarcely hear its sound, scarcely see the imprint of its track; and so it would have turned out, if people had been able to await the passing of the storm. But having for a long time sighed in secret, they began to murmur, and in the end they all began to speak out and shout aloud.

[3] And so our friend [Pompey], unaccustomed to unpopularity, always having enjoyed praise, abounding in glory, now physically disfigured and his morale shattered, does not know in which direction to take himself. In going forward he sees a precipice, in going backwards the charge of inconsistency. The good citizens (*boni*) are hostile to him, the troublemakers (*improbi*) themselves are not his friends. Now see how soft-hearted I am: I did not hold back tears when I saw him on 25 July addressing an assembly (*contio*) about the edicts of Bibulus. For one who before had been accustomed to comport himself in such magnificent style in that spot amid the deep affection of the people and everyone on his side, how humble and dejected he now was, how displeasing not only to those who were present but even to himself as well. [4] What a sight! Pleasing to Crassus alone, not so to the rest. Because he had fallen down from the stars, he appeared to have slipped down rather than gone forward. And just as if Apelles saw his Venus daubed with filth, or Protogenes his renowned Ialysus, each would, I believe, feel great pain, so I did not look upon this man without great pain, one whom I had painted and polished with all the colours of my art, now suddenly disfigured. Although nobody thought I ought to be his friend because of the business with Clodius, my affection for him, however, was so great that no injury

could exhaust it. Thus Bibulus' Archilochian edicts against him are so popular with the people that we cannot pass the place where they are posted for the crowds of people reading them. They are so distressing to Pompey himself that he is wasting away with grief. I find them annoying, by Hercules, because they are torturing a man for whom I have always felt affection, and I am afraid that one so impulsive, so keen to draw the sword and so unused to insult, may give vent to his anger and resentment with full force and feeling.

[5] What will be the end of Bibulus I do not know. As things now stand, he has a remarkable reputation. When he put off the elections to the month of October, because such action is accustomed to fall foul of the wishes of the people, Caesar thought that an assembly (*contio*) could be incited by his speech to march on Bibulus' house. Although he made many highly inflammatory remarks, he could not raise a murmur. In short, they realize that no section of society supports them. There is all the more reason why we have to fear violence. [6] Clodius is hostile to me. Pompey assures me *he* will do nothing against me, but it is dangerous for me to believe him. I am preparing myself for resistance. I hope I will have the full support of all orders. I miss you; moreover, the situation calls for you to meet the crisis. Your presence will add quite considerably in policy, in morale, and lastly, in physical defence, if I see you when the crisis comes. Varro satisfies me. Pompey is an inspired speaker. I hope I shall come out of it at least with considerable honour or at any rate without discomfiture. Rome, between 25 July and 18 October 59 BC.

Cicero, *To Atticus* 2.21 (SB 41)

Cicero's critique of current affairs takes an even more drastic turn towards the end of the year: the *res publica*, which was ailing until a few weeks earlier, is now lost, and the prospect of a traumatic development seems increasingly realistic. Atticus is in Greece, and his friend tries to provide him with some reasoned predictions on what might unfold in the future: much of the attention is focused on Pompey, with whom they both had long-standing ties, and who appears increasingly isolated. Cicero voices his bitter disappointment with Pompey's conduct during the controversial consulship of Caesar: his public endorsement of the land law and of the treatment received by Bibulus may be consistent with his alliance with Caesar and Crassus, but are, in Cicero's view, at odds with his distinguished record of service to the *res publica* and outstanding leadership, and do little to address the fundamental political problem that he now faces: isolation, both from the senatorial order and from the people. The point that Caesar does not have much support in the city is also restated (cf. (c)), and is viewed as a further factor that may lead one to fear violence on a large scale: Caesar and his men might resort to violent means to impose their will. The prediction did not turn out to be accurate – but that does not necessarily mean that Cicero's assessment was altogether ill-founded.

B98   Vettius, *agent provocateur*, 59 BC

[2] But Cicero and Lucullus, not pleased at these events, endeavoured to kill both Caesar and Pompey with the help of a certain Lucius Vettius; they were not able to, but came close to losing their own lives as well. For Vettius, having been denounced first and arrested before he accomplished anything, denounced them; [3] and they would certainly have suffered something dreadful, if Vettius had not accused also Bibulus of being in the plot. But as it was, because, in his defence, Vettius accused this man who had revealed to Pompey what was being done, he was suspected of not telling the truth in the case of the others as well, but of having been suborned as a consequence of some arrangement to make false charges against those of the opposing party. [4] Different people spread different reports about these matters, for nothing at all was proved. When Vettius was brought before the people and named only those I

have mentioned, he was thrown into prison and was treacherously murdered there not long afterwards.

Cassius Dio, Roman History 39.9.2–4

The Vettius affair is a reminder that the unfolding of Catiline's conspiracy was a very recent event, and that the possibility of plot to take the lives of the serving consuls was not a far-flung one; the possibility that prominent individuals could be involved with it was also one that many were prepared to entertain. The allegation that Cicero and Lucullus may have wanted to kill their political opponents will have appeared plausible to some; on the other hand, the possibility that he was an *agent provocateur*, who had been instructed by Caesar and Pompey to spread false accusations against their opponents will have seemed plausible in some quarters. The lack of conclusive evidence and Vettius' sudden death in prison contributed to making the affaire inescapably controversial, and a non-partisan reading of it virtually unviable. – Cicero, *Atticus*, 2.24.2-5 (SB 44), Rome, August (?) 59 BC, deals in detail with this episode.

B99   The Senate tries to conciliate Caesar, 59 BC

… especially since a proposal was several times put to C. Caesar that he should propose the same matters in another way, by which proposal they were for respecting the auspices and for approving his laws.

Cicero, On the Consular Provinces 46

This single piece of evidence apparently records attempts by the leaders of the Senate to get Caesar to re-enact his legislation of 59 BC so as to confirm its legality. They were, in effect, recognizing that their encouragement of Bibulus and his use of *obnuntiatio* in 59 BC had been a mistake and had driven Caesar into opposition. – 'Several times' [Latin *aliquotiens*] is hard to imagine during 59 BC, but could suit the discussion prompted by the opposition of Domitius and Memmius in January 58 BC. However, by the time they made this offer, Caesar, for whatever reasons, had no interest in accepting it.

CIVIC DISRUPTION: 58–52 BC

B100   Cicero prepares for Clodius' offensive, 59 BC

It is clear that our cause will not lack supporters. People are giving assurances, offering personal help, making promises in a remarkable fashion. I have the highest hopes and even higher spirits – hopes that we will prevail, high spirits from the fact that in this state I have no fear of even an accidental mishap. In any event, the situation is as follows. If Clodius gives notice of a prosecution, all Italy will unite and we shall come away with redoubled glory; if on the other hand he tries to proceed by force, I am hopeful that we shall resist with force through the support not only of friends but also of strangers. All are pledging themselves along with friends, clients, freedmen, slaves, even their money. Our old band of loyalists is fired with zeal and affection for us. Those who were previously inclined to be unsympathetic or indifferent are now allying themselves with the loyalists through hatred of the tyrants. Pompey is full of assurances, as is Caesar, but I do not trust them sufficiently to relax any of my preparations. The tribunes are friendly, the consuls are creating an excellent impression, and we have very friendly praetors and highly energetic citizens in Domitius, Nigidius, Memmius, and Lentulus. The others are also loyal citizens, but these outstandingly so. You should therefore have courage and good hope.
Rome, between 25 October and 10 December 59 BC.

Cicero, To Quintus 1.2.16 (SB 2)

After the election of Clodius to the tribunate for 58 BC, Cicero prepares for the imminent political and judicial attack that he is soon to face. In this letter to his brother Quintus he makes a list of those who are prepared to support him: the municipal élites are at the forefront (note the reference to their willingness to leave their towns and come to Rome to take part in a vote in Cicero's favour); Caesar and Pompey are said to be on Cicero's side, but special emphasis is placed on the role that some praetors of the year are prepared to play in stalling Clodius' efforts at that difficult junction.

B101   Tribunate of Clodius, 58 BC

a) Therefore, having laid these foundations for your consulship, three days later while you were looking on and saying nothing, the *lex Aelia* and *Fufia*, the bastions and defences of peace and tranquillity, were overturned by a deadly monster and portent of the *res publica*; associations (*collegia*), not only those which the senate had abolished, were restored, but innumerable new ones were summoned into existence from the dregs of the city and from slaves. By that same man, who was involved in abominable and unheard of sexual debaucheries, that long-established mistress of decency and restrain, the censorship was removed ...

Cicero, *Against Piso* 9

b) [8] I have said that in the consulship of L. Piso and A. Gabinius [58 BC], P. Clodius, tribune of the plebs, enacted four laws that were ruinous for the *res publica*: a corn law, of which Cicero does not make mention at this point (for it was in the highest degree popular), that corn, which was previously given out at six and one third asses for a single *modius*, should be given free of charge; a second that no one should watch the heavens on those days when it was permitted that business be conducted with the people. It was because of this proposal that he says that the *lex Aelia* and *Fufia*, the bastions and defences of peace and tranquillity, had been overturned, since *obnuntiatio*, by which resistance was offered to ruinous laws, which the *lex Aelia* had ratified, had been removed; a third concerning the restoration of associations (*collegia*) and the establishing of new ones which he says have been summoned into existence from the dregs of slaves; a fourth that the censors should pass over no one in reviewing the Senate, nor should they punish anyone with disqualification unless he had been accused before them and condemned by the judgement of each censor; thus by this law of his Cicero says that the censorship, the mistress of decency and restrain, had been overturned.

Asconius, *Commentary on Cicero's Against Piso* p. 8C.12–9C.2

It would be short-sighted to regard the initiative against Cicero and the campaign for his exile as the cornerstone of Clodius' political work during his tribunate. As even the hostile testimony of his harsh critic Cicero makes clear, he put forward a wide-ranging legislative programme, which made an impact on a number of key aspects of the political and social setup of the Republic: a new corn law (which Cicero *did* criticize in *Defence of Sestius* 55 as resulting in a loss of 20% of state revenues); new sets of regulations on the use of religious obstruction in the legislative process (a heavily contentious issue, especially after the recent actions of Bibulus – B94), a law that reinstated the associations (*collegia*) that had recently been abolished on grounds of concern for public order, and a law that limited the discretionary powers of the censors and made the criteria for their review of the senatorial roll more stringent. The potential of the tribunate to set the legislative and political agenda was exploited to the full by a radical and highly capable political operator. Cicero gives heavily partisan accounts of Clodius' programme: it is especially instructive to triangulate them with the explanatory notes that the ancient commentator Asconius provides on the passage of the *Against Piso* quoted here as (b). – For more evidence for corn distributions in the late Republic see B32.

B102   Exile of Cicero, 58/57 BC

a) [15] That year in the *res publica* had already gone by, jurors, when amid great disturbance and fear on the part of many people a bow was stretched – against me alone, as was commonly said by those ignorant of affairs – but in reality against the *res publica* as a whole, by the transfer to the plebs of one reckless madman, who was angry with me but much more keenly hostile to the peace and safety of all. Pompey, a most distinguished man and most friendly to me, while there were many, who were striving to prevent him, had bound Clodius by every precaution, agreement and solemn oath that he would do nothing against me in his tribunate. But that villain, the product of the off-scourings of crimes of all sorts, thought he would not violate his agreement anything like enough if he had not terrified the very person, who had guaranteed another from dangers, with dangers to himself too.

[24] They openly made a pact with a tribune of the plebs that they should receive from him the provinces which they wanted, an army and as much money as they wanted, on the condition that they themselves should first have handed over the *res publica* prostrate and fettered to the tribune; this pact they said when struck could be ratified with my blood. [25] When this was revealed – for so great a crime could not be disguised or hidden – proposals concerning my destruction were put forward by the tribune who at the same time nominated provinces for the consul.

It was at this point that the Senate became alarmed; that you, Roman *equites,* were roused, that all Italy was greatly agitated; and lastly that all citizens of all sorts and orders thought that help should be sought for the highest interests of the *res publica* from the consuls and from their supreme authority, although those two whirlwinds were the only people in the *res publica* apart from that mad tribune, who not only did not bring help to the country when it was plunging headlong to disaster, but were lamenting that it was collapsing too slowly. Day by day insistent appeal was made to them, not only in the complaints of all good men (*boni*) but also by the prayers of the Senate, that they should take up my cause, that they should do something, in short, that they should refer the matter to the Senate. They continued to hound all the most distinguished members of that order by not only refusing but even by making fun of them. [26] At this point when an incredible crowd of people had suddenly assembled on the Capitol from the whole of the city and all of Italy, they all thought they ought to change into mourning and that I should be defended by every means, by individual initiative, since the *res publica* was without official leaders. At that same time, a meeting of the Senate was taking place in the temple of Concord because that very temple revived the memory of my consulship, when the entire order in tears was beseeching the consul with the curly hair; for that other consul, the rough and gruff one, was purposely keeping himself at home. With what arrogance did that filthy pest reject the prayers of the most distinguished order and the tears of the most distinguished citizens! ... You came to the Senate, you, I say, Roman *equites* and all good citizens (*boni*), in mourning garb, and you threw yourselves at the feet of the most foul pimp on behalf of my life. Then, when that brigand rejected your prayers, L. Ninnius, a man of incredible loyalty, mighty courage and determination, brought a proposal before the Senate about the state of the *res publica* and a full meeting of the Senate passed a resolution that it should put on mourning for my preservation ...

[34] And while these same consuls were looking on, a levy of slaves was held in front of the Aurelian tribunal on the pretext of forming associations (*collegia*), when men were enrolled street by street, were organized in military fashion and incited to physical violence, to murder and looting. And with the same men as consuls, weapons were openly carried into the temple of Castor, the steps of the same temple were removed, armed men were in control of the forum and the assemblies (*contiones*), murders and stone throwing were taking place; there was no Senate, there were no other magistrates; one man held all power over all by arms and brigandage, not by some force of his own but, after he had withdrawn the consuls from the *res publica* by a pact on provinces, he was behaving insultingly, he was dominating the scene, he was making promises to some, he was controlling many by terror and fear, even more by hope and promises. [35] Since things were in this state, jurors, since the Senate had no leaders, or had traitors for leaders or rather open enemies, since the equestrian order was being indicted by the consuls, the authority (*auctoritas*) of all Italy was being rejected, some people were being relegated by name, others terrorized by fear and danger, weapons were in temples, armed men in the forum; although these matters were not being hidden by the silence of the consuls, but approved by their words and their vote, although we saw the city not yet overthrown and destroyed, but already captured and overtaken, yet given such great support from good men (*boni*) I would have resisted these great evils, but other fears and other anxieties and suspicions influenced me.

Cicero, *Defence of Sestius* 15, 24–26, 34–35

In his speech in defence of P. Sestius, which he gave in 56, not long after his return from exile, Cicero came back to the issue of his clash with Clodius and of the process that led to the vote on his exile. He identifies the consuls of 58, A. Gabinius (curly hair) and L. Calpurnius Piso (at home), as those who carry a great share of responsibility for his exile: they made a political deal with Clodius, who promised to support the assignment of important and remunerative provincial commands upon the end of their consulship in exchange for their support to the law that provided for Cicero's exile. Cicero had often argued that there was overwhelming opposition to Clodius' plan, and in this passage he restates the point by listing most of the Senate, Pompey, the equestrian order, and the Italian élites among his supporters. However, the connivance of the consuls proves sufficient to Clodius, and in fact it does not just apply to Cicero's exile, but also applies to Clodius' plans to restore the associations (*collegia*), with a view to using them as tools of political violence, intimidation, and coertion. The prospect of civil strife is again looming large, and turns into a key consideration for Cicero, who starts entertaining the possibility that his exile might diffuse the tension in the city.

b) [15.4] Now when Caesar and Pompey spoke such words, not because they had views opposed to each other, but in order to deceive him unsuspectingly, Cicero attached himself to Pompey. [5] For he did not have any prior suspicion of Pompey and was completely confident that he would be saved by him. For many of the others respected and honoured him as one who had saved numerous persons when they were in danger, some from juries and others from their own accusers; [6] and Clodius, in that he was once in the family of Pompey and had once served with him for a long time, did not seem likely to do anything not in accord with his wishes. Cicero expected that Gabinius would be wholly on his side, in that he was particularly friendly to him and Piso too because of his reasonable nature and through his kinship with Caesar.

[16.1] Therefore, on these calculations he hoped to win, since he was now unreasonably confident, even as he had before been terrified without reason; and fearing that he would appear to have made his withdrawal from the city as a result of a guilty conscience, while he said he was considerably obliged to Caesar, he actually listened to Pompey. [2] And thus Cicero was deceived in this way and was preparing as if he were going to gain a great advantage over his enemies. For, in addition to what has already been said, the *equites* assembled on the Capitol and sent envoys on his behalf to the consuls and the Senate, some from their own number, [3] and also the senators Quintus Hortensius and Gaius Curio. And Ninnius gave him help in other ways and urged the people to change their dress, as if for a general calamity. And many of the senators also did this, and would not change before the consuls censured them through an edict.

[4] But the forces of his opponents were more powerful and Clodius would not allow Ninnius to undertake any action on his behalf, nor would Gabinius grant the *equites* access to the Senate, but he drove one of them, because he pressed his case hard, out of the city and he brought an accusation against Hortensius and Curio, because they had been present when the *equites* assembled and had undertaken the embassy. [5] And Clodius brought them before the people and knocked them about with blows at the hands of some prearranged agents because of their embassy. After this Piso, though he seemed well disposed towards Cicero, when he saw that it was impossible for him to be saved by any other means, advised him to slip away secretly in advance. [6] Nevertheless, when Cicero was annoyed at this, Piso came before the assembly as soon as he could (he was frequently unwell) and when Clodius enquired of his opinion about what had been proposed, said: 'No cruel or sad deed pleases me.' Gabinius, too, on being asked the same question, not only did not praise Cicero, but even accused both the *equites* and the Senate.

[17] Caesar, however (for Clodius assembled the people outside the wall because of him, since he had gone off on campaign, and made him arbiter of the proposals), censured the illegality of what had been done concerning Lentulus, [2] but did not, however, approve the punishment proposed in respect of those acts. All his considerations concerning those events, he said, everyone knew (for he had given his vote for saving them) but it was not fitting to propose such a law for events that had passed. [3] That was what Caesar said, while Crassus showed some help for Cicero because of his son, but himself took the part of the plebs. Pompey was promising him his support, but, making different excuses at different times and making frequent journeys from the city on purpose, did not come to his aid. [4] Then Cicero saw this and became afraid; he tried again to resort to arms (among other things he publicly abused Pompey), but he was prevented by Cato and Hortensius, lest civil war might occur as a result. Then at last unwillingly, with disgrace and infamy, he withdrew on the grounds that he had gone willingly into exile as a result of conscience. [5] Before he left, he went up to the Capitolium and dedicated a little statue of Athena, calling it 'Protectress'. He made secretly for Sicily, for he had been their champion and he had great hope that he would be honoured among the communities and individuals and by the governor. [6] When he went into exile, the law took effect: not only did no one oppose it, but those very people who seemed among the foremost working on behalf of Cicero and others gave it their enthusiastic support as soon as he was out of the way. And his property was confiscated, his house was razed to the ground as if it were that of an enemy, and they dedicated its ground to a temple of Liberty. [7] A decree of exile was passed against Cicero himself and staying in Sicily was forbidden; he

was banished four hundred and seventy miles from Rome and it was proclaimed in addition that if he should ever appear within that limit, both he himself and those who gave him welcome might be killed with impunity.

Cassius Dio, *Roman History* 38.15.5 –17

Cassius Dio's account of the events leading to Cicero's exile has the merit of giving a factual summary of the process, and also provides a very different outlook on the events to what we find in Cicero: he appears to have been outwitted by Clodius, Pompey, and Caesar, who managed to isolate him and to overcome any sources of support he might have conceivably relied upon. Both Pompey and Caesar took active steps to make Cicero's punishment possible, without explicitly endorsing it in public (but note Caesar's criticism of the execution of the Catilinarian conspirators). Besides being depicted as a far less skilful operator than he tends to depict himself, Cicero is also cast a somewhat sinister shade: he toys with the idea of unleashing civil strife in order to rescue his position, and is prevented from doing so by two key supporters of his, Cato and Hortensius. His decision to leave has a hypocritical ring to it: it is more an outcome of his political isolation than a selfless sacrifice in the name of civic concord. – Dio also gives a useful summary of Cicero's movements during his exile (about which we are also well informed by Cicero's correspondence) and of how his legal position in Rome changed. The confiscation and destruction of his house is the central subject of his speech *On his house* (*De domo*), which he gave shortly after his return, in 56 BC.

B103   Return of Cicero, 57 BC

I set out from Dyrrachium on the day before the Nones of Sextilis [4 August], on the very day the law concerning me was put to the vote. I reached Brundisium on the Nones [5 August]. My dearest Tullia was there to meet me, on her actual birthday, which was by chance also the foundation day of the colony of Brundisium and of the temple of your neighbour, Salus. This fact was noticed by large numbers and celebrated with great congratulation by the people of Brundisium. On 8 August, while I was at Brundisium, I learned from a letter of my brother Quintus that the law had been carried in the assemblies voting by 'centuries' (*comitia centuriata*) with magnificent support from all ages and orders, with an incredible assemblage of the inhabitants of Italy. Having been most handsomely honoured by the people of Brundisium, I began my journey from there. All along the way delegations gathered with congratulations.

[5] So I reached the outskirts of Rome. My arrival was such that no one of any order known to my *nomenclator* failed to come out to meet me, apart from those enemies who could neither conceal nor deny the fact that they were enemies. When I reached the Porta Capena, the steps of the temples had been filled with the lowest plebeians. When congratulations had been shown me by them with loud applause, similar crowds and applause accompanied me right up to the Capitol and in the forum and on the Capitol itself there was an amazing crowd. On the following day, which was the Nones [5] September, I made a speech of thanks in the Senate.
Rome, about 10 September 57 BC.

Cicero, *To Atticus* 4.1.1–5 (SB 73) (continued in **B107**)

The law providing for Cicero's rehabilitation and return to Rome was passed sixteen months after the beginning of his exile: strong political pressure had been put from an influential section of the senatorial nobility, and many members of the municipal *élites* had also argued that case, but the key factor that made it possible was the decision of Caesar and Pompey to support Cicero's return, as they grew increasingly uncomfortable at Clodius' political and legislative activity. Cicero could safely be expected to vocally oppose any initiative of the former tribune. – In this letter to Atticus Cicero depicts the scene of his return to Rome, a point that he touched upon in other speeches of his, notably those he delivered to the Senate and the people shortly after his arrival at Rome (see also *Against Piso* 51-52). His homecoming is anticipated by the welcome he receives across southern Italy: a display of cohesion and concord that appears to vindicate his long-held commitment to the solidarity of the propertied classes against the threat of political instability. Even the plebs, however, is depicted as part of the collective celebration of Cicero and his achievements, and it is surely significant that it is mentioned in association with the temples of the city of Rome: the gods, on whom the welfare of the political community depends, are also watching. 8 August: the exact day is disputed. – Atticus' house in Rome was in the vicinity of the temple of Salus on the Quirinal: hence 'your neighbour'. – The *nomenclator* was a slave whose task was to remind the master of the names (*nomina*) of the people he met while he was out on political business.

B104   Political violence, 23 January 57

[75] Although the authority of the Senate was being hindered by all sorts of delays, tricks, and unfounded obstructions, the day came at last on which the assembly (*concilium*) of the plebs was to deal with my case: 23 January. The proposer of the bill (*rogatio*), Q. Fabricius, a man who is most friendly towards me, occupied the sacred precinct some time before dawn. Sestius, who is here being tried on public violence charges, was quiet on that day; this agent and defender of my interests did not take a single step, and waited to see the plans of my enemies. How about through whose initiative P. Sestius has been put on trial? How did they conduct themselves? Since they had seized the Forum, the Comitium, the senate-house (*Curia*) at night, with men in arms and a crowd of slaves, they launched an attack on Fabricius, killed several people, and injured many. [76] They violently drove off the tribune of the plebs M. Cispius, an excellent man of great resolve, as he was getting into the forum, and caused a huge massacre, and went about as a group, with swords drawn and bloodied, in every corner of the forum, looking for, and calling out, my brother, an excellent man of great strength, and most devoted to me. He would have happily offered his body to their shots, not in resistance, but in order to die, as he was in great grief and yearning of me – if he had not kept himself alive to sustain the hope of my return. However, he faced the nefarious violence of those criminal brigands and was driven from the speaker's platform (*rostra*), where he had come to beseech the Roman people to provide for the welfare of his brother. He hid in the Comitium, and shielded himself with the bodies of his slaves and freedmen; he defended his own life with the protection afforded by the night and his flight, not by the law and the legal process.

Cicero, *Defence of Sestius* 75–76

Cicero recounts the outbreak of political violence that preceded the vote on the proposal for his return from exile: he depicts the events in a highly unilateral fashion, and the factual accuracy of his version should not be taken for granted. What stands out, and should be retained as a point of great historical significance, is the pace and scale of violence right in the core of the city: getting hold of some crucial sites and keeping control of those is crucial if one is to have the chance to put forward proposals and have them put to the vote of the assemblies. Two aspects are noteworthy: the violation of the prerogatives of the tribune of the plebs, M. Cispius, and the quick, almost casual reference to the killing of a number of people in the same tumult. The commotion does not involve only citizens who fight on different factions, but also slaves and freedmen who are fighting on the side of their patrons. The larger and better trained suite of slaves one had on one's side, the stronger one's hand in this sort of situation could be.

B105   Politics in the *contio*, 57 BC

There were assemblies (*contiones*): turbulent ones summoned by Metellus, reckless one by Appius, and a furious one by Publius. The upshot of all that was that, unless Milo declared negative auspices in the Campus Martius, the election would take place. On 19 November, before midnight, Milo went to the Campus with a large retinue. Although Clodius had a chosen force of runaway slaves with him, he did not have the courage to go to the Campus. Milo stayed until noon, surrounded by the joyful admiration of people and the greatest glory. The campaign of the three brothers was shameful: their violence was outdone and their fury met with comtempt. Metellus, however, asked Milo to declare the auspices to him on the following day in the Forum; he said there was no need for him to go to the Campus at night; he would be in the Comitium at dawn. So on the 20th, Milo came to the Comitium when it was still night time. At dawn Metellus furtively scuttled to the Campus through the byways. Milo tracked him down between the Woods and made his announcement: Metellus turned tail, amidsts the loud and obscene jeers of Q. Flaccus. The 21st was marketday, and for two days there were no gatherings.

On the morning of the 22nd I am writing this three hours before dawn. Milo has already taken up his position on the Campus. ... I gather that Clodius' vestibule is pretty empty: there are a few ragmen without a lantern. They are moaning that it has all been planned by me: they are not aware of how much courage there is in that hero, what degree of intelligence and valour. I overlook some recent divine achievements – but it boils down to this: I do not think there will be an election; Publius will be charged by Milo, unless he is killed first. If he puts himself in Milo's way, I can see that he will be killed by Milo himself. He has no doubts about doing it, and shows no hesitation. He is not frightened about what happened to me. For he will not resort to the advice of envious and treacherous people, or put his faith into an inept nobility.
Rome, 22 November 57.

Cicero, *To Atticus* 4.3.4–5 (SB 75)

This letter to Atticus gives further evidence for the tension that dominates in Rome in late 57: things have not calmed down after Cicero's return. The election for the aedileship, in which Clodius is planning to stand, is imminent, and the main opponent that Clodius is facing at this point is T. Annius Milo, who is mobilizing a crowd of men that is prepared to tackle the force assembled by Clodius. In this phase, however, there is no open confrontation between the two sides: the core of the controversy is whether Milo will take steps to prevent the election by invoking a religious argument. It is also interesting to see that all political activity comes to a halt on two consecutive marketdays. – Cicero's final statement is extraordinary, especially in light of the arguments that he used less than five years later in defending Milo from the charge of having assassinated Clodius: in this letter he expresses the firm view that Milo is in fact determined to kill Clodius should that prove politically necessary. – The election was indeed postponed, and did not take place until the following January: Clodius was successful.

B106   Decision-making in late Republican Rome
[106] Now, unless I am mistaken, the city is in the position that, if you removed the hired gangs, everyone will seem to have the same feeling about the *res publica*. For the will and judgement of the Roman people can be most clearly indicated in three places: at a public assembly (*contio*), in the voting assemblies (*comitia*), and at the assembly for games and the gladiators. What assembly (*contio*) was there in these years, provided it was not corrupt but genuine, wherein the unanimity of the Roman people could not be perceived? Many assemblies (*contiones*) were held concerning me by that most criminal gladiator, to which no one came unless bribed and dishonest; no honest citizen could look upon his ugly countenance or listen to his raving voice. Those were the assemblies (*contiones*) of reckless men, necessarily disorderly. [107] The consul Publius Lentulus held an assembly (*contio*) about me as well; there took place a gathering of the Roman people, all orders, the whole of Italy stood in that assembly (*contio*). He put the case with great weight and eloquence amid such great

silence and approval from all that nothing so popular ever seemed to have reached the ears of the Roman people. Pompey was brought forward by him and showed himself not only the author of my welfare, but also a suppliant of the Roman people. While this man's speech was always impressive and pleasing at assemblies (*contiones*), on this occasion I confidently assert that never had his opinion had greater authority, his eloquence greater charm. [108] In what silence were the other leading citizens of the state heard on the subject of myself! ...

[109] I come now to the assemblies in which people vote (*comitia*), whether for magistrates or on laws. We often see many statutes being enacted. I pass over those, which are enacted in such a way, that barely five people per tribe, and those from another tribe, may be found to cast their votes. That ruination of the *res publica* says he enacted a law against me, whom he labelled 'a tyrant' (*tyrannus*) and 'a robber of liberty'. Who is there to confess that he recorded his vote when the proposal against me was being enacted? But when in the assembly of the centuries, when in accordance with the decree of the Senate (*senatus consultum*) the motion was also being enacted concerning me, who is there who does not publicly declare that he was present and cast his vote for my restoration? Therefore, which cause of the two ought to appear popular? That with which all honest men in the state, all ages and all orders are in unanimous agreement or that to which furies, summoned as it were to the funeral rites of the *res publica*, flock together in flight?

Cicero, *Defence of Sestius* 106–109, with omissions

In his effort to define the terms of the civic concord that enabled him to return to Rome, Cicero also has to address the role and motives of those who have acted against him and still oppose him. He identifies his personal enemy in Clodius and his supporters as 'armed gangs'; however, he also takes a steps further, and argues that different assemblies that are ostensibly of the same kind actually have different significance and meanings: there are *contiones* where people are persuaded by the authoritative arguments of experienced statesmen, and *contiones* where demagoguery and dishonesty prevail; at the same time, there are legislative assemblies where only few citizens cast their votes and assemblies where a high turnout confers greater legitimacy to the resulting deliberations. – Cicero cannot help confronting the fact that Clodius is pursuing his agenda through the established means of constitutional practice: his solution is to argue that the venues through which Clodius pursues his aims betray the *spirit*, if not the form, of proper constitutional practice.

B107 Pompey and the corn supply, 57 BC

[6] The price of grain had risen very sharply and people had gathered in great numbers, first at the theatre and then at the Senate and, at the instigation of Clodius, were shouting that the scarcity of grain was all my doing. A meeting of the Senate was being held during those days about the price of corn and Pompey was being summoned to take charge of the matter in the talk not only of the plebs, but also of the good men (*boni*). He himself wanted it, and the crowds were demanding that I personally should propose it; so, two days later, I put the proposal and made a carefully constructed speech. Although the consulars, apart from Messalla and Afranius, were absent, because, so they said, it was not safe for them to give their views, a decree of the Senate on my motion was passed that discussion be held with Pompey that he undertake the matter and that a law be passed. The decree of the Senate was read out immediately. When the crowd had applauded in this new and stupid manner, when my name was read out, I then made a speech on the invitation of all the magistrates apart from one praetor and two tribunes of the plebs.

[7] On the following day, there were a crowded Senate and all the consulars. They refused Pompey nothing he asked for. When he asked for fifteen legates, he named me first and said I should be his second self in everything. The consuls drafted a law that Pompey be given for a period of five years complete control over the corn supply throughout the world; Messius produced an alternative, which gives him control over all money and adds a fleet, an army and authority (*imperium*) in the provinces superior to that of those who govern them. That consular law of mine now looks modest, while this one of Messius looks intolerable. Pompey says he wants the former, his close friends the latter. The consulars are growling, Favonius in the lead.

[…] Rome, around 10 September 57 BC.

Cicero, *To Atticus* 4.1.6–8 (SB 73) (continued in **B103**)

While political instability is still rife, Rome is also facing a major crisis in its grain supply. The issue is readily politicized. Clodius blames Cicero for it, as large crowds had gathered in Rome to celebrate his return; a section of the crowd, however, is said to be calling for Cicero's direct intervention in the matter. Shortly after his return to Rome, Cicero appears to have regained a meaningful, if not quite central, role in the deliberations of the Senate. He plays a central role in this crisis by advocating that Pompey is given an extraordinary set of responsibilities in managing the grain supply, largely through his connections in the East and with Egypt, and by playing a leading role in drafting the relevant legislation. – The ghost of autocracy, however, is still looming: others argue that Pompey should be given an extraordinary *imperium* overriding that of provincial governors. Although Pompey is publicly rejecting that offer, his friends are supporting it. – The former consuls, the 'consulars', do not appear to play any role in the decision-making process: they are said to be in fear of even attending Senate when the issue is being debated, and yet to be deeply frustrated at the new role acquired by Pompey, whom many of them had long regarded with open hostility. – On this crisis see also Plutarch, *Life of Pompey* 49.4-5, 50; Appian, *Civil Wars* 2.18, 20; Cassius Dio, *Roman History* 39.9.3.

B108   Caesar in Gaul, 58–50 BC: the viewpoint from Rome

a) Because of these achievements reported in a letter from Caesar, a thanksgiving was decreed for fifteen days, which had happened to no one before this time.

Caesar, *Gallic War* 2.35.4 (57 BC)

b) [26] I gave my vote in favour of a thanksgiving of fifteen days. For the *res publica* it would have been sufficient if it had been of as many days as that for C. Marius; for the immortal gods the same thanksgiving as consequent upon the greatest wars would not have been meager; therefore that increase in days was attributed to the standing (*dignitas*) of the man. [27] ... Therefore, in the case of that thanksgiving I voted for, the event itself was allotted to the immortal gods, to the old-established customs of our ancestors and to the interests of the *res publica*, while the dignity of the words, the honour, the novel precedent and the number of days were conceded to the praise and glory of Caesar himself.

Cicero, *On the Consular Provinces* 26–27, with omission

In an otherwise fraught context, news of Caesar's success in Gaul met with robust approval in Rome, not just among the urban populace, but in the Senate too: Caesar clearly took great care in reporting his achievements in official despatches that probably had wider public circulation. The decision to declare fifteen days of thanksgiving to the gods was unprecedented, and its rationale is set out by Cicero in (b): the ensuing ceremonies will have also been invaluable opportunities to gather momentum behing the cause of the war and foster a shared spirit of civic concord. It is remarkable that thanksgivings for Caesar's victories are typically decreed at the end of a year of campaigning (55 BC: Caesar, *Gallic War* 4.38; Cicero, *Balbus*, 61; Dio 39.5; 53 BC: Dio 39.53; 52 BC: Caesar, *Gallic War* 7.90).

B109   Ptolemy Auletes in Rome, 56 BC
a) [2] In this matter these are the facts: Hammonius, the envoy of the king, is attacking us openly with money. The business is being handled through the same creditors as it was being handled when you were here. Any who favour the case of the king – and they are few – all wish the business to be handed over to Pompey. The Senate approves the religious pretext, not because of religion, but through ill will and dislike of that king's bribery.
Rome, 13 January 56 BC.

> Cicero to Lentulus Spinther, *Letters to his Friends* 1.1.2 (SB 12)

b) Concerning the Alexandrian king, a decree of the Senate has been passed that it appears dangerous to the *res publica* for him to be restored 'with a great force'. When that left a dispute whether Lentulus or Pompey should restore him, Lentulus appeared to be gaining his case. For this matter I satisfied my obligation to Lentulus admirably and the wish of Pompey conspicuously.
Rome, 17 January 56 BC.

> Cicero, *Letters to Quintus* 2.2.3 (SB 6)

c) The Senate is not able to meet before the Kalends of February [1 February], as you know, owing to the *lex Pupia*, nor throughout February, unless embassies have been completed or postponed. However, the view of the Roman people is that the pretext of religion has been invented and introduced by those envious of you and your detractors <and this has been taken up by others> not so much to block you as to prevent anyone wanting to go to Alexandria because of a desire for a military force.
Rome, 17 (?) January 56 BC.

> Cicero to P. Lentulus Spinther, *Letters to his Friends* 1.4.2 (SB 14)

The kingdom of Egypt was going through another phase of political instability. The king Ptolemy XII Auletes ('flute-player') had recently been toppled and was in Rome, seeking to persuade the Senate to endorse a military action that would reinstate him into power. As had previously been the case with other client-kings, he was resorting to bribery to steer the deliberations of the Senate in his favour. There was, however, very little appetite for military action in Egypt, and a dispute between Pompey and Cn. Cornelius Lentulus on who should lead the mission was looming on the horizon. A response of the Sibylline Books was being invoked by sectors of the nobility as an argument for not waging any military action: a tribune, C. Cato, put it into the public domain before it was discussed in the Senate (Cassius Dio, *Roman History* 39.14-16.1).

B110   M. Aemilius Scaurus, aedile, 56 BC
a) [8.96] M. Scaurus was the first to put on show at the games of his aedileship a hippopotamus and five crocodiles in a temporary inland waterway.

b) [114] In his aedileship this man constructed a building, the greatest of all ever constructed by the hand of man, not only of temporary duration, but of those intended for all time. This was a theatre: the stage, triple in height, had 360 columns, in a state that had not tolerated, without the disgrace of a very distinguished citizen, six columns of Hymettan marble. The lowest tier of the stage was of marble, the middle of glass – an unheard-of kind of extravagance even afterwards – and the top tier of gilded planks. The columns of the lowest tier, as I have said, were of thirty-eight feet. [115]

There were, as I have indicated, bronze statues between the columns 3,000 in number; the auditorium itself held eighty thousand people, while the theatre of Pompey is quite large enough in seating forty thousand though the city has increased several times in number and the population is so much greater. The rest of the equipment, clothes woven with gold, painted scenery and other props, was so great that when bits and pieces for everyday use that were superfluous were carted to his Tusculan villa and that villa was set on fire by his angry slaves, thirty million sesterces went up in smoke. [116] At any rate he gained one thing from that fire: that no one afterwards was equal to that man's madness.

Pliny, *Natural History* 8.96; 36.114–116

The extraordinary expenses that M. Aemilius Scaurus met during his aedileship in order to fund the construction of a temporary theatre are all the more striking in light of the grain supply crisis that the city faced at the time. They show what efforts some individuals were prepared to make in order to enhance their political prospects in an increasingly competitive environment, and point to a context of striking economic and social inequality. At the same time, they are a further reminder of what astonishing range of luxury goods were available to the most affluent sectors of the Roman élite, and what role they could play in enabling new opportunities for mass entertainment. In addition to the passages above, Pliny mentions the extravagance of Scaurus' theatre at *NH* 36.5-6 (he reused the largest columns in his own house!) and 36.50.

B111   Affairs in Rome, February 56 BC

[1] I wrote to you previously about the earlier news. Now learn what happened afterwards. On the Kalends of February [1 February] embassies were being put back to the Ides [13 February]; on that day the issue was not concluded. On 2 February Milo appeared in court. Pompey was his supporting counsel. M. Marcellus spoke for him at my request. We came off honourably. The case was adjourned to 7 February. Meanwhile, with the embassies put back to the Ides, the business of provinces for quaestors and provisions for praetors was put before the Senate; but, because many complaints about the *res publica* were introduced, no business was transacted. C. Cato promulgated a law to remove Lentulus from his command (*imperium*). His son put on mourning.
Rome, 12–15 February 56 BC.

Cicero, *To Quintus* 2.3.1 (SB 7)

In this period Cicero's brother Quintus was in Gaul, serving on Caesar's staff, and Cicero regularly updated him on current political developments. The information that is conveyed here is on the whole rather unremarkable, but conveys a general sense of a rather ineffective political and constitutional process, especially in the Senate: note the delay with which the foreign embassies are received. The main issue of contention is Lentulus' command in Egypt, which is targeted in a law proposed by Cato.

B112   Meeting at Luca, 56 BC

a) [8] Furthermore, on the Nones of April [5 April] in the consulship of Marcellinus and Philippus, the Senate agreed with me that the matter of the Campanian land be referred to a full meeting of the Senate on the Ides of May [15 May]. Could I have made a greater assault on the citadel of that party, have more forgotten my circumstances, have brought to mind my actions?

When that proposal of mine was uttered, a great stirring of emotion occurred not only among those where it should have but also among those whom I had never imagined it would. [9] When the Senate passed a decree in accordance with my proposal, Pompey, although he had not shown me that he was at all offended, set out for Sardinia and Africa and on the journey went to meet Caesar at Luca. There Caesar made many complaints about my proposal, since he had seen Crassus beforehand at Ravenna and had been stirred up by him against me. It is agreed that Pompey was quite annoyed by it; although I had heard this from others yet I learnt it principally from my brother. Pompey met him within a few days of leaving Luca. 'I was looking for you,' he said, 'how lucky we have met. Unless you deal carefully with your brother, you will have to pay over what you guaranteed me on his behalf.' In short, he made serious complaints, he recalled his services, he recalled his very frequent dealings with my brother himself concerning Caesar's acts and what assurances he had given him concerning me and he called upon my brother himself to witness that what he had done concerning my restoration had been done with the goodwill of Caesar. He asked him to commend Caesar's cause and reputation (*dignitas*) to me, that I should not attack them if I were unwilling or unable to defend them. [10] When my brother had brought me this news and when Pompey had also sent Vibullius to me with instructions that I should keep on hold the matter of the Campanian land until his return, I came to my senses. Rome, December 54 BC.

> Cicero to P. Lentulus Spinther, *To his Friends*, 1.9.8–10 (SB 20)

b) So having crossed the Alps and passing the winter at Luca, there was a large number of ordinary men and women who had made their way there enthusiastically, and two hundred men of senatorial rank, among them Pompey and Crassus, and a hundred and twenty rods of office (*fasces*) of proconsuls and praetors were seen at Caesar's door. Thus having filled all the others with hopes and money he sent them home, while Crassus and Pompey made agreements with him, that they seek the consulship and that Caesar assist them sending large numbers of his soldiers for the vote, and that as soon as they had been elected they would arrange for themselves provinces and armies and confirm Caesar's position for another five-year period.

> Plutarch, *Life of Pompey* 51.3

These two sources give different, complementary insights into the meeting between Caesar, Pompey, and Crassus that took place at Luca, in the south-west of Caesar's province of Cisalpine Gaul, in April 56 BC. Its main consequence was to strengthen and extend the political agreement between the three men, and pave the way for the candidacy to the consulship of Pompey and Crassus for 55 BC. The size and prestige of the retinue of the three men speaks volumes about the influence they had achieved, but also draws attention to the enduring relevance and reach of the coalition that was set against them. – The Luca conference takes place in direct response to the opposition that the implementation of Caesar's agrarian law was finding in the Senate: Cicero was at the forefront of that movement. The reactions of Pompey and Caesar to that development are instructively different. Pompey does not choose the path of direct confrontation, while Caesar conveys his displeasure to Cicero through Quintus Cicero, who is serving under him in Gaul. At the same time, Pompey conveys a critical message to Cicero through an intermediary, his close friend L. Vibullius Rufus. Matters of the utmost political importance could often be entrusted to informal, and yet very effective, channels of communications.

B113   Cicero's reflections, Summer 56 BC

[10] You write that you wish to know what the situation of the *res publica* is: there is the utmost disagreement, but the conflict is unequal. For those who have the greatest strength in resources, arms and power have, it seems to me, actually managed to be stronger in influence as a result of the stupidity and lack of resolution of their opponents. And so, in the face of very little opposition, they have obtained through the Senate everything,

which they thought they could not even attain through the people without disorder. For pay has been decreed to Caesar and ten legates; it has been easily arranged that there should be no successor, in accordance with the Sempronian law. I write to you more briefly because the situation of the *res publica* does not please me. I write to advise you that you learn while your affairs are intact what I, who have been devoted to all letters from my childhood, have come to know more by experience than by learning: that we must not take thought for our security while ignoring our good reputation (*dignitas*) nor for our good reputation (*dignitas*) while ignoring our security.

Rome, late June or July 56 BC.

Cicero to Lentulus Spinther, *To his Friends* 1.7.10 (SB 18)

This letter summarises both Cicero's bleak assessment of the political context in the mid-fifties, and his reflection on the ethical and political response that one should devise in times of traumatic change: the tension between personal safety and moral rigour was bound to become even more relevant in the years to come (cf. also *To his Friends*, 1.8.1–4 (SB 19)). Cicero voices his frustration at the inability of the senatorial nobility to counter the ambition of the three members of the alliance: the crisis that Rome is facing is in fact a wider degeneration of the political élite. – The ten *legati* mentioned in this letter were middle-rank officers that Caesar asked to be appointed to support him in the Gallic campaign and in the consolidation of the Roman administrative presence in Transalpine Gaul.

B114   Second consulship of Pompey and Crassus, 55 BC

a) However, on the day after you set off, I went late at night with Vibullius to Pompey; when I had spoken about the buildings and the inscriptions he gave me a very kind reply, offered great hope, said he wished to speak with Crassus and advised me to do the same. I took the consul Crassus back from the Senate to his house. He took the matter up and said that there was something, which Clodius wanted to obtain at that moment through his and Pompey's agency; he thought that, if I did not prevent him, he could get me what I wanted without argument. I entrusted the whole business to him and said I would be in his hands. Young P. Crassus was present for this conversation; he is very devoted to me, as you know.

[3] On the third day before the Ides of February [11 February] a decree of the Senate was passed concerning electoral malpractice (*ambitus*) on the motion of Afranius, which I had proposed when you were here. But amid loud murmurs from the Senate, the consuls did not pursue the proposal of those who, though they agreed with Afranius, added that praetors should be elected on condition that they were private citizens for sixty days. On that day they clearly rejected Cato. In short, they control everything and that in such a way that they wish everyone to know it.

Rome, shortly after 11 February 55 BC.

Cicero, *To Quintus* 2.8.2–3 (SB 13) with omissions

Cicero discusses the early stages of the consulship of Pompey and Crassus in 55 BC: his assessment is that they are in full control of the political scene, and are now in a position to overcome senatorial opposition on any matter of political significance: in this case, a new measure setting restrictions on electoral corruption. – The first episode discussed in this letter shows that Cicero still has ready access to Pompey and Crassus, whilst not being an ally of theirs. – The presence of 'young P. Crassus', who had been serving in Gaul, signifies the presence in Rome of Caesarian troops for the consular elections. The object of the attempt to keep the praetors as private citizens for two months was to prosecute them for bribery and thereby, perhaps, to get the unsuccessful Cato to replace one disqualified. Hence the unwillingness of the consuls to accept the suggestion; their nominees would be at risk.

b) [42] Pompey and Crassus were elected consuls. But Cato did not give up the fight; he came forward as a candidate and canvassed for the praetorship; for he wished to have a vantage point in the struggles against them and not to stand up against magistrates as a private citizen. [2] But they were afraid of this too, fearing that Cato as praetor would become a match for them as consuls. First of all they convened the Senate suddenly, though many knew nothing about it, and passed a resolution that the praetors-elect should take up office immediately, without leaving the period of time required by law during which there could be legal actions against those who had bribed the people. [3] Secondly, having arranged by this resolution that bribery would not be subject to investigation, they put forward their own clients and friends as candidates for the praetorship, themselves offering bribes and supervising the casting of the votes. [4] But Cato's integrity and reputation proved too much for them again. The majority of the people considered it disgraceful that Cato should be sold by their votes when they would have done better to buy him for the city. So the tribe, which was first called, voted for him. All of a sudden Pompey told a downright and disgraceful lie, declaring that he had heard thunder, and dismissed the assembly. Such events were usually considered inauspicious and nothing could be decided once such an omen occurred. [5] Once again they began large-scale bribery, forcibly ejecting the best citizens from the Campus Martius and got Vatinius elected praetor instead of Cato. [6] It is reported that those who had taken part in this illegal and corrupt election went off home at once like runaway slaves, while a tribune organized a meeting on the spot for the rest, who were standing around in groups and objecting. Cato stood up, as though divinely inspired, and foretold everything that was going to happen to the city. He stirred up the citizens against Pompey and Crassus because, he said, they had plotted these events together and adopted such a policy because they were afraid that Cato as praetor might get the better of them. [7] When finally he went home the crowd, which accompanied him, was greater than that which accompanied all the praetors-elect together.

Plutarch, *Life of Cato the Younger* 42

Cicero's disparaging assessment of the quality of the opposition to Crassus and Pompey is somewhat qualified by this account of Plutarch, who portrays Cato as a formidable critic and credible rival of the consular pair, and discusses at some length the lengths to which they went to thwart the career ambitions of Cato – a figure of unmatched standing within the senatorial nobility, who never reached the consulship. Again, the use of a religious procedure serves to shape the political process. – 42.4 which was first called: The importance of the *centuria praerogativa* is noted in Cicero, *Defence of Plancius*, 49: 'The one *centuria praerogativa* has such great influence that nobody has ever first secured it without being declared consul either in those very elections or, at any rate, in the following year.'

B115   Cicero and Pompey, 55 BC
Cicero to Lentulus Spinther.
My inclination, indeed my love for Pompey is strong enough to make me now feel that whatever is useful to him and whatever he wants is right and true. In my opinion, even his opponents would make no mistake if they gave up fighting, since they cannot equal him. I have another consolation. Everyone agrees that I am entitled either to support Pompey's wishes or to hold my peace or simply to return to my literary studies (and that is my dearest wish). You may be sure that I shall do that, if Pompey's friendship allows me. As for what I had promised myself after attaining the highest public offices and passing through the greatest toils – a high standing (*dignitas*) in the

Senate, freedom in public life – all that has been taken away, not for me in particular, but for everybody: it is now a matter of either giving undignified support to the few or expressing ineffectual dissent.

I am writing all this to you chiefly, so that you reflect on your own position too. The whole system consisting of the Senate, the courts, the whole commonwealth has changed. Tranquillity (*otium*) is what we have to pray for, and the present holders of power seem likely to provide it, if certain people can submit with a degree of patience to their domination (*potentia*). The standing of a consular who plays his strong and courageous part in the Senate is a notion that we must remove from our minds. It has disappeared through the fault of those who lost the Senate the sympathies of a very friendly order and of a most eminent individual.
February (?) 55 BC.

Cicero, *To his Friends* 1.8.2–4 (SB 19)

This letter reflects the viewpoint of a man who has come to terms with a political landscape in which the recent conference at Luca has confirmed the agreement between Caesar, Crassus, and Pompey, and the prospect of a restoration of senatorial authority seems increasingly unrealistic. In spite of the misgivings he had expressed on other occasions (see above, **B97a**, **B97d**), Cicero declares, on the one hand, his personal loyalty towards Pompey and, on the other, makes a general assessment on the direction that the political life of Rome has taken of late. Some individuals are playing a dominant role, and the main challenge, even for someone as distinguished as Cicero, is to negotiate a safe space for oneself in that changed context. Tranquillity, rather than influence, is the aim to which one can reasonably aspire.

B116   Consular legislation of Crassus and Pompey, 55 BC
Thus the consuls arranged to have these matters ratified and after this they imposed harsher penalties on those distributing bribes to anyone, as if they were in some way less in error themselves in that they had obtained office not through money, but by violence. [2] Then they attempted to reduce living expenditure, which had increased to a very great amount, though they themselves advanced to the utmost point of high living and luxury, but they were prevented from having the matter carried and made law because of this very fact. [3] For Hortensius, being among those most fond of spending, persuaded them to lay aside their proposal, by going over the great size of the city and praising them for the great cost of their houses and their magnanimity towards others, thus using their own way of life as an accomplice to his arguments.

Cassius Dio, *Roman History* 39.37.1–3

Another instance of effective opposition to Pompey and Crassus: the elder statesman Hortesius (*cos.* 69 BC) makes the case against the passing of a new law restricting the consumption and display of luxury goods (a so-called sumptuary law, from Latin *sumptus,* 'luxury'). The incident also serves to denounce the ways in which the two consuls use their power, by imposing laws that are at odds with their behaviour.

B117   Restoration of Ptolemy Auletes, 55 BC
[55.1] Around this same time Ptolemy, although the Romans had voted against sending any assistance to him and were even now exceedingly ill-disposed towards him because of the bribery he had employed, was restored and got back his kingdom. [2] Pompey and Gabinius arranged this ... [3] so that Pompey sent orders to Gabinius, then governor of Syria, and the latter organized the campaign; the one acted out of kindness and the other as the result of taking a bribe. They restored the king against

the wish of the people, having no thought either for them or for the oracles of the Sibyl ... [56] Gabinius harmed Syria in many ways with the result that he caused them much more damage than the pirates who were then at their peak ... He was at first planning and preparing a campaign against the Parthians and their wealth ... However, when Ptolemy came with the letter from Pompey, he promised large sums of money both to him and to the army; some he would provide at once, while he would give the rest when he was restored. Gabinius abandoned the business of the Parthians and hastened to Egypt, although the law forbade governors to enter territory outside their own borders or to begin wars on their own responsibility, and although the people and the Sibyl had declared that the man should not be restored ... [57] Berenice was at this time ruling the Egyptians ... [58.3] Having conquered them and having slain Archelaus and many others, Gabinius immediately gained control of all Egypt and handed it over to Ptolemy. And he put to death his daughter and the foremost and richest citizens, because he needed a lot of money. [59] This was how Gabinius restored him; however, he did not send a message home concerning what had been done, in order that he might not himself be the one to announce to them what he had done illegally.

Cassius Dio, Roman History 39.55–59.1, with omissions

The restoration of King Ptolemy had been a matter of debate since the previous year (**B109**): in 55 BC Pompey managed to force the matter and bring about a solution, which was in fact entrusted to the governor of Syria A. Gabinius, who carried out a campaign to Egypt against the limits of his provincial command. Both Dio and Strabo (Strabo, *Geography* 17.1.11) frame their discussion of the Egyptian campaign against the backdrop of a moral crisis in Alexandria and in Rome alike, which also has important religious and political ramifications.

B118   *Lex Trebonia*: provinces for Pompey and Crassus, 55 BC

Nor did Pompey and Crassus behave any better when they were in office. First of all, when people were voting to elect Cato to the praetorship, Pompey dissolved the assembly, alleging inauspicious omens; having corrupted the tribes with bribes, they proclaimed Vatinius instead of Cato. Next, through the agency of the tribune Trebonius they brought forward laws, which gave to Caesar a second five-year period of command, to Crassus Syria and the command against the Parthians, and to Pompey himself the whole of Libya, both the Spanish provinces and four legions.

Plutarch, Life of Pompey 52.2–3

Again, major, long-term provincial commands are assigned to Pompey and Caesar through the intervention of a tribune of the plebs. Pompey did not go to his provinces, but retained control over the troops that were quartered there. – In the Greek sources like Plutarch, 'Libya' usually designates North Africa.

B119   Pompey gets round restrictions on theatres

For often the censors used to destroy theatres as soon as they came into being, in their concern for public morality, since they certainly provided a huge danger of bad behaviour. Therefore Pompey the Great (his theatre alone was greater than him), when he had built a bastion for all disgraceful behaviour, feared unfavourable reaction to his monument from the censors at some point. So he put a temple to Venus at the top and in his edict, calling the people, announced it as the dedication not of a theatre, but of a temple of Venus, 'under which we have added,' he said, 'steps for spectators'.

Tertullian, On Shows 10.4–5

Tertullian, AD c. 160-c. 240 was an early Christian writer, but his concern to condemn pagan Roman behaviour does not make his evidence less useful. Pliny, *NH* 8.20 also speaks of beast shows at the dedication of the Temple of Venus.

B120   Pompey's theatre: a question of language

Tiro Tullius, the freedman of Cicero, wrote in more detail in a letter, in roughly the following terms, "When Pompey was about to dedicate the temple of Victory, whose steps were in the form of the theatre, and to inscribe his name and titles on it, the question came about whether consul 'tertio' or 'tertium' should be inscribed. Pompey most conscientiously referred this question to the most scholarly men of the city, but there was disagreement, with some maintaining that 'tertio' and some that 'tertium' should be written. Pompey therefore asked Cicero to order to be written whichever he thought more correct. Then Cicero was worried about judging the scholars, in case he seemed to be actually rejecting the men whose opinion he rejected. Therefore he persuaded Pompey, that he should write neither 'tertio' or 'tertium', but to abbreviate the word after the second 'T'."

Aulus Gellius, Attic Nights 10.1.7

As well as the amusing linguistic anecdote. Tiro's letter offers contemporary evidence for the dedication of the theatre as a temple of Venus Victrix (Venus the Victorious) and for relations between Pompey and Cicero. Gellius knew other material on this episode: Varro was apparently clear about the distinction and Pompey was accused on indecision.

B121   Dedication of Pompey's theatre, 55 BC

Certainly, if you ask, the shows were extremely elaborate, but not to your taste; for I make that conclusion, in view of my own. For, in the first place, there returned to the stage to honour the occasion those whom I thought had retired from the stage for their own honour ... Now what pleasure do six hundred mules bring in the '*Clytemnestra*' or in the '*Trojan Horse*' three thousand mixing bowls or the varied display armour of infantry and cavalry in some battle? What caught popular amazement would not have brought you any pleasure. [3] ... Now I don't believe you missed the Greek or Oscan shows, especially since you can view the Oscan even in your own Senate. ... Should I think that you who have frowned on gladiators missed the athletes at all? In their case even Pompey himself admits that he has wasted both effort and oil. For the rest two wild beast hunts a day for five days, magnificent, no one denies; but what pleasure can there be for a man of culture when a weak human is torn to pieces by a most powerful animal or a noble beast is transfixed with a hunting spear? ... The last day was that of the elephants. Amid the vulgar crowd there was great amazement at them, but no pleasure; indeed there was even some pity and a sort of feeling that they had some affinity with human kind.
Rome, late August 55 BC.

Cicero to M. Marius, To his Friends 7. 2–3 (SB 24) with omissions

A first-hand account of the inauguration of the theatre of Pompey in August 55 BC: the first permanent theatre in the city of Rome. The extravagance of the programme of performances was a powerful statement on Pompey's influence and prestige, and a reminder of his contribution to the expansion of the empire: the display of the elephants was especially significant in that respect. The shows are worthy of an imperial capital, and they sum up the diversity of Rome's dominions in revealing ways: the performances in Greek and in Oscan show how strongly indebted to other traditions Roman drama was, and how conversant with those traditions a Roman audience could be expected to be. – The comments that the compassion that the combats between men and animals, or the sight of an elephant can inspire offers a valuable insight into wider social attitudes to death and suffering that are often missing in a body of evidence that tends to concentrate on political developments. It is all the more striking in a society where slavery plays such a central role.

B122   Crassus departs for the Eastern front, November 55 BC

But when Ateius, one of the tribunes, proposed to oppose his departure, and many people joined with him, because they were angry that anyone should go out to fight against people who were doing no harm, but were in alliance with them, Crassus became afraid and begged Pompey to stand by him and join in escorting him. [4] For great was his reputation with the crowd. Many people then prepared to stand in his way and shout out against him. When Pompey was seen ahead of him with shining gaze and countenance, he softened them with the result that they yielded in silence as they proceeded through their midst. But Ateius went to meet him and first of all tried to stop him with words and to protest solemnly against his going; then he ordered his attendant to lay hold of him in person and to detain him. [5] When the other tribunes did not allow this, the attendant let go of Crassus, while Ateius ran ahead to the gate and placed a blazing brazier there. When Crassus came to it, Ateius offered incense and poured libations over it; he uttered curses dire in themselves and terrifying, furthermore summoning and calling by name some strange and awful gods.

Plutarch, *Life of Crassus* 16.3–5

Upon his departure for the province of Syria, from which he would soon launch a campaign against the Parthians, Crassus defied the ill omens of the tribune Ateius at the Capuan gate. He would have done well to heed the fig seller at Brundisium *Cauneas* ['Caunean figs!', from Caunus, in Asia Minor or interpreted otherwise *cave ne eas* ('beware of going!': Cicero, *On divination* 2.84)]. There is an impressive series of negative omens accompanying Crassus' Parthian campaign, and constructing a narrative of inescapable death and disaster, only exacerbated by Crassus' inability to recognize signs of divine hostility and act appropriately upon them.

B123   Attacks on Gabinius and his trials, 54 BC

a) You enquire what is happening to Gabinius. We shall know the verdict about 'diminishing the greatness (*maiestas*) of the Roman people' within three days. In that trial he is hard pressed by the hostility of all classes, he is especially damaged by the witnesses; he has the most indolent prosecutors. The jury is varied, the president, Alfius, strict and serious, Pompey vigorous in propositioning the jurors. What will happen, I do not know; however, I do not see a place for him in the commonwealth. My attitude to his ruin – no great concern, to the outcome of things – quite unworried. Rome, 21 October 54 BC.

Cicero, *To Quintus* 3.3.2 (SB 23)

b) Gabinius has been acquitted. Certainly nothing was more inarticulate than the prosecutor Lentulus and his assistants, nothing more disgusting than that jury. But even so, had it not been for the incredible effort and pleas of Pompey, and a rumour of dictatorship, terrifying, he would not have answered even to Lentulus; for even with that prosecutor and that jury, he was thirty-two votes were cast for condemnation out of seventy. At all events, this trial is so notorious that it seems he will be destroyed in the remaining trials, particularly that for extortion (*repetundae*). But you see there is no res publica, no senate, no courts, and no worth (*dignitas*) in any of us. Rome, 24 October 54 BC.

Cicero, *To Quintus* 3.4.1 (SB 24)

Gabinius was prosecuted on a *maiestas* charge upon his return to Rome for breaching his duties as provincial governor, and thus diminishing the greatness (*maiestas*) of the Roman people. From these two letters of Cicero we can follow the development of the case (on which see also Cassius Dio, *Roman History* 39.55.4-5, 59.1-60.1, 62): the prosecutor is criticized for his ineffectiveness, and allegations of corruption are also aired. Pompey is said to be supportive of the prosecution, and to have compelled the defendant to answer the questions of the prosecution (a cursory mention is made to the possibility of Pompey taking up the dictatorship in a situation that some regard as an emergency). Dio takes a different view, and states that both Caesar and Pompey made the case for Gabinius' innocence, and mobilized their supporters accordingly. – The prosecutor was the homonymous son of L. Cornelius Lentulus Niger, praetor at the latest in 61 BC since he was an unsuccessful candidate for the consulship of 58 BC, where Gabinius was elected with Piso. Gabinius was acquitted: 70 votes were cast, 38 for acquittal, 32 for condemnation (see Cicero, *Atticus* 4.18.1 = SB 92).

B124   Death of Julia, 54 BC

It was about the fourth year of Caesar's stay in Gaul when Julia, the wife of Magnus, died. She was the guarantee of the concord between Pompey and C. Caesar, which was already being held together with difficulty as a result of their jealousy of power; and fortune severed everything between the leaders destined for so great a crisis, when the little son of Pompey, born of Julia, also died very shortly afterwards.

Velleius Paterculus, *Histories* 2.47.2

The political affiliation between Caesar and Pompey had been accompanied by the marriage between the latter and Caesar's daughter, in Spring 59 BC: her death in 54 (and that of their baby boy) did not have immediate political consequences, but removed a factor that would have stood in the way of the eventual demise of their alliance.

B125   Electoral scandal, 54 BC

a) [7] Now follow me to the Campus. Bribery is rampant. *'I will give you a signal'*: interest rose on the Ides of Quinctilis [15 July] from 1/3 to 2/3%. You will say 'I am not put out by that'. What a man! What a citizen! All the resources of Caesar are supporting Memmius. With him the consuls have joined Domitius in an agreement I dare not commit to a letter. Pompey growls, complains and is eager for Scaurus: whether that is his intent or a cover is in doubt. None of them stands out *above the rest*; money levels out the good name (*dignitas*) of all. Messalla is languishing, not because he lacks spirit or friends, but a partnership of the consuls and Pompey is blocking him. I think these elections will be protracted. The tribunician candidates have taken an oath to canvass subject to the decision of Cato. They have deposited five hundred thousand HS with him so that, whoever is condemned by Cato, loses it and it is distributed to the candidates.

[8] I am writing this on the day before the elections are thought to be taking place. I shall give you the full story about all the elections on 28 July if they are held and the courier has not set out. If, as is thought, they are without bribery, Cato will have had more influence individually than <all the laws> and all jurors.
Rome, 27 June 54 BC.

Cicero, *To Atticus* 4.15.7–8 (SB 90)

Cicero depicts, here and in the letters from which the two passages below are drawn, some of the political developments of the year 54, especially the buildup of the consular elections for the following year. Disenchantment seems to prevail over any other sentiment: electoral corruption is ubiquitous, and the increase in the interest rate is a consequence of the larger amount of debt that a number of candidates are taking on. Caesar may still be away, but he makes his influence strongly felt in Rome through his support for Memmius; Pompey favours a different candidate, M. Aemilius Scaurus, and the risk of a delay of the vote is considerable, largely because prosecutions of candidates are likely. Cato, who is holding the praetorship, can be expected to vet the candidates very aggressively. – The sentence printed in italics is in Greek in the original text.

b) All who are seeking the consulship have been arraigned for electoral malpractice (*ambitus*): Domitius by Memmius, Memmius by Q. Aculius, a good and well-educated young man, Messalla by Q. Pompeius, Scaurus by Triarius. Great events are afoot, as a consequence of which the end of the men or of the laws is in prospect. Efforts are being made to prevent the courts from taking place. Things seem to be pointing to an *interregnum*. The consuls want to hold elections; the defendants do not want them, especially Memmius, because he hopes to be consul with the arrival of Caesar, but he is remarkably low. Domitius seems a certainty with Messalla. Scaurus has gone cool. Rome, 11 October 54 BC.

Cicero, To Quintus 3.2.3 (SB 22)

Four months later, the risk of a round of prosecutions has proven real: all the leading candidates have been charged with electoral corruption, although attempts are now underway to prevent the trials from taking place, on the one hand, and to postpone the elections, on the other. Some candidates are entertaining the hope of being rehabilitated. The general picture is of a situation where a breakdown in morality is combining with a failing political system.

c) Now learn about the things happening in the *res publica*. The days for the elections are being put off day by day through announcements of unfavourable omens with the widespread agreement of all good citizens (*boni*); the consuls are experiencing such unpopularity because of a suspicion of financial deals arranged with the candidates. All four consular candidates have been charged. The cases are difficult, but I shall do my utmost so that my friend Messalla may be saved, something that is linked up with the salvation of the rest as well.
Rome, 21 October 54 BC.

Cicero, To Quintus 3.3.27 (SB 23)

Cicero takes up the defence of M. Valerius Messalla Rufus (eventually elected consul in July 53 BC), who does not have the support of either Caesar or Pompey; further attempts are made to postpone the elections, and religious arguments are being invoked. There seems to be a clear majority in the Senate for a delay in the vote, although that option is not immune from the risks that a situation of political instability can bring about: the reputation of the serving consuls is undermined by the suspicion of collusion with the prosecuted candidates.

B126   Rome, 54/53 BC
a) I am grieved, my sweetest brother, I am grieved that there is no *res publica*, no courts, that these years which ought to be flourishing with the dignity of a senator are being busied with work in the courts or sustained by literary studies are home; while what I had wanted to have from childhood 'to be best by far and to be pre-eminent over others' has wholly collapsed. Some of my enemies have not been attacked by me, some have even been defended; not only is my mind not free, but neither is my hatred.
Rome, October/November 54 BC.

Cicero, To Quintus 3.5.4 (SB 25)

A powerful statement in a private letter, which has strong political implications: as he reflects on current affairs, Cicero does not just speak of a political crisis, but entertains the much more disturbing notion that the *res publica* is no longer in existence. The explicit reference to 'hatred' is a pointer to a political and psychological climate in which the common ground is being sharply eroded.

b) Business has been postponed, the elections brought to an *interregnum*. There is rumour of a dictator, displeasing to good men (*boni*), while to me what they are saying is even more so. The whole business is both fearful yet going cool. Pompey publicly says he does not want it; previously to me he himself did not say he was unwilling. It seems Hirrus will be the proposer.
Rome, end of November 54 BC.

Cicero, *To Quintus* 3.6.4 (SB 26)

Another pointer of things to come: the failure to perform a basic public act such as the consular elections leads some to denounce a state of crisis, which must be solved by resorting to the dictatorship, a magistracy that is deployed only in a time of emergency, for six months: Pompey is the obvious candidate, but he shows some reluctance, at least in public. He knew, like his contemporaries, that the dictatorship was closely associated with the acts of Sulla in the aftermath of his victory in the Civil War. – On *interregnum* see **L21**.

c) And the consuls, year by year, began to despair of campaigning and fighting anywhere, shut out by the power of the three men. The worst of them regarded the affairs of the state and the elections of their own successors, rather than provincial commands, as the means of making a profit. For these reasons good men completely abandoned holding office, so that on one occasion it happened as a result of such disorder that the *res publica* was for eight months without magistrates, while Pompey purposely disregarded it all, so that they might be in need of a dictator.

Appian, *Civil Wars* 2.19

Appian explains the crisis of 54 BC with the recently introduced prohibition for consuls to take up a provincial command in the immediate aftermath of their magistracy. Since they no longer had that chance of immediate gain, they sought to profit from their role as presiding officers of the consular elections. Moreover, the consulship was more broadly discredited, and more men of questionable reputation and base standards sought the magistracy, hence increasing the margin for prosecutions of candidates. – A sinister note is introduced about Pompey: he coveted the dictatorship all along, and contributed to the climate of disorder in Rome so that the need for a dictator was perceived as more urgent. – On this crisis see Cassius Dio, *Roman History* 40.45-46.

B127   Death of Crassus on the Eastern front, June 53 BC
[31.2] Then the Suren advanced on his horse with his leading men and said: 'What is this? Is the Roman commander-in-chief on foot, while we are riding?' And he ordered them to bring forward a horse for him. [3] But Crassus said that neither he himself nor the other was in the wrong since each was conducting the meeting according to his native custom. Then the Suren said that from that moment there was peace and a truce between King Orodes and the Romans but that they must go forward to the river and put the terms down in writing. 'For you Romans' he said 'are not particularly good at remembering agreements' and he stretched out his right hand to him. When Crassus sent for a horse, he said there was no need; 'for the Great King gives you this one.' [4] At the same time a horse with a gold-studded bridle stood beside Crassus, the grooms lifted him up and sat him astride it. They escorted him, quickening the horse with blows. Octavius was the first to

grab hold of the bridle and after him Petronius, one of the military tribunes, then the rest gathered around the horse and tried to check it, and to drag off those who were pressing down upon Crassus from each side. [5] Jostling, tumult, and then blows took place; Octavius drew his sword and killed the groom of one of the barbarians, while another struck Octavius from behind. Petronius was not in possession of a weapon, but, having been struck on the breastplate, jumped down unwounded. A Parthian, named Pomaxathres, killed Crassus.

[6] Some say it was not he, but that another was the killer and cut off his head and his right hand as he lay there. These are more guesses than known facts. For of those present, some died fighting around Crassus, while others rushed at once up the hill. Then the Parthians came up and declared that Crassus had paid the penalty and the Suren now ordered the rest to come down in confidence; some came down and gave themselves up, while others scattered by night and of these few got away to complete safety. The Arabs hunted down the rest, captured and did away with them. In all twenty thousand are said to have been killed, while ten thousand were captured alive.

Plutarch, Life of Crassus 31.2–6, with omissions

Crassus' campaign to the East was a comprehensive disaster, which made a lasting impression at Rome. Plutarch in the *Life of Crassus* has a very detailed narrative of the Parthian campaign, including a striking sequence of bad omens that accompanied the expedition from its very beginning (see also the 'figs from Caunus' episode mentioned above, **B122**) and a detailed account of the death of Crassus and his men. The account of his demise conveys the sense of the magnitude of the defeat he suffered, but also portrays Crassus meeting his death in a dignified manner, in the face of the treachery of the Suren, the Parthian commander who led the army at Carrhae. Crassus was in fact reluctant to go to a parley with the Suren, trying to encourage his men to wait until dark and attempt escape, but the soldiers were mutinous, and he agreed to hold the conference that proved fatal to him. Carrhae does not just mark the demise of Crassus, but entailed dreadful consequences for thousands of Roman soldiers, who were killed or captured. – The destruction of Crassus' army took place in a year of deep political disruption, and did not fail to make a great impression in Rome. It was, in fact, such a traumatic event that the emperor Augustus could invoke his role in the retrieval of the Roman standards from the Parthians as late as in 20 BC: the handover is depicted on the cuirass of the 'Prima Porta' statue of Augustus.

B128   A further comment on Crassus' death

As to his death, Crassus is free from blame, as he did not surrender to the Parthians, and was not put into chain or duped, but he yielded to the insistence of his friends and fell victim to the treachery of his enemies.

Plutarch, Life of Crassus 38.4

A comment that exonerates Crassus from direct responsibility in the events leading to his death, and stresses the weight of the factors that played up against him: it does not amount, however, to a favourable judgement on Crassus' conduct of the campaign.

THE RUN-UP TO CIVIL WAR

B129   The death of Clodius, January 52 BC

a) [27] Meanwhile, Clodius was aware ... that Milo had a journey, required by religious ritual, by law and by necessity, to Lanuvium on 18 January to elect a priest (*flamen*), because Milo was chief magistrate at Lanuvium. Therefore he himself suddenly left Rome the day before to set an ambush for Milo in front of his estate, as can be shown by events; and such was the manner of his leaving that he abandoned a disorderly assembly (*contio*), in which his madness was missed, which was held that day, which he would never have abandoned had he not wished to be on hand at the place and time of his evil enterprise. [28] Milo, on the other hand, after he he had been in the senate-house that day until the Senate was dismissed, came home, changed his shoes and his clothes, waited a short time while his wife got herself ready, as happens, then left at the moment in time when Clodius would have been able by then to be back, if he was intending to be in Rome that day. Clodius met him, unencumbered, on horseback, with no carriage, with no baggage, without any Greek companions as was his custom, and without his wife, which almost never happened; while this 'conspirator', who, so it is alleged, had organized this journey to commit murder, was riding in a carriage with his wife, wearying a heavy cloak, with a company that was large, heavily laden, with women and a pretty troop of slave girls and boys. [29] He met Clodius in front of his estate about the eleventh hour or not much later. At once several men, with weapons, launched an attack from higher ground; men blocked his way and killed the coachman. When Milo, having thrown aside his cloak, had jumped down from the carriage and was vigorously defending himself, some of those who were with Clodius, having drawn their swords, ran back to the carriage to attack Milo from the rear, while others, because they thought that he was already dead began to attack his slaves who came behind; of those who were resolute and loyal to their master, some were killed, while others when they saw the fighting by the carriage, were prevented from coming to the help of their master and heard from Clodius himself that Milo had been killed and thought that this was indeed the case; the slaves of Milo ... without the order or the knowledge or the presence of their master did what anyone would have wished his slaves to do in such circumstances.

Cicero, Defence of Milo 27–29

b) [31] On 18 January ... Milo set out for Lanuvium, from which free-town (*municipium*) he came and where he was then chief magistrate, to elect a priest (*flamen*) on the following day. Clodius met him around the ninth hour a little beyond Bovillae, as he was returning from Aricia, near the spot at which there is a shrine to the Bona Dea: he had been addressing the town councillors (*decuriones*) of the Aricians. Clodius was riding a horse; about thirty unencumbered slaves clad with swords were following, as was normal for people travelling at that time. With Clodius in addition there were three companions, one of whom, C. Causinius Schola, was a Roman *eques,* and two well-known plebeians, P. Pomponius and C. Clodius. Milo was riding in a coach with his wife, Fausta, the daughter of the dictator Sulla, and his close friend, M. Fufius. A long line of slaves was following them, [32] among them also were gladiators including the well-known Eudamas and Birria. As they were proceeding rather slowly at the very end of the line, they started an altercation with the slaves of

Clodius. When Clodius turned back and looked threateningly upon this tumult, Birria pierced his shoulder with a Thracian hunting spear. When battle had begun, more of Milo's company then came running up. Clodius, having been wounded was brought to the nearest inn at Bovillae. When Milo learned that Clodius had been wounded, since he thought it would be more dangerous for him if Clodius were actually alive, while he would have great relief with him dead, even if he had to undergo punishment, he ordered him to be dragged out. The leader of his slaves was M. Saufeius. Thus Clodius was secretly dragged out and finished off with multiple injuries. His corpse was left in the road because the slaves of Clodius had either been killed or, having been seriously wounded, were in hiding. A senator, Sextus Taedius, who by chance was returning to the city from the country, took it up and ordered it to be carried home in his litter; he himself then went back to the place from which he had set out. The body of Clodius was brought to the city before the first hour of the night and a very large crowd of the humblest plebs and of slaves, in great grief, surrounded the body which was placed in the atrium of his house. Fulvia, Clodius' wife, displayed his wounds with uncontrolled lamentation, and increased indignation at the deed. At dawn on the following day a larger crowd of the same sort assembled, and several men of note were seen, among them a senator, C. Vibienus. It was the house of Clodius on the Palatine, which had been bought a few months before from M. Scaurus. To this same place there hastened the tribunes of the plebs, T. Munatius Plancus, the brother of L. Plancus, the orator, and Q. Pompeius Rufus, the grandson of the dictator Sulla by his daughter. [33] At their encouragement the ignorant mob carried the body down to the forum, naked and muddied, exactly as it had been placed on the litter, so that the wounds could be seen, and placed it on the rostra. There before an assembly (*contio*) Plancus and Pompey, who were supporting the competitors of Milo, stirred up hostility to Milo. The people, led by the scribe, Sex. Clodius carried the body of P. Clodius into the senate-house and cremated it, with benches, platforms, tables and the notebooks of the record clerks. The senate-house itself was set alight by this fire and likewise the basilica Porcia, which adjoined it, was burnt. That same crowd of Clodian sympathizers also attacked the houses of M. Lepidus, the *interrex* (for he had been made a curule magistrate) and that of Milo, who was away; but they driven away from it by arrows. Then they snatched up the rods of office (*fasces*) from the grove of Libitina and brought them to the house of Scipio and of Hypsaeus, then to the estate of Pompey, repeatedly calling upon him, at one moment as consul, at another as dictator. (… *Continued disorder at Rome leads to further interregna and the passing of the 'emergency decree'* (senatus consultum ultimum), *see the start of passage* **B131a** …)

[34] Almost the thirtieth day after Clodius had been killed, Q. Metellus Scipio complained in the Senate against Q. Caepio about this killing of Clodius. He declared that what Milo said in his own defence was false, but that Clodius had set out with twenty-six slaves travelling in order to address the Arician councillors (*decuriones*); that Milo, suddenly after the fourth hour, [35] when the Senate had been dismissed, had hurried to meet him with more than three hundred armed slaves and had attacked him off his guard on the road beyond Bovillae; Clodius had sustained three wounds there and was carried to Bovillae; the inn, in which he had sought refuge, had been stormed by Milo; Clodius had been dragged out unconscious [...*gaps in text*...] and killed on the via Appia and his ring had been pulled off as he was dying. Then Milo had come to his country house, because he knew that the young son of Clodius was on his

Alban estate; since the boy had been previously snatched from danger, he conducted an interrogation of the slave Halicor, in such a way that he cut him up limb by limb; he cut the throats of the foreman and two slaves besides. Of the slaves of Clodius, who had defended their master, eleven had been killed, while only two of Milo's slaves had been wounded; because of these events, on the following day Milo had manumitted twelve slaves who had acted with distinction and had given to the people, tribe by tribe, a thousand asses each to fend off rumours about himself.

> Asconius, *Commentary on Cicero's Defence of Milo* p. 31C.12–35C.16,
> with omissions

These two passages are the fullest surviving accounts of the assassination of Clodius, which occurred at Bovillae, in the vicinity of Rome, in January 52 BC. T. Annius Milo was prosecuted on a murder charge, and Cicero took up his defence: the first passage is a summary of his case. While he could not deny that the gangs of Milo and Clodius had clashed on the Appian Way and that his long-time enemy had lost his life on that occasion, Cicero denied any intention on Milo's part; Asconius, in his commentary on Cicero's speech, sets out a very different version of the events, in which Milo is cast in a much more sinister light and his responsibility is clearly stated, and through which we also learn about the reactions to the assassination in Rome and the political consequences of that event. The fire of the senate-house during Clodius' cremation is a stark illustration of the awful state in which the *res publica* is, and indeed of the complete breakdown of the institutional and political framework through which the city had been ruled for generations.

B130   Justifying the assassination of Clodius, 52 BC

[79] Look at the problem in this way, jurymen: this trial deals, as you know, with the death of Publius Clodius. Picture to your mind, for our thought is free and can bring up what it desires, just as we discern actual objects with our eyes, picture, I say, in your imagination this alternative that I am putting forward to you: suppose I could induce you to acquit Milo, but only on condition that Publius Clodius shall have come to life again. Why those terrified glances? What feelings would he inspire in you if he were alive, seeing that even when he lives no more he has shaken you with a hollow fancy? Again, if Pompey himself, whose character and fortune is such that he has ever been able to achieve what no one else could – if he, I say, had had the choice between proposing an inquiry into Clodius' death and bringing him back from the dead, which, think you, would he have chosen? Even had he been keen on calling him back from the dead for friendship's sake, he would have refrained from doing so, for the sake of the commonwealth. You sit here, then, as the avengers of the death of one to whom you would refuse to restore life, even did you think you had the power; and a law has been proposed for an inquiry into his slaying, although, if he could by the same law have been brought back to life, that law would never have been put forward. If then my client was the killer of such a man as this, could he, in admitting the deed, fear punishment at the hands of the very persons whom he had freed?

[80] The Greeks bestow divine honours upon those men who have killed tyrants (*tyranni*). What have I seen at Athens and in other cities of Greece! What religious rites they established in their honour! What musical compositions and songs! They are worshipped with an observance and commemoration that befits immortal beings. Will you, far from bestowing any distinctions upon the preserver of such a great people and the avenger of such a great crime, even suffer him to be taken to the punishment that befits a criminal? Had he done the deed, he would confess – yes, he would confess

proudly and gladly – that he had done for the sake of everybody's liberty a deed that he would not just confess, but proclaim loud and clear.

Cicero, *Defence of Milo* 79–80

Cicero devotes much of his speech to denying any responsibility on Milo's part for Clodius' death. However, he also explores another side of the argument, and reflects on the political consequences of the assassination of his rival: after saluting it as an altogether positive development, without considering further its lawfulness, he turns to the position of Milo, and, while ostensibly denying his involvement in the events, he notes that *if* he were responsible he should be honoured like the murderers of tyrants are in the Greek world: as a champion of liberty. See also **L33** and, for the circumstances of Cicero's actual speech, its relation to the published version, and the result of Milo's trial, see **G47-G49**.

B131   Pompey appointed sole consul, 52 BC

a) Meanwhile one *interrex* followed another, because consular elections [34] could not be held owing to the very disorders caused by the candidates and their armed gangs. Thus first of all a decree (*senatus consultum*) was passed that the *interrex,* the tribunes and Pompey, who was proconsul and was near the city, *should see to it that the* res publica *suffer no harm,* and that Pompey should hold a levy throughout Italy. He collected a force with the greatest speed. ...

[35] Amid all this [*continued strife between supporters of Milo and Clodius*], since a view was becoming widespread that Pompey ought to be appointed dictator and that the evils of the state could not be cured otherwise, [36] it seemed safer to the *optimates* that he should be appointed consul without a colleague; and when the matter had been debated in the Senate, a decree (*senatus consultum*) was passed upon the proposal of M. Bibulus: Pompey was appointed consul by the *interrex* Servius Sulpicius on the fifth day in the intercalary month before 1 March, and took up his consulship immediately.

Asconius, *Commentary on Cicero's Defence of Milo* p. 33C.25–36C.5, with omissions

Asconius is a key source for the events of the first half of 52 BC. Here he records the passing of the final decree in 52 BC following the death of Clodius and the anarchy in Rome, which the assassination of Clodius had exacerbated. No curule elections had been held: only the *interrex*, and the tribunes, who had been elected, together with Pompey, who was exercising his proconsular command for the corn supply, could respond to the decree. Pompey brought armed forces into the city to suppress the disorder. Even in these circumstances, however, the dictatorship was not revived (see Plutarch, *Life of Pompey* 54.3). The *interrex* (literally, 'between king') was appointed to hold the consulars elections when the consuls were unable to do so during their year of office; it was traditionally a patrician, but the rule was discontinued in the late Republic (see below, **L21**).

b) [20] Many people were talking this matter over with one another, saying that the authority of a single ruler seemed the only remedy for the present ills, but that it was necessary to choose someone powerful and gentle at the same time. By this they meant Pompey, who was then commanding a sufficient army, seemed to be friendly to the people, to be leading the Senate because of his reputation, to be of disciplined and temperate lifestyle, and who was, or was thought to be, easy of access for petitions. He was, so it appeared, displeased at this expectation, but in reality he was secretly doing everything for it and was willing to overlook the disorder of the state and the anarchy consequent upon that disorder ...

[23] The Senate met in fear and they were looking to Pompey to be their dictator immediately; for it seemed to them that present circumstances required such a remedy. But when Cato caused them to change their minds, they appointed him consul without a colleague so that he might have the authority of a dictator, being in sole office, but the accountability of a consul. He was the first consul having two very large provinces, an army, money, and the sole power in the city through being sole consul.

Appian, *Civil Wars* 2.20–23, with omission

The theme of Pompey's dissimulation, which disguises his appetite for power, is not new: see **B126b**. Appian lucidly conveys a sense of the extent of the power reached by Pompey, and establishes a clear link between political influence, control over substantial military contigents, and access to large financial resources.

B132   Pompey's legislation, 52 BC

Then three days later he consulted the Senate about enacting new laws: he promulgated two in accordance with a decree (*senatus consultum*), one concerning criminal violence (*vis*), in which he included and specifically named, the murder which had taken place on the Appian way and the burning of the senate-house and the attack upon the house of the *interrex*, M. Lepidus, the second concerning electoral malpractice (*ambitus*) ... The tribune of the plebs, M. Caelius, one of the staunchest supporters of Milo, tried to block these statutes, on the grounds that the law being passed against Milo was a special law (*privilegium*) and that the lawcourts were being thrown overboard. When Caelius resolutely persisted in his criticism, Pompey became so angry that he said that, he would, if compelled, defend the *res publica* with armed force.

Asconius, *Commentary on Cicero's Defence of Milo* p. 36C.5–17, with omission

Pompey's legislative proposals seem to envisage a strategy of reconciliation: on the one hand, he was determined to secure the punishment of Milo, while, on the other, he intended to sanction those supporters of Clodius who had caused riots in the city after the funeral. When faced with tribunician opposition, however, he does not hesitate to threaten a violent reaction. A *privilegium* was literally a 'special law' – (from *privus* and *lex*): in other words, one that was aimed at a particular case or individual and thus illegal.

B133   Pompey chooses a co-consul, 52 BC

a) He chose as his colleague Quintus Scipio, who was his father-in-law and was on a charge of bribery. [3] For he was by birth the son of Nasica, but by adoption into the family of Metellus Pius was made his heir and bore his name. He gave his daughter away in marriage to Pompey, and received from him in turn the consulship and immunity from prosecution.

Cassius Dio, *Roman History* 40.51.2–3

For the best part of the year Pompey was consul without a colleague; he accepted the appointment of a second consul, Q. Caecilius Metellus Pius Scipio Nasica, only in the final part of his term in office. Dio's criticism is comparable to the arguments used by Cato in 59/58, when Pompey married the daughter of his ally Julius Caesar. Q. Scipio allegedly does not reach the consulship through his merits, but thanks to a marriage alliance.

b) On the Ides of June [13 June] when Pompey was consul for the third time ...
On the Ides of September [13 Sept] when Pompey and Q. Metellus were consuls...

Degrassi, *ILLRP* 1050, 1051

These separate documents which follow the usual Roman custom of given the year by the consul(s) between them show that Pompey was sole consul until at least 13 June 52 BC, while Scipio had become his fellow consul by 13 September.

B134 Legislation of Pompey and law of the ten tribunes, 52 BC

[51.2] To prevent Caesar thinking he had been completely neglected and as a result of this have legitimate cause to be angry with him, he arranged through the tribunes that he should be allowed to seek office even when absent when it was proper in accordance with the law. ...

[56.1] Thus he arranged these matters, and at the same time he renewed the law concerning elections to office, which had somehow been disregarded: it commanded that those, who were canvassing for office, should without fail present themselves before the assembly. He also had a decree ratified which had been passed a short time previously, that those, who had held office in the city, should not be appointed to commands abroad before five years elapsed. [2] Even so, he was not embarrassed that after proposing such measures then, he soon afterwards took Spain for another five years and allowed Caesar to seek the consulship in his absence (for his friends were extremely annoyed at this), as had been voted. Thus he added to the law that permission to do this was only granted publicly and to named individuals. This was in no way different from its not having been prohibited in the first place. For those who had some power would arrange for this to be voted for them.

Cassius Dio, Roman History 40.51.2 and 56.1–2

In spite of his increasing influence in Rome, Pompey cannot quite do without Caesar in this difficult political phase. He therefore orchestrates the passing of a tribunician law that included exceptions to two crucial provisions that he had recently introduced: Caesar was given the privilege to present his candidacy to the consulship without having to return to Rome in person (hence exposing himself to the risk of prosecutions); at the same time, Pompey secures another long-term command in Spain, in spite of rules explicitly providing against continuity between the tenure of the consulship and a provincial governorship. – On this political operation see also Suetonius, *Divus Julius* 26.1–2.

B135 Caesar's provinces, 51 BC

a) [5] Your friend Pompey is open in not wishing Caesar to keep his province with an army and to become consul at the same time. However, he expressed the opinion that no senatorial decree (*senatus consultum*) should be passed at this time; Scipio expressed the opinion that the matter of the Gallic provinces should be referred to the Senate on 1 March with nothing else attached. This opinion depressed Cornelius Balbus, and I know he has complained to Scipio.

Rome, 2 September 51 BC.

Caelius to Cicero, To his Friends, 8.9.5 (SB 82)

b) [9] Furthermore, the following remarks of Pompey, which have brought people considerable confidence, have been noted: he said that he could not without injustice decide about the provinces of Caesar before the Kalends of March [1 March]; but after the Kalends of March he would have no hesitation. When he was asked 'What if some people then use their veto?', he said it made no difference whether C. Caesar was not going to obey the Senate or whether he was arranging for someone not to allow the Senate to pass a decree. 'But what if' asked another 'he wants both to be consul and to keep his army?' He replied very gently: 'What if my son wants to lay into to me with a stick?' With these comments he has made men reckon *that Pompey is having trouble with Caesar*. And so, as I see it, Caesar is willing to settle for one or other of these two conditions: either that he remains and his leave of absence is not used *this year* or, if he can become consul designate, that he leaves his province. [10] Curio is preparing total opposition against him. What he can achieve I do not know; I see, however, that being of the right sentiment, even if he achieves nothing, he cannot come to harm. Rome, early October 51 BC.

Caelius to Cicero, To his Friends, 8.8.4–10 (SB 84)

An alternative translation for '*that Pompey is having trouble with Caesar*' is 'that Pompey has done a deal with Caesar'. '*this year*' is an historical crux.

c) For in the previous year, Marcellus, since he was impugning the reputation (*dignitas*) of Caesar, contrary to the law of Pompey and Crassus, had prematurely put the matter of the provinces of Caesar before the Senate. When opinions had been expressed and Metellus, who was seeking all esteem (*dignitas*) for himself from his hostility to Caesar, put the matter to the vote, a full Senate all voted the other way. The spirits of Caesar's enemies were not broken by these events, but they were given a warning that they had to arrange more critical issues, so that the Senate could thereby be compelled to approve what they themselves had determined.

(Hirtius), Gallic War 8. 53, 1–2

These passages record the onset of a dispute between Caesar and the Senate that will lead to the outbreak of the civil war within about fifteen months. The focus of the controversy is the transition from Caesar's provincial governorship to his candidacy for the consulship, which he was determined to put forward without first returning to the status of private citizen. In Caelius' assessment (conveyed in two letters to Cicero, who was then governor in Cilicia), Pompey is determined not to satisfy Caesar's request; however, he decides to wait until March 50 before taking action, probably because raising the matter any sooner would have been in breach of the law on provincial administration that he had put forward with Crassus during their consulship of 55 BC. The opposite viewpoint shapes the account in book 8 of the *Gallic War*, probably written by Caesar's close associate Aulus Hirtius, who argued that the overwhelming majority of the Senate is in fact on Caesar's side, and that the consul of 51 M. Claudius Marcellus is the leading member of a small clique that is scheming against him. Significantly, Pompey receives no mention. – On this political phase see also Suetonius, *Divus Julius* 28.2-29.1; Cassius Dio, *Roman History* 40.59.

B136   Parthian invasion of the province of Syria, 51 BC
a) A Parthian war is hanging over us. Cassius sent a silly letter, and the letter from Bibulus has not yet arrived. When it is read out I think the Senate will at last be moved to action. For my part I am in great anxiety. If, as I desire, my post is not prorogued, I have June and Quintilis [July] to fear. So be it. Bibulus will hold out for two months, at all events. What will happen to the person I leave behind, especially if it is my brother? But then what about me, if I do not leave so quickly? It is a great 'to-do'. I have agreed with Deiotarus that he should be in my camp with all his forces; he has thirty cohorts of four hundred men equipped with our weaponry and 2,000 cavalry. That will be enough to put up resistance until Pompey arrives; he indicates in a letter he sends to me that this will be his business. The Parthians are wintering in our province. Orodes himself is expected. What more can I say? It is some business. Laodicea, 20 February 50 BC.

Cicero, To Atticus 6.1.14 (SB 115)

Crassus' defeat in Parthia had emboldened the enemy, who attacked the province of Syria in 51: the brunt of the attack was sustained by C. Cassius Longinus, Crassus' former quaestor, who was still in the region. In this letter Cicero, who was still serving in neighbouring Cilicia, weighs up his options, as he might soon be expected to contribute to the counterattack: his hope is that the task will soon be taken up by Pompey, with the endorsement of the Senate. – For more evidence on this campaign and Cicero's reaction to it see *To his Friends* 8.10.1-2 (SB 87)] and *To Atticus* 6.5.3 (SB 119).

b) [1] Then a senatorial decree (*senatus consultum*) was passed that one legion should be sent by Pompey to the Parthian war, another by Caesar; and there was no secret that two legions were being taken away from one man. For Pompey gave the first legion, enlisted from a levy in Caesar's province, which he had sent to Caesar, as though it were one of his. Caesar, however, although there was not the least doubt about the intention of his opponents, sent it back to Pompey and for his own part ordered the fifteenth legion, which he had in Gallia Citerior, to be handed over in accordance with the *senatus consultum*.

(Hirtius), *Gallic War,* 8.54.1–3

The need to mobilize more forces in the East also has immediate repercussions in Rome: both Caesar and Pompey have to discharge one legion each; Pompey, however, picked a legion that he had just sent to Caesar's province. This incident further tarnished the relations between the two men, and was soon to be added to the list of grievances that Caesar had regarding the conduct of much of the Roman political élite towards him. – See also Appian, *Civil War* 2.29-30.

B137   Tribunate of C. Scribonius Curio, 50 BC
a) Caelius to Cicero.
As far as the *res publica* is concerned, the whole struggle has become concentrated upon one issue: the provinces. On this issue Pompey seems, as things stand so far, together with the Senate, to incline to the view that Caesar should leave on the Ides of November [13 November]. Curio has decided to tolerate everything rather than to allow that; he has given up all his other proposals. Our friends, whom you know well, do not dare to push the issue to an extreme confrontation; the scenario of the whole issue is as follows: Pompey, as though not opposing Caesar, but deciding on what he thinks is fair to Caesar, says that Curio is looking for trouble. But he certainly does not want and is obviously afraid of Caesar as consul designate before he has handed over his army. He is being quite badly treated by Curio and the whole of his third consulship is being criticized. I tell you this: if they press hard upon Curio by every means, Caesar will defend his vetoing tribune; if they shrink from that, as they seem likely to, Caesar will stay as long as he wants.
Rome, mid (?) April, 50 BC

Caelius to Cicero, *To his Friends* 8.11.3 (SB 91)

b) Cicero to Caelius.
The situation of the *res publica* concerns me greatly. I support Curio. I want Caesar to be treated with honour. I can die for Pompey, but nothing, however, is dearer to me than the *res publica* itself. You do not make much of your stance in it. You seem to me to be pulled in different directions because you are a good citizen and a good friend.
Side [in Pamphylia], 3 or 4 August 50 BC.

Cicero, *To his Friends* 2.15.3 (SB 96)

By 50 BC it became apparent that the controversy between Pompey and Caesar revolved on the end date of their provincial tenures. A matter of constitutional procedures had serious political implications, and is in turn associated with the workings of a constitutional body, the tribunate of the plebs: C. Scribonius Curio makes clear that he will veto any arrangement that may be unfavourable to Caesar. That stance could present major political problems, but could not be lightly disregarded: hence Cicero's sympathy, at least on grounds of principle, towards Curio's position, which is significantly conveyed in a private letter. – For a favourable summary of Curio's position cf. (Hirtius), *Gallic War* 8.52.4-5; cf. also Appian, *Civil War* 2.26-27, who notes that Curio commanded the admiration of those who felt that Pompey's power was becoming excessive.

c) On high matters of the *res publica* I have often written to you that I do not see peace lasting for a year; and the closer the struggle that has to happen approaches, the more obvious the danger appears. The issue on which they are going to come to battle is this: Pompey has decided not to let Caesar in any way become consul unless he hands over his army and his provinces, while Caesar is convinced that he cannot be safe if he leaves his army. He puts forward the proposal that they both hand over their armies. So it is that their love affair and their odious partnership has sunk not to covert bickering, but is erupting into full-scale war. I am not clear what course to take; I have no doubt that this consideration is also causing you trouble. For I have obligation and friendship with these men, while I love the other cause, but hate the men. ...

[3] I do not imagine that it escapes your notice that in a dispute within the state men ought to follow the more respectable party, so long as the struggle is waged as between citizens and not with force of arms; but when it comes to war and military operations, men should follow the stronger and decide that what is safer is the better. In this dispute I see that Pompey will have the Senate and those who are jurors with him, while all who live in fear or with no good prospect will join Caesar; his army is incomparable. Certainly there is enough time to consider the resources of each side and to choose a side.

Rome, *c.* 8 August 50 BC.

> Caelius to Cicero, *To his Friends* 8.14.2–3 (SB 97), with omissions

The more politically aware minds were by this point in no doubt on the likelihood of imminent conflict: this letter by Caelius starts with a correct prediction and then spells out the stakes, making a thought-provoking distinction between the advantages of sticking to principle and those of choosing the side that is more likely to prevail. The rules that apply to the peacetime political debate do not quite hold valid in the same terms during a civil war.

B138   Illness of Pompey, Summer 50 BC
a) But if he had died two years before men resorted to arms, at the time when the gifts of his theatre and the other buildings that he put around it had been completed and when he was afflicted by a very serious illness in Campania (at which time all Italy offered prayers for that first of all citizens), then fortune would have been denied the opportunity of demolishing him and he would have taken to the underworld unimpaired the greatness which he had possessed in the world above.

> Velleius Paterculus, *Histories* 2.48.2

Cf. also Cicero, *Atticus* 8.16.1 (SB 166) and 9.6.3 (SB 172), where there is mention of decrees passed by Italian *municipia* for Pompey's good health. On the decrees of Italian cities on important political matters see **B146, D5**.

b) After this Pompey suffered a grave illness at Neapolis. When Praxagoras advised the citizens of Neapolis, they offered thanksgiving sacrifices for his recovery. The neighbouring people copied them and the idea made its way through all of Italy and every city large and small held a celebration for many days. [2] No place was able to hold all those who came to meet him from all over, but the roads, the villages and the harbours were filled with people sacrificing and feasting lavishly. Many wearing garlands greeted him with torches in their hands and escorted him showering him with flowers so that his progress and return were a most beautiful and brilliant sight. [3] However, this is said more than anything else to have been the cause that brought about war: for at the same time as the greatness of rejoicing, an arrogance came upon him, which went beyond the calculations from the facts; casting aside the caution for safety which was the basis for his successes and achievements he fell into an absolute confidence and a contempt for the power of Caesar, reckoning that he would not need arms against him nor tedious preparation but that he would destroy him much more easily than he had previously built the man up. [4] In addition to this, Appius came from Gaul bringing the army which Pompey had lent to Caesar; he did much to belittle his achievements there and spread scandalous reports about Caesar; and he said that Pompey was unaware of his own power and reputation, strengthening himself with further troops against Caesar: he would finish Caesar off with Caesar's own troops the moment he was seen, for so great was the hatred of Caesar and the yearning for Pompey among them. [5] In this way, then, Pompey was excited, and because of his confidence he became full of such a great contempt for Caesar that he laughed at those who were afraid of war; as for those who said that if Caesar marched on Rome, they did not see the forces with which they would defend it from him, he smiled and with a relaxed countenance told them not to worry: 'wherever I stamp the earth of Italy with my foot' he said, 'armed infantry and cavalry forces will spring up.'

Plutarch, *Life of Pompey* 57

Plutarch, as ever, is interested in turning points in the lives of his characters, and Pompey's recovery from his serious illness is singled out as the moment in which the overwhelming support he received from the Italian communities and the misleading information that reached him on the mood of Caesar's troops led his misguided decision to rush to war. This flawed political choice is accompanied by increasingly haughty conduct, and by growing contempt towards his former ally Caesar.

B139 The war approaches, 50 BC
The Senate sought the view of each member. And Claudius cunningly divided the motion and enquired separately whether each was in favour of sending successors to Caesar and of taking away his command from Pompey. The majority rejected the latter proposal, but they voted in favour of successors to Caesar. When Curio put the question again, if they were in favour of their both laying down the forces they had to hand, twenty-two disagreed, while three hundred and seventy inclined to the proposal, and the expediency of avoiding conflict. Upon which Claudius at once dismissed the Senate, shouting 'You win, have Caesar as your tyrant (Gk – *despotes*).' [31] Suddenly a false rumour spread among them that Caesar had crossed the Alps and was making for the city; there was great fear and confusion among all and Claudius introduced a proposal that the army in Capua go to meet Caesar as a public enemy. When Curio opposed him on the grounds that the reports were false, he said 'If I am prevented by the vote of the Senate from taking action for the interests of the state, I shall take

action on my own account as consul.' Having said that, he rushed out of the Senate to the suburbs with his colleague and holding out a sword to Pompey said 'I command you, I and my colleague here, to advance against Caesar on behalf of the country. For this purpose we give you the army which is now around Capua or in any other part of Italy and any other forces you may wish to enlist.' Pompey accepted the commands given by the consuls, but added, however, 'if there is no better alternative', either deceiving or scheming even then to appear fair. Curio had no power beyond the city (for it is not permitted for tribunes to go beyond the walls); he lamented among the people what had happened and demanded that the consuls issue an edict that no one yet obey the enlisting by Pompey. When he did not accomplish anything, since the time of his tribunate was running out, and he feared for his life and had given up being able to render help to Caesar, he hastily set out to go to him.

Appian, *Civil Wars* 2.30–31

The Claudii Marcelli made a remarkable showing in the last years of the free republic: Marcus Claudius Marcellus, consul in 51 BC; his cousin, Gaius Claudius Marcellus, consul in 50 BC, and finally Marcus' younger brother, Gaius Claudius Marcellus, consul in 49 BC. The consul of 50 BC was married to Octavia, the sister of the future emperor Augustus. In this passage, the consul of 50 BC is depicted as driving force in the run-up to the conflict: there is a clear majority in favour of an appeasement with Caesar in the Senate, and a tribune is actively arguing Caesar's case; however, Marcellus exploits some unconfirmed (and in fact highly dubious) reports on an imminent invasion of Italy to entrust Pompey with a major recruitment effort. The consuls are effectively devolving their powers to Pompey, in breach of established constitutional practice and against the view of a tribune. Faced with this military mobilization, Curio seeks Caesar's protection: a move that will soon acquire major ideological significance. – Other sources report and discuss these events: see also Plutarch, *Life of Pompey* 58.3-6 with omission; Cassius Dio, *Roman History* 40.46.1-4.

BEYOND THE RUBICON: THE CIVIL WAR

B140   Cicero and Pompey
a) I saw Pompey on 10 December. We were together for perhaps two hours. He seemed to be very happy at my arrival; concerning the triumph he encouraged me, said he was playing his part, and advised me not to approach the Senate until I had concluded the matter so as not to alienate some tribune by giving my views. What more can I say? In this business his conversation could not have been in any way more obliging. Concerning the *res publica* he spoke with me in such a manner as though there were no doubt that we were to have war; nothing to suggest a hope for agreement. He said that, although he had previously felt that Caesar had become completely alienated from himself, he had only very recently decided this for definite; Hirtius, who was one of Caesar's closest associates, had come from Caesar, but had not been to see him; he had arrived on the evening of 6 December, and Balbus had arranged to come to the house of Scipio on the 7th before dawn to discuss the whole business; Hirtius had set out for Caesar in the middle of the night. This to him seemed to be a clear proof of estrangement.
Cumae (?), *c.* 13 December 50 BC.

Cicero, *To Atticus* 7.4.2 (SB 127)

By the end of 50 BC the prospect of a reconciliation between Pompey and Caesar did not appear feasible: this letter conveys Pompey's stated viewpoint in a conversation with Cicero, with whom he appears to be on better terms than had been the case for the best part of the preceding decade. The role of A. Hirtius at this time of great difficulty comes across as especially significant: people (including Pompey) are reading into his behaviour clues on Caesar's current thinking. – Even though the prospect of civil war appears increasingly likely, Cicero is still preoccupied with the award of a triumph for his achievements in Cilicia in the previous year: an opportunity of self-promotion that was eventually denied to him by the Senate, in spite of Pompey's reassurances.

b) [2] I am terribly worried about the *res publica*, and I have found virtually no one who does not think that Caesar should be given what he demands, instead of having to fight. Yes, that demand is insulting, but †better† than was thought. So why should we stand up to him now for the frst time? 'This is certainly no worse' [Homer, *Odyssey* 12.209] than when we extended his five-year term or when we proposed the law that a count could be held for an absent candidate, unless perhaps we gave him these weapons only to fight him now when his is well-prepared. You will say, 'How will you vote?' Not as I am going to talk to you, where my opinion is that anything should be done to avoid it coming to a fight. I shall say the same as Pompey, though I shall not do so in a spirit of humility. But once again it is a great problem for the *res publica* that for me, let alone for anyone else, there is something wrong in going against Pompey in such important matters.
Formiae, *c.* 18 December 50 BC

Cicero, *To Atticus* 7.6.2 (SB 127)

A letter written in mid-December 50 shows how deep Cicero's concern about the prospect of civil war is by that point. Even the prospect of a negotiation and compromise seems far-fetched: Cicero seriously contemplates the need to accept Caesar's conditions unreservedly in order to avert a fatal threat to the survival of the *res publica*, and he claims that many hold the same opinion. A point he makes in passing is especially significant: the established constitutional order has already been seriously undermined by the actions of the senatorial faction to which Cicero belongs, notably by accepting to extend Caesar's provincial command in 55 (the grant of five-year commands to Pompey and Crassus in the same year is left unmentioned). – This text is a reminder of how valuable the evidence of Cicero's letters is: the view that he expresses here is not the one that he is going to state in public, as he is keen to avoid any rift with Pompey. Cicero's attitude to him is highly complex: on the one hand, he is at pains to make clear that his public agreement with Pompey will not be expressed uncritically, 'in a spirit of humility'; on the other, he gloomily points out that disagreeing openly with Pompey has become almost unviable: open political debate is no longer an option, even within the faction that opposes Caesar. The consequences of public dissent are left unspoken, but may be easily imagined. - It is noteworthy that, even as he is discussing a dire political situation of unprecedented gravity, Cicero resorts to a quote from Homer, in the original text of course. Far from being a mere treasure trove of attractive quotes, Greek literature is a resource that gives greater depth to one's reflection on the political turmoil of the time, and the difficult choices that it requires.

c) As for your thinking that I should see Pompey before I came to where you are, it has so happened; for on 25 December he overtook me near Lavernium. We came together to Formiae and we talked privately from the eighth hour [of daylight] till evening. Your question whether there is any hope of a peaceful settlement, as far as I perceived from long and detailed conversation with Pompey, is that there is not even a wish for it. For he reckons that, if Caesar becomes consul, even after having discharged his army, it will be the ruin of the constitution, and he further thinks that when Caesar hears that detailed preparations are being made against him, he will not bother about the consulship this year and will rather retain his army and his province; but if Caesar should leave his senses, Pompey is quite contemptuous of the fellow and confident in his own forces and those of the *res publica*. What more can I say? Although 'the god of war who takes no sides' often came to my mind, yet I was relieved of anxiety listening to a man, brave and experienced and of immensely leadership discussing in political terms the dangers

of a simulated peace. [5] We had to hand a speech of Antony, delivered on 21 December in which there was an indictment of Pompey right from his earliest manhood, a protest about those who had been condemned and a threat of arms. On these matters 'What do you think' he said 'he himself will do, if he comes into control of the *res publica*, when this weak and feckless quaestor of his dares to say such things?' In short, not only did he not seem to be seeking peace, but even to be afraid of it.
Formiae, 25 or 26 December 50 BC.

Cicero, To Atticus 7.8.4–5 (SB 131)

The summary of another conference between Pompey and Cicero shows at least two important themes at work: even Cicero, who had been putting much stock into the prospect of civic concord, is by now speaking 'of the dangers of a simulated peace' (*de pacis simulatae periculis*); moreover, the actions of Mark Antony, by now a tribune of the plebs (though formely a quaestor who had served under Caesar) are exploited as reasons for rushing to war. Pompey is envisaging the emergence of a Caesarean regime in which there will no longer be room for his *dignitas* (and, it is suggested, of many members of the senatorial order). – Antony had issued an attack on the whole of Pompey's career: it is safe guess that his involvement in the Sullan civil war had also been discussed.

B141   Cicero sets out the possibilities

[1] 'Am I to receive a letter from you every day?' you ask. If I have someone to give it to, everyday. 'But you will soon be here in person.' At that time then, when I have arrived, I shall stop. I see that one letter from you has not been delivered to me, one which my good friend, L. Quinctius, was carrying when he was wounded and robbed near the tomb of Basilus. You will, therefore, see whether there was anything in it that I ought to know. [2] And at the same time *you will arrange in careful order a problem,* which is a *real* one.

Since it is necessary either (a) that Caesar's candidacy be granted while he is [absent from Rome] in possession of his army, either through the Senate or through tribunes, or (b) that Caesar be persuaded to hand over his province and his army and that he becomes consul in this way; or (c) that, if he be not persuaded of this, that he puts up with elections being held without his candidacy, but he keeps possession of his province; or (d) that, if he opposes this through tribunes of the plebs, but without taking violent action, matters be brought to an *interregnum*; or (e) that, if because his candidacy is not granted, he leads his army here: then it would be necessary to contend with him with arms, while he makes the start of armed combat (i) either immediately when we are less prepared or (ii) at the elections when his friends' demand that his candidacy be granted in accordance with the law, is rejected: then (i) he would resort to arms simply for this one reason that candidacy was not granted or (ii) for some additional reason, if perhaps a tribune, impeding the Senate or stirring up the people is censured, or has his powers restricted by a *senatus consultum*, or is removed from office, or expelled, or claims to have been expelled; and when he has fled to him for refuge, then war is undertaken, and (i) either the city is to be held or, (ii) if it has been abandoned, he is to be cut off from supplies and from his other forces; which of these evils, one of which must be undergone, would you think the least?

[3] Obviously you will say that he be persuaded to hand over his army and in this way become consul. In every respect this a course of action, which were he to come down to it, nothing could be said against it, and I am surprised that he does not do this

if he does not obtain his request that leave of absence be granted while he retains his army. In our position, however, so some think, nothing is more to be feared than that man as consul. 'But I prefer it so' you say 'rather than with an army.' Agreed, but that very 'so' someone thinks to be a great evil, but there is no remedy for it. It must be conceded if that is what he wants. 'See that man consul a second time whom you have seen in a previous consulship.' 'But at that time when he was weak' he says 'he was stronger than the whole *res publica*! What do you think he will be like now?' And if he is consul, it is certain that Pompey will be in Spain. What a wretched business, if, in fact, the very worst thing is that which cannot be refused, and something which, if he were to do it, would immediately occasion the greatest thanks from good men (*boni*)!

[4] Let us, then, remove this possibility to which they say he cannot be attracted, of the rest which is the worst? To concede to that man what, as he himself declares, is his most impudent demand. For what can be more impudent? 'You have held a province for ten years, which were not granted by the Senate, but by you yourself through violence and faction (*factio*). The time limit, not of the law, but of your own whim, has passed: grant, however, that is was of the law; it is decreed that a successor be sent. You prevent this and say 'Grant my leave of absence.' Grant ours. Are you to have an army longer than the people ordered, against the wishes of the Senate? 'You will have to fight it out, if you do not concede.' Yes we will, with high hope, as the same person says, either of winning or of dying in freedom. If war now has to be fought, at what time depends on chance, with what strategy on circumstances. Thus I am not exercising you on that question. If you have any thought on those things which I have said, let me know: for my part, I am racked day and night.
Formiae, 27 December 50 BC.

Cicero, To Atticus 7.9 (SB 132)

This letter elegantly spells out the various scenarios that the political crisis may conceivably bring about, and the margins that are left for a settlement between the two parties. The internal divisions within the second involved paragraph of this letter are owed to Shackleton-Bailey in his edition of the *Letters to Atticus*, Volume III (in the commentary, p. 310, he provides a diagram). There is, in fact, one outcome that might enable a peaceful settlement: Caesar could dismiss his army and be allowed to run for the consulship straight afterwards. The consensus within the Senate, however, has now shifted towards a clear direction: the very prospect of a second consulship of Caesar is regarded with deep-seated hostility. Many recall his conduct in 59 BC: it is no small paradox that Pompey (by now on the opposite side of the argument) had benefited from, and actively supported, Caesar's actions during that fateful year.

B142   Caesar sets out his case, December 50 BC – January 49 BC
[1] The consuls received the dispatch from Gaius Caesar, but only reluctantly agreed to it being read before the Senate, under extreme pressure from the tribunes. Even so, they could not be persuaded to allow the contents of the dispatch to be put to debate, holding instead a general debate on matters of state. The consul Lucius Lentulus promised that he would not fail the *res publica* and the Senate if that body were fearless and forthright in declaring its political stance, but, if it followed its former course of appeasement towards Caesar and tried to win favour (*gratia*) with him, he would allow self-interest to dictate his policy and would take no notice of any expression of the state's opinion (*auctoritas*); they should remember that he too had claims on Caesar's favour (*gratia*) and friendship. Scipio spoke in the same vein; he said that Pompey would not fail the *res publica,* provided the Senate supported him;

if he hesitated now and did not act with sufficient determination, there would be little point in the senators' changing their minds later and then asking for Pompey's help. [2] Because the meeting of the Senate was being held inside the city and Pompey was near at hand, it seemed that Scipio was acting as his mouthpiece in this speech.

Some had expressed a more moderate opinion. For example, Marcus Marcellus embarked on a speech to the effect that it was not a good idea to put a motion before the Senate on the issue until levies had been held throughout Italy and armies raised. With these for protection the Senate would then be bold enough to carry any resolution it liked in safety and without duress. Again, there was Marcus Calidius, who proposed that Pompey should remove any cause for war by setting out for his provinces. He maintained that Caesar was afraid that Pompey was holding on to the two legions which he had taken from him and was keeping them at Rome to threaten his security. Marcus Rufus, who followed Calidius, took substantially the same line. All three senators were taken to task and severely censured by Lentulus, who declared categorically that he would not put Calidius' proposal; Marcellus was alarmed by the consul's savage criticism and withdrew his opinion. In this way, the harangues of the consul, the fear of a nearby army, and the threats of Pompey's friends coerced that majority of the senators into unwilling acceptance of Scipio's resolution: namely, that Caesar disband his army by a day to be determined; failure to comply with this resolution would result in his being treated as a public enemy. The tribunes Mark Antony and Quintus Cassius opposed their veto. There was an immediate debate on the tribunician veto, and harsh measures were advocated. In fact, the applause of Caesar's enemies rose in proportion to the savagery and cruelty of the views which the various speakers expressed.

[3] Towards the evening the Senate was adjourned and all the members of that body were summoned out of the city by Pompey. The determined received his praise and encouragement for the future, the waverers were rebuked and spurred to action. From all quarters many soldiers from the former allies of Pompey were called out, lured by the prospect of rewards or promotion, and many too were summoned from the two legions surrendered by Caesar. The city, the slope leading up to the Capitol, and even the Comitium were crowded with military tribunes, centurions, and recalled veterans. The consuls, Pompey, and those who maintained old feuds with Caesar mustered all their friends and adherents in the Senate. This vociferous gathering intimidated the weaker senators, rallied the hesitant, and actually made it impossible for the majority to exercise their right to a free vote.

The censor Lucius Piso and Lucius Roscius, a praetor, offered to go to Caesar to inform him of these events and asked for a period of six days for the accomplishment of this task. Several expressed the opinion that envoys be sent to Caesar to put before him the Senate's decision.

[4] All these proposals encountered stubborn resistance from the speeches of the consul Lentulus, Scipio, and Cato. Cato was motivated by his long-standing feud with Caesar and by vexation at his defeat in the consular elections. Lentulus, who was deeply in debt, hoped to obtain a provincial command with an army and bribes from kings seeking official recognition; indeed, among his friends he boasted that

he would be a second Sulla and that supreme power (*imperium*) would fall to him. Scipio was spurred on by the same prospect of a province and an army command; grounds of kinship, he considered, would entitle him to share these with Pompey; at the same time he feared prosecution in the law courts; he was susceptible to the flattery of certain powerful men who at the time had great influence in political affairs and in the law courts; his own vanity and that of these men was a further motive. Pompey himself was driven on by Caesar's enemies and by his determination that no one should equal his own prestige (*dignitas*). He therefore broke with Caesar and was restored to favour (*gratia*) with those who had once been the common enemies of Caesar and himself. Yet the vast majority of these enemies he himself had imposed upon Caesar when he had contracted a marriage alliance with his daughter Julia. He was also influenced by the discredit he had incurred in the matter of the two legions; they had been intended for service in Syria and Asia, but Pompey had turned them into a private army designed to support his own despotism (*dominatio*); he was thus eager for open war.

[5] For these reasons all transactions were carried out in an atmosphere of haste and disorder. Caesar's friends were given no time to inform him of these events. The tribunes of the plebs had no opportunity of protesting at the threat to themselves or even of retaining, by the exercise of their veto, their most basic rights – which even Sulla had left them, but were compelled to take thought for their personal safety only seven days after coming into office. In former times even the most violent tribunes had not customarily to worry about the consequences of their various acts until at least eight months had passed. Recourse was had to the *senatus consultum ultimatum*, which had never previously been proposed even by the most headstrong senators except when the city was virtually on fire and there was a total collapse of public confidence. The decree was dated 7 January. Thus it was that the first five days available to the Senate for meetings since the commencement of Lentulus' consulship (two days had been taken up by business in the Comitia) witnessed the most harsh and hostile decrees regarding Caesar's command (*imperium*) and the position of the tribunes. The latter at once left Rome and made their way to Caesar. He was at Ravenna, awaiting a reply to his very moderate demands and hoping that some sense of human justice might make a peaceful settlement possible.

In this crucial passage, right at the outset of his *Commentarii* on the civil war, Caesar puts forward his case, or indeed denounces the arguments that were used and the steps that were taken by his opponents in waging war against him. The narrative starts somewhat abruptly, without any general background introduction being offered, as if it were addressed to an audience that is already familiar with the main factual developments of the period: Caesar's account may have a factual tone, but is first and foremost an interpretation of a highly controversial set of events. The actions of Pompey and his associates are cast both as an instance of incompetence (cf. the assumption that Caesar's soldiers will soon defect from him) and an unacceptable abuse of power (especially the emphasis on the mistreatment of the tribunes, which enabled Caesar to evoke the precedent of Sulla, and even the violent repressions of the Gracchi and Saturninus). The views of a moderate section of the senatorial order, which were silenced by Lentulus, are punctiliously spelled out: Caesar is very keen to show that the civil war was not inevitable, and was the outcome of a choice made by Pompey and his associates. Sole rulership (*dominatio*) is explicitly singled out as the central aim of Pompey; however, he is also being craftily manipulated by Caesar's enemies within the Senate. The achievements in Gaul and Germany are the cornerstone of Caesar's claim to a consulship, and enable him to establish a most emphatic bond with his soldiers, just at the time when their loyalty is being questioned, and potentially undermined.

[6] On the following days the Senate was convened outside the city. Pompey took the same line as he had indicated through Scipio; he praised the courage and determination of the Senate; he described his forces: he had ten legions in a state of readiness; furthermore he had been reliably informed and knew for certain that Caesar's soldiers were disaffected towards him and could not be persuaded to defend or follow him. Proposals about remaining matters were at once put to the Senate; a levy should be held throughout Italy; Faustus Sulla should without delay be sent to Mauretania; money from the treasury should be given to Pompey to use; it was proposed too that Juba should be an ally and friend. The consul Marcellus refused to allow this for the moment; the tribune of the plebs, Philippus, blocked the proposal about Faustus. About the other matters, senatorial decrees were issued. Provinces were decreed to private citizens, two consular, and the rest praetorian. Syria fell to the lot of Scipio, Gaul to L. Domitius. Philippus and Cotta were passed over by private arrangement and their lots were not cast. Praetors were sent to the remaining provinces. They did not wait, (as had happened in previous years) for a vote to be put to the people about their commands (*imperia*), but departed wearing their military cloaks after formal expression of their vows. The consuls – something that had never happened before this time – left the city and private citizens had lictors in the city and on the Capitol contrary to all ancient precedents. Levies were held throughout Italy, weapons were requisitioned, moneys were exacted from the free-towns (*municipia*), were removed from shrines: all the laws of gods and men were confounded.

[7] When Caesar learned of these events he addressed a meeting of his soldiers (*apud milites contionatur*). He recalled all the injuries done to him by his enemies over the years: he complained that Pompey had been drawn away from him and perverted by them through jealousy and disparagement of his reputation, though he himself had always been well disposed to the high office (*honor*) and standing (*dignitas*) of Pompey. He complained that a novel precedent had been brought into the *res publica*: that the tribunician veto was being marked with censure and crushed by armed force; in recent years it had been restored by armed force. Sulla had stripped the power of the tribunes of everything but had left the veto intact; Pompey, who had the credit for restoring those powers, which had been lost, had now taken away even those, which it had kept before. Whenever it was decreed that *the magistrates should see to it that the* res publica *suffer no harm* – by these words and this decree of the Senate the Roman people were summoned to arms – this had happened in the case of laws harmful to the state, of violence by tribunes, of secession by the people, of the seizure of temples and the heights; and he explained that these precedents of a former age had been made good by the deaths of Saturninus and the Gracchi. None of these things had happened at this time, none had even been contemplated (no law had been promulgated, no business with the people had been started, no secession had occurred). In nine years under his leadership they had brought the greatest good fortune to the *res publica*, they had won very many battles, they had pacified all Gaul and Germany: now he encouraged them to defend the name and the importance (*dignitas*) of his command from his enemies. The soldiers of the thirteenth legion, which was there – for he had summoned it at the outbreak of the troubles, the rest had not yet arrived – shouted out that they were ready to avenge the wrongs done to their commander and to the tribunes of the plebs.

Caesar, *Civil War* 1.1–7

In this crucial passage, right at the outset of his *Commentarii* on the civil war, Caesar sets out his case, or indeed denounces the arguments that were used by his opponents in waging war against him. The actions of Pompey and his associates are cast both as an instance of incompetence (cf. the assumption that Caesar's soldiers will soon defect him) and an unacceptable abuse of power (see esp. the emphasis on the mistreatment of the tribunes, which enabled Caesar to evoke the precedent of Sulla, and even the violent repressions of the Gracchi and Saturninus). The achievements in Gaul and Germany are the cornerstone of Caesar's case, and enable him to establish a most emphatic bond with his soldiers, just at the time when their loyalty is being questioned, and potentially undermined.

B143   The eve of civil war
a) The first book on the civil war
The causes of civil war and its beginnings are described, also the disputes over sending a successor to C. Caesar, since he said he would not dismiss his army, unless Pompey dismissed his. And it includes the actions of C. Curio, tribune of the people, first against Caesar, then for Caesar. When a decree of the Senate had been passed that a successor to Caesar should be sent, M. Antony and Q. Cassius, tribunes of the people, were driven from the city since they were attempting to block this decree of the Senate by their veto. The consuls and Pompey were ordered by the Senate to see to it that the *res publica* should suffer no harm. C. Caesar entered Italy with his army to prosecute a war against his personal enemies. He captured Corfinium together with L. Domitius and P. Lentulus, set them free, and drove Pompey and his supporters from Italy.

Livy, *Summaries* 109

b) Titus Livy, one of the most distinguished [historians] for his style and his accuracy, praised Pompey in such high terms that Augustus used to call him a 'Pompeian'. But this did not affect their friendship.

Tacitus, *Annals* 4.34

c) [3] Nothing was left by Caesar that could be tried for the sake of preserving peace, but nothing was accepted by the Pompeians, since one consul was more bitter than was right, and the other, Lentulus, could not be safe while the *res publica* was safe, and since M. Cato insisted that they ought to die before the *res publica* accept any terms from a citizen. The stern old-fashioned Roman would praise the party of Pompey, the prudent would follow that of Caesar; they would reckon the one side more prestigious, the other more formidable. [4] When finally all the things that Caesar had demanded had been rejected, even though he was content just to retain the title to the province with, but a single legion, they decreed that he should enter the city as a private citizen and should, in his candidacy for the consulship, submit himself to the votes of the Roman people. Caesar concluded that war had to be fought and crossed the Rubicon with his army.

Velleius Paterculus, *Histories* 2.49.3–4

Velleius wrote under Tiberius, and his praise extends to Tiberius' adoptive father, Augustus and *his* adoptive father, Julius Caesar. Opponents of the Julio-Claudians usually therefore get very rough treatment in his history. At the same time, like others in the early imperial period, he was sympathetic to Cato and especially Pompey (compare Lucan, and Livy the 'Pompeian' – **B143b**): this passage combines praise for Pompey with the conclusion that Caesar was in the right.

d) But when Pompey began enlisting, some did not heed the call, while few gathered reluctantly and without enthusiasm; the largest numbers shouted out for a settlement of the dispute. For Antony read out a letter of Caesar's before the people, forcibly defying the Senate, containing proposals attractive to the crowd. For he proposed that they should both leave their provinces, dismiss their military forces and put themselves in the hands of the people and render accounts of what they had done. [3] But Lentulus, who was by then consul, would not convene the Senate; Cicero, who had recently arrived from Cilicia, was trying to arrange a settlement that Caesar should leave Gaul and give up all the rest of his army and wait for a second consulship with two legions and Illyricum. [4] When Pompey was not content with that, the friends of Caesar were persuaded to give up one of the two legions. But when Lentulus offered resistance and Cato shouted out that Pompey was again being mistakenly deceived, the settlement came to an end.

Plutarch, *Life of Pompey* 59.2–4

In this version of the events, Pompey is depicted as a rather marginal figure in the context of the final stage of the negotiations: Cato and Lentulus play a central role in precipitating events and precluding any last-ditch reconciliation; Cicero's attempt proves ineffective; there is some willingness on Caesar's side, but it proves irrelevant in an increasingly polarised context. – For a closely comparable version, focusing on Caesar, see Plutarch, *Life of Caesar* 30.3-31.

e) [2] As soon as Antony entered upon office he was of no small help to those who were managing affairs on behalf of Caesar. [4] For first of all he blocked the consul Marcellus in handing over to Pompey the soldiers who had already been assembled and in allowing him to enlist others by issuing an edict that the assembled force should sail to Syria and bring help to Bibulus who was fighting the Parthians, and that those whom Pompey was enlisting should not be under his orders. [5] Secondly, when the members of the Senate would not accept Caesar's letters or allow them to be read, he read those out himself, having the power to do so because of his holding office, and he caused many to change their opinion, since Caesar appeared from what he wrote to be making just and moderate requests. [6] Finally, when two questions were put to the Senate, one whether Pompey should dismiss his forces, the second whether Caesar should, with few ordering Pompey to lay down arms but all but a few ordering Caesar to, Antony got up and asked whether Pompey and Caesar together should not lay down arms and dismiss their forces. [7] They all accepted this proposal enthusiastically, and praising Antony loudly demanded that they should vote upon it. [8] Since the consul refused, the friends of Caesar put forward other demands, which seemed to be reasonable; these Cato vehemently opposed and Lentulus, who was consul, drove Antony out of the Senate. [9] As he was going out he uttered many curses against them; putting on the garments of a slave and, with Quintus Cassius, hiring a cart, he set out for Caesar. As soon as they came into his presence they cried out that there was no longer any order among those controlling affairs in Rome, since it was not possible for tribunes to enjoy freedom of speech, but anyone speaking on behalf of justice was driven out and risked his life.

Plutarch, *Life of Antony* 5

This account follows the same broad interpretation of the crisis as the version contained in the *Life of Pompey*, but focuses more closely on the contribution of Mark Antony to the case that some were still making on Caesar's behalf. The violation of the prerogatives of the tribunes of the plebs was a central part of the argument that Caesar deployed to justify his action against Pompey and the Senate.

f) [2] But when he saw that more determined action was being taken and that the consuls-elect were on the opposing side, he entreated to the Senate in a letter that the privilege given to him by the people should not be taken away from him; or that all other commanders should also relinquish their armies. He was confident, so people thought, that he would more easily summon his veterans, as soon as he wished, than Pompey would new recruits. He then concluded an agreement with his opponents that, having dismissed eight legions and given up Transalpine Gaul, two legions and the province of Cisalpine Gaul should be conceded to him or even one legion with Illyricum until such time was he became consul. [30] But when the Senate did not intervene and his opponents said that they would not make any agreement concerning the *res publica*, he crossed into Cisalpine Gaul and, having conducted assizes, halted at Ravenna intending to take vengeance by war should any violence have been taken by the Senate against the tribunes using their vetoes on his behalf.

[2] This, at any rate, was his pretext for civil war. However, people thought that there were other reasons. Pompey used to say that, since Caesar was not able to pay with his private resources for the completion of the projects that he had begun nor to satisfy the expectation of the people which he had made about his arrival home, he wanted to create turmoil and confusion everywhere. [3] Others said he was afraid that he would be compelled to render account of those actions that he had taken in his first consulship against the auspices, the laws and tribunician vetoes; while M. Cato used repeatedly to say in public and on oath that he would prosecute Caesar as soon as he had dismissed his army; while people commonly predicted, that if he returned as a private citizen, he would plead his case before the jurors surrounded by armed guards following the precedent of Milo. [4] Asinius Pollio lends further credence to this view, recording the exact words that Caesar spoke when at the battle of Pharsalus he looked over his slaughtered and defeated enemies: "This is what *they* wanted; despite all my great achievements, I, Gaius Caesar, would have been condemned had I not sought help from my army." [5] Some think that he was taken by the practice of giving orders (*imperium*), and having weighed up his own strength and that of his enemies he took the chance of seizing despotism (*dominatio*), something that he had desired from early years. Cicero seems to have thought this, for in the third book of his *On Duties* he has Caesar say 'If law is to be overturned, it should be overturned for the sake of monarchic rule (*regnum*). In other matters you should cultivate piety (*pietas*).'

[31] Therefore when news was brought that the veto of the tribunes had been set aside and that they had fled the city, he at once sent some cohorts ahead in secret so that no suspicion should be aroused.

Suetonius, *Divus Julius* 29.2–31.1

Suetonius gives a wide-ranging summary of the factors that may have led Caesar to embark on the civil war. On the one hand, he summarizes the circumstances that triggered his clash with the Senate; Caesar's correspondence is again regarded as a major part of the process. On the other, Suetonius brings in some alternative explanations, including the first-hand account of Caesar's comment to Pollio in the aftermath of the battle of Pharsalus, which was no doubt recorded in Pollio's lost historical work (*Fragments of the Roman Historians* 56 F3a – and compare **154b**). – The reference to Cicero, *On Duties* is 3.82: 'Those who pay no attention to all that is morally right and honourable, so long as they gain power, are they not doing exactly the same as the man who wanted to have as a father-in-law one through whose audacity he might himself be powerful? It seemed to him advantageous to be most powerful through another's unpopularity; he did not see how unjust to his country and how disgraceful this was. While the father-in-law himself always had these Greek verses on his lips. . .' The son-in-law is Pompey, husband of Julia, daughter of Caesar. The quotation is a gloss on Euripides, *Phoenissae,* line 524.

g) Caesar reached Ravenna, which was next to Italy and the last town in Caesar's province. Embracing Curio and expressing his thanks for what he had achieved, he gave consideration to the present circumstances. Curio indeed thought he should summon his entire army at that moment and lead it against Rome, but Caesar still wished to try for a settlement. Thus he instructed his friends to agree on his behalf that he would give up his other provinces and forces, but would keep just two legions and Illyricum with Cisalpine Gaul, until he was elected consul. When this seemed satisfactory to Pompey, but the consuls prevented it, Caesar sent a letter to the Senate and Curio hastening three hundred miles in three days, Curio handed it over to the new consuls as they were entering the senate-house on the first day of the year. The letter contained a formal account of what Caesar had done from the beginning and a proposal that he was willing to lay down his command at the same time as Pompey, but that, while Pompey still kept his command, he would not lay down his; he would come at once with speed to avenge his country and himself. At this, as though it were a declaration of war, they all shouted out aloud that Lucius Domitius should be his successor. And Domitius at once set off with 4,000 men from the levy.

[33] Antony and Cassius were tribunes after Curio, and they approved the proposal of Curio. The Senate still more contentiously reckoned that the army of Pompey was its protector, that of Caesar its enemy. The consuls, Marcellus and Lentulus, ordered Antony and those with him to leave the Senate lest, even though they were tribunes, they might nonetheless suffer something untoward. At which very point Antony shouted aloud, got up angrily from his seat and called upon the gods to witness that his holy and inviolate office was being assaulted and that they, introducing a proposal, which they thought to be of benefit, were being driven out with violence, though they had committed no murder or foul deed. Having said this, he stormed out like a man possessed, prophesying war, slaughter, proscriptions, flight, confiscation and all the other disasters, which were going to overtake them, calling down dire curses on those responsible for this situation. Curio and Cassius rushed out with him; for indeed an army of Pompey was already visible standing around the senate-house. They immediately set off at great speed for Caesar, by night, hidden in a hired cart, donning the clothes of slaves. And Caesar displayed them to the army just like this and stirred them up by saying that after having achieved so much they were being reckoned public enemies and that such men as had spoken on their behalf were being driven out disgracefully.

Appian, *Civil Wars* 2.32–33

Appian's account also emphasizes the unwillingness of the Senate to resume any meaningful negotiation, and stresses the role of the three tribunes, whose rushed escape from Rome is turned both into an illustration of the disorder from which the city is seized and into a powerful argument that Caesar can use, first and foremost, to mobilize the loyalty of his soldiers.

B144   Cicero reaches Rome, January 49 BC
Cicero to Tiro.
I approached the city on 4 January. There came out to meet me on the road a welcome such that nothing could be more magnificent. But I have fallen into the very flame of civil disorder, or rather war; though I could, so I think, have found a remedy for it.

The desires of certain men were an impediment (for on each side there are people who desire to fight). Certainly Caesar himself, our friend, had sent a threatening and harsh letter to the Senate and was being impudent in that he wished to hold on to his army and province against the wish of the Senate, and my friend Curio was urging him on. Our friend Antony and Q. Cassius, though not expelled by any force, have set out for Caesar with Curio, after the Senate had given to the consuls, the praetors, the tribunes of the plebs and to us who are proconsuls the task that we see to it '*that the* res publica *suffer no harm*'. Never has the state been in such danger, never have wicked citizens had a leader more ready. To be certain on this side too preparations are afoot. This is being done through the authority and commitment of Pompey who is – rather late – beginning to be afraid of Caesar.

Outside Rome, 14 January 49 BC.

Cicero, *To his Friends* 16.11.2 (SB 143)

Cicero's take on the political and moral stakes of the crisis and of the conflict that is about to unfold is clearly summarized in this letter to his freedman and secretary Tiro. Cicero was not in the city when the tribunes left to join Caesar: his understanding of the decree of the Senate that provides for drastic action against Caesar is that even those who, like him, have proconsular rank are entrusted with the response to Caesar. As his reference to the warm welcome he received upon his return, Cicero appears to regard himself as a figure of enduring significance in the politics of his time. There is a passing, but firm criticism of Pompey for not having responded with sufficient swiftness and sense of urgency to Caesar's machinations. – 'Our friend Antony' is of course sarcastic.

B145   Caesar's case for civil war, February 49 BC

[22] Some hours before dawn Lentulus Spinther communicated from the wall with our sentinels and guards: he wanted to meet with Caesar, if possible. Permission was granted, and he was released from the town [Corfinium]; Domitius' soldiers did not leave his side until he was escorted into Caesar's presence. He discussed his own welfare with him, prayed and pleaded that Caesar spare him, reminded Caesar about their old friendship, and listed the favours he had done him, which were extraordinary: Caesar had enabled Lentulus' election to the pontifical college and his provincial command in Spain after his praetorship, and had supported his bid to the consulship. Caesar interrupted him: he said that he had not left his province with harmful intent, but to defend himself from the insults of his enemies, to restore the tribunes of the plebs, who had been expelled from Rome in connection with this affair, to their proper standing, and to liberate himself and the Roman people from the oppression by a faction (*factio*) of few men. Encouraged by his words, Lentulus requested permission to come back to Corfinium. He said his ability to obtain Caesar's consent to his safety would give hope to others: not a few people were so terrified that they felt driven to make exceedingly harsh plans for their own lives. Once permission was granted, he departed.

Caesar, *Civil War* 1.22

The brief speech with which Caesar responds to the surrender of P. Cornelius Lentulus Spinther, a former consul who has in charge of the Pompeian garrison quartered at Corfinium, offers a neat summary of the arguments that Caesar invoked to justify the conflict with Pompey: the wish to see his merits duly recognized went hand in hand with the defence of the rights of the tribunes and, though that, with a wider claim to a commitment to freedom. Caesar's ambition to set the *res publica* free from the rule of a faction is echoed (no doubt deliberately) in the opening statement of Augustus' *Res Gestae* (1.1), where of course reference is made to another civil war, that of the late forties.

B146   The position of two Italian communities in the civil war, January 49 BC
[12] Meanwhile, Caesar was informed that the praetor Thermus was holding the town of Iguvium with five cohorts, and was fortifying it; he was also told that the sentiment of all the people of Iguvium toward him was very positive. Caesar sent Curio with the three cohorts that he had at Pisaurum and Ariminum. Having found out about his imminent arrival, Thermus, distrusting the community's sentiment, withdrew his cohorts from the town and fled. His soldiers abandoned him on the march and returned home. Cicero recovered Iguvium with great and general goodwill. Having been informed about these developments, being confident in the goodwill of the free-towns (*municipia*), Caesar withdrew the cohorts of the thirteenth legion from garrison duty and headed for Auximum, a town that Attius was holding with the cohorts that he had brought within its walls. Attius was also recruiting troops through the whole of Picenum by sending senators from town to town.

[13] Having learned of Caesar's imminent arrival, the town councillors (*decuriones*) of Auximum went to see Attius Varus in their numbers. They told him that the business was not for them to adjudicate upon; that they could not tolerate C. Caesar, a commander who had obtained such great achievement on behalf of the commonwealth, being barred from the town and its fortifications, nor could the rest of their townspeople put up with that; moreover, they said that Varus should take consideration of the future and his danger. Being disturbed by their words, Varus led out the garrison that he brought into town, and fled. A few soldiers of Caesar's advance-guard chased him and compelled him to stop. After a fight began, Varus was deserted by his men; not a small part of the soldiers went home, the rest reached Caesar, and with them there was, as a captive, the senior centurion L. Pupius, who had earlier had the same rank in Pompey's army. Caesar praised the soldiers of Attius, let Pupius go, thanked the people of Auximum, and promised to remember their deed in the future.

Caesar, *Civil War* 1.12–13

The merits that the citizens of Auximum (modern Osimo) credit Caesar with are of course those of the Gallic victory: Caesar's dry narrative stresses that they understood the weight of his claim to have his *dignitas* recognized better than his rivals and opponents in the Senate. The townsmen conduct themselves as a free-governing community, which takes its stance in the civil war after assessing the respective merits of the two parties of the conflict. The attitude of Pompey's soldiers, who are ready to abandon their army as soon as things become difficult, stands in sharp contrast with the politically aware and morally responsible behaviour of the citizens of Iguvium and Auximum. The position taken by the people of Auximum is all the more remarkable in light of their connection with Pompey: an inscription dating to his third consulship (52 BC) shows that he was a patron of the *municipium* (*ILLRP* 382 = EDCS-17300434). – The reference to the Gallic victory occurs in other moments of the Civil War, and indeed of its aftermath: the reverse of a *denarius* struck in 48 or 47 showed images of trophies from the Gallic campaign and of a bearded prisoner seated with the hands tied behind his back (*RRC* 452/4).

B147   Priestly symbols on a *denarius* of Caesar, 49 BC

Obv: Pontifical emblems (*cullulus, aspergillum,* axe, and *apex*).
Rev: Elephant trampling a dragon
          CAESAR.

> *RRC* 443 = Ghey, Leins & Crawford 2010, 443.1.12 = BM 2002,0102.4405

This coin issue was struck in the early phase of the civil war, possibly before the arrival at Rome: it mentions Caesar without reference to his official status, but makes prominent reference to his role as *pontifex maximus*, and therefore to his central position in the religious life of the *res publica* (another priestly symbol, the *lituus*, appears in other coins struck by Caesar or his associates in this period: *RRC* 456, 458, and 467, where the legend is COS.TERT.DICT.ITER.AVGVR PONT.MAX, 'consul for the third time, dictator for the second time, augur, *pontifex maximus*', 46 BC). The image on the reverse – the elephant that tramples a dragon – is rather more elusive: it is likely to be a reference to the victory that awaits Caesar and his army, and which will in turn benefit the city as a whole.

B148   Pompey's coinage, *denarius* of 49 BC

> *RRC* 447.1a = Ghey, Leins & Crawford 2010, 447.1.2 = BM R.8856

Obv: Bust of Jupiter, wearing a diadem
          VARRO.PRO.Q. [Varro proquaestor]
Rev: Sceptre upright; on left, dolphin, on right, eagle
          MAGN.PRO.COS. [Magnus proconsul]

> *RRC* 447/1a = Ghey, Leins & Crawford 2010, 447.1.2 = BM R.8856

Pompey also had to fund his war effort, and duly struck his own coinage: the existence of two competing sets of coinage in this period is the clearest illustration that two alternative states were facing each other. This coin issue, like others produced under Pompey's watch in this period, was struck by one of his aides, the proquaestor Varro (possibly a son of the great polymath M. Terentius Varro). The use of an official title, for both Varro and Pompey, is a clear pointer to a wider claim to constitutional legitimacy. The animals depicted on the obverse might be a reference to the reach of Pompey's command, which encompasses land and sea (cf. the inscription from Ilion, below **E11d**).

B149   Caesar's conciliatory message, March 49

Caesar to Oppius and Cornelius.

I am very glad that in your letter you express such strong approval of the proceedings at Corfinium. I shall happily follow your advice, all the more so because I had of my own accord decided to conduct myself in the mildest possible way and to endeavour to reconcile Pompey. Let us try whether by this means we can regain the goodwill of all, and enjoy a lasting victory, seeing that others have not managed to escape hatred by cruelty, or to make their victory endure, except only L. Sulla, whom I am not going to imitate. Let this be the new method of victory: to protect ourselves with mercy and generosity. As to how that is to be done, some options occur to me, and many can be found. I am asking you to give these matters some thought.

I have captured N. Magius, the prefect of Pompey. I have of course followed my established practice and immediately released him. Two prefects of the engineers of Pompey have already fallen into my hands and have both been released. If they wish to be grateful, they will have to encourage Pompey to prefer being a friend of mine, rather than a friend of those who who have always been the most bitter enemies of his and of mine, through whose tricks the commonwealth has come to its current predicament. *c.* 5 March 49.

Caesar, *Letter in Cicero, To Atticus* 9.7c (SB 175)

As he was leading his army through peninsular Italy towards Rome, Caesar did not fail to make contact with a number of prominent figures within the Senate, both restating his case for war and mooting the prospect of a reconciliation with Pompey, before the prospect of fully-fledged conflict became ineluctable. Cicero's correspondence yields the text of a letter that Caesar addressed to two close friends of his, C. Oppius and L. Cornelius Balbus: the latter forwarded it to Cicero, who in turn appends it to a letter to Atticus. The message that Caesar wishes to impress is focused on clemency and reconciliation, and quotes the recent developments at Corfinium as an example of the strategy that he is intending to pursue. The reasons that led Balbus to hand the text to Cicero are obvious: Caesar's message was intended to gain support within the camp of Pompey's supporters. The reference to Sulla is especially significant, as it lent itself to an obvious comparison with Caesar's case: they both led victorious armies towards Rome at the end of a major campaign. Caesar, however, pledges to follow an altogether different course of action to Sulla's. – The 'prefects of the engineers' (*praefecti fabrum*) are figures of great significance in the late Republican armies, as they operate in close cooperation with the commander, and are appointed directly by him: showing clemency towards a prefect of Pompey is therefore a clear message of personal goodwill that has strong political implications.

B150   Rapidly changing situation

[1] 'What is this, I ask you? What is happening? I am in darkness.' 'We hold Cingulum,' he says 'we have lost Ancona. Labienus has deserted Caesar.' Are we talking about a commander of the Roman people or Hannibal? What a mindless wretch of a man, who has never seen even the shadow of what is honourable. And yet he says he is doing all these things for the sake of his status (*dignitas*). Where on earth is status (*dignitas*), except where there is honour and morality? Is it then honourable to have an army without any authorization from the people, to seize cities of Roman citizens in order to have an easier access to the fatherland, to plot cancellation of debts, return of exiles,

six hundred or so other crimes so as to possess the greatest of all deities – tyranny (Gk: *tyrannis*)? Let him have his fortune for himself! By Hercules, one bout in the sunshine with you I should prefer to all kingdoms (*regna*) of that sort, [2] or rather to die a thousand times rather than think once about anything of that sort. 'But what if you were to wish it?' you ask. Come, who is there who may not be allowed to wish? But I reckon it to be more wretched to wish this very thing than to be crucified. One thing is more wretched than that, to obtain what you have so wished. But enough of this: for I am happy to theorize with you amid these vexations.

[3] Let us return to our friend. For heaven's sake, what sort of a strategy does Pompey's seem to you? This is my question – why has he abandoned the city? For I am at a loss. Nothing seemed more preposterous at that time. Are you to abandon the city? Would you do the same then if the Gauls were coming? 'The *res publica* does not consist of house walls', he says. But it does of altars and hearths.
Formiae, 21 (?) January 49 BC.

Cicero, *To Atticus* 7.11.1–3 (SB 134)

As the previous letter in the collection of the correspondence with Atticus makes clear (7.10 = SB 133), Cicero's reservations on Pompey's leadership became increasingly strong. Caesar is making significant inroads across peninsular Italy, and Cicero readily suggests the attractive comparison with Hannibal, the foreign invader that had most captivated Roman historical imagination. Faced with this threat to the survival of the city, Pompey has chosen to leave Rome and organize the resistance elsewhere: in doing so, however, he has also relinquished the temples of the gods, and fatally undermined the bond between the community of the Roman citizens that he is supposed to lead and the city from which they stem. – A similar puzzlement over Pompey's conduct is also voiced in the following letter, 7.12 (SB 135), where Cicero also seeks his friend's advice on how best to look after the interest of his family at a time that is becoming increasingly fraught with risks. The position of his wife Terentia and his daughter Tullia was of special concern to him (*To his Friends*, 14.18 [SB 144] and 14.19 [SB 145]). – On the defection of Labienus to Pompey see also *To Atticus* 7.13a.2-3 (SB 137).

B151 Caesar writes to Cicero, March 49

[1] Although I have nothing to write to you, I am sending this letter so that I do not miss a day. They say that Caesar will stay the night of the 27th at Sinuessa. A letter from him was delivered to me on the 26th, in which he now counts on my 'resources', not, as he said in his former letter, on my 'help.' Since I had written applauding his clemency at Corfinium, he has replied as follows: Caesar *imperator* to Cicero *imperator*.

[2] 'You rightly surmise about me (I am well known to you) that of all things I abhor cruelty the most. I have taken great pleasure from the incident in itself, and your approval of my action gives the utmost joy. I am not bothered by the fact that those who were released by me are said to have left in order to wage war against me once again. Nothing pleases me better than that I should be true to myself, and they to themselves. [3] As for yourself, I hope I shall find you in Rome, so that I can avail myself of your advice and resources in all matters, as usual. I should say to you that I find your [son-in-law] Dolabella a most pleasant fellow. I am all the more in debt towards him on this account; he would not be able to do otherwise. He is a man of great kindness, good feeling, and goodwill towards me.'
Formiae, 26 March 49.

Cicero, *To Atticus* 9.16 (SB 185)

The letter conveyed by Balbus (see above, **B14**) had the intended effect: Cicero sent Caesar a message of congratulations on his conduct at Corfinium, and Caesar duly replied stressing his commitment to leniency and moderation, and his hope to find Cicero in Rome: a thinly veiled invitation not to embrace Pompey's cause. – P. Cornelius Dolabella, Cicero's son-in-law, was on Caesar's camp: that connection was not unprecedented; Quintus, Cicero's brother, had been serving on Caesar's staff during the Gallic campaign.

B152   Gloomy news from Capua

[1] You hear about our misfortunes before I do; for they leak out from that place. There is nothing good for you to look for from here. I reached Capua on 5 February, just as the consuls had ordered. On that day Lentulus arrived late. The other consul had not arrived at all on the 7th. For I left Capua on that day and stayed at Cales. From there I despatched this letter the following day before dawn. These are the things I learnt while I was at Capua. There is nothing in the consuls, there is no levy anywhere; for the recruiting officers do not *dare to show their faces*, since *he* is here, while on the other side our leader is nowhere, is doing nothing and they are not enlisting. For not only is the will lacking but also hope. Our Gnaeus (what a wretched and unbelievable business!), how utterly down he is! There is no spirit, no plan of action, no forces, no commitment. I shall pass over those matters, the most disgraceful flight from the city, the most timid meetings in the towns, lack of intelligence not only about his opponent but also of his own forces. What on earth is this? [2] On 7 February the tribune of the plebs C. Cassius arrived at Capua, brought instructions that the consuls should go to Rome, take the money from the inner treasury, and leave at once. Having abandoned the city they are to return; with what military protection? Then they are to depart; would they be allowed? The consul wrote back to him that he should first go to Picenum. But that has been completely lost; no one knows this except me, as a result of a letter from Dolabella. I have no doubt that Caesar will be in Apulia very soon, and that our Gnaeus will be on board ship.

[3] What I am to do is a big *question*, but it would not have arisen, by Hercules, had not everything been done so very disgracefully and had I not been kept from any part in the action, but the question of what is fitting for me. Caesar himself encourages me to work for peace, but the letter was prior to beginning to rush headlong. Dolabella, Caelius say I give him great satisfaction. A remarkable *dilemma* tortures me. Help out with advice, if you can, and look after things there as far as you are able. Amid such confused circumstances, I have nothing to write: I await your letter.
Cales, 8 February 49 BC.

Cicero, To Atticus 7.21 (SB 145)

The consuls of 49 had summoned a meeting of the partisans of the Senate at Capua, in which Cicero took part: this letter conveys his dismay at the lack of a coherent strategy, whether on Pompey's part or of the serving consuls. A reasonable call is made by a tribune to seize the treasury from Rome before Caesar gets hold of it: that option, however, appears increasingly less viable. – The context, however, is becoming increasingly more complex: Caesar is seeking to make inroads among his opponents, and has approached Cicero directly, by letter, urging him to make an attempt to favour reconciliation. The developments, however, are proceeding fast: even Caesar's invitation to favour concord risks being overcome by the events. – Cicero was also in epistolary contact with Pompey in this period: see *To Atticus* 8.1 (SB 151) and 8.11 (SB 161, where the text of one of his letters to Pompey is preserved).

B153 Cicero's reactions to Caesar

[1] All my interest is in the news from Brundisium. If he has come upon our Gnaeus here, there is a faint hope for peace; if he has crossed over first, fear of a deadly war. But do you see upon what sort of a man the *res publica* has fallen, how shrewd, how vigilant, how well prepared? If, by Hercules, he kills no one, and also does not take anything away from anyone, he will be most highly regarded by those who feared him most. [2] The men of the free-towns (*municipia*) have much conversation with me, the country people too; they care absolutely nothing about anything other than their fields, their little farmsteads, and their little moneys. And see how things have turned: that man they used to have confidence in before, they fear, while they now love the man they used to be afraid of. By what great errors and faults of ours this has happened I cannot contemplate without distress. I have written to you what I think is hanging over us and I now await your letter.

Formiae, 1 March 49 BC.

Cicero, *To Atticus* 8.13 (SB 163), with omission

By early March 49, Cicero contemplates Caesar's impressive progress across Italy, and comes to terms with the position of strategic advantage that he is enjoying across Italy: he can now turn the choice of exercising restraint into a major asset, which will earn him the gratitude and support of the members of the municipal élites, whom Cicero blames for being more preoccupied with their personal position and financial welfare than with the prosperity of the *res publica*. – At the same time, Cicero is now moderately open to the option of a reconciliation between Caesar and Pompey: the two men, however, did not meet at Brundisium.

B154 Cicero assesses Caesar and Pompey

[2] … The one is ablaze with madness and wickedness and does not allow them any respite, but it grows more intense day by day; he has just expelled his adversary from Italy, now he is trying to hunt him down in one direction, in another to strip him of his province and he no longer refuses but in a certain way demands that he be called tyrant (*tyrannus*), just as he actually is. [3] The other, the one who did not even raise me up when I was prostrate before his feet, who said he could do nothing against the wishes of this man, having escaped from the hands and sword of his father-in-law, is preparing war by land and sea, not an unjust war certainly but not only righteous but also necessary, deadly for his citizens if he does not win, disastrous if he does win.

[4] I do not place the achievements of these very great commanders nor even their fortune before my own; certainly they seem to be at their very peak, while mine seems buffeted and more difficult. For who can be happy when the fatherland has been deserted or overwhelmed through their actions? And if, as I am advised by you, we have rightly said in that book that nothing is good except what is honourable and nothing is evil except what is disgraceful, then certainly each of these men is most wretched; for each of them the safety and reputations (*dignitas*) of their country has always come behind their own despotism (*dominatio*) and personal advantages.

Cumae, 14 April 49 BC.

Cicero, *To Atticus* 10.4.2–4 (SB 195)

This letter provides a valuable insight into Cicero's own views on the conduct of the two protagonists of the conflict: his disparaging assessment is not surprising in light of the comments he makes elsewhere in his correspondence, but is here interestingly linked with a philosophical problem that he had discussed in a different context, his recent work *On the State* (3.38b), where the tension between personal happiness and the difficult predicament of the *res publica* received close attention.

**B155   Cicero's son-in-law, Dolabella, writes to him from Caesar's camp
in Greece**

[1] If you are well I am happy. I am well and Tullia is in good health. Terentia has
been less well, but I am certain she has now recovered. Furthermore, all your affairs
here are in excellent order.

Although at no time ought you to have suspected that it was for the sake of party rather
than your own sake that I was advising you either to join Caesar and me or at least to
retreat into inactivity; in present circumstances, especially now victory is tending in
our direction, I cannot possibly be thought of as doing anything except to be advising
you because I cannot dutifully remain silent. My dear Cicero, you will please accept
these words whether you approve or disapprove of them, so that you judge them
conceived and written by one most well disposed and devoted to yourself.

[2] You are aware that Pompey is secure neither through the glory of his name nor of
his achievements, nor through client kings and nations whom he used continually to
boast about and further that what happens to all the lowest people that they can escape
honourably cannot happen in his case; driven from Italy, the provinces of Spain lost,
his army of veterans captured, now finally surrounded with siege-works, something
which I am inclined to think has never happened to any other of our commanders.
Wherefore, consider in view of your good sense, what he can hope for or what you can
do for him; for you will most easily adopt the course which will be most advantageous
for yourself. I ask this of you: that, if he now avoids this danger and takes refuge in his
fleet, you take thought for your own interests and finally be a friend to yourself rather
than to anyone else. You have now satisfied the claims of the duty of friendship; you
have satisfied the claims of party and of that *res publica* of which you approved. [3]
What remains is that we should be where the *res publica* now is, rather than, while
going after the old one, be in none at all. So, my dearest Cicero, if by chance Pompey
is driven from this locality too and is forced to make for other regions, I would like
you to retreat to Athens or to some peaceful community. If you are going to do this,
I would like you to write to me so that I can wing my way to you, if by any means
I can. Whatever requests are required concerning your status (*dignitas*) from the
commander, given Caesar's kindness, it will most easy for you to obtain them from
him yourself and, anyway, I think my pleas will possess not a little influence with him.

It will be a mark of your good faith and kindness to see that the courier I have sent to
you can return to me and brings me back a letter from you.
Caesar's camp near Dyrrachium, May 48 BC.

Cornelius Dolabella to Cicero [*To his Friends* 9.9 (SB 157)]

The civil war of 49 BC had caused divisions within families, as is always the case with internal strifes (see
above, **B9**): Cicero's son-in-law, P. Cornelius Dolabella, had joined Caesar and had a significant role in his
camp. In this letter, which dates to three months before the battle of Pharsalus, Dolabella invites him to
abandon Pompey, arguing that he has now fulfilled his obligations towards his old friend, and that he should
now concentrate on his best personal interest. That will enable him to make, in due course, a valuable
contribution to the *res publica*.

B156 Battle of Pharsalus

Pompey had been besieged at Dyrrachium in Epirus (modern Durazzo in Albania) but had successfully broken the siege, albeit missing the chance of a decisive victory (Plutarch, *Pompey* 65.5). His forces moved to Thessaly (N. Greece). Caesar's troops were outnumbered, maybe by as much as 2:1 (Appian, *Civil Wars* 2.70), but lack of supplies forced Caesar to fight at Pharsalus, where his battle tactics achieved a decisive victory. His own detailed account is *Civil War* 3.30–99. Asinius Pollio's contemporary account is lost, except for his quotation of Cicero's reaction, which Plutarch gives in a Greek translation (**B156b**) and Suetonius in apparently the exact Latin words (in **B143e**), but it is likely to have formed the basis for the account of Appian, *Civil Wars* 2.70–82 as well as Plutarch, *Pompey* 67–72 and *Caesar* 42–46. Livy's account survives only in summary (a) although it was probably a major source for Lucan's epic, poetical account in book 7 of his *Civil War.*

a) Pompey was besieged by Caesar at Dyrrachium, but stormed Caesar's fortifications slaughtering very many of those defending them, and lifted the siege. The war moved to Thessaly where Pompey was defeated in pitched battle at Pharsalia. Cicero, someone by nature least suited to warfare, remained in Pompey's camp. Caesar pardoned all those on the opposite side who had surrendered unconditionally to the victor.

Livy, Summary 111

b) When Caesar came to Pompey's camp and saw lying there the bodies of the enemy who had already been killed, and those still being killed, he gave a groan and said, "This is what *they* wanted – to force me to the point where I, Gaius Caesar, the victor in such great wars, would have been condemned if I had dismissed my army." This is what Asinius Pollio says are the words which Caesar spoke at that time in Latin, which Pollio wrote in Greek.

Plutarch, Life of Caesar 46.1 = Asinius Pollio, FRH 56 F3

c) In Pompey's camp one could see planted bowers, an abundant display of silver, tents floored with freshly cut turf, the tents of Lucius Lentulus and of some others covered with ivy, and much else that indicated excessive luxury and confidence in victory, so that one could easily reckon that they had had no fear about the outcome of the day, since they had been pursuing unnecessary pleasures. Yet these men had been accusing Caesar's most wretched and long-suffering army of luxury, while it had always been lacking every item of basic necessity. Pompey, as our men were now within the rampart, having got hold of a horse and removed his commander's insignia, rushed out of the camp through the rear gate and, spurring his horse, headed for Larissa.

Caesar, Civil War 3.96

At the end of his account of the battle of Pharsalus, Caesar takes the time to describe what he and his men found in Pompey's camp, which was by then deserted: his emphasis on the display of wealth in what should be a military setting are revealing of their flawed moral and political credentials, and is put in stark contrast with the austere and sober climate of Caesar's army – an army where 'traditional' Roman virtue is upheld. The brief sketch of the situation in Pompey's camp is immediately, and tellingly, followed by the report of Pompey's hasty escape from the battlefield. – The Lentulus who is mentioned here is the same man whom Caesar pardoned at Corfinium in the early phase of the war (**B145, B149**); he joined Pompey at the earliest opportunity (see above **B156**).

B157 *Libertas* **on coinage, 48 BC**

Obv: Laureate head of *Libertas*
LIBERTATIS [Of Liberty]

Rev: Roma seated on a pile of arms, wearing helmet, holding sceptre in her right
hand and placing the left foot on a globe; flying Victory crowning Roma
C.VIBIVS.C.F.C.N. [Gaius Vibius, son of Gaius, grandson of Gaius]

RRC 449/4 = Ghey, Leins & Crawford 2010, 449.4.6 = BM 2002,0102.4451

This coin issue was struck by C. Vibius Pansa Caetronianus, an associate of Caesar who held the consulship
a few years later, in 43 BC, and lost his life in the battle of Mutina: the imagery he resorts to here stresses, on
the one hand, an image of victorious Rome that extends her reach across the whole world (note the presence
of the globe) and, on the other, the commitment of Caesar and his side to the restoration of civic liberty, here
depicted in its personification (see above the claim that Caesar made at Corfinium, **B145**, **B149**).

B158   Pompey's death, 48 BC
After his defeat at Pharsalus and the loss of most of his army, Pompey fled to Egypt to seek help from King
Ptolemy. Instead he was murdered on the shore of Egypt and his body mutilated, an episode so notorious
that it seems even to prompt an allusion in Virgil's *Aeneid* in the description of the death of Priam of Troy, as
well as narrative accounts: Appian, *Civil Wars* 2.84–86; Plutarch, *Pompey* 77–80; Velleius, *Histories* 2.53

a) Cicero's reaction
[3] I am distressed to hear of my Tullia's illness and physical weakness. I can see that
you are taking great care of her, and I am most grateful for that.

About Pompey's end I never had any doubt. The hopelessness of his position had
become so obvious to all kings and peoples that I expected this to happen wherever
he went. I cannot but feel sorry for his fate. [4] I knew him for an honest, upright, and
principled man ... [5] As for L. Lentulus, he had set his eyes upon Hortensius' house
and Caesar's property in the suburbs and at Baiae. The same sort of thing is of course
going on at this end, only with them there was no limit to it. All those who had stayed
in Italy were counted as enemies. [6] However, I would like to talk about this some
day, when I have less on my mind.
Brundisium, 27 November 48 BC.

Cicero, *To Atticus* 11.6.3–6 (SB 217), with omission

A dry, if balanced assessment of Pompey and his character, which leaves their previous political dealings
on the background, or indeed sets them within the wider context of his values and personality, placing the
emphasis on the man himself.

b) Priam's death in Virgil's *Aeneid*

This was the end of Priam's fortunes; this was the death that was fated him
That he should see Troy burnt and Pergamum brought down,   555
He who once had been the proud ruler of the peoples
And lands of Asia. He lies, a huge trunk on the sea-shore,
His head ripped from his shoulders, a nameless corpse.

Virgil, *Aeneid* 2.554–558

Virgil, through Aeneas, is here describing the death of the king of Troy. Midway through line 557, the
description seems to change from Priam killed in his palace by a sword-thrust in the side to that of a
headless corpse on a sea-shore (for further parallels see A.M. Bowie, "The Death of Priam: Allegory and
History in the Aeneid," CQ 1990, 471-480).

B159 Republican resistance to Caesar in North Africa and Spain, 47–45 BC
a) *Denarius* of Metellus Scipio

Obv: Laureate head of Africa right, wearing elephant's skin; on right, corn-ear;
       below, plough
       Q.METELL SCIPIO.IMP [Quintus Metellus Scipio *imperator*]
Rev: Hercules standing facing, one hand on hip, resting arm on club draped with
       lion's skin EPPIVS LEG.F.C [Eppius saw to it in his capacity as legate]

    RRC 461 = Ghey, Leins & Crawford, 2010, 461.1.7 = BM 2002,0102.4560

b) *Denarius* of Cato

Obv: Bust of Roma, draped, hair tied with band
       ROMA; M.CATO.PRO.PR [Marcus Cato propraetor].
Rev: Victory seated right, holding *patera* and palm-branch
       VICTRIX [(Rome) victorious].

    RRC 462b = Ghey, Leins & Crawford 2010, 462.1b = BM 2002,0102.4564

c) *Denarius* **of Gnaeus Pompeius (son of Pompey the Great), 46–5 BC**

Obv: Head of Pompey, right
        CN.MAG.IMP (Gnaeus Magnus, *imperator*)
Rev: Female figure with turreted crown (city of Corduba) welcomes soldier
        disembarking from ship
        PR.Q. M.MINAT.SABIN (M. Minatius Sabinus, proquaestor)

        RRC 470 = Ghey, Leins & Crawford 2010, 470.1.1 = BM 1867,0101.1306

The coalition of Caesar's opponents that survived the defeat of Pharsalus rallied its forces in North Africa and mounted effective resistance there until Caesar's victory at Thapsus in February 46. The coin issues a) and b) were struck by the two most prominent members of that faction, Q. Metellus Scipio (*interrex* in 53, consul in 52 – here aided by his legate Eppius) and the Younger Cato. Their iconography points to the themes of prosperity and victory (see the references to Hercules and the goddess Victoria); the personification of Africa is no doubt intended to mobilize local support. The most politically significant feature, however, is the choice of these two champions of established Republican tradition to strike coinage in their own name: note the emphasis on their legal status, *imperator* and *propraetor* respectively. Even after their defeat at Thapsus and the death of Cato, Gnaeus Pompeius, elder son of Pompey the Great, continued to resist with forces in Spain, until his defeat at the battle of Munda in March 45 BC. His coin issue (**B159c**) was struck in Spain, evoking his father, local support for the Pompeian forces, and the legal *proquaestor* whose name appears.

B160   Suicide of Cato, April 46
a) [67.1] Having had a bath, he had dinner with many people, seated, as was his custom after the battle; for he never reclined except when sleeping. All his companions and the magistrates of Utica had dinner with him. [2] And after the dinner the drinking involved intellect and charm, as the different arguments of the philosophers circulated one after another until there the enquiry into the so-called paradoxes of the Stoics came up: that the good man alone is free and that all the bad are slaves. [3] When at this point, as expected, the Peripatetic objected, Cato broke in forcefully and raising his voice loudly and harshly developed his argument at very great length, displaying astonishing vehemence so that no one could be unaware that he had determined to put an end to his life and to release himself from present troubles. [4] Therefore, when after his speech there was silence and dismay among all, Cato, trying to revive them and to allay their suspicion, once more put in questions and thoughts about present circumstances as though he was afraid for those who were sailing and afraid for those who were making their journey across a waterless and hostile desert.

[68.1] Having brought the dinner to an end, he took his usual after-dinner stroll with his friends. He gave appropriate instructions to those in command of the guards and, having embraced and taken farewell of his son and each of his friends more affectionately than had been his previous custom, he retired to his room. [2] Again he caused suspicions about what was going to happen. Having entered his room, he lay down and took out the dialogue of Plato 'On the Soul'. When he had gone through most of it, he glanced up above his head; he saw that his sword was no longer hanging there (his son had secretly removed it while he was having dinner). He called a household slave and asked him who had taken his sword. [3] When the slave gave no reply, he went back again to the book. A little while later, as though with no concern or haste, he ordered the slave to fetch it. [4] There was some delay and no one brought the sword. Having finished the book, he then summoned the slaves again one by one and raised his voice louder, demanding his sword. [5] Having struck one slave on the mouth and bruised his hand, he shouted out angrily that he was being betrayed by his son and the household slaves unarmed into the hands of the enemy. Eventually his son ran in with his friends and falling on his knees embraced his father, pleading with him in tears. [6] Cato got up and looked at them sternly, 'When and where have I been convicted of insanity without knowing of it? No one explains to me and tries to make me change my mind on matters about which I am alleged to have made a wrong decision, but I am prevented from using my own judgement and I am disarmed. [7] Why, my dear boy, don't you bind your father and tie his hands behind his back so that when Caesar comes he will find that I am not able to defend myself. [8] I do not need a sword against my own life when it is possible to die holding my breath for a short while or smashing my head against the wall.'…

[70.8] But when Butas had gone out, he drew his sword and stabbed himself in the stomach. The inflammation of his hand weakened the blow somewhat and he did not manage to kill himself at once, but in his death-throes fell from the bed and made a noise by knocking over a geometrical abacus that was lying beside the bed. His household slaves heard the noise and shouted out; his son together with his friends rushed in at once. [9] They were horrified to find him covered in blood with most of his entrails protruding, but still alive and with his eyes open. The doctor approached him and tried to replace the entrails, which were uninjured, and to sew up the wound. [10] When Cato revived and realized this, he pushed the doctor away, tore his entrails with his own hands, opened the wound again, and died.

Plutarch, Life of Cato the Younger 67–70, with omissions

Cato the Younger took his own life in April 46 at Utica, in North Africa, after the defeat suffered at Caesar's hands at Thapsus in February. Plutarch's account casts the decision of the great Republican champion as the philosophical choice of an individual who is not prepared to live under a tyrant, and prefers death to the prospect of having to accept Caesar's clemency. Plutarch depicts that action as a decision that is taken in the face of great adversity and against the opposition of his relatives and friends, in the name of a higher principle. – 'Who more justly took up arms, it is a sin to know; each protects himself with a powerful judge: the victorious cause pleased the gods, the vanquished pleased Cato' (Lucan, *Civil War* 1.126–128).

B161   Celebrating Cato under Caesar's watch, 46 BC
As to the *Cato*, it is a problem worthy of Archimedes. I cannot work anything out which your companions would read not with enjoyment, but with equanimity. Even if I were to keep clear of the speeches he gave in the Senate and his whole set of political views and strategies, and chose simply to praise his seriousness of purpose

and steadfastness, they would hate to hear even that. But no genuine eulogy of that remarkable man is possible without paying tribute to the way he foresaw our present state of affairs and endeavoured to avert it, and abandoned his life rather than witness it in action.

Tusculum, May (?) 46 BC.

Cicero, *To Atticus* 12.4.2 (SB 240)

Cato's political legacy readily became a matter of controversy, a mere few weeks after his suicide. Cicero wrote a piece in Cato's defence, which does not survive. We hear about the difficulties he faced in writing that text from a letter to Atticus: he compared the task to a difficult mathematical problem that would have required the ingenuity of a great scientist like Archimedes of Syracuse (*c.* 287–212/211 BC). Cicero faced the conundrum of praising Cato without confronting Caesar too directly or causing him offence; the 'companions' of Atticus to whom he alludes are in fact Caesar's supporters (Caesar himself was not in Rome at the time). At the same time, Cicero was quite clear that it was not possible to praise Cato without acknowledging his political position (for a less positive assessment of Cato's politics see above, **B143c** and **B143d**). A few months later, after his retun to Rome, Caesar wrote and published a riposte to Cicero's tract, entitled *Anticato*; that work does not survive either, although it is mentioned by Suetonius (*Divus Julius* 56.5) and Plutarch (*Life of Cicero* 39.2; *Life of Caesar* 3.4, 54.3–6); he also wrote a letter to Cicero, in which he firmly criticized Cato, whilst praising the literary qualities of Cicero's work (we hear about it from Cicero himself: *To Atticus* 13.46.2 = SB 338).

CAESAR'S VICTORY

B162   Reforms of Julius Caesar, 48–44 BC

[40.1] Turning from these matters to putting the state of the *res publica* in order, he corrected the official calendar (*fasti*), long thrown into disorder the fault of the pontiffs (*pontifices*) as a result of their free rein in intercalating, to such an extent that the festival days of harvests did not coincide with summer nor those of the vintage with autumn; he synchronized the year with the course of the sun so that it was of three hundred and sixty five days and so that with the intercalary month removed one day should be intercalated each fourth year. [2] In order that the arrangement of seasons might for the future fit in with the Kalends of January [1 January], he inserted two extra months between November and December; that year in which these arrangements were established was of fifteen months, including the intercalary month, which in accordance with custom had occurred in that year. [41.1] He filled up the number of the Senate, he recruited patricians, and he increased the number of praetors, aediles, quaestors and minor magistrates too; those deprived of the rank through the action of the censors or condemned for electoral bribery by verdict of jurors he restored. [2] He shared elections with the people in such a way that, with candidates for the consulship excepted, of the remaining number of candidates, one half whom the people wished should be publicly decided, while the other half would be those whom he himself had selected. He would make them known through notes circulated around a tribe with a brief message: 'Caesar dictator to this or that tribe: I commend to you so-and-so that he hold his magistracy (*dignitas*) through your vote.' He also admitted to political office the sons of the proscribed. He reduced the jury courts to two categories, the equestrian and the senatorial order; the tribunes of the treasury (*tribuni aerarii*), which used to be the third, he removed.

[3] He conducted a review of the people neither according to the usual custom nor place, but by districts (*vici*), through the proprietors of the tenement blocks and from the three hundred and fifty thousand receiving corn from the state he cut it down to one hundred and fifty thousand; and so that no fresh assemblies for the purpose of review should be held whenever required, he arranged that each year a selection by lot by the praetor should be held for the place of those who had died from among those who had not been included on the register. [42.1] With eighty thousand citizens having been distributed to overseas colonies, so that the population of the city, which had been depleted, might be kept up, he prescribed by law that no citizen older than twenty years or less than ten<?>, who was not under military oath, should be continuously absent from Italy for more than a three-year period, nor should any son of a senator travel abroad unless he was in service with a military commander or on the staff of a magistrate, nor should those who were cattle farmers have less than one third freeborn youths among their herdsman. To all those who practised medicine at Rome and were teachers of liberal arts he granted citizenship so that they would more willingly live there and others would be attracted there too. [2] Concerning debts, having dispelled expectation of their cancellation, in the end he decreed that debtors should satisfy their creditors by means of an assessment of their property at the value at which they had purchased it before the civil war, with deduction from the principal of any interest which had been paid in cash or pledged in the account books; by these terms about a quarter of the money on loan was lost. [3] All the associations (*collegia*), apart from those of ancient foundation, he broke up. He increased the penalties for crimes; and since the wealthy involved themselves in crime because they went into exile with the family estates intact, he fined murderers of near relatives, so Cicero writes, with the loss of all their goods, murderers of others with the loss of half. [43.1] He dispensed the law with the greatest thoroughness and rigour. He even removed from the senatorial order those convicted of extortion (*repetundae*). He dissolved the marriage of a man of praetorian rank, who had immediately married a woman two days after divorce from her husband, although there was no suspicion of adultery. He introduced customs dues on imported goods. He banned the use of litters, likewise crimson garments and pearls, except for specified people and age groups on specific days. [2] He made a point of enforcing the law against extravagance, posting guards at various points around the market, to confiscate and convey to him forbidden delicacies, sometimes having secretly despatched lictors and soldiers to enter and remove from the dining room any delicacies that his guards had failed to notice, even if they had already been served.

[44.1] He entertained designs, more numerous and greater day by day, for adorning and administering the city, and also for the expansion and protection of the empire: in particular, he planned to build a temple to Mars, larger than any other existing temple (having filled up and levelled the surface of a lake on which he had previously staged the spectacle of a naval battle), and to build a theatre of enormous size resting against the Tarpeian rock; [2] to codify civil law, and from the vast and diffuse body of laws to select the best and indispensable ones and concentrate them in a very few volumes; to provide the public with the largest possible Greek and Latin libraries, giving Marcus Varro the task of collecting and classifying; [3] to drain the Pomptine marshes and to empty the Fucine lake; to build a road from the Adriatic along the ridge of the

Apennines as far as the Tiber; to drive a canal through the isthmus of Corinth; to curb the Dacians, who had poured into Pontus and Thrace; and shortly to wage war on the Parthians through Armenia Minor, but not to engage them in battle before he had tested them out. [4] Such were his activities and projects when death cut him short.

Suetonius, *Divus Julius* 40–44.4

This detailed overview of the political acts of Caesar after his victory in the Civil War is powerful illustration of the extraordinary range and quality of the projects on which he embarked. The most controversial aspects of the late Republican political debate were addressed, and in a number of cases ambitious, long-term solutions were put forward: the decision on the membership of the Senate, the civic magistracies, the membership of the juries of the criminal courts, the foundation of new colonies, the role of associations (*collegia*) in Roman politics (most of them were abolished), and measures that provided some relief to debtors, addressing an issue that was all the more urgent in the aftermath of the civil war. The reordering of the Roman public calendar aims to put an end to its discretionary management, which until then had been the prerogative of the pontifical college: the creation of a year of fixed length (set at 365 days) was therefore a political operation, which has shaped the way in which time is organized in a great number of cultures, to our day. The wide-ranging programme put in place by Caesar could be passed speedily because of his position as dictator, and is closely identified with an agenda that sets out to bring a general resettlement to the affairs of the city and of the empire alike: it cannot be mechanically identified with a *popularis* agenda (in spite of Caesar's political background), and certainly not with an 'optimate' one. The great monumental programme on which Caesar embarks is a central part of it, and is compounded by intervention in sanitation infrastructure and in road building. The military campaigns that Caesar carries out in this period, and the planned offensive against the Parthians belong in this wider programme of pacification and development, in which Caesar emerges as a figure of unrivalled importance, who acts in a fully monarchic logic.

B163   Caesar and Venus on *denarius*, 47–46 BC

Obv: Head of Venus right, wearing a diadem.
Rev: Aeneas left, carrying a statue of the goddess Pallas (*Palladium*) in his hand and Anchises on his shoulder
CAESAR.

RRC 458/1 = Ghey, Leins & Crawford 2010, 458.1.13 = BM 2002,0102.4549

This coin issue marks the first appearance of Venus on Caesar's coinage. Caesar's clan, the *gens* Julia, had long claimed descent from Venus' son, the Trojan prince Aeneas, who, according to a well-established mythical tradition, had landed on the shores of Latium at the end of a long journey, following the destruction of Troy. The connection between Caesar and Aeneas, who is here portrayed as he rescues his old father Anchises during the sack of Troy by carrying him on his shoulders (an act of ultimate filial piety), is explicitly stressed. The mythical connection with Troy enabled the Julii to claim a special place in the history of Rome, reaching back to a time that predated the foundation of the city; it also establishes a distinctive association with the Greek world. Venus appears on other later coin issues struck by Caesar or his close associates (*RRC* 463, 465/3 and 6, 468). – The Trojan theme will of course be central to much of the ideological discourse developed by Augustus: Virgil's great epic poem, the *Aeneid*, plays a cardinal role in that connection.

B164   An appeal to restore the *res publica*, 46 BC

[23] It is for you and you alone to revive all that you see lying in ruins around you, inevitably shattered and overthrown by the violent shock of war. Law courts have to be reorganized, credit re-established, licentious passions checked, and the birth rate raised. Everything that is now in a state of disintegration and collapse needs to be knit together by rigorous legislative measures ... [24] All these are the war wounds that you have to heal – and no one can heal them but yourself. ... [25] As it is, on the contrary, the welfare of every Roman citizen and the whole state has become dependent on what you do. And to this day so far are you from having completed your greatest achievements that you have not even laid the foundations of all that needs to be planned.

[27] This phase, then, still awaits you. This act of the drama has not yet been played. This is the programme to which you must devote all your energies: the re-establishment of the constitution, with yourself the first to reap its fruits in profound tranquility and peace. And then, if you wish, after you have paid your country what you owe her, after you have fulfilled your debt to nature itself, after you have really had your fill of life – then and then only may you talk of having lived long enough.

Cicero, *On behalf of Marcellus* 23–24, 25, 27

The ethical and political problems that we found spelled out in the previous passage became all the more pressing after Caesar's victory, and after the pardon that Cicero received from him, allowing him to return to Rome and to the Senate. Adjusting to the new reality whilst retaining some meaningful role and a semblance of dignity was not a simple challenge. Oratory was again the main channel through which Cicero could hope to exert some degree of influence: the speech he gave on behalf of his friend M. Claudius Marcellus (consul in 51 BC), an associate of Pompey is an attempt to cast Caesar in the role of a clement victor of a devastating war, who must now take upon himself the task of rebuilding the *res publica* through firm and inclusive action. It is also a case for the need to restore a semblance of constitutional order, and of refraining from any temptation to set up an autocratic regime. The success of his attempt to engage with the changed political context and define a role for Caesar that was not altogether incompatible with Republican tradition has been much debated by modern scholars. There is little doubt that it was carried out with much ingenuity.

B165   Caesar's head on *denarius*, 44 BC

Obv: Wreathed head of Caesar, right; behind, *lituus* (augur's staff)
        CAESAR.DICT.QVART. [Caesar dictator for the fourth time]
Rev: Juno Sospita in chariot right, holding reins, shield and spear
        M.METTIVS.

RRC 480/2a = Ghey, Leins & Crawford 2010, 480.2.1 = BM R.9060

The presence of Juno on this coin issue struck by Marcus Mettius, a close associate of Caesar, shows that Venus was not the only deity with which he asserted a connection. The most remarkable feature, however, is the presence of Caesar's portrait on the coin issue: an unprecedent development in the history of Roman coinage, which brings to completion a process that had arguably started with Sulla, four decades earlier (see above, **B17**). The laurel wreath on Caesar's head is a reference to the privilege to wear one that was bestowed upon him by the Senate in the previous year (Cassius Dio, *Roman History* 43.43.1; cf. Suetonius, *Divus Julius* 45.3). The extraordinary presence of Caesar's head is somewhat balanced by two relatively usual details: the mention of his official title, which enables a precise dating of this coin issue, and the familiar presence of the *lituus* (see above, **B17**, **B39**). – Cf. 480/19, where the wreathed head of Caesar is accompanied by the *lituus*, the *apex* (a peaked hat routinely used by priests), and the title of *parens patriae* ('father of the fatherland').

B166   A grand and onerous visitor, January 45 BC

[1] What a guest, such an imposition for me, but not one to be regretted! For it was really quite enjoyable. But when he arrived at Philippus' in the evening of the second day of the Saturnalia, the house was so filled with soldiers that scarcely was there a dining-room vacant where Caesar himself could eat: all of two thousand men. I was really quite concerned what would happen the following day; but Barba Cassius came to my help, and he posted guards. Camp in the ground; the house was defended. *He* was at Philippus' house on the third day of the Saturnalia until the seventh hour, and he admitted no one; he was, so I think, on accounts with Balbus. Then he went for a walk along the shore; after the eighth hour he took a bath; then he heard about Mamurra, his face did not change. He was anointed; he took his place at table. He was taking a course of emetics and so he ate and drank heartily and agreeably, from a lavish and well–prepared meal and not only that but

> well cooked and garnished,
> with good conversation and, to tell the truth, with pleasure.

[2] Furthermore his company were entertained quite lavishly in three dining rooms. Nothing was wanting for the less grand freedmen and the slaves. For the grander I offered choice entertainment. In sum we showed ourselves men of refinement. However, the guest was not the sort of person to whom you would say: 'Do please come again when you are back this way.' Once is enough. There was nothing of substance in the conversation, much on literary topics. In sum, he was pleased and was agreeably satisfied. He said he would be one day at Puteoli, and another at Baiae.

There you have my entertainment, or quartering; troublesome to me, as I said, but not vexatious. I shall be here for a short while, and then I shall go to Tusculum.
When he went past the house of Dolabella, and nowhere else, the whole body of armed men rode to his left and right. [I have heard] this from Nicias.
Puteoli (?), 19 December 45 BC.

Cicero, To Atticus 13.52 (SB 353)

This letter is not just evidence for a revival in the relationship between Caesar and Cicero after the end of the civil war, and for Cicero's return into the political community: he receives a visit from Caesar at one of his country villas, and that is in itself a sign of his standing, even though the two men discuss their shared literary interests, rather than political matters. What is arguably even more significant is the size of the retinue that surrounds Caesar on his travels: a sign of the complexity of the circle of friends and associates that surround him, which serves both as an indicator of his unrivalled influence and of the contribution that Caesar's circle has in the functioning of government. The fact that Caesar can impose the presence of dozens of 'friends' to his distinguished host is in itself a powerful political statement. – The lines quoted in the letter are a quotation from the second century BC poet Lucilius. – Nicias was a grammarian from Cos, who was on friendly terms with Cicero and Dolabella: Cicero heard from him about the continuation of Caesar's journey.

B167 Honours to Caesar and their reception, 46–44 BC

a) However, other deeds and words of his outweighed these so that it is reckoned that he abused his power and was justly killed. For not only did he accept excessive honours: successive consulships, a perpetual dictatorship, a prefecture of morals, as well as the *praenomen* 'Imperator' and the *cognomen* 'Father of his Country', a statue displayed among the kings, and a raised seat in the theatre; but he also allowed honours to be decreed him greater even than is right for human station: a golden seat in the senate-house and in front of the *rostra*, a wagon and a litter in the procession to the circus, temples, altars, statues next to those of the gods, a seat of honour (*pulvinar*), a priest (*flamen*), *Luperci*, and a month named after him; indeed, there were no honours which he did not receive and give as he wished.

Suetonius, *Divus Julius* 76.1

Suetonius summarizes the extraordinary range of honours that were bestowed upon Caesar after his victory in the civil war: they did not just draw attention to the fact that his power was effectively that of a monarch, but heavily suggested that the status of Caesar was not merely human. The creation of a priest (*flamen*) of the cult of Caesar is the most powerful indication that he was being worshipped as a god during his lifetime. *Luperci* were the young aristocratic 'priests' at the Lupercalia festival (see **B168**). Suetonius leaves his readers in no doubt that the string of honours he received was carefully directed by Caesar himself, and was not the product of flattery from Caesar's associates.

b) [4.1] The honours that were given him after those which have been mentioned were such and so many; although they were not proposed and ratified all at the same time, they will be related one by one. [2] They first of all voted that he should always ride even in the city itself, dressed in triumphal garb; and that he should sit on the magistrate's chair everywhere except at the games. For then he had the honour of watching on the tribunes' bench and in the company with those who were tribunes of the moment. [3] They bestowed on him the 'spoils of honour' (*spolia opima*) to offer at the temple of Jupiter Feretrius, just as if he had killed some enemy commander-in-chief with his own hand; and further always to have laurel-bearing lictors and to ride into the city on horseback from the Alban Mount after the Latin Festivals. [4] In addition to such honours as these, they named him father of his country and they stamped that on the coinage; they voted to offer public sacrifices on his birthday and ordered that in the towns and in all the temples in Rome there should be a statue of him; [5] and they set up two on the *rostra*, one for his having saved the citizens, the other for his having delivered the city from siege, with the crowns customary for such achievements. They decided to build a temple of Concordia Nova on the grounds that they were at peace through him and to hold an annual festival in her honour. [5.1] When he had accepted these, they assigned him the task of filling in the Pomptine marshes and of cutting a channel through the isthmus of the Peloponnese and of constructing a new senate-house, since the Hostilia, though rebuilt, had been demolished; [2] the pretext was that the temple of Fortuna was to be built there, which Lepidus actually completed when he was master of the horse, but the real reason was so that the name of Sulla should not be preserved on it but that another one constructed afresh might be called, the Julian, just as they named the month, in which he had been born, Julius, and one of the tribes selected by lot Julian. [3] And they voted that he should be censor alone and for life; that he should enjoy the privileges granted to tribunes so that if anyone should insult him in word or deed, he should be forfeit to the gods and held accursed; while his son, should he produce or even adopt one, should be appointed a *pontifex*. [6.1] Since he was happy with these honours, he was given a gilded chair and clothing which the kings had once worn, and a guard of *equites* and senators; and furthermore they decided that prayers should be offered each year on his behalf; that they should swear by his fortune, that everything to be done by him in the future should be ratified. [2] After this they dedicated to him, as to a hero, a quinquennial festival, and a sacred minister of the games of Pan, a third priestly college which they called the Julian, and in the gladiatorial games an individual day every time both in Rome and in the rest of Italy. [3] When he was pleased with these they voted that his gilded chair and his crown studded with stones and woven with gold should be carried into the theatres just like those of the gods and his chariot brought into the chariot races. And finally they addressed him directly Jupiter Julius and decided that a temple be consecrated to him and his clemency, having appointed Antony as their priest, like some *flamen Dialis* (priest of Jupiter).

[7.1] And, at the same time as these, they also voted what show their temper most revealingly when they granted him to construct his tomb within the *pomerium*. The decrees concerning these matters they inscribed on silver *stele* in gold letters and they placed them beneath the foot of Capitoline Jupiter, showing him quite distinctly that he was human. [2] For they had begun to honour him so that he might be reasonable; but as they went on, when they saw that he was happy with what they were voting (for apart from a few honours, he accepted them all) different people were all the time proposing different honours in excess, some flattering him excessively, while others were ridiculing him. [3] Indeed some ventured to allow him to have sexual intercourse with as many women as he wished, because he still had relationships with many women even then, although he was fifty years old. Others and they were the majority, did this because they wanted to bring upon him envy and indignation as soon as possible in order that he might be the more quickly destroyed. [4] And this actually happened.

Cassius Dio, Roman History 44.4–7.4

c) [107] There were some who thought about conferring upon him the title of king, but as soon as he learned about that he forbade it with threats, saying that it was an inauspicious name, on account of the curse of their ancestors. He dismissed the praetorian cohorts that had been serving as his bodyguard since the wars, and showed himself only with the ordinary civil escort. While he was thus transacting business before the *rostra*, the Senate, preceded by the consuls, each one in his official robe, brought the decree awarding him the honours mentioned above [*Civil Wars* 2.106]. He greeted them with his right hand, but did not rise when they approached, nor while they remained there; yet that also offered his detractors a pretext for accusing him of aspiring to the title of king. He accepted all the honours, except the ten-year consulship. As consuls for the ensuing year he designated himself and Antony, his master of the horse, and he appointed Lepidus, who was governor of Spain, but was governing it through his friends, master of the horse instead of Antony.

Appian, Civil Wars 2.107

Other sources for this period single out the range of honours received by Caesar as one of the great historical problems of the time. Cassius Dio gives an even fuller overview of the tributes he received, but takes a different view from Suetonius: he contends that some in the Senate contributed to this climate of celebration of Caesar in order in order to cast a sinister light upon him, and implicitly denounce him as a tyrant. – This list is recorded under 44 BC. Elsewhere Dio records other honours: for 46 BC, 43.14; for 45 BC, 43.43.1; 43.44.2; 43.45. Other (less detailed) accounts of these events are Livy, *Summaries* 116; Florus, *Summary of Roman History* 2.13.91; Plutarch, *Life of Caesar* 57.1.

B168   The Lupercalia incident, 15 February 44 BC

It was the festival of the Lupercalia, of which many authors write that it was celebrated by shepherds in ancient times, and that it is connected with the Arcadian Lykaia. Many of the noble youths and of the magistrates run through the city naked, striking with good humour and laughter those they meet with leather thongs. Many of the magistrates' wives also purposely get in their way, and put out their hands to be struck like children at school, convinced that the pregnant will thus be helped to an easy labour, and the barren to conceive. Caesar was attending this ritual, seated upon the *rostra* on a golden throne, arrayed in triumphal attire. Antony was one of the runners in the sacred race, as he was consul. When he entered the forum and the crowd made way for him, he carried a diadem, around which a laurel crown was tied, and offered it to Caesar. There was some applause, not much, but slight, as prearranged. Caesar pushed it away, all the people applauded; when Antony offered it again, few applauded; when Caesar declined it again, everyone applauded. The attempt having thus failed, Caesar rose to his feet, ordering the wreath to be carried up to the Capitol. However, his statues were seen adorned with royal diadems, and two of the tribunes, Flavius and Marullus, went up to them and tore the diadems down; after discovering those who had first hailed Caesar as king, they led them to prison... Caesar was furious, and dismissed Marullus and his colleague from office, and in his attack against them he insulted the people as well, for again and again he called the men 'Brutuses' and 'Cumaeans'.

Plutarch, *Life of Caesar* 61, with omission

Many found Caesar's power disturbingly close to that of a king, and therefore at odds with the long-standing Republican tradition that firmly rejected monarchy. Four weeks before Caesar's assassination a puzzling incident took place at a major religious festival: a crowd of men led by Mark Antony, arguably the closest and most trusted associate of the dictator, offered him the title of king, represented by the diadem, a headband that was the widely used symbol of kingship in the Hellenistic world. Caesar turned down the offer, much to the delight of the crowd: it remains unclear whether the offer was concerted in advance with Caesar (as seems likely), whether it was an episode of unsolicited flattery, or even a gesture that was intended to undermine him and mobilize opposition around him (as some have suggested). – Plutarch firmly favours the first view, and suggests that it was an attempt on his part to test the ground. His reaction to the conduct of the tribunes appears to corroborate this assessment; it is all the more extraordinary in light of the role that the defence of tribunician rights had played in Caesar's case for civil war. – The Latin *Brutus* means 'stupid', but is also the name of the nobleman who led the uprising against Tarquinius Superbus in 509 BC; the inhabitants of Cyme, in Aeolia, had a reputation for not being very bright. – Concerns over Caesar's monarchic aspirations are also at the forefront of the account in Suetonius, *Divus Julius* 79-80 and Appian, *Civil Wars* 2.112-113.

THE IDES OF MARCH AND THEIR AFTERMATH

B169   An account of the Ides of March

[82] As he took his seat, the conspirators gathered around him as if to pay their respects, and straightway Tillius Cimber, who had assumed the lead, approached him, as if he wanted to ask him something; when Caesar put him off to another time with a gesture, Cimber grabbed his toga by both shoulders; then, as Caesar cried 'Why, this is violence!', one of the Cascas stabbed him from one side, just below the throat. [2] Caesar caught Casca's arm and ran it through with his stylus; as he tried to leap to his feet, he was stopped by another wound. When he realized that he was attacked on every side by drawn daggers, he wrapped his toga around his head, and at the same time he drew down its lap to his feet with his left hand, in order to fall more decently, covering the lower part of his body too. In this way he was stabbed with twenty-three wounds, uttering merely a groan at the first stroke, and not a word, although some have related that, when Marcus Brutus rushed at him, he said in Greek, 'You too, son?' All the conspirators ran off, and he lay there for some time; finally three slaves put him on a litter and carried him home, with one arm hanging down. According to the physician Antistius, of so many wounds none turned out to be mortal, except the second one, which he had taken in the chest. The conspirators had planned to drag the body of the victim to the Tiber, confiscate his property, and revoke his official decisions, but they abandoned that plan through fear of the consul Marcus Antonius, and of Lepidus, the master of the horse.

Suetonius, *Divus Julius* 82

The killing of Julius Caesar on the Ides of March [15 March] 44 is one of the best-known and most intensely debated political assasinations in history: much ink has flowed since antiquity on who was privy to the conspiracy, and on what or who could have stopped it: there is an ample tradition on the signs that occurred in the days preceding the Senate meeting in which the attack on Caesar was due to take place, and on the attempts that were made to alert Caesar to the plot, even as he was making his way to the meeting of the Senate (see also Plutarch, *Caesar* 63–65). This took place in a meeting room within Pompey's theatre complex (Plutarch, *Caesar* 66.1, who notes [66.7] the irony that Caesar fell at the feet of a statue of Pompey). What is perhaps most striking about this extraordinary development is that Caesar, the most powerful man in Rome, was unaware of a plot involving about sixty individuals, several of whom were very close to him (Decimus Brutus, one of the leading conspirators, was in his residence on the Ides). This circumstance is so peculiar that it has led some to speculate that Caesar did not do anything to stop his assassination, either out of fatalism, or even because he was bent on some self-destructive spiral. It is best to avoid speculation.

B170   The motives of Caesar's killers: a critical viewpoint

[1] Caesar did all this as a preliminary step to the campaign that he was going to lead against the Parthians. However, a baleful frenzy fell upon certain men because of their envy of his advancement and their hatred of the fact that he had been preferred to them. It unlawfully killed him, adding a new name to infamy; it scattered the decrees to the winds and revived the Romans seditions and civil wars after a state of harmony. His assassins, to be sure, said that they had shown themselves at once destroyers of Caesar and liberators of the people, but in truth they impiously conspired against him, and they threw the city into civil strife when at last it was being correctly ruled.

Cassius Dio, *Roman History* 44.1

The conspiracy against Caesar included a number of individuals with very diverse political and personal backgrounds: some were disillusioned or disgruntled associates of Caesar, while others were former associates of Pompey, whom Caesar had pardoned and enabled to resume a distinguished political career – notably C. Cassius Longinus and M. Junius Brutus, who both held the praetorship in the year 44 BC. The unintended consequence of the Ides was a civil war that led to the onset of autocracy, but the chief aim of the conspirators was to restore Republican freedom by taking the life of someone that they regarded as a tyrant. The criticism voiced by Cassius Dio reflects a viewpoint that is inequivocably favourable to Caesar, but also draws attention to a fundamental problem presented by the initiative of the conspirators: they killed a serving magistrate, whose power had full constitutional and religious legitimacy (note the term 'impiously'), who was unarmed and without defence.

B171   Caesar's assassins and *Libertas*
a) *denarius* 44 BC

Obv: Head of Libertas
        LIBERTAS. [Liberty]
Rev: Togate figure walking between two lictors carrying *fasces* and preceded by
        an attendant;
        BRVTVS [L. Junius Brutus, cos. 509 BC]

        RRC 433/1 = Ghey, Leins & Crawford 2010, 433.1.6 = BM 2002,0102.4364

b) *aureus*, 43–42 BC

Obv: Head of *Libertas*, wearing diadem
        LIBERTAS [Liberty], M.AQVINIVS.LEG. [M. Aquinius, legate]
Rev: Tripod with cauldron, decorated with two laurel branches
        C.CASSI; PR.COS. [C. Cassius, proconsul]

        RRC 498 = Ghey, Leins & Crawford 2010, 448.1.1 = BM R.9234

c) *aureus,* **43–42 BC**

Obv: Head of *Libertas*, wearing diadem
       LEIBERTAS [Liberty]; C.CASSI. IMP. [C. Cassius, *imperator*]
Rev: Jug and *lituus* (augur's staff)
       LENTVLVS SPINT. [(P. Cornelius) Lentulus Spinther]
       RRC 500/2 = Ghey, Leins & Crawford 2010, 500.2.1 = BM 1884,0425.466A

d) *denarius,* **43–42 BC**

Obv: Head of Brutus right, bearded.
       BRVT.IMP; [Brutus, imperator]; L.PLAET.CEST. [L. Plaetorius Cestianus]
Rev: *Pileus* (felt hat) between two daggers
       EID.MAR. [Ides of March]
       RRC 508/3 = Ghey, Leins & Crawford 2010, 508.3.2 = BM 1855,0512.40

Between 43 and 42 the coalition of the so-called Liberators, the leaders of the conspiracy that took Caesar's life, established a strong political and military presence in the Greek-speaking provinces. The ruthless confiscations that Brutus and Cassius carried out enabled them to get hold of a considerable amount of financial resources, which partly offset the manpower gap with the armies mobilized by the Triumvirate. The coinage produced by the Liberators is a symptom of the emergence of a Roman alternative State in the East. Brutus and Cassius did not refrain from placing their names on the coinage they struck, but they made prominent references to the cause in whose name they had arranged the assassination of Caesar: Republican liberty. (d) emphatically celebrates the Ides of March as the moment when the city was restored to freedom: the presence of the *pileus*, the cap that freed slaves used to wear, encapsulates that message in the most immediate terms. The fact that Caesar was a magistrate and a *pontifex maximus* when he was assassinated is glossed over, and a claim to traditional piety is asserted through the references to the symbols of lawful *imperium*, the *fasces*, and to the those of the augurate, the jug and the *lituus*.

B172   Cicero on Brutus and Caesar, Spring 44
[2] Now, please do not refrain from the effort of writing news (I am expecting much), including whether the report about Sextus can be taken as established, but especially about our Brutus. My present host tells me that Caesar used to say about him: 'It is

a great question what he wants; but whatever he wants, he wants it badly.' He had formed that impression when Brutus spoke in support of Deiotarus at Nicaea: he had found his speech forceful and bold. Matius has also told me (I am writing things down as they occur to me) that recently, when I came to see Caesar at Sestius' request and was sitting waiting to be summoned, Caesar said: 'I must be a most hated man: Marcus Cicero is sitting waiting and cannot get to see me at his own convenience. If there is an easygoing man, it is him. And yet I do not doubt he hates me.' This and much else of the same sort.

From Matius' house, near Rome, 7 April 44.

Cicero, *To Atticus* 14.1.2 (SB 355)

Cicero's correspondence in the period following the Ides is especially engaging and rich in detail, as it charts the fast-moving political developments of an age of deep disruption: it also provides a number of anecdotes that would hardly find a place in other kinds of evidence. This letter to Atticus records two (reported) sayings of Caesar, one on Brutus, and one on the unwelcome consequences of the restrictions to access to him; the latter seems to reflect a degree of discomfort with the consequences and the demands of the quasi-monarchic position he had gained.

B173   Political violence in the aftermath of the Ides
[118] After the murderers had perpetrated such a crime, in a sacred place, on someone whose person was sacred and inviolable, there immediately was a flight throughout the senate-house and throughout the whole city. Some senators were wounded in the tumult, and others were killed. Many other citizens and foreigners were also killed, not with premeditation, but because such things happen in public commotions, out of the mistakes of those into whose hands revolts end up. For the gladiators, who had been armed early in the morning for that day's shows, ran from the theatre into the fenced areas surrounding the senate-house. The theatre itself was emptied by the disturbance, in haste and terror, and the markets were plundered. Everybody closed their doors and prepared for defence from the roofs. Antony fortified his house, as he guessed that the conspiracy was targeting him as well as Caesar. Lepidus, the master of the horse, who was in the forum at the time, learned about the events and ran to the island in the river where he had an infantry legion, which he moved to the Campus Martius so that it could be better prepared to execute Antony's orders; for he left the command to Antony, who was a closer friend of Caesar, and also a consul.

Appian, *Civil Wars* 2.118

Rome had witnessed a number of episodes of political violence even before the outbreak of the Civil War of 49-48, and the pattern resumed on the Ides of March, hours after the assassination of Caesar: there appears to be a serious risk to the safety of the other serving consul, Antony, who is rescued by the intervention of the men of Lepidus, the deputy of Caesar on the dictatorship. The initial cooperation between the two leading associates of Caesar enables them to mount a counteroffensive, and restore some order in the city, after hours of uncontrolled turmoil, in which a number of people had lost their lives.

B174   Cinna the poet, March 44 BC
[3] There was a certain Cinna, however, a friend of Caesar, who, so they say, had a strange dream the previous night. He dreamed that Caesar was inviting him to dinner, and he was trying to excuse himself; Caesar, however, led him along by the hand, although he did not wish to go and was resisting. [4] When Cinna heard that the body of Caesar was being cremated in the forum, he rose up and went there to pay respect,

although his vision had caused him some misgiving and he was in a fever. [5] As soon as he was seen, one of the crowd asked another what this man's name was, and he was told that he was Cinna. This was passed along, and there was an angry shouting all over the place, as they cried that this man was one of Caesar's killers: [6] for among the conspirators there was a man who bore the same name. They assumed that this was the same man: the crowd rushed upon him and tore him in pieces there and then.

Plutarch, *Life of Caesar* 68.3–6

This episode is revealing of the tension and confusion that dominate in Rome in the aftermath of the Ides, and of how strong the potential for episodes of unbridled political violence could be. Cinna's literary work survives only in fragments, but its influence on the poets of his generation (notably Catullus) and of the subsequent one is well attested. Moreover, the poet can safely be identified with C. Helvius Cinna, who held the tribunate in 50 BC (see T. P. Wiseman, *Cinna the Poet and other Roman Essays*, Leicester 1974, 44-58). He was probably from Brixia (modern Brescia) in Cisalpine Gaul, a region where Caesar had far-reaching political connections.

B175   Caesar's will

At the request of his father-inlaw, Lucius Piso, his will was unsealed and read in Antony's house: Caesar had made it on the previous Ides of September [13 September 45 BC] at his residence near Lavicum, and had put it in the care of the chief of the Vestals. Quintus Tubero states that, from his first consulship until the beginning of the civil war, he used to nominate Pompey as his heir, and to read this out to the assembled soldiers. [2] In his last will, however, he named three heirs, his sisters' grandsons, Gaius Octavius to three-fourths of his estate, and Lucius Pinarius and Quintus Pedius to share the remainder. At the end of the will, he also adopted Gaius Octavius into his family and gave him his name. He named several of his assassins among the guardians of his son, in case one should be born to him, and Decimus Brutus even among his heirs in the second degree. He left his gardens near the Tiber for their common use to the people, and three hundred sesterces to each man.

Suetonius, *Divus Julius* 83

The opening of Caesar's will opened a new political phase in the aftermath of the Ides, as it mobilized loyalty and sympathy towards his legacy in the Roman populace, and provided for the adoption of young Gaius Octavius: a decision that was to have major political implications – he would henceforth call himself *Caesar*; modern scholarship calls him 'Octavian' to distinguish him from Julius. In fact the legal basis for all this is exceptionally shaky. Julius Caesar could have made his legacy to Octavius conditional on Octavius adopting Caesar's name. Or he could have adopted Octavius as his son while he was alive. But he could not adopt him as his son in his will, since being adopted meant acknowledging the *patria potestas* (full legal powers of a father) of another man – powers that would inevitably be ended by death. So Octavian's claim to be Julius Caesar's son (rather than just taking his name) was a very moot one. Opponents like Brutus (e.g. in Cicero, *To Friends* 1.16) continue to call him Octavius, as does Cicero himself, **B177c**, and it may be that at some stage special legislation was needed to validate Octavian's claim to be Julius Caesar's son.

The decision to appoint the Roman people as heir to a considerable share of his fortune is not just a restatement of Caesar's long-standing political loyalties (cf. above, **B93a**) it was also a powerful indicator of the monarchic status that Caesar had carved out for himself in the final years of his life, and a function of the extraordinary wealth that he had gathered, which placed him in a position of unrivalled financial strength. The political developments of the late Republic and the trend towards autocracy must also be explained against the background of unprecentended accumulation of wealth in some quarters of the Roman élite, which was largely a consequence of the making of the empire.

B176 Antony after the Ides of March, 44–43 BC

[16.1] At this state of affairs, the young Caesar came to Rome, a son of the late Caesar's niece, as has been said, who had been left heir to his fortune. He was staying at Apollonia when Caesar was assassinated. [2] The young man immediately went to greet Antony as his father's friend, and reminded him of the moneys deposited with him. For he was under obligation to give every Roman seventy-five drachmas, as Caesar had provided in his will. [3] But Antony, at first despising him as a mere youngster, told him he was out of his mind, and that in his complete lack of good judgment and of friends he was taking up a crushing burden in the succession of Caesar. [4] When the young man refused to listen to this, and demanded the money, Antony continued to do and say many things to insult him. [5] For instance, he opposed him in his campaign for the tribunate, and when he attempted to dedicate a golden chair in honour of his father [Caesar], according to a decree of the Senate, Antony threatened to take him to prison unless he stopped seeking popular favour. [6] When, however, the young man made common cause with Cicero and all those who hated Antony, and through them obtained the support of the Senate, while he himself obtained the favour of the people and gathered the soldiers of Caesar from their colonies, then Antony started to fear him and came to a conference with him on the Capitol. They were reconciled.

[7] Afterwards, as he was asleep that night, Antony had a strange vision. It seemed to him, namely, that his right hand was hit by a thunderbolt. A few days later, a report reached him that Caesar was plotting against him. [8] Caesar offered explanations, but did not convince him. So once more their enmity was in full strength, and they were both hurrying about Italy, trying to bring into the field by large sums of money that part of the soldiery that was already settled in the colonies, and to have the edge over the other in winning the support of the part that was still in arms.

[17.1] Cicero, who was the most powerful man in the city, and was inciting everybody against Antony, persuaded the Senate to vote him a public enemy, to send Caesar the rods of office (*fasces*) and other insignia of the praetorship, and to dispatch Pansa and Hirtius to drive Antony out of Italy. [2] These men were consuls at that time, and in a clash with Antony near the city of Mutina, at which Caesar was present and fought on their side, they defeated the enemy, but fell themselves. [3] Many woes befell Antony in his flight: the greatest was famine. But it was his nature to be at this best when in an evil predicament, and when he was unfortunate he most resembled a good man.... [5] Antony, however, was at this time an admirable example to his soldiers, after such a life of luxury and extravagance as he had led, happily drinking foul water and eating wild fruits and roots. Bark was also eaten, it is said, and animals never tasted before were their nourishment as they crossed the Alps.

Plutarch, Life of Antony 16–17, with omissions

A concise summary of the personal and political position of Antony in the aftermath of the Ides, where seizing control of Caesar's political legacy quickly proves a difficult operation, and the competition he faces from young Octavian (Caesar) soon proves very intense: the alliance between 'young Caesar' and the sectors of the senatorial nobility that had opposed his adoptive father has the effect of isolating Antony, and of leading to a military action against him. Cicero's influence is somewhat overstated here; the background of the so-called 'War of Mutina' (April 43), in which the dispute between Antony and Decimus Brutus over the governorship of Cisalpine Gaul played a central role, is heavily compressed. Plutarch, who has a keen interest in the virtues and flaws of his characters, also comments on the outstanding military leadership, which also has moral implications: as he is extravagant and decadent in peacetime, he can be formidably disciplined and restrained on campaign, and build a strong connection with his soldiers through that conduct.

B177   Cicero after the Ides of March
a) Cicero to L. Minucius Basilus.
I congratulate you, I am delighted. I love you, I look after your interests: I want to be loved by you and to be informed of how you are, and of what is being done.

Cicero, *To his Friends* 6.15 (SB 322)

This brief note may be the earliest surviving reaction of Cicero to the Ides of March: a message possibly written on the Ides, in which Cicero, who was not part of the plot, addressed his unreserved appreciation to a member of the conspiracy. Lintott, *Cicero as Evidence,* 304 notes: 'the very fact that it has survived suggests that those who first edited Cicero's letters thought it worth including precisely because they took it to be reference to the conspiracy'.

b) [1] The day before yesterday I sent you a longer letter; now in answer to that which I have received most recently. I should wish, by Hercules, that Brutus was at Astura. You write about the lack of discipline of these people. Did you expect otherwise? For my part I expect even greater. For when I read a public speech about 'so great a man', about 'so distinguished a citizen' I cannot endure it. And yet the things are already a laugh. But remember that is how the custom of reckless speeches is nurtured so that these, not heroes, but certainly future gods, are enjoying everlasting glory, not without envy, not even without danger. But they have a consolation in the consciousness of a very great and glorious deed; what is there for us, who with the king dead are not free? But fortune will look to these things, since reason is not at the helm.

[2] ... Balbus, Hirtius and Pansa are here with me. Octavius has just arrived, and is actually at the house of Philippus next door; he is completely devoted to me. Lentulus Spinther is with me today; he departs early tomorrow morning.
Puteoli (?), 21 April 44 BC.

Cicero, *To Atticus* 14.11.1 (SB 365)

This letter shows Cicero's reservations with the strategy that the assassins of Caesar are pursuing in the aftermath of the Ides of March, as well as his irritation towards Antony's attempt take up the legacy of Caesar. He also mentions the conversations he is having with distinguished former partisans of Caesar such as Balubus and Hirtius, whom he is hoping to bring into a new coalition that is committed to the primacy of the Senate, while not dismissing altogether the political legacy of Caesar. In this context, the young great-nephew of Caesar, C. Octavius has also returned to Italy from Epirus, where he was getting ready for the campaign against the Parthians. Cicero seems confident, here and elsewhere, on his ability to steer the political choices of that young, inexperienced man: it will soon become clear that young 'Caesar Octavianus' was willing and able to act as an independent political player. – Astura was then a small island off the coast of Latium; it is now a peninsula.

c) My dear Atticus, I am afraid that the Ides of March will have given us nothing except a feeling of happiness and recompense for our hatred and grief. What news is brought me from Rome! What events I see here! *O deed that was noble, yet incomplete*!

You know how much I love the Sicilians and how I declare that I am honoured to have them as my clients. Caesar gave them much – and I did not object, though making them Latins was intolerable. But anyway … look how Antony has received a large sum of money and established a law passed in the assembly under the dictator, under which the Sicilians are Roman citizens – something never mentioned when in his lifetime. Isn't the case of our Deiotarus similar? He is certainly deserving of any kingdom – but not through Fulvia. Six hundred cases are similar. Anyway I return to this: are we not in some way going to get our way in a case as well known, as well attested, as well supported as that of Buthrotum? There is more chance there the more he does such things.

Octavius is here with us, very respectful and very friendly. [2] His followers call him Caesar, but Philippus does not, so neither do I. I do not think he can be a good citizen: so many people surround him who threaten us with death. They say that the current situation is intolerable. What do you think when the boy gets to Rome where our liberators cannot be safe? They shall always be famous, and happy in the knowledge of their deed. But we, unless I am mistaken, we will be lying discarded. Therefore I long to go 'far from the sons of Pelops', as the saying goes. Nor do I have any liking for the consuls designate who have even forced me to speak in public, so that I am not even allowed to rest even while at the baths. But this is because I am too approachable. For that was once almost a necessity, but now, however things are, it is not the same. Puteoli, 22 April 44 BC.

Cicero, To Atticus, 14.12.1–2 (SB 366)

Only a few weeks after the assassination of Caesar, Cicero reflects on the increasingly likely possibility that the removal of the Dictator, which many (including him) had saluted as a turning point, may have solved none of the political problems of the day. Mark Antony is still one the serving consuls, and Cicero reports his recent attempt to grant the Roman citizenship to the inhabitants of Sicily, who had recently been granted the Latin status (the scope and reach of that decision remain unclear). The underlying accusation that is being levelled at him is that he has sold legal privileges in exchange for bribes. – This letter provides evidence for the first encounter between Cicero and young Octavius after the Ides: Caesar's adoptive son is making a point of spending some time with him in Campania, before making his way to Rome, where he will soon make his claim to Caesar's inheritance. Cicero's initial attitude towards him is ambiguous: he is struck by the respect that the young man is showing towards him, but is also sceptical of his ability to conduct himself as a true Republican. An elusive reference is made to the influence of some advisors. Cicero is increasingly doubtful about his own perspectives: he feels that he will be an increasingly isolated voice in the Roman political perspectives. His advice, however, is still being sought by the consuls designated by Caesar for the following year, A. Hirtius and C. Vibius Pansa, who are rather dismissively mentioned here. – The sentence in italic is a literary quotation from a lost Greek text that cannot be identified.

d) [2] You defend the Bruti and Cassius in such a way as if I am finding fault with them; I cannot praise them enough. I put together the faults of the circumstances not of the men. For with the tyrant (*tyrannus*) removed I see the tyranny (*tyrannis*) remains. For things are being done which he was not going to do … We are now obeying the notebooks of the man to whom we ourselves could not be slaves …

[3] But let us pass over what is past; let us protect those men carefully and securely and, as you advise, be satisfied with the Ides of March; they have indeed given to our friends, godlike men, an entrance to heaven, but they have not given the Roman people freedom. Recall your words. Do you not remember that you declared aloud that all was lost if he were honoured with a funeral? You did indeed speak wisely. And you see what has developed as a result. [4] As for what you write that Antony will bring

forward a proposal about provinces on the Kalends of June (1 June), that he himself have the Gauls and that the time for both of them be extended, will it be possible for a decision to be made freely? If it is possible, I shall be happy that freedom has been recovered; if it is not possible, what has this change of master brought me other than the happiness with which I beheld the just death of a tyrant? You write that looting is taking place at the temple of Ops. I too saw it at that time. We have indeed been freed by great men, but we are not free. Thus the praise is theirs, the fault is ours. Then you encourage me to write history, so that I may gather together the great crimes of those by whom even now we are hard pressed. Shall I not be able to praise those very men who have used you as a witness to their wills? And the small change, by Hercules, does not move me, but it is not a nice thing to hound with insult men who, whatever sort they are, wish one well.

Puteoli, 28–29 April 44 BC.

Cicero, *To Atticus* 14.14.2–4 (SB 368), with omission

Caesar's willingness to work with some friends of Caesar does not change his judgement on the actions of the late dictator, or indeed on the merits of his assassins towards the *res publica*: he explicitly regards them as 'great men', and appears to be casting blame on the political élite more broadly for not having done enough to change the power balance after the great opportunity presented by the Ides of March. The implicit, but clear target of his polemic is of course Mark Antony, whom he regards as the most dangerous continuator of Caesar's regime.

e) [8] But it will not escape your notice as a very learned man that, if Caesar was a tyrant, which to me at any rate seems to be the case, on the matter of your moral stance it can be argued in either of two ways: in the one which I am accustomed to use, that your loyalty and kindness should be praised since you hold dear a friend even though he is dead; or in the other which some people use that the freedom of one's country (*patria*) should be put before the life of a friend. Would that my arguments from those conversations had been relayed to you! Who more willingly and more often than I recalls those two greatest acts which are to your renown: that you were the most influential advocate of not venturing civil war and of acting with moderation in victory. In this I have found nobody who did not agree with me.

Rome, mid October (?) 44 BC.

Matius to Cicero, *To his Friends*, 11.27.8 (SB 348)

This letter conveys the viewpoint of a friend of Caesar, C. Matius, a man of equestrian standing, who makes a valuable point about the enduring loyalty that some felt towards the late dictator, and of the political damage that allegations of tyranny could create, in a context where the potential for further divisions is rife.

B178   Cicero on Antony, 2 September 44 BC

Mark Antony's speech on that day was a fine one, and his goodwill was conspicuous; peace was established through him and his sons with our most distinguished citizens. And what followed was in keeping with these early developments. He invited the most prominent men in the city to the debates that he held on the *res publica* in his own house; he made favourable reports to our order; nothing was found in C. Caesar's notebooks that was not known to everyone; he answered with outstanding thoroughness the questions that were put to him.

Cicero, *Philippics* 1.1.2

Between 44 and 43 Cicero gave a series of speeches against Mark Antony, which go under the title of *Philippics*, after the series of speeches that the Athenian orator Demosthenes gave against Philip II, king of Macedon. Most of these speeches are violent attacks on Antony, who is cast as a corrupt tyrant, who has no place in the political community. However, in the first speech, which he gave in the Senate in early September, he is still open to the possibility of an appeasement between the factions in the *res publica*, and has complimentary words about Antony's handling of the political legacy of Julius Caesar in the aftermath of the Ides.

B179   Political factions (*partes*), 1 January 43

[31] Therefore I propose, conscript fathers, that no mention be made of envoys; I think the matter should be attended to without delay, and I propose that it should be carried out straight away: a state of tumult should be declared, a suspension of public business (*iustitium*) should be decreed, military attire should be assumed, a levy should take place, all exemptions from service being suspended in Rome and in the whole of Italy, except for Gaul. [32] If this is done, the very belief and reputation of our severity will prevail upon the mindless arrogance of that criminal gladiator. He will feel that he has embarked on a war against the *res publica*, and will get to experience the energy and strength of a Senate that has unity of purpose; for now he claims that there is clash of factions (*partes*) going on. Which factions? One side has been defeated, the other is in the midsts of C. Caesar's faction; unless we think that the faction of Caesar is being taken on by the consuls Pansa and Hirtius, and by his son C. Caesar. This war does not stem from a division between the factions (*partes*), but from the nefarious hopes of our most vicious citizens, for whom our assets and fortunes have been marked down and are already being distributed according to each individual's whim.

Cicero, *Philippics* 5.31–32

This passage offers a rather typical example of Cicero's polemic against Antony: the epithet 'gladiator' is revealing of his wider attempt to exclude his opponent from the number of respectable citizens (see above, **B66**, **B106**). It is also interesting for the attempt it provides to chart the new political situation in Rome: Antony is claiming that was is going on is an ordinary clash of *partes* (groups with different political views), while Cicero contends that Antony is facing the opposition of any decent man, including some very prominent associates of Caesar. The faction that Cicero identifies as the defeated one is probably that of Pompey's followers. The aims of Antony and his followers are merely predatory: Cicero is making the case for not having any further talks with Antony, who is besieging Decimus Brutus at Mutina, in Cisalpine Gaul, and that a levy be carried out across Italy, with a view to launching an immediate military action. His view was not accepted, and an embassy to Antony was dispatched: however, a military action was eventually launched, leading to the so-called war of Mutina, in April 43 (see above, **B176**).

B180   Octavian and Julius Caesar's comet, July 44 BC

[94] A comet is worshipped in only one place in the world, a temple in Rome, having been judged by the Divine Augustus to be greatly propitious to himself. It appeared at the beginning of his career, at games that he was celebrating to Venus Genetrix not long after the death of his father Caesar, as a member of the priestly college which Caesar had founded. [94] Indeed he made his joy clear in these words in [*gap in the text*]: 'On the very days of my games, a comet was visible for seven days in the northern region of the sky. It rose about the eleventh hour of the day [*i.e. at dusk*], and was both clear and visible from all lands. The people believed that by this star was signified the fact that Caesar's soul (*anima*) had been received among the immortal gods, for which reason this emblem was added to the image of his head, which we soon afterwards consecrated in the Forum.' This is what he said in public; with inner joy he interpreted it as having been born for him, and that he was born in it. And, truth be told, it had a salutary effect for the world.

Pliny the Elder, *Natural History* 2.93–94

This passage contains one of the most substantial quotes from the lost autobiographical work of Augustus (*Fragments of the Roman Historians* 60 F1), which comprised thirteen books and provided an account of his life until the Cantabrian War that he fought in the Iberian peninsula in 26/25 BC (see Suetonius, *Augustus* 85.1). The appearance of a comet in the sky of Rome during a major religious festival that was directly associated with Julius Caesar enabled Octavian to make a religious claim that had major political implications: Caesar had risen to heaven, and his deification was now complete. After the Ides of March the cult of *Divus Julius* had been in practice discontinued, with the support of Antony and Lepidus; the comet of July 44 enabled Octavian to prepare its revival. Being able to assert that he was the son of a god entailed obvious advantages, which he was ready to reap in the years to follow. – Pliny makes an interesting comment on the gulf between Octavian's public statements and his personal views: he regarded the comet, first and foremost, as a sign that foreboded his own rise to power. No suggestion is made, however, that Octavian was privately sceptical on the value of the sign, and that he devised an interpretation intended to manipulate or defraud the public opinion.

B181   Octavian's irritation towards Cicero, Spring 43

Decimus Brutus to Cicero.

My affection for you and your services to me compel me to do what I do not do for myself: being afraid. There is something that has often been said to me and which I do not dismiss – of late Labeo Segulius, a man of great consistency, tells me that he has been with Caesar and there has been much talk of you. He says that Caesar does not complain about you, to be sure, except that he said what you are said to have said about him: 'the young man must be praised, honoured, and got rid of.' He added that he is not up for being got rid of. Eporediae, 24 May 43 BC.

> Decimus Brutus to Cicero, *To his Friends* 11.20.1

The relationship between Cicero and Octavian had ostensibly been excellent since the latter's return to Rome in the aftermath of the Ides of March (see above, **B177**). This letter by Decimus Brutus, one of the Caesaricides, issues a warning to the elder statesman: Octavian is said to have caught wind of Cicero's views about him, and to have privately criticized him. Octavian's irritation forebodes the events that occurred six months later, after the creation of the triumvirate.

B182   Rumours on the death of the consuls, April 43 BC

When, in this war [of Mutina], Hirtius in battle, and Pansa shortly afterwards, died of their wounds, a rumour spread that their deaths were Octavian's work, his intention being that, after Antony's escape, with the *res publica* bereft of the consuls, he alone would take over the victorious armies. Pansa's death was certainly suspicious enough for Glyco the doctor to be arrested for having put poison in the wound. Aquilius Niger adds that the other consul, Hirtius, had been killed by Octavian himself in the commotion of the battle.

> Suetonius, *Augustus* 11

Not even Octavian's victory could obliterate a highly hostile tradition on his alleged involvement in the deaths of the consuls of 43 BC at the battle of Mutina: an event from which he unquestionably drew considerable advantage. The possible responsibility of Glyco for Pansa's death does not of course indicate Octavian's involvement. Suetonius does not appear to lend any credibility to this version, whilst nonetheless reporting it; nothing else is know about the work of the author from which he drew his information on Hirtius' death (*Fragments of the Roman Historians* 67, F1).

C. THE TRIUMVIRAL PERIOD (AND BEYOND)

C1   The formation of the Triumvirate, October 43 BC

[2] Octavian and Antony met near the city of Mutina on a small, hollow island in the river Lavinius, reaching a friendship from enmity. They each had five legions of soldiers, whom they stationed opposite each other; they then both proceeded with 300 men towards the bridges over the river. Lepidus himself went before them, inspected the island, and waved his military cloak as a signal to them to proceed. Each then left his three hundred men with their friends on the bridges, and advanced to the middle of the island in plain sight, and there the three men sat together in council – Octavian in the centre, because he was consul. They conferred for two days until night, and came to these decisions: that Octavian should resign the consulship, and that Ventidius should take it for the rest of the year; that a new magistracy for the settlement of the civil conflicts should be created by law, with powers analogous to those of the consuls, and that Lepidus, Antony, and Octavian should hold it for five years; this title seemed preferable to that of dictator, perhaps because of the law of Antony that abolished the dictatorship. They should at once nominate the yearly magistrates of the city for the following five years, and divide the provincial commands: Antony would have the whole of Gaul, except for the region near the Pyrenees, which was called Old Gaul; this, along with neighbouring Spain, was assigned to Lepidus; Octavian was to have Libya, Sardinia, and Sicily, and all the islands in the vicinity.

[3] In such a fashion the three men divided up the dominion of the Romans among themselves, postponing only the assignment of the regions beyond the Adriatic Sea, since Brutus and Cassius were in control of those, but they established that Antony and Octavian were to wage war against them. Lepidus was to be consul the following year and to remain in Rome to attend to what was required there, governing Spain through others. He was to keep three legions in the vicinity of Rome, while Antony and Octavian would divide up the remaining seven between themselves, three to Octavian, four to Antony, so that they would each have twenty for the war. In the meantime, they raised the hopes of the army for a military victory, along with other gifts, with the promise of settling colonies in eighteen Italian cities, which, standing out on the others for wealth, for the fertility of their land and the beauty of the houses, would be divided up among them, as if they had been conquered in war. These were various cities, and the most famous ones were Capua, Rhegium, Venusia, Beneventum, Nuceria, Ariminum, and Hipponium. Thus the most beautiful parts of Italy were being marked out for the army; however, they decided to destroy their enemies first, and so that they would not be disturbed as they were settling the internal situation, while having to fight an external war. Having reached these decisions, they put them in writing: then Octavian, in his capacity as consul, announced them to the armies, without mentioning those who would have been put to death. Having heard the decisions, they sang a victory song and embraced each other to mark the reconciliation.

Appian, Civil Wars 4.2–3

What is sometimes called the 'Second Triumvirate' should in fact be understood as *the* Triumvirate, as it led – unlike the alliance between Caesar, Pompey and Crassus – to the setting up of a new magistracy, the triumvirate 'for the establishment of the commonwealth' (*rei publicae constituendae*), which was created under the *lex Titia* in November 43 BC. For five years the triumvirs enjoyed a set of powers that were unprecedented in the history of the Republic, and placed them in a political and constitutional position that prevailed over that of the consuls. The precedents of Sulla and Caesar dissuaded them from reviving the dictatorship, and prompted the devising of a new magistracy, which fundamentally altered the constitutional setup of the Republic, and arguably led to its demise. As Appian's account makes clear, the agreement reached by Octavian, Antony and Lepidus is chiefly a reconciliation among three military leaders, which involved their armies, and was indeed enabled by their enthusiastic support: the pledge to embark upon a set of colonial assignments across Italy was the cornerstone of the new political setup. The arrangements between the triumvirs completely bypassed the Senate: the factor that enabled them and made them sustainable was the presence of the army across Italy, and indeed in the immediate surroundings of the city. Its implications, however, had wider imperial significance: the division of the provincial commands among the triumvirs is another major breach from Republican practice – possibly the most significant one.

C2   The text of the proscription decree, November 43 BC

[8] The proscription decree read in these terms: 'Marcus Lepidus, Marcus Antonius, and Octavius Caesar, elected by the people to order and regulate the commonwealth, declare what follows. If the criminals had not obtained the forgiveness they begged for, because of their disloyalty, and if they had not become enemies of their benefactors after having obtained it, they would not have killed Gaius Caesar, who had spared them out of compassion after having defeated them in war, made them friends of his, and raised to public offices and honours, and covered them with gifts; nor would we be compelled to resort to these measures against those who attacked us and declared us enemies. Now, though, on the evidence of the attacks against us and from which Gaius Caesar suffered, seeing that evil does not let itself be conquered by generosity, we prefer to strike our enemies first, rather than suffer at their hands. No one should consider our actions unjust, cruel, or disproportionate, if they reflect on what Caesar has suffered and on what we have suffered. Although Gaius was dictator and chief priest, although he had defeated and subjugated the peoples that were most fearsome to the Romans, and had sailed the unsailed sea beyond the Pillars of Heracles, the first among the men, discovering regions unknown to the Romans, they murdered him in the middle of the sacred senate building before the eyes of the gods, stabbing him twenty-three times: men who had been captured by him in war and spared, and some of them included in his will as heir to a share of his fortune. After this crime, instead of punishing the guilty, the others dispatched them to magistracies and provincial governorships, through which they seized the resources of the commonwealth, with which in turn they are gathering an army, while they are asking barbarians that have always been enemies of the empire to provide them with another force. They have burned down, destroyed or razed to the ground the cities subjected to the Romans that did not obey their orders; they have terrified the others, mobilizing them against the fatherland and against us.

[9] We have already punished some of them; you will see that the rest will soon pay their dues, with the help of the god. But, although the best part of the work has been brought to completion by us or is well underway (the affairs in Spain, in Gaul, as well as here at home), one task is left: waging war overseas against those who killed Gaius. In getting ready to fight a war in your interest far away from here, it does not seem safe, neither for us nor for you, to leave behind the other enemies, who will take advantage of our absence and will seize the opportunities afforded by the war; nor is it prudent to dither on account of these people in such an urgent situation, but to get rid of all of them, who have begun the war against us when they voted us and our armies enemies.

[10] They intended to eliminate many thousands of citizens, without considering the punishment of the gods and the condemnation of men. We will not treat harshly a multitude of people, nor will we declare enemies all those who have opposed us or have been plotting against us, and we will give no consideration to wealth, means, or reputation. We will not kill as many people as those that another dictator before us killed, who was also involved in a civil war to redress the commonwealth, and was named 'Fortunate' because of his success – although it is inevitable that three men should have more enemies than a single one. On the contrary, we will kill only the worst ones and those who are most responsible of everything that has happened. And we shall do that for your sake, no less than for ours. It is inevitable that, if we are in disagreement among ourselves, all of you, who are in the middle, should greatly suffer, and it also inevitable that some comfort be given to an army that has been abused, upset, and declared an enemy by our common enemies. Even though we could arrest without notice those whom we have decided to strike, we have decided to make their list public, rather than capturing them out of surprise. We are doing this for your sake, so that the soldiers do not behave in an unrestrained manner towards innocent people, overwhelmed by anger, but they refrain from striking others, in accordance with the orders, having at hand a list of people identified by name.

Let fortune be kind, then: no one shall harbour or hide anyone among those whose names are listed below, or shall accompany him anywhere, or shall let himself be corrupted by his riches. Who shall be detected saving, aiding, or colluding with them, we shall add him to the list of the proscribed, without accepting any pretext or excuse. Those who shall kill the proscribed shall bring us their head: a free man will receive 25,000 Attic drachmas for each head; a slave will receive 10,000 drachmas and the citizenship status of his master, as well as his own individual freedom. Informers shall receive the same rewards. No mention will be made in the official records of those who will capture the proscribed, so that their identy is not divulged.'
This was the decree of the Triumvirs, translated from the Latin language into Greek.

Appian, *Civil Wars* 4.8–10

This extraordinary passage records a text of what purports to be the Greek translation of the decree with which the triumvirs announced a round of proscriptions (the second one in Roman history, after those carried out by Sulla in 82/81 BC) and set out the ways in which these were to be carried out. Its authenticity has been questioned, but is now accepted by most scholars: there are no decisive arguments standing against it. The whole document is predicated on the assumption that there is a group of enemies that have committed a crime (the assassination of Caesar) and have so far escaped punishment: the triumvirs declare their intention to make them atone for their misdeeds. The endorsement of the people is strongly asserted at the outset, the assistance and endorsement of the gods is assumed without discussion, and the proscriptions are regarded as the preliminary stage of a wider military effort, which will be the necessary step to defeat the enemies not just in Rome, but more widely across the empire. The themes of loyalty and treason permeate the whole document, and are set out as the fundamental principles upon which the proscriptions are based: the assassins of Caesar are traitors; those who will abet the escape of the proscribed will also be considered as traitors to the *res publica*, and will receive the same punishment. On the other hand, considerable financial rewards are identified for those who will inform on the proscribed: the clause even applies to the slaves, who are promised freedom if they enable the capture on their master. – The process that is set out here is as sophisticated as it is ruthless in its operation; yet the triumvirs make a public commitment to restraint and moderation, and state their intention to kill fewer people than had been the case with the Sullan proscriptions. The unfolding of the massacre was soon to tell a different story: according to Appian (4.5), about 300 senators and about 2,000 members of the equestrian order were included in the list.

C3   Scenes from the proscriptions, 43/42 BC

A freedman concealed a proscribed man in a tomb, but he could not endure the horror of the grave; he therefore moved him to a modest little house that he had rented. A soldier was lodged near him, and the man, who could not tolerate that fear either, switched from cowardice to the most wonderful audacity. He cut off his hair and ran a school in Rome until peace returned.

Volusius was proscribed during his aedileship and, since he had a friend who was initiated into the mysteries of Isis, he asked him to lend him his robe, put on a linen garment reaching to his feet, put on the dog's head and as a priest of Isis he made the journey to Sextus Pompey.

The people of Cales protected Sittius, one of their fellow-citizens who had spent much for them, making use of a vast personal fortune: they gave him an escort, they threatened his slaves, they prevented the soldiers from approaching their walls, until the danger became less significant; they then sent envoys to the triumvirs and obtained that Sittius not be deported to another part of Italy, but be allowed to stay in his motherland. Sittius was the first or the only man who was an exile in his own motherland.

Varro was a philosopher and a writer of history, and had been a good soldier and a commander; he was proscribed, probably because he was an enemy of monarchy. His friends were keen to give him shelter and competed for that. Calenus won, and hosted him in a villa where Antony used to stop on his travels. Yet no slave, either of Calenus or of Varro, ever revealed that Varro was there.

Appian, *Civil Wars* 4.47

The proscriptions are a major development of political and social history, which must be understood against the background of specific constitutional arrangements. They also generated, however, a stream of striking anecdotes, which drew attention to the emotional and moral implications of a project of large-scale violence: the string of examples listed by Appian include two cases of a successful escape, in which the ingenuity of the solutions devised by the victims is testimony to the might of the attack they were under, the remarkable story of Publius Sittius, who was saved by the intervention of his fellow-citizens, and the predicament of Varro, a great intellectual of his time (see **H25–H30**), who was rescued by the solidarity of his friends. – For another remarkable example cf. the so-called *Laudatio Turiae* (below **K13**).

C4   Cicero's death, December 43 BC

[17] T. Livy's account: 'Cicero had left the city before the arrival of the triumvirs, being certain (as was the case) that he could no more be snatched from Antony than Cassius and Brutus could be snatched from Caesar. First he fled to his property at Tusculanum, then set out across country to Formiae to board ship from Caieta. He put out to sea several times from there, but sometimes adverse winds brought him back, sometimes he could not bear the tossing of the ship as the waves rolled under it. Finally he felt tired of flight and of life: returning to his villa on higher ground, just over a mile from the sea, he said, "May I die in the fatherland (*patria*) I have often saved." It is well known that his slaves were ready to fight bravely and loyally for him, but that he ordered them to put down his litter and quietly to submit to the compulsion of unjust fate. He leant out of the litter, offered his neck unflinchingly and had his head cut off. This did not satisfy the brutal cruelty of the soldiers. They also cut off

his hands which they blamed for having written criticism of Antony. So his head was taken back to Antony in Rome, and placed, at his command between the two hands on the Rostra, where as consul, where frequently as ex-consul, where that same year in his speeches against Antony, his voice had been heard and admired for its eloquence as no human voice had ever been admired. People could hardly raise their gaze to look through their tears at his slaughtered limbs.' ...

This is the *epitaphion*, to use the Greek word, of Livy on Cicero: [22] 'He lived for sixty-three years, so that, if violence had been absent, his death could not seem premature. His talent was fortunate both in its works and in the rewards of those works; he himself long experienced good fortune; but in the long course of good fortune, he was at times struck by blows: by exile; by the collapse of the faction (*partes*) on whose side he had stood; by the death of his daughter; by so sad and bitter a death. He endured none of all his adversities as was worthy of a man except his death; to one making a true assessment this could have seemed less undeserved, because he had suffered no more cruel a fate from a victorious enemy than he would himself have brought about had he shared the same good fortune. However, for whoever weighs up his vices against his virtues, he was a great and memorable man and to rehearse his praises would need a Cicero as a eulogist.' As Livy is by nature the fairest judge of all great talents, he had accorded the fullest testimony to Cicero.

Livy, book 120, quoted by Seneca the Elder, *Declamations, Suasoria* 6.17 and 22

b) [24] Asinius Pollio, too, who has recorded the very brave death of Verres, the opponent in court of Cicero, is the only one of all to narrate the death of Cicero in a spiteful manner, but though unwillingly, he has nonetheless given him full testimony. 'Therefore about this man's works, so many and so great, which will last for all time, it is superfluous to make mention of his talent and his industry. Nature and fortune deferred to him equally, seeing that good looks and sound health stayed with him to old age; then a long period of peace, which suited his talents, was granted him; for with the processes of law being enforced with the rigour of an earlier age, a very large number of men guilty of wrongdoing emerged, many of whom he preserved unharmed through his advocacy and thus obliged to him; then through the great service of the gods and through his own judgement and hard work the circumstances both of his canvass for the consulship and his conduct of it were most fortunate. Would that he could have borne success with greater moderation and adversity with greater courage! For when each of them befell him, he thought they could not change. Thus heavy storms of envy broke out against him and the confidence of his enemies in attacking him was the surer; he used to look for quarrels with greater vigour than he pursued them. But since perfect virtue has fallen to the lot of no mortal, judgement has to be made of a man based on the greater part of his life and character. And I would judge that he did not even meet with a death to be pitied, if he himself had not thought death so wretched.' I can tell you for certain that there is nothing more eloquent in his histories that this piece I have related so that he seems not to have praised Cicero, but to have competed with Cicero.

Seneca the Elder, *Declamations, Suasoria* 6.24–25

The death of Cicero received memorable accounts in several lost historical sources on the late Republic (Seneca also quotes in full the accounts of Aufidius Bassus, Cremutius Cordus and Bruttedius Niger), in which it was singled out both as a moment of great significance in itself and as the end of any prospect of Republican freedom. Even Asinius Pollio, whose outlook on Cicero and his legacy was distinctly hostile, did have to engage with the intellectual and political contribution of that man to the history of his time. – Antony ordered for Cicero's remains to be put on display on the *rostra*, the very tribunal from which Cicero had often spoken to great acclaim: the gruesome scene was powerfully described by the historian A. Cremutius Cordus (d. AD 25); the passage survives thanks to an extensive quotation in Seneca the Elder (*Declamations, Suasoria* 6.24 = *Fragments of the Roman Historians* 71 F1).

C5   Augustus on Cicero

I gather that Caesar [Augustus], a long time afterwards visited one of his grandsons; since the boy had in his hands a book of Cicero, he was frightened and tried to hide it beneath his tunic. But Caesar saw it and took the book. He read a great part of it as he stood and then gave it back to the lad, saying: 'An eloquent man, my boy, eloquent and a lover of his country.'

Plutarch, *Life of Cicero* 49.5

A telling anecdote on the shrewd and lucid engagement with the past – even its less convenient facts – of which Augustus was capable after his victory. Cicero was not an altogether unlikely reference point for a regime that claimed to be based on the restoration of the *res publica*.

C6   The Triumvirs and Caesar's legacy, 43 BC
a) *denarius*

Obv: Head of M. Antony, right, bearded; behind, *lituus*
        M.ANTON.IMP. [Mark Antony *imperator*].
Rev: Laureate head of Caesar, right., behind, jug
        CAESAR.DIC. [Caesar dictator]

RRC 488/1 = Ghey, Leins & Crawford 2010, 488.1.2 = BM R.9125

b) *aureus*

Obv: Head of Octavian, right, bearded
C.CAESAR.IMP. [Gaius Caesar *imperator*]
Rev: Laureate head of Caesar, right
C.CAESAR.DICT.PERP.PONT.MAX. [Gaius Caesar, perpetual dictator, *pontifex maximus*]

RRC 490/2 = Ghey, Leins & Crawford 2010, 490.2.1 = BM 1864,1128.8

Caesar's major innovation of including his own portrait on coinage was readily taken up by those who competed over his political legacy: in 43 both Antony and Octavian produced issues in which their portraits and their claims to military distinction featured prominently. That is hardly surprising if one bears in mind that the main recipients of that coinage output were the soldiers serving under their command. A long, fierce struggle for power was looming on the horizon: however, the competing coin issues produced by the two men shared a dominant feature: the portrait of Caesar crowned with a laurel wreath (the same iconography that was used in early 44 in Caesar's late coinage, see **B165**), accompanied with references to the official status he had upon his death – a pointed reference to the legitimacy of Caesar's position, and a tribute to a man whose memory was widely cherished by the armies that were then serving under Antony and Octavian.

C7   The formation of the Triumvirate: numismatic evidence, 43–42 BC
a) *aureus*: **Antony and Octavian**

Obv: Head of M. Antony right, bearded; behind, lituus (augur's wand)
M.ANTONIVS.III.VIR.R.P.C. [M. Antony, triumvir for settling the *res publica*]
Rev: Head of Octavian right, bearded
C.CAESAR.III.VIR.R.P.C. [Gaius Caesar, triumvir for settling the *res publica*]

RRC 492/1 = Ghey, Leins & Crawford 2010, 492.1.1 = BM R.9137

b) *aureus*: **Antony and Lepidus**

Obv: Head of M. Antony right, bearded; behind, *lituus* (augur's wand)
        M.ANTONIVS.III.VIR.R.P.C (Mark Antony, triumvir for settling the
        res publica)
Rev: Head of Lepidus right; behind, *aspergillum* and *simpulum*; around,
        inscription. M.LEPIDVS.III.VIR.R.P.C (Marcus Lepidus, triumvir for
        settling the *res publica*)

> *RRC* 492/2 = Ghey, Leins & Crawford 2010, 492.2.1 = BM 1848,0819.80

These impressive gold issues celebrate the establishment of the Triumvirate: they were struck by Antony in Cisalpine Gaul, Antony and his fellow triumvirs portrayed on each side of the coin, with their new official title given great prominence. Octavian struck a virtually identical issue, with his portrait on the obverse and that of Antony on the reverse (*RRC* 493). Lepidus similarly struck *aurei* and *denarii* in 42 BC with his portrait on the obverse and Octavian's on the reverse (*RRC* 495). Lepidus accompanies the reference to his status as triumvir with a mention of his position as *pontifex maximus*, which he gained after Caesar's death.

C8   Formation of Triumvirate: epigraphic evidence
a) Triumvirate on *Fasti Colotiani* **(List of Consuls), Rome**
[M. A]emilius, M. Antony, Imp(erator) Caesar, IIIvirs for settling the *res publica* from 27 Nov to 1 Jan in 6 years' time.

> Fasti Colotiani = *Inscr. Ital.* 13.1.18 = EJ page 32 = EDCS-59100092*

This is a well-preserved list of consuls from between 45 and 12 BC found in the Colotian Gardens in Rome. M. Antony's name was erased then reinscribed. The entry appears below the names of the consuls for 43 BC, so the triumvirs' term was from 27 Nov 43 to 1 Jan 37.

b) Augustus records his triumvirate in the *Res Gestae*
In this same year [43 BC], moreover, the people appointed me consul, after both consuls had fallen in war, and triumvir for settling the *res publica*.

> *Res Gestae* 1.4

c) Letter of Antony to the *Koinon* **of Asia**
Mark Antony, imperator, triumvir for settling the *res publica* to the Commonwealth (*koinon*) of Greeks of Asia, greetings.

> EJ 300 = Sherk *RDGE* 4.85

Papyrus, datable by the rest of the letter (not given here) to 42/1 or 33/2 BC.

C9 Two letters from Brutus to communities in the Greek East

a) Brutus to the Patarans, early 42 BC

Damasippos, the Rhodian admiral, so I have learned from Hermodoros the Samian captain, fled with two cataphracts after the fall of Rhodes and appeared in your largest harbour. The fact that he put in there I do not consider any fault of yours: but if, after he has put in, you allow him to escape further to any other place on earth, I will count it against you both as injury and as treachery.

Letters of Brutus [21 Jones]

b) Brutus to the Cyzicenes, Summer-early autumn 42

Your ambassadors met me as I was leaving for the war and begged to be exempted from the alliance, excusing you on the ground of your impoverishment and your lack of public funds. The need being so urgent, it would be proper for you to send further help even now, even if you did not give it before, because the timing would make the service more valuable. But since you seem to entertain an unfavourable expectation of the war, I am pleased by the impoverishment you allege (since on the contrary I would have been annoyed to hear that you were wealthy, treacherous as you are). Your fighting men I will no longer consider allies, but subordinates and recalcitrant. You surely must be aware that it would be strange (for you) to share in any victory in war that may occur, when to the best of your ability you have betrayed us into the utmost impoverishment.

Letters of Brutus [30 Jones]

A collection of thirty-five Greek letters attributed to M. Junius Brutus survives in several manuscripts, and Plutarch's *Life of Brutus* also makes reference to a collection of Brutus' letters (2.5-8). Most of the letters are addressed to a number of Greek communities with which Brutus had dealings during the civil war. Their authenticy has been much debated: whatever view one may take on this point, these letters were seen in antiquity as credible examples of how a Roman commander might conceivably address a Greek community in the late Republican context. Brutus' language revolves heavily on the themes of loyalty and obedience, and starkly emphasizes the pressures under which cities found themselves in the age of the civil wars, especially in provincial contexts.

The text printed here follows the recent edition in C. P. Jones, 'The Greek Letters Ascribed to Brutus', *Harvard Studies in Classical Philology* 108 (2015) 195-244.

C10 Opposition to triumviral assignments in Italy, 41 BC

Meanwhile, as soon as Caesar had left Sentinum and Gaius Furnius, who was defending the walls, had set off and pursued him a long distance, Rufus unexpectedly attacked those who were inside, and captured the city, sacked and burned it down. The people of Nursia came to terms without having suffered any ill treatment; when, however, after burying those who had fallen in the battle they had had with Caesar, they inscribed on their tombs that they had died struggling for their liberty, they were fined by a huge sum, so that they abandoned their city and at the same time all their territory.

Cassius Dio, *Roman History* 48.13.6

In 41 BC Octavian had to address significant opposition to the land assignments that the agreement underpinning the triumvirate entailed: the city of Nursia in Sabine country was a hub of especially staunch resistance, and took on Octavian's army in open battle (for the early stages of the operations in Sabine and Umbria cf. 48.13.2). Octavian did not pursue the destruction of the city, and accepted an agreement at first: their decision to set up a memorial in honour of those who had lost their lives in battle, however, prompted a harsh reaction on his part. Dissenting voices had to be silenced, whether by imposing terms of peace or by sheer repression. – The neighbouring city of Perusia, which L. Antonius and his associates had elected as their base, suffered an even grimmer fate: it was captured, destroyed by fire, and most of its inhabitants were killed (48.14). The civil war of 49/47 took place mainly outside Italy; the conflicts of the triumviral period had a much stronger impact on the peninsula. For the second time in two years, an Italian city gave its name to a war: the 'War of Perusia', after the 'War of Mutina' of 43 BC (see above, **B176**).

C11   Lead sling-shot from Perusia, 41/40 BC

Octavius, you suck cock. Legion X, Equestrian.

CIL 11.6721.9a = Ashmolean Latin Inscriptions 428 = EDCS-47900410

The text (FELAS / OCTAVI / LE X E) of this sling-shot launched by the soldiers of the Tenth Legion, besieged by Octavian's forces at Perusia, has recently been re-read. It shows opponents of Octavian using his original name, 'Octavius', rather than the name 'Caesar' he claimed, accompanied by a Latin obscenity. See http://blogs.ashmolean.org/latininscriptions/2016/12/21/felas-octavi-the-roman-bullet-that-changed-sides-podcast-9/

C12   Octavian and the Italian sanctuaries, 41 BC

Thus the negotiations failed: Octavian and Lucius had resolved upon war and by now issued bitter edicts against each other. Lucius had an army of six legions of infantry, which he had recruited when he took up his consulship, and Antony had eleven, which were under the command of Calenus; they were all in Italy. Octavian had four legions at Capua, and the praetorian cohorts about his person. Salvidienus led six more legions from Spain. Lucius had financial resources from Antony's provinces, where there was not a state of war. But war was raging in all the provinces that fell within Octavian's remit, except Sardinia; for that reason he borrowed money from the temples, graciously promising to return it – from the Capitoline temple at Rome, from those of Antium, of Lanuvium, of Nemi, and of Tibur, in which cities there are to this day the most plentiful repositories of sacred money.

Appian, *Civil Wars* 5.24

Appian devotes an important section of book 5 of the *Civil Wars* to the War of Perusia (5.14-49), in which the scale of the conflict emerges very powerfully: the fund-raising effort that Octavian undertook before starting the campaign is revealing of how demanding it was likely to prove. His control over Italy enabled him to access the resources of a number of major sanctuaries, which were not merely important religious centres, but significant economic players in their own right, typically in control of considerable land resources and immune from taxation. While seizing their assets would have amounted to a religious offence, borrowing them in order to fund a campaign was an acceptable, or at least defensible, practice. – Q. Salvidienus Rufus was at the time one of Octavian's closest associates. He took part in the war against the Liberators, was put in chage of Spain, and was then recalled to Italy when the Perusine War began. He eventually fell from grace and was sentenced to death in 40 BC, in the aftermath of the Brundisium agreement, after trying to defect to Antony.

C13   Reconciliation between Octavian and Antony, *aureus*, September 40 BC

Obv: Head of Octavian right, bearded
CAESAR, IMP [*imperator*].
Rev: Head of Antony right.; behind,
ANTONIVS, IMP [*imperator*]

RRC 529/1 = Ghey, Leins & Crawford 2010, 529.1.2 = BM 1864,1128.229

After the Perusine War, and months of grave tensions between Octavian and Antony, which seemed likely to lead to a wider, fuller military confrontation, the two men met at Brundisium and initiated talks, heeding the call of their entourages, and more widely of their armies, who wanted a reconciliation; the outcome was an agreement under which Octavian controlled the West, Antony the East, and Lepidus North Africa. The reconciliation was celebrated in several coin issues. This *aureus* features the portraits of Octavian and Antony, but no longer refers to their position as triumvirs; the emphasis is on their role as military commanders. Constitutional realities are increasingly less significant.

C14   A letter of Octavian to Plarasa/Aphrodisias, 39–38 BC
[? Imperator Caesar, son of Divus Julius, designated consul] for the second and [the third] time, (one) of the Triumvirs for settling the *res publica*, to the magistrates, council and people of the Plarasans and Aphrodisians, greetings. If you are well it would be good; I too am in good health, together with the army. Solon, son of Demetrius, your ambassador, who has taken the greatest care over the business of your city, has not only been satisfied by the administrative arrangements that have been made, but has also urged us to send you from the public records these copies of the edict, the decree of the Senate, the treaty, and the law that relate to you. For this I praised him, approved him the more, held him as one of my acquaintances and gave him the appropriate privileges, thinking him deserving of honour from us; and I congratulate you on the possession of such a citizen. The copies of the privileges that relate to you that are subjoined; I wish you to register them among your public records. Letters of Caesar.

Aphrodisias and Rome, no. 6

This inscription tells a story that is in many ways the reverse of the scenario sketched by the letters of Brutus (**C9**): not one of punishment and retaliation, but one of loyalty and rewards. It is the opening text of a series of documents that were received by the city of Plarasa/Aphrodisias in the Triumviral period, confirming the connection of the community with Octavian and restating an impressive set of privileges. The connection between the goddess Aphrodite and the *gens* Julia plays a central role in shaping the connection with a city that is so obviously linked with the cult of the goddess. – It is likely that this letter was written by Octavian (the opening section of the text no longer survives, and had to be supplemented): the reference to the army is noteworthy. A leading citizen of Aphrodisias who acted as a diplomatic intermediary with Octavian is credited with a central role. The letter was eventually inscribed and displayed in public; the text in which we read it is a copy that was inscribed and put on display in the early third century AD.

C15   The changing position of Sextus Pompey, Summer 44 – end of 43

a) Antony also proposed that Sextus Pompey, the son of Pompey the Great, still much loved by everyone, should be recalled from Spain, where he was still under attack by Caesar's praetors, and that he should be paid millions of Attic drachmas from the public treasury in compensation for his father's confiscated property, and be appointed commander of the sea, just as his father had been, in charge of the Roman ships, wherever situated, for immediate service. The astonished Senate accepted each of these decrees with enthusiasm and commended Antony the whole day long; for nobody seemed to them to be more devoted to the republic than Magnus, and hence nobody was more sorely missed.

Appian, *Civil Wars* 3.4

b) These are instances of the extreme misfortunes that occurred to the proscribed: instances in which some were saved against all expectation and at a later period raised to distinguished positions are more pleasant to me to relate, and will be more useful to my readers, as they show that they should never despair, but that hope will always remain to them. Some (those who were able to do so) fled to Cassius or to Brutus, or to Africa, where Cornificius upheld the republican cause (*demokratía*). Most of them, however, went to Sicily, because of its proximity to Italy, and because Sextus Pompey was glad to receive them. He showed the most admirable commitment on behalf of those unfortunate men, sending envoys that invited everybody to come to him, and offering to those who could save the proscribed, both slaves and free people, twice as much the rewards that had been offered for killing them. His small boats and merchant ships met those who were escaping by sea, and his triremes sailed along the shore, making signals to those wandering there, and saving whomever they happened to find. Sextus himself met the new arrivals and provided them right away with clothing and other necessary items. To those among them who were worthy he assigned tasks in his army and his fleet. Later, when he started negotiating with the triumvirs, he did not strike a treaty without including in it those who had found shelter with him. In this way he was most useful to his unfortunate motherland, and from this he gained a high reputation of his own, in addition to that which he had inherited from his father, and not inferior to it.

Appian, *Civil Wars* 4.36

c) [17.1] For Sextus, having left Spain at the time already referred to in accordance with his agreement with Lepidus, had been appointed admiral a little later, and, although he had been removed from office by Caesar, he nevertheless held on to his fleet and made the bold resolution to sail to Italy. However, when Caesar's associates had secured control of Italy, [2] he learned that he had been convicted as one of the murderers of Caesar's father, he stayed clear of the mainland, but sailed about among the islands, keeping a close watch on the events and securing food supplies without resorting to crimes; for, since he had not taken part in the assassination, he expected to be rehabilitated by Caesar himself. [3] However, when his name was actually posted on the tablet and he gathered that the proscription edict applied to him too, he abandoned any hope of being restored by Caesar, and made preparations for war. He built triremes, welcomed the deserters, drew the pirates to his side, and took up the protection of the exiles. [4] By these means he became powerful in a short time, and seized control of the sea off Italy; he raided its harbours, towed away the ships, and carried out plundering raids. Since these activities went well for him, and enabled him to obtain soldiers and money, he sailed to Sicily and got hold Mylae and Tyndaris without a struggle, although he was driven away from Messana by Pompeius Bithynicus, who was then in charge of Sicily. [5] Nonetheless, he did not withdraw altogether from it, but attacked the region, prevented the importation of supplies, and won over those who came to the rescue of the Sicilians by inducing in them the fear of suffering a similar fate, and by ambushing others and harming them. He also formed a connection with the quaestor, and got hold of his funds; finally he took Messana, and Bithynicus too, on the understanding that he should have equal authority to him. [6] He did not harm Bithynicus at the time, but he took away arms and money from the citizens. Next he won over Syracuse and some other cities, and gathered more soldiers and a very strong fleet from those. Quintus Cornificius also sent him a force from Africa.

Cassius Dio, *Roman History* 48.17

The coalition that had rallied around Pompey came to an end shortly after Pharsalus. However, Pompey's sons, Gnaeus and Sextus, retained a strong position in Spain, where they fought a war against Caesar in early 45 (see **B159c**). Gnaeus lost his life in that campaign, while Sextus continued the struggle: after the Ides of March, his rehabilitation became part of a wider reconciliation attempt between Caesarians and Liberators (a). He was entrusted by the Senate with the charge of the fleet and the protection of coastal Italy: his control over the sea soon turned into a long-term strategic asset. However, in November 43 he was included in the proscriptions list: his strong military presence in Sicily enabled him to draw the energies of many of the proscribed, and to gain control over sea communications between the island and Rome, and notably of the corn supply of the city (b) and (c). Against all odds, within a few years Sextus and his alternative state became a political and military force that the triumvirs had to reckon with. The shifts in his political and legal predicament (from runaway to lawful holder of an official post, from proscribed to recognized political partner of the triumvirs) are powerful testimony to unstable nature of politics in the triumviral period, and to the weight that control over military forces had in that context.

C16   *denarius* of Sextus Pompey, 43–40 BC

Obv: Head of Neptune, right; hair tied with band, with trident over shoulder
        MAG.PIVS.IMP.ITER. [Magnus Pius, *imperator* twice]
Rev: Trophy with trident above and anchor below, prow-stem on left and
        ornamental stern on right, two heads of Scylla at the base
        PRAEF.CLAS.ET.ORAE.MARIT.EX.S.C [prefect of the fleet and of the
        maritime coast by decree of the Senate]

RRC 511/2b = Ghey, Leins & Crawford 2010, 511.2,4 = BM 2002,0102.4791

Sextus Pompey's coinage is not just testimony to the financial and logistical significance of the structure that he had established in Sicily and Sardinia. It also sheds light upon the ways in which Sextus defined and represented his own position. This legend of this issue stresses that he had received the official task of overseeing the coastline of Italy and the fleet by the Roman Senate in the aftermath of the Ides; it also shows that he had inherited his father's name, *Magnus* (Great), whilst also using another one, *Pius* (Pious): the pointer to military distinction was accompanied by an assertion of piety towards the gods. Perhaps unsurprisingly, the deity with which Sextus asserted a special connection was Neptune: a fitting acknowledgement of the importance that his fleet and his maritime achievements had in securing him an influential position.

C17   The pact of Misenum, Summer 39 BC

[1] Now Sextus Pompey was holding Sicily, was ravaging Italy, and, with his many pirate ships, which were under the command of Menas the pirate and Menecrates, had made the sea unsafe for sailing. However, he was thought to be well disposed towards Antony, since he had given shelter to Antony's mother when she fled from Rome with Fulvia, and it was decided to make terms with him. [2] They met him at the promontory and mole of Misenum, near the sites where Pompey's fleet was anchored, and the forces of Antony and Caesar were drawn up. [3] After it had been agreed that Pompey should have Sardinia and Sicily, should keep the sea clear of robbers, and should send to Rome an agreed amount of grain, they invited each other to dinner.

Plutarch, *Life of Antony* 32.1–3

In the summer of 39 a short-lived reconciliation was reached between the triumvirs and Sextus Pompey: his control over Sicily and Sardinia received official confirmation, while he agreed to fulfil some obligations on the grain supply of the city of Rome and the policing of the Central Mediterranean. The agreement was not based on any consideration of principle, of course: it recognized the overall strategic situation, and brought some respite to the increasingly difficult situation in Rome and Italy. – Antony's mother, Julia Antonia, had fled Italy with Fulvia after the war of Perusia. During the proscriptions she sheltered her brother Lucius, who had been included in the triumvirs' list, and she eventually secured his pardon by sternly confronting Antony himself: see Appian, *Civil Wars* 4.37.

C18   The government of Sextus Pompey, Lilybaeum (modern Marsala), Sicily.

Under Magnus Pompey Pius son of Magnus, imperator, augur, consul designate, L. Plinius Rufus, son of Lucius, *legatus pro praetore*, praetor designate, supervised the building of the gate and towers.

ILLRP 426 = EDCS-14700098*

It would be misguided to dismiss Sextus Pompey as the leader of a 'pirate state': he was in charge of a significant portion of the Mediterranean World for nearly a decade, and he was also involved with the demands of government. This inscription records a public work carried out by his associate Plinius Rufus in the city of Lilybaeum some time after the Misenum agreement. – Cicero had served as quaestor in that same town nearly four decades earlier.

C19   Gaius Caesar Octavianus, son of a god

Obv: Head of Octavian, bearded, right
        CAESAR, DIVI.F. [Caesar, son of a god]
Rev: Wreathed head of Caesar, right
        DIVOS IVLIVS [Divus Julius]

RRC 535 = Ghey, Leins & Crawford 2010, 535.1.4 = BM 1872,0709.433

This bronze coin issue from the triumviral period stresses a point that is often voiced in Octavian's political discourse: his loyalty to the memory of Julius Caesar is not just a political statement and an example of his filial piety, but has implications that are greatly advantageous to the triumvir, as they stress his direct connection with a god. It is not by chance that Antony did not show any interest in continuing the cult of Divus Julius in the aftermath of the Ides of March: he knew what benefits it could yield to his rival. The formation of the triumvirate, which had the loyalty to Caesar as its central political and moral justification, made the revival and further promotion of the cult an inescapable necessity – and one that turned into Octavian's favour.

C20   Renewal of triumvirate, 37 BC

The triumvirate set up by the *lex Titia* (see **C1**) lapsed on 1 Jan 37, though the triumvirs continued informally in office, as agreed by Antony and Octavian in the summer and authorized retrospectively later that year. Suet. *Aug.* 27.1 agrees with Augustus about a 10-year continuous period.

a) [37 BC] M. Aemilius [Lepidus], son of M(arcus) [II], M. Antonius, son of M(arcus) II, Imp(erator) Caesar [son] of Divus, [IIIvirs for settling the *res publica]*

Fasti Capitolini Consulares (Capitoline Consul List) = *Inscr. Ital.* 13.1.59 =
EJ page 33

b) I was one of the triumvirs for settling the *res publica* for ten consecutive years.

Res Gestae 7.1

c) To M(arcus) Lepidus, three times hailed as Imperator, pontifex maximus, IIIvir for s(ettling) the *r(es) p(ublica)* for a second time, twice consul, patron [of the colony], by decree of the town councillors (*decuriones*).

ILLRP 1276 = EDCS-13302651

d) Imperator Caesar, consul designate for a third time, twice IIIvir for settling the *res publica*, built the wall and towers.

EDCS-04600006* = *Inscr.Ital.* 10.4.21

Inscription from the port city of Tergeste (Trieste, NE Italy), datable from Octavian's titles, to 33 BC.

C21   War between Sextus Pompey and Octavian

[4] At this time, and even earlier, Sextus and Caesar went to war with one another: for since they had made their agreement, neither of their own free will nor by choice, but by necessity, they did not respect it at any point in time, but immediately quarrelled, having broken the truce. [5] They would have gone to war in any case, even if they had not found any pretext: their causes, however, were the following. Menas, who was still in Sardinia at the time, like a sort of praetor, was suspected by Sextus because of the release of Helenus, and because he had been in touch with Caesar. He was also being slandered by people of his own rank, as they were jealous of his power. [6] Therefore, he was summoned by Sextus, the pretext being that he should give an account on the grain and the money of which he had been in charge. He did not obey, but he captured and killed the men that had been sent for that purpose; then, after negotiating with Caesar, he delivered him the island, the fleet along with the army, and himself. [7] Caesar was pleased to see him, because he said that the Sextus was giving refuge to deserters in violation of the agreements, was building triremes, and had garrisons in Italy. Not only did he not give up Menas on Sextus' request, but went even further and held him in great honour, decorated him with golden rings, and enrolled him in the equestrian order.

Cassius Dio, *Roman History* 48.45.1–7

The Misenum agreement recognized the strength of Sextus Pompey and secured a short-term stabilization of the Western and Central Mediterranean. However, Cassius Dio, our best-informed source for this period, is very clear that the conflict between Octavian (then in charge of Italy) and Sextus was inevitable. The defection of Menas is merely a twist that precipitates developments. – Menas (also known as Menodorus) was a freedman of Sextus: he belongs in a series of naval commanders of Greek origin that are attested in the late Republican period, when it was still common for Rome to resort to the expertise of Greek officers in sea warfare (see **L26** for the case of Asclepiades of Clazomenae in the Social War, and the position of Seleucus of Rhosus, who was awarded the Roman citizenship and a number of privileges by Octavian for his involvement in the war against Sextus: *RDGE* no. 58).

C22   Sextus Pompey's escape, 36 BC

Pompey was informed about the defection of the infantry while he was on the road. He changed his attire from that of a commander to that of a private citizen and sent orders to Messana to put on board of the ships whatever could be put. It had all been prepared long before. He summoned Plenius from Lilybaeum in a hurry, with the eight legions that he had, with a view to fleeing with those. Plenius hurried to obey his instructions, but other friends, garrisons, and soldiers were deserting, and the enemy was sailing into the strait. Pompey did not wait even for Plenius in the well-fortified city, and fled from Messana, with his seventeen ships, towards Antony, as he had had saved his mother in similar circumstances.

Appian, *Civil Wars* 5.122

After meeting a crushing defeat at Naulochus, in which Octavian's close friend M. Vipsanius Agrippa played a crucial role, Sextus Pompey fled with his warships, hoping to reach Asia Minor and to be able to persuade Antony to join forces against Octavian. The parallel with his father's escape from the battlefield at Pharsalus (see **B156c**) is obvious, and yet left implicit: note the detail of the change of attire. Sextus' plan would soon prove unviable: he was captured the following year by Amyntas, a governor of Antony, and executed shortly afterwards. – Appian, *Civil Wars* 5.143 relates the events and has a balanced assessment of his historical achievements and significance. – The 'Plenius' (*Plenios*) mentioned by Appian is the L. Plenius Rufus mentioned in the inscription from Lilybaeum (see **C18**).

C23   The fall of Lepidus, 36 BC

[11.2] Lepidus attacked Messana and, after being let into the town, set fire to part of it and pillaged other parts. When Caesar, having ascertained this, quickly arrived and put up resistance, Lepidus came out of the city in fear; he set his camp on a strong hill, and voiced grievances about the treatment he had received. He set out all the slights that he thought he was receiving, [3] demanded all the rights that had been granted to him according to the terms of their first alliance, and lay his claim on Sicily, on the grounds that he had taken part in its conquest. He sent some men to Caesar with these grievances, and called upon him to accept an arbitration: [4] he had the forces that he had brought over from Africa, those that had been left behind in Messana, as he had been the first to enter the city and had mooted to them some hope of a political change.

[12.1] Caesar, however, did not respond to that, but, since he felt that justice was entirely on his side and in his weapons, being stronger than Lepidus, he immediately moved against him with a few men, with the aim of shocking him with that sudden action, as Lepidus lacked any energy, and of winning over his soldiers. [2] He got into their camp, as they formed the impression that he was coming in peace, on account of the small number of men that surrounded him. However, as he spoke in way that was not to their liking, they got angry and attacked him, even killing some of his men, although he managed to save his life, having quickly obtained reinforcements. [3] After this, he came against them once again with the whole army, and having enclosed them within their entrenchment, he began a siege. Fearing capture, and without starting a collective revolt, on account of their respect for Lepidus, they privately deserted him in groups, as individuals, and changed their loyalty. Thus he was compelled to become a suppliant to Caesar, on his own initiative, wearing the dress of mourning. [4] He was therefore deprived of any authority, and he could not live in Italy without a guard. As to those who had been involved on Sextus' side, the equestrians and the senators were punished, except for a few, while of the rank and file those of free condition were drafted into Caesar's camp, and those who had been slaves were returned to their masters for punishment; if no master could be found, they were impaled. As for the cities, some surrendered voluntarily and received a pardon; those who resisted were punished.

Cassius Dio, *Roman History* 49.11–12

A dry account of the events that led up to the breach in relations between Octavian and Lepidus, in the aftermath of the victory against Sextus: as soon as Lepidus was deserted by his soldiers, his political position was untenable, and his influence had vanished. Remarkably, Octavian let him retain the senior religious post of *pontifex maximus* until his death, in 13 BC, devising sophisticated methods to enable the activity of the pontifical college without requiring his direct involvement. The brief notice on the fate encountered by the supporters of Sextus is also significant: the decision to return the slaves to their masters is intended as a strong message that law and order are being restored (cf. **B42b** on Pompey's massacre of the runaway slaves at the end of the Spartacus War). – The city of Messana (modern Messina) is on the strait that separates Sicily from the Italian peninsula.

C24   The rise of P. Ventidius Bassus, consul suff. 36 BC

After the conquest of Asculum, Cn. Pompeius, father of Pompey the Great, subjected P. Ventidius, still a child, to the eyes of the people at his triumph. This is the Ventidius who later celebrated a triumph in Rome over the Parthians and, through the Parthians, over the shade of Crassus that lay miserably on enemy soil. In the same way in which as a captive he had shuddered at the prison, as a victor he filled the Capitol with his good fortune. He was also extraordinary in having been elected praetor and consul in the same year.

Valerius Maximus, Memorable Deeds and Sayings 6.9.9

The triumviral period marks the emergence of a number of individuals of great military ability, mostly of municipal origin, who obtained high office in spite of being of their rather undistinguished background: Q. Salvidienus Rufus, T. Statilius Taurus, and M. Vipsanius Agrippa. P. Ventidius Bassus was one of Antony's most trusted associates, and obtained major success against the Parthians in 38 BC; he also reached the office of consul suffect in 36 BC. He was the son of one of the leaders of the Italian coalition that had taken on Rome in 91 BC, and as a child had been displayed in the triumph of Cn. Pompeius Strabo in 89: the extraordinary path that took him to high office and enabled him to celebrate his own triumph did not fail to command interest, and is revealing of the scale of political and social change that late Republican Italy went through in barely more than half a century.

C25   The encounter between Antony and Cleopatra, 41 BC

As he was making preparations for the Parthian war, he sent to Cleopatra, ordering her to meet him in Cilicia, in order to make answer to the charges that were levelled at her of raising and giving to Cassius a large amount of money for the war. However, Dellius, Antony's envoy, when he saw Cleopatra's appearance, and noticed her brilliance and cleverness in conversation, immediately perceived that Antony would not so much as think of doing such a woman any harm, but that she would acquire the greatest standing with him. He therefore resorted to subservience, and to inducing the Egyptian to go to Cilicia 'decked out in finery' (as Homer would say [*Iliad 14.162*]), and not to be afraid of Antony, who was the most agreeable and humane of commanders. She was persuaded by Dellius, and judging by the proofs which she had previously had through her associations with Gaius Caesar and Gnaeus, the son of Pompey, she hoped that she would more easily conquer Antony. For those men had known her when she was still a girl and inexperienced in affairs, but she was going to visit Antony at the very time when women have the most brilliant beauty and are at the peak of their intellectual power. Therefore she provided herself with many gifts, much money, and such ornaments as her high standing and prosperous kingdom made it reasonable for her to take, but she left putting her greatest confidence in herself, and in the magical arts and charms of her own person.

[26] Although she received many letters of summons both from Antony and from his friends, she so despised and laughed at the man as to sail up the river Cydnus in a barge with gilded poop, its sails spread purple, the rowers pulling back their silver oars to the music of flutes, accompanied by pipes and lyres. She reclined beneath a canopy embroidered with gold, adorned like Aphrodite in a painting, while boys like Cupids in paintings stood on either side and fanned her. Likewise the most beautiful of her servants, attired like Nereids and Graces, were also stationed, some at the rudder handles, and others at the ropes of the sails. Wonderful perfumes from many incense offerings spread along the river banks. Of the inhabitants, some escorted her on both sides, directly from the river, while others came down from the city to behold the sight. The crowd in the marketplace gradually streamed away, until finally Antony, seated on his tribunal, was left alone. And a rumour spread everywhere that Aphrodite had come to Dionysus for the good of Asia.

Plutarch, Life of Antony 25–26

The first encounter between Antony and Cleopatra readily turns into much more than a diplomatic conference between a Roman magistrate and the queen of a vassal state: the Egyptian queen stages a masterly performance, in which the weight of a long-standing tradition of political and religious ceremonials at the court of Alexandria played a central role. Antony had also been receiving divine honours in the Greek East, as Pompey and Caesar had before him: ruler-cult had been a strong local tradition throughout the Hellenistic period. The meeting was thererefore also the encounter between two gods: Plutarch stresses the impact it had on those that witnessed it, whilst also depicting it as the beginning of a personal association between the Roman magistrate and the Egyptian queen, which would shape the history of the following decade, and in which Cleopatra puts her seductive powers to the service of a bold and ambitious political strategy. – There is no mention of her looks in Plutarch's account: the emphasis is on her conversation and intellectual power.

C26   Conflicting accounts, 35–33 BC

[54] As for Octavia, she was thought to have been treated in an insulting manner; when she returned from Athens, Caesar ordered her to reside in her own house. However, she refused to leave the house of her husband: she even asked Caesar himself, unless on other grounds he had resolved to wage war upon Antony, to ignore Antony's treatment of her, since it would be an unspeakable thing for the two greatest commanders to plunge the Romans into civil war, the one for the love of a woman, and the other out of resentment on behalf of another. These were her words, and she confirmed them by her actions. For she lived in their house, just as if he were there, and she looked after his children, not only those to whom she herself had given birth, but also those of Fulvia, in a noble and splendid manner; she also received such friends of Antony as were sent to Rome to seek office or on business, and helped them to obtain from Caesar whatever they needed. Without meaning it, however, she was damaging Antony with this conduct, for he was hated for wronging such a woman. He was also hated for the distribution which he made to his children at Alexandria: it was regarded as spectacular and arrogant, and to betray a hatred of Rome. After filling the gymnasium with a crowd and placing on a tribunal of silver two thrones of gold, one for himself and the other for Cleopatra, and other lower thrones for his sons, first he declared Cleopatra Queen of Egypt, Cyprus, Libya, and Coele Syria, and that she was to share her regal power with Caesarion. Caesarion was believed to be a son of the former Caesar, by whom Cleopatra was left pregnant. Secondly, he proclaimed his own sons by Cleopatra Kings of Kings: to Alexander he assigned Armenia, Media and Parthia (when he should have subdued it), to Ptolemy Phoenicia, Syria, and Cilicia. At the same time he also presented his sons: Alexander in Median garb, which included a tiara and an upright turban, Ptolemy in military boots, cloak, and a woolen hat carrying a diadem. For the latter was the dress of the kings who came after Alexander, the former that of the Median and Armenian kings. When the boys had embraced their parents, one was given a bodyguard of Armenians, the other of Macedonians. Cleopatra, indeed, both then and at other times, assumed in her public appearances a robe sacred to Isis, and was addressed as New Isis.

[55] By disclosing these things to the Senate and by frequently denouncing them before the people, Caesar tried to rouse the crowd against Antony. Antony, too, kept sending counter-accusations against him. The main allegations he made were, in the first place, that after taking Sicily from Pompey Caesar had not assigned a part of the island to him; secondly, that after borrowing ships from him for the war he had not returned them; thirdly, that after ejecting his colleague Lepidus from office and stripping him of any distinction, he was keeping for himself the army, the territory, and the revenues that had been assigned to Lepidus; finally, that he had colonized

almost the whole of Italy to the advantage of his own soldiers, and had left nothing to the soldiers of Antony.

Plutarch, *Life of Antony* 54–55

When the relationship between Cleopatra and Antony began, he was married to Fulvia; it continued even after her death (40 BC) and his marriage with Octavia, the sister of Octavian, which was decided shortly afterwards in an effort to revive the faltering alliance between the two men. Antony's treatment of Octavia was readily exploited by Octavian as evidence that he had lost sight of traditional Roman virtues and had entered an alliance with a foreign monarch: it turned into a powerful argument in favour of Octavian's claim to the status of champion and protector of Rome and Italy, and of the attempt to depict Antony as the enemy of the *res publica*. Accounts of Antony's lifestyle at the court of Alexandria played a crucial role, and the story of the so-called 'Donation of Alexandria', in which Antony had allegedly distributed the empire among Cleopatra and his children, was the centerpiece of that attempt. Antony did respond to those allegations, placing the emphasis on Octavian's disloyalty: it is a safe guess that, had he won at Actium, a very different story of Octavian's conduct in the Thirties would have survived to posterity. – It is noteworthy, though not altogether surprising, that Antony's treatment of Octavia and Cleopatra played such a significant role in the *political* case that was mounted against him. His private life was, in fact, a highly political matter: throughout the Republican period the dividing lines between the two domains had been very different to what we are accustomed in modern times. – According to Suetonius, *Life of Augustus* 69.2, Mark Antony confronted Octavian on his own sexual conduct in a private letter, which he sent some time before the breakdown in their relationship and to which the biographer had access: he admitted in very explicit terms his liaison with Cleopatra, and went on to list the names of several mistresses of his ally, rival, and soon-to-be enemy. In making that point, Antony was also denying that Cleopatra could in any way be regarded as his wife.

C27   War declaration, 32 BC

This led the Romans, who were indignant, to believe that the other reports in circulation were also true: that, if Antony should win, he would bestow their city upon Cleopatra and transfer the seat of the empire to Egypt. And they became so angry at this that everybody, not only Antony's enemies or those who were not siding with either man, but even his closest friends, condemned him severely; for in their displeasure at what was being read and in their eagerness to counter Caesar's suspicion towards them, they spoke in the same way as the rest. They deprived him of the consulship, to which he had been elected, and of all his authority. They did not formally declare him an enemy, because they feared that his associates would also have to be regarded as enemies, should they not abandon him. However, by this action they showed their attitude more forcefully than with any other means. They voted pardon and praise to those who had taken his side if they would abandon him, and declared war outright on Cleopatra, put on their military cloaks, as if he were close at hand, and went to the temple of Bellona, where they performed all the rites preliminary to war in the customary fashion through Caesar as fetial priest. These were formally against Cleopatra, but in fact against Antony.

Cassius Dio, *Roman History* 50.4.4–5

The association between Antony and Cleopatra provided Octavian with a compelling argument in mobilizing support across Italy: he shrewdly depicted it as a threat to the survival of the empire (notably by envisaging the move of the capital from Rome to Alexandria), and argued that what was looming was not a civil war, but a conflict against a foreign power, and a monarchic one at that. The point was further impressed by the choice to give a central role in the process that led to the war declaration to an ancient priesthood, the *fetiales*, who were traditionally in charge of the ceremonies that opened and concluded a war: Octavian joined that priestly college and carried out a ritual outside the temple of Bellona in that capacity. As Octavian did on many other occasions, religious tradition (whether genuine or invented) was put to the service of highly bold, and indeed subversive, political operations.

C28   The coinage of Antony and Cleopatra, 32 BC

Obv: Head of Mark Antony right; behind, Armenian tiara
ANTONI.ARMENIA.DEVICTA [Of Antony, after the conquest of Armenia]
Rev: Bust of Cleopatra, right, draped and wearing diadem; before, prow
CLEOPATRAE.REGINAE.REGVM.FILIORVM.REGVM. [Of Cleopatra, queen of kings and of sons of kings]

RRC 543/1 = Ghey, Leins & Crawford 2010, 543.1.3 = BM TC, p237.2 CleMA

As ever, when a war effort is looming suitable amounts of coinage must be produced: this coin issue, which was produced by Antony's mint, shows that the association between him and Cleopatra was publicly and officially asserted by the late thirties. The legends are in Latin, suggesting that this coinage was chiefly intended to be used by Antony's troops: his victories in Armenia (34-33 BC) are given emphasis, while Cleopatra's regal status is compounded by the mention of the 'sons of kings', a category that includes Caesarion, the son of Cleopatra and Julius Caesar, and the children she had had with Antony. The preoccupations and aims that appear to underpin the so-called Donation of Alexandria emerge here. Stressing the importance of Caesarion, Caesar's natural son, was also a chance to further undermine the position of Caesar's adoptive son, Octavian.

C29   The oath of Italy, 32 BC

The whole of Italy of its own accord swore an oath of allegiance to me, and demanded me as its commander for the war in which I conquered at Actium. The Gallic and Spanish provinces, Africa, Sicily and Sardinia swore the same oath of allegiance.

Augustus, *Res Gestae* 25.2

Octavian carried out a masterful political operation in the build-up of the war against Antony and Cleopatra: he presented it as a conflict with an external enemy, the Egyptian queen, effectively overshadowing the fact that it was, first and foremost, a civil war. The promotion of the traditional Roman and Italian values against the corrupt ways of a foreign monarch and her degenerate Roman associate was at the core of the case he built: the oath that all the communities of Italy and of the Western province made in 32, declaring their allegiance to him, played a major role in corroborating it. The prominent role it has in Augustus' overview of his achievement, published only after his death in AD 14, is further proof of the significance it had in his strategy: far from being a mere political statement, it was a solemn political and religious act that bound the civilian people of Italy and the province to his cause on a deep personal level, as if they were serving in arms under him. – On this phase of the war preparations see also Cassius Dio, *Roman History* 50.6, who conveys a clear sense of how large and ambitious the war effort was.

C30   Octavian and the political élite, 32 BC

[4] But Caesar was encouraged by this, and wished to make use as soon as possible of the enthusiasm of his army, which was magnificently trained, and to wage war in Greece near his rival's strongholds, rather than in Italy and in the vicinity of Rome. [5] Therefore he gathered at Brundisium all his troops of any value, and all the men of influence, senators and equestrians alike: he wished to make the soldiers cooperate

with him and keep the others from starting a rebellion, as they might do if left by
themselves, but mainly with the aim of showing to the whole world that the largest
and strongest element among the Romans were in sympathy with himself. [6] From
Brundisium he ordered to all of them to take along a set number of servants and also
(soldiers excepted) to carry with them their own supplies. He then crossed the Ionian
Sea with the whole contingent. He was not leading them to the Peloponnese or against
Antony, but towards Actium, where the greater part of his rival's fleet was docked,
to see if he could anticipate Antony by gaining possession of it, willing or unwilling.

Cassius Dio, *Roman History* 50.11.4–12.1

As he is getting ready for the campaign that will lead to the victory at Actium and the annexation of Egypt,
Octavian rallies the support of the 'men of influence' in Italy, as well as of his army: the strict instructions
that he gives them on the number of servants and the amount of supplies that they are expected to bring
with them shows how his position is no longer that of a commander who gathers the support of his peers
within the senatorial élite, as would have been the case even for the best part of the first century BC, but that
of a leader who is in a position to dictate the terms on which his associates are to lend their support to him.

C31   Octavian's victory at Actium, 2 September 31 BC

At the centre you could see the fleets, wrought in bronze,   675
And the Actian war, there see the battle-lines drawn,
And all Leucate boiling with war, and the waves sparkling with gold.
On one side was Augustus Caesar, leading the Italians
To battle together with Senate and People, the Penates
And the great gods, standing on the high poop, while from his brow   680
Twin flames shot joyfully upward, and on his helmet his father's star appeared.
On the other wing, Agrippa, with the winds and the gods on his side,
Stood aloft, leading his line, and – that proud badge of war –
His temples adorned with the ships' beaks of the naval crown
On the other side, with barbarous arms and a motley array,   685
Antony, returned in conquest from the eastern peoples and the Red Sea,
Brought Egypt into the battle, the might of the Orient, far-away Bactria,
While (for shame!) an Egyptian wife followed behind.
The fleets charged into battle; the whole sea foamed,
Shattered with oar strokes and the bow-waves of three-toothed prows.   690
They made for open water. Now you would think that the isles of the Cyclades,
Torn loose, were sailing the seas or mountains colliding in battle
With towering mountains – so vast were the turreted decks of the ships,
On which men hastened to battle. Blazing tow and flying steel
Were scattered everywhere by hands and weapons, while with fresh   695
Slaughter Neptune's fields grew red. In the midst the queen summoned
Her squadrons with the Egyptian rattle, but failed even yet
To see the twin snakes waiting at her back. Her gods, misbegotten,
Of every kind, even barking Anubis, ranged against Neptune,
Minerva, and Venus, brandished their armaments. At the heart   700
Of the struggle, engraved in iron, Mars raged, and
From the skies the grim Furies, and Discord, delighting
In her garment divided, ran riot; behind her Bellona

Followed, bloodily flailing. Above and surveying it all,
Actian Apollo was drawing his bow. For terror of this, all,   715
Egyptian and Indian, Arab and Sabaean, were turning to flight.
The queen herself could be seen, having summoned the winds,
To be opening her sails and now, even now, to have loosened the ropes.
Amid carnage, and pale at the prospect of death, the fire-god
Had portrayed her carried along by the waves and the north-west wind.   720
Opposite, the Nile, grieving with his mighty body, was stretching out
His folds and with all his robes was calling back the defeated
To his watery bosom and the secret retreats of his streams.

Virgil, *Aeneid* 8.675–713

There are a number of ancient accounts of the battle of Actium: most claim that Antony bravely fought for victory until the end (Velleius Paterculus, *Histories* 2.84-86; Plutarch, *Life of Antony* 62-68; Florus, *Roman History* 2.21), while Cassius Dio (*Roman History*, 50.11-35, esp. 50.15, 30-4) claims that Cleopatra had persuaded Antony to seek withdrawal by sea before the battle. They all concur, however, in the basic factual point that the battle marked the comprehensive victory of Octavian in the civil war. We find a memorable illustration of the significance of the battle in a passage of Virgil's great epic poem, the *Aeneid*, in which an extensive description is given of the shield that the god Vulcan made for Aeneas, the Trojan prince who went on to found a new city on the shores of Latium from which the founders of Rome will eventually hail (see LACTOR 17, G38, whence this translation is drawn). The shield features scenes of the future history of Rome, and the battle of Actium and Octavian's later triumph have an especially prominent role. There is no place for Antony in this account of the battle: the clash is between Italy and Egypt, between a virtuous military leader and a foreign, monstrously wealthy queen, between the gods of Rome, among whom Apollo is especially prominent, and those of Egypt. The closing reference to the Nile forebodes the conquest of Egypt that will shortly follow the victory at Actium.

C32   Octavian's decisions after Actium, 31 BC

Caesar now punished the cities by seizing their money and taking away what was left of the authority over their citizens that their assemblies still had. He deprived all the princes and kings, except Amyntas and Archelaus, of the territories that they had received from Antony; he also deposed Philopator, the son of Tarcondimotus, Lycomedes, the king of a part of Cappadocian Pontus, and Alexander, the brother of Iamblichus. The latter, because he had secured his kingdom as a reward for accusing his brother, he led in his triumphal procession and afterwards put to death.

Cassius Dio, *Roman History* 51.2.1–2

After Actium Octavian did not pursue the same strategy of systematic clemency that his adoptive father had embraced: the defeat of Mark Antony involved a comprehensive resettlement of the Greek East, where a host of kingdoms on the fringes of the empire were under the control of friends and clients of his defeated rival. Most of them were deposed, and Alexander of Emesa received an especially harsh punishment. (But see also LACTOR 19, M39 for a family tree showing many descendants of Mark Antony ruling over kingdoms friendly to Rome under the Julio-Claudian emperors and beyond.) These measures paved the way for a much more assertive intervention in Egypt, which was carried out in 30 BC: Octavian annexed it to the empire as a province with special status, under the watch of a prefect of equestrian standing, personally appointed by himself.

AN EPILOGUE: THE ADVENT OF MONARCHY

C33   Regime change or restoration?

[1] In my sixth and seventh consulships [28–27 BC], after I had put an end to civil wars, although by everyone's agreement I had power over everything, I transferred the *res publica* from my power to the control of the Roman Senate and people. [2] For this service, I was named Augustus by a decree of the Senate and the doorposts of my house were publicly clothed with laurels, and a civic crown was fastened above my doorway, and a golden shield was set up in the Julian senate-house; through an inscription on this shield the fact was declared that the Roman Senate and people were giving it to me because of my valour, clemency, justice, and piety. After this time I excelled everyone in influence (*auctoritas*), but I had no more power (*potestas*) than the others who were my colleagues in each magistracy.

Augustus, *Res Gestae* 34

In this crucial passage of the long autobiographical text written by the emperor Augustus and published after his death, in August AD 14, the old statesman reflects – speaking in the first person – on the moment that marked the political settlement at the end of a long season of civil war: the power-sharing arrangement between the victor of the war and the Senate, in which Caesar Octavianus' new political and constitutional position was defined, and he acquired a new name, *Augustus*. Remarkably, the man that is rightly regarded as the first Roman emperor denies having created a monarchic regime. His emphasis is on the restoration of the traditional order, in which the Senate and the people have a central role, and magistracies are held by individuals who hold the same degree of power. Augustus shifts the emphasis from his power (*potestas*), which he claims to be no greater than that of any other lawfully elected magistrate, to his influence and prestige (*auctoritas*), which has no rivals: what determines it, though, is precisely his commitment to the traditional constitution, and his willingness not to establish a monarchic regime in Rome. This claim to a commitment to tradition and established constitutional practice, of course, concealed a very different reality, in which Augustus did have unmatched power and influence, and where the basis of his political hegemony was a highly innovative, creative, and indeed subsersive use of unequalled wealth, wide-ranging military power base, and channels of political communication that encompassed the whole Empire.

C34   The end of a regime

In the seven hundred and twenty-fifth year since the foundation of the City, and during the consulship of Caesar Augustus *imperator*, then consul for the fifth time (with Sex. Appuleius), Caesar returned from the East as a conqueror. On the sixth of January, he entered the City in a triple triumph. It was at this time, when all the civil wars had been put to sleep and brought to an end, that he first had the gates of [the temple of] Janus closed. On this day Caesar was first saluted as Augustus. This name, which everyone up to that time had held inviolate and to which other rulers hitherto had laid a claim, signifies that the assumption of the supreme power over the world was allowed by law. From that time on, the highest power of the state resided and remained in one man. The Greeks call this type of government *monarchìa* ('monarchy', 'rule of one').

Orosius, *History against the Pagans* 6.20.1–2

As noted at the outset, any attempt to firmly date the end of the Republic reflects a degree of subjective judgment, and is not immune from potential limitations. 31 BC marks the defeat of Antony and Cleopatra, although their demise did not occur until the following year. The definition of the political and constitutional role of the victor of the civil war, however, was accomplished only in January 27 BC, when a comprehensive power-sharing agreement between Octavian and the Senate was devised: within that complex settlement Octavian was also granted the name *Augustus* (see **C33**). The Christian author Orosius, who wrote a history of Rome that relied heavily on Livy, makes a lucid assessment of the events of 27, and attaches considerable significance to the bestowal of the name: originally an adjective meaning 'consecrated, venerable', the name also established a connection between Octavian and augury, a major aspect of Roman public religion. Interestingly, the new name of Octavian is singled out as a sign that a new regime has emerged, and that the republic has been replaced by a monarchy.

C35   Tacitus surveys the *res publica*

[1.1] At the beginning kings held the city of Rome. Liberty and the consulship were established by Lucius Brutus. Dictatorships were resorted to when occasion required. The power (*potestas*) of the *decemviri* lasted only two years; the consular authority (*ius*) of the military tribunes was short-lived. Cinna's despotism (*dominatio*) was brief, as was Sulla's. The sway (*potentia*) of Pompey and Crassus quickly yielded to Caesar, and the armed might of Lepidus and Antony to Augustus, who, under the name of princeps, took the whole state, exhausted by civil discords, into his rule (*imperium*).

[2.1] After the deaths of Brutus and Cassius, the republic no longer had an army. Pompey had been defeated in Sicily, Lepidus disposed of, and Antony killed. As a result even the Julian side had only Caesar left to lead them. He laid aside the title of triumvir and presented himself as a consul, content to defend the people by virtue of the tribunician power (*ius*). Thereafter, once he had seduced the soldiery with gifts, the people with corn, and everyone with the delights of peace, he gradually increased his power, arrogating to himself the functions of the senate, the magistrates, and the law. He faced no opposition, since the bravest souls had died in battle or fallen victim to proscription, while the surviving nobles enjoyed a wealth and status which increased in proportion to their servility; and having profited by revolution, they preferred present safety to the insecurity of the past. [2.2] The provinces too had little objection to the prevailing state of affairs. They had lost faith in the rule (*imperium*) of the senate and people, having suffered at the hands of rival governors and avaricious magistrates, and having been denied the protection of the laws, which were constantly subverted by violence, intrigue, and finally corruption.

Tacitus, *Annals* 1.1–2, with omission

Tacitus, the great historian of the early Principate, opens his *Annals* with a heavily compressed summary of the demise of the Republic, in which a sequence of men of great influence and ambition is brought to a close by the rise of Octavian: his key ability is identified in his seductive ability and his talent to offer rewards and attractive prospects to different sectors of Roman society, in exchange for their willingness to accept his autocratic rule. The central tradeoff is between the end of political liberty and the advent of a new season of peace and tranquility, after decades of turmoil and violence.

PART 2: KEY THEMES

D. ROME AND ITALY

The story of the Roman empire must be understood against the background of the conquest of Italy and of the integration between Rome and Italy. As we saw in the opening section of this volume, the tensions over the occupation and distribution of land in the Italian peninsula, on the one hand, and the controversy over the inclusion of the Italian Allies into the Roman citizen body, on the other, are the defining issues of the early first century BC. They retain considerable significance throughout the late Republican period, well into the Triumviral period: Octavian bases his case for waging war against Cleopatra and Antony on the need to uphold the values and interests of Italy. This section includes some evidence for the complex relationship between Italy and Rome in the first century BC, notably on the role that local communities carried on playing in an increasingly integrated political context.

D1   Loyalties of a municipal man

[3] *Marcus*: For my part, when it is possible to be away for more days, especially at this time of year, I make for the beauty and the healthy climate of this place; however, it is seldom possible. But in fact another reason also gives me pleasure, which does not apply to you, Titus.

Atticus: And what, I ask you, is that reason?

Marcus: Because, to speak the truth, this is my own and my brother's real fatherland (*patria*). Here is the most ancient stock from which we are descended; here are our family religious objects (*sacra*), here our family, here many traces of our ancestors. In brief: this house, as you now see it, was made more substantial through the energy of my father; since he was of weak health, he passed almost all his time here in literary pursuits. But in this very place, while my grandfather was alive and the house was small and old-fashioned, like that house of Curius among the Sabines, I tell you I was born. And so something exists and lies hidden in my mind and consciousness, so that this place gives me perhaps more pleasure, just as that wisest of men is said to have refused immortality so that he could see Ithaca again …

[5] *Atticus*: I too am absolutely delighted to have got to know it. But that remark that you made a moment ago that this place – for I assume you were speaking about Arpinum – is your real fatherland: what did you mean? Do you, then, have two fatherlands, or is there one that we share? Unless, perhaps, the fatherland of wise old Cato was not Rome, but Tusculum.

Marcus: I think, by Hercules, that both Cato and all those who come from the free-towns (*municipia*) have two fatherlands, one from nature, the other from citizenship (*civitas*): just as that Cato, though he was born at Tusculum, was taken into citizenship of the Roman people, and so, though he was by birth a Tusculan and by citizenship a Roman, he had one fatherland of place, another of law. ... But it is necessary that that one takes precedence in our affection from which the entire citizen body (*civitas*) has the name of *res publica*, for which we ought to die and to which we should give ourselves completely, and in which we ought to place and, as it were, to consecrate everything we have. But the one that gave us birth is almost as sweet as the one that received us. Thus I will never deny that this is my fatherland, though that one is the greater and this one contained within it [... (*gap in text*) ...] has two citizenships (*civitates*), but reckons them one citizenship.

Cicero, *On the Laws* 2.2–5

Cicero's *On the Laws,* like its model, Plato's *Laws* is set in dialogue form, between Cicero, his brother and Atticus. The tradition of independence and self-government that predates (and presupposes) the enfranchisement of the Allies has far-reaching ideological implications. In this passage Cicero does not make a point that applies just to his own experience or that of his brother Quintus: on the contrary, he seeks to establish a general principle defining the two-fold sense of belonging that one can have, both to the hometown and to a greater political entity (both described here as *patria* – fatherland). These concerns were of course enhanced by the demands of the aftermath of the Social War, but had deeper roots: Cicero singles out the exemplary case of a major figure of the early second century BC, Cato the Censor (234-149 BC), who hailed from the small town of Tusculum and achieved great political prominence at Rome.

D2   The importance of a municipal background

But let us come to the main and starting point of this matter concerning the birth of each of you. [19] You are from the very old free-town (*municipium*) of Tusculum, from which there are very many families of consular rank, among them the Iuventii, – there are not as many from all the rest of the *municipia* – while my client here is from the *praefectura* ('settlement without urban status', 'district') of Atina, not so ancient, not so distinguished, not so close to the city. How much difference would you want this to make to electoral prospects? Firstly, do you think that the people of Atina or those of Tusculum show the greater support to their fellow townspeople? The former – for I can easily know this because I am a close neighbour – were delighted in an amazing way when they saw the father of this excellent and most distinguished man, Cn. Saturninus here, become aedile, then praetor, because he was the first person to have brought curule office not only into that family but also into that district (*praefectura*); the latter – I believe, because it is a *municipium* stuffed with ex-consuls, for I know for certain that they are not spiteful people – I have never thought were particularly delighted by the public office (*honor*) of their own people. [20] We have this situation: our *municipia* have it. What shall I say about myself, what about my brother? Our holding of public offices (*honor*) has received the support, I might almost say, of the very fields and hills. Now when do you see someone from Tusculum boasting about that M. Cato, a leader in every virtue? Or about Ti. Coruncanius, from his *municipium?* Or about the many Fulvii? No one says a word. But whenever you come upon someone from Arpinum, even if you may not wish it, you will nonetheless have to listen to something, perhaps, about us, but certainly about C. Marius. First of all, therefore, my client here had the enthusiastic support of his own people, while you had just as much as could be among men already saturated with people holding public offices (*honor*). [21] Secondly, the fellow members of your *municipium*, very distinguished though they are, are nonetheless few in number when they are compared with those of Atina; the district (*praefectura*) of my client here is full of the most stout-hearted men such that no other in the whole of Italy can be said to be more so; you see the mass of them here now, members of jury, in grief and mourning to make supplication to you. Very many Roman *equites* are here, very many tribunes of the treasury (*tribuni aerarii*) – for we have dismissed from the court the plebs which was in full attendance at the election – what strength, what value (*dignitas*) did they contribute to this man's candidature? For they did not <only> bring him the tribe Teretina, about which I shall speak elsewhere, but they brought him status (*dignitas*), they made him the focus of all eyes and provided him with a solid, tough and conscientious crowd of supporters. For *municipia* are much influenced by association with their neighbours.

Cicero, *Defence of Plancius* 19–21

Cn. Plancius, *eques* and *novus homo,* as Cicero, followed a full traditional senatorial career: he was mess-mate (*contubernalis*) with A. Torquatus in Africa (69 BC); he served with Q. Metellus in Crete (68 BC), was military tribune with C. Antonius in Macedonia (62 BC), and was finally elected quaestor for 58 BC, where he served under a relative from Atina, L. Saturninus, in Macedonia, giving practical assistance to the exiled Cicero. He had an uneventful tribunate in 56 BC. He was curule aedile in 55 or 54 BC and was successfully defended by Hortensius and Cicero when charged with electoral bribery under Crassus' law of 55 BC by M. Iuventius, an unsuccessful candidate. – Cicero took up his defence in that case. Plancius was from the small town of Atina; his counterpart, Laterensis, is a citizen of Tusculum. Like Cicero, they are men of municipal background that have achieved some prominence at Rome; the advocate stresses Plancius' ability to cultivate his local connections, which is not just an electoral asset (the citizens of Atina can cast their vote in Rome), but a symptom of his political rectitude. Cicero also makes the interesting point that the inhabitants of small towns tend to support the candidacies of their fellow-citizens more keenly than the inhabitants of larger centres tend to do. Tusculum has produced a number of senior magistrates over the decades, and its citizens tend to take a less keen interest in elections than those of less distinguished towns. – The reference to Plancius' voting district, the tribe Teretina, points to the importance that the connections with neighbouring communities could have for the prospects of candidate of municipal descent.

D3   Being the citizen of a *municipium*

A *municeps* is, as Aelius Gallus says, one who was born a free man in a free-town (*municipium*). Again, one who, though from a different kind of men, performed a duty. Again, one who in a *municipium* has been freed from servitude to a *municeps*. However, Servius the son used to say that in the beginning they had been those who had become Roman citizens on this condition, that they always kept their *res publica* separate from the Roman people, the Cumani, Acerrani, Atellani, who <were both Roman citizens, and served in the legions, but did not take up public offices>.

Festus, On the meaning of words 126.16–24 Lindsay

The definition of what a *municipium* was, and what rights, duties, and privileges its citizens had, especially vis-à-vis Roman citizens, was a complex matter of debate, especially in the decades following the Social War and the inclusion of the Allies into the citizen body. This entry from the work of the lexicographer Sextus Festus Pompeius (probably later second century AD) provides a definition of *municeps* that stresses three important points: the strong connection between freedom and citizenship; the notion that the status of citizens entails some duties; and the principle whereby *municipia* are communities that retain a separate institutional setup from Rome, notwithstanding their ties and obligations. – Festus is here engaging with the view of two antiquarian authors of the late Republican period, Aelius Gallus and Servius; the problem had clearly attracted much attention. For other definitions of *municipium* and *municeps* see Paul the Deacon, *Summary of Festus* p. 117.5-12, 155.7-19, and Aulus Gellius, *Attic Nights* 16.13.6-9.

D4   Municipal support for a defendant, 66 BC

They did not send their laudatory decree in documents, but wished the most honourable men, whom we all know, to be present here in large numbers and to praise Cluentius in person. There are here present people from Ferentinum, men of the greatest renown, and Marrucini likewise of equal status (*dignitas*); from Teanum in Apulia and from Luceria you see Roman *equites,* most honourable men, here to praise him; from Bovianum and from the whole of Samnium have been sent not only the most handsome expressions of praise, but men of the greatest distinction and noblest birth have also come with them. Now as for those who have estates, who do business, who keeps herds in the territory of Larinum, honourable men of the greatest distinction, it is difficult to say how concerned they are, how anxious. Few men, in my view, are so respected by a single individual as this man is by the whole community here.

Cicero, Defence of Cluentius 197–198

Criminal trials in Republican Rome usually involve significant performative elements, as Cicero's speeches often make apparent. At the same time, the political and social background of the case can play a crucial role in steering the jury's deliberations. Defendants and plaintiffs would often be surrounded by crowds of friends and associates, who asserted their support with their presence. In his defence of Cluentius (see above, **B29**) Cicero takes the time to list the men from Larinum and from a number of neighbouring communities that came to Rome to show their admiration for the defendant. The connection with Larinum is geographical, as well as economic (note the reference to transhumance); Cicero stresses that they are men of distinguished birth and of considerable wealth who are preoccupied with the social order of their territory, and regard his client as someone who can make a contribution to it through his influential role in his hometown. – Their decision to attend in person is singled out as noteworthy: a decree in praise of Cluentius had been passed at Larinum, but they decided to deliver it and restate its message in person.

D5   Decree of the citizens of Placentia in honour of Cicero, 58 BC

Cicero says that the Placentines have deserved very well of him, because they too passed decrees honouring Cicero greatly and competed in this respect with the whole of Italy, when action was taken to bring about his return from exile.

Asconius, *Commentary on Cicero's Speech Against Piso*, p. 3C.20–23

The communities of Roman Italy could take a direct interest in political developments at Rome, and had the tools to make their position heard: Cicero, for instance, gratefully acknowledged the support of a number of Italian cities that passed decrees calling for his return from exile, and singled out Placentia, in Cisalpine Gaul, as an especially vocal supporter of his cause.

D6   A world of self-governing communities: the law from Furfo, 58 BC

Lucius Aienius, son of Lucius, and Quintus Baebatius, son of Sextus, dedicated the temple of Jupiter Liber at Furfo, on 13 July (Quinctilis), during the consulship of Lucius Piso and Aulus Gabinius, in the month of Flusaris, on the fifth comitial day, having presented these laws and these limits of the site: that the outer mouldings, which are made of stone for this temple, and that the staircase, which is to be refurbished in stone, near the temple the columns stand on this side of the staircase leading towards the temple, and the posts and the beams. That it is to be lawful and compliant with divine law to touch, repair, cover, remove, drive in, clean, use iron, move forward, and move back into place [objects within the sacred precinct]. That what is given, presented, or dedicated to this temple, it be permitted to use or sell it; when it has been sold, it is to be secular (*profanum*). That the sale or lease shall be the task of whomever the district (*vicus*) of Furfo has elected as aedile, provided that they feel that they are selling or leasing that object without crime or impiety; no one else is to have this power. That whatever money is received, it may be used to purchase, rent, lease, or give, so that the temple may be improved and more handsome. Any money used for those purposes is to be secular, provided there is no fraud involved. Any objects bought with the money, bronze or silver, for this temple, should be subject to the same regulations as if they had been dedicated. If someone steals something sacred in this place, there shall be a fine set by the aedile at whatever amount he wishes. This fine can be matter of an absolution or a conviction by the majority [of the people of] the district of Furfo, the Fificulani and the Taresuni (???). If anyone sacrifices at this temple to Jupiter Liber or to the Genius of Jupiter, the skins and hides shall belong to the shrine.

ILLRP 508 = EDCS-14804538*

Roman Italy is a world of self-governing communities, which retain and protect their independence in spite of their close ties with Rome and with other cities. Much of the evidence for the workings of local government in the Roman world is epigraphical, and records the work of local magistrates and the decisions of local senates; much of local government activity takes place within the context of communities that have urban status, but in rural settings there is evidence for non-urban settlements: *pagi, vici, praefecturae*, and *fora*. – This inscription is a rare record of local government for the late Republican period (most of the surviving evidence dates to the Principate): the *vicus* (district) of Furfo (near modern Barisciano, L'Aquila) produced a detailed set of regulations on the use and upkeep of a temple of Jupiter Liber. This text shows a thorough effort to define the distinction between what belongs in the religious domain and what pertains to the secular; at the same time, it makes powerfully clear that the regulating and handling of religious affairs in the Roman world is a responsibility of the political community. This is a cardinal principle of Roman religion, which may be seen both in Rome and across the empire. – The translation provided here follows the text and the interpretation in U. Laffi, 'La *lex aedis Furfensis*', in *Studi di storia romana e di diritto,* Rome 2001, 515-544. – For a definition of 'secular' (*profanum*) see Paul the Deacon, *Summary of Festus,* p. 299.11: 'one calls *profanum* what is not bound by the religious regulations of a temple'.

D7 Cicero and Clodius at Ostia

The Se[na]te and the Roman pe[op]le gave [wa]ll[s and gates] to the c[olony of O]stia. The consul Marcus [Tulliu]s C[icer]o [built them and overs]aw the works. The [tribune of the plebs] Publius Cl[o]d[ius Pul[cher co]mplet[ed them and app] rov[ed the work [...] [x and x saw to the refurbishment of] this gate, which old age had ruined [...]

CIL 14.4707 =EDCS-11900483*

The translation of the text is based on the reconstruction provided by F. Zevi (*Année Épigraphique* 1997, 253) of fragments of two almost identical inscriptions from the Porta Romana at Ostia. The inscription records a major public work in the colony of Ostia, which was decided in Rome, carried out by Cicero during his consulship of 63 BC, and brought to completion by Cicero's arch-enemy, the tribune Clodius, whose strong interest in Ostia was driven by the importance of the port of the city as in the corn supply of Rome. The inscription may be dated to the late first century AD on the basis of its lettering and overall layout: it commemorates the involvement of two major figures in late Republican history with the affairs of the city, and was probably produced when the gate was refurbished, a century and a half or so after its inauguration. – Roman Italy is a world of self-governing communities, but the direct intervention of the Roman *res publica* in sites of major economic and strategic significance was possible: in this case, the consul himself was personally involved with the construction of the defence infrastructures of a port town that was key to the long-term welfare of Rome.

E. ROME AND THE EMPIRE

One of the most fascinating aspects of the history of the late Republic is the tension between internal political disruption and imperial expansion. The evidence presented in this section sheds light on some inter-related areas, which are intended to convey a measure of the increasing complexity of the workings of provincial administration in the late Republican period: it ranges from Sicily under Verres to the Greek East under Pompey, and it then turns to some specific themes, such as the development of Roman law in the provinces, the struggle against piracy and Mithridates in the East, and the assignments of high-profile provincial commands to prominent political figures of the late Republican period.

VERRES

E1   Verres' governorship of Sicily, 73–71 BC

[13] With this man as praetor, the people of Sicily did not have possession of their own laws or of the decrees of the Roman senate, or of the common rights of all nations. Each of them in Sicily has only as much as escaped the attention of this avaricious and intemperate ruffian, or been left over when his greed was glutted. For the space of three years, nothing was legally decided except on the nod of this creature, nothing so belonged to anyone's father or grandfather that it might not be taken away by the courts on the order of Verres. Countless sums of money were forced from the estates of the farmers by a novel and nefarious practice; the most loyal allies were considered as enemies, Roman citizens were tortured and executed like slaves, the guiltiest criminals were freed from the courts by paying sums of money, the most honourable and honest men were prosecuted in their absence, condemned and banished with their cases unheard; strongly fortified harbours, the greatest and most secure cities were left open to robbers and pirates, Sicilian soldiers and sailors, our allies and friends, were starved to death; excellent fleets, strategically located, were to the great disgrace of the Roman people, lost and destroyed. [14] The most ancient works of art, some of them from the wealthiest of kings, which they wished to adorn the cities, others from our commanders, who, when victorious, gave or restored them to the communities of Sicily in the hour of victory – this same praetor stripped and despoiled them all. Not only did he do this in the case of public statues and works of art that he treated thus, but he also pillaged the holiest and most venerated shrines; in fact, he has not left the people of Sicily a single god whose workmanship seemed to him any more artistic or ancient; in the matter of his adulteries and scandals, I am deterred by a sense of decency from recalling his acts of wanton wickedness: and besides, I do not wish, by recalling them, to increase the misfortune of those whose children and whose wives it was not possible to keep safe from outrage of this lecherous scoundrel.

Cicero, *Against Verres* 1.13–14

The powerful portrait of the former governor of Sicily C. Verres that Cicero produces in the early section of his first speech, which was delivered at Verres' corruption trial in August 70, is predicated on the assumption that he is subverting the well-ordered world of the province of Sicily, and that he stands as a fatal threat to healthy civic coexistence. There is a clear strategy at play here, as well as a series of important political points on what amounts, in Cicero's vision, to the constituent parts of a solid political reality: from the treasury to the respect of citizenship rights, to the defence of shrines and the protection of families: the theft of sacred property is significantly mentioned just before adultery among the crimes allegedly committed by Verres.

E2   Verres' three-year plan

He used to claim that he would never be convicted of plundering his province as he had a promise of support from a powerful friend; he was not making money just for himself, but had so planned his three years' governorship of Sicily that he would think he was doing very nicely if he could put one year's profit into his pocket, could hand over the second year's to his patrons and the men who were to defend him in the courts, and could keep back the entire profit of his third year, the richest and most lucrative of all, for distribution as bribes to his jurors.

Cicero, *Against Verres* 1.40

It is immaterial whether this statement was indeed made by Verres: it is voiced in court, and must have had a ring of plausibility to it; no doubt some Roman magistrates thought and acted along similar lines. The three-year term of Verres enables him to plan a strategy of ruthless exploitation of the province, through which he will also secure *de facto* immunity from any later prosecution upon his return. – We should of course allow for Cicero's understandable attempt to overstate the nature and significance of the challenge he was facing in prosecuting Verres, as he was beginning to make a case that could prove crucial to his later political prospects.

E3   The consuls check Verres' activities in Sicily, 72 BC

And so in the Senate Cn. Lentulus and L. Gellius, the consuls, immediately declared that a resolution should be passed in the Senate *that men in the provinces should not be prosecuted on capital charges in their absence* and they informed the Senate in full detail about the case of Sthenius and the iniquity and cruelty of this creature. There was present in the Senate Verres, this man's father, and with tears in his eyes he kept asking each individual senator to have mercy on his son; however, he did not have much success since feeling in the Senate was unanimous. Opinions were expressed: *whereas Sthenius has been prosecuted in his absence, it is agreed that no trial of him is to take place in his absence, and, if any has taken place, it is agreed it shall not be valid.*

Cicero, *Against Verres* 2.2.95

L. Gellius and Cn. Cornelius Lentulus Clodianus were the consuls of 72 BC. The texts in *italics* are those of the resolutions of the Senate, which Cicero is quoting as corroborating evidence. Sthenius had his house stripped of its numerous works of art by Verres, and then publicly opposed his intention to remove public and sacred works of art evincing the uncontrolled fury of the governor. His case is being considered in a senatorial debate. For the full details see Cicero, *Verrine*, 2.2.82-118; Verres' habit of ignoring the rights of Roman citizens residing in the province of Sicily is denounced right at the outset of the speech, and is a major feature of the case against him, and of the overall depiction of his character: far from being a merely juridical point, it is an allegation that is intended to depict Verres as someone who does not understand what being a citizen is actually about.

THE GREEK EAST

E4   Law on praetorian provinces: attempts to remedy provincial
abuses *c.* 100 BC

[lines 1–15 = Cnidos Copy, Column III] [... there is to be] a decree of the Senate [concerning any ...,] king and peoples and there is to be a vote concerning each matter. No one, in contravention of those measures which are in the statute which M. Porcius Cato as praetor passed three days before the *Feralia*, is knowingly with wrongful deceit to draw up (an army) or march or travel outside his province, for whatever reason, no matter when he shall arrive, nor is any magistrate or promagistrate to travel or proceed outside the province in command of which province it is or shall be appropriate for him to be according to this statute, except according to a decree of the Senate, except for purposes of transit or for reasons of state, and he is without wrongful deceit to restrain his staff.

[lines 10–15 = Delphi Copy, Block C] [...] The magistrates now in office, except for tribunes and governors, within the five days [next after] the people pass this statute, and whoever shall hereafter hold a magistracy, except for governors, whoever of them [shall be] in Rome, within the five days next [after each of them] shall take up his magistracy; they are to swear by Jupiter and the ancestral gods to do all the things that have been laid down in this statute and to see to it that they are put into effect and not to do anything contrary to this statute nor to act so that anyone else do so nor to act otherwise than as is (written down) in this statute in order that it may be put into effect.

[lines 15–19] No one is to do anything contrary to this statute knowingly with wrongful deceit, and whatever it is appropriate for anyone to do according to this statute he is to do it. No one is to act, to the effect that evasion of this statute be compassed, knowingly with wrongful deceit, and no one is to act or intercede to the effect that what is appropriate according to this statute be not done. Those for whom it is appropriate to act or swear are to act and swear to the effect that (nothing) be not observed or be observed otherwise than is written down in this statute. And whoever acts or intercedes contrary to this statute, and whatever he fails to do according to this statute or if he does not swear according to this statute, it shall not be possible for him to go unpunished nor is it any the less lawful <for whoever>may wish to sue him.

[lines 19–24] If anyone should do anything contrary to this statute, and if anyone for whom it is in any respect appropriate to act <or to swear> according to this statute should fail to act or swear, or if anyone should compass evasion of this statute or should act in any other way otherwise than is written down in this statute or intercede, or offend, with wrongful deceit, he is to be fined two hundred thousand sesterces for each offence which he may commit. And if anyone fail to do something except as is written down in this statute or do something otherwise than is prescribed in this statute, he is to be obliged to pay this sum to the people. As for this sum, whoever wishes, who is a freeborn member of this state, for whom it is lawful to propose a fine and to sue according to this statute, he is to have action and suit and he is to prosecute before the person responsible for these matters.

[lines 24–30] And no magistrate or promagistrate is to act so that the matter be not judged nor is he to block this sum being at issue and being sued for and the trial taking place and the sum being exacted. Whoever contrary to this should act or block or intercede, likewise for each offence he is to be condemned to pay, as if he had acted contrary to this statute or as if he was required to do something according to this statute and had failed to do it, {likewise he is to be condemned to pay} as is written down above. Whatever sum be sued for according to this statute, if this sum, whenever it be sued for, from whomever it be sued for, be not [paid, the same] praetor, before whom anyone may have gone for a pre-trial, [likewise] is in such a way to appoint a court, insofar [as it shall be possible, that the person] from whom (the sum) may be sued for [according to this] statute [pay] the people [without demur.] And he [...this] matter [...] judges [...]? [...]

Roman Statutes 1.12

Two copies of the Greek translation of a detailed statute on provincial administration dating to the second century BC have been found at Delphi and Cnidos respectively. The fact that the law was translated is a clear indication that its provisions were of direct interest to the residents of the provincial communities in the Greek East, and indeed to some allies of Rome in the region. The section of the text that records the backers of the proposal does not survive, but it may be placed with a fair degree of confidence in the age of Saturninus and Glaucia (103-100 BC): its underlying principle is that the powers of provincial governors must be exerted in strict compliance with the law passed by the people, and the degree of detail of this text shows that little room was left to the personal discretion of the governor; moreover, clear sanctions are envisaged for those who breach the terms of the law, and they are to be directly accountable to the people, rather than the Senate. The developments of the late Republican period show that the concerns that underpin this law were not entirely misplaced: provincial commands were repeatedly used to build or consolidate the power base of ambitious promagistrates. – *Feralia*: 21 February, a feast on which offerings were made at the tombs of the dead.

E5   Mithridates' letter to Arsaces

[1] 'King Mithridates to King Arsaces greetings. All who, when their own affairs are prospering, are asked to join an alliance for war, ought to consider whether it is possible to be at peace at that time; then, whether what is sought is morally right, safe, glorious or disgraceful. [2] If you could enjoy permanent peace, if the enemy were not quick to seize their chance and most wicked and there were not to be outstanding glory if you defeated the Romans, I would not dare to seek an alliance but would hope in vain that my misfortunes would be associated with your prosperity. [3] And the very things, which seem able to hold you back, your anger with Tigranes because of the recent war and my own lack of success – will, if you are willing to make a realistic estimate, give you the greatest encouragement. [4] For Tigranes being open to attack will agree to whatever alliance you want; in my case, though Fortune has stolen much from me, she has given me the habit of giving good advice; and, since I am not at my strongest I provide an example, such as is desirable for those who are flourishing, of how you may arrange your own affairs better.

[5] Now the Romans have one reason for making war against all nations, peoples, and kings, and it is an old one: an insatiable desire for empire (*imperium*) and riches. This first induced them to make war against king Philip of Macedon, under the pretence of friendship, while they were being hard pressed by the Carthaginians. [6] When Antiochus came to Philip's help, they diverted him through a trick with the surrender of Asia; and soon afterwards, when Philip had been crushed, Antiochus was stripped of all his territory this side of the Taurus and of ten thousand talents. [7] Then Perses, Philip's son, after many battles with varying results, was taken into their protection before the gods of Samothrace. These cunning inventors of treachery, because they had granted him his life by an agreement, killed him by keeping him from ever sleeping. [8] Eumenes, whose friendship they make a great boast of, they first betrayed to Antiochus as the price of peace; afterwards they treated him as the custodian of captured territory and by their exactions and their insults reduced him from a king to the most wretched of slaves; then they impiously forged his will and led his son Aristonicus in triumph like an enemy because he had tried to win back

his father's kingdom; Asia was besieged by these same people. [9] Finally, when Nicomedes died, they plundered Bithynia although a son had without doubt been born of Nysa, whom he had called his queen.

[10] Why should I mention my own case? Separated on all sides by kingdoms and tetrarchies from their empire (*imperium*), because it was said that I was rich and would not be a slave, they provoked me to war through Nicomedes. I was not unaware of their wrongdoing and had previously cited as evidence what happened to the Cretans, who alone were free at that time, and to king Ptolemy. [11] And so in revenge for the wrongs I suffered, I drove Nicomedes out of Bithynia and recovered Asia, the spoil of king Antiochus, and freed Greece from the yoke of slavery. [12] Archelaus, the vilest of slaves, impeded my designs by betraying my army. Those whose cowardice or crooked cunning kept them out of the fighting so that they might be safe through my efforts are now paying the most savage punishment: Ptolemy is putting off war day by day through bribery, the Cretans have been assaulted once and will have no end except their own annihilation. [13] In my case, when I realised that battles had been put off rather than peace granted because of their own internal troubles, I then began the war again, though Tigranes, who too late accepts what I said, disagreed; you were too far away and all the others had submitted; and at Chalcedon I routed Marcus Cotta, the Roman commander, by land and by sea and deprived him of a first-class fleet. [14] At Cyzicus I stayed besieging the town with a large army for a long time while provisions failed, since none nearby gave support; and at the same time the winter kept me from the sea. Thus, through no action of the enemy, I tried to return to my own kingdom and lost the pick of my army, with my fleets being shipwrecked at Parium and Heraclea. [15] With my army reconstituted at Cabera and with several battles between Lucullus and myself, shortage of supplies again came upon both of us. To him lay available the kingdom of Ariobarzanes untouched by the war, while I withdrew to Armenia, all the places around me having been devastated. The Romans followed not me but their habit of subverting all monarchies; and, because in mountainous country they prevented a huge force from battle, they are now boasting of the imprudence of Tigranes as if it were a victory.

[16] Now, I ask you, consider whether you think that with our defeat, you will be stronger to resist or that there will be an end to the war? I know very well that you have great resources of men, weapons, and gold; and for that reason I am after you as an ally, while the Romans are after you as plunder. But it is my intention, while the kingdom of Tigranes is intact, to put an end to this war with my troops <skilled in war>, far from home, with little trouble and through our efforts, since in this enterprise we can neither conquer nor be conquered without danger to yourself. [17] Or do you not realise that the Romans, now that the Atlantic has put a limit to their expansion westwards, have turned their armies in this direction? That from the beginning they own nothing except what they have plundered: home, wives, lands and empire (*imperium*)? That they were once refugees, without homeland, without parents, but have become established as the scourge of the world? That nothing human or divine prevents them from pillaging and exterminating friends and allies, those situated near and far, weak and strong; and from considering as their enemies all not slaves to themselves, and – above all – monarchies? [18] For few want freedom, the majority want fair masters (*domini*); we are suspected as rivals and people who will in time exact vengeance. [19] But you yourself, who have Seleuceia, the greatest of cities, and the kingdom of Persia famed for its riches,

what do you expect from them except treachery now and war later? [20] The Romans turn their weapons against all, most keenly upon those whose defeat will bring the most spoils; by daring and by deceit, by breeding war from war they have become great: [21] through this practice they will destroy everything or they will fall in battle, a thing that is not difficult if you in Mesopotamia and we in Armenia surround an army, without provisions, without support, and safe hitherto only through good luck or our own shortcomings. [22] And fame will attend you as the one who went out to help great kings and overwhelmed the robbers of the nations. [23] This is what I urge and advise you to do; and not to prefer putting off your own ruin as a result of mine rather than becoming victor by alliance with me.'

Sallust, *Histories* 4.67 McG = 60 R.

One of the longest fragments of Sallust's *Histories* is a letter purportedly written by Mithridates to Arsaces, the king of Parthia, urging him to join forces with him in the war against Rome and her ally Tigranes, king of Armenia. While it is conceivable that there were political and diplomatic contacts between the two men, the text we read in Sallust is certainly a free construction of the historian, and should be read against the backdrop of his reflection on the role of wealth in the history of Rome and his wider assessment of the impact of the Roman empire. The letter expresses a very critical view of the nature and consequences of the Roman conquest of the Mediterranean, which echoes specific aspects of Mithridates' political discourse (cf. **B12**), and conjures up to sketching an abrasively critical assessment of the historical trajectory of Rome, in which the traditional claim to 'good faith' (*fides*) is comprehensively subverted, and treachery is singled out as the fundamental principle. We should certainly not conclude that Sallust endorsed these views, but it is noteworthy that he nonetheless chose to voice them in his work, both as an opportunity to confer greater depth to his historical account and as a way to raise further questions about the nature of the empire that Rome controls.

E6   Antonian Law on the Termessians, 68 BC

[Col. I, line 36] Whatever free men or slaves the citizens of Termessus Maior in Pisidia [Col. II] lost in the Mithridatic War, the magistrate or promagistrate, who shall have jurisdiction over this matter and to whom the parties shall go for a pre-trial hearing concerning this matter, is to administer justice over this matter and is to appoint trials and procedures for recovery in such a manner that they may be able to recover them.

[lines 6] No magistrate or promagistrate or legate or anyone else is to introduce soldiers into the town of Termessus Maior in Pisidia or into the territory of Termessus Maior in Pisidia for the purpose of wintering nor see that anyone introduce soldiers thither or that soldiers winter there, unless the Senate shall have decreed with mention of the town's name that soldiers be brought into winter quarters in Termessus Maior in Pisidia; nor is any magistrate or promagistrate or legate or anyone else to see, or order, that they in fact give or provide anything or that in fact anything be taken from them, except what it is or shall be appropriate for them to give or provide according to the *lex Porcia* (Law of Porcius).

Roman Statutes 1.19 = EDCS-20000144

The emphasis of Mithridates' letter in Sallust (**E5**) is on the ruthlessly acquisitive and exploitative nature of Roman power in the Greek East: a point that is corroborated by a broad range of parallel evidence. However, it is worth questioning the picture further. The statute from which this quotation is drawn is one of the many legal texts in which the relationship between Rome and a city in a provincial setting was defined and a set of mutual obligations was codified. The Roman world is largely a world of self-governing communities, in the Republic as well as under the Empire: the law on the status of the city of Termessus in southern Asia Minor includes clear provisions that rule out (under normal circumstances) the presence of Roman troops in the city – The lex Porcia was an earlier statute on provincial administration, probably passed in 121 BC, which regulated the requisitions that a magistrate could make from an allied community. The free status of Termessus owes much to the loyalty of the city to Rome during the First Mithridatic War, and the statute contains a clause on the process through which redress for the losses suffered during the war is to be sought, with the direct involvement of a Roman promagistrate: a symptom of the significance that was accorded to this matter.

E7   The demands of the empire, 66 BC

You yourself, Quintus Hortensius, gravely and elegantly spoke against Aulus Gabinius, when he put forward a law on the appointment of single commander against the pirates; from this very spot you spoke at length against the same law. Now, by the immortal gods, I beseech you – if your opinion had carried greater weight (*auctoritas*) with the Roman people than their welfare and genuine cause, would we be having this glory and this present power across the whole wide world? Or do you say that the empire existed at a time when the envoys, quaestors and praetors of the Roman people were being captured? When we were prevented from having any private and public communication with all of our provinces? When every sea was so tightly closed to us that we could not carry out any private or public business overseas?

Cicero, On the Manilian Law / On Pompey's Command 52–53

Cicero in his speech proposing giving special command to Pompey for the campaign against Mithridates (see **B4, B5, B12, B13**) makes the rhetorical point that Rome's extensive overseas empire had made it absolutely vital to eliminate the pirates (achieved by Pompey the previous year, also with special command, also opposed by Hortensius). He is taking on Hortensius, one of the most talented orators of the time and a much-admired rival of his (see **G39**), by stressing how remarkable Pompey's achievements are and how flawed the decision not to grant him the commands against the pirates would have been: Hortensius was wrong a year back, and his advice should not be followed now either. Hortensius' view of how the empire should be run - without conferring full powers upon an individual, even in a dire emergency - is dismissed as 'obsolete': on this occasion, Cicero is arguing for the need to innovate established practice in provincial government and in wider constitutional matters; he took a very different view at other moments of his career. In many ways, the end of the Roman Republic should be studied against the background of the tension between innovation and tradition, and through the consequences (planned or unintended) that the attempts to resolve such tension had. - Note the repeated references to 'public' and 'private' business that Cicero makes here: he is forcefully stressing that the empire can yield substantial rewards on many levels, and that taking active steps to stabilize it is truly in everybody's best interest.

E8   Roman discredit in Asia Minor

[65] It is hard to convey, Romans, how much we are hated among foreign peoples, because of the greedy and insulting conduct of the men whom we have dispatched to them over the last few years, holding official command (*imperium*). What temple do you suppose has been held as sacred by our magistrates, which community inviolable, which house sufficiently protected and defended? They seek out rich and flourishing cities, through which they might find an opportunity for war to satisfy their desire for plunder… [67] Do you think that any community has been 'pacified' and still remains wealthy? That any state is wealthy and seems pacified to these people? The coastal regions, Romans, asked for Pompey's appointment not just because of his military glory, but also on account of his restraint: for they saw that governors, barring a few exceptions, were making fortunes on a yearly basis out of public funds, and that we were not obtaining any results with our so-called fleets, except for incurring even greater damage by our defeats.

Cicero, On the Manilian Law / On Pompey's Command 65–67, with omissions

E9   Pompey extends the Roman Empire

Pompey in this one war having cleared out the lairs of the pirates, having destroyed the greatest king, and having engaged in battles, besides the Pontic war, with Colchians, Albanians, Iberians, Armenians, Medes, Arabs, Jews and other eastern nations, extended the Roman empire as far as Egypt. He did not advance into Egypt itself, although it was in a state of revolt against the king and the king himself invited him and sent him gifts and money and clothing for his whole army. He either feared the greatness of the kingdom, which was still a prosperous one, or wished to guard against the envy of his enemies, or the prohibition of oracles or through other considerations. ... Of the subjugated nations he left some autonomous for the sake of an alliance, while others immediately became subject to the Romans, and others he distributed to kings – to Tigranes, Armenia; to Pharnaces, Bosporus; to Ariobarzanes, Cappadocia and the other provinces mentioned before: to Antiochus of Commagene he handed over Seleucia and parts of Mesopotamia that he had overrun. He made Deïotarus and others tetrarchs of the Gallograecians, who are now the Galatians bordering on Cappadocia. He made Attalus dynast of Paphlagonia and Aristarchus dynast of the Colchians. He also appointed Archelaus priest of the goddess at Comana, which is a royal power. Castor of Phanagoria he made a friend of the Roman people. To others he gave much territory and money.

Appian, *Mithridatic Wars* 114

Appian's overview of Pompey's settlement of the East stresses the range of different options to which he resorted, not least by stressing the significance of his decision not to conquer Egypt: the predicament of the last surviving Hellenistic kingdom remained an important issue of Roman politics for three more decades. Conquest was not the only tool that Pompey used: he was in fact willing to bestow or renew privileges, including that of self-government, on communities that he regarded as loyal, and did not hesitate to resort to a number of client-kings on the fringes of the territories that he had conquered, notably in Armenia, in the Crimea, and in Palestine.

E10   Pompey founds cities in the East

[28] Near this place Pompey founded a city in Lesser Armenia, Nicopolis, which even now survives and is well peopled.

[30] Both rivers [the Lykos and the Iris] meet somewhere near the middle of the valley and at their junction is situated a city, which the first founder called Eupatoria after his own name. Pompey, coming upon it half finished, adding to it territory and settlers, called it Magnopolis.

[38] Now after the territory of the Amisenians up to the Halys is Phazemonitis, which Pompey called Neapolitis, declaring the settlement at the village of Phazemon a city and calling it Neapolis.

[40] Mithridates ... not only took Bithynia at the first assault, but also took possession of Asia as far as Caria and Lycia. And here too a place was named as a city, that is, Pompeiopolis.

Strabo, *Geography* 12.3.28, 30, 38, 40

There is abundant evidence, both literary and epigraphical, for the city foundations carried out by Pompey in the East, especially in Asia Minor: Strabo, who was from that region, is an especially valuable source.

These new settlements were unlike the colonies that were founded in Italy during the Republican period, including those installed for Sulla's veterans. They were created by the initiative of an individual and were not related to the *res publica* by any specific legal arrangement. They no doubt served the purpose of securing a more effective control of the territory, as well as providing the communities of a region with a clearly identifiable political centre; in some cases there were entirely new foundations, while in others (such as Eupatoria/Magnopolis, in passage b) they were created at the sites of existing centres. Moreover, as the names of several of them emphatically show, they were intended as a tribute to Pompey's achievements, following a pattern that is well attested throughout the Hellenistic period, when city foundations are a customary feature of regal power. Nicopolis = 'Victory-City'; Magnopolis = 'Great-City' i.e. 'City of Pompey the Great'; Neapolis = 'New-City'; Pompeiopolis = 'City of Pompey'. With these initiatives Pompey was beginning to tread – at least in the Greek East – ground that was distinctly monarchic.

E11   Honours paid to Pompey in the Greek East

a) The People (honour) their saviour and founder Pompey, son of Gnaeus, the Great, *imperator* for the third time, who destroyed those who had seized the inhabited world by his wars on both land and sea. [...*gap*...] ... Dorotheos, (son) of Hegesandros, of Olynthos made (the statue).

from Mytilene, *SIG*³ 751

b) The people of Athe[ns and the Society] of Worshippers of Pompey [in Delos (dedicate this statue of)] Pompey [the Great, son of] Gna[eus,] *imperator*, [to Apollo.]

from Delos, Durrbach, *Choix* 162

c) The People (honour) Pompey the Great, son of Gnaeus, *imperator* for the third time, patron and benefactor.

from Miletus, *Milet* 1.7.253

d) The people and [the youth] (honour) Pompey the Great, son of Gnaeus, *imperator* for the third time, patron and benefactor of the city, because of his [piety] towards the goddess [...] and his benevolence towards the people, having freed men from the barbarian wars [and the] dangers of pirates, and having established peace and safety both by land and sea.

from Ilion, SEG 46.1565, *c.* 66 BC

e) The people (honour) Pompey the Great, son of Gnaeus, *imperator* for the third time, saviour and benefactor of the people and of the whole of Asia, guardian of land and sea, because of his valour and his [bene]volence towards them.

from Miletopolis, ILS 9459, *c.* 66 BC

Inscribed dedications to prominent Romans, usually promagistrates to whom a honorific statue is devoted, are a customary feature of the late Hellenistic period, in Greece as well as in Asia Minor. For Pompey there is a strikingly high number of dedications, and the references to his achievements against the pirates are especially prominent (see a) and b)). The economic and social benefits that a number of coastal communities gained from his success were very significant. – The presence at Delos of what may be a cultic association in honour of Pompey is not altogether surprising, and has precedents not just in the rest of the Hellenistic monarchies, where ruler cult is widely attested, but also in the dealings between Greek cities and Roman governors: in the 90s the cities of the province of Asia celebrated a festival called *Moukieia*, in honour of the governor of Asia Q. Mucius Scaevola.

E12   Death of Mithridates, 63 BC

[112] And Mithridates died. ... He lived sixty-eight or sixty-nine years, and of these he was king for fifty-seven years; for the kingdom came to him when he was an orphan. He subdued the neighbouring barbarians and brought under his control many of the Scythians, and waged war vigorously against the Romans for forty years, during which time he frequently conquered Bithynia and Cappadocia, overran Asia, Phrygia, Paphlagonia, Galatia, and Macedonia. He invaded Greece ... and ruled the sea from Cilicia to the Ionian Sea, until Sulla confined him again to his paternal kingdom after destroying one hundred and sixty thousand of his soldiers. In spite of meeting with so great disaster he nonetheless renewed the war with ease. He engaged with the best commanders in battles. He was defeated by Sulla, Lucullus, and Pompey, though he got much the better of them many times. Lucius Cassius, Quintus Oppius, and Manius Aquilius he captured and took around with him as prisoners, until he killed the latter as being the cause of the war, while the others he surrendered to Sulla. He defeated Fimbria, Murena, the consul Cotta, Fabius, and Triarius. He was always high-spirited and indomitable even in misfortune. Indeed, even when defeated, he would leave no opportunity for attacking the Romans and left no avenue of attack untried. He made alliances with the Samnites and the Gauls, and he sent legates to Sertorius in Spain. He was often wounded by enemies and others in conspiracies, but he never left off on that account, even when he was an old man. ... He was bloodthirsty and cruel to all – he killed his mother, his brother, three sons and three daughters. ... He cultivated Greek learning, and thus became acquainted with the religious cults of Greece, and he was fond of music. In most things he exercised self-control and he was capable of toil and hardship. He gave in only to pleasures with women.

[113] Such was the end of Mithridates, called Eupator and Dionysus. When the Romans learned of his death, they held a festival because they had been delivered from a difficult enemy.

Appian, *Mithridatic Wars* 112–13

We know that a number of intellectuals lived and worked at Mithridates' court, and that historical accounts in which the king received a favourable assessment were produced in antiquity (notably by Metrodoros of Scepsis, who was nicknamed *Misorhomaios,* 'Roman-hater': Pliny the Elder, *Natural History* 34.34). However, the surviving literary tradition is comprehensively hostile, the letter to Arsaces in Sallust's *Histories* (see above, **E5**) being a partial exception. Appian, who devoted a whole work to the Mithridatic Wars, reflects on the character of the king after recounting his death (he committed suicide in Crimea, in 63 BC, in order to escape capture: see e.g. Appian, *Mithridatic Wars* 111). His assessment, while unreservedly negative from a political standpoint, insists on the king's resourcefulness, and on the many talents he displayed in his relentless struggle against Rome: a peculiar combination of natural talent and intellectual power, sustained by an excellent education. – The mention of an alliance with the 'Samnites' is a reference to the contacts that probably took place between Mithridates and the Italian Allies during the Social War.

E13   Cicero's military operations to parade the *imperium Romanum*, 51–50 BC

When these operations had been completed, I led my army to Pindenissum, a town of the free Cilicians. It occupied a very high and well-fortified position and was inhabited by people who had never obeyed even kings. Since they were giving refuge to fugitives and were awaiting the arrival of the Parthians with very great eagerness, I thought that it was a matter concerning the reputation of our empire (*imperium*) to check their impudent behaviour, so that the spirits of the rest, who are not sympathetic to our empire (*imperium*), might also be more easily broken. I surrounded them with a rampart and a ditch, I hedged them in with six forts and an extensive camp, attacked them with a ramp, mantlets and towers. I used many siege-engines and many archers. With great effort on my part and without any inconvenience or expense on the part of our allies, I completed the operation on the fifty-seventh day; with the result that, when all parts of the city had been demolished or fired, they were compelled to come under my control. All quarters of the city were demolished or burnt down and they were compelled to yield to me. Their neighbours, the Tebarani, were equally impudent and wicked. After the capture of Pindenissum I received hostages from them; I sent the army into winter quarters; I put my brother Quintus in charge of the business of quartering the army in villages, which had either been captured or not properly settled in peace.

Tarsus, end of 51 or beginning of 50 BC.

Cicero to M. Cato, To his Friends 15.4.10 (SB 110)

This operation of Cicero's and the thinking behind it might be compared with Caesar's in Gaul (**E43**). This extract is part of a long letter to Cato in which Cicero is seeking Cato's support for the possible award of a triumph at the end of his governorship in Cilicia: his attempt was unsuccessful. In this letter Cicero discusses what may be termed as an act of pre-emptive warfare: there was the prospect of a Parthian offensive in that area, and the city of Pindenissum had been harbouring fugitives from the neighbouring territory. Although the community had a long tradition of civic independence and had not carried out acts hostile to Rome, it became the target of a comprehensive attack, which was intended, perhaps primarily, to send a message to other communities in the region that had not expressed their full loyalty to Rome. Cicero is keen to show how effective and economical his efforts were, and stresses that this intensive – if low-scale – attack did yield immediate results: the neighbouring community handed hostages to the Roman army.

LAW IN THE PROVINCES

E14　Reflections on the *imperium Romanum*

[26]…But, as long as the empire of the Roman people was maintained by acts of kindness, not of injury, wars were waged in the interest of our allies or over the empire (*imperium*); wars did not end in a harsh manner or only with what was necessary; the Senate was a harbour and refuge of kings, tribes, and nations; [27] and our magistrates and commanders were eager to gain the highest praise from this one thing alone, if they should have defended our provinces and our allies with fairness and good faith; and so it could more truthfully be called a protectorate (*patrocinium*) of the world rather than an empire (*imperium*).

This custom and practice we had already begun gradually to modify previously; but after the victory of Sulla, we abandoned it completely; for it had ceased to be the case that any action against our allies seemed wrong, when such great cruelty took place against citizens. For that reason, in his case a dishonourable victory followed an honourable cause; for when he had planted his spear in the forum and was selling the property of men who were good (*boni*), men of substance and, at the very least, Roman citizens, he dared to say that 'he was selling his spoils.' There followed one who, in an impious cause, with an even more infamous victory, was to confiscate the property not of individual citizens, but to encompass whole provinces and regions in one single law of ruin. And so, when foreign peoples had been oppressed and ruined, we have Massilia being carried in a triumphal procession, to serve as proof that the empire (*imperium*) had been lost; and we saw a triumph being celebrated over a city without which our commanders would never have gained a triumph for their wars beyond the Alps. I could mention many more nefarious acts against our allies, if the sun had ever seen one more infamous than this particular one.

Cicero, *On Duties* 2.26–28

Cicero's philosophical treatise on duties was composed in the autumn of 44 BC, at a time of frenetic political and intellectual activity. In this important passage he reflects on the uneasy links between the development of the empire and the dramatic changes in Roman internal politics. He sketches a schematic and ideologically loaded account whereby until Sulla the empire is run in scrupulous observance of principles of fairness and loyalty, and is more a form of protectorate than an actual empire. After the Sullan proscriptions, in which Roman citizens were treated like foreign subjects, there was a sea-change in the way politics was conducted at Rome (cf. Sallust, *Catiline's War* 11.4–5 on new attitudes to wealth after Sulla: L36b). Caesar, who is not explicitly named, is the obvious target of even harsher criticism: he would have turned the whole empire, including Rome, into a subject land. His behaviour towards the city of Massilia (Marseilles), an old ally of Rome that Caesar besieged and conquered during the civil war (cf. *Civil Wars* 1.34–2.22), receives especially polemical comments.

E15   Verres in Sicily

When he had organized these considerable and fruitful sources of profit from the cases, which he had arranged to hear and to try with his council, that is, with his own staff, he then lighted upon a limitless method for seizing countless sums of money. His courts were of the following composition: they were made up of Roman citizens, if the parties were Sicilians, although Sicilians ought to have been appointed according to their statutes; while, if the parties were Roman citizens, Sicilians made up the courts. [32] [...] But so that you may comprehend his whole scheme of trial procedure, acquaint yourselves first with the rights of the Sicilians, then with the procedure of this fellow.

The Sicilians possess the legal right that when a citizen has a case with another citizen they contend at law in their own city and subject to their own statutes; when a Sicilian had a case with a Sicilian not of the same city, the praetor should appoint judges for it by lot in accordance with the decree of P. Rupilius, which he laid down as a result of the decree of the ten legates, which they call the *lex Rupilia*. [*Further arrangements involving Roman citizens and Sicilians are then described.*] [33] When this fellow was praetor, all these rights were not only thrown into confusion, but also completely taken away from both Sicilians and Roman citizens. First of all their own rights; in the case where a citizen was at law with another citizen he appointed as judge anyone who suited himself, his herald, his soothsayer, his doctor; of if the court had been constituted according to their statutes, and they had come to one of their own citizens as judge, he was not allowed any freedom to make his decision: acquaint yourselves with the edict of the fellow, by which edict he brought all courts under his control [...] [34] No judges were ever selected from the Romans residing in the communities (*conventus*), or proposed from the businessmen. Such was the source of judges, as I say, his own staff, not the staff of Q. Scaevola – not that he was accustomed to appoint from his own staff – but the staff of C. Verres.

Cicero, *Against Verres* 2.2.31–34, with omissions

The administration of justice is one of the main duties of a provincial governor and is tightly regulated by the law under which the province is governed (for Sicily, that was the *lex Rupilia*, dating back to 132 BC).

At the same time, it can be a unique opportunity for a ruthless governor to profit from his position. Verres' handling of the process is here depicted in heavily polemical terms. His actions fall short of any expectation that could be set on a governor: they do not look after either the interests of the provincials or those of the Roman businessmen that resided in the province. His courts were staffed by people recruited from his inner circle, in a consistent pattern of unrestrained cronyism. – Cicero describes at length and in lurid detail Verres' judicial irregularities during his period as governor: the case of Heraclius of Syracuse, 2.2.35–42; of Sopater of Halicyae 2.2.68–75; of Sthenius of Thermae, 2.2.83–118; the collection of corn, 2.3.25–28; the case of P. Gavius, a Roman *eques*, 2.5.160–163 (**L32**). Such episodes show clearly that neither Roman citizens nor provincials had any reliable defence, against the power (*imperium*) of a governor, if he chose to abuse it. Q. Mucius Scaevola had been a model of capable and restrained governor in the province of Asia: 'Nor is the glory of Q. Scaevola [...] any less illustrious. He governed Asia so scrupulously and so firmly that the Senate in its decree proposed Scaevola as an example and model of administration for magistrates going out that that province in the future.' (Valerius Maximus, *Memorable Deeds and Sayings* 8.15.6). The date of his governorship is disputed: 97 BC, as propraetor, or 94 BC, as proconsul (cf. **E1–E3**).

E16   Cicero returns from his quaestorship, 74 BC

[64] I have no fear, judges, of coming across as having too high a concept of myself, if I say a word about my quaestorship… Let me say it out loud: I can state that at the time I thought that people in Rome did not speak of anything other than my quaestorship. I had dispatched a huge quantity of corn at a time of most severe scarcity; the unanimous view was that I had been civil towards the money-lenders, fair towards the traders, restrained towards the allies, and most scrupulous in every aspect of my duties; the Sicilians had contemplated bestowing unprecedented honours upon me. [65] Therefore I left the province with the hope that the Roman people would offer me all sorts of distinction. But on my way back from the province I happened to arrive at Puteoli, intending to make the journey by land, as many affluent people are usually there; I nearly fell over, judges, when someone asked me on what day I had departed from Rome, and whether there was any news. When I replied that I was on my way back from my province, he said, 'Why, of course, you come from Africa, do you not?' 'No,' I answered, in a somewhat prickly fashion, for I was now most irritated, 'from Sicily.' At this point someone else added, as if he knew it all, 'What! don't you know that this chap has been quaestor at Syracuse?' To cut my story short: I set aside my irritation, and made myself just one of those who had come for the waters.

Cicero, Defence of Plancius 64–65

An amusing anecdote, which Cicero quotes several years after the event, as a sobering reminder of how little impact one's involvement in provincial administration could have in Rome or across Italy: it took much more than a successful stint in a province to enable a steady rise to political prominence.

E17   Caesar in Cisalpine Gaul

a) Caesar himself set out for Gallia Citerior to conduct assizes. [58/57 BC]

Caesar, Gallic War 1.54.3

b) He himself, having completed the assizes in Gallia Citerior, set out for Illyricum. [55/54 BC]

Caesar, Gallic War 5.1.5

c) Having dealt with these matters and completed the assizes (in Illyricum), he returned to Gallia Citerior. [55/54 BC]

Caesar, Gallic War 5.2.1

Caesar's *Commentarii* on the Gallic campaigns are mostly focused on military developments, but they do not fail to devote some attention to the wider range of activities carried out by Caesar in his capacity as governor: the administration of justice in Cisalpine Gaul, a province that was largely pacified in the fifties and where Caesar tended to spend the winter, and in Illyricum, receives brief, but meaningful mentions. Caesar makes a point of not having disregarded civil affairs even in the most critical phases of a demanding military effort.

E18   Cicero in Cilicia, 51 BC

I composed my edict in Rome. I added nothing except what the tax-collectors (*publicani*) asked me to, when they had come to me at Samos, that I should transfer as many words from your edict into mine. The chapter, which deals with reducing the expenses of the communities, was very carefully written. In this chapter there are some innovations, contributing to the well-being of the communities, in which I take very great delight. But the part which has caused some suspicion to arise that I sought to offend you, was passed on from previous magistrates. [...] When I was at Laodicea, and at Apamea, and at Synnada, and at Philomelium, and at Iconium (I spent time in all these towns), all deputations of this sort had already been nominated. All the same I want you to know that I made no ruling for the reduction or cancellation of such expenditure on deputations except at the request of the leading men of the communities, to avoid expenditures of a far from necessary kind, leading them into the sale of taxes and those very harsh impositions (you will know to what I refer), the poll tax and the door tax.

In camp near Mopsuhestia (in Cilicia), 8 October 51 BC.

> Cicero to Appius Claudius, *To his Friends* 3.8.4–5 (SB 70), with omissions

Cicero, who has taken charge of the province of Cilicia, is responding to the complaints of his predecessor, Appius Claudius, about his interference with deputations of provincials that were planning to appear before the Senate in Rome to offer praise for Appius' administration of the province. Cicero claims to have imposed a limit on the expenditure for these diplomatic missions in order to bring them some relief in what remains a context of heavy taxation. – Cicero had set out these restrictions in the edict under which the province was to be run under his governorship: he conscientiously drafted it even before reaching his province, partly reproducing sections of the edict used by his predecessor, and partly in consultation with the tax-collectors that operated in the province. Cicero's commitment to the interests of the equestrian order was strongly confirmed during his provincial tenure.

E19   A territorial controversy between two Spanish communities, 87 BC: the Contrebia tablet

Let those of the Senate of Contrebia who shall be present at the time be the judges. If it appears, with regard to the land that the Salluienses purchased from the Sosinestani for the purpose of making a canal or of channelling water, which matter is the subject of this action, that the Sosinestani were within their rights in selling to the Salluienses against the wishes of the Allavonenses; then, if it so appears, let those judges adjudge that the Sosinestani were within their rights in selling to the Salluienses that land which is the subject of this action; if it does not so appear, let them adjudge that they were not within their rights in selling. Let those same persons who are written above be the judges. If the rules of the Sosinestan community were to apply, then, in the place where the Salluienses most recently and officially put in stakes, which is the subject of this action, if it would be permissible within their own rights for the Salluienses to make a canal through the public land of the Sosinestani within those stakes; or if it would be permissible for the Salluienses within their own rights to make a canal through the private land of the Sosinestani in the place where it would be proper for the canal to be made, so long as the Salluienses pay the money to the amount that would have been placed on the land where the canal might be brought; then, if it so appears, let those judges adjudge that it is permissible for the Salluienses within their own rights to make the canal; if it does not so appear, let them adjudge that it is not permissible for them to do so within their own rights. If they were to adjudge that it is permissible for the Salluienses to make the canal, then, on the arbitration of five men, whom a magistrate [or the magistracy?] of Contrebia shall have assigned from his [or their] Senate, let the Salluienses pay money from public funds for the private land where the canal shall be brought. Gaius Valerius Flaccus son of Gaius, *imperator*, established the right of judgement. They pronounced the opinion: 'Whereas the right of judgement in the matter that is the subject of this action is ours, we give judgement in favour of the Salluienses.'

When this adjudication was made, these were the magistrates of Contrebia: [... (*various names*)...]. [...]assius, son of Eihar, the Salluiensian, presented the case for the Salluienses; Turibas, son of Teitabas, the Allavonensian, presented the case for the Allavonenses. Transacted at Contrebia Balaisca, on 15 May, L. Cornelius and Cn. Octavius being the consuls.

Année Épigraphique 1979, 377 = EDCS-08901025

This bronze tablet from Contrebia (modern Botorrita, near Zaragoza) records the resolution of a controversy involving three Spanish communities over the legal status and use of land in which three communities had a stake, and on the location at which the envisaged construction of a canal should take place. The role of the Roman governor to which the communities turned seeking a resolution, C. Valerius Flaccus, was to appoint a panel of adjudicators, who are to provide a solution to the controversy: the matter was solved in terms that reveal the mastery of a complex legal terminology and thinking, and were accepted as authoritative by all parties. – A contingent of Salluienses is attested serving in the army of Cn. Pompeius Strabo in 90 BC: an inscription recording a citizenship grant in their favour survives (see **L25**). For an edition and a clear discussion of the document from Contrebia see J. S. Richardson, 'The *Tabula Contrebiensis*: Roman Law in Spain in the Early First Century B.C.', *JRS* 73 (1983) 33-41.

E20   Pompey's exercise of patronage in Spain
a) The case of Cornelius arises, jurors, from that statute which L. Gellius and Cn. Cornelius enacted in accordance with a decree of the senate: by this statute we see that it was confirmed that those should be Roman citizens to whom Pompey awarded citizenship individually in accordance with the decision of his advisory council.

Cicero, *Defence of Balbus* 19

L. Gellius Publicola and Cn. Cornelius were the consuls of 72 BC. Cicero is here defending Cornelius Balbus, who in 56 BC was accused of illegal citizenship. Pompey had held a five-year proconsular command over the two provinces of Spain from 54 BC, renewed for a further five years in 52 BC. In 49 BC the Pompeian commanders in Spain decided to withdraw to 'Pompeian' territory.

b) And so Afranius and Petreius decided themselves to leave the districts and to transfer the war to Celtiberia. [3] This decision was also influenced by the fact two different sorts of communities had existed at the time of the war with Sertorius: the vanquished were afraid of the name and authority of the absent Pompey, while those who had remained in friendship, had been given great rewards and had a high regard for him.

Caesar, *Civil War* 1.61

c) Although Caesar was being summoned back to Italy by many pressing circumstances, he had nevertheless decided not to leave behind any part of the war in the Spains, because he was aware of the many favours and the wide patronage of Pompey in nearer Spain.

Caesar, *Civil War* 2.18.7

E21   Roman justice in Spain

As for the governor himself, he passes his winters in administering justice in the regions by the sea, and especially in New Carthage and Tarraco, while in the summer time he goes the rounds of his province, always making an inspection of the things that require to be put right.

Strabo, *Geography* 3.4.20

In his discussion of the Iberian provinces Strabo, writing under Augustus/Tiberius, shows governors continuing to carry out their customary jurisdictional duties, according to an annual pattern that was already in use under the Republic, and was employed as a matter of course unless there was a pressing military emergency.

E22   Incompatibility of State and private business

Cicero to Cornificius.

My good friend C. Anicius, a man endowed with every good quality has been granted a special embassy (*libera legatio*) to Africa for the sake of his private business affairs. I would like you to help him in every possible way and do all your utmost so that he may complete his business as smoothly as possible; in particular, what he values most highly, I recommend his worthiness (*dignitas*) to your good offices and I request of you what I myself used to do in my province, without being asked: I granted all senators lictors. This was something which I had been given and had known to have been frequently done by men of the highest standing. And so, my Cornificius, you will do this and you will see to his status (*dignitas*) and well-being in all regards for my sake. I shall be most grateful. See that you take good care of your health.

Rome, 44 or 43 BC.

Cicero to Cornificius, *To his Friends* 12.21 (SB 429)

This recommendation letter (one of the many that survive in Cicero's correspondence) sheds light on a common practice in the late Republican period: senators would often travel to a province on private business, after being granted the title of *legatus* ('envoy', 'ambassador') by the Senate, hence gaining the right to travel at the State's expense and with a special status. In this text Cicero asks Q. Cornificius, the governor of the province of *Africa Vetus,* to afford special protection to his friend C. Anicius by granting him use of his lictors, the attendants who normally escort the governor and the members of his staff as they carry out their business. – The apparent frequency of this practice shows how geographically widespread the economic interests of the members of the Senate could be, and how blurred the distinction between public and private business could become. There is indeed some evidence for a *lex Julia* setting a time limit on the duration of *liberae legationes* ('free embassies'): Cicero, *Atticus*, 15.11.4 (SB 389), June 44 and Suetonius, *Divus Julius* 42.1.

E23   Octavian's restrictions on the movements of senators, 28 BC

[6] In addition to these measures he forbade all members of the Senate to go outside Italy, unless he himself should order or permit them to do so. This restriction is still observed down to the present day, for no senator is allowed to leave for the purpose of

visiting any place, except Sicily and Narbonese Gaul. [7] Since those parts are close at hand and the inhabitants are unarmed and peaceful, those who have any possessions in those parts are given the right to go there to visit them, without asking for permission.

Cassius Dio, *Roman History* 52.42.6–7

We have seen how significant the role of the presence of members of the senatorial order in the provinces was during the Republic, and what significance it might have on furthering their political position in Rome: it was, not least, a major opportunity for them to pursue valuable economic opportunities, and form new power bases across the empire. Against this background, it is not surprising to see Octavian taking active steps to limit the mobility of the senators across the empire, and to confine their movements to Italy.

PIRACY IN THE MEDITERRANEAN, 78–66 BC

E24   Publius Servilius Vatia Isauricus, 78–75 BC

a) To Cilicia and Pamphylia was sent P. Servilius after his consulship, an energetic man. He subdued Cilicia, attacked and captured very famous cities in Lycia, among them Phaselis, Olympus and Corycus [in Cilicia]. Having also attacked the Isauri, he brought them under rule and brought an end to the war in a period of three years. He was the first of all Romans to make a march in the Taurus. Returning he received a triumph and earned the name of Isauricus.

Eutropius, *Abridgement of Roman History* 6.3

b) Servilius, son of Gaius, *imperator*, defeated the enemy, captured Isaura Vetus and sold the captives. Whether it is a god or goddess who protected Vetus Isaura, he fulfilled his vow.

Sherk, *Rome and the Greek East to the Death of Augustus* 67B

Publius Servilius Vatia Isauricus, consul in 79 BC, held a proconsular command in Cilicia from 78 to 75 BC. He had a twofold task: to deal with the pirates infesting the south-east Aegean, in particular Lycia and Pamphylia and secondly to re-establish Roman presence inland so as to maintain communication with Cappadocia and guard against threats from Mithridates. – The remarkable Latin dedication under (b) records the performance of a ritual by Servilius, who fulfilled the vow he had made to the patron deity of Isaura Vetus as he set out to attack the city: his victory was seen as proof that the god (whose name and gender are unknown to Servilius) had deserted the city, and had joined the Romans. The dedication was therefore a highly aggressive claim to divine favour, and indeed a powerful gesture of religious appropriation.

E25   Julius Caesar and the pirates

[1.4] Caesar spent a short time in Bithynia with King Nicomedes; then, on the voyage back, was captured near the island of Pharmacusa by the pirates who had already by that time taken control of the sea with a great deal of equipment and countless small vessels. [2.1] When they initially asked for a ransom of twenty talents, he laughed at them for not knowing whom they had taken prisoner, and agreed that he would give them fifty. Then he sent his companions each to different cities to procure the money. Left on his own with just one friend and two slaves amongst the Cilicians, the most murderous people, he treated them with such contempt that whenever he wanted to sleep he would send someone to tell them to be quiet. [2] For thirty-eight days, as if they were not his gaolers but his royal bodyguard he joined in their games and their exercise without any hesitation. He wrote poems and some speeches using them as his audience: those who were not impressed he would call to their faces uneducated barbarians and often threatened with a smile to hang them. [3] They enjoyed this and put his outspokenness down to a certain inexperience and childishness. The ransom arrived from Miletus. He had no sooner paid it and been set free than he manned ships and put to sea from Miletus harbour against the pirates. He caught them, still at anchor near the island, and captured almost all of them. The money he took as booty, the men he put in prison at Pergamum … *(but not convinced that the governor of Asia would act properly)* … Caesar left the governor to do as he pleased, returned to Pergamum, took the robbers out and crucified them all, just as he had often said on the island that he would do, they thought as a joke.

Plutarch, *Life of Caesar* 1.4–2.3

Suetonius, *Divus Julius* has the same story and similar details. It can be approximately dated to between 77 and 75 BC.

E26   M. Antonius (Creticus), 73–71 BC
a) As for Antonius, while he was doing many things against the welfare of our allies and contemplating doing more against the interests of the provinces, death overtook him.

Cicero, *Against Verres* 2.3.213

b) This is the M. Antonius who through the influence of the consul Cotta and the intrigue of Cethegus obtained unlimited authority (*curatio infinita*) of the whole sea coast, and plundered both Sicily and all the provinces, and in the end when waging war on the Cretans died.

Gronovian Scholiast, p. 259 Stangl

M. Antonius Creticus, father of Marcus Antonius (Mark Antony the triumvir), married Julia, the sister of Julius Caesar. He was given an *imperium infinitum* (unlimited command) against the pirates; he held it from 74 to 72/71 BC, campaigning firstly along the Ligurian coast of Italy and of Spain and later against Crete. Velleius (*History,* 2.31.3) reports that his *imperium* was the same as that which Pompey would have later. – The Gronovian scholiast describes him as not only a scoundrel himself, but with the worst colleagues (p. 202 Stangl). He was disastrously defeated by the Cretans and made a peace with them. Many members of the Senate looked with hostility upon such commands, as the opposition to the proposal of Gabinius in 67 BC makes clear, and he did not enjoy the support and the huge forces that were assigned to Pompey a few years later.

E27   Crete and the pirates: Q. Caecilius Metellus (Creticus), 68–65 BC
[98] Quintus Metellus as proconsul was charged with the war against the Cretans and besieged the city of Cydonia. … [99] Q. Metellus, proconsul, sacked Cnossus, Lyctus, Cydonia and a very large number of other cities. … [Book 99] also contains the campaigns waged against the Cretans by Metellus and the letters of Metellus and Pompey dispatched by each in their turn. Q. Metellus complains that the glory of his achievements is being diverted away from himself in advance in that Pompey has sent his legate to receive the surrenders of the cities. Pompey explains that he had to do this. [100] … Q. Metellus, with the Cretans completely subdued, gave laws to the island, which had previously been free.

Livy, *Summaries* 98, 99,100

Q. Caecilius Metellus, *cos.* 69 BC, was given the province of Crete (with Achaia) and entrusted with the campaign against the pirates. Pompey's achievements on a much more important and demanding front, that of Asia Minor, overshadows his substantial achievements: the restoration of Roman control over Crete was no mean feat.

E28 The impact of piracy

[20.1] Pirates always used to harass those who sailed the sea, just as robbers did those who dwelt on land. ... [2] But previously they used to plunder by land and sea, in certain places and only during the summer season, in small groups; but now, from the time when war was waged everywhere and continuously at the same time, when many cities had been ruined, while punishments hung over all the fugitives and there was no freedom from fear for anyone, very many had turned to plunder ... [4] For while the Romans were busily engaged with their enemies, the pirates had flourished greatly, sailing about to many places and adding to their number all who were like themselves with the result that some of them, in the manner of allies, were able to bring help to many others. [21.1] ... When those wars had ended, the pirates did not cease their activities, but did a great deal of harm to the Romans and to their allies on their own account. For they did not sail in small numbers, but with great fleets, and they had commanders so that they gained a great name; [2] they used to seize and rob first and foremost those who sailed on the sea (and they no longer allowed the winter season to be safe for them, but as a result of their daring, their experience and their success they made voyages at that time too without fear) and then those who were in harbours. [3] For if anyone dared to sail out against them, he was almost always defeated and perished, but even if he was victorious, he was then unable to capture any of them because of the speed of their ships; and so returning in a short time as if they had been victorious they would ravage and set ablaze not only farms and fields, but also whole cities; while some places they settled so as to make them winter quarters and naval bases as if in a friendly land.

[22.1] As their operations progressed, they used to advance inland and they would do much harm to those who did not even use the sea. And they dealt in this way not only with their alliance overseas but also with Italy itself. [2] For thinking that they would have greater profits from that country and that they would make all the rest more frightened, if they not did hold off from that land too, they sailed against other cities there and against Ostia itself and they fired the ships and sacked everything. [3] And finally, since no attention was being taken of them, they established settlements on land and disposed of all the men they did not kill and all the booty they took without fear as if they were in their own homeland. [4] Although different people plundered in different places (for the same people were not able to do harm over the whole sea at the same time) they nonetheless showed such friendship to one another that they sent money and assistance even to those completely unknown as though to their closest relations. [5] And this was not the least reason for their strength that they all honoured those who paid court to any of them and they all ravaged those who came into collision with any of them.

[23] The power of the pirates grew to such an extent that the war against them became serious, unceasing, and unpredictable, and without quarter. Indeed the Romans used to hear of these matters from time to time and did witness some of them (for some of

their imports did not come in to them and the corn supply was cut off completely); [2] they did not however give great thought to these matters when they should have but they used to send out fleets and commanders as they were roused at some moment by individual reports but they would achieve nothing. However, they caused their allies all the more distress for these very reasons until they were desperate. Finally they assembled and deliberated for many days over what they ought to do. [3] Worn out by the continuous dangers and seeing that the war against the pirates would be a great and long one, and reckoning that it was not possible to campaign against them all at once or individually (for they helped one another and there was no way they could drive them off everywhere at the same time) they were at a complete loss and in great despair of in any way putting matters straight.

Cassius Dio, Roman History 36.20.1–23, with omissions

By the seventies BC Rome had revived and strengthened a complex system of economic and fiscal exploitation of the Greek East, chiefly of the province of Asia. However, that capability did not entail a complete, or indeed even a robust control of the territory that was in principle subject to Roman rule. Cassius Dio's overview of the rise and success of piracy in the Eastern Mediterranean establishes a causal link with the long string of military conflicts that took place in the region, and clearly stresses that Rome did not have the ability to contain the consolidation of the pirates' forces: in fact, Dio suggests that Rome lacked the local knowledge to chart and pursue the initiatives of the pirates, who appear to create a structure that may be plausibly compared with that of a state, and began to present a real risk to the Italian peninsula, including the major port of Ostia. – For another powerful overview of the rising power of the pirates in the Eastern Mediterranean and a discussion of their association with King Mithridates see Appian, *Mithridatic War* 91-93.

E29   Command against the pirates: Pompey the Great, 67 BC

[96] Pompey himself sailed with a varied force and much armament, expecting that he would need it for all kinds of fighting and sieges against precipitous peaks. But he needed none of it; for the pirates were struck with fear at his fame and his force and hoped that if they did not come to battle they might obtain humane treatment; first of all those who held Cragus and Anticragus, the greatest strongholds, and after them the Cilicians of the mountains and then all one after another gave themselves up and at the same time they surrendered many weapons, some ready, others being forged, and ships, some still on the stocks others at sea; bronze and iron collected for them, and sail cloths and ropes and timber of all sorts; and a host of prisoners, some for ransom, others bound to their tasks. Pompey burned the timber, put the ships to sea, released the prisoners to their home countries; and many of them found their cenotaphs there on the assumption that they were among the dead. Those pirates, who seemed most to have come to this state, not through wickedness, but through poverty, because of war he settled at Mallos and Adana and Epiphaneia or at any other desolate or poorly populated town in Cilicia Tracheia. Some of them he also sent away to Dyme in Achaia. Thus the war against the pirates, which was thought would be very difficult, was, thanks to Pompey, of few days' duration. He took seventy-one ships by capture, three hundred and six surrendered by them, and about one hundred and twenty towns and strongholds and other stations. About ten thousand pirates were carried off in battle.

Appian, Mithridatic Wars 96

Appian gives a detailed account of the preparations for Pompey's campaign against the pirates and the establishment of the military and logistical infrastructures that would make it possible. The conflict turns out to be rather uneventful, and is not so much resolved by military action: it is brought to completion by a political and economic settlement that provides a long-term solution to the economic predicament of the defeated pirates.

E30 Enactment of the Gabinian law, 67 BC

[24.5] Pompey, who was very eager to command, because of his own ambition and the enthusiasm of the people, no longer now regarded this command to be an honour but failure to obtain it to be a dishonour; seeing the opposition of the powerful (Gk: *dunatoi*), he wanted to appear to be under compulsion. [6] He was always in the habit of pretending to desire least the things he wanted; and on this occasion more so, because of the jealousy if he were of his own accord to lay claim to the command, and because of the glory if he should be appointed against his will as the one most worthy to command. [... (*There follows a speech from Pompey and a reply from Gabinius*)...]

[30] When Gabinius had spoken in such manner, Trebellius tried to speak in opposition. When he did not gain permission to say anything, he opposed the taking of the vote. [2] Gabinius was therefore annoyed; he delayed the voting regarding Pompey and introduced another motion concerning Trebellius himself. The first seventeen tribes to give their decision voted that Trebellius was acting wrongly and ought no longer to be tribune. When the eighteenth was on the point of voting the same way Trebellius finally just about kept silence. [3] Roscius, seeing this, did not dare to utter a word, but raising his hand aloft bade them choose two men, so that he might in this way cut off a little of Pompey's power. As he was giving this gesture with his hand, the crowd gave a loud and threatening shout so that a crow flying above their heads was startled and fell as if struck by lightning. [4] When this happened Roscius kept not only his tongue, but his hand motionless as well.

[*Gabinius then persuades Catulus to come forward and speak; he opposes so much power being given to one man and urges that the regular magistrates deal with the problem.*]

[36a] Catulus, one of the *optimates*, had said to the people: 'If he fails when sent out on this task – as tends to happen in many encounters, especially on the sea – what other man will you find to take his place for the more necessary tasks?' Thereupon the whole crowd, as if by some agreement, cried out and exclaimed: 'You!' Thus Pompey secured command of the sea and of the islands and of the mainland for fifty miles inland from the sea.

Cassius Dio, Roman History 36.24.5–6, 30, 36a

The decision to grant Pompey a command against the pirates was not as foregone a conclusion as Cicero's discussion in the speech on the Manilian law would suggest. Dio's account shows that the proposal of the tribune Gabinius was opposed by another tribune of the plebs: this hurdle was overcome by the remarkable combination of a threat to depose his rival (through a legal device that recalls the removal of M. Octavius in 133 BC) and of the prospect of using political violence against any opponents, including the tribune L. Roscius Otho, who suggests a possible compromise. Even the opposition of Q. Lutatius Catulus, one of the most prominent members of the Senate, is overcome by suggesting the prospect of the command being granted to Catulus if Pompey were to be unsuccessful. – Chapter 36a is drawn from Xiphilinus' summary of Cassius Dio's *Roman History*. Other versions of these events may be found in Plutarch, *Life of Pompey* 35-36 and Asconius, *Commentaries* p. 72C.8–21.

E31   Cicero celebrates Pompey's achievements, 66 BC

Or do you think that there is any shore anywhere so desolate that news has not reached it of that day when the entire Roman people, packing the forum and filling all the temples, from which this spot can be seen, demanded Pompey alone as commander for a war that was common to all nations? ... On the very day on which he was placed in command of the naval war by you, grain immediately became cheap, after a period when it was very scarce and expensive, on the hope and reputation of one man, to a degree that prolonged peace could barely have achieved when the corn lands were at their most fruitful.

Cicero, *On the Manilian Law / On Pompey's Command* 44

In the mid-first century BC the spread of information across the Mediterranean world was a much slower and messier process than is the case in the modern world: however, the links between knowledge and power, and between rumour and political developments are as strong a factor in the world of the late Roman Republic as they are in our time. Dio (**E28**) insists on the consequences that the poor knowledge of the pirates' movements has for Rome; in this passage Cicero emphasizes the reach of Pompey's reputation, and claims that the very news of his appointment to the campaign against the pirates led to a reduction in the price of grain, as it prompted the wide expectation that the war would be won. Although the role of rhetorical exaggeration must be recognized, this notice is a strong hint of a scenario of close interdependence across different regions of the Mediterranean empire.

THE EASTERN FRONT, 87–63 BC

E32   Asia: propraetorship of L. Licinius Murena, 84–81 BC

[64] Murena had been left behind by Sulla with the two legions of Fimbria to settle the rest of the affairs of Asia, but he sought trifling pretexts for war because of a desire for a triumph ... against the tribes of the Bosporus Mithridates constructed ships and made ready a large army; such was the great size of the force that it quickly gave rise to a rumour that it was not being assembled against the tribes of the Bosporus but against the Romans ... when Archelaus learned this he was afraid and fled to Murena. He spurred him on and persuaded him to attack Mithridates first. Murena advancing through Cappadocia attacked Comana, a large town subject to Mithridates, which had a rich and sacred temple, and killed some of the king's cavalry. When envoys of the king put forward the treaty, Murena replied he did not see a treaty; Sulla had not had it written out. ... Having said this Murena immediately began looting and he did not even hold back from the temple moneys. He spent the winter in Cappadocia. [65] Mithridates sent to Rome – to the Senate and to Sulla – bringing charges over what Murena was doing. In the meantime, Murena, having crossed the Halys ... overran four hundred villages; the king did not go to meet him but awaited the ambassadors. Murena returned to Phrygia and Galatia laden with much plunder where Calidius, sent from Rome as a result of the complaints of Mithridates, did not hand over a decree, but said publicly in the hearing of all that the Senate ordered Murena to show consideration to the king since he was in alliance. Having said this, Calidius was seen in private conversation with Murena who in no way relaxed his aggression, but then attacked the territory of Mithridates. So Mithridates, thinking that open warfare was being waged by

the Romans ... crossed the river and got the better of Murena in all respects ... the king attacked him and losing many men he fled over the mountains to Phrygia ... [66] He drove all of Murena's garrisons out of Cappadocia ... Sulla did not deem it right to make war on Mithridates when he was in alliance. Aulus Gabinius was sent out to tell Murena that the previous statement was correct – not to make war on Mithridates – and to reconcile Mithridates and Ariobarzanes with one another ... thus the second war between the Romans and Mithridates came to an end in about the third year.

Appian, *Mithridatic Wars* 64–66, with omissions

A summary of the so-called Second Mithridatic War, which was in fact a short conflict, in which the lack of formal ratification in Rome of the peace agreement between Sulla and Mithridates, and the personal ambition of Licinius Murena bring about a revival of the conflict. Mithridates' swift response shows that the defeat against Sulla had not deprived him of substantial military capability. Murena returned to Rome in 81 BC and celebrated a triumph: Appian's account casts doubts on the effectiveness of his war effort. Clearly he and Sulla had different views on the policy to be pursued in relation to Mithridates and equally clearly the Senate did not control a provincial official: a concerning sign of later developments in the Republican period. Calidius' actions – in public and in private – seem to betray differences of opinion in Rome, but the late 80s were disturbed times. Indeed, though an embassy came from Mithridates to Rome, after the death of Sulla, to seek to ratify the Peace of Dardanus, the Senate did give the ambassadors audience.

E33   Mithridates and Pompey, 66–63 BC

a) And while he was still in Cilicia they appointed him commander of the war against Mithridates with the same powers, having absolute authority, to make agreements and to make war as he wished and to make whoever he so judged friends and enemies of the Romans.

Appian, *Mithridatic Wars* 97

b) [3] The members of the aristocratic group ... privately exhorted and encouraged one another to attack the proposal and not to give up their freedom... [4] But when the time came, they were afraid of the people and the rest abandoned the cause, but Catulus criticized the proposal and the tribune at length; but in fact he persuaded nobody ... [5] The proposal was nevertheless ratified, so they say, by all the tribes and Pompey, who was not present, was not far from having all the powers which Sulla possessed after he had conquered the city by arms and war.

Plutarch, *Life of Pompey* 30.3–5, with omission

The operations of Pompey against Mithridates and in the East are related in Plutarch, *Life of Pompey* 30-46; Cassius Dio, *Roman History* 36.42.4-44.2; 45-54; 37.1-23; Appian, *Mithridatic Wars* 97-121.

PROVINCIAL COMMANDS, 58–51 BC

E34   Caesar seeks a suitable province, 59 BC

From all the number of provinces Caesar chose Gaul rather than any other since it was ideal material for his financial advantage and for the chance of triumphs. Admittedly, in the beginning he received Cisalpine Gaul with the addition of Illyricum under the *lex Vatinia*; a little later he received Comata too through the Senate, since the fathers were afraid that if they themselves refused the people would give him this too.

Suetonius, *Divus Julius* 22

Another case of a major provincial command being granted through a piece of tribunician legislation. Gallia Comata 'long-haired Gaul' (known also as Transalpine Gaul) signified un-Romanized Gaul beyond the boundaries of the province of Cisalpine Gaul. As is well known, this is the province where Caesar made the greatest impact and to which he devoted most of his energies: it was not part of his original brief. – See also Cassius Dio, *Roman History* 38.8.5.

E35   Cicero attacks Vatinius for his law assigning provinces in 59 BC

You had deprived the Senate of its power to decree a province, its discretion to choose a commander, its control over the treasury: the Roman people never sought these functions for itself and it never tried to take away from the Senate the direction of high policy. But I admit that in other matters something like this has happened. Rarely, but it has nevertheless happened that the people chose a commander: who ever heard of legates without a senatorial decree? Before you no one did that; after you a Clodius straight away did the same thing in the case of two monstrous creatures in the *res publica*. Hence you should be sacrificed in a more dire and dreadful way, because not only have you wounded the *res publica* by what you have done, but also by the example you have set; not only are you yourself an unprincipled rascal, but you have also wished to teach others.

Cicero, *Against Vatinius* 36

A passage of great historical interest: in his bitter attack on Vatinius, Cicero spells out the powers that the Senate can reasonably be expected to exert in matters of provincial administration. It is also significant that a link is established with the later actions of Clodius, who had unduly favoured the consuls of 58, Gabinius and Calpurnius Piso, in a similar case (see **B102a** where a political trade-off secures the consuls remunerative provincial commands in exchange for their acquiescence to Clodius' political and legislative programme, in which the proposal for Cicero's exile had a central part.). Cicero identifies a tradition of irresponsible tribunician politics in the fifties, with which Caesar is implicitly, but firmly linked. In fact the predicament of Pompey in 67 and 66 BC (**E30**) shows how valuable the support of a tribune of the plebs could be to an individual who intended to secure a coveted provincial command. Note the use of sacrificial terminology, which is all the more loaded in a context of looming political violence.

E36   M. Cato's extraordinary command in Cyprus, 58–56 BC

But with them I do at least have something to discuss: in your case, on the other hand, what is this gross impudence that you dare to say that no extraordinary appointment should be given to anyone? It was you who, by a wicked law, without any investigation of the case, confiscated the property of Ptolemy, king of Cyprus, brother of the Alexandrian king, while he was reigning with equal legitimacy; you who implicated the Roman people in the crime; you who organized the patronage of this command (*imperium*) to seize the kingdom, the goods and the fortunes of a man whose father, grandfather, and ancestors had enjoyed the friendship and alliance with us; you who put M. Cato in charge of bringing to Rome his money and, if he should defend his rights, of waging war. [21] You will say: 'What a man! The most upright, the most wise, the most courageous, the most patriotic, with a remarkable and almost unique claim to fame through his virtue, his sound judgement and his way of life.' True, but what is all this to you, for you say that in the *res publica* no one ought to be given any extraordinary appointment? And in fact in this case I show up no more than your inconsistency: for it was not for that man's worth (*dignitas*) that you were promoting him in this matter, but you were getting him out of the way for your criminal enterprise.

Cicero, *On his House* 20–21

In a speech delivered in 56 BC Cicero confronts a problematic political development that had intervened two years earlier: M. Porcius Cato, one of the most prominent and authoritative members of the conservative section of the senatorial order, was entrusted with the task of organizing the new province of Cyprus, and the main backer of that assignment was Clodius. The partnership of the two men stands as a warning against assuming that men of different political persuasions and allegiances could not possibly cooperate, and that rigid ideological divides apply in the late Republican period. It also questions the picture of Clodius that Cicero often sketches, that of a disreputable individual who does not belong in the number of honest citizens and with whom no decent man can possibly form a partnership. Cicero solves the problem with a shrewd rhetorical twist: Clodius wanted Cato, the most virtuous man in Rome, away from the city, and plotted to grant him that overseas posting. Cato's willingness to accept it at a time of great political crisis remains unexplained. – Whatever the political background of his provincial assignment might have been, Cato appears to have upheld the highest standards of integrity and fairness during his tenure: so was argued, at least, in the lost historical work of Munatius Rufus, who served under him at Cyprus (quoted in Valerius Maximus, *Memorable Deeds and Sayings* 4.3.2; see *Fragments of the Roman Historians* 37 F1).

E37 Caesar in Gaul: Ariovistus and the Germans

[42] When Ariovistus learned of Caesar's approach, he sent envoys to say that as regards his earlier demand about a meeting, it was now possible for him to do this. … [43.1] There was a wide plain and within it a quite large mound of earth. This spot was about equidistant from the camps of Ariovistus and Caesar. [2] They came to meeting here as had been arranged. Caesar halted the legion, which he had put on horseback, two hundred paces from the mound. [3] Ariovistus likewise halted his cavalry at the same distance. Ariovistus demanded that they should speak on horseback and that they should each bring ten men with them. [4] When they reached the spot Caesar began his speech by recalling his own and the Senate's favours to Ariovistus. He had been called 'king' by the Senate, called 'friend' and many gifts had been sent. This had happened to few others and Caesar explained that such favours were customarily granted in return for signal services. [5] Though he had neither access to the Senate nor a just claim, through the favour and generosity of himself and the Senate, he had gained these rewards. [6] He explained too how longstanding and just were the reasons for the friendship existing between themselves and the Aedui; what decrees of the Senate had been passed concerning them, [7] how often and what honours these conferred, how the Aedui had at all time held the foremost position among the Gauls, even before they had sought our friendship. [8] It was the custom of the Roman people to wish their friends and allies to be deprived of nothing that belonged to them but to add to their favour (*gratia*), status (*dignitas*), honour (*honor*): who could allow them to be deprived of what they had brought to the friendship of the Roman people? [9] He then made the same demands which he had given in the instructions to the envoys: Ariovistus should not make war on the Aedui or their allies; he should return the

hostages; if he could not send any part of the Germans back home, he should at least not allow any more to cross the Rhine.

[44] Ariovistus replied briefly to Caesar's demands, but proclaimed at length his own abilities … [6] As for the mass of Germans he was bringing across the Rhine, he was doing this in self-defence not to attack Gaul: evidence of this fact was that he would not have come had he not been asked, that he had not attacked but defended himself. [7] He had entered Gaul before the Roman people. Never before this time had an army of the Roman people gone outside the territory of the Gallic province. [8] What did Caesar want with him? Why did he enter what belonged to Ariovistus? This Gaul was his province just as the former was ours. Just as it would not be right to make any concession to him if he attacked our territories, so we were wrong in that we were impeding him in what was rightfully his. [9] As for his statement that the Aedui had been called brothers, he was not such a barbarian or so unversed in affairs as not to know that in the most recent war against the Allobroges the Aedui had not brought help to the Romans nor themselves used the help of the Roman people in those squabbles, which the Aedui had had between themselves and the Sequani. [10] He had to suspect that, with this feigned friendship, Caesar, because he had an army in Gaul, had it to crush him. If he were not to go away and lead his army back from these regions, he would treat him not as a friend, but as a public enemy. [11] If he killed him he would be doing something pleasing to many nobles and leaders of the Roman people: he knew this for certain through envoys of those people themselves, all of whose thanks and friendship he would gain by Caesar's death. [12] But if he withdrew and handed over to him free occupation of Gaul, he would recompense with a considerable reward and would, without any effort or risk on Caesar's part, complete any wars Caesar wished to wage.

[45] Caesar spoke at length on the matter of why he could not leave the business in hand: neither his nor the Roman people's custom allowed him to abandon loyal allies nor did he judge that Gaul belonged more to Ariovistus than to the Roman people.

Caesar, *Gallic War* 1.42–45.1, with omissions

Much of Caesar's work in the first year of his Gallic campaign involved addressing the threat presented by the Germani and their leader Ariovistus: formally a friend of the Roman people, he had been clashing with another allied community, the Aedui, and sought to expand into their territory; the Aedui had therefore sought the Roman intervention. Caesar had had early exchanges with Ariovistus, in which he urged the Germani to withdraw from their newly acquired position, and effectively claimed equal stading by his initial refusal to meet halfway with Caesar (Caesar, *Gallic War* 1.34-36). Ariovistus' attitude towards Caesar and his requests remains very firm even when the two men meet in person, after Caesar's decision to move his army towards the positions occupied by the Germani. On this occasion Ariovistus seeks talks with Caesar, but insists on conducting them on horseback; he then responds to Caesar's lengthy discussion of the favours carried out for the Germani by stating his merits and his entitlement to promote his own interests. He goes as far as suggesting that Caesar's attitude may be disingenuous, and conceals the intention to launch an attack on him. He then makes an even more extraordinary claim: he knows that some people in Rome want Caesar dead, and they have indeed conveyed that preference to him. In making this claim, Ariovistus is suggesting that the assassination of the legitimate Roman promagistrate would not necessarily undermine his relationship with Rome. This detail is also of major political significance to Caesar, who wrote the *Commentarii* with the central aim to shape the reception of his Gallic campaign in Rome, both in the Senate and beyond: suggesting that some are plotting his demise amounts to sending a divisive and aggressive political message to his fellow-citizens.

E38   Caesar on the Rhine, July 55 BC

[16] Having brought to completion the German campaign, Caesar decided that the Rhine had to be crossed, for many reasons: the most compelling one was that, since he saw that the Germans could be so easily induced to come into Gaul, he wanted to make them fear for their own fortunes too, once they would understand that the Roman army had the ability and the courage to cross the Rhine.

Caesar, *Gallic War* 4.16.1

The Rhine remained a highly meaningful landmark throughout the Gallic campaign as the 'natural' boundary between Gaul and Germany. Its moral and psychological significance is arguably even greater, and is further confirmed by the later Roman attempts to expand beyond it, notably in the early Principate.

E39   Ptolemy and Egypt, 56 BC

[2] Meanwhile, Ptolemy the king of Egypt, who had left Alexandria because of a fit of anger and a quarrel with the citizens, was sailing to Rome in the hope that Pompey and Caesar would restore him with an armed force. He wished to meet Cato and sent a messenger to him, in the hope that Cato would come to him. [3] However, Cato happened to be occupied in purging his bowels at the time, but told Ptolemy to come to him if he wished. When Ptolemy came, Cato did not go to meet him or even rise to his feet, but greeted him as any normal visitor and asked him to sit down. At first Ptolemy was somewhat put out by this reception and was amazed at the plain and simple surroundings of Cato in contrast with his stern and haughty character. [4] But when he began to converse about his own situation, he listened to words that were forthright and full of good sense. Cato criticized him and explained what great happiness he had given up, and to what humiliation, hardship, corruption, and greed he was exposing himself at the hands of those who held power at Rome. Their demands would scarcely be satisfied if the whole of Egypt were turned into cash. Cato advised Ptolemy to sail back and be reconciled with his people; he was himself ready to sail with Ptolemy and assist him in the reconciliation. [5] Then Ptolemy, as though brought to his senses by Cato's words after some fit of madness or delirium, recognized the man's truthfulness and intelligence and became eager to make use of his sound advice. However, his friends made him change his mind again; but as soon as he reached Rome and came to the door of one of the magistrates, he groaned at his mistaken policy, because he had scorned the words not of a good man, but of the oracle of a god.

Plutarch, *Life of Cato the Younger* 35.2–5

This anecdote relates a meeting between the king of Egypt, Ptolemy XII, and Cato the Younger, in which much is made of Cato's ability to speak the truth and to uphold much higher standards of conduct than his contemporaries: Plutarch suggests that his moral credentials are the reason that leads the king to seek his advice. He even goes as far as stating that Cato's wisdom is comparable to the lore of a divine oracle. In his assessment, a potential Roman intervention in Egypt would just be an opportunity for some members of the Roman élite to enrich themselves; the only opportunity Ptolemy has to regain power is to seek an accommodation with his subjects. What underlies Cato's assessment is a negative view on the role of client kingdoms, both on the territories they rule and on the political competition in Rome. – Ptolemy XII Auletes (the flute-player); he was the son of Ptolemy XI Alexander II and a mistress, and succeeded on the latter's death in 80 BC. He was confirmed in his kingdom and recognized as a friend and ally of the Roman people, probably in 59 BC, on the payment of a sum of 6,000 talents to Caesar and Pompey. In attempting to collect the money he was driven out by his citizens and made his way to Rome – his meeting with Cato occurred during this journey – to seek support to his attempt to regain power in Alexandria.

E40   Cicero supports Caesar's retention of his Gallic provinces, 56 BC

[32] The Gallic War has been fought under Gaius Caesar's command, conscript fathers; before we merely repelled attacks. Our commanders always thought that those peoples had to be beaten back, rather than attacked. Even the famous C. Marius, whose divine and outstanding valour came to our rescue amidst great losses and deaths of the Roman people, repelled large contingents of Gauls that were streaming into Italy – but did not himself reach into their cities and countries. Recently that great ally of my labours, dangers, and counsels, C. Pomptinus, a man of outstanding strength, put an end with his battles to a war that was suddenly waged by the Allobroges and fomented by this criminal conspiracy; he tamed those who had attacked us, then satisfied with that victory and having freed the commonwealth from fear, he retired. I can see that C. Caesar's strategy has long been a different one. For he did not think that he should fight by himself against those that he saw in arms against the Roman people, but that the whole of Gaul must be brought under our rule. [33] He therefore has taken on in battle the fiercest people of the Germani and the Helvetii and has defeated them with outstanding success; the rest he has terrified, repelled, tamed, and accustomed them to be obedient to the rule of the Roman people. Our commander, our soldiers, and the arms of the Roman people have made their way into regions and peoples that no written work, no spoken word, no report had previously made known to us. All that we used to hold of Gaul, conscript fathers, was a path through it; the rest was held by peoples that were either enemies of this empire, or disloyal, or unknown, or known to be savage, barbarous, and warlike – peoples that anyone would have liked to see crushed and tamed. From the very beginning of this empire of ours no wise man has failed to regard Gaul as the greatest danger to this empire. However, on account of the violence and number of those people, we have never before engaged in a conflict with them as a whole. We have always resisted them when we have been attacked: now we have reached the point when the limit of our empire and that of those lands are the same. [34] Nature, not without a degree of divine favour, had once protected Italy with the Alps as its rampart: for if that entry port had opened to savage crowds of Gauls, this city would have never offered a seat and an abode to the greatest empire. Let the Alps sink now! For there is nothing beyond those high mountains all the way up to Ocean that Italy should dread. No more than one or two summers can tie the whole of Gaul to us with eternal chains, either of fear or hope, punishment or rewards, arms or laws. But if we leave this work unfinished and unrefined, the might of Gaul, much as it has been cut down, will pick up again one day and will revive to bring about a new war.

Cicero, *On the Consular Provinces* 32–34

The sixties and the fifties are an age of great imperial expansion, and this comment of Cicero in a speech of 55 BC is an early attempt to make sense of the consequences of Caesar's victories in Transalpine Gaul: until 58 BC the Roman rule in Gaul did not extend beyond a network of roads, and the rest of the region was in foreign, and potentially hostile hands; Cicero also stresses their demographic strength. On the one hand, Caesar's achievements receive an emphatic celebration; on the other, they are justified in light of the real threat of a new attack on Italy.

E41   Cato opposes the proposal of Trebonius, 55 BC

[33.2] Now Gaius Trebonius, a tribune, proposed that to the one should be given Syria and the neighbouring lands, to the other the two Spains, for there had recently been some disturbance there, to govern for a period of five years; they should employ as many soldiers as they wished, both citizens and allies, and should make war and peace with whomsoever they pleased. [3] Many took offence at this ... The consuls, fearing that they might utterly fail in what they were doing, won over their opponents on the condition of extending Caesar's command also for three more years – to reveal the real truth. [4] However, they did not propose anything on his behalf to the people until their own arrangements had been confirmed ... [34.1] On the other hand, Cato and Favonius with two tribunes and some others as their helpers, resisted all that was being done by the consuls. But as they were few in number fighting against many, they spoke out to no purpose. [2] And Favonius, who obtained from Trebonius only one hour for his speech in opposition, used it up complaining without purpose against the very limitation of his time. Cato, for his part, received two hours to make his speech. [3] He devoted his efforts to criticism of present conditions and the general state of affairs, as was his custom, and so exhausted his time before he had spoken about any of the proposals before them, not because it was impossible for anything to have been said on these matters too; but in order that he might be silenced by Trebonius while still appearing to have something more to say and thus accuse him in the matter too. He well understood that even if he used up the whole day, he could not persuade them to vote anything he wanted. [4] Thus, when ordered to be silent, he did not stop immediately, but was pushed and dragged from the assembly. He then came back and, though finally having been ordered to be taken to the prison, he did not restrain himself.

[35.1] That day was used up in this way so that the tribunes were not able to speak at all...[3] Thus Gallus feared that someone might keep him from the forum on the next day or do something worse. He went into the senate-house in the evening and spent the night inside, because of the safety of the place and so that he could leave there at dawn to join the crowd. [4] Trebonius caused him to spend both the night and most of the day there to no purpose, having locked all the doors of the senate-house. Others, having occupied the place of the assembly in advance during the night, barred Ateius, Cato, Favonius and the others with them from entering. [5] When Favonius and Ninnius somehow got inside unobserved, while Cato and Ateius, having climbed on some of those who standing around and being lifted up by them, declared an omen from the sky so as to dissolve their meeting, the attendants of the tribunes drove them both out, wounded others who were with them, and even killed some. [36] The law was passed in this way.

Cassius Dio, Roman History 39.33.2–36.1, with omissions

Dio provides a reasonably detailed account of the process that in 55 BC led to the passing of law under which new provincial commands were assigned to Crassus and Pompey, who also were the serving consuls of that year: again, a tribune of the plebs, Trebonius, took the lead in that process. Cato and others, including two tribunes, Ateius Capito and Aquilius Gallus, oppose the bill. They do not just present a set of political arguments, but resort to a number of obstruction techniques: first by hindering and delaying the debate in the Senate, then by invoking a religious argument, and claiming that they saw signs of divine hostility in the sky. In both instances their objections are silenced by the violent reaction of Trebonius' supporters: in the later incident their intervention even leads to the death of some of their opponents. – Plutarch, *Life of Cato the Younger* 43. 1–7 records this incident in similar terms.

E42   Cato attacks Caesar's actions in the Gallic war

Caesar had attacked warlike nations and overcome them at great risk. He was rumoured to have set upon the Germans during a period of truce and to have killed three hundred thousand of them. The rest of the citizens called for the people to offer sacrifices for the good news, but Cato insisted that they should hand over Caesar to those who had been wronged; they should not turn the curse upon themselves or allow it into the city. [2] 'Nonetheless,' he said, 'let us sacrifice to the gods that they will not inflict punishment for the folly and madness of the commander upon the soldiers, and that they will spare the city.' [3] As a result of this Caesar wrote a letter and sent it off to the Senate. When it was read out it contained a good many accusations and insults against Cato. He stood up and without anger or hostility but apparently in reasoned and well-prepared terms showed how the accusations against him were nothing but abuse and scurrility and a rather childish and boorish act on Caesar's part. [4] Then he dealt with Caesar's plans from the beginning, revealing his whole policy not as an enemy, but as an accomplice and a collaborator. He explained that it was not the sons of the Britons or the Celts, but Caesar himself they ought to fear, if they had any sense. [5] He so moved and stirred people that the friends of Caesar regretted having read his letter in the Senate and having provided Cato with the opportunity to make remarks that were just and accusations that were true.

Plutarch, *Life of Cato the Younger* 51.1–5

Caesar's handling of the Gallic campaign became a matter of serious controversy in the final part of the war: Cato denounced his conduct towards the Germans, invoking religious arguments that must have been especially weighty and potentially damaging, as they were deployed against the *pontifex maximus*, who is eventually denounced as even more dangerous than an external enemy. Caesar responds to the allegations in writing: Plutarch's remark on the intemperate nature of his riposte is at odds with the measured tone and coldly manipulative outlook of what survives of the *Commentarii*. – Cato's attempt met with the effective opposition of Caesar's allies, but was the opening act of a persistent controversy over Caesar's Gallic command, which was a central feature of the run-up to the civil war of 49 BC. Note the hostile actions of the consul M. Claudius Marcellus in 51 BC (Suetonius, *Divus Julius* 28.2-29.1).

E43   Speech of Critognatus, 52 BC

[12] 'What, then, is my proposal? To do what our ancestors did in a war, in no way of equal magnitude, with the Cimbri and the Teutones: besieged in their towns and constrained by a similar lack of provisions they sustained their lives on the bodies of those who seemed, because of age, useless for war and they did not surrender to their enemies. [13] Even if we did not have a precedent for such action, I should, nevertheless, judge it a most splendid thing to be established for the cause of freedom and to be handed on to our descendants. [14] Now in what respect was that war like this one? Gaul had been devastated, the Cimbri, having inflicted great disaster, did in the end, however, leave our territory and make for other lands; they left us our rights, our laws, our lands and our liberty. [15] But the Romans – what else are they after, or what else do they want, if they are not induced by envy: to settle in the lands and the states of those whose noble reputation and prowess in war they have come to recognize and to put on them the yoke of perpetual slavery? For they have waged wars on no other terms. [16] But if you do not know what is happening among distant nations, then look round and see neighbouring Gaul, which, reduced to the status of

a province, its rights and laws completely changed, subjected to the axes, is being crushed with perpetual slavery.'

Caesar, Gallic War 7.77, 12–16

Critognatus, a man of high birth and great prestige among the Arverni, is speaking in a council of Gallic leaders within the besieged Alesia: some have counselled surrender, others a breakout. He proposes grim resistance and lambasts the Romans. At various points in his account Caesar gives dry factual information on the consequences of his victories and on the toil that his defeated enemies had to suffer. In this passage, however, he takes a step further, and briefly takes a Gallic viewpoint, and indeed that of an enemy that is not prepared to surrender, because he is convinced that the aims of the Romans are those of a predatory opponent, who always embarks on a war with the ambition to achieve a comprehensive, merciless victory. Caesar is not necessarily endorsing this viewpoint; yet, attributing it to an enemy amounts to a statement on the emotional impact that his presence has had on the local communities. – For a comparable instance, cf. the letter of Mithridates in Sallust's *Histories* (see above, **E5**), and the speech of the Caledonian chief, Calgacus in Tacitus, *Agricola* 30.5.

F. THE IMPERIAL ECONOMY

It would be mistaken to regard the Roman empire as a military and political construction whose making was driven mainly by economic motives: the existence of the empire, however, brought about an unprecedented degree of economic interdependence across the Mediterranean world. The sources collected in this section shed light on this phenomenon from two angles: the financial dealings in the provincial settings, and the migration from Rome and Italy to various corners of the empire, in the East and in the West. Both processes had a considerable impact not just in the provinces, but in Italy as well, and are an important part of the background to the fall of the Roman Republic.

CREDIT AND DEBT IN THE PROVINCES

F1   M. Brutus' financial dealings in Cyprus

[11] To be brief: in order to stand by my word to him, when the Salaminians came to me at Tarsus and Scaptius was with them, I ordered them to pay the money. They spoke a lot about the contract and a lot about the injuries Scaptius had done them. I refused to listen to them; I encouraged them, I even asked them to complete the business in response to my acts of kindness towards their community and finally said I would use force. They not only did not refuse, but said it was on my account they were paying; since I had not taken what they were accustomed to give the governor, they were paying in a way from my account, and even somewhat less in the case of Scaptius' account than in that of the governor's levy. … [13] You have my case. If Brutus does not approve it I do not know why we should have regard for him; but his uncle will certainly approve, especially as a decree of the Senate was recently passed (I think, after you had left) in the case of creditors, that one percent simple interest should be calculated as the legal rate.
Laodicea, 15 February 50 BC.

Cicero, *To Atticus* 5.21.11 and 13 (SB 114)

There is widespread evidence for the involvement of many members of the equestrian order as money-lenders in the Greek East, but we know that some senators were involved in that sort of remunerative activity. Several letters of Cicero from the late fifties attest the transactions between M. Junius Brutus, who played a crucial role in the conspiracy against Caesar a few years later, and the city of Salamis, the largest city on the island of Cyprus; when Brutus' debtors found themselves unable to pay back what they owed, they sought the mediation of Cicero, who was then governor in Cilicia. Brutus emerges as a ruthless and aggressive creditor, who did not refrain from applying very high interest rates. Cicero was far from hostile to him, but in this case he shows a degree of impatience towards his requests, and in this letter to his friend Atticus he stresses the tension between Brutus' attitude and the position held by his uncle M. Porcius Cato, who held a more conciliatory attitude towards debtors, and had recently backed a Senate decree that set a low limit on the rates that creditors could charge. As the decisions of Lucullus in the late seventies show, the debate on how to limit the margins of profit for creditors was not a new one, and was closely linked with different strategies on how to manage (and, ultimately, exploit) the Empire.

F2   Debt problems of the Allobroges

At this same time at Rome Lentulus, just as Catiline had instructed, was working either on his own initiative or through others on any whom he believed to be suitable for revolution either through character or circumstance, and not only citizens, but men of any sort provided that they would be of use in war. [40] Accordingly, he gave to one P. Umbrenus the job of seeking out the envoys of the Allobroges, and, if he could, urge them to become allies in the war, thinking that, being overwhelmed with personal and public debt, and furthermore because the Gallic nation was by nature warlike, they could easily be won over to such a course. ... [41] The Allobroges were for a long time uncertain what course of action to take. [2] On the one side, was their debt, their love of war, and great rewards to be hoped for in the event of victory; but on the other side were greater resources, courses of action that were safe, sure rewards in the place of uncertain hope. [3] As they turned over these matters, the good fortune of the state finally won through. [4] And so they revealed the whole matter, just as they had come to learn of it, to Q. Fabius Sanga, whose patronage their state mostly used.

Sallust, *Catiline's War* 39.6-40.1, 41.1-4

The problem of debt among provincial communities was not confined to the Greek East: it plays a significant role in the demise of Catiline, when the conspirators seek to persuade a Gallic community, the Allobroges, to join them, in the hope that their difficult financial situation will lead them to take a radical course of action. The detail of the background context are unclear, but it is reasonable to assume that the Allobroges had creditors in Rome, and that they might have been able to get a cancellation of their debts had they sided with the winning side. Their difficult financial situation eventually did not prove a strong enough factor to sway them, and their decision to give evidence to the Roman government proves crucial to the repression of the conspiracy (cf. Sallust, *Catiline's War* 44–48). – Debt is also crucial in shaping the motives of other members of the conspiracy: compare in particular the position of the former Sullan veterans in Etruria.

THE ITALIAN DIASPORA

F3   Massacre in Asia, 88 BC
[22] In the meantime Mithridates built a large number of ships for an attack upon Rhodes, and wrote secretly to all his satraps and city governors that on the thirtieth day thereafter they should set upon all Romans and Italians in their towns, and upon their wives and children, and their freedmen of Italian birth, kill them and throw their bodies out unburied, and share their goods with king Mithridates. He threatened to punish any who should bury the dead or conceal the living, and proclaimed rewards to informers and those who should kill persons in hiding. To slaves, who killed or betrayed their masters, he offered freedom; to debtors, who did the same to their creditors, the remission of half their debt. These secret orders Mithridates sent to all the cities at the same time. When the appointed day came disasters of the most varied kind occurred throughout Asia. [... *(Lurid and gory details follow)*...]

[23] Such was the awful fate that befell the Romans and Italians in Asia, men, women, and children, their freedmen and slaves, all who were of Italian blood; by which it was made very plain that it was quite as much hatred of the Romans as fear of Mithridates that impelled the people of Asia to commit these atrocities. But they paid a double penalty for their crime: one at the hands of Mithridates himself, who ill-treated them perfidiously not long afterward, and later at the hands of Cornelius Sulla.

Appian, *Mithridatic Wars* 22-23

The development that enabled Mithridates' early success in Asia Minor was the overwhelming support he encountered in the Greek cities of the region: he was widely welcomed as the liberator from a predatory foreign ruler, and his pledge to exempt the cities from taxation for the next five years certainly made his rhetoric of autonomy and civic freedom very credible. One of his main preoccupations, however, was to make sure that no reconciliation between the Greek city-states and Rome was possible in the foreseeable future, and he resorted to a device that secured that aim in the most traumatic way: he ordered the citizens of those communities to kill all the Roman and Italian residents. Many Italian tradesmen who were based in the area were also involved in tax-collection and money-lending activities, and were therefore seen by many as desirable targets. – The massacre of the Italians had tens of thousands of victims, and entailed far-reaching political and economic consequences: it caused a major rift with Rome, which was not overcome even after Sulla's victory and offered ground for his strategy of retaliation against the cities of Asia Minor; at the same time, it caused a huge loss of capital and assets, from which major financial difficulties in Italy ensued.

F4   Debts of a Greek city, 71/70 BC

Since Numerius and Marcus Cloatius, sons of Numerius, Romans, foreign ambassadors (*proxenoi*) and benefactors of our city, from the very beginning have continued to act justly both toward our city and, privately, toward those of the citizens who approached them (with a request), omitting nothing of zeal and ardour, because of which at appropriate times the city gratefully made public mention and voted suitable honours for them, in the years of Lachares' magistracy when they were negotiating our release from the obligations of the first loan; and in the year of Phleinos' magistracy, when concerning the second loan of 3,965 drachmas, which the city had borrowed in the year of Damarmenos' magistracy, they accepted the People of Athens as arbitrator in the time of Marcilius and then after being implored by the citizens, they permitted the payment of what the citizens persuaded them; and in the year of Biadas' magistracy, when, asking for it as a personal favour from Publius Autronius (Paetus) and Lucius Marcilius, who were their guests whom they had put up at their own expense, they successfully pleaded for the city to be spared the soldiers and other considerable burdens imposed by the legates, through which actions they brought relief to the city, the aforementioned legates having done this entirely as a favour to them; and they have often brought into goodwill and support for the city many of the (Roman) leaders, the legate Gaius Julius (Caesar) and the legate Publius Autronius (Paetus) and the legate Fulvius, doing all these things out of their goodwill toward the city and its citizens; and when there had been imposed on our city an order for grain by Gaius Gallius and for clothing by Quintus Ancharius according to (the requisition) allotted to our city, they used all their zeal and ardour and went to intercede with them in order that our city might not have to contribute, but might be exempted; and in this they succeeded, and we did not have to contribute; whoever of our citizens has approached them with a private request, or has had any need, they have done everything for everybody, making themselves available without evasion in every critical situation; and in the year of Timokrates' magistracy, when Antonius had come here and our city had need of cash and nobody else was willing to enter into contract with us, they loaned us 4,200 drachmas under contract at interest of four drachmas (= 4%), and being approached by the People in the year of Nikaretidas' magistracy with a request to accept simple interest, they granted us instead interest of two drachmas (= 2%) and relieved the city of the payment of over 1,500 drachmas from the money owed.

SIG[3] 748 = Sherk, *Rome and the Greek East to the Death of Augustus*, no. 74

This inscription from Gytheum, in the Southern Peloponnese, sheds light on the political and economic predicament of a relatively small town in the aftermath of the Mithridatic War. It records a decree in honour of two Roman residents of the city, the Cloatii brothers, probably of Campanian origin, who had lent money to the community and later agreed to charge reduced interest rates and to decrease the amounts owed to them. Moreover, they agreed to act as hosts to some Roman magistrates who happened to dock at the city's port, both doing a service to the reputation of the community and sparing it a considerable expense. – The Cloatii did not have a formal connection with the city and were not in a position to hold the local magistracies: while their decision may have also been driven by good economic sense, as it increased the chances of their credit being paid back in due course, it should also be read as an indicator of their personal connection with Gytheum and of wider preoccupations in late Republican society (not just within the political élite) about the impact of the empire on its subjects. – *Antonius* is Marcus Antonius Creticus, commander 72/71 BC, against Cretan pirates, by whom he was defeated and obliged to make peace. Marcilius, C. Julius Caesar [the later dictator] and P. Autronius Paetus, convicted of bribery in the consular elections of 66 BC, all appear to have been his *legati*. – Proxeny is an institution attested throughout the Greek world: the status of *proxenos* was bestowed by a community upon a non-citizen, and expressed a formal relationship of friendship between the *polis* and *proxenos*.

F5   Lucullus and the Sullan settlement of Asia, 70 BC

Lucullus now turned his attention to the cities of Asia, in order that, while he was free from military operations, he might deal in some way with laws and justice; because these had been lacking for a long time, unspeakable and unbelievable misfortunes were prevalent in the province; it was being plundered and reduced to slavery by the tax farmers and moneylenders; they were being forced to sell individually their handsome sons and their unmarried daughters, and to sell publicly their votive offerings, pictures, and sacred statues. [2] For them the end was being assigned to their creditors and becoming slaves, but before this worse experiences: tortures of rope, rack, and horse; standing under the open sky in the burning heat of the sun, or in the cold; being pushed into mud and ice, with the result that slavery seemed to be the casting off of burdens and peace. [3] Such were the evils that Lucullus found in the cities and within a short time he freed those who were being wronged from them all. For, in the first place, he ordered that the monthly rate of interest should be calculated at one per cent, and no more; in the second place, he cut off all interest greater than the principal; third, and most important of all, he fixed that the lender might receive as interest a quarter of the income of his debtor, and that a lender who added interest to the principal was deprived of the whole; [4] with the result that in a period of less than four years all debts were paid and properties given back to their owners unencumbered. This public debt arose from the twenty thousand talents, with which Sulla had fined Asia; and twice this amount had been paid back to the moneylenders, but had now been calculated by them with interest and had reached a hundred and twenty thousand talents. [5] Thus these men raised an outcry against Lucullus in Rome, on the grounds that they had been dreadfully treated, and they stirred up some of the tribunes with bribes against him, being men of great influence and having got many of those who were active in politics in their debt.

Plutarch, Life of Lucullus 20

The massacre of the Italians was readily exploited by Sulla in the aftermath of the war against Mithridates. His need to secure resources to deploy in the civil war that awaited him in Italy was one of the considerations that led him to impose a hefty war indemnity on the communities of the province of Asia, which were forced to borrow money at high interest rates from Roman money-lenders in order to face the pressing demands that had been set on them. That led to a significant economic crisis, which had very significant political ramifications. Fifteen years later, during his governorship of Asia, Lucullus sought to allay the crisis by putting a cap on the interest rates that could be charged on loans: it was a measure that earned him gratitude in the province and had positive economic implications, but had very heavy consequences for his political prospects in Rome, as it triggered the enmity of large sectors of the equestrian order, from which came the money-lenders that had been affected by his measures.

F6   Importance of the province of Asia to the Roman economy

[14] Now, if it was for the sake of our allies that our forefathers ... waged war ... how much more eager should you be ... to defend at one and the same time not only the safety of your allies but also the standing (*dignitas*) of your empire (*imperium*), especially as it is a matter of the greatest of all provincial taxes? For the taxes from all the other provinces, citizens, scarcely contribute enough for us to protect those very provinces, while Asia, on the other hand, is so rich and fertile that it easily surpasses all other lands in the productiveness of its fields, the variety of its fruits, the vastness of its pastures and in the vast volume of its exports. And so, citizens, if you wish to hold on to what is useful for war and the value (*dignitas*) of peace, you must defend this province not only from calamity but also from the fear of calamity. [15] For in all other matters, when a calamity occurs, then loss is sustained; but in the matter of provincial taxation, it is not only the arrival of trouble but also the very fear of it that brings calamity. For when enemy forces are not far away, even if no incursion has been made, nonetheless the herds are abandoned, agriculture is forsaken, and merchants take a rest from sailing the seas. Thus tax revenue cannot be maintained from harbours, from tithes, or from grazing; consequently, the revenue of a whole year is often lost through one single rumour of danger and fear of war. [16] Finally, then, what do you think is the state of mind of those who pay us taxes, or those who organize their collection and enforce their payment, when two kings with enormous forces are hard by, when one inroad of very brief duration by cavalry can take away the tax revenue of a whole year, when the tax-collectors (*publicani*) reckon that the very large number of employees they have in the salt-pans, in the fields, in the harbours and the guard posts is in great danger. ...

[17] This war affects the property of many Roman citizens; you must give careful attention to them, citizens, as befits your wisdom. For the tax-collectors (*publicani*) have transferred their businesses and resources to that province; their circumstances and their fortunes ought in itself to be a matter of concern to you. For, if we have always considered that taxes are the sinews of the *res publica*, then we shall certainly say that that order, which organizes their collection, is the foundation of all the other orders. [18] Next, from all the other orders energetic and industrious men are some of them personally engaged in business in Asia, and you ought to take care of their interests in their absence; some have large sums of their money invested in that province. Your human kindness requires you to prevent a large number of citizens from calamity, your wisdom to see that the calamity of many citizens cannot be separated from the *res publica*. For in the first place it is of little use that you later recover through victory the revenues that have been lost to the tax-collectors (*publicani*); for there will not be an opportunity for the same men to recover them on account of the calamity nor a willingness on the part of others on account of their fear [19] Secondly, we certainly ought, having been taught by calamity, to keep in our memory what the same Asia and that same Mithridates taught us at the beginning of the war in Asia. For we know that at exactly the time when a large number of people lost great sums of money in Asia, credit collapsed in Rome because payment had been made impossible. For it is not possible in one state (*civitas*) for a large number of people to lose their property and fortunes without dragging more people with them into the same calamity; keep the *res publica* from this danger. For, believe me, what you see for yourselves, that this credit

and this system of finances, which is in operation in Rome, in the forum, is closely tied and bound up with those finances of Asia. They cannot go into free fall without finances here being undermined and crashing in the same movement.

Cicero, *On the Manilian Law / On Pompey's Command* 14–19, with omissions

In the speech to the people setting out the case for Pompey's Eastern command, Cicero insisted at some length on the unparalleled economic advantages for Romans presented by the rule over the province of Asia. Although no quantitative information is provided, the audience is left in no doubt on the scale of the rewards that the province generates. Against this background, the case for pre-emptive military action is made: Rome cannot afford even the prospect of political instability in the region, as it would undermine the effective exploitation of the province. Moreover, Cicero stresses that many Roman citizens reside in Asia Minor and have considerable investments there, whose collapse would have significant repercussions in Rome: the massacre of 88 BC (see **F3**) had already given a stark illustration of this degree of interdependence between Italy and the Greek East. Hence the need for a swift military intervention: the experience with Mithridates of two decades earlier stands as a powerful warning against the risk of inaction.

F7   Export of gold

[67] Although gold used to be exported annually on the Jews' account from Italy and all our provinces to Jerusalem, Flaccus ordained by decree that it should not be exported from Asia. Who is there, jurors, who cannot genuinely praise this action? Not only on many occasions before, but also during my consulship the Senate decreed with the greatest severity that gold ought not to be exported. To resist this barbarian superstition was an act of firmness; and to pay no attention to the crowd of Jews, which sometimes gets excited in assemblies (*contiones*), in the interests of the *res publica* was an act of the utmost gravity. But it will be said that Pompey, when Jerusalem was captured, did not lay a finger on anything from the temple.

Cicero, *Defence of Flaccus* 67, with omissions

In praising the decision of his client L. Valerius Flaccus to forbid the export of gold from the province of Asia during his governorship, Cicero makes an important indirect point about the frequent circulation of gold from Italy and other regions to Jerusalem, where it is brought to the Temple. Circulation of wealth is therefore not just from the provinces to Rome, in an empire that is becoming increasingly interconnected. At the same time, Cicero records the concerns of the Senate on the export of gold from Italy and of the attempts that were made to curtail it: the tone of Cicero's discussion suggests that they were not altogether successful. – Pompey was in Jerusalem in the final part of his Eastern campaign, when he reorganized Judaea (Josephus, *Jewish Antiquities* 14.4.74-76). Cicero praises his restraint in his dealings with the temple.

F8   Governing a province: Cicero to his brother Quintus, 60/59 BC

[32] Now the tax-collectors (*publicani*) bring considerable difficulty to your wishes and your efforts. If we oppose them, we shall be separating from ourselves and the *res publica* a class which has done us great service and which through our efforts has been joined with the *res publica*; on the other hand, if we go along with them in everything, we shall have been allowing the people with whose safety and interests we ought to be concerned to suffer utter ruin. If we are willing to consider things honestly, then this is the one difficulty in your command (*imperium*). ... [33] How much bitterness the issue of the tax-collectors (*publicani*) brings to our allies, we have realized from our own citizens who, in the matter of abolishing the customs duties (*portoria*) in Italy, recently complained not so much about the dues as about some wrongs at the hands of the customs officers. I can, therefore, well imagine what happens to our allies in far away places, now that I have heard the complaints from citizens in Italy. For you to

manage things in such a way that you satisfy the tax-collectors (*publicani*), especially when they have made a bad contract, and that you do not allow the allies to be ruined, seems to require some almost superhuman quality – that is *yours*.

Now in the first place, what is most painful for the Greeks, that they are taxpayers, ought not to seem painful for the simple reason that, without the empire (*imperium*) of the Roman people, they themselves by their own institutions were in the same position through their own doings. Now they cannot refuse to accept the name – *publicanus* – since they themselves were unable to pay the tax, which Sulla had fairly allotted them, without the *publicanus*. That the Greeks are not more lenient in exacting taxes can be realized from the fact that the Caunians and all the islands assigned to Rhodes by Sulla recently had recourse to the Senate requesting that they should pay taxes to us rather than to the Rhodians. And so those who have always been taxpayers ought not to shudder at the name *publicanus*, nor can those who have not been able to pay through their own arrangements refuse to accept it, nor can those who have asked for it refuse. [34] At the same time let Asia consider this: that no calamity of foreign war or internal quarrels would have been far away from it, were it not contained within this empire (*imperium*); then, since this empire (*imperium*) cannot be maintained by any means without taxes, let Asia be content to pay the cost of permanent peace and tranquillity with some part of its revenues.
Rome, end 60 BC or beginning 59 BC.

Cicero, To Quintus 1.1.32–34 (SB 1), with omission

When his younger brother Quintus took up a provincial command in Asia Minor, Cicero wrote a lengthy letter in which he offered detailed advice on how to approach the task at hand, and in which he does not simply provide technical advice, but also discusses the conduct to be had towards provincial subjects, and comes back to political issues that others had confronted in the recent past. The difficulties of achieving good standards of clean government without alienating the *publicani* were experienced by Lucullus in the late seventies; on the other hand, the deep-seated resentment of the provincial communities towards the tax-collectors was an issue that could not overlooked (a). The pressures under which the cities of Asia were dated back to the age of Sulla at least (b), but Cicero argues that harsh tax-collecting was not just a Roman prerogative, and quotes an example drawn from the practice at Rhodes. – The final point on the link between taxation, the functioning of the empire, and peace, may be read as disingenuous or manipulative, but it is also presupposed by a clear and mature vision of what the remit of a public power is, and of what the demands of the running of a state are.

F9   Roman tax-collectors and fiscal regulations in the province of Asia, 75 BC
Whatever persons [or whatever things] a *publicanus* (tax-collector) from Asia into Asia imports or exports (i.e., within Asia), in relation to anything on which the consuls L. Octavius and C. Aurelius leased out the *telos* (tax), on this [he is] not [to pay] tax, on a ship and the equipment of a ship, and on slaves and on everyone male or female, whom they bring from home or send for, on books, [tablets and everything] on which there is writing, and on anything by which they are maintained, and on animals which anyone brings from home for the sake of this journey, on these [things] he is not to pay customs duty (Gk: *telos* = Latin *portorium)*.

Whatever ore is exported from Asia to Rome according to the law on mining, on this ore and on the vessels in which it is contained, they are to [give the collector] four *asses* per hundred pounds; more in tax is not to be owed on these things. If anyone in contravention of these provisions [holds up these vessels] with wrongful deceit, so that the ore is not transported, then the collector is to be liable to the shipper for double the amount which has been held up.

The Customs Law of Asia, lines 74–81

A lengthy Greek inscription from Ephesus records the text of the customs law of the province of Asia. It is a text of great historical importance, as it offers a unique insight into the workings of Roman provincial government, and especially of how economic and fiscal matters were handled in one of the most remunerative provinces of the Empire (see **F6**). The Ephesus inscriptions records a law that was passed in AD 62, under the Flavians, but the core of the text dates back to a much earlier period: the opening section was probably drafted not long after the creation of the province of Asia (133 BC), and several clauses were added later, and can be safely dated from the mentions of the serving consuls. The text quoted here was added in 75 BC, after the consuls had drawn up new terms for the work of the tax-collectors (*publicani*) in the province. It details exemptions for the tax-collectors themselves, who are immune from taxation on any items pertaining to their official tasks, and sets out specific instructions on the exportation of metal; it makes reference to a law on mining that is not otherwise attested. Quite apart from the valuable technical information it provides, this text is a remarkable example of the balance between continuity and innovation in the practice of the Roman government, and of the level of detail and complexity that it entailed. – The text of the law is in Greek, as is the case with most official documents from the Greek East, but translates a lost Latin original.

F10 Traders in Gaul

a) ... that under this praetor Gaul was overwhelmed with debt. From whom do they say that loans for such enormous sums of money were made? From the Gauls? Absolutely not. From whom, then? From Roman citizens who are engaged in business in Gaul. Why do we not hear their statements? Why are none of their accounts put forward in court? I harry the prosecutor and press him hard, jurors; I harry him, I say, I demand witnesses ... Gaul is packed with businessmen, full of Roman citizens. None of the Gauls does any business without a Roman citizen of Rome; not a penny is moved without the account books of Roman citizens.

Cicero, *Defence of Fonteius* 11

The predicament of the Allobroges in 63 BC (see **F2**) shows that debt was a major concern to that community: see also Sallust, *Catiline's War* 40.4. A speech delivered by Cicero in 69 BC gives further depth to the economic context of that crisis: the spiral of debt was generated by the willingness of Roman tradesmen based in Southern Gaul to lend their money in exchange for high interest rates. The picture sketched by Cicero is one of a province in which there are huge margins of profit for Roman investors, and in which the main fronts of expoitation are controlled by private individuals, rather than by the *res publica*.

b) Of all these the Belgae are the bravest, because they are furthest from the culture and the civilized way of life of the province and because traders least frequently come and go to them, importing those things which tend to make men weak and womanish.

Caesar, *Gallic War* 1.1.3

c) The Gauls are extremely addicted to the use of wine and fill themselves with the wine which is brought into their country by merchants, drinking it unmixed; and since they partake of this drink without moderation in their craving for it, when they are drunk they fall into a stupor or a state of madness. Consequently many of the Italian traders, induced by the love of money which characterizes them, believe that the love of wine of these Gauls is their own stroke of good luck. For they transport the wine on the navigable rivers by means of boats and through the level plains on wagons; and they receive for it an incredible price. For in return for a jar of wine they receive a slave, getting a servant in return for a drink.

Diodorus, *Library of History* 5.26.3

The presence of Roman merchants, who could also act as money-lenders if and when required, was not limited to the territories that were under direct Roman rule. There is clear, independent evidence for the involvement of traders in the central and northern regions of Transalpine Gaul well before the coming of Caesar's troops: both Caesar and Diodorus of Sicily establish a clear, and no doubt facile, link between the influx of new commodities and the debasement of the moral character of the indigenous populations. The spread of wine trade plays a major role in this context, and the link between wine and slave trade suggested by Diodorus points to an avenue of connectivity between the Mediterranean and the inland regions of the European continent.

F11   Italian traders in the Greek East
a) The Italians and the Greeks who are doing business at Delos (honour) Lucius Munatius Plancus.
Agasias son of Menophilos, from Ephesus, made (this).

ILLRP 360 = EDCS-24700020

b) The Italians that are doing business at Argos (offer this) to Q. Caecilius Metellus, son of Gaius, *imperator*.

ILLRP 374 = EDCS-24900077*

c) [The Roman citizens] who are doing business at Cos (honour) the community of Cos on account of its piety towards Gaius Julius Caesar, *pontifex maximus*, father of the fatherland and god, and for its benevolence towards them.

ILLRP 408 = EDCS-08200657

A considerable number of inscriptions record the presence of Roman traders and money-lenders in the Greek East, both as individuals and as members of corporate groups: the three texts selected here focus on the latter category of cases, and shed light on three different moments of the Roman presence in the Eastern Mediterranean. The inscription in honour of L. Munatius Plancus, a legate of Sulla who visited Delos in 87 during the First Mithridatic War, is bilingual: the dedication put up by the traders is in Latin, while the signature on the base of the statue dedicated to Plancus is in Greek, and records the name of the artist who made it, and who hailed from Asia Minor. Plancus earned the gratitude of Roman and Greek traders alike for his contribution to the stabilization of a major port in the Eastern Mediterranean, which Mithridates' offensive had severely harmed. The second inscription celebrates Q. Caecilius Metellus Creticus, consul in 69, who led a campaign in Crete in the following year. However, it does not come from the island where Metellus concentrated his operations, but from an important city of mainland Greece: the traders that were based there no doubt benefited from, and were grateful for, his efforts in reducing the impact of piracy in the Aegean. The dedication from Cos dates to the final months of Julius Caesar's life, and attests a cult of Caesar in the island of Cos, off the coast of Asia Minor (there is no apparent tension between Caesar's divine status and his role as *pontifex maximus*). The local community of Roman citizens recognized and paid tribute to the devotion that the people of Cos showed towards Caesar: it was a statement of civic concord and, at the same time, an indirect homage to Caesar and an acknowledgement of his new, unprecedented status.

F12 Slave market in Delos

Now it was [Diodotus] Tryphon and the worthlessness of the successor kings who by succession were then ruling Syria and Cilicia at the same time, which caused the Cilicians to organize the operations of the pirates in the first place; for others organized revolution together as he had done, and, with brothers disagreeing with one another, made the country subject to any who might attack it. The export of slaves more than anything else encouraged them to the evil business, being extremely profitable; for they were easily captured and the market, not at all far away, was large and very wealthy, namely, Delos, with a capacity to accept and to dispatch ten thousand slaves on the same day; with the result that there was a saying about this: 'Merchant, sail in, unload, all is sold.' The reason for this was that after the destruction of Carthage and Corinth the Romans became rich and used many domestic slaves; the pirates seeing this easy source of profit blossomed in huge numbers, themselves plundering and trading in slaves.

Strabo, *Geography* 14.5.2

Much of the slave trade in the Greek East had long been enabled and sustained by the capture of prisoners in military campaigns; as Strabo notes, however, the demand for slaves became even greater at Rome in the aftermath of the victories of Carthage and Corinth, and the end of large-scale military operations in the East. The supply of slaves for the Roman market was secured largely by contingent of independent seafarers, mostly based on the coast of Cilicia, who are usually mentioned as 'pirates' in the surviving evidence, with a clear hostile slant; much as they might have seemed unsavoury allies, and even though Strabo's reservations on their trade were not isolated, they played a key role, and were the main suppliers of the great slave-market at Delos, an island whose port had been exempted from taxation since 166 BC.

F13 Crassus and his slaves

[4] Observing that the conflagration and collapse of buildings were natural and familiar fatalities in Rome, because buildings were too large and too close together, he proceeded to buy slaves who were architects and builders. Then, when he had over five hundred of these, he started buying burnt down houses, and houses adjoining those that had burnt down, which their owners would sell off at a low price out of fear and uncertainty. In this way the largest part of Rome came into his possession. [5] However, although he owned so many craftsmen, he did not build any house for himself other than his own; indeed, he used to say that men who were fond of building were their own ruin, without any need for other foes. And although he owned a great number of silver mines, and highly valuable land with labourers on it, one might nevertheless regard all these assets as nothing compared with the value of his slaves; [6] so many and so capable were the slaves he possessed, — readers, copyists, silversmiths, administrators, table servants; and he himself oversaw their education, he taught them with care, and he was fully persuaded that the foremost duty of the master was to care for his slaves as the living tools of the management of a household.

Plutarch, *Life of Crassus* 2.4–6

Plutarch devotes close attention to the wealth of Crassus and how he gathered it: owning a large number of slaves was far from untypical for someone of his standing, but the care with which Crassus managed his slaves as the most valuable form of investment, on account of the key role that they could have in the effective running of a household, is noteworthy. Crassus' approach to investment, whether in real estate, mining, or land, is both careful and shrewd, and is accompanied by an outlook that does not prioritize the growth of the patrimony, but its long-term sustainability.

F14   Slaves as economic actors
Flaccus, (slave) of Rabirius has examined (this) on 1 April, in the consulship of
Decimus Silanus and Lucius Murena.

CIL 1².911 = *ILLRP* 1026 = EDCS 24701311

This *tessera nummularia* may firmly be dated to the early spring of 62 BC: it is a small ivory token, a few
centimetres long, pierced with a hole: it was meant to be attached to a bag to certify that the contents
(usually money) had been duly checked (see below **L23**). The involvement of a slave in this basic, but
crucial financial operation is especially noteworthy, and belongs within a wider context of involvement of
slaves in economic activity.

F15   Atticus' income and estates in Epirus
When the great increase in his wealth occurred, he changed nothing of his daily style
of life and displayed such moderation that neither on the two million sesterces, which
he had inherited from his father, did he live with insufficient splendour, nor on the ten
million did he live in greater affluence than to begin with, but with both fortunes stayed
on the same level. [3] He had no park, no luxurious villa near Rome or by the sea, nor
any country estate in Italy, but for those at Arretium and Nomentum, but all his income
consisted of his properties in Epirus and the city. From this it can be realized that it was
his custom to measure his use of money not by amount, but by sound reasoning.

Nepos, *Life of Atticus* 14.2–3

T. Pomponius Atticus, the close friend and correspondent of Cicero, was a man with strong connections
in the senatorial order, and of considerable political influence, but he always remained a member of the
equestrian order: his biographer Nepos gives some valuable detail on the extent of his personal fortune,
and emphasizes his reluctance to spend large amounts of money or display his wealth through the status-
symbols that were fashionable in some sectors of the élite. Moreover, the base of his fortune was not located
in Italy, but in Epirus (roughly corresponding to modern Albania): a relatively more stable region in the
difficult political context of the late Republic.

F16   An alternative Roman State in Spain
[14.1] As a result of these operations Sertorius was admired and loved by the barbarians.
With Roman weapons and battle formations and signals, he removed the frenzied and
savage element of their courage and made of their strength an army instead of a great
band of robbers. [2] Furthermore, using silver and gold without stint, he equipped their
helmets and adorned their shields; by teaching them to wear flowered cloaks and tunics
and providing the money for these things and joining with them in love of beautiful
things he won great popularity with them. [3] What most won them over was his
treatment of their children. For he assembled the noblest boys from their tribes in Osca,
a large city, and set over them teachers of Greek and Roman studies: ostensibly he was
educating them, on the assumption that he would give them a share in administration
and government, when they became men, while in fact he made them hostages. [4] Their
fathers were amazingly delighted seeing their sons in purple-bordered togas, going back
and forth to school in very smart attire, and Sertorius paying the fees for them, and
conducting frequent examinations, distributing prizes to those who deserved them, and
presenting them with gold necklaces, which the Romans call *bullae*...

[15.1] And it was not only by the Iberians that he was cherished, but also by the
soldiers from Italy. [2] At any rate when Perpenna Vento, from the same faction (Gk:
stasis) as Sertorius, arrived in Spain with large sums of money and a considerable

force and decided to wage war against Metellus on his own independently, his soldiers became discontented and there was much talk in the camp of Sertorius, which distressed Perpenna who was crazy about noble birth and wealth. [3] However, when news came that Pompey was crossing over the Pyrenees, the soldiers snatched their weapons and the military standards and raised an uproar against Perpenna, ordering him to lead them to Sertorius; [4] if he did not, they threatened to abandon him and proceed to a man able to save himself and to save them. [5] Perpenna gave in and led them and joined with Sertorius bringing fifty-three cohorts. ...

[22.5] But the magnanimous character of Sertorius was shown, firstly, in his giving the name of Senate to the senators who fled from Rome and spent their time with him, in appointing quaestors and praetors from among them, and in arranging all such matters in accordance with ancestral customs; [6] and, secondly, in his using the arms, wealth, and the cities of the Iberians, while not even so much as discussing his yielding some part of supreme authority to the Iberians themselves, but in his appointing Romans as commanders and commanders over them, on the grounds that he was recovering freedom for the Romans and not strengthening them against the Romans. [7] For he was a man who loved his country and had a strong desire to return home from exile.

Plutarch, *Life of Sertorius* 14.1–4; 15.1–5; 22.5–7

Plutarch is deeply fascinated with the character and talents of Q. Sertorius, and that is his main focus in the biography that he devotes to him: an important section of his narrative is devoted to the steps Sertorius took to build a new political and military entity – a State, by all intents and purposes – in the Iberian peninsula: a Roman construction, but one that was set against the *res publica*. His ability to combine Italian and indigenous contingents is especially remarkable, as much as the clear hierarchical principle on which that was based. His attempt to build an institutional framework resembling that of the *res publica*, including a Senate made up of exiles, is revealing of his ambition, his long-term intentions, and the capability of the entity he had created.

F17   Roman civilians in Gaul

a) Caesar waited a few days near Vesontio for corn and provisions. As a result of enquiries by our soldiers and reports from Gauls and traders who declared that the Germans were physically huge, incredibly courageous and skilled in arms (they said that they had often met them in battle and not been able even to look them in the face or in the eye) a sudden panic seized the whole army so great that it seriously disturbed their senses and morale.

Caesar, *Gallic War* 1.39.1

b) They killed the Roman citizens who had settled there to do business – among them one C. Fufius Cita, a respectable Roman *eques*, who was in charge of the corn supply on the order of Caesar – and plundered their property. [2] Report of this was quickly conveyed to all the states of Gaul. For whenever something important or significant happens, they make it known by shouting through the fields and the districts; others in their turn take this up and pass it on to their neighbours, as then happened.

Caesar, *Gallic War* 7.3.1–2, with omission

c) Noviodunum was a town of the Aedui situated in a favourable position on the banks of the river Liger. [2] Caesar had conveyed all his Gallic hostages, his corn, his funds, and most of his own baggage and that of the army to this place. [3] He also sent here a large number of horses bought for this war in Italy and Spain. [4] When Eporedorix and Viridomarus arrived at Noviodunum and learned of the situation of their state ... the two of them thought that so great an advantage should not be let slip. [5] So they killed the guards at Noviodunum, and the men who came there to do business, and shared out the money and horses among themselves. ... [7] They set the town on fire so that it might not be of any use to the Romans. [8] They carried away on boats all the corn, which they could at short notice; the rest they ruined by river, water and fire.

Caesar, *Gallic War* 7.55.1–8, with omissions

Securing effective and frequent supplies of corn is a major concern for any army, and is a recurring preoccupation for Caesar during his Gallic campaign: the three passages quoted here show that the concern was as strong in the early phase of the war (a) as it was in the final months (b and c). A member of the equestrian order is directly entrusted with the gathering of corn, no doubt because of his valuable local knowledge of the territory; Roman tradesmen in Gaul also prove crucial in the early stages of the conflict in gathering valuable information on the Germani – not so much about their movements and aims, but rather their outward appearance. – Passage c) emphatically shows how strong the connection between army and corn is: Caesar moves that resource along with his camp, and when the Aedui manage to break into Noviodunum their main target is the corn, which they seize as soon as their attack has been carried out. Caesar soon regained ground, but the aim pursued by his enemies is telling.

F18   Recruitment in the provinces by Caesar
a) As Caesar was expecting a more serious disturbance in Gaul, he arranged to conduct a levy through his legates M. Silanus, C. Antistius Reginus, and T. Sextius; [2] at the same time Caesar requested the proconsul, Pompey, to order the troops he had sworn in as consul from Cisalpine Gaul to muster and proceed to him. ... [4] When Pompey satisfied this obligation ... Caesar's legates swiftly concluded the levy and before winter was over three legions had been formed and brought to him.

Caesar, *Gallic War* 6.1.1–4, with omission

Caesar's military effort in Gaul spanned across nearly a decade, and required the mobilization of robust contingents: the *Commentarii* record various recruitment efforts on Caesar's part, which were carried out mostly in Cisalpine Gaul (a), where Caesar used to spend the winter months. That such a high number of men could be drafted to serve in the army is revealing of the attractiveness of the prospect of military activity in a province that had not yet been fully conquered and the rewards it could yield. – There was in principle a close link between a legion and the magistrate that had recruited it. In the run-up to the civil war between Caesar and Pompey, one of the legions quartered in Gaul was diverted to Pompey on the Senate's instructions – see **B136b**.

F19   Recruitment of Horace in Athens
Athens added a little more of the liberal arts so that I would distinguish between the straight and the crooked and amid the woods of the Academy seek the truth. But harsh times drove me from that pleasant place, and the surge of civil war bore a callow youth to arms that would not be a match for the muscle of Caesar Augustus.

Horace, *Epistles* 2.2.43–48

In this passing, but very meaningful reference to his youth the poet Horace (Q. Horatius Flaccus) recalls the days he spent pursuing literary and philosophical studies in Athens, where he attended the Academy, a school founded by Plato, and acknowledges his decision to join the army of the Liberators, which had its core force in the Greek East: although he fought on the losing side, after the end of the war he was able to establish a personal relationship with Octavian and to reach literary prominence in Rome.

G. LAW, LAWYERS AND LAWCOURTS

One of the most original and influential aspects of Roman culture is the degree to which law developed as an independent and complex domain of intellectual activity. The development of Roman jurisprudence is a crucial aspect of the cultural and intellectual history of the Republic, and is directly linked with the political, economic, and social developments of the age that coincided with the construction of the Mediterranean empire. The following section aims to provide a general introduction to the development of Roman law in the late Republican period, and its connection with the workings of Roman administration: the census is a valuable case-study in this respect, and offers a valuable example of the far-reaching ties between Roman law and Roman politics. The role that the activity in the lawcourts could play in enabling one's social and political rise is another facet of these connections: the career of Cicero is a striking, but by no means isolated case.

THE MAKING OF ROMAN LAW

G1   A condensed history of Roman law

[26] For us, Romulus had exercised rule as it pleased him; then Numa bound the people by religious sanctions and by the law of the gods, and some laws were devised by Tullus and Ancus. But it was principally Servius Tullius who was the enactor of inviolable statutes, with which even kings complied.

[27] When Tarquinius had been driven out, against the factions (*factiones*) of the fathers the people made many provisions to protect freedom and strengthen concord; the board of ten men (*decemviri*) was created and, having sent for all outstanding laws from wherever they could be found, the Twelve Tables were composed, the culmination of equitable law. For statutes followed, although sometimes against evil-doers as a result of an offence, more often however they were enacted by force because of disagreement between the orders, and for obtaining unlawful offices or for driving out famous men or for other disgraceful aims. Hence the disturbers of the plebs, such as a Gracchus and a Saturninus; and equally Drusus, a briber in the name of the Senate; the allies were deceived in their hope and cheated through the veto. And not even in the Italian war, then in the civil war, did this practice discontinue without many different laws being voted for, until the dictator L. Sulla, having abolished and reversed previous statutes, when he had added many more, brought about a lull in this process, but not for long; at once there were the turbulent proposals of Lepidus and not much after the restoration to the tribunes of their licence to stir up the people however they wished. Thereafter trials (*quaestiones*) were enacted not only for matters of communal import, but against individual persons; with the *res publica* at its most corrupt, most statutes were enacted.

Tacitus, *Annals* 3.26–27

Tacitus discusses the origins and development of law and law-making in Rome within his treatment of the legislation on celibacy enacted by Augustus, and makes a thought-provoking point on the development of legislation in the Republican period, where he sees a paradoxical correlation between the increase in the number of pieces of legislation being passed and the rise of political instability: statutes are often passed for reasons of political expediency and, far from bringing clarity and a stronger rule of law, they make a crucial contribution to an increasingly disrupted political context. – The Gracchi and their opponent Livius Drusus are placed at the beginning of this process; tribunician legislations and political prosecutions (which are, at least in principle, tools to keep the powerful under check) are regarded as the key factors of instability, and indeed of corruption.

G2   Sources of law

a) [67] … Customary law is considered to be that which by the agreement of all the long passage of time has been approved without statute. In it there are some laws which are themselves now fixed through the passage of time. There are many others in this class but by far the largest part is that which the praetors have been accustomed to issue in their edicts. Some kinds of law have now become fixed by custom; this kind includes agreement, equity, and precedent. [68] An agreement is that which among those who enter into it is thought to be so legally binding that it is said to prevail in law. Equity is what is fair and just to all. Precedent is that about which a decision has previously been made on the opinion of some person or persons. Statute laws will have to be learned from statutes. Therefore from these parts of law it will be necessary to give attention to what seems to develop for each case from the case itself or from a similar case or from a greater or lesser case and to draw it out by examining carefully each individual part of law.

Cicero, *On Invention* 2.67–68, with omissions

Statute legislation, which is passed by vote a popular assembly, is not the only decision that has force of law in the Roman Republic: in this passage of his early rhetorical work, Cicero discusses other 'sources of law', which include custom, and which plays an important role in the edicts issued by the praetors at the beginning of their term in office, in which the principles that they will follow in dispensing justice are set out. Cicero writes at a time when the Roman legal science is becoming increasingly sophisticated and complex: the notion of custom is unpacked into three complementary principles (agreement, equity, and precedent), which are carefully defined in this text. – It is noteworthy that these basic legal notions are discussed in a work that is intended for the use of aspiring orators: a good legal training is of course essential to those who want to make a name for themselves in the lawcourts.

b) Now the laws of the Roman people consist of statutes, decrees of the people (*plebiscita*), decrees of the Senate (*senatus consulta*), constitutions of the emperors, edicts of those who possess the right to issue edicts (*ius edicendi*), and the responses of jurisprudents.

Gaius, *Institutes* 1.2

This passage of the imperial jurist Gaius neatly sums up the various 'sources of law' in ancient Rome, and shows that various kinds of texts could have force of law, or could at least be invoked in support of a certain legal argument. Even the advice of established legal experts ('jurisprudents') could be numbered among the sources of law.

c) *Atticus*: Is it, then, not from the edict of the praetors, as many now think, nor from the Twelve Tables, as our predecessors thought, but from deep within the recesses of philosophy that you think the discipline of law is to be drawn?
Marcus: Now we are not in this discussion, Pomponius, looking for how we are to give an opinion in a matter of law, nor what response we are to give to some consultation; important though that matter may be, as indeed it is, and it has been maintained in the past by many distinguished men, and is now maintained by one with the greatest authority and knowledge, but in this debate of ours we must embrace the whole subject of universal law and statutes, in such a way that this civil law (*ius civile*), as we term it, is confined within a certain small and narrow space. It is the nature of law that we must expound and that has to be traced back from the nature of man; statutes by which states ought to be governed must be considered; then those laws and commands of peoples, which have been compiled and written down, must be

dealt with; among these what are called the civil laws (*iura civilia*) of our own people will not escape notice either.

Cicero, On the Laws 1.17

The debate on the sources of law shows that sound legal thinking in the Roman world is not just about the effective interpretation of a body of legal texts. On the one hand, it is necessary to be conversant with the philosophical dimension of the law; on the other, it is important to be familiar with the legal production of a number of states, beyond Rome. 'Civil law', which applies in the *res publica*, is merely a part of a much wider social and cultural process, with which Cicero's philosophical dialogue engages in its reflection on the laws of a well-ordered political community. – *One with the greatest authority and knowledge*: probably the great jurist Servius Sulpicius Rufus.

d) The civil law (*ius civile*) is that which comes from statutes, decrees of the people (*plebiscita*), decrees of the senate (*senatus consulta*), decrees of the emperors, and the authority of the jurists.
[1] The praetorian law is that which the praetors introduced to support or to supplement or to correct the civil law (*ius civile*). It is also termed *ius honorarium*, so named with reference to the *honos* (office) of the praetor.

Digest 1.1.7; 1.1.7.1 (Papinian)

This definition of the law and its parts by the imperial jurist Papinian (AD 142–212) gives further complexity to the notion of *ius civile*, and stresses the role that the praetors can have in correcting and sharpening the *ius civile*, and in applying it according to discretional criteria.

G3   Public and private law

Moreover no long discussion is needed to explain why I think that the orator must also be acquainted with state laws (*iura publica*), which is exclusively concerned with the state (*civitas*) and the empire (*imperium*), and also with the records of past events and the precedents of antiquity. For just as in cases and proceedings related to private interests, his language must often be borrowed from the civil law (*ius civile*), and, as we have said already, a knowledge of the civil law (*ius civile*) is indispensable to the orator; so, in public cases, alike in the lawcourts, in popular assemblies (*contiones*) and in the Senate, all this recalling of old times, the authority of state law (*ius publicum*), and the principles and knowledge of administration of the *res publica* should be material, as it were, at the disposal of those orators involved with the *res publica*.

Cicero, On the Good Orator 1.201

In this passage of one of his rhetorical works, Cicero points out an important general principle. A good Roman orator cannot be just a gifted public speaker or an effective advocate: he must be thoroughly conversant with the complexity of the law, both public and private. Even the discussion of a case in a lawcourt requires a clear understanding of the wider legal and constitutional framework within which it takes place. This wider awareness is all the more essential to the orators who are involved with the political debate of their time.

G4   Edicts

a) Now the right of issuing edicts is possessed by the magistrates of the Roman people. But the most important right is that of the two praetors, the urban and the peregrine, and those who preside over jurisdiction in the provinces; likewise the edicts of the curule aedile and those quaestors, who have jurisdiction in the provinces of the Roman people.

Gaius, Institutes 1.6

Much of Roman law in the Republic was codified and enforced through the edicts that some magistrates, especially the praetors, issue at the beginning of their office: although much of the contents of the edict did not change year by year, the magistrate had in principle full discretion. Gaius' summary also draws attention to the role that praetors and quaestors that were deployed in the provinces had in the administration of justice in the territories under their watch.

b) [119] And just as he started, on becoming praetor designate, to compile his whole edict to suit the wishes of those who were trading law with him for their own advantage, so, during his actual magistracy he would make decisions contrary to that very edict without any scruple. That is why L. Piso filled many notebooks with those cases where he used his veto because that man, Verres, had made a decision inconsistent with his own edict. I do not think you have forgotten what a mass of people, what a queue there was that used to gather before the chair of Piso; had Verres not had him as a colleague he would have been stoned in the forum.

Cicero, *Against Verres* 2.1.119

This passage from the Second Verrine touches upon the alleged abuses of power committed by Verres during his praetorship (74 BC), and accuses him of having violated the terms of his own edict. His colleague in the praetorship, L. Calpurnius Piso, played an important moderating function in blocking a number of decisions that were inconsistent with the edict.

c) Then Cornelius proposed another statute that praetors should administer justice in accordance with their standing edicts (*edicta perpetua*). Although no one dared to offer resistance, many people were against it. This action took away the opportunity for influence from praetors who, in their eagerness to gain favour, had become accustomed to administer justice without consistency.

Asconius, *Commentary on Cicero's Defence of Cornelius* p. 59C.7–11

The risk of illegitimate interpretations of the terms of the edict was not just relevant to Verres' corruption case: an attempt to contain it was made in a statute presented by Cornelius, tribune of the plebs in 67 BC, who sought to restrict the praetors by binding them to a 'perpetual edict' that could not change on a yearly basis: however, the praetors retained their prerogative to grant or refuse lawsuits (*actiones*) in individual cases.

G5   Promulgation and legislation

a) [13] At last the tribunes of the plebs entered office. The assembly (*contio*) of Publius Rullus was eagerly awaited because he was the initiator of the agrarian statute and was behaving more aggressively than the rest of the tribunes ... I was waiting for the fellow's statute and his *contio*. At the start no statute was proposed; he ordered a *contio* to be summoned on the day before the Ides [12 December 64]. A large crowd gathered in eager anticipation. He made a speech, lengthy certainly and with very fine words. I thought it had one fault: in that vast gathering no one could be found to understand what he was saying. ... Nevertheless, the more alert among those, who had stood in the *contio*, surmised he wanted to say something about the agrarian statute. At length, while I was still consul designate, the law was posted in public. On my instruction, a number of copyists gathered simultaneously and brought me a transcript of the statute.

Cicero, *On the Agrarian Law* 2.10–13, with omissions

As Tacitus noted (**G1**), statute legislation was closely linked to the political context in which it was put forward. A tribune of the plebs who intended to propose a new bill would typically present it to a popular assembly before formally submitting it to the consideration of the *comitia tributa*: that was the key occasion in which the case for the proposal would be set out and support would be mobilized. In this polemical passage Cicero describes the process through which Servilius Rullus put forward an agrarian law that Cicero strongly contested: first there was a speech (with which Cicero takes issue on rhetorical grounds), and only at a later stage was the text put on public display ('promulgated'). Cicero, who is a serving consul, gets access to the text from a transcript drawn up by some copyists. – Cf. Cicero, *Philippics* 1.24 on Caesar reading out his laws at public gatherings.

b) But you yourself wrote that Clodius had posted for public information on the doorpost of the senate-house a clause of his statute concerning me that it should not be permitted for a motion either to be proposed or to be discussed. Thessalonica, 17 August 58 BC.

Cicero, To Atticus 3.15.6 (SB 60)

Putting the text of a bill on public display was a political act of clear significance as well as a legal requirement, even in a context where many voters were illiterate. As this brief reference in a letter of Cicero shows, Clodius also resorted to this device.

c) Glaucia, a loathsome man but clever with it, was in the habit of advising the people to pay attention to the first line when some statute was being read out; if it were 'Any dictator, consul, praetor, master of horse' they should not bother; they might know it had nothing to do with them; but if it were 'whoever after the passage of this statute' they should beware lest they were being made liable to some new court.'

Cicero, Defence of Rabirius Postumus 14

Some bills were not just displayed in their written version, but were also read out in public: the few surviving texts of Roman statutes show that they were often very complex and detailed documents. Servilius Glaucia, the great political agitator of the second century BC, gave his audience a helpful tip on how to gauge the political agenda of a bill from its opening clause. 'Whoever after the passage of this statute' suggests that the bill does not apply predominantly to magistrates and public bodies, but has a wider, in principle more egalitarian focus.

G6 Depositing proposals and statutes in the treasury

Let those who do public business observe the auspices; let them pay attention to the public augur; when proposals have been promulgated let them keep them *preserved* [*?on record*] in the treasury (*aerarium*).

Cicero, On the Laws 3.11

A corrupt text where '*preserved*' (? on record) is a conjecture, which is supported by a scholiast on Cicero, Sestius, 135 as follows: 'The Junian and Licinian Law, passed in 62 BC at the instigation of the consuls Licinius Murena and Junius Silanus, provided that it should not be lawful for a statute to be brought secretly into the *aerarium*, since statutes were stored in the *aerarium*' [Stangl p. 140]. At any rate, it reflects a concern on Cicero's part with the proper preservation of legal texts – not just the bills that were passed, but those that were promulgated too. – M. Porcius Cato, as quaestor in 64 BC, kept a close watch on deposits in the treasury: Plutarch, *Cato the Younger*, 17. 3 = B56.

G7 *Trinum nundinum* and *satura*

a) Rutilius writes that the Romans instituted market days (*nundinae*) so that for eight days the rustics might do their work in the fields, but on the interval of the ninth day they might come from the country to Rome to do market business and to approve statutes; and so that resolutions and decrees might be put with the people being more numerous – these were published on the third market day and easily became known to individuals and the people as a whole. Whence too is derived the custom that statutes were promulgated on the third market day (*trinum nundinum*).

Macrobius, *Saturnalia* 1.16.34

This late antique source provides a helpful summary of the principle of the *trinum nundinum* ('three market days', i.e. seventeen days), whereby a continuous period of time had to elapse between the promulgation of a bill and the vote on it. Rome was not a democracy, but the principle was that the popular assemblies were crucial sources of legislation, and had to base their deliberations on careful reflection.

b) It was perhaps at the sixth hour of the day that ... I complained about certain matters to do with the *res publica* ... at the ninth hour on that very same day your adoption took place. If, when the interval in the case of all other legislation must be three market-days (*trinum nundinum*), an interval of three hours is sufficient in the case of an adoption, then I find no fault at all; but if the same interval has to be observed, the Senate judged that the people were not bound by the statutes of M. Drusus, since they had been passed contrary to the *lex Caecilia Didia*.

Cicero, *On his House* 41

Cicero declared that the *trinum nundinum* was not observed when it was proposed that Clodius be adopted a plebeian and its enactment followed within hours. – The *lex Caecilia Didia* of 98 BC banned statutes which dealt with different subjects in one bill. This was known as a *lex satura* ('hotchpotch' law: Festus explains *satura* as 'a kind of food composed of varied ingredients and a law crammed with many items; thus in the *sanctio* of statutes it is added 'let [none] *per saturam* either abrogate or derogate.'[Festus, p. 314M)].

c) The tribunes of the plebs made a proposal concerning provinces contrary to the acts of C. Caesar. He decreed a two-year period, they a six-year period. Did the Roman people accept this law too? Well? Was it promulgated? Well? Was it not carried before it was written down? Did we not see something accomplished before anyone suspected it was going to happen? [8] Where was the *lex Caecilia Didia*? Where the promulgation involving three market days (*trinum nundinum*)? Where the punishment under the recent *lex Iunia* and *Licinia*? Can *these statutes* be valid without the destruction of the all the rest?

Cicero, *Philippics* 5.7–8

The provisions on the *trinum nundinum* and the *lex Caecilia Didia* against 'hotchpotch' legislation (see note above) are also relevant in the polemic of Cicero against Mark Antony in 44 BC, after the assassination of Julius Caesar in 44 BC. Like Clodius, Antony openly disregards the restrictions that are set to the law-making process, and to the interaction between a political leader and the popular assembly.

G8   The form of a bill (*rogatio*)
The wording of this bill (*rogatio*) is as follows: 'Would you wish, would you order that L. Valerius be the son of L. Titius as rightly and lawfully as if he had been born of that father and the mother of his family, and that Titius have the power of life and death over Valerius which a father has over a son. This, just as I have stated it, I so ask of you, citizens.'

Aulus Gellius, *Attic Nights* 5.19.9

A statute takes the form of a question (*rogatio,* from *rogare*, 'to ask') that is put to the Roman people by the proposing magistrate. The text quoted by Gellius is a rather straightforward one, which deals with the potential adoption of a patrician into a plebeian family; many statutes were of course much longer and more complex than the example used here.

G9   Statute legislation and provincial magistrates

I pass over his leaving his province, his leading an army out of it, his waging war on his own initiative, his entering a kingdom without the order of the Roman people or of the Senate – acts, which not only very many ancient statutes, but also the *lex Cornelia maiestatis* and the *lex Julia de pecuniis repetundis* most plainly forbid.

Cicero, *Against Piso* 50

The reference is to the restoration of Ptolemy Auletes to his throne in Alexandria in 55 BC by A. Gabinius, then governor of Syria, who is accused of having breached a number of statutes, including recent pieces of legislation by Sulla (the *lex Cornelia maiestatis* – Cornelius' law on diminishing power of Rome, i.e. limiting the power of provincial magistrates, 81 BC) and Caesar (the *lex Julia de pecuniis repetundis* – Julius' law on corruption, 59 BC): it was not uncommon for a law to come back to issues that were covered in previous pieces of legislation, whether to restate an established point or to mark an explicit departure from previous practice. – Note the reference first to the 'order of the Roman people' and then '[that] of the Senate'.

G10   Legislation of C. Gracchus, Sulla, Caesar and Pompey

[18] Is there anything that may so properly be called the act of one who has been involved in a civilian capacity in power and authority in the *res publica* as statute? Ask for the acts of Gracchus: the Sempronian statutes will be produced. Ask for the acts of Sulla: the Cornelian statutes will be produced. What were the acts that made up the third consulship of Pompey? Without doubt his statutes. If you were to ask Caesar himself what he had done in Rome as a civilian, he would answer that he had passed many fine statutes.

Cicero, *Philippics* 1.18

A passage that asserts the close identification between major political figures and the pieces of legislation which they promoted, and still bear their name as a result, and shows at the same time how contentious statutes could still be even long after their passing.

G11   Codification

a) The consul Pompey was the first person to want to organize the reduction of the laws into books, but he did not continue through fear of his critics. Then Caesar began to do it, but was killed before [he could].

Isidore, *Etymologies* 1.5.1

b) He intended to reduce the civil law (*ius civile*) to a fixed limit and from the immense and diffuse mass of statutes to bring together in a very few books all that were best and necessary.

Suetonius, *Divus Julius* 44.2

The upkeep of public records is a growing preoccupation of the Roman élite in the late Republic; Isidore, a late antique source, suggests that an attempt to produce a sort of a legislative 'code' was made by Pompey and Caesar, who both failed, for different, if perhaps not altogether unrelated reasons: the 50s and 40s BC are an age in which concerns over the excessive influence of an individual were clearly strong in several quarters. Creating a selection of the 'best and necessary' legislation was inevitably going to be a contentious step, which ran against established practice.

G12   Law and society

[70] Now the person who thinks that civil law (*ius civile*) should be despised is tearing apart the bonds not only of judicial procedure, but also of the interests and life of all; the person who criticizes those who interpret the law, if he says they are inexperienced in law, is disparaging men, not the civil law (*ius civile*): if he thinks that one should not submit to the jurists, then it is not men he is injuring, but he is bringing about the ruin of statutes and law. Therefore you must most certainly bear in mind that nothing in the state is to be kept hold of with greater care and attention than the civil law (*ius civile*). For once this has been removed, there is no criterion by which anyone can establish what is his and what is another's; there is no criterion such as may be fair for all and one and the same for all. ... [73] Now what exactly is this civil law (*ius civile*)? Something such that it cannot be bent by influence, nor broken by power, nor corrupted by money; but if it be overwhelmed, or even abandoned or not guarded with sufficient care, then there is nothing which anyone may reckon he possesses with security, nothing he will inherit from his father, nothing he will leave for his children. [74] For what point is there in possessing a house or a country estate left by one's father or properly acquired by some means, if it is uncertain whether you can keep hold of what you possess by right of conveyance? If the law is inadequately protected? If it cannot be maintained by civil and public statute against some private interest? What benefit, I ask, to possess a country estate, if the rights of boundaries, possession, of water and roads, which have been more fittingly described by our ancestors, can be upset and changed on any consideration? Believe me, in the matter of these same possessions a greater inheritance has come to each one of us from law and statutes than from those by whom all those very goods have been left to us. For that a country estate comes to me can be brought about by the will of anyone; that I keep hold of what has become mine cannot happen without the civil law (*ius civile*). An estate can be bequeathed by one's father: but uninterrupted title to the estate, that is the end of worry and risk of lawsuits, is not bequeathed by a father but by statutes ... [75] Wherefore the public heritage of law, which you have received from your ancestors, you ought to keep hold of with no less care and attention than the heritage of your private property: not only because this private property is protected by the civil law (*ius civile*), but also because an inheritance is abandoned with loss for an individual, while law cannot be lost without great loss for the state.

Cicero, *Defence of Caecina* 70–75, with omission

The case of A. Caecina is a complex civil dispute: it was heard in 69 BC and it involved a member of a prominent Etruscan family. As he makes his way through an intricate set of legal problems, Cicero finds the scope for full-scale celebration of the merits and importance of *ius civile*: his focus here is on what we also call 'civil law', i.e. on matters of ownership and inheritance, which play a central role in Caecina's affair, but the political implications of his argument are many and far-reaching: *ius civile* is an intellectual domain that responds to rational and transparent principles, which can secure the orderly unfolding and development of civic life and social relations, and is under the care of a group of carefully trained experts. The defence of private property that is such a central concern of *ius civile* is closely related, in Cicero's assessment, to the protection of public freedom. Far from entailing a merely technical expertise, law has a crucial political dimension.

CENSUS AND CITIZENSHIP

a) THE ROMAN CENSUS

G13a   Cicero on the office of censor

Even the office of censor, which before used to seem disagreeable to the people, is now clamoured for, is now become popular and capable of getting applause.

Cicero, *Against Caecilius* 8

G13b   Ancient commentary on Cicero

Even the office of censor: Censors were customarily appointed every fifth year to regulate the customs (*mores*) of the political community (*civitas*). The censors would mark citizens in the following manner: one who was a senator was expelled from the Senate; one who was an *eques* was deprived of his public horse; one who was a plebeian was transferred from the list of Caerites and was made an *aerarius*, and in consequence was not in the register of his own voting tribe (*centuria*) but remained a citizen only in the sense that in accordance with his personal liability he made payments termed *tributum*.

pseudo-Asconius, *Commentary on Cicero's Speech Against Caecilius* 8, p. 199 Stangl

This brief note by an ancient commentator on the *Verrines* gives a very helpful overview of the main duties of the censors, and of the strong integration between their administrative responsibilities and their general oversight over the morals of the city. One of their key tasks is to keep a general overview of social mobility within the community: those who are deserving of being enrolled in a higher order can expect to receive due recognition, while those who do not fulfil the duties entailed by the senatorial status can legitimately be struck off the roll.

G13c   Aulus Gellius on the censors' mark

[16.13.7] *Caerites*: 'We have been told the citizens of Caere became the first townspeople (*municipes*) without the right of suffrage and that it was granted them to take on the honour of Roman citizenship, but to be free of its tasks and burdens in return for receipt and guardianship of the sacred objects during the war with the Gauls. Hence, vice-versa, those were named 'tablets of Caere' on which the censors ordered those to be recorded whom they deprived of their votes by way of their *mark*.'

[4.12.1–2] Noteworthy instances in ancient records of marks and punishments of the censors. If anyone had allowed his land to become overgrown through neglect and did not give it sufficient care and attention and had neither ploughed nor weeded it or had allowed his orchard or vineyard to become derelict, this was not without punishment: the censors would make him an *aerarius*. [2] In like manner, if any Roman *eques* was seen to have a thin or not well-groomed horse, he was marked for 'lack of polish'; this word has the meaning as if you were to say 'lack of care'.

Aulus Gellius, *Attic Nights* 16.13.7 and 4.12.1–2

G14   Ritual end of the censorship

[86] Now I shall first put down some things from the censors' records:
When by night the censor has gone into the precinct (*templum*) to take the auspices, and a message has come from the sky, let him command the herald to call the men:

'May this be good, fortunate, happy, and salutary for the Roman people, the Quirites, and for the well-being of the *res publica* and for the government of the Roman people, the Quirites, and for me and my colleague, for our integrity and for our magistracy: all the citizen foot soldiers under arms and private citizens, those in charge of all the tribes, issue a summons to assemble (*inlicium*) hither to me, should anyone wish a reckoning to be given either for himself or for another.'

[87] The herald summons them first in the *templum*; afterwards he summons them likewise from the walls. When it is light, the censors, the scribes, and the magistrates are anointed with myrrh and ointments. When the praetors and the tribunes of the plebs and those who have been called to the summons have come, the censors cast lots with each other, which of them shall conduct the final purification ritual (*lustrum*). When the *templum* has been determined, then after that he who is to perform the *lustrum* conducts the assembly (*inlicium*).

Varro, On the Latin Language 6.86–87

The census was not merely an administrative procedure that had to be carried out for military and financial purposes. Its moral significance was further corroborated by the involvement of the censors with a number of important public rituals: they were expected to take auspices before performing their duties and duly seek signs of divine consent to the activity they were about to carry out. This passage of Varro's treatise on the Latin language describes the augural ritual that took place before the citizens who were due to be enrolled by the censors were formally summoned. – A *templum* is not just a temple, but any sacred precinct; *inlicium* is an archaic word used in the formula for summoning the 'meeting' to assess citizens by the censor. In regular usage '*contio*' was used. The *lustrum* was a ceremony that marked the final stage of the census, normally the year after the censors entered office.

G15   Consequences

The judgement of the censor exposes the condemned man to almost nothing except embarrassment. And so, as the entire judgement quite simply involves someone's name, that censure has been called *ignominia* (un-naming, disqualification).

Cicero, On the State 4.6a

G16   Public display: *recognitio/transvectio equitum*, 70 BC

[4] It is the custom for Roman *equites,* whenever they complete the military service for the time required by the law, to bring their horse to the forum in front of the two men whom they call censors, and having enumerated each of the commanders and commanders under whom they have served and given an account of their military service, to be discharged. Honour and dishonour are given out according to the career of each.

[5] At that time the censors Gellius and Lentulus were seated in their place and the entry of the *equites* being examined was in progress, when Pompey was seen making his descent from above down to the forum, having all the distinctions of his office, but leading his horse by his own hand. When he was near and was plainly visible, having ordered the lictors to stand aside, he led his horse to the tribunal. [6] The populace (Gk: *demos*) was amazed and in complete silence, while awe and delight at the sight took hold of the magistrates. Then the senior magistrate asked him: 'I enquire of you, Pompey the Great, if you have completed all the military service according to

the law?" 'I have completed it all' he replied 'and all under my own command.' On hearing this, the populace (*demos*) gave a loud shout and it was no longer possible to restrain their shouts of delight, but the censors got up and escorted him to his home, pleasing the citizens who followed and applauded.

Plutarch, *Life of Pompey* 22.4–6

This anecdote provides a neat combination of tradition and sharp innovation. The ritual display before the census of the members of the equestrian order who had completed their military duties was an established feature of the census and its significant spectacular dimension. In the census of 70 BC the consul Pompey, who was still a member of the equestrian order, as he had not previously held any public office in spite of his extraordinary military record, took part in the *recognitio equitum* (an overview of the equestrian order) and gave an answer to the customary question of the censors in which his unprecedented position was neatly summarized. The occasion enabled him publicly to emphasize his distance from the senatorial order, and was duly saluted as a pointed political statement by the crowd that witnessed it.

b) THE CENSUS IN THE FIRST CENTURY BC

One of the most significant aspects of the census in the first century BC is that between 70 BC and 28 BC, when Octavian conducted a census, no census was completed with the *lustrum*. The resulting difficulties are considerable: the citizen list will have become wildly inaccurate; membership of the Senate after Sulla became automatic upon holding the quaestorship; the revision of the senatorial and equestrian rolls (*lectio senatus* and *recognitio equitum*) were presumably not carried out, but the statute of Clodius in 58 BC would suggest that the censorial *nota* had been in use since 70 BC. Such censors as were elected must have dealt with public contracts, as, for example, in 61 BC, with the reaction of the *publicani*.

G17   Cn. Cornelius Lentulus Clodianus, L. Gellius Publicola, 70 BC

Cn. Lentulus and L. Gellius, the censors, conducted a severe census, removing 64 men from the Senate. When the *lustrum* had been completed by them, 900,000 citizens were enrolled.

Livy, *Summaries* 98

The removal of 64 members of the Senate is remarkable: it is virtually equal proportionately to the removal of 32 members in 115 BC, the last recorded total, and in both cases an ex-consul was among those removed: P. Cornelius Lentulus Sura, consul 71 BC, who would re-establish himself, become praetor in 63 BC, and be the leading Catilinarian conspirator to be executed in 63 BC. Also expelled from the Senate was C. Antonius Hybrida, later consul in 63 BC with Cicero, who (according to a later source) 'had plundered the allies, defied a judicial enquiry, sold his estates because of the magnitude of his debts, and did not have control of his own property' (Asconius, p. 84C.22-25). The importance of the census of 70 BC cannot be overemphasized: large numbers of new citizens must have been enrolled, the local notables (*domi nobiles*), with the wealth and leisure to make their presence felt in the voting assemblies (*comitia centuriata*). Hence, perhaps, the reluctance of the *boni* to allow another complete census and *lustrum*, and the attempt of Caesar and Crassus to arrange the enfranchisement of Cisalpine Gaul, against the redoubtable opposition from the likes of Catulus.

G18   Q. Lutatius Catulus, M. Licinius Crassus, 65 BC

[3] The censors were also at variance with one another concerning the people living beyond the Po: one wished to admit them to citizenship, while the other did not, so that they did not carry out any of their other duties, but resigned their office. [4] And because of this their successors too did nothing in the following year, since the tribunes hindered them over the roll of senators, in fear that they themselves might be expelled from the Senate. [5] Meanwhile all those in Rome, except those inhabiting

what is now Italy, were expelled on the motion of a tribune Gaius Papius, since they were becoming so numerous and they did not seem suitable to live with citizens.

Cassius Dio, *Roman History* 37.9.3–5

One of the stated aims of Papius' law was to pursue false claims to Roman citizenship: the poet Archias from Antioch and L. Cornelius Balbus from Gades were prosecuted in 62 and 56 respectively, and their status as Roman citizens was challenged in two separate court cases. We have good insights into their predicaments through the defence speeches that Cicero gave on their behalf. – On the censorship of Crassus and Catulus see Plutarch, *Life of Crassus* 13.1.

G19   Census of 61 BC
In that year the censors enrolled all those who were in office into the senatorial order, and beyond the number.

Cassius Dio, *Roman History* 37.46.4

This is the sole evidence for censors in 61 BC. Their names are unknown, but one was possibly C. Scribonius Curio, consul 76 BC. Cicero states that Cotta and Curio reached the highest office in the *res publica* without giving entertainments (*On Duties* 2.59). L. Julius Caesar, consul 64 BC, is another possibility. It was presumably they who arranged the contract with the tax-collectors (*publicani*) which would prove very controversial (**B86**).

G20   Clodius' statute on the censors' *nota*, 58 BC
a) For laws were passed ... to the effect that the censorial examination, that is to say, the verdict so authoritative, of a most hallowed institution, should be removed from the *res publica*.

Cicero, *Defence of Sestius* 55, with omission

b) *That the censorial examination:* He is making an enumeration of the Clodian statutes, of which this was one: that it should not be permitted to the censor to pass over anyone in reading out the roll of the Senate unless that person was known to have been condemned.

Bobbian Scholiast on Cicero, p. 132 Stangl

Note the important qualification introduced by the commentator: the senators who were convicted did not escape the exclusion from the order.

G21   M. Valerius Messalla Niger, P. Servilius Vatia Isauricus, 55 BC
I would very much like to know whether the tribunes are blocking the census by invalidating the days (for that is the rumour here), what they are doing in general about the censorships, and what they are thinking about doing.
Cumae, 27 April 55 BC.

Cicero, *Atticus* 4.9.1 (SB 85)

Cicero mentions a delay in the elections for the censorship: there is evidence that he considered running for that prestigious office. At the beginning of October 57 BC he had written to Atticus [4.2.6 (SB 74)], saying that he had told Pompey that he would not object if he were appointed a *legatus* provided he was in no way impeded. He would have been willing to accept any *libera legatio* (see **E22**) had he not wished to leave open for himself the possibility of standing in elections for censors, which the consuls of 56 BC were expected to hold. In the event the political shenanigans of 56 BC impeded elections of curule magistrates.

G22   Censors mark Tiber boundaries

M. Valerius, son of Marcus, grandson of Manlius, Messalla and P. Servilius, son of Gaius, Isauricus, censors, in accordance with a decree of the Senate, fixed this boundary

ILS 5922c = EDCS-17700536

After their election to the consulship, Pompey and Crassus arranged the election of other magistrates, including P. Servilius (*cos.* 79 BC) and M. Messalla (*cos.* 61 BC) as censors. During the Republic the censors had oversight of the banks of the Tiber and in 54 BC the river overflowed, causing serious flooding: whence the boundary marker. Some eighteen similar markers of these censors have been found at different spots on the banks of the Tiber. This one was restored by later officials. These censors were still in office in mid-54 BC (see Cicero, *To Atticus* 4.16.8 [SB 89], about 1 July 54 BC: 'I suppose you are not interested asking about the *lustrum*, which has been given up as hopeless'). Valerius Maximus (*Memorable Deeds and Sayings* 2.9.9) records that Messalla had been lightly wounded by the censorial *nota* but later sought and gained censorial power.

G23   Appius Claudius Pulcher, L. Calpurnius Piso Caesoninus, 51/50 BC

I almost forgot what the most important item to write about was. Do you know that censor Appius is performing marvels here, that he is dealing most rigorously with matters of statues and pictures, with the size of estates, and with debt? He is convinced that the censorship is like a skin treatment or washing soda; for he wants to wash away the dirt, but he is opening all his own veins and vitals. Run, by gods and men, and come as soon as you can to laugh at these happenings – legal proceedings concerning the *lex Scantinia* taking place before Drusus, Appius taking action over paintings and statues. Rome, *c.* 8 August 50 BC.

Caelius to Cicero [*To his Friends* 8.14.4 (SB 97)]

Appius intended to take action against Curio and Caelius; Piso protected Curio, Caelius was prosecuted under the *lex Scantinia*, but responded with a countercharge on the same statute against Appius as he told Cicero a few months later (*To his Friends* 8.12.3 (SB 98)). The precise remit of the *lex Scantinia* is problematic: it apparently covered sexual assault. Drusus can be assumed to be an obvious flouter of the *lex*, and not really in charge of trials concerning it - but Caelius' point here is about Appius' hypocrisy – he allegedly plundered Greece for his own art collection too, so should not be investigating the art collections or sexual behaviour of others. He did strike off the historian Sallust for sexual immorality (*Invective against Sallust* 19) or more probably for acting against Cicero and Milo as tribune in 52 BC.

G24   Octavian, 28 BC

I revised the membership of the Senate three times, and in my sixth consulship [28 BC] I conducted a census of the population with Marcus Agrippa as my colleague. I performed the ceremony of purification (*lustrum*) forty-two years after the last one; in this census 4,063,000 individual Roman citizens were registered.

Augustus, *Res Gestae* 8.2

This is the first census since the 70 BC one for which a population figure survives. Various attempts have been made to explain the huge increase in the number of registered citizens. Some have argued that the census of 28 included all Roman citizens, possibly including women and children, rather than just male citizens eligible for military service. Others have attached great importance to the decentralization of census operations that is attested through other sources: citizens were no longer expected to turn up before the censors in Rome, but could be enrolled in their hometowns. Several scholars have argued that census operations had become more accurate by the end of the Republican period. The recent citizenship grant to the communities of Cisalpine Gaul (see **L30**) may have also played an important role. No one envisages the population of Roman Italy quadrupling within half a century, but there is substantial disagreement among scholars on whether the population count in first century BC Italy was 'low', 'high', or somewhere in between. Whichever solution one chooses to favour conjures up a different picture of the demography, and therefore of the economic and social history, of Roman Italy (cf. above, **L30**, for Appian's comment on *dusandria* in the Gracchan period).

JURISTS

G25   A survey of Roman jurists

[39] Then there were Publius Mucius and Brutus and Manilius, who laid the foundations of civil law (*ius civile*). Of these Mucius left ten books, Brutus seven, Manilius three: the writings of Manilius are extant. Two of them were consuls, while Brutus was praetor. Publius Mucius was also *pontifex maximus*. [40] They were followed by Publius Rutilius Rufus, who was consul in Rome and proconsul in Asia, Paulus Verginius and Quintus Tubero, that Stoic student of Pansa, who himself was consul. There was at the same time Sextus Pompeius, the uncle of Gnaeus Pompeius, and Coelius Antipater, who composed histories, but devoted greater effort to oratory than to the knowledge of the law. Also Lucius Crassus, brother of Publius Mucius, who was called Munianus; he Cicero says was the most accomplished of the jurists. [41] After them there was Quintus Mucius, the son of Publius, *pontifex maximus*. He was the first to arrange the civil law (*ius civile*) by categories reducing it into eighteen books. [42] Mucius had many students, but of particular importance were Aquilius Gallus, Lucilius Balbus, Sextus Papirius, Gaius Iuventius: Servius says that of these Gallus was of the greatest influence with the people. ... [43] Now while Servius Sulpicius occupied first place in pleading cases or certainly second after Marcus Tullius he is said to have approached Quintus Mucius to consult him on a matter concerning a friend of his; when Servius had not fully understood his reply (*responsum*) concerning the law, he had asked Quintus a second time. When the *responsum* had been given by Quintus Mucius and he still did not grasp it, he had been upbraided by Quintus Mucius along these lines: for he said it was a disgrace for a patrician and a noble pleading cases to be ignorant of the law with which he was involved. Stung by this insult, as it were, Servius devoted himself to civil law (*ius civile*) and studied for the most part with those whom we have mentioned: trained by Lucilius Balbus, instructed most of all by Aquilius Gallus, who lived at Cercina. That is the reason many books of his were completed at Cercina and are extant. When he had died on an embassy, the Roman people set up a statue to him in front of the *rostra,* and it exists today in front of the *rostra* of Augustus. Many of his works are extant; he left around one hundred and eighty.

[49] And, let us note in passing that before the time of Augustus the right publicly to give expert rulings (*ius respondendi*) was not granted by the emperors, but those who had confidence in their studies used to give responses to those who consulted them; and they did not invariably give signed rulings (*responsa*), but would often write themselves to judges, and give testimony on behalf of those who consulted them.

Digest 1.2.2.39–43, 49 (Pomponius)

The *Enchiridion* ('Handbook') of the imperial jurist Pomponius, which survives in the first book of the Digest, provides a lengthy chronological overview of the greatest Roman jurists. Its main ambition is to convey a sense of the distinction and richness of an intellectual tradition that goes far back into the early days of the Republic. The passage quoted here covers the period from the mid-second century BC to the Augustan period. The emphasis is on the increasingly more important role that expert rulings (*responsa*) had in securing the standing of the jurists. With Augustus, the right to give *responsa* is granted by the emperor; in the Republican period authoritative *responsa* could be conveyed by judges and play an important role in judicial proceedings. The point was already made by Cicero in *Orator* 1.212, where the ability to give *responsa* is singled out as the distinctive form of expertise that a jurist can claim. – *Responsa* were not, however, the only form in which legal knowledge was codified and transmitted: note the extensive production of Aquilius Gallus.

G26   Consultations

For there is no doubt that the house of a jurist is the oracle of the whole state. The proof of this is the door and the forecourt of Q. Mucius here; in spite of his very weak health and his now advanced age, it is thronged daily by a vast crowd of citizens and by the brilliance of the most distinguished citizens.

Cicero, On the Good Orator 1.200

This passage refers to Q. Mucius Scaevola, augur, praetor in 120 BC, governor of Asia, and consul in 117 BC (see also **G27**). Cf. also Cicero, *Philippic*, 8.31: 'I recall, senators, Q. Scaevola, the augur, during the Marsic war, though in extreme old age and his health broken, every day as soon as it became light, gave the opportunity to all to come and see him; nor did anyone during that war see him in his bed; and the feeble old man was the first to come to the senate-house'. – This text shows how the expertise of a jurist is closely linked with social status and has direct political implications: the house where some lawyers receive those who wish to consult them is also a manifestation of their prominence, and the crowd of those who attend it is testimony to their prestige; the old age and frailty of Mucius is emphasized by Cicero in sharp contrast with the enduring sharpness of his intellect.

G27   Q. Mucius Scaevola

a) There was Q. Scaevola, a contemporary and colleague, of all men the most learned in the study of civil law (*ius civile*), the most shrewd in talent and intelligence, the most polished and fastidious in diction, and indeed, as I am accustomed to say, among jurists the best orator, among orators the best jurist.

Cicero, On the Good Orator 1.180

'As for Scaevola, we know well enough the elegance of his oratory from the speeches, which he left' (Cicero, *Brutus*, 163). In the defence of his *legatus*, P. Rutilius, who was accused of extortion in the province of Asia, a *cause célèbre* (Cicero, *Brutus*, 115): 'Q. Mucius spoke, precisely and clearly, with a careful finish, as was his custom, but with nothing of the vigour and resources, which a trial of that kind and the importance of the case demanded'.

b) He was the first to arrange civil law (*ius civile*) by categories reducing it into eighteen books.

Digest, 1.2.2.41 (Pomponius)

c) Indeed Q. Scaevola, *pontifex maximus*, used to say that, in all cases of arbitration, the greatest force existed in those in which the phrase 'in accordance with good faith' was added; and he thought that the phrase *good faith* had very wide application; it was involved in trusteeships, in partnerships, in trusts, in mandates, in buying and selling, in hiring and in letting, activities by which communal life is bound; in these matters it required a great judge to decide what each individual ought to be answerable for to another, especially when in very many cases there were counter legal actions.

Cicero, On Duties 3.70

These three passages draw attention to three major aspects of the legal achievements of Q. Mucius Scaevola (cos. 95): the balance he struck between legal knowledge and rhetorical skill; his attempt to systematize the study of law according to rational categories; and the care with which he pursued the study of matters of detail, which involved a careful reflection on the language in which legal problems are presented, and was very much in keeping with the other two defining aspects of Scaevola's work.

G28   C. Aquilius Gallus

Canius was furious; but what could he do? For C. Aquilius, my colleague and friend, had not yet introduced the *formulae* concerning *wrongful deceit*. When asked what 'wrongful deceit' was in these specific *formulae*, he used to respond: 'When one thing had been pretended, another done.' Quite splendidly defined, as one would expect from a master of definition.

Cicero, On Duties 3.60

Attention to matters of language and definition was also a distinctive aspect of the work of C. Aquilius Gallus (*c.* 116-*c.* 44 BC), and is a symptom of the consolidation and development of Roman jurisprudence in the first half of the first century BC. – In *Defence of Caecina*, 77–79, Cicero makes use of a legal argument devised by Aquilius, and emphasizes at some length the prestige that he enjoyed in the city of Rome, establishing an intriguing correlation between his expertise and his character ('he is so just and good a man, that he seems to be a jurist by nature, not by training; he has such experience and understanding that it seems that from the *ius civile* not only has he derived some knowledge, but goodness too').

G29   Ser. Sulpicius Rufus
a) the case of Murena

[19] Servius followed his military service with me here in the city, giving responses, preparing documents, drawing up *formulae* of security – a life full of anxiety and vexation; he learned civil law (*ius civile*), he got little sleep, he worked hard, he was on hand for many, he put up with the stupidity of many, he endured their arrogance, he stomached those who were difficult. He lived for the wishes of others not for his own. Great praise and gratitude is shown by men when one person works hard in a profession so as to bring benefit to many... [23] Since you seem to me to be hugging your knowledge of jurisprudence as if it were a darling daughter, I shall not allow you to be so mistaken as to think that this whatever-it-is that you have taken such pains to learn, is in any way outstanding. I have always felt that other qualities – self-control, dignity, uprightness, integrity, and all the others – have made you thoroughly deserving of the consulship and every other office. I shall not say that you have wasted your time in learning civil law (*ius civile*), but I shall say that there is no secure road to the consulship in your profession. For all the skills, which win for us the support of the Roman people, must have a prestige which impresses and a usefulness which pleases them. [24] The greatest prestige is with those who have outstanding distinction in warfare, because everything, which concerns the empire and the condition of the state, is thought to be defended and upheld by them; and the greatest usefulness, since we are able to enjoy not only the *res publica*, but also our own possessions as a result of their decision and danger. The ability in speaking – to be able by judgement and by eloquence to influence the minds of the senate, the people, and those who act as jurors – which has often carried weight in electing a consul, is also important and full of prestige. A consul is sought who can at times check the frenzies of the tribunes, who can calm the passions of the people, who can resist bribery. It is not surprising if, because of this ability, men, even those

that were not *nobiles*, have often reached the consulship because they were good orators, particularly since the same ability produces the widest influence, the firmest friendships and the greatest popularity. There are none of these, Sulpicius, in that profession of yours. [25] Firstly, prestige cannot exist in such a narrow field of knowledge; for the subject matter is insignificant, almost entirely involved in single letters or in divisions between words. Secondly, even if among our ancestors there once was some respect for your profession, it has come into complete contempt and disregard with the publication of your secrets.

Cicero, Defence of Murena 19–25, with omission

In the case against Murena, Cicero's counterpart was the most capable and distinguished jurist of his time, Ser. Sulpicius Rufus, who also happened to be a long-time personal friend of his. However, Cicero did not refrain from launching a personal attack on Sulpicius, which, whilst being tinged with irony, made some abrasive points on the gap of prestige and significance between jurisprudence and other forms of knowledge and expertise that have more immediate political repercussions, notably military leadership and oratory (the lack of military distinction was always a pressing, if largely unspoken, concern to Cicero, who based his credentials on his rhetorical ability).

b) [152] At this point Brutus said: 'Are you actually saying, are you putting our friend Servius ahead even of Q. Scaevola?' 'Yes, I do think so, Brutus,' I replied 'there was great experience of civil law (*ius civile*) in Scaevola and in many others, but in this one man there was skill; he would never have achieved this through knowledge of the civil law (*ius civile*) had he not learnt besides the skill which taught to divide the universal into the particular, to set forth what lies hidden by defining, to make clear the obscure by interpreting; first of all to see the ambiguous, then to make clear distinctions, and finally to possess a standard by which true and false may be judged and what consequences follow from what propositions and what do not. [153] For he brought this skill, the greatest of all skills, like a light, to the unsystematic rulings (*responsa*) and court proceedings of others.' 'You seem to me,' he said 'to be talking about dialectic.' 'You understand correctly' I said, 'but he further added to this a knowledge of letters and an eloquence of speaking, which can most easily be perceived from his writings, which are beyond compare.

Cicero, Brutus 152–153

In the more sedate setting of a treatise on rhetoric, Cicero gave a much more positive assessment of Sulpicius' contribution to Roman intellectual life: he developed the teachings of Scaevola and his predecessors to an unprecedented degree of sophistication and complexity, and showed how closely integrated the study of law is to the exploration of complex philosophical issues, while retaining a keen interest in eloquence and literary matters. Cf. also the tribute to Sulpicius pronounced shortly after his death in February 43 (*Philippics* 9.10–11).

c) Cicero to Sulpicius
[3] I will do nothing arrogant; nor shall I encourage you, a man endowed with such knowledge and disposition, to return to those skills to which you have given your earnest application from your earliest years. [4] I shall just say this, something of which I hope you will approve: when I saw that for that skill, which I had studied, there was no place either in the senate-house or in the forum, I turned all my effort and attention to philosophy. For that branch of knowledge of yours, in which you have

achieved singular distinction, there is left no more place than for mine; wherefore I do not advise you, but I have convinced myself that you are engaged in the same subjects, which even if they do not bring advantage, take one's mind away from anxiety.
Rome, first half September 46 BC, or perhaps earlier.

Cicero to Sulpicius, *To his Friends* 4.3.3–4 (SB 202)

Sulpicius had joined the faction of Pompey in the civil war, and did not return to Italy for over two years after Pharsalus. In this letter Cicero confronts a problem that he and Sulpicius shared: both the skills in which they excelled (eloquence and jurisprudence) are no longer meaningful in a context that is dominated by one individual. Cicero reports to have turned his attention towards philosophy, and most of his production in this period is indeed taken by major philosophical works. Although he does not give his friend specific advice, he appears to suggest that a similar path may be open to someone of Sulpicius' intellectual calibre. – Note the focus on *personal* tranquillity and safety with which the letter ends. Cicero's preoccupation with the decline of *ius civile* did not fade away with Caesar's assassination, but was even deepened by the traumatic developments of the months following the Ides of March (see *On Duties*, 2.65, written in the autumn of 44: 'as with public offices, as with every grade of status (*dignitas*), the brilliance of this knowledge has been destroyed.

d) Sulpicius to Cicero

[1] When I received the news of your daughter Tullia's death, I was indeed as much grieved and distressed as I was bound to be, and looked upon it as a calamity in which I shared. ... [2] Think how Fortune has dealt with us up to now. Reflect that we have had snatched from us what ought to be no less dear to human beings than their children – country, honour, rank (*dignitas*), every political distinction (*honor*). What further pain could be inflicted by this particular loss? ... [3] But, it will be said, after all it is an evil to lose one's children. Yes, it is: only it is a worse one to endure and submit to the present state of affairs. ...

[4] I want to mention to you a circumstance that gave me no small comfort, in the hope that it might also prove capable of diminishing your sorrow. On my journey back from Asia, as I was sailing from Aegina toward Megara, I began to survey the localities that were on every side of me. Behind me was Aegina, in front Megara, on the right Piraeus, on the left Corinth: towns which at one time were most flourishing, and now lay before my eyes in ruin and decay. I began to reflect to myself: 'Hah! Do we mere men feel indignant if one of us perishes or is killed – we, whose life should be shorter – when the corpses of so many cities lie in helpless ruin? Will you please, Servilius, restrain yourself and remember that you were born a mortal man?' Believe me, I was not a little strengthened by that reflection.
From Athens, mid-March 45.

Sulpicius, Letter to Cicero, *To his Friends* 4.5.1–4 (SB 248), with omissions

This letter of condolence from Sulpicius to Cicero is an extraordinary document of intellectual history. The death of Tullia, Cicero's beloved daughter, becomes the opportunity to reflect on the dreadful state of the *res publica*. Sulpicius had fought against Caesar: although he had been pardoned and had since been involved with the provincial government of Greece, his private views remained heavily critical. The sight of formerly great Greek cities affords him the opportunity to reflect on how all things human are bound to come to an end, and on the need to come to terms with one's mortality. No other writings of comparable length by Sulpicius survive: this letter gives a sense of how considerable the loss of his work is.

G30 **Horace consults Trebatius Testa**
To some people in satire I seem too sharp and to stretch
My work beyond the law; another party thinks whatever
 I have composed to be without vigour, and that a thousand
Verses like mine can be run off in a day. Trebatius, lay down
What I am to do. '*You should take a rest.*' Not compose verses   5
At all, you're saying? '*That's what I'm saying.*' Well, I'm damned,
If that were not best: but I cannot sleep. '*Let those who need deep*
Sleep, oiled, swim three times across the Tiber,
And at nightfall let them have a body soaked in strong wine.
But if so great a passion for writing seizes you, be bold   10
To write the deeds of unconquered Caesar, to win many
Rewards for your toils.' That's what I want, dear sir, but strength
Fails me: for it is not anyone who can describe battle-lines
Quivering with javelins or Gauls dying with broken spear,
Or wounded Parthian slipping from his horse.   15
'*But you could write about a just and brave man*
Like wise Lucilius about Scipio.' I shall not fail
When the occasion arises: except at the right time, the words
Of Flaccus will not come to the attentive ear of Caesar,
Who, if you wrongly wheedle, will, fully secure, kick back.   20
'*How much more correct this, than to harm in hostile verse*
Pantolabus the chic idler and Nomentanus the playboy,
While everyone fears for himself, though he is untouched,
And hates!'

                              Or whether peaceful old age   57
Awaits me or death is hovering with black wings,
Rich, poor, in Rome or, if chance so order, in exile,
Whatever shall be the colour of life, I shall write. '*My boy,*   60
I fear you may not live long, and that some powerful friend
Of yours may strike you with cold.'

                              Whatever I am, although
Below the census and talent of Lucilius, yet unwilling   75
Envy will admit that I have till now lived with the great,
And while seeking to drive teeth into a fragile being will
Stumble upon a tough one; unless you, learned Trebatius, in
Any way disagree. '*For my part I cannot even split a hair on this;*
But nonetheless be warned, lest perhaps some business   80
Strike you through ignorance of the sacred statutes:
Whoever shall compose harmful poems against another, it's the law
And the court.' So be it, whoever compose harmful poems; but what if
Anyone composes good poems praised by Caesar as judge? If anyone
Barks at one deserving reproaches, while blameless oneself?   85
'*The documents will dissolve in laughter, you will go away discharged.*'

                              Horace, *Satires* 2.1.1–23, 57–62, 74–86

The poet Horace imagines himself in dialogue with the noted jurist C. Trebatius Testa, whose *responsa* to him are printed in italics. Trebatius was a friend of Cicero, who recommended him to Julius Caesar (Cicero, *To his Friends* 7.5 = SB 26) and to whom he dedicated his *Topica*. Some thirteen letters of Cicero to Trebatius survive in the collection of *To his Friends* 7.6-18 (SB 27–39) from May 54 BC to June 53 BC. His time in Gaul on campaign with Caesar was not entirely happy as the letters reveal. He would later enjoy the favour of the emperor Augustus. – Horace's playful and fictional interaction with the jurist is indirect, but revealing evidence of the significance of jurisprudence as a major source of authoritative knowledge, which is not narrowly limited to legal matters, but can encompass moral and social questions. The shadow of Caesar (Octavian, in this context) emerges at the end of our passage, where Trebatius concedes that, whilst personal attacks are not allowed in poetry, they can be laughed off if Caesar endorses them.

G31   Jurist and advocate

But this topic is more important for hypothetical cases, which occur in court proceedings, when the question is asked what is fact or what has happened or what will happen or what can possibly happen. [51] And such is the outline of this specific topic. This topic suggests that the question be asked what has happened before the event, what at the same time, what after it. 'This has nothing to do with the law, it's for Cicero', our friend Gallus used to say if someone brought some issue to him, which involved a question of fact.

Cicero, *Topics* 50–51

This anecdote about Aquilius Gallus suggests another area of tension between law and oratory, and the very different degrees with which they are preoccupied with factual accuracy. Again, it is not by chance that it is told in a highly technical philosophical work; in the *Defence of Murena* Cicero had wittily claimed that jurists are usually would-be orators who have failed to achieve distinction and have switched to a less demanding trade (29).

G32   Advocacy

Again, this rule of duty is to be carefully observed that you never summon an innocent man to court on a capital charge; for that cannot possibly be done without committing a crime. For what is so devoid of human feeling as to direct to the ruin and destruction of good men the eloquence bestowed by nature for the safety and protection of mankind? And yet, while this action is to be avoided, in the same way we should not as a matter of scruple be unwilling to defend a guilty man on occasions, provided he is not wicked and depraved; for people expect it, custom permits it, humanity also accepts it. It is always the business of the judge in a trial to find out the truth; it is sometimes the business of the advocate to maintain what is plausible, even if it be not strictly true; I should not venture to write this, especially since I am writing about philosophy, if the same point was not acceptable to Panaetius, the strictest of Stoics. Then, too, glory and popularity are most often won by defence cases, and all the more so, if it ever happens that help is brought to a person who appears to be oppressed and overwhelmed by the resources of someone powerful, as I have often done on other occasions: when I was a young man I took up the case of Sextus Roscius against the power of Lucius Sulla, then a figure of dominant power; as you know, the speech survives.

Cicero, *On Duties* 2.51

In this passage Cicero treads some potentially treacherous ground. The reference to capital cases was bound to remind some of his readers of his controversial role in the repression of Catiline's conspiracy. His discussion of the commitment to truth that an advocate should uphold is also deeply relevant to his career development, as he took up a number of high-profile cases that had served his political prospects, in which the position of his client could legitimately be regarded as very weak, and in which he was at the very least economical with the truth (e.g. the defence of Cluentius or that of Milo). His attempt to provide different definitions for the roles of the judge and the advocate is however part of a wider reflection on the place of law in Roman society, and indeed beyond: Cicero hastens to note that the great Stoic philosopher Panaetius from Rhodes – a major influence on him, especially in *On Duties* – is in fundamental agreement with his position.

G33   Ideal orator for the lawcourt

I wish this to be the case with the orator: when it has been reported that he is going to speak, the space on the benches be occupied, the tribunal be full, the scribes be courteous in giving and giving up places, the circle of bystanders be made up of many different people, the judge be alert and attentive; when the person who is going to speak rises, silence will be signalled by the circle of bystanders; then there will be frequent expressions of approval, much applause; peals of laughter when he wants them, when he wants, tears; with the result that a person who sees these events from some way off, even if he does not know what is taking place, will nevertheless understand that the speaker is finding favour and that there is a Roscius on stage.

Cicero, *Brutus* 290

An extraordinary vignette of the moments that precede the beginning of a major speech, and in which a lawcourt is suddenly populated for us by figures that are usually overlooked. Far from being the passive recipient of a message, the audience of a speech is a crucial factor in its success: Cicero's assumption is that it takes a *good* orator to achieve the degree of control over the audience that he sketches (cf. Cicero, *Best On the Ideal Orator*, 1. 3: The best orator is the one who instructs, delights and moves the minds of his audience. It is his duty to instruct, it is a compliment to delight and it is essential to move). – Roscius was one of the most successful actors of the time: cf. Cicero's speech in his defence, the *Pro Roscio Comoedo*.

G35   Prosecutors

[3] And so, just as to live the life of a prosecutor and to be induced by reward to bring defendants before the courts is very close to robbery, so to drive out a person seeking the ruin of the state is to be compared with the defenders of the country and for this reason the leading men in the *res publica* did not decline this element of duty and distinguished young men also have been considered to give surety to the *res publica* by the prosecution of evil citizens, because they did not appear either to hate rascals or to provoke animosities, except through a confidence in their own sound mind: [4] and this was done not only by Hortensius, the Luculli, Sulpicius, Cicero, Caesar and very many others, but also by the two Catos.

Quintilian, *The Orator's Education* 12.7.3–4

The early imperial rhetorician Quintilian reflects on the ethical dimension of the task of the prosecutor: while there is the risk that a prosecutor might be driven by questionable motives, the prosecution of 'evil citizens' is a duty that benefits the state and can mark a major step in the career of a junior politician. – L. Lucullus, as a young man brought an action against Servilius, augur, the prosecutor of his father (Plutarch, *Life of Lucullus* 1.1); Julius Caesar against Dolabella, a supporter of Sulla (Plutarch, *Life of Caesar* 4.1). They are examples of young prosecutors. Cicero similarly mentions such prosecutions by Caelius in his defence of him (*Defence of Caelius* 78).

G36   M. Antony and L. Licinius Crassus

So now we have reached Antony and Crassus. For I reckon that these were the greatest orators and in them for the first time the ability to express oneself well and properly in Latin reached a level equal to the glory of the Greeks. [139] All details came to the mind of Antonius, and all was set in its proper place where it could have the greatest effect and force ... His memory was perfect, there was no suggestion of practising; he always appeared to come forward to speak without preparation, but he was so well prepared that, when he spoke, the jurors sometimes seemed not to have been sufficiently prepared for being on their guard. [140] His actual words had not been chosen with the greatest refinement; so he lacked the reputation for speaking with precision; not however that he spoke with any trace of vulgarity, but he lacked that distinction in the use of words which is proper to the orator. ... [143] Equal in rank with him some placed L. Crassus, while others placed Crassus ahead. On this fact, however, all were of the same opinion that no one who had either of these two as an advocate would need the talent of anyone else. For my part, although I attribute to Antonius all that I have said above, I nevertheless set down my considered opinion that nothing could have been more perfect than Crassus. He possessed a most imposing presence, and combined with this presence the wit and style befitting an orator, not offensive or smart; he spoke Latin accurately, carefully, elegantly without fuss; his exposition and presentation were remarkable; in discussing matters to do with civil law (*ius civile*), with equity, or with right he had a good supply of arguments and analogies. [144] Just as Antony possessed incredible ability in creating probabilities, in allaying or in exciting suspicions, so in interpretation, in definition, in setting out equity no one was more resourceful than Crassus.

Cicero, Brutus 138–144, with omissions

M. Antonius, grandfather of the *triumvir*, was consul in 99 BC, censor in 97 BC and augur from 87 BC, until his death at the hands of the Marians in 82 BC. He is one of the leading participants in Cicero's *On the Good Orator*, where (1.172) it is said of him: 'The power of the natural talent of Antony seems incredible, almost unique and godlike; even if it were to be deprived of its knowledge of the *ius civile*, it would easily be able to protect and defend itself with all the other weapons of its practical wisdom'. L. Crassus was consul in 95 BC, censor in 92 BC, and died in 91 BC. He is another leading speaker in *De oratore* (*On the Ideal Orator*), which is set in 91 BC, only a few days before his death. His speech in support of the *lex Servilia iudiciaria* in 106 BC is said to mark the date when Latin eloquence first reached its maturity (Cicero, *Brutus* 161). – In the portraits of these two extraordinary orators and legal thinkers – the greatest of the generation before his own – Cicero draws attention to their unique blend of natural talent (whether memory, diction, or commanding presence) and outstanding technical expertise.

G37   Publius Sulpicius

[203] For Sulpicius was really the most imposing, and, so to speak, the most tragical orator among those I heard. His voice was powerful, and yet sweet and dazzling; his gestures and the movement of his body were beautiful, but in such a way that one would think that he had been trained for the forum, not for the stage. His language, rapid and voluble, was neither redundant nor superabundant. He wanted to imitate Crassus; Cotta preferred Antonius, but lacked his force, and Sulpicius did not have the wit of Crassus. ... [205] The surviving speeches that bear the name of Sulpicius are viewed as texts written by my contemporary P. Cannutius (a man of non-senatorial rank, in my view most eloquent) after the death of Sulpicius. We do not have a single speech of Sulpicius, and I often heard him say that he neither had the habit of writing speeches nor was he able to write any ...

Cicero, Brutus 203, 205

For Sulpicius, influential tribune in 88 BC, see **A11**. This passage gives a neat summary of the qualities that one could expect to find in an orator, and further confirmation of the political power of the spoken word. It also shows that the history of Roman oratory is not just the history of the speeches that were committed to a written form and eventually published: Sulpicius is a great orator notwithstanding his inability (or unwillingness) to write his speeches down. His reputation as model of powerful public speaker was such that Cannutius allegedly set out to create a compilation of his speeches.

G38 Marcus Licinius Crassus

a) However, I shall first introduce some others, if you don't mind, beginning with M. Crassus, who was the contemporary of Hortensius. Now he had been equipped with moderate training, with even more limited natural ability, but by hard work and application, and because he also used his care and influence to the winning of cases, he was for some years among the leading advocates. In his speeches there was pure Latin diction, no commonplace language, material carefully put together, no ornamentation nor any brilliance, however; much imagination, but little vigour of voice, so that everything would be spoken in the same monotonous strain.

Cicero, *Brutus* 233

b) Concerning culture he gave most attention to public speaking, it being of use for many people; and having become among the best public speakers among the Romans, through care and toil he surpassed those most gifted by nature. They say that there was no case so trifling or despicable to which he came without preparation; but often, when Pompey and Caesar and Cicero were reluctant to get up and speak, he would fulfil all the tasks of an advocate. And for this reason he became more pleasing as being a caring person and one willing to help.

Plutarch, *Life of Crassus* 3.2

c) Giving up any attempt to become equal with Pompey in military matters, he sank himself into politics; by determined efforts, by advocacy, by lending money, by helping in canvassing and by asking questions for those who were seeking some public office, he acquired power and reputation matching that which Pompey had as a result of his many great military campaigns.

Plutarch, *Life of Crassus* 7.2

Crassus was one of the major political figures of his time: his influence is usually attributed to his extraordinary wealth, but there is evidence for his rhetorical ability and his ability to impress and mobilize his audiences (Plutarch, *Life of Crassus* 3.2). Even Cicero, whose assessment of Crassus' oratory is qualified, recognizes the care and expertise that he put into his speeches, and to good effect; Plutarch makes clear that focusing on oratory was a deliberate strategy on Crassus' part, when he realized that it was the most effective way of raising his political profile and widen his connections. Defence speeches played a significant role. Crassus defended Macer in 66 BC (Plutarch, *Life of Cicero* 9.1-2), Murena in 63 BC (Cicero, *Defence of Murena* 10), Sestius in 56 BC (Bobbian Scholiast, p. 125 Stangl), Caelius in 56 BC (Cicero, *Defence of Caelius* 18, 23), and L. Cornelius Balbus in 56 BC (Cicero, *Defence of Balbus* 17, 50).

G39 Hortensius and Cicero

a) [301] Hortensius began to speak in the forum when he was quite young: very soon he began to be employed in more important cases. Although he had started in the period of Cotta and Sulpicius, who were ten years his seniors, when Crassus and Antony were then at their height, then Philippus, afterwards Julius, in renown for public speaking he was compared with these very orators. In the first place, he possessed a memory so retentive as I think I have known in nobody else, so that what he had practised by himself beforehand he could without a script reproduce in the same words with which he had thought it out. This was a great help and he made such use of it that he remembered his own words prepared beforehand and written down, without anyone recalling them, in their entirety, together with all those of his opponents. [302] He was fired with such a zeal that I have seen no one with a more intense eagerness for learning. He allowed no day to pass without speaking in the forum or practising public speaking outside the forum. Very often he would do both on the same day. He brought a genre of speaking to the forum that was far from ordinary, two things in which he had no equal: divisions and recapitulations of the matters about which he was going to speak, a retentive memory of all that had been said against him and what he himself had said. [303] In vividness of language he was fastidious, good in putting words together, resourceful in deploying them. He had achieved this through consummate natural ability and unremitting practice. He would remember a case by heart; he would make sharp divisions and would rarely pass over anything in a case that needed confirmation or refuting. His voice was strong and pleasant, his movement and gesture were more studied than was enough for an orator. Thus when he was at his peak, Crassus had died, Cotta was exiled, and the courts were interrupted by war, I came to the forum.

Cicero, *Brutus* 301–303

This is the lengthiest appraisal of the exceptional talents of Q. Hortensius Hortalus (114-50 BC), who was the greatest orator of the generation that came of age in the nineties (cf. *Orator* 3.228-230), that Cicero provided in his works: the central quality that enables Hortensius to shine is his memory, which enables him to achieve full control over his material, and to present it in the most compelling and accessible fashion, by resorting to careful and effective divisions of his argument. Training and effort, however, also play a very significant role in helping Hortensius to put his personal qualities to the service of his case. – Cicero regards Hortensius as the best orator of his time *before* his arrival on the scene.

b) And Cicero thinks that delivery is the one dominant element in speaking ... but Q. Hortensius was the strongest of all. Evidence for this fact is that his writings are so far below his reputation as the leading orator for a long time, then for some time as the rival of Cicero, and finally, for the remainder of his life, the second. So it appears that something gave pleasure while he was speaking that we do not find when we are reading him.

Quintilian, *The Orator's Education* 11.3.8

An interesting glimpse into the later reception of Hortensius' speeches, which were published during his lifetime and studied for several generations to come: Quintilian comments that those texts do not quite live up to the reputation that Hortensius had among his contemporaries, and makes a plausible suggestion on the quality of his delivery (cf. Gellius, *Attic Nights* 1.5.2, for the view that Hortensius had theatrical ability). – Hortensius undertook a number of important defence cases: C. Verres (70 BC); with Cicero, C. Rabirius (63 BC); Murena (63 BC); Sulla (63 BC); Flaccus (59 BC); Sestius (56 BC) and Scaurus (54 BC). Cicero, *To Atticus* 1.16 (SB 16) is critical of his role in the trial of Clodius resulting from the Bona Dea affair.

G40   Oratory in the late Republic
[10] In oratory, then, if you should care to look into types, you would come across almost as many forms of talent as of physical appearance. But there were some sorts of oratory, which through the circumstances of the times were of rougher manner, but which in other respects already betrayed great force of talent. In this class were men

like Laelius, Africanus, Cato and the Gracchi. ... [11] Let L. Crassus and Q. Hortensius occupy the middle type. Then let a huge growth of orators, of no great difference in age, blossom forth. Here we shall find the force of Caesar, the talent of Caelius, the subtlety of Calidius, the accuracy of Pollio, the dignity of Messala, the probity of Calvus, the gravity of Brutus, the penetration of Sulpicius and the asperity of Cassius.

[12] But we have in M. Tullius not just a Euphranor, outstanding in a large variety of arts, but a man of outstanding eminence in all those things in which anyone is praised. Nonetheless, men of his own times had the audacity to assail him with criticisms: too bombastic, Asianic, exuberant, excessively repetitive, sometimes dull in his jokes, in his composition affected, without restraint and almost, what can hardly be, effete. [13] And after he had been done away with in the triumviral proscriptions, all those who hated him, who envied him, who competed with him, even those who flattered the powers of the time, attacked one who was not going to reply. Yet that man, who is thought by some jejune and arid, could not be maligned by his own personal enemies except for his excessive ornamentation and superabundant talent. Both charges are false: but let the latter opportunity for spreading lies be closer to the truth.

Quintilian, The Orator's Education 12.10.10–13

Quintilian had just (12.10.1-10) provided a quick history of Greek art, including mention of Euphranor (4th century BC) as uniquely talented in painting and sculpture as well as other cultural pursuits. He moves on here to a quick overview of the most authoritative orators of the late Republican period, dividing them into categories that define their rhetorical expertise, but are also suggestive of their character and the approach with which they took part in the political life of their time. Cicero receives especially warm praise, partly in response to the criticism he received from some unnamed contemporaries of his: although he is in many ways a *classic* author in the history of Roman eloquence, his rhetoric did not fail to cause sharp controversy – just like his politics.

G41 Decline of oratory

a) [67] The subject has reminded me that I should at this point also deplore the temporary cessation, not to say, demise of eloquence; and I should not fear to do so, if I did not appear to be making some complaint on my own behalf. Many orators have been done to death; in few do we see any hope; in far fewer any ability; in many just presumptuousness.

Cicero, On Duties 2.67

b) [39] (*Tacitus describes unfavourably procedures and customs of his own day.*) But the orator needs noise and applause, and as it were a theatre; such occurred every day for the orators of old, when people alike in number and distinction packed the forum, when groups of clients and tribes and deputations from the free-towns (*municipia*) and a good part of Italy were present to support those who were in danger, when in very many judicial proceedings the Roman people believed that what was being judged was of importance to them. It is well known that C. Cornelius, M. Scaurus, T. Milo, L. Bestia, and P. Vatinius were accused and defended before a concourse of the whole state so that the very enthusiasm of the partisan people was able to excite and fire even the most frigid orators. And, by Hercules, that is why speeches of this sort are extant so that those who produced them are themselves ranked by no other criteria more than their speeches.

[40] Then too the incessant assemblies (*contiones*), the right granted to harass all the most powerful individuals and the actual glory of personal hostilities, when very large number of able speakers did not keep off Publius Scipio or Lucius Sulla or Pompey, when they used the ears of the people, like stage actors for attacking the leading citizens – as is the nature of malice – what eagerness they applied to the talented, what firebrands for orators!

Tacitus, *Dialogue on Oratory* 39–40

Writing towards the end of the Republican period, Cicero reflects on the decline of eloquence and the general debasement of the wider political conversation: since there are fewer capable orators, the overall quality of the debate suffers as a result. – At the end of the first century AD Tacitus stages a dialogue on the crisis that oratory is going through under a monarchic regime in which debate and controversy are actively curtailed, and rhetorical expertise plays a far less significant role in determining one's career advancement than had been the case in the Republic. A number of major cases that were heard in the last century of the Republic are listed as examples of the interest and controversy that oratory could mobilize: significantly, the involvement of people from the Italian communities is singled out. Popular gatherings, the *contiones*, are singled out as moments in which the powerful can be placed under robust scrutiny, and in which oratory plays a very significant role, on both sides of the argument. In the *Brutus* (46) Cicero had regarded eloquence as a major stabilizing force, 'the ally of tranquillity and as it were an offspring of the well-ordered state': Tacitus gives a much more problematic picture.

LAWCOURTS

G42   Trial of Verres, 70 BC

[35] But as things stand, Hortensius, since you take so much pleasure in the despotic power (*imperium*) you now enjoy over our courts of law, and since there exist men who seem almost deliberately to court the hatred and ill-will of the Roman people, and who feel no shame at their outrageous behaviour and the ill-repute it brings them, but rather wish it to continue, I declare publicly that, though the task I have undertaken may well be difficult and dangerous, I still consider it to be one to which I may properly devote all the resources of my age and energy. [36] The whole senatorial order is suffering from the unprincipled and unscrupulous conduct of a small minority and is crushed by its poor reputation in the law courts. I therefore declare publicly that I shall attack these men; my hostility to them will be bitter, implacable, and unremitting. This is the task which I claim as mine by right, to which I shall devote myself when aedile, – a fitting task, indeed, for the position of trust to which the Roman people has appointed me from 1 January, signifying thereby its wish for me to guide its deliberations about affairs of state and the treatment of wicked and criminal men. This is the spectacle which I promise to the Roman people as the fairest and finest of my aedileship. Here is advance notice of my intention. I advise all those who have made a practice of employing bribery to pervert the course of justice – all who have offered or contributed money, have accepted money, or have acted as agents or go-betweens in any way – to heed it carefully; their backers too, men who have unscrupulously lent their support to this process. I warn these foul criminals not to meddle in this trial, not even to think of doing so. [37] Next year Hortensius will be consul, enjoying supreme command (*imperium*) and power: I shall be aedile, little more than a private citizen. Yet the promise I now make is of such significance and its fulfilment will be

so welcome to the Roman people that the consul himself when matched against me on this issue shall seem to be of less importance – if this is possible – than a private citizen.

I shall bring to your notice, in full and incontrovertible detail, the whole story of the disgraceful crimes committed in the courts during the ten years since control of the juries was transferred to the Senate. [38] I shall inform the Roman people of the fact that for the period of equestrian control of the courts, for an unbroken period of almost fifty years, there was not one case, jurors, not a single case in which the faintest suspicion attached to any member of the equestrian order that his verdict had been influenced by receipt of a bribe; but that, once the Senate recovered control of the courts and the power of the Roman people over individual senators was removed, Quintus Calidius declared when found guilty that a man of praetorian rank could not decently be convicted for less than three million sesterces; that, when Quintus Hortensius was praetor in charge of the extortion court, the damages assessed after the conviction of the senator Publius Septimius included a sum to cover his receipt of bribes when serving as a juror. [39] Nor are these the only cases. It was established beyond any possibility of doubt that Gaius Herennius and Gaius Popilius, two senators convicted of misappropriating public funds, and Marcus Atilius, who was convicted of treason, had all accepted bribes when serving as jurors. Again, when Gaius Verres was urban praetor and was organizing the system by which jurors are allotted to the courts, it came to light that certain senators voted against a defendant whose case they had not heard and thus secured his conviction, and that one particular senator who was serving as a juror accepted money both from the defendant for distribution on his behalf to other jurors, and also, in the very same case, from the prosecutor to vote against the defendant. [40] And what of the notorious case in which the verdicts of the jurors who were under oath were recorded on tablets of different coloured wax? How can I find words to express my horror that this should happen in Rome and with a jury of senators? It is a disgraceful and damaging stain upon the honour of the entire senatorial order. These crime will, I assure you, all receive my most strict and careful attention.

You can imagine then what my attitude will be if I have reason to believe that any such offence has been committed in this case. What make me particularly suspicious – and I can produce many witnesses to the truth of this statement – is something Gaius Verres was frequently heard to say in Sicily in the presence of many people. He used to claim that he would never be convicted of plundering his province as he had a promise of support from a powerful friend; he was not making money just for himself, but had so planned his three years' governorship of Sicily that he would think he was doing very nicely if he could put one year's profit into his pocket, could hand over the second year's to his patrons and the men who were to defend him in the courts, and could keep back the entire profit of his third year, the richest and most lucrative of all, for distribution as bribes to his jurors. [41] This prompts me to repeat a remark which I made recently before Manlius Glabrio while exercising my right to reject jurors and which, I understand, made a great impression on the Roman people. I said that I though a time would come when our foreign subjects would send deputations to Rome to request the repeal of the extortion law and the abolition of the court concerned with this offence. The provincials think, you see, that if the courts were abolished, each governor would extort from them only so much as he considered sufficient for his own use and his children's; whereas now, with the courts in the state they are, each governor takes enough to satisfy himself, his patrons, his advocates, the praetor who presides over his trial, and his jurors – there is no end to it, in fact. They believe they could satisfy the demands of the most rapacious of governors, but that they are totally unable to pay the sum necessary to ensure the acquittal of a man whose guilt is beyond doubt. [42] What a tribute this is to our legal system! What a splendid reputation we senators enjoy! Our allies want to abolish the extortion court, which our ancestors established to protect them! Do you imagine that Verres would ever have felt so confident about the outcome of this trial if he did not share this low opinion of you? You have greater reason to hate him – if this is possible – than the rest of the Roman people, for he clearly considers you as rapacious, as wicked, and as corrupt as himself.

[43] In the name of the gods, jurors, do not neglect this situation. Think how it may develop. I warn you publicly that in my opinion this opportunity to free the whole senatorial order from the unpopularity and disgrace under which it now labours has been given you by the gods. You must not refuse it. Nobody believes any longer in the strict impartiality of our legal system or its freedom from corruption; its very existence has come to seem a farce. And so, we are despised by the Roman people and held in contempt, crushed by the weight of a scandal that has too long continued. [44] This too was the only reason why the Roman people were so keen to see the tribunes enjoy their full powers once more. Yet the restoration of tribunician power was only the ostensible object of its demands: what it really wanted was to recover control of the courts. The wise and distinguished Q. Catulus realized this. When he was asked his opinion in the debate on Pompey's motion that the power of the tribunes should be restored he began by declaring with the full weight of his influence (*auctoritas*) that the senators were exercising their control of the courts in an inefficient and immoral way. He pointed out that if the senators serving the courts had been prepared to meet the expectations of the Roman people, the loss of tribunician power would never have been felt so keenly. [45] Again, when Pompey himself made his first public speech as consul-elect, outside the city, and declared – as was generally expected – that he would restore the power of the tribunes, one could hear an encouraging murmur of approval from the crowd. But when he went on to say in that same speech that the provinces had been ravaged and plundered by their governors, that the courts were an offence against morality and justice alike, and that he intended to deal with the situation – then it was not just a murmur: a full-throated roar showed that this was what the Roman people really wanted. [46] The eyes of the world are now upon you. Each and every one of you is being watched to see how well he keeps his juror's oath and how effectively he protects our laws. Men see that since the tribunician law was passed, one senator has so far been convicted, a man of very modest resources, and though they find nothing to criticize in his conviction, nothing has yet occurred to rouse their great enthusiasm. After all, there is nothing praiseworthy about a spotless conscience when nobody has the means or the inclination to corrupt it. [47] In this trial you will judge the accused; the Roman people will judge you. This is the case, which will decide whether senators will ever convict a wealthy man even when his guilt is clear.

Cicero, *Against Verres* 1.35–47

The case against Verres was politically charged and marked a major moment in the making of Cicero's career: that was clear to many when it was heard, and Cicero did not conceal its far-reaching political implications. In fact, he set out to show that the significance of the case far exceeded his own ambitions and indeed the crimes committed by Verres: it was an opportunity for a jury of senators to show their willingness to convict a member of their order at a time when many were calling for the end of senatorial control over the courts, shortly after the abolition of the Sullan reform of the tribunate, which had been decided a few months earlier, with the support of the consul Pompey and the relative acquiescence of an authoritative senator like Q. Lutatius Catulus (*cos.* 78 BC). Politicizing a legal case was a perfectly acceptable, and indeed helpful, move on Cicero's part. – Public interest and personal advancement seem to serve as mutually reinforcing drivers. The prosecution is also an opportunity for Cicero take on in court Q. Hortensius Hortalus, who is widely regarded as the best orator of his time: he makes pointed reference to Hortensius' prestige and seniority, and to his status as consul designate for the following year. However, Cicero has also been elected to a magistracy, albeit a lesser one, the aedileship, and the mandate he has received from the Roman people serves a further prompt to look after and champion their interests in a corruption case. Vigilant and firm action against dishonest governors and jurors will be a defining feature of his tenure as aedile, and will set higher standards for the senatorial order as whole (so he claims).

G43   Trials of C. Manilius
a) On a charge of extortion (*repetundae*), 66 BC

And after this, when a case was prepared against Manilius by the powerful (Gk: *dunatoi*) and he was eager to gain time for the case, Cicero did everything against him (for he was praetor and had presidency of the court) and with reluctance put him off to the following day, offering as a pretext that the year was coming to its end. [2] And when the crowd was annoyed by this he came into the assembly, having been compelled by the tribunes of the plebs so he alleged; he railed against the Senate and promised to speak on behalf of Manilius. As a result of this he gained a bad reputation generally and was called a traitor. But a tumult followed immediately and prevented the court from being convened.

Cassius Dio, *Roman History* 36.44.1–2

An example of a legal case in which strong political concerns were at stake: according to Dio a faction of the Senate ('the powerful, the rich') was targeting the tribune Manilius, and Cicero briefly connived with them, although his position as presiding praetor was supposed to be impartial; he then changed his attitude towards the defendant when he was put under pressure to do so at a public gathering.

b) On a charge of *maiestas*, 65 BC

For when C. Manilius after the year of his tribunate, which he had conducted in a most turbulent manner, was going to answer an accusation concerning 'diminishing the greatness (*maiestas*) of the Roman people', he arranged through conspiracy with a crowd to blockade the same Minucius, his accuser. When he was blockaded, L. Domitius here brought him help by gathering a large body of good men (*boni*).

Bobbian Scholiast, p.119 Stangl

An example of violence, or at least a very real threat of it, obstructing the course of justice, and preventing a prosecutor from bringing his case against Manilius for abuse of power: the crisis is solved by the intervention of a rival gang, rallied by a faction of the Senate. See also **G44** below.

G44   Trial of Cornelius, 65 BC

Manilius had disrupted his trial by means of gangleaders; then, because both consuls were presiding at his trial in accordance with a decree of the senate (*senatus consultum*), he made no reply and was condemned. Immediately Cominius took heart again … and renewed his prosecution of Cornelius under the law of 'diminishing the greatness (*maiestas*) of the Roman people'. The case was heard with great public interest. Cornelius was terrified by the fate of Manilius and brought few companions into the court so that not even a shout arose from his counsel.

The foremost men in the state, who had the greatest influence in the senate, gave hostile evidence against him: Q. Hortensius, Q. Catulus, Q. Metellus Pius, M. Lucullus and M'. Lepidus. This was their testimony: they had seen Cornelius as tribune reading out aloud a text in front of the *rostra*, something which no one was thought to have done before Cornelius. They wanted it to appear that they judged this matter to be of particular relevance to the charge of diminishing the tribunician greatness (*maiestas*); for if tribunes were permitted to do this, the tribunician veto would be virtually removed. Cicero could not deny that this had happened. He therefore took refuge in this point that he said that because a text had been read by a tribune this did not mean that the power of the tribunes had been diminished thereby. A reading of the speech itself will make clear with what skill and knowledge of oratory – such that he did not offend the dignity (*dignitas*) of the most distinguished citizens against whom he was speaking and yet did not let the accused be injured by their prestigious influence – and with what restraint he handled a case which was so difficult for others. He did have some help, because, as I have said above, Cornelius, apart from an uncompromising opposition to the wishes of the foremost citizens, in the rest of his life had done nothing to incur any great disapproval, and in addition, because Globulus who had used the veto was supporting Cornelius, and – something which I have also said – because Cornelius had been the quaestor of Pompey the Great. This brought benefit among two decuries – that of the Roman *equites* and the tribunes of the treasury (*tribuni aerarii*) and among the majority of the third section too – the senators, with the exception of those who close friends of the foremost in the state. The case was conducted before a large gathering, with great public interest in what the outcome would be … they noticed that evidence was being given by leading persons and that the accused was admitting what they said. The speech of the accuser, Cominius, is extant. It is quite worth having to hand not only because of the speeches of Cicero on behalf of Cornelius, which we possess, but also for its own sake. Cicero, as he himself indicates, spoke for four days in defence of Cornelius; it appears that he brought these proceedings together in two speeches. The praetor, Quintus Gallius, presided in this court.

Asconius, Commentary on Cicero's Defence of Cornelius p. 60C.10–62C.5,
with omissions

This note by Asconius, in his commentary on the (largely lost) speech of Cicero on behalf of Cornelius, who was prosecuted for 'diminishing the greatness (*maiestas*) of the Roman people' in 65 BC, gives a reasonably thorough background of the case and records its outcome and the developments that led to it. It shows how complex and eventful a criminal case could be: the accusation against Cornelius had considerable political implications, because it revolved on the limits to the power of the tribunes; the trial attracted considerable interest; and the considerations that led to the formation of majority in support of Cornelius. The jury consisted of senators, equestrians, and tribunes of the treasury, and it is striking to see that the intervention of a number of distinguished senators was not sufficient to persuade most of the senatorial jurors to lend their support to the prosecution case – the senatorial order is a far less cohesive body than is often claimed. – Cominius, who took up the prosecution against Cornelius, was of municipal origin. On the Cominii, see Cicero, *Defence of Cluentius* 100: 'P. and L. Cominii, Roman *equites*, honourable men and skilled speakers'; Cicero, *Brutus* 271: 'Roman *equites*, my friends, who have recently died, P. Cominius, from Spoletium, who was the accuser when I defended Cornelius. His style of speech was methodical, spirited and fluent.'

G45 Senate and *equites* clash over bribery legislation

We are here involved with a weak *res publica*, wretched and changing. For I believe you have heard that our *equites* have almost separated from the Senate; first of all they were very annoyed that a promulgation had been made in accordance with a senatorial decree that there should be a judicial investigation concerning those who had taken money to give verdicts. By chance I was not present when the decision had been taken on the matter, and I realized that the equestrian order was annoyed, but did not say so openly. I upbraided the Senate, so I thought, with great authority; in a cause that was certainly not respectable I was stern and eloquent.

Rome, 5 December 61 BC.

Cicero, *To Atticus* 1.17.8 (SB 17)

The preoccupation of preserving some political solidarity between the Senate and the equestrian order, which he regarded as the only sources of stability in the *res publica*, is often stated in Cicero's writings. Tensions over the control on the criminal courts were a major focus of controversy, and had been since the age of Gaius Gracchus (see *Against Verres* 1.38): the episode that is discussed in this letter reflects an attempt of the Senate to curb corruption among the jurors. This was regarded by the equestrian order as a hostile initiative: as the letter makes clear, Cicero was uneasy with that approach, but he argued against the initiative of the Senate because he regarded the upkeep of relations between the two orders as a far greater priority. He also wanted to retain political support within the equestrian order and was keen not to alienate its sympathy (cf. *To Atticus* 2.1.8 = SB 21, June 60 BC).

G46 Regulations for the courts, 55 and 52 BC

a) The praetor L. Aurelius Cotta passed a judicial law some years before at the time when Verres was being accused by Cicero [70 BC]. By this law the courts were shared between the Senate, the Roman *equites* and the tribunes of the treasury (*tribuni aerarii*). Then, later, Pompey, in his second consulship [55 BC], when this speech was made, promulgated a law that, contrary to prior practice, jurors chosen from the wealthiest census rating among the centuries, but equally from the same three orders, should decide the case.

Asconius, *Commentary on Cicero's Speech Against Piso*, p. 17C.4–10

b) Then he promulgated two statutes in accordance with a decree of the Senate, one concerning violence (*vis*)... the second concerning electoral malpractice (*ambitus*). The penalty was more severe and the procedure of trials shorter. Each law gave instructions that witnesses be produced first, then on one and the same day closing speeches be given by the plaintiff and the defence in such a way that two hours be given the plaintiff, three to the defence.

Asconius, *Commentary on Cicero's Defence of Milo*, p.36C.6–13, with omission

The running of the law courts remained a major focus of interest in the late Republican period. Asconius provides evidence for two pieces of legislation that were passed in 55 BC: a law restricting access to the juries to the wealthiest members of the three orders that were entitled to membership; and one setting out clear restrictions on the sequence of procedures that had to be followed during a trial, and on the amount of time that plaintiffs and defendants were allowed to use.

G47   The trial of Milo, 52 BC: an alternative account

[*Milo is simultaneously on trial for violence* (vis) *and for electoral malpractice* (ambitus)] [39] Lucius Domitius Ahenobarbus was the president of the court for *vis* and Aulus Manlius Torquatus of the court for electoral malpractice (*ambitus*). Both ordered the accused to appear before their respective court on 4 April…

[40] On the first day C. Causinius Schola was produced as a witness against Milo; he said he had been with Clodius when he had been killed and he exaggerated the enormity of what had been done as much as he could. When M. Marcellus began to question him, he was so terrified by the great rumpus from the mass of Clodian supporters, that fearing extreme violence he was given refuge by Domitius on the tribunal. For this reason Marcellus and Milo himself begged for protection from Domitius. At that time Pompey was sitting near the treasury and had been disturbed by the same shouting; and so he promised Domitius that on the following day he would come down with a guard and so he did. The supporters of Clodius, frightened by this action, allowed the statements of the witnesses to be heard in silence during the two days. M. Cicero and M. Marcellus and Milo himself questioned them. Many of those who lived at Bovillae gave testimony about the events that had taken place there; they said that the innkeeper had been murdered, the inn stormed, the body of Clodius dragged out into the open. Some virgins from Alba too stated that an unknown woman had come to them to pay a vow on the instruction of Milo, because Clodius had been killed. The last to give their testimony were Sempronia, the daughter of Tuditanus and mother-in-law of Clodius, and his wife Fulvia; by their tears they greatly moved those who were present. When the court had been dismissed about the tenth hour, T. Munatius encouraged the people at an assembly (*contio*) to be present in force on the following day and not to allow Milo to slip from their grasp, and to make clear their feelings and their grief to those who were going to cast their voting tablet. On the following day, which was the last of the trial, [41] 8 April, shops had been closed throughout the city; Pompey placed guards strategically in the forum and about all the approaches to the forum. He himself took up position in front of the treasury as on the day before, surrounded by a picked detachment of soldiers. Then the selection by lot of the jurors from the first day was made; afterwards the silence throughout the forum was as complete as could be in any forum. Then within the second hour the prosecutors, the elder Appius and M. Antony and P. Valerius Nepos began to speak. They used their two hours in accordance with the law.

Cicero alone responded to them. Although some people thought that the charge should be rebutted on the grounds that the killing of Clodius had been in the interest of the *res publica* – M. Brutus followed this line in that speech, which he composed on behalf of Milo and published as if he had delivered it – Cicero did not think, in the case of anyone who might be condemned in the public good, that that very same person could be also be killed without trial. And so as the prosecutors had made the basis of their case that Milo had arranged an ambush for Clodius, since this was false – for that altercation had begun by chance – Cicero seized hold of this point and argued on the contrary that Clodius had laid an ambush for Milo, and his whole speech had regard to that issue. But it was well known, just as I have said, that battle had taken place that day not through the deliberate intent of either of them but had in fact happened by chance and from the altercation between slaves had developed in the end to that killing. However, it was well known that each of them had often threatened the other with death, while the larger number of slaves escorting Milo than Clodius made him suspect, but the Clodians had been the more ready and prepared for battle than Milo's slaves. When Cicero began to speak he was greeted with such a noisy reception by the Clodians, who could not hold themselves in check in spite of fear of [42] the soldiers who were standing around. Thus he did not speak as resolutely as he was accustomed to. There survives what was taken down from his speech: he wrote the one that we read with such polish that it can rightly be thought of as his best.

Asconius, *Commentary on Cicero's Defence of Milo* p. 39C.5–42C.2, with omission

Asconius' account gives an extensive overview of the events that unfolded during Milo's trial in April 52: notice the multiple charges which Milo faced. The level of intimidation that the supporters of Clodius imposed on the jury and on the defence advocate was extraordinary, even by the standards of a period in which the threat of political violence was very frequent indeed. The involvement of Pompey, who does not directly take part in the proceedings, but keeps a close watch on what is going on in the forum, is also noteworthy: he supported the prosecution of Milo, in spite of his past differences with Clodius. - Asconius is especially interested in bringing out the difference between the account of the facts of the case produced by Cicero in his speech, the version of the prosecution, and the likely development of the events that took place in Bovillae in January 52. – He also draws attention to the considerable differences between the speech that Cicero delivered on the day and its published version, which is probably one of his finest works. An important political aspect of Cicero's case is worth stressing: he did not argue that Clodius deserved to be killed because of his political positions, but that Milo had acted in self-defence. He therefore steered clear from the argument that had been used in December 63 in support of the execution of the Catilinarian conspirators. – On the crisis of 52 see also Cassius Dio, *Roman History* 40.48.2–49.4. On Cicero's apparent nervousness on this occasion Plutarch, *Life of Cicero* 35.2-4 and Cassius Dio, *Roman History* 40.54.2-3 (see below, **G49**).

G48 Verdicts on Milo

Fifty-one jurors voted: twelve senators condemned him, six acquitted; thirteen *equites* condemned, four acquitted; thirteen tribunes of the treasury (*tribuni aerarii*) condemned, three acquitted. The jurors seemed to have been aware that at the outset Milo had not known that Clodius had been wounded, but they had realized that, after he had been wounded, he had been killed on the order of Milo... [54] It was declared that Milo had been condemned above all through the efforts of Appius Claudius. On the following day Milo was indicted and condemned, in his absence, on a charge of electoral malpractice (*ambitus*) before Manlius Torquatus ... A few days later he was condemned on a charge of violation of the law on associations (*de sodaliciis*) before M. Favonius. Then he was again condemned on a charge of violence (*vis*), in his absence, before L. Fabius. Within a very few days Milo set out for exile in Massilia.

Asconius, *Commentary on Cicero's Defence of Milo* p. 53C.19–54C.20, with omission

The breakdown of the jury votes in favour of Milo's conviction shows that, although the overall tally was the most important result, attention was also paid to how the three components of the jury had voted. Asconius also reports three more convictions that Milo received in the following days: the charge *de sodaliciis* ('on the associations') related to the formation of an organized group of supporters, no doubt for the purposes of political violence.

G49   Milo's reaction

[3] When Milo read the speech sent to him by Cicero, during his banishment, he wrote back that it was fortunate for him that those words had not been pronounced in court; for he would not be eating such fine red mullets in Massilia, where he was living in his exile, if a defence of that kind had been put forward. [4] This he wrote, not because he was pleased with his condition – indeed, he made many efforts to secure his return – but as a joke on Cicero, because the orator, after saying nothing useful at the time of the defence, had composed and sent to him fruitless words, as if they could then be of any use to him.

Cassius Dio, *Roman History* 40.45.3–4

Milo left Rome before the end of his trial, and spent several years in Massilia (modern Marseilles), a Greek city in Southern Gaul: the anecdote related by Cassius Dio is clearly hostile to Cicero, as other aspects of Dio's narrative, and also draws attention to the comfortable, and indeed privileged life that Milo could lead even after his conviction and hurried departure from Rome.

H. INTELLECTUAL LIFE

Law is a major aspect of Roman intellectual life, and its development in the first century BC is part of a wider process, through which the cultural debate and production in Rome became increasingly more diverse and complex. The encounter with Greek culture is central to it: this was especially apparent in the development in the domains of rhetoric and philosophy, and was crucially enabled by the presence of Greek teachers in Rome and the mobility of Roman students to the Greek East. It was therefore, in a way, a product of the empire. Greek influences, however, are not the only factor worthy of attention. On the contrary, the most ambitious minds of the late Republican period set out to devise Roman approaches to the various forms of intellectual discourse: this is apparent from Cicero's philosophical and rhetorical works, from Lucretius' Epicurean poem, and even from the vast, mostly lost body of work produced by Varro on an extraordinarily wide range of problems.

EDUCATION AND RHETORIC

H1   The death of Hortensius, 50 BC

[1] When on leaving Cilicia I had come to Rhodes and word was brought to me of the death of Q. Hortensius, I was more deeply affected by it than anyone suspected. For I saw myself deprived of a friend who was bound to me by ties of pleasant companionship and by the exchange of the many good offices of a friend, and I grieved that in the death of so distinguished an augur the dignity of our college had suffered loss. Thinking of this I recalled that I had been elected to that body on his nomination and his sworn statement of my worth; and that I had been inducted into its ranks by him, so that, in accordance with augural tradition, it was my duty to regard him as a father. [2] It distressed me too, that in the great absence of wise and patriotic citizens there had gone from us a great man, in fullest sympathy with me on all questions of public policy, at a time most inopportune for the interests of the state, leaving us to lament the loss of his authority and wise experience. I grieved moreover to have lost in him, not, as some may have thought, a rival jealous of my forensic reputation, but rather a comrade and fellow-worker in the same field of glorious endeavour. [3] If in arts of lesser moment history records that famous poets have manifested grief for the death of fellow poets, how much more must I have felt the death of one with whom rivalry was more glorious than to have been quite without a rival? – The more so since his official career was never challenged nor crossed by me, nor mine by him. Quite the contrary: each of us was helped by the other with the exchange of suggestion, advice, and the offices of a friend.

[4] His life was one of uninterrupted felicity, and he departed it the more opportunely for himself than for his fellow countrymen. He fell at a time when, had he lived, he would have found himself able only to mourn for the *res publica*, not to help it. He lived as long as it was possible for a good citizen to live an honourable and happy life. To our own misfortune and loss, then, let us confine our grief, if grieve we must; but as for him, let us not think of his death with pity, but rather with gratitude for its timeliness; and as often as we recall this illustrious and truly happy man, let our thoughts be fixed with affection upon him and not with self-love upon ourselves. [5] For if this be our grief, that we can no longer enjoy his presence, it is a sorrow which it behoves us to bear with reason, and to beware lest we entertain it, not out of love for

him, but from loss of some advantage to ourselves. If on the other hand our hearts are troubled as though he had suffered some calamity we fail to recognize with adequate gratitude the supreme felicity of his life and death. [6] For were Hortensius alive today he would doubtless have occasion, along with other good and loyal men, to mourn the loss of many things; but one pang he would feel beyond the rest, or with few to share it: the spectacle of the Roman forum, the scene and stage of his talents, robbed and deprived of that polished eloquence worthy of the ears of Romans or even of Greeks.

Cicero, *Brutus* 1–6

The opening section of the *Brutus*, a rhetorical work of Cicero in which much attention is devoted to the history of Roman oratory, discusses the recent death of Q. Hortensius Hortalus, a major political figure of his own time, and one of the greatest public speakers of his generation (see **G39**). Cicero discusses at great length the extent of his intellectual debt to Hortensius, and stresses the many mutual ties they had, notably their membership of the augural college (one of the main public priesthoods in Rome) and their shared pursuit of eloquence, which led them both to seek not just excellence in Rome, but a standard that was comparable to that of Greek rhetoric. – Both Hortensius and Cicero were very heavily involved with the politics of their time, and Cicero takes the chance to reflect on the state of the *res publica* at the time of Hortensius' death, suggesting that the passing of a man like Hortensius coincides with a moment of deep, and fundamentally unwelcome, transformation in the history of Rome.

H2   Importance of appealing to the public in oratory

[183] Here Atticus interrupted: 'Now for what reason do you say 'in your own judgement and in that of the general public'? In approving or disapproving of an orator is the judgement of the common people always in agreement with that of those qualified to judge? Or is it not rather that some are approved by the crowd while others are approved by those who are qualified to judge?' 'You ask a pertinent question, Atticus,' I said, 'but you will hear from me an answer that not all the general public may perhaps approve of.' [184] 'Would you be concerned at that, provided you are to gain the approval of Brutus alone?' he asked. 'Very true,' I said, 'for I would prefer that this discussion about approving or disapproving an orator please you and Brutus, while I should want my eloquence to be approved by the people. For the orator who speaks in such a way that he is approved by the crowd is inevitably approved by the learned. Now I shall judge what is right and wrong in speaking, provided that I am one with the ability and knowledge to judge. What sort of orator a man is can simply be judged from what he achieves by speaking. [185] For there are three things, in my opinion at least, which are to be achieved by speaking: that the hearer should be informed, that he should be pleased, and that he should be emotionally moved. By what qualities in an orator each of these is achieved or through what failings an orator either does not attain them or amid them even slips up and falls, some expert practitioner will judge. Now whether or not an orator succeeds in so affecting his audience in the way that he wishes is normally judged by the assent of the crowd and public approval. That is why there has never been disagreement between the experts and the general public about the good or the bad orator.'

Cicero, *Brutus* 183–185

Cicero devoted a considerable part of his work to the discussion of rhetorical theory, and notably of what makes one a good orator: in this passage he explores, through the framework of a fictional dialogue with his friend Atticus, the tension between the attributes of an effective orator who meets the approval of the people and those of an orator who commands the respect of the educated. His contention is that both audiences can be persuaded and impressed at the same time, and that an orator who managed to achieve an effective combination of persuasiveness and ability to move and entertain is likely to impress the widest section of his audience, regardless of their background. One can therefore be an effective political operator without forsaking moral standards and literary ambition.

H3 Writing of speeches

Some orators merely out of inertia have left nothing written, not being inclined to add a task at home to their exertions in the forum – for of course most orations are written after, and not for, delivery.

Cicero, *Brutus* 91

We know that a large body of written speeches circulated in Republican Rome; what survives of Cicero's production is merely a portion of the large set of material that was available at the time. This brief passage has a twofold importance: it shows that many published speeches did not necessarily reflect closely the version that had been delivered orally (see **G47** end), and it points out that many public speeches were never published in written form, and never became part of the historical tradition on the time in which they were delivered.- Even those who set out to write the history of the late Republican period at that very time had to deal with the limitations of their evidence.

H4 Oratory in Italy

Among the allies and Latins there were some who were also esteemed orators, such as Q. Vettius Vettianus, of the Marsi, whom I knew personally, a man of wisdom and experience, and brief of speech; Q. and D. Valerius of Sora, neighbours and friends of mine, not so much admired for their eloquence as for their acquaintance with Greek and Latin letters; C. Rusticelius of Bononia, a trained and practised speaker, with a natural gift of ready speech. But the most eloquent of all outside the city was T. Betutius Barrus of Asculum, some of whose orations delivered there are extant. Very well known too is his speech delivered at Rome against Caepio, to which reply was made through the mouth of Caepio by Aelius, a writer of speeches for many, though no orator himself.

Cicero, *Brutus* 169

The aftermath of the Social War witnessed the gradual rise to prominence of a number of individuals of municipal origin, many of whom were active in the courts in Rome, and in some cases reached senatorial status. Some of them attained some distinction as orators, and are duly recorded by Cicero, who is elsewhere rather scathing about the rhetorical ability of some municipal men (e.g. *Brutus* 242). At least one of the men mentioned here, Betutius Barrus, also published a collection of speeches.

H5 Expulsion of Latin rhetoricians from Rome, 92 BC

Then some years after that decree of the senate, Gnaeus Domitius Ahenobarbus and Lucius Licinius Crassus the censors issued the following edict for restraining the Latin rhetoricians: 'It has been reported to us that there be men who have introduced a new kind of training, and that our young men frequent their schools; that these men have assumed the title of Latin rhetoricians, and that young men spend whole days with them in idleness. Our forefathers determined what they wished their children to learn and what schools they desired them to attend. These innovations in the customs and principles of our forefathers neither please us nor seem proper. Therefore it seems necessary to make our opinion known, both to those who have such schools and to those who are in the habit of attending them, that they are displeasing to us.'

Aulus Gellius, *Attic Nights* 15.11.2

The close interrelation between oratory and politics in the Roman world means that the teaching of rhetoric is not a neutral practice, but one that may at times become the focus of attention on the part of those in power. In 92 BC, a few months before the outbreak of the Social War, the expulsion of a group of rhetoricians from the city of Rome is attested: the contents and methods of their teaching are not specified in the surviving evidence, but it is abundantly clear that there were concerns within the senatorial order that prompted a repressive initiative. – Much debate has revolved around the adjective 'Latin', and the role that the activity of such a group of rhetoricians could play in a context where tensions on the status of the Italian Allies were rife.

GREEK INTELLECTUALS IN ROME

H6   Philo of Larissa, Academic philosopher, 159/8–84/3 BC
a) In the consulship of Sulla and Pompeius [Rufus: 88 BC] … Philo, the head of the Academy, along with a group of loyal Athenians, had fled from Athens because of the Mithridatic war and had come to Rome. Filled with enthusiasm for the study of philosophy I gave myself up wholly to his instruction.

Cicero, Brutus 306

b) [3.1] When his schooldays were over he attended the lectures of Philo of the Academy who, of all the pupils of Clitomachus, was the most admired by the Romans for his eloquence and most loved for his character ... [3.3] He retired into the life of a scholar and philosopher, going on with his studies and associating with Greek scholars until the time came when Sulla seized power and it looked as though the political situation had become rather more settled.

Plutarch, Life of Cicero 3.1–3, with omission

Many young members of the Roman political and social élite sought high-level rhetorical and philosophical instruction in the Greek East, and would spend extended periods at the school of an established teacher, whether in Athens or elsewhere. The First Mithridatic War, however, led to the forced displacement of some notable exponents of the Greek intellectual élite: in 88 BC Philo, the great master of the Academy, left Athens, which had fallen under the control of the anti-Roman forces, and taught in Rome, where he made a lasting impression on Cicero, who was by then in his late teens.

H7   Antiochus of Ascalon, Academic philosopher, *c.*130–*c.*69/68 BC
When I was proquaestor at Alexandria, Antiochus was in my company, and Antiochus' friend, Heraclitus of Tyre, was at Alexandria already; for he had been for many years a pupil both of Clitomachus and Philo, and was undoubtedly a person of some standing and distinction in the school of philosophy in question, which after having been abandoned is now being revived; I often used to hear Antiochus arguing with Heraclitus, both however in a gentle manner.

Cicero, Academica 2.11

Service in the provinces could also be an opportunity to gain exposure to ongoing trends in Greek culture: in this passage of a philosophical dialogue by Cicero, Lucullus recalls his time in Alexandria during the Mithridatic War (87/86), when he was sent to Egypt to raise a fleet: on that occasion he met the renowned philosopher Heraclitus of Tyre, who engaged in earnest discussion with Antiochus of Ascalon (125-68 BC), by then already a friend of the Roman magistrate – it is unclear in what circumstances they had met.

H8 Posidonius of Apamea, polymath, *c.*135–*c.* 51 BC

a) In Rhodes he studied oratory with Apollonius, the son of Molon, and philosophy with Posidonius.

Plutarch, *Life of Cicero* 4.5

b) As a matter of fact, however, I am no new convert to the study of philosophy. From my earliest youth I have devoted no small amount of time and energy to it, and I pursued it most keenly at the very periods when I least appeared to be doing so, witness the philosophical maxims of which my speeches are full, and my intimacy with the learned men who have always graced my household, as well as those eminent men (*principes*), Diodotus, Philo, Antiochus, and Posidonius.

Cicero, *On the Nature of the Gods* 1.6

c) At any rate, it is said that Pompey, upon arriving at Rhodes on his expedition against the pirates (immediately afterwards he set out against Mithridates and the tribes that extended as far as the Caspian sea), happened to attend one of the lectures of Posidonius, and that when he went out he asked Posidonius whether he had any orders to give; that Posidonius replied: 'ever be most brave, and pre-eminent over others.' Add to this that among other works he also wrote the history of Pompey.

Strabo, *Geography* 11.1.6

Posidonius was a tremendously prolific and versatile intellectual, whose importance in the philosophical and political debate of his own time is hard to overestimate: his writings covered a broad range of themes and literary genres, his philosophical work was widely admired and studied, not just by those who shared his Stoic convictions, and his historical work, which survives to us only in fragments, played a major role in shaping the tradition on the last century of the Republic. He was originally from Apamea, in Syria, but spent most of his life in Rhodes, where he became a citizen of considerable standing and influence. – His influence was considerable also in some quarters of the Roman political élite. Cicero attended his lectures and spoke of him with great admiration; Pompey made sure to meet him and seek his advice during his visit to Rhodes. Posidonius duly recognized his high political standing, and is said to have devoted an historical work to his achievements.

H9 Apollonius Molon, rhetor, early first century BC

[312] At this time [81 BC] I devoted myself to study with Molon; for he happened to come to Rome during the dictatorship of Sulla as the member of a diplomatic mission to the Senate on the reimbursement of Rhodes… [326] However, not content with them [*i.e. the teachers Cicero had met in Athens*], I went to Rhodes and attached myself to Molon, whom I had already heard at Rome: he was eminent, not merely as an advocate in actual cases and a writer of speeches for others, but he was especially able in criticizing and amending flaws, and wise in his whole system of teaching. He set out to repress, if possible, the redundance and excess of my style, which had a youthful impetuousness and lack of restraint, and to restrain it, so to speak, from overflowing its banks. Thus I returned, after an absence of two years, not only better trained, but almost transformed. My voice was no longer overstrained, my language had cooled off, my lungs had got stronger, and my body had gained weight.

Cicero, *Brutus* 312, 326

Both Posidonius and Apollonius Molon lived and worked in Rhodes, and Strabo singles them out in his overview of the notable citizens of Rhodes (14.2.13). Like Posidonius, Molon was not a native of the island, as he came from Alabanda, in Asia Minor. His influence in his adoptive city is shown by his participation in the embassy that visited Rome in 81 BC, with a view to seeking some concessions in the aftermath of the Mithridatic War. That was the first occasion in which the Senate allowed a foreign ambassador to speak in Greek, without the help of an interpreter (Valerius Maximus, *Memorable Deeds and Sayings* 2.2.3; Plutarch, *Cicero* 4): a sign of his personal prestige, as well as perhaps of a gradual change of attitude towards the Greek-speaking subjects of the Empire and the status of the Greek language in a political setting. – Cicero's comments on the rewards of the instruction he received from Apollonius offer a valuable overview of the qualities that a young orator is expected to master as he is about to embark on the profession.

H10   Xenocles of Adramyttium, rhetorician, second-first centuries BC

Another inhabitant of Adramyttium was the famous orator Xenocles, who belonged to the Asiatic school and was as able a debater as ever lived, having even made a speech on behalf of Asia before the Senate, at the time when it was accused of Mithridatism.

Strabo, *Geography* 13.1.66

The aftermath of the Mithridatic War presented the élites of the province of Asia with the formidable challenge of regaining some degree of favour with Rome, and allaying the impact of the punitive fine decreed by Sulla. Resuming a viable interaction with the Roman government, notably with the Senate, was a task that required the intervention of the best political minds and the most skilful speakers of that generation: Strabo here records a speech that the orator Xenocles (on whom see also Cicero, *Brutus* 316) gave to the Senate on behalf of the whole province, attempting to justify its conduct after Mithridates' invasion: it is unclear what effect, if any, his intervention had, but it is nonetheless remarkable that the audience in the Senate took place at all, shortly after the end of the war.

H11   Tyrannio of Amisus, grammarian and scholar, early first century BC

Rome also contributed much to this [*errors in the texts of Aristotle*]; for immediately after the death of Apellicon, Sulla, who had captured Athens, carried off Apellicon's library to Rome, where Tyrannio the grammarian, who was fond of Aristotle, got it into his hands by paying court to the librarian, as did also certain booksellers who used bad copyists and would not collate the texts – a thing that also takes place in the case of other books that are copied for selling, both here and at Alexandria.

Strabo, *Geography* 13.1.54

The story of the encounter between Roman and Greek culture is not just one of mobility of intellectuals: it is also, perhaps even predominantly, about the mobility of texts, the circulation of Greek literature in Rome and Italy, and its lively and complex reception. The episode recalled by Strabo in this brief passage is a moment of great significance in the intellectual history of the West: the arrival at Rome of the library of the Athenian philosopher Apellicon, which included a large selection of works of Aristotle that had not circulated in Rome until then, and which did not fail to make an impression in the educated quarters. The production of new copies of Aristotle's work was intended to satisfy such appetite for knowledge, but led to a gradual debasement of the quality of the texts of Aristotle at the hands of careless copyists.

ROMAN STUDENTS OF GREEK PHILOSOPHY

H12   T. Pomponius Atticus
[4] When Sulla came to Athens, on his way back from Asia, he kept Pomponius by his side as long as he was there, captured by the young man's civility and learning. He spoke Greek so well that he seemed a native Athenian; his Latin was so agreeable that its grace seemed, so to speak, innate, not acquired. He also recited poetry, both in Greek and in Latin, so well that nothing further could possibly be added... [3] He stayed at Athens for quite a number of years: he devoted as much effort to his family fortune as the conscientious head of a household (*paterfamilias*) should, and devoted all the rest of his time either to literature or to the commonwealth of the Athenians; nonetheless, he fulfilled his duties towards his friends in Rome, for he regularly attended their elections. ... [5] When affairs at Rome reverted to calm, he returned, I think, when L. Cotta and L. Torquatus were consuls [65 BC].

Nepos, *Life of Atticus* 2.2–4.5, with omissions

Atticus' decision to move to Greece (see **B7**) was driven by the traumatic political developments of the early eighties, and was quickly followed by the relocation of most of his economic and financial interests away from Italy. – His biographer Nepos expands at some length on the level of cultural and linguistic assimilation that he reached a mere few years after his move to Athens. His bilingualism also has political implications: he was as keenly interested in Roman politics as he was involved with the affairs of Athens. – Atticus returned to Italy only in 65 BC, in a phase of relative tranquility in Rome, but he retained close ties with Greece for the rest of his life.

H13   M. Tullius Cicero
Arriving at Athens I spent six months with Antiochus, the wise and famous philosopher of the Old Academy, and with him as my guide and teacher I took up again the study of philosophy, which from my early youth I had pursued, had made some progress in, and had never wholly let drop. But at the same time at Athens I continued zealously with rhetorical exercises under the direction of Demetrius the Syrian, an experienced teacher of eloquence not without some reputation.

Cicero, *Brutus* 315

Shortly after his defence of Roscius of Ameria, Cicero decided to leave Rome and spend a period of study in Greece: the political situation in Italy had probably become potentially insidious for him. In Athens he pursued both philosophical and rhetorical studies, under the direction of two of the most established teachers of the time; from another recollection of that happy stay (*On Ends – De finibus*, 5.1) we gather that other young Romans, including Atticus, as well as Cicero's brother and cousin, were studying at Athens in that period.

H14   L. Licinius Lucullus
[4] However, the things in Lucullus' career that deserved the honour of a national celebration have fairly well won their tribute of fame in both Greek and Latin records. But my knowledge of these facts about his public life I share with many persons; the following more private details I have often learnt from him in company with few others – for Lucullus was more ardently devoted both to letters of all sorts and to philosophy than persons who did not know him supposed, and indeed not only at an early age but also for some years during his proquaestorship, and even on military service, when military duties are usually so engrossing as to leave a commander not

much leisure when actually under canvas. But as Philo's pupil Antiochus was deemed the chief among philosophers for intellect and learning, he kept him in his company both when quaestor and when a few years later he became *imperator*, and having the powerful memory I have spoken of already he easily learnt from frequent repetition doctrines he would have been quite capable of learning from a single hearing. Moreover, he took a marvellous delight in reading the books about which Antiochus used to discourse to him.

Cicero, *Academica* 2.4

In this passage Cicero speaks in approving terms of Lucullus' keen interest in Greek culture and stresses the importance of his long-standing connection with Antiochus of Ascalon: Lucullus comes across as a serious and effective student, who had a deep appreciation of the potential and significance of Greek philosophy.

H15   M. Junius Brutus
From there Brutus put to sea and sailed to Athens. Here the people welcomed him eagerly and extolled him in public decrees. He dwelt with a certain guest-friend (Gk: *xenos*), attended the lectures of Theomnestus the Academic and Cratippus the Peripatetic, discussed philosophy with them, and was thought to be wholly given up to literary pursuits.

Plutarch, *Life of Brutus* 24.1

The pursuit of intellectual interests during a stay at Athens was not just the prerogative of young members of the political élite: in the aftermath of the Ides of March, M. Junius Brutus left Italy and went to the Greek East in the hope of rallying forces and launching a counteroffensive against the Caesarians. During his stay at Athens he took the chance to attend lectures on philosophical topics; he conducted himself as a committed lover of things Greek, and the people of Athens were ready to assert their connection with him and exploit the potential political implications of his philhellenism.

H16   Quintus Cicero and the Greeks of Asia
a) [6] Your province consists of a native population that is the most highly civilized in the world and of Romans who are either tax-collectors (*publicani*) ... or wealthy businessmen who think they owe the safety of their money to my consulship ... [7] As for the Greeks, when they look at you leading the life you do, they will think you are a character from history or a divine being come down from heaven into the province. Rome, end 60 or beginning 59 BC.

Cicero, *To Quintus* 1.1.6–7 (SB 12), with omissions

In his long set of recommendations to his brother ahead of his governorship in Asia, Cicero gives a broad brush assessment of the attitude of the population of the province: the Greeks will admire the frugality and decency of Quintus, as they are so accustomed to greedy and unrestrained Roman magistrates, while the *publicani* based in the province will accord Quintus the same gratitude and appreciation that Cicero claims to have earned in Rome, especially during his consulship. There is a strong, and perhaps surprising, degree of correlation between political developments in Rome and the climate that one may expect to encounter in the provinces.

b) Furthermore, much caution is called for with respect to friendships, which may arise with certain among the Greeks themselves, apart from the very few who may be worthy of the Greeks of old. Nowadays a great many of these people are false, unreliable, and schooled in over-complaisance through long servitude. My advice is to admit them freely to your company in general and to form ties of hospitality

and friendship with the most distinguished; but too close intimacies with them are neither respectable nor trustworthy. They do not dare to oppose our wishes and they are jealous not only of the Romans, but also of their fellow countrymen.
Rome, end 60 or beginning 59 BC.

Cicero, *To Quintus* 1.1.16 (SB 1)

A scathing comment on the character and attitude of the Greek residents of the province: Cicero warns against the effects that close dealings with the subjects can have to the reputation and effectiveness of a governor. It is conceivable that the legacy of hostility and mistrust left by the Mithridatic War is still playing a part in shaping this prejudice.

H17 Attractions of Epicurus

[68] Someone will no doubt ask, 'How do you come to know all this?' Well, I do not propose to describe any individual in such a manner as to insult him, especially if he be a man of parts and learning, a class with which I could not be angry, even if I wished. There is a certain Greek who lives with him, a man whom, to tell the truth, I have found to be a very gentlemanly fellow, at any rate as long as he is in company other than Piso's, or is by himself. This man met our young friend Piso, who even then wore a scowl as if he resented the existence of the gods, and was not averse to his friendship, especially as the other eagerly sought him; he so far gave himself up to his company that he absolutely lived with him and scarcely ever left his side. I am speaking not to an ignorant audience, but, as I think, in an assembly of learned and accomplished gentlemen. You have of course heard it said that Epicurean philosophers assess the desirability of anything by its capacity to give pleasure – whether rightly or wrongly is no concern of ours, or at any rate not relevant to the present issue – it is, however, a dangerous argument to put before a young man of only moderate intelligence, and one that often leads to disaster. [69] Accordingly, as soon as the lewd Piso heard pleasure praised so highly by so great a philosopher, he did not pick and choose; he so stimulated all his pleasurable sensations, and raised such a whinnying to welcome his friend's arguments, that he plainly thought he had found in the Greek not a professor of ethics but a master of the art of lust. The Greek at first drew distinctions as to the meaning of the precepts; but, as the proverb says, 'a cripple had got the ball'; he insisted on what he had received, he stuck to the letter of his lesson, and would have it that Epicurus was an eloquent fellow; and indeed he does, I believe, assert that he cannot conceive any good apart from bodily pleasure. [70] To make a long story short, the Greek was far too charming and complaisant to have any notion of standing up to an *imperator* of the Roman people.

Now the Greek of whom I am speaking had at his finger-tips not only philosophy but other accomplishments too, which Epicureans are said commonly to neglect; he proceeded to compose a poem, so witty, neat, and elegant that nothing could be cleverer. Anyone who wishes is free to find fault with him for this poem; but let him do so gently, not as with a low and bare-faced rogue, but as with a poor little Greek, a parasite, a poet. When he came upon Piso, or rather fell in with him, he was just beguiled, a Greek in a strange land as he was, by the same savage scowl as has beguiled so many sages and so great a society as our own. Once in the toils of friendship, there was no drawing back for him, and, what was more, he wished to avoid the reproach of fickleness. In response to request, invitation, pressure, he wrote reams of verse to Piso and about Piso, giving expression in lines of perfect finish to all his lust and immoralities, all his varied dinners and banquets, all his adulteries; [71] and in these poems anyone who wishes can see the fellow's life reflected as in a mirror.

Cicero, *Against Piso* 68–71

Cicero was an outspoken critic of the Epicurean philosophy, its theological vision, and the message of disengagement from politics that it advocated. In this speech, delivered against L. Calpurnius Piso in 55 BC, he focuses at some length on the Greek poet and philosopher who lived as a guest in Piso's house: even Cicero concedes that the literary and intellectual qualities of this man are outstanding, and his portrait is not altogether unsympathetic, although the audience is left in no doubt on the sycophantic nature of the relationship with his patron. – Piso's guest may be identified as Philodemus of Gadara, who came to Rome around 75 BC and died between 40/35 BC, probably at Herculaneum. A considerable amount of his writings has been found as charred papyri in a villa in Herculaneum that may have belonged to Piso, his friend and patron.

H18   The spread of Epicureanism in Italy

The study of wisdom is certainly long-standing among us; however, I do not find the name of any philosopher before the time of Laelius and Scipio that I could single out individually: in the younger days of those men we find that Diogenes the Stoic, and Carneades the Academic, were sent as ambassadors by the Athenians to the Senate. ... [6] So that of that true and elegant philosophy which is upheld to this day among the Peripatetics, having been derived from Socrates, and by the Stoics, although they express themselves differently in their disputes with the Academics, there are virtually no Latin records, or very few of those – whether this is because of the magnitude of the task itself, or because people were otherwise occupied, or because they concluded that these studies could not be entrusted to the ignorant. When everyone else was being silent, C. Amafinius arose and spoke. When his books were published, the crowd (*multitudo*) was moved, and turned towards this doctrine, either because it was very easy to understand, or because they were enticed by the seductive thought of pleasure, or because they got hold of what was offered them, since there was nothing better. [7] After Amafinius, as many people who held the same views wrote a great deal, they also occupied the whole of Italy: that these arguments should be so easily learned and approved of by the uneducated, is the greatest proof that they were not written with a great deal of subtlety; they think that this is the prop of their doctrine.

Cicero, *Tusculan Disputations* 4.5–7, with omissions

In this passage, written in 45 BC, Cicero reflects on the impact of Greek thought in Rome: while conceding that Rome has not produced original thinkers, he stresses that philosophical studies have been practised since the mid-second century BC; he regards the visit (on official business) of two distinguished Athenian masters in 155 BC as a defining moment. Yet, few have set out to write about philosophical matters in Latin: a notable exception is the work of Gaius Amafinius, a follower of Epicurus, who probably lived at least a generation before Cicero, and whose Latin works made a considerable impact not just in Rome, but across Italy. Cicero, who is no admirer of the Epicurean doctrines, regards Amafinius' success as indirect evidence that his thought is not especially sophisticated. Cicero's choice of words is striking: he speaks of a 'crowd' of people, many of whom are said to have very little education, taking an interest in philosophy.

H19   Lucretius expounds Epicurean philosophy

a) Mother of the sons of Aeneas, delight of men and gods,
Life-giving Venus, you who, beneath the gliding constellations of the sky,
Make teem with life the ship-bearing sea and the fruit-bearing land,
Since it is through you each species of living creature
Is conceived and having come forth looks upon the light of the sun;   5
You, O goddess, it is you the winds flee, you and your arrival
The clouds of heaven flee; for you the skilful earth sends up
Sweet flowers; for you level waters of the ocean smile,
And the sky, now grown calm, shines with beams of light.
For as soon as the sight of spring day has been revealed   10
And the breeze of life-giving Zephyr is unloosed and grows strong,
First of all birds of the sky mark you, goddess and your
Entry, struck in their hearts by your power.
Then the herds of cattle gambol wildly in the rich pastures
And swim across swift streams; each thus captured by your charm   15
Follows you eagerly wherever you proceed to lead it.
Then over seas and mountains and gushing rivers,
And the leafy dwellings of birds, and the verdant meadows,
Striking into the hearts of them all an alluring love
You make them eager to reproduce their breed according to their species.   20
Since it is you alone, O goddess, who govern the birth of things,
And since without you nothing comes forth to the radiant shores of light,
And nothing happy, nothing lovable is created,
I am keen that you be a partner in writing these verses,
Which I am trying to compose on the nature of things   25
For our son of Memmius whom you, goddess, at all time
Have wished to excel, endowed with all things.
Wherefore, goddess, bestow an everlasting charm upon these words.
Meanwhile make the savage deeds of warfare
Over all seas and lands fall asleep and be still.   30
For you alone are able to help mortals with tranquil peace,
Since Mars mighty in arms rules the savage deeds
Of war; and he often lets his body sink into your lap,
Conquered entirely by the eternal wound of love,
And thus looking up at you with his shapely neck leaning back,   35
Gasping at you, goddess, he feeds his greedy gaze with love
And upon your lips his breath is hanging as he reclines.
And you, O goddess, embracing him as he lies there
Upon your holy body, pour sweets words from your lips,
Seeking for the Romans, famed one, calm peace.   40
For I cannot do work at this unfavourable time for our country
With mind at ease, nor can the famed son of Memmius
In such circumstances be wanting to the common safety.   43

Lucretius, *On the Nature of Things* 1.1–43

b) For I am going to treat of the whole law of heaven,
And of the gods for you and I shall reveal the origins of things,   55
Whence nature creates all things, increases and nurtures them
And whither the same nature destroys and breaks them up again;
And in rendering this account, it will be my custom to call them
Matter and procreative bodies for things, and to name them the
Seeds of things and regularly to use the name first bodies for   60
These same things, because from those first things are all derived.
When the life of men lay for all to see, foully grovelling
Upon the ground, crushed beneath the weight of religion,
Which displayed her head from the regions of the sky,
Hovering over the mortals with horrible appearance,   65
A Greek man was the first that dared
To raise mortal eyes against it, and the first to oppose it;
Neither the reputation of the gods nor thunderbolts
Could quell him, not the sky with menacing murmur,
But all the more they goaded the eager courage of his mind,   70
So that he should desire to be the first to shatter the tight bars of nature's gates.
Therefore, the lively power of his mind prevailed,
And he proceeded far beyond the flaming walls of the world,
And he went through the immeasurable space
With his mind and his spirit; whence he returns victorious, bearing his prize,   75
The knowledge of what can come into being,
Of what cannot, how each thing has limited power, a measure, a deep-set boundary.
Therefore religion is now in her turn subjugated and trampled over,
Victory lifts us high up to heaven.

Lucretius, On the Nature of Things 1.54–79

c) Wherefore of the things above I must give   127
A proper account, by what principle the movements
Of the sun and moon occur, and by what force the things
That happen on earth; then, no less important, with fine reason   130
We must see of what the soul and the nature of the mind is made up;
And what is the thing which, while we are awake, blocks our minds
And makes us fear when affected by illness or buried in sleep
So that we seem to perceive and to hear before our very eyes those
Whose bones the earth embraces, after they have met death.   135
Nor do I fail to understand that my task is difficult,
To make clear the obscure discoveries of the Greeks in Latin verse,
Especially since we often have to deal with new words
Because of the poverty of the language and the novelty of the subject matter;
But still your valour, and the expected pleasure   140
Of your agreeable friendship persuades me to take this task up,
And leads me to spend the tranquil nights in wakefulness,
Seeking by what words and what kind of poetry
I may at last be able to display clear lights before your mind,
Whereby you may see into the depth of hidden things.   145

Lucretius, *On the Nature of Things* 1.127–145

In the mid-first century BC a poet called T. Lucretius Carus wrote a poem in which he set outs the principles of Epicureanism: its contents were drawn from the writing of Epicurus himself, but were presented in highly innovative and creative terms. Six books of this work, whose title was *De rerum natura* ('On the nature of things'), survive. Hardly anything is known about Lucretius' biography and background; the poem is addressed to a young prominent member of the Roman nobility, C. Memmius, who held the praetorship in 58 BC: a further indication that Epicurean philosophy was also of interest to individuals who were actively involved in politics. The three programmatic passages from Book 1 that are quoted here give a sense of the ambition of the poem, which was intended as a strong, all-encompassing account of the functioning of the universe. The liberating power of philosophical knowledge is asserted in the strongest terms, and is set up against the oppressing influence of religion (*religio*), notably the traditional worship of the gods: Epicurus is cast as the first man who had the courage to aspire to a superior degree of knowledge. Although Epicureanism advocates the withdrawal from active political engagement, its overall vision has far-reaching political implications, especially because of its critique of traditional religion. Criticizing *religio*, however, does not amount to embracing atheism: the poem is opened by an invocation to Venus, the goddess of Love and, more broadly, of peaceful and fruitful coexistence. – Lucretius approaches his brief as an example of serious philosophical writing, which is set out in verse form, as is often the case in the Greek tradition, rather than in prose. His comment on the limitations of the Latin language, which has not yet developed a full philosophical vocabulary, is especially poignant, and draws attention to a wider literary and cultural problem that is also acknowledged and discussed in some of Cicero's philosophical writings (see below, **H23**).

H20 Lucretius according to Cicero

[3] Lucretius' poems are just as you write, with many flashes of intelligence, but much artistry too – but [we shall talk of that] when you come.
February 54 BC.

Cicero, *To Quintus* 2.9.3 (SB 14)

This is the earliest contemporary reference to Lucretius and his work: Cicero had no sympathy for Epicureanism, but his admiration for the great Epicurean poem (or indeed 'poems', *poemata*, as he refers to it) is expressed in unequivocal terms. There has been much speculation and debate on the nature of their relationship and on the role that Cicero may have played in supporting the edition and publication of the *De rerum natura*. At any rate, the work had a profound influence on the following generations of poets: Virgil, Horace, and Ovid all show a deep and detailed knowledge of Lucretius'.

H21 Philosophy gone rogue: Cicero attacks Vatinius, 56 BC

You have the habit of calling yourself a Pythagorean, and of concealing your savage and barbarous ways behind the name of a most learned man. Tell me: even though you were engaged in unknown and illicit rituals, you used to evoke spirits from the underworld, and you appeased the *Manes* (Spirits of the Dead) with the entrails of young boys, what perversity of the mind, what madness has led you to show contempt for the auspices through which this city was founded, and by which the whole *res publica* and the empire are ruled, and to declare to the Senate, at the beginning of your tribunate, that the responses of the augurs and the haughtiness of their college would not be an obstacle to your actions?

Cicero, *Against Vatinius* 14

The former tribune P. Vatinius gave evidence against P. Sestius, a tribune of 57 who had been one of the most vocal and effective advocates of Cicero's return from exile, and was prosecuted in the following year (see above **B104**). The speech with which Cicero attacked Vatinius survives: one of the arguments that the orator deploys against him is his allegiance to the philosophical doctrines of Pythagoras of Samos (*c.*

570 - *c.* 495 BC). The Pythagoreans believed in the immortality of the soul and in reincarnation after death: Cicero alleges (it is unclear on what grounds) that Vatinius sought to recall the souls of the dead from the underworld, and even engaged in human sacrifices. Vatinius' allegiance to a foreign philosophical doctrine is here exploited as the pretext to cast him as someone who is plotting for the demise of traditional religion, and therefore of the political community itself. At the same time, Cicero stresses that what Vatinius allegedly did is not consistent with the Pythagorean doctrine: his stated philosophical allegiance is no more than a smokescreen. – A couple of years after launching this vicious attack, Cicero agreed to defend Vatinius from criminal charges of electoral malpractice: as he makes clear in a letter to P. Cornelius Lentulus Spinther (*To his Friends* 1.19.19 = SB 20, December 54), Pompey had orchestrated their reconciliation, and Caesar had subsequently insisted that he take up Vatinius' case. As ever, Cicero's work as an advocate is firmly embedded in the political context of the time.

H22   Nigidius Figulus

The age of Marcus Cicero and Gaius Caesar had few men of outstanding eloquence, but had two towering figures in wide-ranging learning and in the broad set of arts by which humanity is instructed: Marcus Varro and Publius Nigidius. The records of knowledge and learning left in his writings by Varro are widely known and are in general use. The discussions of Nigidius, however, are not so popularly known, but their obscurity and subtlety have caused them to be neglected, as if they were of little use. A case in point is what we read a short while ago in his work entitled *Grammatical Notes*, from which I drew a few extracts to show an example of the nature of his writings. In discussing the nature and the order of the letters, which grammarians call vocals [dipthongs], he wrote the following words, which I leave unexplained, in order to exert my readers' concentration: 'a and o', he says, 'are always first, i and u are always second, e both follows and precedes: it precedes in *Euripus*, it follows in *Aemilius*'.

Aulus Gellius, *Attic Nights* 19.14.1–5

Gellius emphatically pays tribute to the importance of the intellectual work of P. Nigidius Figulus, whom he places on a par with Varro: like Varro, he was both a tremendously productive scholar and a figure of some political distinction, who reached the praetorship in 58 BC. The range of his production may be gleaned from the titles of dozens of lost works, which shows a keen interest in philosophy, mathematics, science, and music: separate disciplines, of course, but intellectual pursuits that were much more closely and more obviously related to each other in antiquity than is the case in modern times. He was a committed proponent of the doctrines of Pythagoras, and the expertise in cosmological matters that was apparent in many of his writings was informed by his philosophical interests. Even Gellius, who strongly admires his work, concedes that it could make difficult reading. The text that is summarized and partly quoted in this passage reflects an interest in the balance between the parts and the whole that is in keeping with his philosophical allegiance, and from which wider philosophical principles are then drawn: in this specific case, a general rule on the position of vowels within dipthongs.

H23   Acculturation and translation

[4] A more difficult task therefore is to deal with the objection of those who profess a contempt for Latin writings as such. What astonishes me first of all about them is this, – why should they dislike their native language for serious and important subjects, when they are quite willing to read Latin plays translated word for word from the Greek? Who has such a hatred, one might almost say for the very name of Roman, as to despise and reject the *Medea* of Ennius or the *Antiope* of Pacuvius, and give as his reason that though he enjoys the corresponding plays of Euripides he cannot endure books written in Latin? What, he cries, am I to read *The Young Comrades* of Caecilius, or Terence's *Maid of Andros*, when I might be reading the same two comedies of Menander? [5] With this sort of person I disagree so strongly, that, admitting the

Electra of Sophocles to be a masterpiece, I yet think Atilius' poor translation of it worth my while to read. 'An iron writer' Licinius called him; still, in my opinion, a writer all the same, and therefore deserving to be read. For to be entirely unversed in our own poets argues either the extreme of mental inactivity or else a refinement of taste carried to the point of caprice. ... But given a noble theme, and a refined, dignified and graceful style, who would not read a Latin book? Unless it be someone ambitious to be styled a Greek out-and-out, as Albucius was greeted by Scaevola when the latter was praetor in Athens... [10] Mucius' sarcasm was however deserved. But for my part I can never cease wondering what can be the origin of the exaggerated contempt for home products that is now fashionable. It would of course be out of place here to attempt to prove it, but in my opinion, the Latin language, so far from having a poor vocabulary, as is commonly supposed, is actually richer than Greek. When have we, that is to say, when have our competent orators or poets, at all events since they have had models to copy, ever lacked any of the resources of the florid or the chaste style?

In my own case, just as I trust I have done my duty at the post to which the Roman people appointed me, by my political activities and by the toils and dangers I have undergone, so it is assuredly incumbent upon me also to use my best endeavours, with such zeal, enthusiasm and energy as I possess, to promote the advancement of learning among my fellow-countrymen. Nor need I be greatly concerned to join issue with any who prefer to read Greek, provided that they do actually read it and do not merely pretend to do so. It is my business to serve those who desire to enjoy literature in both languages, or who, if books in their own are available, do not feel any great need of Greek ones.

Cicero, On Ends (De finibus) 1.4–5, 9–12, with omissions

The greatest contribution that Cicero made to the culture of his time was his endeavour to write about philosophical topics in Latin: philosophy had a long and distinguished tradition in Greek, but the operation of discussing it in a different language was as innovative as it was bold. It was also an operation with strong political connotations, which implied a positive assessment of the place of Rome in the wider imperial context. In this passage Cicero makes two important points: it is reasonable for a Latin-speaking audience to expect to find discussions of important topics in Latin; and, in spite of what Lucretius claimed, the Latin language is not intrinsically less equipped than Greek to provide a discussion of complex matters. The intellectual context in which Cicero puts forward his effort to write about philosophy in Latin is a comfortably bilingual one, in which both idioms have their rightful place, and readers are equally interested and well-versed in both languages, and open to the value of the literary production in both.

H24   Composing *On the* Res publica [*De re publica*]

As for your question what I have done about those books that I had begun to write when I was on my estate at Cumae, I have not been idle nor am I but I have already made frequent changes to the whole plan and outline of the writing. For two books were already completed, in which during the nine-day festival which occurred in the consulship of Tuditanus and Aquillius [129 BC], the discussion was constructed by me with Africanus, shortly before his death, and Laelius, Philus, Manilius, <P. Rutilius>, Q. Tubero and the sons-in-law of Laelius, Fannius and Scaevola; the conversation was divided over nine days and into nine books about the best form of the state and the best citizen. The work was being put together quite splendidly and the high status (*dignitas*) of the men was bringing considerable weight to the dialogue. When these books were read to me on my property at Tusculum, with Sallustius listening, I was advised by the latter that discussion about these matters could be much more authoritative if I myself spoke about the *res publica*, especially since I was not a Heraclides of Pontus, but a consular and one who had been involved in the greatest affairs in the *res publica*; what I was ascribing to men so ancient would seem to be made up; in those books of mine which were about the theory of public speaking I had tactfully removed the orators' discussion away from myself, but had nonetheless assigned it to those I had seen; finally Aristotle speaks himself what he writes about the state and the outstanding person.

[2] He quite impressed me, and all the more because I was not able to touch upon the momentous disorders in our state, because they were later in time than the age of those who were the speakers. At that time I was following this precise course so that I did not give offence to anyone by entering upon our times. But now I shall both avoid that danger and also speak myself with you; however, I shall also send to you, if I come to Rome, what I had begun. For I think you will realize that those books have been abandoned by me not without a good deal of heartburn.

Tusculum, end October/beginning November 54 BC.

Cicero, To Quintus 3.5.1–2 (SB 25)

This letter to Quintus records a stage in the composition of the philosophical dialogue on the ideal state, in which Cicero contemplated casting himself as a character: he was urged to do so by his friend Sallustius (not to be confused with C. Sallustius Crispus, the historian), who reminded him that he was a former consul, not merely a writer and thinker (Heraclides of Pontus, *c.* 388-*c.* 310 BC, was one of the foremost Greek intellectuals in the fourth century BC). Cicero, however, stuck with the strategy he had chosen, setting the dialogue in 129 BC: precisely because it dealt with significant and contentious political issues, it was desirable to distance it from the political reality of the day, and place it in a relatively distant, albeit still quite relevant, past. – Cicero resumed the writing of the dialogue, and took nearly three years to complete it – an unusually long time by his standards. A letter from his friend Caelius of June 51 BC (*To his Friends*, 8.1.4 (SB 77)) suggests that the work met with a warm initial reception in learned circles.

VARRO'S PLACE IN ROMAN CULTURE

H25   The works of Varro

a) [9] 'What you say, Varro, is true,' I rejoined, 'for we are wandering and straying about like visitors in our own city, and your books led us, so to speak, right home, and enabled us at last to realize who and where we were. You have revealed the age of our native city, the chronology of its history, the law of its religion and its priesthood, its civil and its military institutions, the topography of its districts and sites, the terminology, classification and moral and rational basis of all our religious and secular institutions, and you have likewise shed a flood of light upon our poets and generally on Latin literature and the Latin language, and you have yourself composed graceful poetry of various styles in almost every metre, and have sketched an outline of philosophy in many departments that is enough to stimulate the student though not enough to complete his instruction.'

Cicero, Academica 1.9

b) An incomplete list of Varro's works
So Varro wrote: 45 books of *Antiquities*, 4 *On the Life of the Roman People*, *Imagines* (pen portraits of famous people) 15, *Logistorici* (enquiries into words) 76, *On the Latin Language* 25, *Academic Disciplines* 9, *On Latin Speech* 5, *Problems in Plautus* 5, *Annals* 3, *On the Origin of the Latin Language* 3, *On Poetry* 3, *On the Origins of Drama* 3, *On Theatrical Performances* 3, *On Theatrical Records* 3, *On Descriptions* 3, *On Different Styles of Writers* 3, *On Libraries* 3, *On Readings* 3, *On Similar Words* 3, *Embassies* 3, *Persuasive Speeches* 3, *On Pompey* 3, *Monographs* 10, *On Characters in Plays* 3, *On Civil Law* 15, *Summary of 42 books of Antiquities, in* 9 books, *Summary of 15 books of Imagines* in 4 books, *Summary of 15 books on the Latin Language* in 9 books, *On Elements of Numbers* 4 books, *On Farming* 3 books, *On Looking after one's Health* 1 book, *Autobiography* 3 books, *Types of Philosophy* 3 books, *City Matters* 3 books, *Menippean Satires* 150 books, *Poetry* 10 books, *Speeches* 22 books, Tragicomedies 6 books, *Satires* 4 books; and very many others, a list too long to count. I have copied out barely half the list and that is too boring for my readers.

Jerome, *Epistles* 33.1–2 (Varro, *Fragments of the Roman Historians* 52 T1).

Cicero's exploration of new domains of knowledge was by no means isolated: the late Republic is an age of lively intellectual developments as much as it is one of deep political disruption. M. Terentius Varro was the author of an unrivalled cluster of antiquarian work, most of which is lost to us: the fragments that do survive convey a clear sense of its richness and diversity. His treatments of *Roman Antiquities* and *Divine Antiquities* receive special praise from Cicero in the opening section of the *Academica*, a philosophical work in which Varro is one of the characters who take part in the dialogue: the metaphor with which Varro is thanked for his ability to help his readers find their whereabouts enables us to catch a glimpse of the range of problems that he covered, spanning from the foundation of the city to its topography, which was in turn inextricably linked with the religious landscape and the relationship between the city and its gods. The boundaries of what Roman culture was, or had the potential to become, were tested and redefined by Varro's work. Varro was not just the most learned man of his time: he was also a writer of great technical expertise, who was at home in several literary genres, whether in prose or verse. His formidable output did not fail to impress readers in antiquity, including early Christian thinkers and scholars like Augustine and Jerome; the latter's amazement at the range of his work seems mixed with a degree of irritation. Much of Varro's work must have still been accessible in full in Late Antiquity, although it seems unlikely that Jerome had access to all the titles he lists in this passage.

H26   Varro's intellectual and military distinction
The only statue of a living person to be placed in the library founded in Rome by Asinius Pollio, the earliest one in the world established from war spoils, was that of Marcus Varro. A leading orator and citizen gave that crowning distinction to one individual, chosen from the multitude of great minds that were at work at the time. It was no less a tribute, in my view, than when Pompey the Great awarded to the same man a naval crown for his deeds in the war with the pirates.

Pliny the Elder, *Natural History* 7.115

Varro was both an intellectual of extraordinary range and ability and a member of the senatorial nobility, who achieved senior public offices and some military distinction: Pliny the Elder, who pursued a similar, if less impressive career in the mid-first century AD, reflects on his achievements in both areas. The choice to put up a statue in his honour in the first public library in Rome seems an apt tribute to Varro's major contribution to making Roman culture both more systematic and more diverse. The library was inaugurated by C. Asinius Pollio, who was apparently following up plans devised a few years earlier by Julius Caesar, and funded it from the spoils of his campaign that he had carried out against the Illyrians in 39 BC. Caesar's original project entailed Varro's direct involvement: he was to be entrusted with the task of ordering an unparalleled collection of Greek and Latin texts (Suetonius, *Divus Julius* 44.2).

H27   Cicero and Varro: literary and social conventions

I have followed your prompt and finished some pretty clever books addressed to Varro – but I am waiting for your answer to my questions: first, how you knew that he coveted a dedication from me, when, in spite of being an extremely prolific writer, he has never taken the initiative; and next, whom he was jealous of. If he is not jealous of Brutus, he certainly cannot envy Hortensius or those who speak in *On the State*. Please make that clear to me, especially whether you still hold the view that I should send him what I have written, or whether you think it is not necessary. But let us talk about this in person.
Arpinum, 28 June 45 BC.

                                                                    Cicero, *To Atticus* 13.18.2 (SB 325)

Cicero and Varro are without a doubt among the most original intellectuals of their generation: they were on very good personal terms, although never close; they both chose Pompey's side in the Civil War, were pardoned by Caesar, and were both included on the proscription list of the triumvirs, although Varro, unlike Cicero, managed to survive the manhunt. In 45 BC Cicero dedicated his philosophical treatise *Academica Posteriora* to Varro: a sign of great respect, which Cicero felt Varro would have warmly welcomed. From this letter, in fact, we gain the impression that Varro might have been slightly offended by Cicero's failure to dedicate him one of his previous works. Even a seemingly innocuous and uncontroversial choice like the dedication of a philosophical work could have social, and broadly speaking political, implications that would normally be lost to us, if we did not have access to Cicero's correspondence.

H28   Varro and the number seven

[13] Varro says that the physicians who use music as a remedy state that the veins of men, or indeed their arteries, are set in motion according to the number seven, and that this treatment they call 'harmony through four' because it results from the harmony of four tones. [14] He also thinks that the phases of danger in diseases are more violent on the days which are made up of the number seven, and that those days seem to be, as the physicians call them, 'critical'; namely, the first, second, and third week. [15] And Varro does not fail to mention a fact that adds to the power and influence of the number seven: that those who decide to die of starvation do not meet their death until the seventh day. [16] Varro wrote such things about the number seven as a result of painstaking investigation. But he has also brought together in the same place others that are rather trifling: for example, that there are seven wonderful works in the world, that the old sages were seven, that the traditionally prescribed number of rounds in the races in the circus is seven, and that seven commanders were chosen to attack Thebes. [17] Then he adds in that book the further point that he had entered upon the twelfth heptad of his age, and that until that day he had completed seventy heptads of books, of which a great number were destroyed when his library was ravaged, at the time of his proscription.

                                                                    Aulus Gellius, *Attic Nights* 3.10.13–17

This passage offers an example of how Varro's work is known to us: mostly through quotations or summaries in later work, usually from the imperial period, such as Aulus Gellius' diverse compilation known as *Attic Nights*. Gellius is here interested in the role that the number seven plays in Varro's thought: the collection of examples, many of which are drawn through empirical observation, reflects an attempt to create a systematic body of knowledge encompassing a wide range of domains, from medicine to music, from art to philosophy and literature, and showing a degree of intellectual ambition that is not previously attested in Roman culture, and is not merely driven by the ambition to match or replicate the great achievements that Greek culture could lay claims to.

H29 Varro and the Latin language
[109] I had arranged six books on the ways in which Latin names were assigned to things for our own use; I dedicated three of these to Publius Septumius, who was my quaestor, and three to you, of which this is the third – the first three are on the doctrine of the origin of words, the second three on the origins of words. Of those which precede, the first roll contains the arguments, which may be offered as to why etymology is neither a branch of learning nor a useful pursuit; the second contains the arguments why it is a branch of learning and is useful; the third states what the nature of etymology is. [110] In the second three books, which I sent to you, the subjects are likewise divided up as follows: first, that in which the origins of words for places are set forth, and for those things that are usually located in specific places; second, with what words times are designated and those things that are done in times; third, the present book, in which words are draws from the poets in the same way as those that I have mentioned in the other two books were drawn from prose writings.

Varro, *On the Latin Language* 7.109–110

Varro's best-attested work is a treatise on the Latin language. Of 25 books, books 5 and 6 survive, books 7-10 are partly extant, the rest lost. The dedicatee of this section of the work (books 5-10) was Cicero. This extract conveys a sense of how systematically arranged it was, and what a prominent role etymology played in his discussion: the underlying principle is that, if one succeeds in grasping the origins of a language, one can expect to achieve a deeper understanding of its fundamental principles and its inner workings.

H30 Varro on theology
Next, what is the meaning of his statement that there are three kinds of theology, that is, of the account that is given about the gods? And that of these one is called mythical, another physical, and the third, civil? If Latin usage allowed, we should call the first kind that he envisages 'fabular'. But let us call it 'fabulous', for the term 'mythical' is derived from 'fables', since in Greek a fable is called *mythos*. The second kind may be called 'natural', as is already accepted in common usage. Varro himself gives a Latin name to the third kind, that of 'civil'. Then he says: 'They call 'mythical' the theology that is used chiefly by poets, that used by philosophers 'physical,' and that used by political communities 'civil'.

Augustine, *City of God* 6.5.1

Varro's great treatise on *Divine Antiquities* survives in a heavily fragmentary state, and much of what we know about its coverage and argument derives from Christian sources, which have an explicitly hostile agenda towards the pagan religious view that underpins Varro's discussion. Augustine has a polemical discussion of the notion discussed by Varro of three kinds of theology, which serve different purposes: one for the political domain, one suited for philosophical discussion and reflection, and one that serves the needs of poetry and literature. Arguing that there are three different ways of talking about the gods does not mean that they are not taken seriously, and that they are an empty figment of human imagination or a tool of political domination: on the contrary, Varro argued that religion is a complex domain, and that a range of different approaches to the divine is needed if its complexity and importance is to be appreciated to the full. – On this problem, which predates Varro and has a rich history in Hellenistic philosophy, see also *City of God* 4.27.

K. WIVES AND DAUGHTERS IN LATE REPUBLICAN SOCIETY AND POLITICS

This section does not set out to offer a comprehensive overview of the evidence for the social position of women in late Republican Rome: the task would require robust engagement with archaeological and iconographical evidence that would not fall within the remit of this sourcebook. Moreover, the epigraphical evidence for the Republican period is far less abundant than is the case for the Principate, and that limits our appreciation of major aspects of the social history of the period, including the role of women in public and private contexts. – What follows provides an overview of the evidence for some remarkable women that hailed from families belonging to the Roman political élite: they appear, first and foremost, as wives, daughters, or sisters, but they also come across, in a number of cases, as weighty political players in their own right. Most of what we hear about them reflects a male viewpoint – the preconceptions and agendas of the men that produced the texts in which these women are mentioned. However, their voices are not altogether lost, and their very presence in sources that are so heavily shaped by the preoccupations of men strongly shows that the presence of women in society cannot simply be explained away as an irrelevance, but is a force that must be reckoned with.

K1 Women and political participation

What does a woman have to do with a public meeting (*contio*)? If ancestral custom is to be observed, nothing. But when domestic quiet is stirred by the waves of sedition, the authority of ancient practice is subverted, and the compulsion of violence has greater force than persuasion and the precept of restraint.

Valerius Maximus, *Memorable Deeds and Sayings* 3.8.6

This brief comment by Valerius Maximus, the author of a compilation of morally improving stories who lived under the emperor Tiberius, draws attention to an interesting tension: on the one hand, there was a deep-seated tradition that regarded any form of political involvement of women with suspicion; on the other, women could and did participate in political developments, especially at times of crisis. On this assessment, the last century of the Republic is a moment that has unique potential for the political participation of women: indeed, as the following pages will show, there are a number of significant examples.

K2 The wives of Pompey the Great

a) [1] Admiring Pompey because of his virtue [Gk: *aretê*] and considering him a great asset for his own affairs, he [Sulla] became eager to attach Pompey to himself through marriage by some means or other. [2] With Metella, his wife, being in agreement, they persuaded Pompey, having got rid of Antistia, to take as his wife Aemilia, the step-daughter of Sulla, the daughter of Metella and Scaurus, who was already living with a husband and at that time with child. Thus the circumstances of the marriage were typical of a tyranny and suited the times of Sulla rather than the character of Pompey, in that Aemilia was being given in marriage to him when she was with child by another man, [3] while Antistia was being driven out in dishonour. Her case was tragic, because she had recently lost her father because of her husband; for Antistius had been murdered in the senate-house, for Pompey's benefit, because Antistius was thought to be a partisan of Sulla. Her mother, looking upon the events, had committed suicide so that this misfortune was added to the tragedy concerning this marriage and, by Zeus, Aemilia had no sooner become part of Pompey's house than she died in childbirth.

Plutarch, *Life of Pompey* 9.1–3

Marriages had long been valuable opportunities to establish or strengthen political connections within the Roman nobility – although it was misguided to view them merely as such. – Sulla is here said to have masterminded the marriage between Pompey and his step-daughter, as a way of consolidating his ties with a young man who had played an important role in determining his success during the Civil War: his decision has a monarchic (or, as Plutarch puts it, tyrannical) flavour, as it seems to prefigure the inclusion of Pompey in a dynasty. – The marriage, however, was tragically cut short by Aemilia's death in childbirth, which Plutarch places within a broader pattern of loss that also affects Antistia.

b) For Mucia, his wife, had been unfaithful during his absence abroad. While Pompey was far away, he paid no attention to the report. But when he was near Italy and, so it seems, considering the charge at his leisure with rather more careful thought, he sent her notice of divorce, neither at that time having written nor later explaining the reasons for which he divorced her. But the reason has been written in the letters of Cicero.

Plutarch, Life of Pompey 42.7

In fact, apart from a passing reference in *To Atticus* 1.12.3, there is no other reference to the matter in Cicero's letters. Pompey's third marriage, to Mucia, was not a happy one: it is notable that Pompey starts taking an interest in her infidelity only when he is about to return to Italy, and (one can reasonably assume) Mucia's behaviour could be positively damaging to his reputation.

c) [3] Cato had two nieces of marriageable age and Pompey proceeded to ask for the elder one as a wife for himself and the younger one for his son. Some say that it was not for Cato's nieces, but for his daughters that the marriage proposal was made. [4] When Munatius told Cato and his wife and sisters about this, the women were overjoyed by the proposed relationship in view of the greatness and reputation of Pompey. But Cato, stung by the proposal, without hesitation or deliberation, said straight out, [5] 'Go, Munatius, go and tell Pompey that Cato is not to be captured with ease through the women's apartments.' ... [6] At these words the women were angry, while Cato's friends found fault with his answer as ill-mannered and arrogant. ... [9] If we are to judge by what happened it seems that Cato was wholly wrong in not accepting the marriage alliance, but in letting Pompey turn to Caesar and contract a marriage which, by combining the power of Pompey and Caesar, all but overturned the Roman state and destroyed the constitution.

Plutarch, Life of Cato the Younger 30.3–9, with omissions

Cato's indignant refusal to enter a marriage alliance with Pompey is not just portrayed as an example of his ability to put principle before political expediency; it is also a reaction that sets him apart from the majority of his contemporaries. Plutarch shows characteristic interest in a biographical incident that reveals a core aspect of Cato's character, while also having major political implications.

d) Julia, the daughter of Caesar, had been promised to Caepio and was about to marry him in a few days. Totally unexpectedly, Pompey married her; he promised his own daughter to Caepio to appease his wrath, though she had been previously betrothed to Faustus, the son of Sulla. Caesar himself married Calpurnia, the daughter of Piso.

Plutarch, Life of Pompey 47.6

The political alliance struck between Caesar and Pompey in 60 BC was quickly followed by the marriage between Pompey and Julia, which, in spite of its obvious political background, was a happy union, cut short by Julia's death in childbirth in 54 BC.

K3 Terentia, the wife of Marcus Cicero

a) The rest of the women were terrified at this [portent of an altar fire relighting], but the Vestal Virgins ordered Terentia, the wife of Cicero, to go as quickly as possible to her husband and order him to carry out his decisions on behalf of the country, on the grounds that the goddess was giving him a great light for safety and for renown. [3] Terentia, who was not otherwise one of mild spirit or lacking in courage but an ambitious woman, as Cicero himself says, a person more to share in political business with himself than to share domestic concerns with him, told him this and urged him on against the conspirators.

Plutarch, *Life of Cicero* 20.2–3

Plutarch reports a tradition that credits Cicero's wife, Terentia, with a leading role in the repression of Catiline's conspiracy: she conveys to her husband the interpretation that the Vestals gave of a prodigy that had taken place as they were performing a sacrifice. On that occasion Terentia follows the instructions that she had received from the priestesses, but Plutarch uses the anecdote as an example of her ability and ambition to influence the political choices of her husband. This portrait of Terentia can of course be constructed as a damning evidence of Cicero's character and leadership.

b) [2] Now certainly Cicero did not appear to be giving evidence for the sake of the truth, but to be speaking in defence of his own wife, Terentia. [3] For she had a hatred of Clodius because of his sister, Clodia, on the grounds that she wished to marry Cicero and was attempting this through a certain Tullus, who was a companion and close friend of Cicero; his frequent visits to Clodia and his close attendance upon her since she lived nearby caused Terentia to be suspicious. [4] Being of a difficult nature and ruling Cicero, she urged him to attack Clodius and give evidence against him.

Plutarch, *Life of Cicero* 29.2–4

Cicero's decision to give evidence against Clodius in the *Bona Dea* trial of 62 BC was a turning point in his political career, as it marked the beginning of the enmity between the two men. Plutarch relates a tradition in which Terentia's jealousy and personal resentment towards Clodius and his sister Clodia was the factor that led Cicero to make a choice that was to prove very damaging.

c) From Tullius to his dear Terentia and Tullia and Marcus greetings.
[1] I send you letters less often than I can, because, while every moment is wretched for me, when I write to you at home or read your letters I am so overcome with tears that I cannot bear it. ... But if the present evils are fixed, then I certainly want to see you, my life, as soon as I can, and die in your embrace, since neither the gods whom you have worshipped so piously nor the men to whom I have devoted myself have returned us thanks. ... [3] Am I to ask you to come – a sick woman, physically and spiritually exhausted? Am I *not* to ask then? Am I to be without you? I think I should put it like this: if there is any hope of my return, you must build it up, and help the cause. But if, as I fear, it is all over, then see that you come to me any way you can. Be sure of one thing: if I am with you, I shall not seem to have been completely destroyed. ... [6] For the rest, dearest Terentia, bear up with all the dignity you can muster.
Brundisium, 29 April 58 BC.

Cicero, *To his Friends* 14.4.1–6 (SB 6), with omissions

d) All the annoyances and anxieties with which I kept you in the most miserable state, something that is most annoying to me, and my little Tullia, who is sweeter to me than my life, I have set aside and discarded. I realized what their cause was the day after I left you. I threw up pure bile during the night. I was at once so relieved that some god seemed to have produced the cure. To that god you will certainly make satisfaction piously and purely as is your custom.

Cicero, To his Friends 14.7.1 (SB 155)

During his exile (58-57 BC) Cicero wrote a remarkable series of letters to Terentia, from which two examples are quoted here: they do not just show a striking willingness of Cicero to project an emotional persona, and a great deal of personal affection towards Terentia and the rest of the family, who was suffering a moment of great difficulty. They also show the deep confidence that Cicero expresses towards the ability of his wife to run the household in his absence, and indeed to help the cause of his return to Italy.

e) [1] But he was prevented by many public and private affairs, which he did not wish for, and by misfortunes, the majority of which seem to have been of his own doing. [2] For, first of all, he divorced Terentia having been neglected by her during the war, so that he was sent out lacking the necessary victuals and not even when he returned to Italy did he find her considerate. [3] For she did not come to him, while he spent a long time in Brundisium; and when his daughter, who was just a young girl, came the long journey, she did not provide her with a fitting escort, nor means for the journey, but in addition stripped and emptied Cicero's house of everything by her many massive debts. Now these are the most plausible pretexts given for the divorce. [4] Terentia denied these pretexts and Cicero himself provided her with a clear defence by not long afterwards marrying a young girl through love of her youth: so Terentia spread it abroad, while Tiro, Cicero's freedman, has written, it was for the sake of the means to pay off the debts. [5] For the girl was very rich and Cicero, having been left her legal guardian, had charge of her property. Owing many tens of thousands he was persuaded by his friends and relatives to marry the girl, in spite of his age, and to be rid of his creditors by using her resources. [6] But Antonius, recalling the marriage in his replies to the *Philippics*, says that he threw out the wife with whom he had grown old, and at the same time wittily joking about Cicero's domestic life as unbusinesslike and unmilitary.

Plutarch, Life of Cicero 41.1–6

The marriage of Cicero and Terentia did not survive the difficult phase of the Civil War of 49-47 BC; the increasing distance between them is also apparent in some of the letters that Cicero sent his wife at the time. The divorce was bitter, and different explanations were given for the end of a marriage that had been very happy: the circumstances that led to the split and Cicero's decision to remarry shortly after the divorce were exploited against him by his enemies, chiefly by Mark Antony.

K4   Praecia, mistress of Publius Cethegus

There was a certain woman then in Rome, Praecia by name, whose reputation for beauty and wit filled the city. In other respects she was in no way better than a common whore, but, as a result of using her associates and companions for the political ambitions of her friends, she added to her other charms the reputation of being a true friend and a person who got things done. She thus acquired very great influence. [3] When Cethegus, who was then also at the height of his fame and controlling the city, was drawn into her company and became her lover, power in the city came entirely into her hands. No public business was carried out unless Cethegus was in favour; Cethegus did nothing unless Praecia ordered it. This woman, therefore, Lucullus fawned upon with gifts and flattery (it was doubtless a great reward for a swaggering and pompous woman to be seen joining zealously with the ambitions of Lucullus) and he at once had Cethegus praising him and endeavouring to obtain Cilicia on his behalf.

Plutarch, *Life of Lucullus* 6.2–3

This anecdote emphasizes, in terms that are ideologically charged, the influence that some women could have in steering or influencing political developments, notably by supporting the establishment of new political ties between individuals that had been part of opposite factions: Lucullus, who needed the support of Cornelius Cethegus in order to obtain a prestigious and potentially profitable command in the Greek East, resorted to Praecia as an intermediary, who in turn regarded her connection with an ambitious and capable political operator like Lucullus as a boon to her reputation and influence.

K5   Chelidon, mistress of C. Verres
[120] Now, I beg you, jurors, recall the wanton behaviour of that man in his administration of justice, what inconsistencies of decisions, what trafficking, how empty the houses of all those who are regularly consulted about civil law (*ius civile*), how full and crammed the house of Chelidon; whenever there was an approach to him by that woman, a whisper in his ear, at one moment he used to call back those among whom he had already made a judgement and change his decision, at another among others he would, without any scruple, give an opposite decision to those most recent decisions he had given shortly before.

Cicero, *Against Verres* 2.1.120

As is the case with Terentia and Praecia, a woman who has great influence over her husband or lover can be cast as a destabilizing presence, with questionable morals and no sense of what her rightful place in society is. At the same time, her role can be seen as evidence for the shortcomings of the man that is the target of her efforts. In Cicero's account Chelidon, Verres' lover, has great power over a man who is supposed to exert the power of a Roman magistrate and dispense justice fairly, but is unable to do so with any decency and consistency: during his tenure in Sicily, there was no need to consult legal experts ahead of a hearing before the governor, as obtaining Chelidon's favour was all that mattered.

K6   Women in the Catilinarian conspiracy, 63 BC
a) But there was in the conspiracy Q. Curius, a man of no humble birth but deep in crime and disgrace, whom the censors had removed from the senate because of scandal. [2] This man possessed no less foolishness than recklessness; he did not keep silent about what he had heard, nor did he conceal his own crimes either. He had not the slightest scruple about what he said or did. [3] He had long had an affair with a woman of noble birth, Fulvia; since he was less pleasing to her, because, through poverty, he was less able to be lavish, he began suddenly to boast and to promise seas and mountains and sometimes to threaten her with a sword if she were not submissive to him; finally he began to behave more assertively than had been his custom. [4] But Fulvia, when she got to know the reason for the unusual behaviour of Curius, did not conceal such a danger to the *res publica*, but, without giving the source, told several people what she had heard by various means about the conspiracy of Catiline.

Sallust, *Catiline's War* 23.1–4

b) [24.3] At that time Catiline is said to have won over to his side many men of every sort, and even some women, who at first had met their enormous expenses by prostitution, but later, when age had set a limit to their income but not to their extravagance, had run up huge debts. ... [25.1] Now among these women was Sempronia, who had often committed many crimes with the daring of a man. [2] In birth and beauty, in her husband too and children, she was fortunate enough; a woman well read in Greek and Latin letters, able to play the lyre and dance more skilfully than is necessary for an honest woman, and having many other accomplishments which minister to luxury. [3] But there was nothing that she held so cheap as modesty and chastity; you could not easily decide whether she was less sparing of her money or her name; for her sexual desires were so fervid that she sought men more often than she was sought by them. [4] Even before this, she had often broken her word, repudiated her debt, been a party to murder; extravagance and poverty had driven her headlong. [5] Nevertheless she was a woman of no mean talent; she could write verses, tell jokes, and converse with modesty, with tenderness, or with wantonness; in fine, she possessed considerable wit and charm.

Sallust, Catiline's War 24.3–25, with omission

Two women play a central role in Sallust's account of the conspiracy of Catiline. Fulvia is crucial to the foiling of the plot itself: she is the mistress of one of the conspirators, who decides to disclose what she knows about his involvement, effectively enabling the consul Cicero to begin his investigation and setting the machinery of repression into motion (see **B74**). Sempronia has a far less significant place within the development of the plot, and makes just one appearance in Sallust's account, where she is singled out as a revealing example of the sort of perverse combination of talent and depravity that is typical of many members of the conspiracy, including Catiline himself, and is a symptom of a wider moral crisis that has far-reaching political implications. – The pointed references to her literary knowledge and interest in music and dance are telling of a persistently awkward attitude toward departures from a traditional and subdued model of femininity, even in the increasingly sophisticated world of the late Republican élite. She was the wife of D. Junius Brutus, consul in 77 BC.

K7   Aurelia, mother of Julius Caesar

a) [4] For in the past, each person's son, born of pure parentage, was brought up not in the tiny room of a hired nurse, but in the lap and bosom of his mother, whose greatest praise was to protect the home and devote herself to her children ... [6] In this manner we have heard Cornelia took charge of the upbringing of the Gracchi; Aurelia, that of Caesar; Atia, that of Augustus: in this way did they rear the leading children.

Tacitus, Dialogue on Oratory 28.4–6, with omission

In this passing reference in Tacitus' dialogue on the decline of oratory in the Principate one finds an instance of the model of femininity that women like Sallust's Sempronia are criticized for having rejected: the mothers of Julius Caesar and Augustus are singled out as models of devotion to their children, as well as Cornelia, the mother of the Gracchi. – Aurelia was the daughter of L. Aurelius Cotta, consul 119 BC, and sister of L. Aurelius Cotta, tribune of the plebs 95 BC and praetor *c.* 90 BC. She thus belonged to the plebeian nobility and was probably the cousin of the three Aurelii Cottae - Gaius, Marcus and Lucius, consuls respectively in 75, 74 and 65 BC.

b) Publius Clodius was a man of patrician birth and conspicuous for wealth and eloquence. In violence and wantonness he was second to none among those infamous for wickedness. [3] This man was in love with Pompeia, the wife of Caesar, and she was not unwilling. But close watch was kept on the women's apartments and Aurelia,

Caesar's mother and a woman of discretion, followed the young woman closely and always made their meeting difficult and full of danger.

Plutarch, *Life of Caesar* 9.2–3

After the death of his first wife in 69, Caesar married Pompeia in 67 BC, who happened to be a granddaughter of Sulla. Aurelia's vigilance and keen interest in the stability of her son's marriage is implicitly singled out both as an instance of her motherly virtue and an indication of her moral superiority to her daughter-in-law.

c) At the time ... Pompeia was celebrating the festival of the Bona Dea and Clodius, who was still beardless and young, put on a dress and, taking the instruments of a lute girl, went to the house looking like a young woman. [2] Chancing upon open doors he was taken in by a maidservant, who was in the conspiracy ... an attendant of Aurelia came upon him ... [3] The women were panic-stricken. Aurelia put an end to the secret rites of the goddess and covered up the sacred objects. Then she ordered the doors to be closed and went about the house with torches, searching for Clodius. [4] He was found where he had taken refuge in the room of the girl with whose help he had entered the house. When they saw who he was, he was driven out through the doors by the women.

Plutarch, *Life of Caesar* 10.1–4, with omissions

In spite of Aurelia's best efforts, the relationship between Pompeia and Clodius became close enough for the latter to be caught in the house of the *pontifex maximus*, dressed as a young woman, as a ritual that only women could attend was taking place. Aurelia takes the decision to stop the ceremony, in the full knowledge that a scandal would ensue: the ritual has been violated, and appropriate action must be taken. The gesture with which she covers the objects used in the ritual is a pointed reference to her piety.

K8   The wives of Julius Caesar
a) Cornelia was the daughter of the Cinna who had once held sole power at Rome. When Sulla gained overall power, not being able either by hopes or by fear to induce Caesar to divorce her, he confiscated her dowry.

Plutarch, *Life of Caesar* 1.1

Sulla's failed attempt to bring the marriage to an end is an example of his aim to take comprehensive revenge on his enemies, and make sure that they shall not even have any descendants, who might in some way be willing and able to take up their political legacy. The anecdote is of course also intended to put Caesar in a rather flattering light. Cornelia died in 68 BC; Caesar's decision to give a eulogy for her is also noteworthy (Plutarch, *Life of Caesar* 5.4). The daughter that was born from that marriage, Julia, later married Pompey the Great.

b) Caesar divorced Pompeia at once, but when he was summoned to testify at the trial, said he knew nothing about the accusations being spoken against Clodius. [9] Since his statement appeared strange, the prosecutor asked, 'Why, then, did you divorce your wife?' 'Because,' replied Caesar, 'I thought my wife ought not even to have been under suspicion.'

Plutarch, *Life of Caesar* 10.8–9

A famous anecdote, also related in Suetonius, *Divus Julius*, 74.2, which follows Caesar's unilateral decision to repudiate his wife after the Bona Dea scandal. Caesar's comment is not just an example of the high concept he had of himself and his standing: it also enabled him not to give damning evidence against Clodius, whom he regarded as a significant and potentially valuable political player.

c) [7] But Caesar, making more use still of the power of Pompey, for he had a daughter betrothed to Servilius Caepio, engaged her to Pompey and said he would give the daughter of Pompey to Servilius, though she herself was not unbetrothed either, having been promised to Faustus, the son of Sulla. [8] A little later Caesar married Calpurnia, the daughter of Piso, and he got Piso elected consul for the following year, although at this point Cato called loudly on men to witness and shouted that it was not tolerable when the empire (*imperium*) was being prostituted away by marriages and by men introducing one another to commands and armies and magistracies through women.

Plutarch, *Life of Caesar* 14.7–8

Caesar's marriage with young Calpurnia, his third wife, was part of a political agreement between him and her father, which enabled the latter to the elected to the consulship for 58 BC. Cato, who had refused forming a marriage alliance with Pompey a few years earlier (**K2c**), publicly denounced the practice of accompanying political alliances with marriage arrangements, arguing that they made a mockery of the due political process. This comment, while having some factual basis, could be applied to other moments of the political history of the Roman Republic, and not just to the time when Pompey, Crassus, and Caesar formed their alliance. – Cf. also Appian, *Civil Wars* 2.14.

d) [8] After that, sleeping, as he was accustomed, beside his wife, all the doors and windows of the house flew open at the same time. Distracted by the noise and at the same time by the light of a brightly shining moon, he perceived that his wife was in a deep sleep but uttering unclear sounds and inarticulate groans from her sleep. [9] In fact she appeared bewailing and holding in her arms her murdered husband. ... [10] And so when it was day, she begged Caesar, if it were possible, not to go out, but to postpone the senate; but if he thought next to nothing of her dreams, she begged him to inquire through other divination and sacred rites about the future. [11] Some suspicion and fear did, it seems, possess him. For he had not before noticed any superstition characteristic of a woman in Calpurnia, but he then saw her in great anxiety. [12] When the priests, after many sacrifices, told him the omens were unfavourable he decided to send Antony and put off the Senate.

Plutarch, *Life of Caesar* 63.8–12

A number of omens are said to have occurred in the run-up to the Ides of March, and some did present themselves directly to Caesar. The dream that his wife Calpurnia recounted to him on the morning of the Ides was very vivid, and deeply struck him: he even came to the decision to call off the Senate session, only to be persuaded by one of the conspirators, Decimus Brutus, who was in his house that morning, that postponing the session would have cast him in an unfavourable light. – The view that women are more superstitious than men is widely voiced in classical literature: it is that very prejudice that persuades Caesar to take Calpurnia's dream seriously, since she did not usually seem to have time for superstition.

K9   Marcus Porcius Cato: marriage and women

[24.4] It appears that Cato was wholly unfortunate in the women of his household. For this Servilia had a bad reputation because of her affair with Caesar; and the behaviour of the other Servilia, also Cato's sister, was even more disgraceful. [5] She had married Lucullus, a man of the highest renown among the Romans, and she had borne him a child. She was divorced because of her scandalous conduct. [6] But, most shameful of all, not even Atilia, Cato's wife, was clear of such failings: although she had borne him two children, he was obliged to divorce her because of misconduct.

[25.1] Then he married Marcia, daughter of Philippus, a woman of good reputation. Everyone has much to say about her. ... [3] Among Cato's many adherents and admirers there were some who were more distinguished and renowned than others, and these included Quintus Hortensius, a man of outstanding reputation and of noble character. [4] Now Hortensius wanted to be not only a companion and associate of Cato, but, somehow or other, to join all his house and family in a kinship alliance with Cato. Cato's daughter, Porcia, was married to Bibulus and had borne him two sons. Hortensius tried to persuade Cato to give him Porcia in turn, as being fertile soil for the production of children. [5] In the opinion of men, he said, such an action was unconventional, but by natural law it was honourable and for the good of the state that a woman in the prime and vigour of life should not lie idle and let her fertility pass nor, by producing more than sufficient children, overburden and impoverish a household which did not want them. [6] By sharing their descendants among worthy men they could produce an unfailing supply of virtue, spread among the families, and cause an intermingling of the state within itself by family ties. [7] If Bibulus was completely devoted to his wife, Hortensius said he would give her back as soon as she had borne him a child, and he would then be more closely connected with Bibulus himself and with Cato because they would have children in common. [8] Cato replied that he liked Hortensius very much and valued a family tie with him, but thought it out of place to talk about marrying his daughter who had been given to another man. [9] Then Hortensius changed his tack, took off the mask and did not hesitate to ask for Cato's own wife, since she was still young enough to bear children and Cato had enough heirs. [10] And one cannot say that he acted like this in the knowledge that Cato paid no attention to Marcia, for they say that she happened to be pregnant at the time. [11] Now Cato, seeing the eagerness and desire of Hortensius, did not refuse, but said that Philippus, Marcia's father, must also agree. [12] So Philippus was asked to give his consent; but he would not give Marcia in marriage except with Cato himself present to join in giving the bride away. [13] Although this took place at a later date, I decided to mention it in advance here, seeing that I was recording the facts about the women in Cato's family.

Plutarch, *Life of Cato the Younger* 24.4–25, with omission

Plutarch devotes a rather lengthy section of his biography of Cato to the women in his family, partly as a way of complementing what he says elsewhere about his attitude to 'political' marriages. His sisters (half-sisters, in fact, both called Servilia: see above [24.4]) and his first wife committed adultery. His second marriage, with Marcia, the daughter of L. Marcius Philippus (*cos.* 56), had an extraordinary development: Cato agreed to divorce her so that she could marry Q. Hortensius Hortalus, who was very keen to form a kinship bond with Cato and had first asked him for his daughter's hand. Cato may have objected to the link between political alliances and marriage arrangements, but Hortensius' intention to form an association with him was certainly politically motivated, and Cato's decision not to break the engagement of his daughter and M. Calpurnius Bibulus is motivated by concerns that are both social and, broadly speaking, political. – Hortensius' pledge to divorce Porcia as soon as she gave birth to a child is revealing of a driving factor in how many of the Roman nobility approached marriages: these are, first and foremost, the opportunity to perpetuate one's family name and to secure the survival of the family's fortune. Cato understands that concern well, and on that basis he decides to let Hortensius marry his wife.

K10   Servilia, mother of Brutus

a) But above others, Caesar loved Servilia, the mother of Marcus Brutus, for whom during his last consulship he purchased a pearl worth six million sesterces and during the civil war, besides other gifts, knocked down at a very cheap price some extensive estates that were under auction. With many being amazed at their cheapness Cicero very wittily remarked: 'A better purchase than you realize with a third knocked off!', for Servilia was even procuring her daughter, Tertia, for Caesar.

Suetonius, *Divus Julius* 50.2

Servilia was the daughter of Q. Servilius Caepio, who was praetor in 91 BC and died in 90 BC. She married M. Junius Brutus, tribune of the plebs in 83 BC and an opponent of Sulla, who was executed by Pompey after surrendering at the siege of Mutina in 77 BC. The couple had one son, Brutus, who later became a major figure in the conspiracy against Caesar. She and her sister were half-sisters to M. Porcius Cato (see above, **K9**): this Servilia exercised considerable influence over Cato (Asconius, *Commentaries* p.19C.24-25). The long association between Caesar and Servilia makes the famous 'You too, my son' pronounced (in Greek: Suetonius, *Divus Julius* 82.3) on the Ides of March all the more poignant, although there is no evidence whatsoever that Caesar may have been the natural father of Brutus. The gifts that Caesar made to Servilia are historically more instructive, as they show both a pattern of huge private expenditure (the pearl) and a willingness to make use of the power secured at an age of political and social disruption to obtain direct personal advantage (the purchase of the estate). – Cicero's comment is based on a rather distasteful pun: *Tertia* means 'third'.

b) I arrived at Antium before midday. My arrival was pleasing to Brutus. Then before a large audience, with Servilia, Tertulla and Porcia, he asked me what he should do. Favonius too was present. I advised what I had been contemplating on the way, that he should take on the supervision of the corn from Asia; there was nothing remaining for us to do except to see he was safe: on this the defence of the *res publica* itself depended. When I had entered upon this speech, Cassius arrived on the scene. I repeated the same points. At this moment, with brave face certainly – you might say he was breathing Mars – he said he would not go to Sicily. 'Was I to have accepted an insult as if it were a favour?' 'What are you going to do, then?' I enquired. He then said he would go to Achaia. 'What about you, Brutus?' I asked. 'I'll go to Rome' he said, 'if you agree.' 'I don't at all; for you will not be safe.' 'But supposing I could be, would you be in favour?' 'Yes, certainly, and that you should not go to a province either now or after your praetorship; but I am not going to be the one to advise you to commit yourself to the city.' I stated what, I am sure, comes to your mind, why he would not be safe in the city. [2] Then in lengthy conversation they complained, and Cassius above all, about the opportunities let slip and they sharply accused Decimus. To this I said they ought not to go on and on about the past, but I agreed nonetheless. And when I started to talk about what ought to have been done, nothing new but what everyone else was saying every day, not however touching that topic that someone else besides ought to have been dealt with, that they should have summoned the Senate, stirred up the people more strongly when they were ablaze with enthusiasm, taken over the *res publica* entirely, your friend exclaimed: 'Well indeed, I have never heard anyone saying this!' I restrained myself. But it seemed to me that Cassius would go (for Servilia promised she would see to it that the supervision of the corn would be removed from the decree of the Senate) and our friend Brutus was quickly forced to withdraw from his empty talk in which he had said he wished to be in Rome. For he decided that the games might be held in his name in his absence. It seemed to me that he wished to set out for Asia from Antium.
Antium (?), *c.* 7 June 44 BC.

Cicero, *To Atticus* 15.11.1–2 (SB 389)

This remarkable extract from Cicero's correspondence (repeated in another letter a few days later, Cicero, *To Atticus* 15.12.1 = SB 390) shows a political meeting taking place at a private house, in which Brutus and Cassius discuss their options in the increasingly difficult aftermath of the Ides of March, and seek Cicero's advice. His view is that the city is not a safe place for Brutus, as he would become a likely target of Caesar's friends. Cicero is already urging the elimination of Antony – he is the 'someone else' that is alluded to. There are signs of an impending divide among the conspirators: Decimus Brutus is accused of not having having effectively used the legions that were under his command in Cisalpine Gaul. Remarkably, Servilia is in the room, and her presence is not a silent one (as it is ostensibly the case with Porcia, the wife of Brutus and a daughter of Cato, and Tertulla): she states that she has the influence to bring about a significant change in a decree of the Senate, and will make sure that the reference to entrust the task of securing the corn supply to Brutus and Cassius is removed. Her influence is therefore not limited to the circle of her son's immediate political friends, but reaches into sectors of the political élite that are not necessarily friendly to him.

K11   Clodia, sister of Publius Clodius Pulcher

[30] There are two charges: one about gold, one about poison, in which one and the same person is involved. Gold was taken from Clodia, poison was sought to be given to Clodia, so it is said. All the other matters are not charges, but slander; they belong rather to unruly abuse than to a criminal lawcourt. 'Adulterer, pervert, bribery agent', such is abuse, not accusation. For there is no foundation for these charges, no basis; they are insulting remarks, recklessly blurted out by an angry accuser without any backing. [31] But as for the two charges I have mentioned, I see the person responsible, I see the source, I see a definite individual and fountainhead. Caelius needed gold: he took it from Clodia, he took it without a witness, and he had it as long as he wanted. I see the strongest evidence of a remarkably close friendship. He wanted to kill the same woman: †he sought poison, he pestered her slaves, he prepared the drink, he fixed the place, and he brought it secretly.† Here, on the other hand, I see a violent hatred has come into existence with a most cruel rupture. In this case, jurors, our entire concern is with Clodia, a woman not only of noble birth but also of notoriety; about whom I shall say nothing except what is necessary for rebutting the charge. [32] But you realize, in view of your remarkable understanding, Cn. Domitius, that our concern is with this woman alone. If she says that she did not lend the gold to Caelius, if she does allege that the poison was not obtained by him for her, we are behaving in an outrageous manner if we name the mother of a family (*materfamilias*) in terms other than what the virtue of married women demands. But if with this woman removed, no charge nor resource is left for the prosecutors to attack Caelius, what else is there for us, his advocates, to do, except to repel those who are attacking him? Indeed, I should do that with all the more vigour, did not personal animosities come between me and that woman's husband – I meant to say brother: I always make that mistake. I will act with moderation, then, and go no further than my duty to my client and the case itself compels me. Indeed I never thought that I should have to engage in quarrels with women, especially with a woman whom everybody has reckoned to be the friend of all rather than the enemy of anyone.

[33] But first of all I shall inquire of herself, whether she prefers me to deal with her in a severe, solemn, and old-fashioned way, or in a relaxed, easy-going, modern way. If in that grim mode and method, then I must call back from the underworld one of those bearded men of old – not with the modern type of goatee beard that she delights in, but a rough one, like those we see on old statues and busts – to rebuke the woman and speak on my behalf, so that she may not perhaps get angry with me. Let me therefore call up some member of this very family of hers: most suitably, that

famous Caecus, for he will feel the least sorrow since he will not see her. [34] If he appears, this, I am sure, is how he will deal with her; this is what he will say: 'Woman, what have you to do with Caelius, with a mere youth, with an outsider? Why have you been so friendly with him that you lent him gold, or so hostile that you were afraid of poison? Did you not see that your father, had you not heard that your uncle, your grandfather, your great-grandfather, your great-great grandfather and your great-great-great grandfather were consuls? Lastly, did you not know that you had recently married Q. Metellus, a most illustrious and most courageous man, most devoted to his country, who as soon as he had stepped over the threshold surpassed nearly all his fellow-citizens in courage, glory and status (*dignitas*)? When from a family of the highest nobility you had married into a most illustrious house, why was Caelius so closely connected with you? Was he a kinsman? A relative by marriage? A friend of your husband? He was none of these. What was it then if not some reckless passion? If the portrait-busts (*imagines*) of the men of our family did not influence you, did not my own descendant, that famous Q. Claudia, prompt you to emulate the renown of our household in the glorious achievements of its women? Did not that famous Vestal virgin Q. Claudia prompt you, who, embracing her father in his triumph, did not allow him to be pulled down from his chariot by a hostile tribune of the plebs? Why has your brother's vice influenced you more than the virtues of your father and your ancestors repeated right down from my times not only by the men but also by the women of our house? Was it for this that I broke up the peace with Pyrrhus, so that you might strike deals for your disgusting love affairs? Was it for this that I brought water into Rome, so that you might use it for your incestuous debauches? Was it for this that I built a road so that you might frequent it accompanied by other women's husbands?'

Cicero, *Defence of Caelius* 30–34

†This portion of the text is corrupt: 'he sought poison, he pestered whom he could, he got hold of it, he fixed the place, and he brought it' is an alternative reading to the OCT translated above.

In 56 BC Cicero took up the defence of M. Caelius, a young nobleman who had been charged with having taken part in several episodes of political violence (*vis*). He decided to focus his case on circumstances in which Caelius' former lover, Clodia, was directly implicated, and to devote much of his energy to a lengthy attack on Clodia and her character, casting her as a manipulative individual who cast her spell over a young and inexperienced man who was not to blame in any way. Clodia was the sister of P. Clodius Pulcher, the former tribune towards whom Cicero had a deep-seated, well-known, and strongly reciprocated enmity. The passage quoted above does not fail to mention that connection, and does so in abrasive terms, effectively suggesting that they had an incestuous bond. Cicero's operation is quite straightforward: he claims that the whole case against Caelius rests on his association with Clodia, and that his main brief is therefore to denounce her flaws. Cicero makes much of Clodia's distinguished ancestry, and resorts to a well-rehearsed rhetorical device by imagining a polemical speech that Appius Claudius Caecus [**Caecus** = 'Blind', hence Cicero's pun at the end of section 33], the censor of 312 BC, would address to his descendant. – The comment on the influence that the portraits of the ancestors can have on a member of the nobility is especially significant. The contributions that Appius Claudius made to the development of civic life in Rome (the Appian Way, the aqueduct) are set against the immoral and intrinsically destabilizing adulterous acts of Clodia. – Cicero's strategy is questionable in several respects, but has the merit of offering an example of how personal attacks could be used in a court of law, and sketches a model of perverted and corrupt femininity that sheds light on the wider problem of the role that women were expected to play in the conventional élite morality of the late Republican period. Some years previously Cicero had unsuccessfully approached Clodia to seek her help in deterring her brother-in-law, Metellus Nepos, tribune of the plebs 62 BC, from attacking Cicero's handling of the Catilinarian conspiracy (Cicero to Metellus Celer, *To his Friends* 5.2.6 (SB 2)).

K12 Porcia, the wife of M. Junius Brutus

[3] Porcia, who, as has been said, was a daughter of Cato, was the wife of Brutus, who was her cousin. She had been married, but her previous husband had died. Brutus married her when she was still a young woman and had a boy, whose name was Bibulus, from her previous husband. And a small booklet containing reminiscences of Brutus, written by him, is preserved. [4] Porcia, being affectionate and loving her husband, full of good sense, did not attempt to ask her husband about his secrets until she had put herself to the following test. [5] Taking a small knife with which barbers cut nails and having put out of the bedroom all the attendants, she made a deep gash in her thigh so that a copious flow of blood resulted; after a short time violent pains and shivering fevers seized her as a result of the wound. [6] When Brutus became anxious and distressed, Porcia, then in the height of her pain, conversed with him as follows: [7] 'I, Brutus, being the daughter of Cato, was given to your house, not as a concubine sharing only your bed and your table, but to be a partner of your joys and a partner of your woes. [8] All your acts in respect of the marriage are without fault; but what demonstration or gratitude can there be on my part if I am not to bear with you your secret suffering or thoughts which require trust; [9] I know that a woman's nature appears weak to bear a secret; but there is a certain amount of strength for character in good upbringing and excellent company. [10] It is my good fortune to be a daughter of Cato and wife of Brutus. I had trusted less in these previously, but I now know that I am invincible to pain.' [11] Having said this she revealed the wound to him and explained her test. He was amazed and stretched his hands upwards, prayed to the gods to grant him to complete the deed and to appear a husband worthy of Porcia. And then he tried to bring his wife back to health.

Plutarch, *Life of Brutus* 13

Porcia had been married first to M. Calpurnius Bibulus, consul in 59 BC, by whom she had a son. Brutus married her in 45 BC (see Cicero, *To Atticus,* 13.10.3 (SB 318), 13.11.1 (SB 319), and 13.17.1 (SB 324)). This anecdote stresses the extraordinary resilience and commitment of Brutus' wife: a theme that has an important narrative function in Plutarch's biography, as it is part of the build-up to the assassination of Caesar, but is also intended to draw attention to the depth of Brutus' connection with an extraordinary woman, to whom he is also related by blood, and who is in turn closely related to the late Cato (an aspect that no doubt Brutus stressed in his own lost 'small booklet'). Porcia's resilience in the face of pain and adversity is part of a distinguished Republican tradition. – Cf. also Cassius Dio, *Roman History* 44.13.2–14. Porcia died not long afterwards: Cicero, *To Brutus* 1.9.2 (SB 18), dated to the end of June (?) 43 BC, offers his condolences to Brutus on the death of his wife. Valerius Maximus (*Memorable Deeds and Sayings,* 4.6.5) attributes her death to suicide, and mistakenly places it after Philippi.

K13 A wife in the triumviral proscriptions, 43–42 BC

[Col. 1.27] Rare are the marriages which last long enough to be ended by death, not cut short by divorce: [for it befell] us, that it was extended into its 41st year without animosity. If only our long-continued [marriage] had undergone [its final] change through my lot, as it was fairer that I as the older partner yield to fate.

[Col. 2.2a] You provided support for my flight [by selling] your ornaments, when you [took] all the gold and pearls from your body and handed them over to me and then you enriched me in my absence with slaves, money, and income, [having cunningly deceived] my enemies' guards. [6a] [You pleaded for my life in my absence], something which your courage encouraged you to try. The clemency [your words won] from those against whom you argued protected [me]. [And yet always] your words were uttered with strength of spirit. ...

[11] And yet I shall confess that the bitterest experience in my life was felt on your behalf, after [I had now been restored] as a citizen to my country through the favour and judgement of the absent Caesar Augustus, [when] Marcus Lepidus, his colleague who was present, was accosted [by you] about my recall [and] you, prostrate on the ground [at his] feet, not only were not raised up, but were dragged away and manhandled like [a slave], your body covered in bruises. Yet with a most steadfast [spirit you kept reminding him] of Caesar's edict with his congratulation on my recall, and, despite having heard insulting words and having received cruel wounds, you openly [declared these things] so that the instigator of my dangers might become known. [Soon this affair] damaged him.

CIL 6.41062 = EDCS-60700127*

An extraordinary inscription from Rome records the text of the eulogy that a man of senatorial rank gave in honour of his late wife: it is a unique document of the vicissitudes of a family in the triumviral period. The extracts quoted here pay tribute to the role that the lady played in supporting her husband after his name was included on the proscription list, and the successful efforts she made in securing his pardon: the description of her meeting with Lepidus is especially vivid. The ability that she shows in managing the family fortune and putting resources to good use is a salutary warning against dismissing the role of women in the economic domain. – The inscription is often referred to as *Laudatio Turiae* ['Praise of Turia'], as some scholars have identified this pair with the Turia and Q. Lucretius Vespillo, mentioned in Valerius Maximus, *Memorable Deeds and Sayings* 6.7.2; cf. also Appian, *Civil Wars* 4.44: the hypothesis, however, is speculative. For translation of the whole inscription, see LACTOR 17, T37.

K14   Hortensia's exemplary speech, 42 BC

Hortensia, daughter of Q. Hortensius, pleaded the cause of women before the triumvirs resolutely and successfully, when the order of matrons had been burdened by them with a heavy tax and none of the men had the courage to lend them his advocacy. Reviving her father's eloquence, she obtained the remission of the greater part of the charge. Q. Hortensius then lived again in his female progeny and inspired his daughter's words. If his male descendants had chosen to follow her example, the great heritage of Hortensian eloquence would not have been cut short with the single speech of a woman.

Valerius Maximus, *Memorable Deeds and Sayings* 8.3.3

Valerius Maximus records the memorable speech of Hortensia, the daughter of one of the greatest orators of the late Republican period (see **H1**), who undertook the plea of a group of matrons before the triumvirs. The status of the 'order of matrons' mentioned here is controversial; it is unlikely to be a technical expression. However, it is clear that Hortensia made her case on behalf of a considerable number of women: Appian, *Civil Wars* 4.32–34 records the controversy and gives a version of Hortensia's speech. 1,400 'of the richest women' were required by the Triumvirs to produce an assessment of their wealth and make a contribution to the forthcoming military campaign against the Liberators. – Valerius' praise seems double-edged: on the one hand, Hortensia is very effective, shows greater courage than her male contemporaries, and exceeds the merits of her descendants; on the other, her rhetorical ability is said to have been 'inspired' by her late father, rather than being the product of her own talent and ingenuity.

K15   Fulvia, wife of Mark Antony

[5] For having left off that dissolute sort of life, he turned to marriage, marrying Fulvia who had been wedded to the tribune Clodius; no little woman concerned with spinning or with housekeeping, nor thinking herself worthy to have power over a husband who was a private citizen, but wishing to rule a ruler and to command a commander, [6] with the result that Cleopatra owed tuition fees to Fulvia for making Antony subject to the power of a woman, taking him over completely manageable and trained from the start to pay attention to women. [7] Not that Antony did not try to make her merrier by joking and playing the lad.

Plutarch, *Life of Antony* 10.5–7

Marcus Antonius (Mark Antony), later *triumvir*, was Fulvia's third husband and there were two sons of the marriage, Antyllus and Iullus Antonius. Plutarch establishes a pattern in Antony's personality, as he often does with his characters: he was vulnerable to falling under the control of a woman, well before the beginning of his relationship with Cleopatra. – Fulvia had previously been married to Publius Clodius, tribune of the plebs in 58 BC. By him she had a son and a daughter, P. Clodius and Claudia, the latter being for a short time the first wife of the future emperor Augustus (on her role in the aftermath of Clodius' death see Asconius, *Commentaries* p. 32C.20-22 and 40.18-21). She then married Gaius Scribonius Curio, tribune of the plebs in 50 BC, of which union there was one son. Cicero hints at an intrigue involving Antony in the house of Clodius during his tribunate when he was married to Fulvia: 'Also even at this time he was up to something in Clodius' house – he best knows what I mean.' (*Philippics* 2.48). Cicero also makes mention of the violent deaths of Fulvia's previous husbands Clodius, killed on the Via Appia in January 52 BC, and Curio, killed in Africa while fighting on behalf of Caesar against Juba, king of Numidia in 49 BC: 'Who was ever heard abusing my consulship except yourself and Publius Clodius, whose fate awaits you, as it awaited Gaius Curio, since you have that in your house which proved fatal to them both?' (Cicero, *Philippics* 2.11). Elsewhere Cicero would characterize her 'as cruel as she was greedy' (*Philippics* 13.18). Fulvia became a figure of some importance after the death of Caesar in 44 BC, and played a significant role in the build-up of the so-called Perusine War in 41 BC, when she proved a skilful political operator, considerably weakening the political position of Octavian in Rome and Italy (see **K16**). Velleius Paterculus (*Roman History* 2.74.3) has a brief, striking comment that casts her as an extreme, disturbing figure: 'Fulvia, the wife of Antony, who had nothing of the woman in her except her sex, was creating turmoil everywhere through armed violence'. The significance of Fulvia in the political events of her time is also shown by the obscene references to her that were inscribed on slingshots that were found at Perusia (*ILLRP* 1106 = EDCS-24900044 and 1112 = EDCS-24900051) and by the equally lewd verses that Octavian allegedly wrote about her during his youth, heavily alluding to Antony's infidelity towards her (quoted in Martial, *Epigrams* 11.20).

K16   Fulvia's influence, 41 BC

The following year Publius Servilius and Lucius Antonius became consuls in name, but the consuls were in fact Antonius and Fulvia. She, the mother-in-law of Caesar and wife of Antony, held Lepidus of no account because of his sluggishness, and managed affairs herself, so that neither the Senate nor the people carried out any business contrary to her wishes.

Cassius Dio, *Roman History* 48.4.1

While Antony was busy in the Greek East, attending to a campaign against the Parthians that ultimately proved unsuccessful, his cause in Italy was effectively championed by his brother, L. Antonius, and especially by his wife Fulvia, who proved very capable in mobilizing public opinion against Octavian, whose position she sought to undermine at a time when the land confiscations he was carrying out across Italy were attracting considerable dissent. – Cassius Dio focuses his comment on the remarkable circumstance of a woman who reached a level of influence that could fairly be compared to that of a serving consul. The 'Caesar' that is mentioned here is Octavian, who was briefly married to Fulvia's daughter, Clodia Pulchra.

L. POLITICS IN THE LATE REPUBLIC

One of the overarching aims of this volume is to bring the study of the Roman Republic beyond a narrow consideration of the political history of the period. This final section, however, brings the focus back on Roman politics, only to seek to further the appreciation of its sheer complexity, and to draw attention to the complex interplay between political practice (the ways in which politics is done, and the political struggle is regulated) and political culture (the ways in which politics is thought about and debated). Some familiar aspects of the late Republican period – mounting political violence, increasingly fierce and dysfunctional political competition, the crisis of traditional institutions, the debates and controversies over citizenship and the rights it entailed – will receive further attention in what follows, and their mutual connections will receive close attention. The final section on the army will mark a return to the theme with which this sourcebook began: the connection between citizenship, land, and military service, and its enduring political significance.

POLITICAL CULTURE

L1   Roman debts to the Greeks

But if the lot had put you in charge of Africans or Spaniards or Gauls, uncivilized and barbarian nations, it would still have been the duty of a civilized man such as yourself to take thought for their interests and to serve their advantage and welfare; but since we are, in fact, governing a race of men among whom not only does civilization itself exist, but from which it is thought to have come to others, we certainly ought to grant that above all to those from whom we have received it. [28] For I shall not be ashamed to say this, especially since there can be no suspicion of laziness or levity in that life and those achievements of mine, that all the things that I have achieved I have gained from those studies and arts which have been handed down to us in the writings and teachings of Greece. So, apart from the common debt which is owed to all men, we seem in addition to owe it to this stock of men in particular that we should wish to exhibit among those very people by whose precepts we have been taught what we have learnt from them.

Rome, end 60/beginning 59 BC

Cicero, *To Quintus* 1.1.27–28 (SB 1)

In the letter that he addresses to Quintus in preparation for his governorship of Asia, Cicero discusses the duties of the good provincial governor, and makes a number of points of principle on the ethics of ruling and the duties that one should fulfil towards the subjects. However, he also makes a specific point: ruling communities of Greeks entails engaging with the deep cultural and intellectual debt that Rome has towards Greek culture, notably towards Greek political thought. Since they share that important background, the members of the Greek élites will be able to recognize and duly appreciate the conduct of a benevolent and principled governor.

L2   Contrast between Roman and Greek assemblies

[15] Bless that famed tradition and teaching, which we received from our forefathers, if we could but maintain it! But somehow it is now slipping from our hands. Now those most wise and most upright men of ours did not want there to be any power in an assembly (*contio*); what the plebs might approve or the people might order, when the assembly (*contio*) had been cleared out of the way, when the divisions had been distributed, when the orders, the classes and the age groups had been sorted by tribe and by century, when the proposers had been heard; when the proposal had been promulgated for many days and understood, they wished it then to be ordered or to

be forbidden. [16] All public affairs of the Greeks, on the other hand, are conducted through the recklessness of a public assembly (*contio*) sitting down. As a result ... that ancient Greece, which once flourished with its wealth, its power (*imperium*), and its glory, collapsed through this one fault, the unrestrained liberty and licence of assemblies (*contiones*).

                                                    Cicero, *Defence of Flaccus* 15–19

In his defence of Flaccus (62 BC) Cicero takes a disparaging view of the quality of the political life and debate in the Greek cities of Asia Minor, which are depicted, on the whole, in a heavily critical fashion, as cities where demagoguery and manipulation often play a central role. The memory of the Mithridatic War and of the treatment that the Greeks of Asia had inflicted upon the Italians who resided in the province is still looming large in the text, and is shrewdly exploited to the service of Cicero's client. – In this passage Cicero makes a point of great historical interest, drawing a sharp distinction between the Roman practice, whereby the will of the people is restrained and channelled through a number of institutional filters, and popular gatherings (*contiones*) have no constitutional status; and the Greek context, in which popular assemblies have a central role, and a potentially destabilizing one: the people in assembly cannot be trusted to make consistently reliable decisions, and not to turn their freedom into licence – in other words, not to take decisions that affect the interests of the established political and economic élites.

L3   The tribal assembly elects the aediles

[3.2.1] At the elections for aediles, under a hot sun, when I and Q. Axius, a senator, a member of my tribe, had cast our votes and wished to be on hand for the candidate, whom we were supporting, when he returned home, Axius said to me: 'while the votes are being sorted, would you like us to make use of the shade of the Villa Publica rather than [... *the text here is hopelessly corrupt* ...] [2] So we proceeded and came to the villa. There we came upon Appius Claudius, sitting on a bench so that he was on hand to be consulted if need should require.

[3.5.18] While we were conversing, shouting arose in the Campus. While we, old hands at elections, were not surprised that this happened as a result of the enthusiasms of the voters, yet we still wished to know what the reason was. Pantuleius Parra came to us and told us that by the recording tablet, when they were sorting the votes, a man had been caught throwing voting tickets into the ballot box and had been dragged off to the consul by the supporters of the other candidates. Pavo got up, because the man who was caught was said to be the observer for his candidate.

[3.7.1] Meanwhile Appius' official (*apparitor*) came from the consul with a message that the augurs were being summoned. He left the Villa.

[3.17.1] Meanwhile Pavo returned to us and said: "If you want to weigh anchors, the votes have been cast and the casting of lots for the tribes is taking place. The herald has begun to call out whom each tribe has elected aedile." Appius got up at once in order to congratulate his candidate on the spot and then go off to his estate. As they were getting up, we were looking back because we knew that our candidate was coming too. ... [3.17.10] That is the limit of our discussion. There was a noise on the right, and our candidate, with the broad striped toga, came into the Villa, aedile elect. We went to meet and congratulate him and escorted him to the Capitoline. From there he went to his home and we to ours.

                                    Varro, *On Agriculture* 3.2.1–2; 5.18; 7.1; 17.1; 17.10

This is a remarkable passage, which belongs in a treatise on agriculture written by the great polymath M. Terentius Varro (see **H25–H30**): it provides a brief, but remarkably vivid account of the election of the aediles, which took place in the *comitia tributa*. Varro and a fellow-senator hear about the development of the election in the Villa Publica near the Campus Martius, where the vote is taking place, and take an interest in the event when they hear a clamour from the Campus: someone has been accused of trying to tamper with the vote, no doubt on behalf of a candidate. That does not prevent the election from being carried to completion: the successful candidate is duly declared aedile elect, in the presence of the augurs, and his first act is to ascend the Capitoline Hill. – The apparitor is an official attendant of a magistrate: in this case, his task is to announce to those near the Villa that the outcome of the election is about to be announced.

L4   The Roman Forum – the centre stage of Roman politics
a) Did you dare to enclose so many Roman citizens in the prisons for foreign criminals and malefactors? Did the thought of the lawcourt, of the assembly (*contio*), of this crowded gathering, which is now looking upon you with so hostile and unfriendly a gaze, did these things never enter your mind? Did not the reputation (*dignitas*) of the Roman people, far away though it was, nor the sight of this crowd ever enter your mind or your imagination? Did you never think you would return to the gaze of these people here, never come into the forum of the Roman people, never be subject to the power of the laws and the courts?

Cicero, Against Verres 2.5.143–144

b) But I am inclined, jurors, to think that this experience has been of more benefit to me than if everyone had congratulated me. For when I realized that the ears of the Roman people were somewhat hard of hearing, while their eyes were alert and sharp, I stopped thinking about what people would hear about me; I saw to it afterwards that they saw me everyday in person, I lived in the public eye; I frequented the forum; neither sleep nor my doorkeeper kept anyone from meeting me. Thus if I have any reputation, and I do not know how great it is, it has been won in Rome, it has been acquired in the forum.

Cicero, Defence of Plancius 66

Two classic statements in which Cicero identifies the Forum as the main focus of political activity in Rome: the place where citizens are persuaded and mobilized, where magistrates exert their power, and where those who seek or aspire to public office are judged through their daily conversation with their fellow-citizens. As the admonishment to Verres reminds us, it is also the place where the crimes and misdemeanours of citizens that have fallen short of their duties towards the commonwealth come under the scrutiny of the citizen body. – These statements are of course heavily shaped by rhetorical and partisan concerns, and serve specific purposes in the cases Cicero is making, but they reflect some fundamental assumptions about Roman political culture that deserve to be taken seriously.

L5   'A *popularis* consul', 63 BC
[3] I am the first *novus homo* whom you have made consul for a very long time, the first, one might almost say, within living memory. Under my leadership you have stormed the citadel which the nobility had fortified so carefully and kept under such close guard, and have shown that in future you wish its gates to stand wide open to the claims of merit. It is not simply that you have made me consul, in itself a great honour, but that you have done so in a way few *nobiles* in this city have ever become consul and, before me, no *novus homo*. Certainly, if you consider what happened to other *novi homines*, you will find that those who reached the consulship at their first attempt stood for election many years after they had been praetor, when they were well past the minimum age set by law, and that they all owed their success to continual

effort and to a happy choice of the right year to stand; but those who were candidates at the minimum age were never elected on their first attempt. I am the only one of all the *novi homines* we can remember who both stood for office at the minimum age and was elected at the first attempt. These facts make it impossible for anyone to claim that the honour (*dignitas*) which I have received from you was snatched from some other candidate or won only after continual requests; I stood for the consulship at the correct point in my career, and my success must be seen as the reward of merit.

[6] My object, however, must be to ensure that all my actions and all my decisions are greeted with praise for your action in deciding to elect me consul, and I consider that I should be prepared to suffer any fate rather than fail in this. What makes my task as consul even more difficult and dangerous is that I have decided that I should not follow the same rules or act on the same principles as previous holders of this office. Some of them, indeed, have gone to great lengths to avoid coming here and speaking to you face to face, while the others have done so only reluctantly. As for me, the promise I am about to make you here, where it is an easy thing to say, I have already made in the Senate where such language seemed quite out of place; as I said there in my first speech, on 1 January, I shall be a *popularis* consul.

[7] I realise that I owe my election, in which I far outstripped men of the highest nobility, not to the support of a group of powerful men nor to the far-reaching influence of a small minority, but to the will of the entire Roman people. It is inevitable, then, that both now in my year of office and throughout the rest of my life I shall be seen to be on the side of the people. But in attempting to explain the true force and meaning of this phrase 'a *popularis* consul' I stand in great need of your understanding, for a dangerously misleading impression of its meaning is now becoming current, caused by the hypocritical claims of a group of men who attack and frustrate the true interests and well-being of the people while making it the object of their speeches to win a reputation as *populares*. [8] The state for which I assumed responsibility on 1 January was, I know, deeply affected by terror and anxiety. There was no limit to the fears of good men (*boni*), nor to the confident expectations of the troublemakers (*improbi*); every sort of disaster and calamity was considered possible. It was reported that all kinds of revolutionary plots against the present form of government and against the freedom you now enjoy were either being started or had been in progress from the time when I became consul designate. There was no feeling of confidence in public life, but its loss was due not to some sudden crushing disaster but to suspicion, to disorder in the law courts and to the invalidating of decisions already reached in them. There was a general feeling that the aim behind all this was the re-establishment of despotism (*dominatio*) in some new form, that these men would not be satisfied with constitutional authority (*imperium*), on however grand a scale, but were bent on tyranny (*regnum*).

[9] Since I not only suspected these things but also perceived them clearly – for they were not being done in secret – I declared in the senate that in this office I would be a *popularis* consul. For what is so *popularis* as peace? Not only do those, to whom nature has given feeling, seem to take delight in it but even buildings and fields. What is so *popularis* as freedom? You see that not only men but also wild animals long for it and put it ahead of everything else. What is so *popularis* as leisure (*otium*)? It is so pleasurable that you, your ancestors and all the bravest men think that the greatest

labours must be undertaken so that they may at some time enjoy leisure (*otium*), especially if combined with authority (*imperium*) and rank (*dignitas*). Moreover it is for this reason that we owe our forebears especial thanks and praise, because it is as a result of their labour that we are able to enjoy leisure (*otium*) without risk. How can I not be a *popularis*, therefore, when I see all these things, citizens? Peace abroad, the freedom proper to your race and name, leisure (*otium*) at home, in a word all the things which are dear and precious to you assigned to my trust and, in a way, to the guardianship of my consulship? [10] Nor, citizens, ought you to consider something welcome or *popularis*, some promulgation of free handouts, which can make a fine show with words but which cannot possibly be brought about without exhausting the treasury; nor should you consider *popularis* such things as disruption of the lawcourts, instability of court judgements, restoration of the condemned; such are usually the death-throes of states already doomed and ruined. Nor should those who promise lands to the Roman people, whether they are plotting some secret scheme while they are putting it forward with hope and specious pretence, be reckoned *populares*.

Cicero, *On the Agrarian Law* 2.3, 6–10

In his first speech to the people upon taking up the consulship, Cicero made the case against the agrarian bill recently put forward by the tribune Servilius Rullus – not an easy brief. He preceded his speech with a preliminary statement that said much both about his political biography and his broader political vision, and in doing so broke the ground for the rather uneasy case he was about to make. He stressed that he was a new man, without senatorial ancestors, who owed his rise to the consulship to his own merits and to popular favour; he then insisted on his ambition to be supportive of the needs and requests of the people (*popularis*), without resorting to demagogic strategies. In making this claim, he also puts forward a view of what he thinks truly serves the interests of the people: peace and political cohesion are to be prioritized, and radical political acts, such as expensive funding schemes and a political use of the courts, must be avoided. Having defined his brief and the true interests of the people in these terms, he can now concentrate on what he regards as the flaws and dangers of Rullus' plan.

L6 The duties of a consul, 63 BC

[3] Wherefore, if it is the duty of a good consul, when he sees everything by which the *res publica* is supported being shaken and uprooted, to offer his assistance to the fatherland, to aid the pursuit of the common welfare and fortunes, to invoke the loyalty of his fellow-citizens, to regard his own welfare as less important than his own – then it is also the duty of good and brave citizens (such as you have shown yourselves to be in all the moments of the history of the *res publica*), to block all the access routes of civil strife, to fortify the bulwarks of the *res publica*, and to regard the consuls as the holders of the highest power (*summum imperium*), and the Senate as the holder of the advice; and finally to judge those who have followed their guidance worthy of praise and honour, rather than of condemnation and punishment.

Cicero, *Defence of Rabirius Charged with High Treason* 3

During his consulship Cicero took up the defence of the elderly senator Gaius Rabirius, who had been prosecuted for his involvement in the events leading to the assassination of Saturninus and Glaucia, nearly four decades earlier (see **B61**, **X2**): the trial had obvious political implications, and Cicero addressed them firmly in his speech. The events of 100 BC had been triggered by a decree of the Senate, which entrusted the consuls with whatever action may be necessary in order to restore public order: the serving consul of 63 BC insists at length on the need for close cooperation between consuls and Senate, and on the duties that consuls have towards the 'good and brave citizens': the rhetoric of the *popularis* consul is replaced by the image of a consul whose chief loyalty is to tradition and stability.

L7   *Optimates* and *populares*, March 56 BC

[96] There have always been two groups of men in this state who have been eager to be involved in affairs of state and to play a pre-eminent part in them; of these groups one wanted themselves to be considered and to be *populares,* the other *optimates*. Those who wanted what they did and what they said to be pleasing to the crowd (*populus*) were considered *populares*, while those who acted in such a way that their policies found favour with the best people (*optimi*) were considered *optimates*. [97] Who, then, are all these best people? In number, if you ask, they are countless, for we could not otherwise remain stable; they are the leaders of state policy, they are those who follow their line, they are the members of the greatest orders, to whom the senate-house is open, they are the Romans from the free-towns (*municipia*) and from the countryside, they are those engaging in business, they are even freedmen *optimates*. The number of this group, as I have said, is spread far and wide, and of varied background; but the group as a whole, to remove error, can be briefly outlined and defined. *Optimates* are all those who are not guilty of crime, who are not evil by nature, who are not raving mad, who are not encumbered in their domestic affairs. So then let them be those – this breed as you have termed them – who are innocent of crime and of sound mind and well established as regards their domestic affairs. Those who serve the wishes, the interests, and the views of these men in governing the *res publica*, the defenders of the *optimates* and the *optimates* themselves, are reckoned the most important and the most distinguished citizens and the leaders of the state. [98] What then is the objective for these men who govern the *res publica*; that on which they must concentrate their attention and towards which they must direct their course? It is what stands far above all else and is most desirable for all men of sound mind, all good men (*boni*), all the well-off – peace (*otium*) with honour (*dignitas*). Those who want this are all *optimates*, those who bring it about are thought the foremost men and the saviours of the state; for it is not right and proper that men be so carried away by the honour (*dignitas*) of playing a part in public affairs that they do not make provision for peace (*otium*), nor that they should concentrate on any *otium* which is at variance with honour (*dignitas*).

Now these are the foundations of this peaceful honour (*otiosa dignitas*), these are the components which must be guarded by the leaders and defended even at the risk of their lives: the observances of religion, the auspices, the powers of magistrates, the authority of the senate, the statutes, the custom of our ancestors, the courts, jurisdiction, credit, the provinces, the allies, the renown of the empire (*imperium*), the military, the treasury. [99] To be the protector and the patron of these many great elements requires a man of great spirit, of great ability and of great resolve. For amid so large a body of citizens there is a very great number of men who either through fear of punishment, being conscious of their crimes, are seeking revolution and political changes in the *res publica*; or who, because of some innate madness, thrive on discord among citizens and violent political disorder; or who on account of the embarrassed financial position of their family affairs would rather go down in the flames of conflagration affecting all than just themselves. When they have got men to protect and to advance their desires and their crimes, storm waves arise in the *res publica*, so that those who have demanded for themselves the governance of their fatherland must exercise vigilance and must do their utmost, with all their knowledge and diligence, so that, having preserved those foundations and components about which I spoke earlier, they may hold on to the course and reach that harbour of peace (*otium*) and honour (*dignitas*).

[100] If I were to deny, jurors, that this course is stormy, difficult, and full of dangers and snares, I should be telling a lie, and all the more so because I have not only always known the statement to be true, but have myself experienced these dangers more than other men.

The forces which attack the state are greater than those which defend it. Men who are naturally reckless and desperate are set in motion by a mere nod, and then their own natural disposition hurries them forward against the state without prompting. But respectable men (*boni*) for some reason are slower to act; they neglect the initial stages and are eventually aroused at the last moment only by sheer necessity, and sometimes this hesitation and slowness of movement leads to a situation in which, for all their desire to preserve civil harmony (*otium*) even at the cost of some loss in personal standing (*dignitas*), they end up without either.

[101] Of those who would like to be thought defenders of the state the unreliable desert and the timid are useless. The only ones who stand firm and endure everything for the state are men of the character of your father, M. [Aemilius] Scaurus, who from the time of C. [Sempronius] Gracchus and Q. Varius resisted all attempts at revolution and was never shaken from his purpose by any violence, threats, or unpopularity. Or like Q. [Caecilius] Metellus, your mother's uncle; during his censorship, he censured L. [Appuleius] Saturninus, who was then at the height of his power in the popular cause, in the face of a violent and angry crowd refused to admit to the citizen lists an imposter claiming to be a Gracchus, and was the only man who refused to swear to obey a law which he had judged to be illegally proposed; after all this, he preferred to leave Italy than to abandon his principles. Or again, leaving aside examples from the past – though there are many, as one would imagine from the extent of our power (*imperium*) – and without mentioning any who are still alive, men of the quality of the late Q. [Lutatius] Catulus, who was neither driven from his course by the threat of danger nor enticed from it by the blandishments of office.

[102] In the name of the immortal gods I beg you to imitate these examples, if you seek honour (*dignitas*), praise and glory; these examples are glorious, they are superhuman, they are immortal; they are proclaimed in men's stories, entrusted to the archives of history and transmitted to posterity. The task involves hard work, I do not deny it; and the perils, I admit, are great; as Atreus so truly says in the play of Accius,
> '*Many are the snares for the honourable*' (*boni*);

but
> '*To lay claim to something which many people envy and to seek to gain is sheer folly, unless you are prepared to work hard and employ the greatest care*'.

I wish Accius had not also provided a quotation for our worthless citizens to seize on:
> '*Let them hate, provided that they fear*'.

for the precepts given in our youth in those other words are splendid.

[103] But this *optimate* system of governing the country was formerly more dangerous when it often happened that the desires of the masses or the interests of the people did not coincide with the national interest. When Lucius Cassius introduced a law about the use of a secret ballot, the people thought that its own freedom was at stake; the leaders of the state disagreed and feared the impetuosity of the masses and the licence which the ballot offered, for the interests of the *optimates* were at stake. Tiberius Gracchus proposed a land bill which pleased the people and seemed likely to put the fortunes of the lower classes on a secure basis, but the *optimates* opposed it vigorously because they saw that it was leading to discord and thought evicting the rich from the estates they had held for so long was no better than robbing the state of its champions. Gaius Gracchus introduced a corn law; the plebeians were delighted because they were being presented with food on a generous scale and without having to work for it, but respectable citizens (*boni*) opposed it because the thought that it invited the plebs to abandon hard work for idleness, and because they saw that it was a drain upon the treasury.

[104] In my own lifetime too there have been many issues, which I omit intentionally, which were the subject of dispute as the desires of the people conflicted with the advice of our leading men (*principes*). But at the present time there is no longer any reason why the people (*populus*) should disagree with the élite and their leaders (*principes*). The people makes no demands, is not eager for revolution, and is delighted with the peace (*otium*) it now enjoys, with the prestige (*dignitas*) enjoyed by all the *optimates*, and with the glory of the whole state. Those who wish to incite the Roman people to sedition and riot can no longer arouse them by offers of largesse, because the plebeians have passed through the stage in which the dangerous course of insurrection and strife seemed appropriate and now embrace peace (*otium*); this is why these instigators of strife and riot are now reduced to hiring audiences for their public meetings. Their object is not to make speeches and proposals which their audience want to hear; no, by bribery and corruption they ensure that the audiences seem at least to want to hear whatever they say.

[105] Surely you do not imagine that the Gracchi or Saturninus or any of those people who were considered *populares* in time past ever had hired audiences at public meetings? None of them did, because the official distributions and the prospect of advantage offered by the proposal of some law excited the multitude without any need of bribery. Accordingly in those days the *populares* did indeed give offence to thoughtful and respectable people, but to judge from the demonstrations of popular approval they had considerable support: they were applauded at the theatre, the voters supported their proposals, and their names, speeches, expression and gait were objects of popular affection. Their opponents were thought to be important and distinguished men, but, although they carried great weight in the Senate and had particular influence with the respectable (*boni*), they were not acceptable to the multitude. Their desires were often thwarted by the popular vote. If ever any one of them was applauded he would fear that he had made some mistake. And yet in matters of real importance it was by the influence (*auctoritas*) of such men that this same people was most swayed.

Cicero, *Defence of Sestius* 96–105

Like the texts quoted under the previous entry, this passage must be read, first and foremost, within the context of the speech in which it belongs: it is not a piece of serious political thinking, and does not belong in a philosophical treatise, but is part of a defence speech, in which the discussion of political matters is inextricably linked to the need to secure the acquittal of Cicero's client. Cicero is making a point about the political divides in the city, and quickly turns those political differences into moral ones: the distinction between *optimates* and *populares* is soon elided by the point whereby anyone, regardless of his origins, can aspire to be an optimate. The central focus of the political divide identified by Cicero is the willingness to bear the interest of the *res publica* in mind, rather than pursuing a partisan or lf-serving agenda. The gap between this model and the portrayal of the *popularis* consul in the speech on the agrarian law of 63 (see above, **L5**) is far narrower than has often been recognized. – The second part of Cicero's argument, however, is possibly even more interesting than the fundamental distinction he draws: he envisages the rise of a man who will act as the guardian and guarantor of the new political arrangement based on 'peaceful dignity': there are forces that threaten social and political stability, which can become especially dangerous if they manage to rally behind an effective leader (Clodius is no doubt at the forefront of Cicero's mind here). This point entails a potentially tricky paradox: urging the emergence of a Republican 'first man', a *princeps*, can readily turn into a fatal threat to the Republican order that Cicero wishes to defend. Indeed, Cicero is keen to stress the aspects of continuity with the Republican past: the list of great men who stood up to defend the Republic from the likes of the Gracchi and Saturninus is intended to set models of exemplary conduct that can serve as a valuable inspiration in the struggle against Clodius and his associates (who are not explicitly mentioned here, but are clearly central to Cicero's argument). Cicero appears to be constructing a tradition of political conduct that is favourable to the plight of the people, and sets the interest of the people against that of the senatorial nobility: the law on secret ballot of 137 BC is regarded as its starting point, but the Gracchi are sharply opposed to the political agitators of Cicero's day, who lack their authoritativeness and moral standards, and bribe their supporters in backing them, especially at public meetings. – This passages sheds light most interestingly upon an often overlooked dimension of Roman Republican politics: the role that public gatherings (political and not) had in the making of public opinion. Theatre shows could be as significant as the *contiones* summoned by a magistrate: note the reference to the competing readings of lines of plays by the poet Accius (section 102): some of his best-known lines were turned into political slogans by different factions; Cicero is clearly disapproving of the attempt of those he terms *populares* to exploit one of his lines for their own political aims.

L8   A philosophical definition of *optimates*

For all who have the power (*potestas*) of life and death over the people are tyrants (*tyranni*), but prefer to be called kings (*reges*), like Jupiter the Best. However, when a certain number of men, through their riches or birth or some other resource, hold the *res publica*, that is a faction (*factio*) – but they are called *optimates*. Yet, if the people are supremely powerful (*plurimum potest*) and everything is administered according to their wishes, that is called liberty, but in fact it is licence. But when one fears the other, a man fears another man and an order fears the other, then, since no one has confidence in their own strength, a sort of pact takes shape between the people and the powerful (*potentes*); from that state of affairs emerges this combined sort of political regime, which Scipio was praising. Thus, the matter of justice is neither nature nor desire, but weakness. For we must choose among three options: to do injustice and not to suffer it, or to do it and suffer it, or else neither to do it nor to suffer it.

Cicero, *On the* Res Publica 3.23

Cicero's interest in the political culture of his time is not just apparent in his political speeches: it also informs the whole of his philosophical production. One of the characters of his dialogue *On the* Res Publica (which survives only in fragments), Lucius Furius Philus (consul in 136) voices a critical viewpoint on the nature and aims of the nobility, and argues that their power is based on privilege, rather than merit; at the same time, he warns against the risks of unrestrained popular government. The solution he envisages is one in which the nobility and the people balance each other out, and a sort of 'mixed' constitution emerges: the case for this political regime is also made by Scipio Aemilianus elsewhere in this work, and is of course central to the assessment of the Roman 'constitution' in the sixth book of Polybius' *Histories*. – The notion of 'faction' (*factio*) receives especially hostile emphasis: far from having a neutral meaning, it denotes a clique of individuals that are not led by honourable aims (for a similar use of the term by Caesar, see **B145** and by Augustus in the very first statement of his *Res Gestae*, 'I liberated the *res publica* which had been oppressed by a despotic faction').

L9   Portrait of a Roman nobleman

[139] Quintus Metellus, in the speech that he delivered at the funeral of his father Lucius Metellus, pontiff, twice consul, *dictator*, master of the horse, member of the fifteen-man board for land assignments, who was the first man who led a procession of elephants in a triumph, having captured them in the First Punic War, left it in writing that his father had achieved the ten greatest and best things in whose quest wise men spend their lives: [140] he wanted to be a first-rate warrior, an excellent orator, a commander of the highest valour, to be in charge of matters of the greatest importance under his own auspices, to achieve the greatest honour, to be supremely wise, to be deemed the most eminent senator, to achieve great wealth through good means, to leave behind many sons, and to enjoy the highest distinction in the city (*civitas*). These things had befallen upon his father, and to no one else since the foundation of Rome.

Pliny, *Natural History* 7.139–140

The range of the Elder Pliny's reading is astounding, and encompasses a great number of works that are lost to us. He had access to the text of the eulogy delivered in 221 BC by Quintus Caecilius Metellus in honour of his father Lucius, who was consul in 251 and 247. This source lies well beyond the chronological remit of this volume, but it is of significance to our understanding of the late Republican context. The summary provided by Pliny lists the ten aims that, in Metellus' opinion, a man of high standing had to set himself, and offers an especially valuable insight into the set of key values that were asserted by the Republican nobility. Metellus' bold claim on the unprecedented extent of his father's achievements is also an instance of the strongly competitive nature of the Roman élite discourse – an aspect that becomes increasingly prominent in the last century of the Republic.

POLITICAL ASSOCIATIONS

L10   Associations (*Collegia*), 64 BC

a) Its beginning was the Crossroad Games (*ludi compitalicii*), which were then put on for the first time after the consulship of L. Julius and C. Marcius [91 BC], contrary to the authority of this order; When a certain tribune of the plebs had ordered the officials (*magistri*) to put on the games with his support, contrary to a decree of the senate (*senatus consultum*), Q. Metellus ... as consul designate, while a private citizen ordered them not to take place and by his influence (*auctoritas*) secured the point which he was not yet able to through the power of office (*potestas*). You, when the day of the *compitalicii* had fallen on the Kalends of January [1 January], you allowed Sex. Clodius, although he had never before worn the senator's toga (*toga praetexta*), to put on the games and flit around in a *toga praetexta*.

Cicero, *Against Piso* 8

b) In the consulship of L. Julius and C. Marcius... by a decree of the Senate the associations (*collegia*) that seemed to have been [organized] contrary to the interests of the *res publica* were abolished. The officials (*magistri*) of the *collegia* used to put on games just as the local officials (*magistri vici*) put on the Crossroad Games (*ludi compitalicii*), dressed in the *toga praetexta*; which games were broken up with the abolition of the *collegia*. Then six years after they had been abolished, P. Clodius, tribune of the plebs, with the enactment of a statute, restored the *collegia*. He directed the odium and the charge of their restoration on Piso because, when he was consul, he allowed Sex. Clodius in the *toga praetexta* to hold the games on 1 January before the statute was carried. He was a very close associate of Clodius and the leader of the Clodian gangs... At that time too L. Ninnius, a tribune of the plebs, attempted to prevent these games. Two years before the *collegia* were restored, Q. Metellus Celer, when consul designate, had prohibited the local officials (*magistri vici*) from holding the *ludi compitalicii*, so Cicero records, although the *ludi* were to be held with the backing of a tribune of the plebs; I have not come across the name of this tribune.

Asconius, *Commentary on Cicero's Speech Against Piso* p. 7C.9–26, with omission

In his speech against Piso of 58 BC Caesar discusses his role in aiding Clodius' initiative to restore the *collegia*, private associations of a political, professional or religious kind, which had been outlawed in 64 under a decree of the Senate. The *collegia* were linked with the performance of games. In 61 BC, by force of his influence, the consul designate Metellus Celer stopped the illegal holding of games, although those were backed by an unnamed tribune of the plebs. – 'Organized' is a textual emendation.

L11   Clodius restores the *collegia*, 58 BC
[55] Recall all the other baneful events of that year ... for laws were passed ... that the associations (*collegia*) should be restored contrary to the decree of the Senate, not only the old established ones, but that innumerable new ones should be enrolled by one gladiator ...

Cicero, *Defence of Sestius* 55, with omissions

In a polemical overview of the policies enacted by Clodius during his tribunate, Cicero includes a law for the re-establishment of the *collegia*, which undid the provisions of the senatorial decree of 64 BC. His implication is that Clodius intends to use these associations as paramilitary gangs. – Note the derogatory epithet 'gladiator', which Cicero will later use against Antony too (see *Philippics* 3.18 and 5.32, above **B179**).

ELECTIONEERING

L12   *Ambitus/largitio*: traditional practice
[44] For you must not think, Laterensis, that the measures dealing with electoral malpractice (*ambitus*) that the Senate has submitted to the will of the people had for their object the abolition of electoral rivalry, interest and popularity; there have always been good men (*boni*) who have not scrupled to desire popularity among their fellow-tribesmen. ... [45] Nor must we impose upon our children a veto which will forbid them to court the respect and affection of their fellow-tribesmen, or tell them that it is wrong for them to secure for their friends the votes of their tribes, or to look for a like service from their friends in their own elections. ... Such a course I have myself adopted, when it has been required by the exigencies of my own candidature. ...

[47] For just as I show that Plancius is a popular man in his tribe, and that he has become so by showing kindnesses to many, by acting as security for many, and by

procuring official posts for several through his father's interest and popularity, and finally that by his own merits, his father's, and those of his ancestors, he has included the whole district (*praefectura*) of Atina in the circle of his universal beneficence, so it lies with you to prove that he was an agent with whom illicit payments were deposited, that he gave out money (*largitio*), that he took down names in a written list and that he subdivided the tribal members.

Cicero, *Defence of Plancius* 44–45, 47 with omissions

In his speech in defence of Plancius, Cicero straddles a careful line of argument on the legitimate ways of securing electoral support: the legislation on electoral corruption is intended to limit abuses, but does not remove the significance of the bonds that candidates can and wish to consolidate with their potential voters, especially in their hometowns and in their tribes (i.e. electoral districts): Cicero celebrates the fact that Plancius is able to command the support of a whole community. Building such networks of support and patronage does not amount to corruption, but requires all the craft of a skilful political operator.

L13   Corruption in the consular elections for 53 BC

[2] The consuls are now subject of intense scandal, because the candidate C. Memmius read out in the Senate the agreement which he and his fellow candidate had made with the consuls: that, if they were elected consuls, they would both give them 4,000,000 sesterces if they did not provide three augurs to declare that they had been present when a law passed by popular assembly (*lex curiata*) was enacted, which had not been enacted; and two consulars to declare that they had been present at the drafting of a resolution making provision for the consular provinces when there had been no meeting of the Senate at all. This deal was said to have been made not with words, but through the account books of many persons with names and full details; it was produced by Memmius at the suggestion of Pompey with the names erased. Appius is exactly as he was: certainly no worse off. His colleague has collapsed and is obviously, I say it, laid low. [3] Memmius, however, with the break-up of the agreement against the wish of Calvinus has clearly gone cold and all the more because we understand that the revelation of Memmius is most displeasing to Caesar. Our friend Messalla and his fellow candidate Domitius have been most generous with the people. Nothing more popularly appreciated. They are sure consuls.
Rome, 1 October 54 BC.

Cicero, *To Atticus* 4.17.2–3 (SB 91)

The election of the consuls of 53 was preceded by a major corruption scandal, triggered by the revelations of the candidate C. Memmius, who claimed that he had agreed to circumvent some religious and administrative restrictions with the consuls of 54. Some documentary evidence was brought to the attention of the Senate, and Pompey played the role of someone who was working to enable the disclosure of relevant evidence. The entity of the sum involved is very significant.

L14   Legislation against bribery
a) Calpurnian statute *de ambitu*, 67 BC

Such were the events in the consulship of Acilius [Glabrio] and [Calpurnius] Piso [67 BC]; in addition a statute was enacted by the consuls themselves against those convicted of bribery with regard to magistracies: none of them should hold office, or be a member of the senate, but that they should also incur a fine in addition.

Cassius Dio, *Roman History* 36.38

In 81 BC Sulla passed a statute on electoral bribery by which the guilty were not allowed to seek office for ten years. It proved inadequate. The *lex Calpurnia* soon gained a reputation of extreme severity and the extension of legislation to include the bribery agents (*divisores* – 'those who distributed the cash') was a change of real substance. It seems also to have removed the *ius imaginum* (the right to display portrait busts of distinguished ancestors in their houses and at funerals) from the convicted (Cicero, *Defence of Sulla* 86).

b) A decree of the Senate, 64 BC

Since the scope for electoral malpractice (*ambitus*) was increasing without restraint day by day on account of the excessive recklessness of Catiline and Antonius, the Senate had decreed that a statute concerning electoral malpractice (*ambitus*) with even increased penalties should be proposed, and the tribune of the plebs, Q. Mucius Orestinus, had vetoed this proposal.

Asconius, *Commentary on Cicero's Defence of Milo* p. 83C.6–9

A remarkable case of a tribune vetoing a proposal of the Senate for a law against corruption: according to Asconius (p. 86C.1), he was colluding with Catiline, who must have had reasons to fear that the law would be used to launch a prosecution against him in the run-up to the elections.

c) Proposal of the consul M. Tullius Cicero on electoral malpractice (*ambitus*), 63 BC

You said that on my proposal the Senate passed a decree that it be deemed a contravention of the statute of Calpurnius if men were paid to meet candidates, if their companions were hired, if places were given to the tribes indiscriminately at the gladiatorial games and if dinners were given indiscriminately.

Cicero, *Defence of Murena* 67

This passage shows that a statute passed in 149 BC (the *lex Calpurnia*) still provided the basic regulatory framework on corruption matters: the Senate could pass decrees through which the offence was more carefully defined. – Note the overlap between the practices listed here and those mentioned by Cicero in the speech for Plancius (see **L12**)

DISRUPTED ELECTIONS

L15   Pompey's campaign fund, 61 BC

[12] Now elections are in prospect; into them, against the wishes of all, our Magnus is thrusting Aulus' son and in his cause he is fighting not with authority (*auctoritas*) and influence (*gratia*), but with those methods by which Philip said all fortifications could be stormed provided that a donkey laden with gold could get up to them. That consul, like the second actor, is said to have undertaken the business and to have the bribery agents (*divisores*) in his house. I do not believe that, but two vexatious decrees of the Senate have now been passed, which are thought to have been directed at the consul at the instance of Cato and Domitius: one that it be permissible for searches to be made of the houses of magistrates, the second that a person at whose house bribery agents (*divisores*) are living is acting against the interests of the *res publica*. [13] Lurco, a tribune of the plebs, a magistracy at enmity with the Aelian law, has been released from the Aelian and Fufian laws so that he can propose a law about electoral

malpractice (*ambitus*) which he, as a man with a limp, has promulgated with good auspices. And so the elections have been put off until 27 July.
Rome, early July 61 BC.

Cicero, *To Atticus* 1.16.12–13 (SB 16)

In this letter Cicero speaks candidly of Pompey's willingness to use his wealth to steer political developments; the analogy with Philip of Macedon is an uncomfortable one, as it likens Pompey (who has just returned from the East) to a king. Rumours and suspicions are rife, and also affect the serving consuls. The imminent presentation of a bill on electoral law is likely to delay the elections for the new consuls; Quintus Metellus Celer and Lucius Afranius were eventually returned.

L16   The aftermath of Luca, 56/55 BC

[41] After this, Pompey and Crassus met Caesar who had crossed over the Alps. They made a decision to canvass together for a second consulship. Once established in office they would have Caesar voted another period of office of the same duration and for themselves the most important provinces with sums of money and military force. [2] This was a conspiracy to share out power and to overthrow the constitution. [3] Many good men were at that time preparing to canvass for the consulship. When they [Pompey and Crassus] were seen in the hustings, they put off all the others, apart from one, Lucius Domitius, the husband of Porcia, the sister of Cato. Cato persuaded him not to stand down or to withdraw on the grounds that the contest was not about the consulship, but about the liberty of the Romans. [4] In fact, word went around the sensible elements still in the city that they must not permit Pompey and Crassus to unite their power so that the consulship became oppressive and overwhelming, but that one of them should be kept out of that office. [5] So they joined forces in support of Domitius, encouraging him and urging him to continue his opposition; many of those keeping silent through fear would support him at the vote. [6] Fearing this very thing, Pompey and his supporters laid an ambush for Domitius as he was going down at dawn by torchlight to the Campus Martius. [7] The torchbearer, who was standing beside Domitius, was the first to be struck and fell down dead. After that the others suffered injuries and fled, except for Cato and Domitius. [8] For Cato held Domitius back, although he himself had been wounded in the arm and urged him to stand fast and, as long as they had breath, not to give up the struggle against tyrants (Gk: tyrannoi), who were showing clearly, in making their way to the consulship by such crimes, how they would use that office. [42] However, Domitius did not withstand the danger, but sought the refuge of his house for safety. Pompey and Crassus were elected consuls.

Plutarch, *Life of Cato the Younger* 41–42.1 (continued in **B114b**)

This episode shows two political dynamics of the utmost interest in the aftermath of the Luca conference of 56 BC, in which the agreement between Pompey, Crassus, and Caesar was revived. First, a coalition gathers around an alternative candidate, and all the other contenders withdraw in order to maximize his chances of success. Secondly, Pompey does not hesitate to resort to violence and intimidation in his effort to thwart any viable competition: the assassination attempt fails, but Domitius leaves the contest. Plutarch focuses heavily on the role of Cato, who is again cast as a paragon of virtue.

BREAKDOWN IN LAW AND ORDER

L17   Unrest, January 62 BC

Meanwhile Nepos had introduced a proposal that Pompey should be summoned back with his army [for he was still in Asia] on the pretext of bringing order to the existing situation, but actually in the hope of himself gaining power through Pompey amid the disturbances he was causing because Pompey supported the plebs. The senate prevented this proposal being adopted. [2] For in the first place, the tribunes Cato and Quintus Minucius vetoed the proposals and stopped the clerk, who was reading the motion. Then when Nepos himself took the document in order to read it himself, they snatched it away from him. When even so he then attempted to speak without notes, they stopped his mouth. [3] As a result of this a battle took place between them with sticks and stones and even with swords; others joined in bringing help to one side or the other. The senators therefore convened in the senate-house that very day. They changed their dress and entrusted the consuls with the protection of the city, *'that it might suffer no harm'*. [4] At this Nepos then again took fright and immediately departed from their midst. Having issued some written statement against the Senate, he set out for Pompey, although he was not permitted to pass any night out of the city.

Cassius Dio, *Roman History* 37.43.1–4

The conspiracy of Catiline provides the background for a proposal of the tribune Metellus Nepos, which advocated a recall of Pompey to Italy to deal with the emergency: it met with widespread opposition within the Senate, which somehow anticipated the difficulties that Pompey would soon encounter in those circles. The constitutional and political position of the tribune is also significant: after his public clash with some of his fellow-tribunes, the Senate does not hesitate to envisage violent actions against him, and he decides to leave the city and join Pompey: a move that we shall also see in early 49 BC, when Curio and Antony joined Caesar. On this episode see Plutarch, *Life of Cato the Younger* 26–29.1 and Suetonius, *Divus Julius* 16.

L18   Caesar's agrarian statute, 59 BC

[6] However, Bibulus would not give in but, gaining the added support of three tribunes in his struggle, prevented the enactment of the law; finally when no other pretext for delay was left him, he declared a cessation of legal business (*iustitium*) for all the remaining days of the year during which the people could not meet in assembly in accordance with the laws. [2] Then Caesar, giving him short shrift, announced a fixed day so that enactment might take place on it; the plebs seized possession of the forum during the night. Bibulus came up with those he had got ready and forced his way through towards the Temple of the Dioscuri, from where Caesar was speaking to the people, some giving way out of respect, [3] others thinking he was not going to oppose them. When he reached the top and tried to speak in opposition, he was himself pushed down the steps and his rods of office (*fasces*) were shattered, and the tribunes and others suffered blows and injuries. [4] Thus the law was passed.

Cassius Dio, *Roman History* 38.6.1–4

The passing of Caesar's agrarian law was made possible by the political decision to overlook the religious opposition invoked by Bibulus, and to remove him physically from the forum when he refused to withdraw his opposition. It is noteworthy that the support of three tribunes for Bibulus does not appear to influence the conduct of Caesar's supporters: they are removed from the platform along with Bibulus, whose *fasces*, a symbol of official power, were broken in a gesture of deep symbolic significance.

L19 Attempts to prevent the return of Cicero by violence, 57 BC

a) If Q. Fabricius had been able to carry through against violence and sword what he had attempted to do concerning me, then I should have recovered my position in the month of January; goodwill prompted him towards my salvation, violence held him up, your authority called him back.

Cicero, *After his Return, to the Senate* 22

b) Although the resolution of the Senate was being hindered by all manner of delay, of farce and of chicanery, the day for the assembly to deal with my case finally arrived, 23 January. The author of the proposal, my very good friend Q. Fabricius, seized the *rostra* some time before daylight. Sestius, the man who is the defendant on the charge of violence, was on that day inactive: the advocate and defender of my cause did not take the initiative; he waited to see the plans of my enemies. Well now, how did these men on whose decision Sestius is summoned to court conduct themselves? Since they had seized the Forum, the Comitium, the senate-house in the dead of night with armed men, the majority of them slaves, they made an attack upon Fabricius, laid hands upon him, killed some people and wounded many.

Cicero, *Defence of Sestius* 75

c) [2] And as a result of this many other disorderly things happened; in the actual voting Clodius, knowing that that plebs would be in favour of Cicero, took the gladiators that his brother prepared in advance for the funeral games of Marcus, his relative, and burst into the assembly, wounded and killed many. [3] Thus the proposal was not ratified.

Cassius Dio, *Roman History* 39.7.2–3

Cicero denounces in emphatic terms the use of violent methods by Clodius to prevent the vote of a law for this rehabilitation; the circumstance is confirmed by Cassius Dio, a source that is usually unsympathetic towards him. The episode is remarkable, but far from exceptional, especially in the fifties. Violence could also be deployed to force the vote on a piece of legislation, curtail any dissent, and overcome any procedural opposition: the bills put forward by Sulpicius in 88 (see above **B5**) and Caesar in 59 (see **L18**) are cases in point, and their legitimacy was contested on those very grounds.

L20 Trial of Milo, 56 BC

[4] So I think things are now moving to a climax. For Pompey realizes this and he shares his knowledge with me that a plot is being hatched against his life, that C. Cato is being supported by Crassus, that funds are being made available to Clodius and that each of them is being encouraged by him, by Curio, by Bibulus and by the rest of his detractors; he must take vigorous precautions so as not to be caught unawares since the crowd that attends the assemblies (*contiones*) has become completely alienated from him, the nobility is hostile, the Senate is not sympathetic and the young men are ill disposed. And so he is getting himself ready; he is summoning men from the countryside. Clodius is also strengthening his gangs; a troop is being got ready for the Quirinalia. For that occasion we are much superior because of Milo's own forces, but a large troop is expected from Picenum and Gaul, so that we may all make a stand against Cato's proposals concerning Milo and Lentulus.
Rome, 12–15 February 56 BC.

Cicero, *To Quintus* 2.3.2–4 (SB 7)

This extract from a letter of Cicero to his brother Quintus sheds light on the volatile political climate of the year 56 BC: Crassus and Pompey appear to be set against one another, although they will soon renew their agreement with Caesar at Luca; Clodius and Milo are rallying their forces in Rome and across Italy, and there is considerable potential for large-scale political violence. C. Cato (tribune of the people in 56 BC and probably a second cousin of [M. Porcius] Cato the Younger) is leading an attack against Milo and Lentulus through two separate bills; the initiative for the recall of Lentulus from his governorship in Cilicia fails, and the bill against Milo is dropped after the Luca conference, when Pompey renews his agreement with Crassus and Caesar, and tensions with Clodius subside.

L21 Deliberate violence delays the consular elections, 56 BC

[27] They came to an agreement because they realized they had no other hope of achieving their aims as private citizens, but if they were consuls and consequently were controlling affairs themselves, in emulation of Caesar, they expected they would be a counter to him and would quickly become superior to him, as two against one. [2] And so they put aside all the pretence whereby, if any of their associates encouraged them to seek the magistracy, they declared they no longer wished to be consuls, and they went after it openly although they were previously supporting others in their canvass. [3] When they canvassed for it outside the period specified in the laws and some others and the consuls themselves in particular (for Marcellinus had some clout) made it obvious they would not allow them to be elected, they arranged for the consular elections not to take place in that year, urging on others and Gaius Cato in particular, so that, with the appointment of an *interrex*, they might seek and win the office in accordance with the laws…

[29] Meanwhile, Clodius quickly jumped over to the side of Pompey in a hope that, if he were to co-operate with him in achieving his aims at that time, he would make Pompey completely his own. He came before the crowd in his normal dress, having made no change in response to the decree, and made a speech attacking Marcellinus and the others. [2] Thus, when there occurred considerable annoyance on the part of the senators at this, Clodius left the people in the middle of his speech and rushing to the senate-house came close to being killed. For when the Senate came out to meet him, he was prevented from going inside, [3] and at that moment, hemmed in on all sides by the *equites*, he would have been torn to pieces, had he not cried out aloud and called upon the crowd for help. Many ran to him carrying fire to set the senate-house alight, if they should do him any harm. Thus he was saved, after having come so close to being killed. [30] Pompey was in no way panicked by these events, but on one occasion rushed into the senate-house doing what he could to oppose the Senate, which was about to take a vote. He prevented it from being ratified. When Marcellinus afterwards asked him in public if he really desired to be consul, in the hope that he would shrink from admitting that he was a serious candidate, he replied that he did not want the office at all for the sake of the law-abiding citizens, but he was contending for it very seriously because of the trouble-makers. [2] So he was now striving for it openly; Crassus too was asked and likewise did not admit it, but did not deny it either; as was his custom, he adopted a middle position, saying that he would do whatever was for the interest of the state. Marcellinus and all the rest were fearful of their preparation and their opposition and no longer frequented the Senate. [3] Since the number required in accordance with the laws for holding any vote concerning elections did not assemble, it was not possible to pass any measure at all concerning them, but the year thus passed away.

Cassius Dio, *Roman History* 39.27–30.3, with omissions

The agreement of Luca in 56 BC had far-reaching implications, but its implementation was not straightforward: there was opposition to the election of Pompey and Crassus to the consulship, and they had to plan their election by resorting to an elaborate ploy, publicly denying any interest in the post, and seeking to postpone the vote, in the hope that the climate might become more favourable to their candidacy. Clodius, in the meantime, had repositioned himself, showing his support for Pompey in the face of considerable senatorial hostility. Dio stresses that one of the factors that led Pompey and Crassus to seek the consulship was to strengthen their position towards their ally Caesar.

L22 Violence over elections, 53 BC

[24] Since P. Clodius had decided to harass the *res publica* in his praetorship with all manner of crime and saw that the elections of the previous year had been so dragged out that he would not be in office for many months; since he did not view this position of high office as others did but wanted to avoid L. Paulus, a citizen of distinguished quality, as a colleague and to have a complete year to tear the *res publica* apart, he suddenly abandoned his own year and transferred himself to the following year not because of some religious scruple, as happens, but so that he should have, as he himself used to say, a full and complete year to hold office as praetor, that is to overthrow the *res publica*. [25] It occurred to him that his praetorship would be lame and enfeebled with Milo as consul; he saw moreover that he was going to be consul with the full agreement of the Roman people. He betook himself to Milo's competitors, but in such a way that he alone directed their whole electoral campaign, even against their wishes; that, as he frequently used to say, he took their complete elections on his shoulders. He would assemble the tribes, he would act as agent, he would enrol a new Colline tribe with a register of the most depraved citizens. The more chaos he created, the more, day by day, Milo gained in strength. When the fellow, every ready for every wicked scheme, saw that a man of the greatest bravery, most hostile to himself, was a certain consul and realized that that fact had often been made clear through conversations, but also through the votes of the Roman people, he began to act openly and to say publicly that Milo ought to be killed. [26] He had summoned from the Apennines coarse foreign slaves through whom he had plundered state forests and harassed Etruria; you saw them. The business was not in the least concealed. For he would frequently say in public that the consulship could not be taken from Milo, but his life could. He often intimated this in the Senate, he said it in an assembly-speech (*contio*); furthermore, when M. Favonius asked him what hope he had in his madness with Milo alive, he replied that within three days, or at most a fourth, that man would be dead.

Cicero, *Defence of Milo* 24–26

A central argument of Cicero' case in favour of Milo at his trial for the assassination of Clodius is that the 'patrician tribune' had long been aiming to kill Milo, and had sought to prevent him from attaining the consulship: since Clodius was coveting the praetorship, he was determined to prevent his rival from reaching the top public office. There was no scope for peaceful coexistence in Clodius' view – or so Cicero claims.

L23 A plebeian *interrex*, 13 June 53 BC

C. Octavius tested (this) on the Ides of June, with Q. Metellus *interrex*.

CIL 1.2663c = *ILLRP* 1046 = EDCS 24700159

This extract is an inscription on a *tessera nummularia*, a token or ticket usually attached to a bag of coins by a slave giving his name, the day, the month and the year in which he tested and approved the contents. In this instance the banker himself tested the contents (see above **F14**). – C. Octavius may well be the grandfather of Augustus: 'M. Antony reproaches him [Augustus] with having.... a grandfather who was a banker' (Suetonius, *Augustus* 2.3). Q. Metellus was an *interrex* in 53 BC, when consuls were not elected until July; his full name was Q. Caecilius Metellus Pius Scipio and he was a plebeian, although *interreges* ought to have been patricians: a further sign of the unprecedented stress under which the traditional institutions of the Republic are in this period. The editor of *ILLRP*, Attilio Degrassi, notes that the year was indicated by the *interrex*, there being no consuls – the usual indication of the year.

L24   Barricades in Rome, 48 BC

For Dolabella, in despair of obtaining any pardon from Caesar, desired to accomplish some terrible deed before perishing, hoping thus to gain lasting renown; thus there are actually some men who become infatuated with the basest deeds for the sake of fame! From this motive he, too, caused confusion generally, even promising that on a certain specified day he would enact his laws in regard to debts and house-rents. On receipt of these announcements the crowd erected barricades around the Forum, setting up wooden towers at some points, and put itself in readiness to cope with any force that might oppose it. At that, Antony led down from the Capitol at dawn a large body of soldiers, cut down the tablets containing Dolabella's laws and afterwards hurled some of the trouble-makers from the very cliffs of the Capitoline. However, not even that stopped their quarrelling. Instead, the greater the number of those who perished, the greater disturbance did the survivors make, thinking that Caesar had become involved in a very great and difficult war. And they did not cease until he himself suddenly appeared before them; then they reluctantly quietened down.

Cassius Dio, *Roman History* 42.32–33

The year 48 BC is largely associated with the battle of Pharsalus and the conclusion of the Civil War, which mostly took place outside Italy: the political and social situation in Rome, however, was as tense as it had been before the outbreak of the war. P. Cornelius Dolabella, the son-in-law of Cicero, put forward policies and measures that were intended to bring about debt relief, attracting considerable and vocal support from sectors of the Roman populace: in this particular instance, a barricade was mounted in the city: not even the repression carried out by Mark Antony in his capacity as master of the horse (*magister equitum*) stopped the riot, which was inspired by a clear political aim: to secure the direct intervention of Caesar on the matter. Upon his return to Rome, he pardoned those involved in the riots. – Dio appears to regard the crowd that was involved in the barricades as a mere tool in Dolabella's hands: the economic and social significance of the issues on which the protest was based suggests that those who took part had deeper and more urgent motives than the wish to support the position of a political patron.

CITIZENSHIP: INTEGRATION AND EXCLUSION

L25   Pompeius Strabo's citizenship grant to Spanish horsemen, November 89 BC

Gnaeus Pompeius, son of Sextus, *imperator*, made Spanish horsemen (Roman) citizens on account of their valour, (in the camp) near Asculum on 17 November, according to the Julian law. On the advisory board (were): [sixty names follow]... The Salluienses squadron: ... [thirty names follow]

Gnaeus Pompeius', son of Sextus, *imperator*, in the camp near Asculum presented the Salluienses squadron on account of their valour with a small silver spear, plate, torque, armlet, chest-plates, and a double ration of corn.

ILLRP 515 = EDCS-19900038*

This bronze inscription from Rome records a collective citizenship grant that Cn. Pompeius Strabo made to a squadron of Spanish horsemen who fought under his orders during the Social War (see also Velleius 2.21.1): the Julian law of 89 BC, which provided for the citizenship grant to the Italians who had stayed loyal to Rome, provided the legal framework for that concession, which was accompanied by a set of gifts to each soldier. – The inscription also records the names of the members of the advisory board (*consilium*) of Pompeius Strabo and of the beneficiaries: the staff of Strabo included his son Cn. Pompeius (better known to posterity as Pompey the Great), M. Aemilius Lepidus (the consul of 78), and L. Sergius Catiline. – A descendant of the members of the *turma Salluitana*, P. Otacilius Arranes, is attested a generation later as a municipal magistrate at Casinum (modern Montecassino), in Latium Adiectum: his Roman name still betrays his Celtiberian origins (*CIL* 1².3107 = EDCS-26500762).

L26 Decree of the Senate (*senatus consultum*) on Asclepiades and his associates, 78 BC

In the consulship of Quintus Lutatius Catulus, son of Quintus, and Marcus Aemilius Lepidus, son of Quintus and grandson of Marcus, when the urban and peregrine praetor was Lucius Cornelius Sisenna, son of […] month of May. The consul Quintus Lutatius Catulus, son of Quintus, consulted the Senate in the Comitium on 20 May. Witnesses present at the writing were Lucius Faberius, son of Lucius, of the tribe Sergia, Gaius, son of Lucius, of the tribe Popiilia, Quintus Petillius, son of Titus, of the tribe Sergia. Whereas the consul Quintus Lutatius Catulus, son of Quintus, said that Asclepiades, son of Philinos, the Klazomenian, Polystratos, son of Polyarkos, the Karystian, Meniskos, son by adoption of Eirenaios, who was Meniskos son of Thargelios, the Milesian, as […] had been present in (their) ships at the beginning of the Italic war, had given to our state valiant and faithful service, and that he wishes, if it seems good to him, to send them back to their countries in accordance with the decree of the Senate, that to reward their fine accomplishments and brave deeds for our state, they might receive honour; concerning this matter (the senators) have decreed as follows: Asclepiades, son of Philinos, the Klazomenian, Polystratos, son of Polyarkos, the Karystian, Meniskos, son by adoption of Eirenaios, who was previously Meniskos son of Thargelios, the Milesian, are to be called fine and good men and friends (of Rome). The Senate and the people of the Romans consider that their deeds have been good, brave and loyal to our state; for this reason the Senate decides that they, their children and their descendants are to be in their own cities immune from all liturgies and from financial contributions; if any taxes have been levied on their properties since they left in the service of our state, these (taxes) are to be given back and restored in full; if any of their fields, houses or properties have been sold, since they left their home land in the service of our state, all of these are to be returned to them in full; if any fixed day for payment of debts has passed, since they left their homeland in the service of our state, this is not to be detrimental to them, and for this reason no debt owed to them is to be less valid, nor is it to be any less lawful for them to sue or exact payment (of debts); whatever inheritances have come to them or their children by chance, these they are to fully hold, possess and enjoy; whatever lawsuits they, their children, their descendants or their wives may bring against another person, or if other persons bring lawsuits against them, their children, their descendants or their wives, these men, their children, or their wives are to have the right of choice: if they wish of having the case decided in their own cities by their own laws, or before a magistrate of ours with Italian judges, or in a free city, one which has remained constantly in the friendship of the people of the Romans, wherever they may prefer, there the trial about these matters is to be held; if any judgments have been made about them in their absence, since they left their homeland, the situation is to be restored to what it was before and a trial is to take place afresh according to the decree of the Senate; if their cities owe any public debt, they are not to be obliged to contribute towards these debts; our magistrates, any of them who will farm out (the contracts for) Asia and Euboea or impose taxes on Asia and Euboea, are to take care that these men are not obliged to give anything; the consuls Quintus Lutatius and Marcus Aemilius, one of them or both, if it seems good to them, are to take care that these men be entered on the roll of friends (of Rome) and that they be permitted to set up a bronze tablet of friendship on the Capitolium and to perform a sacrifice, and (the consuls) are to instruct the urban quaestor to provide gifts for them according to the official roll, to rent a lodging and to send furnishings; if they desire, concerning their own affairs, to send envoys to the Senate or to come themselves, permission is to be granted to them, their children and descendants to come as envoys or to send them; the consuls Quintus Lutatius and Marcus Aemilius, one of them or both, if it seems good to them, are to send letters to our magistrates who are in charge of the provinces of Asia and Macedonia and to their (city) magistrates, that the Senate wishes and considers it just that these things be done in this fashion as may appear to them to be timely in keeping with the interest of the state and their own good faith. Decreed. (Tablet) of Asclepiades (son) of Philinos the Klazomenian, of Polystratos (son) of Polyarkos the Karystian, of Meniskos (son) of Eirenaios the Milesian.

ILLRP 513 = Sherk, *RDGE* no. 22 = EDCS-01000001*

There is reasonably good evidence for citizenship grants to individuals from the Western provinces in this period; less so for those from the Greek-speaking provinces. Around 62 BC Pompey granted the Roman citizenship to his friend Theophanes of Mytilene (Cicero, *Defence of Archias* 24), who also wrote an historical work about his achievements in the East. About fifteen years earlier, in 78 BC, a decree of the Senate was passed bestowing a set of legal privileges to three Greeks of Asia Minor, Asclepiades from Klazomene, Polystratos of Karystos, and Meniskos of Miletos, who had served with distinction in the Social War: they were formally declared 'friends of the Roman people' and added to the list that was preserved on the Capitol, in Rome. The privileges that the three Greeks were granted were fiscal and legal, but did not include the full set of protections and rights to which Roman citizens were entitled. – The beautiful bronze inscription found at Rome has a Latin text (fragmentary), followed by an almost complete Greek text. The text given here follows the edition in A. Raggi, '*Senatus consultum de Asclepiade Clazomenio sociisque*', *ZPE* 135 (2001) 73–116.

L27 Plotian bill on the return of the supporters of Lepidus, 70 BC
a) Also he brought about a return to the citizenship (*civitas*) for the brother of his wife, L. Cinna, and those who had followed Lepidus in that discord between citizens and who, after the death of the consul, had taken refuge with Sertorius, by means of Plotius' bill (*rogatio*) and he himself made a speech on the matter.

Suetonius, *Divus Julius* 5

b) Now he caused an amnesty to be given to all who had been with Lepidus and Sertorius; then he arranged that safety be granted to all those from that time, who had been left over from those who had been proscribed by Sulla; and he later brought them back from exile and he bestowed honours and offices upon all those who had been put to death by him.

Cassius Dio, *Roman History* 44.47.4

Caesar gave support to the followers of Lepidus and Sertorius in 70 BC, who must have had among their number new citizens resulting from the Social War; the sons of the proscribed were not so fortunate, because they had to wait until 49 BC for the full restoration to the citizen body. Hardly anything is known about the specifics of the law and its proponent, Plotius or Plautius, who might be the same person who put forward the agrarian bill mentioned in **B89**.

L28　　The sons of the proscribed, 60s BC

a) ... but great preliminary struggles awaited the consulship of Cicero. For in the first place those who were prevented from holding office by the laws of Sulla, and they were neither few nor weak, sued for offices and tried to win the favour of the people, making many charges against the tyranny of Sulla which were just and true, indeed, but disturbing the government at an improper and unseasonable time.

Plutarch, *Life of Cicero* 12.1

b) For the tribunes joined with Antony the consul, who was very similar to them in character; one of them was for supporting the sons of those proscribed by Sulla for magistracies, while another was for giving to Publius Paetus and to Cornelius Sulla, who had been convicted with him, the right to be in the Senate and to hold office.

Cassius Dio, *Roman History* 37.25.3

The legacy of the Sullan proscriptions is still open in the late sixties, during Cicero's consulship of 63 BC, as he himself admitted, see **B78** [4]: the descendants of the proscribed are pushing for their full inclusion in the citizen body and the grant of the right to be elected to public office. The example mentioned by Dio (b) shows how divisive the issue still was, and how readily it could be turned into a matter of political positioning, especially for a relatively junior, if influential, political figure like a tribune of the plebs.

L29　　Individual citizenship grants

Again, did not Gnaeus Pompeius, the father of Pompey, after his outstanding achievements in the Italian War, bestow citizenship (*civitas*) upon Publius Caesius, a Roman *eques*, a good man, still living, a citizen of Ravenna and a member of an allied state? And did not Gaius Marius grant the same status to two whole cohorts of men from Camerinum? And did not that most distinguished man Publius Crassus bestow it upon Alexas of Heraclea, a citizen of that community (*civitas*) with which an almost unique treaty is thought to have been concluded at the time of Pyrrhus, during the consulship of Gaius Fabricius? Again, did not Lucius Sulla bestow the citizenship (*civitas*) upon Ariston of Massilia?

Cicero, *Defence of Balbus* 50

In 56 BC Cicero took up the case of L. Cornelius Balbus, a notable from the Spanish city of Gades who had been granted the Roman citizenship by Pompey and whose claim was challenged in court. In setting out his argument Cicero mentions a number of comparable precedents of individuals who received the Roman franchise by concession of a Roman magistrate: the examples he quotes date from the late second century BC, and suggest a clear link between military achievement and the benefaction conferred by a magistrate. Such grants are of course quite different in intent and purpose to the grants of Roman citizenship that were bestowed upon a whole community, as was the case after the Social War.

L30　　Cisalpine Gaul

a) Cn. Pompeius Strabo, father of Pompey the Great, established the Transpadane colonies. This he did, not by introducing new colonists (*coloni*); the existing inhabitants of the towns simply stayed put, with Pompey giving them the Latin right (*ius Latii*), that is to say that they were to have the same right as any other Latin colony, namely that men there might acquire Roman citizenship by standing for local office in their own hometown.

Asconius, *Commentary on Cicero's Speech Against Piso* p. 3C.7–12

b) Comum was a modest settlement, but Pompeius Strabo, the father of Pompey the Great, established a settlement when it had suffered ill-treatment at the hands of the Rhaeti situated above it. Then Gaius Scipio added three thousand; then Divus Caesar added five thousand to the settlement, of whom five hundred were the most famous of the Greeks; and to these he gave the citizenship (Gk: *politeia*) and enrolled them among the colonists. However, they did not settle there, although they left behind to the foundation their name [*Novum Comum*].

Strabo, *Geography* 5.1.6

Communities that had previously had Latin status were given full Roman citizenship by the Julian statute of 90 BC; a law by Cn. Pompeius Strabo conferred the Latin status upon communities north of the Po, creating a pathway to Roman citizenship for the office-holding members of their élites (on the Latin right see note on **A3**) – Strabo's testimony on Comum shows that the development of some settlements in Cisalpine Gaul unfolded over several generations, and owed much to the direct involvement of major political figures in Rome: Caesar's role in the affairs of Cisalpine Gaul is especially significant, and must be understood against his background of his governorship in the province.

L31   Proposal of the tribune C. Manilius to enfranchise freedmen, 67 BC
a) Now at that time when Gaius Manilius, a tribune of the plebs, supported by a force of freedmen and slaves, was proposing the most reckless statute that freedmen should have the right of voting in all the tribes. ... Domitius had forced his way in and had broken up the meeting in such a way that many of the supporters of Manilius were killed.

Asconius, *Commentary on Cicero's Defence of Milo*, p. 45C.12–17, with omission

b) But Mallius came close to prosecution. For on the last day of the year and towards evening, having organized some of the crowd, he gave to the class of freedmen the right to vote with those who had freed them. But then on the following day, on the first day of the month on which Lucius Tullus and Aemilius Lepidus entered upon their consulship, the Senate voted to reject it.

Cassius Dio, *Roman History* 36.42.3

Dio uses 'Mallius' for 'Manilius'. – The voting rights of freedmen were a controversial political issue. In the first century in 88 BC P. Sulpicius and in 87 BC L. Cornelius Cinna had tried without success to distribute freedmen among all the tribes (see LACTOR 13, *From the Gracchi to Sulla*, under the respective years). Not only would their votes be influential in the *comitia centuriata* but their gratitude for this added influence would redound to the credit of the author of the measure. The proposal was revived in 67 BC, in a very different political context, under the initiative of a tribune: it also met with firm senatorial opposition. – Cf. the tradition on the discovery of statutes providing for the same measure among Clodius' papers after his death: Asconius, *Commentaries* p. 52C.18–21.

CIVIL RIGHTS AND POLITICAL REPRESSION

L32   Verres abuses the freedom of Roman citizens

[161] Verres suddenly ordered Gavius to be flung down, stripped naked and tied up in the open market-place, and rods to be got ready. The unhappy man cried out that he was a Roman citizen, a townsman of Compsa; that he has served in the army under a distinguished Roman *eques*, L. Raecius, who was engaged in business at Panormus and could assure Verres of the truth of his story. To this Verres replied that he had discovered that Gavius had been sent to Sicily as a spy by the leaders of the runaway slaves, a charge which was brought by no informer, for which there was no evidence, and which nobody saw any reason to believe. He then ordered the man to be flogged severely all over his body.

[162] There in the open marketplace of Messana a Roman citizen, gentlemen, was beaten with rods; and all the while, amid the crack of falling blows, no groan was heard from the unhappy man, no words came from his lips in his agony, except 'I am a Roman citizen'. By thus proclaiming his citizenship he had been hoping to avert all those blows and shield his body from torture; yet not only did he fail to secure escape from those cruel rods, but when he persisted in his entreaties and appeals to his citizen rights, a cross was made ready, yes, a cross, for that hapless and broken sufferer who had never seen such an accursed thing till then.

Cicero, *Against Verres* 2.5.161–162

Allegations of abuse against Roman citizens in the province of Sicily are an important aspect of the case against Verres: Cicero here quotes the unfortunate case of Gavius, who hailed from the Campanian town of Compsa. His status as Roman citizen would have normally made him immune from a public beating at the hands of a Roman magistrate: the only justification that could be given for inflicting that treatment upon him was to deny that he was citizen, and indeed Verres claimed that he was a member of Spartacus' slave army, or at least an abettor of it. – The episode took place at Messana, the city of the strait, in the late seventies, as the slave war was raging in the southern part of the peninsula, and there were pressing concerns that Spartacus' men might be able to make a breakthrough into Sicily.

L33   Justifiable homicide

[72] The charge concerning the death of Clodius, jurors, does not cause me any concern; I am not so demented or so ignorant and unaware of your views that I do not know what you feel about the death of Clodius. If I were unwilling so to rebut the charge as I have rebutted it, it would still be open to Milo to shout aloud and to tell the glorious lie – with impunity I killed him! I killed not a Spurius Maelius, who by lowering the price of corn and by wasting his own resources, because he appeared to be showing excessive favour to the plebs, came under suspicion of seeking to be king; not a Ti. Gracchus who, through civil strife, removed a colleague from office – their killers have filled the whole world with the glory of their names – but a man – for he would dare to say it, since he had liberated his country at his own risk – whose unspeakable adultery on the holiest couches of the gods, women of the most noble birth had detected.

Cicero, *Defence of Milo* 72

Cicero devotes the best part of his case in favour of Milo to argue that he was not responsible for the assassination of Clodius. At one point, however, he argues that even had Milo killed his enemy and were to admit to it, he would be entitled to impunity: he eliminated a man who was a danger to the *res publica* and had violated the rites of Bona Dea. He singles out the precedents of Spurius Maelius and Tiberius Gracchus as instances of great men who were lawfully killed because of the great danger they presented to the community (cf. the much more positive judgement he expressed about the Gracchi elsewhere: *On the agrarian law* 2.10); Clodius had accomplished far less significant actions, but was nonetheless a threat that it was justifiable to remove.

L34   Constitutional and moral questions, 49 BC

[1] However, not to surrender myself wholly to bitterness of spirit, I have chosen some *theses* as it were, which are both political and topical, with the object of distracting my mind from its griefs and to keep it busy on the question at issue. This sort of thing:-

[2] Ought a man to remain in his country under a tyranny? Ought he to strive for the overthrow of a tyranny by every means, even if the existence of the state is going to be endangered thereby? Ought he to beware of the overthrower lest he be set up as a tyrant? Ought he to try to help his country under a tyranny by taking opportunity as it comes and by words rather than by war? Ought a statesman to live quietly in retirement while his country is under a tyranny or ought he to take every risk for freedom's sake? Is it right to make war against one's country and blockade it when it is under tyrannical rule? Ought a man to enrol himself on the side of the best citizens even if he does not approve of overthrowing a tyranny by war? Ought he in politics to join in the danger of his friends and benefactors even though he does not approve of their actions in capital matters? Ought a man who has rendered his country great service and has on that account brought himself irreparable suffering and hostility voluntarily to incur danger on his country's behalf, or may he be allowed to think of himself and his family, giving up political opposition to those in power?

[3] Practising myself upon these questions and setting out the arguments on either side, now in Greek now in Latin, I take my mind for a while off my troubles and at the same time ponder matters of relevance.
Formiae, 12 March 49 BC.

Cicero, *To Atticus* 9.4 (SB 173)

The outbreak of the civil war between Caesar and Pompey marked the beginning of a phase that was likely to end with the victory of a would-be autocrat. Cicero chose Pompey's camp, after much deliberation, and was mindful of what the conflict would in due course bring about. In this letter we see him pondering a number of philosophical questions that were suggested to him by the ongoing political developments, and had much wider ethical resonance. Political involvement and philosophical reflection are closely linked throughout Cicero's life, especially in his final years: this text is a powerful illustration of that. The presence of Pompey and Caesar is clearly recognizable in all the questions that occur to him. – Significantly, what is underlined in this extract is written in Greek: a language that remains, even for Cicero, a master and champion of Latin prose, a very congenial vehicle for philosophical speculation and debate, especially in informal settings.

THE ARMY

L35   C. Marius recruits *proletarii*, 107 BC

Meanwhile Marius himself enlisted soldiers, not in the traditional manner nor from the assembly-group, but just as anyone was willing, for the most part individuals that were enrolled as mere persons.

Sallust, *The War against Jugurtha* 86.2

C. Marius allowed the drafting of volunteers into the army he recruited during his first consulship, in 107 BC, ahead of the campaign against the Numidian king Jugurtha. He also lifted any surviving restrictions based on property qualifications: this reform, while not insignificant, was less radical than some modern scholars have argued, since the limit had already been lowered earlier in the second century BC. Moreover, volunteers had been drafted in Scipio Aemilianus' campaign against Numantia (134 BC); on the other hand, at times of manpower shortage conscription was occasionally revived (e.g. during the Social War and the Civil Wars of the forties and the thirties). – Marius' recruitment practices enhanced a general trend in late Republican history that is both clear and historically significant: opening the army to the poor could pave the way to the emergence of semi-professional armies, made up of people with few economic prospects beyond military service, fiercely loyal to their commanders, keenly aware of the material rewards of campaigning, and driven by strong economic interests.

L36   Sulla marches against Rome and against Mithridates, 88 BC

a) They ordered him to be confident and to lead them to Rome. He was delighted and led six legions at once. And the leaders of the army, apart from one quaestor, ran off separately to Rome not accepting he should lead an army against the country; envoys meeting him on the road asked why he was advancing with arms against the country. He answered, in order to liberate it from tyrants.

Appian, *Civil Wars* 1.57

Sulla was the first to lead his army against the city; the identity of the quaestor is unknown, although some have identified him with L. Licinius Lucullus, while the leaders will have been officers, *legati*, or military tribunes. Here is manifest the close bond between the legionary soldier and the commander.

b) [5] There was the additional fact that L. Sulla had treated the army which he had led in Asia, in order to make it loyal to himself, with extravagance and with excessive lavishness. Delightful places, pleasures had easily softened the warlike mentality of the soldiers when they were doing nothing; [6] it was there that the army of the Roman people first grew used to making love and drinking, to wonder at statues, pictures, embossed vessels, to steal these from private and public sources, to plunder shrines, to defile everything sacred and profane. [7] Thus it was that these soldiers, when they gained victory, left nothing remaining for the defeated. Success wearies even the minds of wise men; still less might those of corrupt character restrain their victory.

Sallust, *Catiline's War* 11.5–7

Sallust identified in Sulla's Eastern campaign a turning point in Roman history: not so much for its military and political consequences, but because of the impact that Sulla's lax standards of discipline had, and because of the acquisitive mentality that became widespread among his troops.

L37   L. Valerius Flaccus and C. Fimbria against Mithridates: the 'Fimbrians', 86 BC

[1] Lucullus, with the legion which had been enlisted by him in Italy, crossed into Asia. There he came upon the rest of the forces, all of which had long been corrupted by greed and high-living, and the Fimbrians, as they were called, who had become difficult to handle through their growing used to lack of discipline. [2] These were the men who with Fimbria had removed Flaccus, the consul and commander, and had then betrayed Fimbria to Sulla, wilful and lawless men, warlike and resolute with experience of war. In a very short time indeed Lucullus cut out their insolence and turned around the rest. Then for the first time, so it seems, they experienced a genuine commander and leader; previously they were subject to demagogic flattery, being accustomed to campaign as the fancy took them.

Plutarch, *Life of Lucullus* 7

Since the Fimbrians had been enlisted in 86/5 BC, they had experienced almost two decades of continuous service. Some would volunteer to serve with Pompey: Pompey, therefore, decided that he had to make war, made general preparations and enrolled in addition the Valerians (Cassius Dio, *Roman History* 36.46.1).

L38   L. Licinius Murena, governor of Transalpine Gaul, 64 BC

But the province of L. Murena brought him many expressions of gratitude together with an excellent reputation. On setting out he conducted a levy in Umbria. The political situation allowed him the opportunity to exercise generosity, as a result of which he linked to himself the many tribes which are made up from the towns of Umbria.

Cicero, *Defence of Murena* 42

The governor of a province was authorized by decree to hold a levy while proceeding to his province and would thus conduct it somewhere in Italy on the route; the aim was not to recruit a full army, but to bring an already existing force up to strength. Murena, the propraetor on his way to Transalpine Gaul, was able to exercise favours which redounded to his advantage at the time of the consular elections in 63 BC.

L39   Views of the Roman army

a) The most depressing feature of this war is what Antony is promising to his bandits: first of all, town houses – for he confirms he will divide up the city – then he will lead them from all the gates and settle them wherever they want. All the Cafos, all the Saxae and the rest of the vermin which is following Antony are marking out for themselves the best houses, estates, villas at Tusculum and Alba. And furthermore these rustics, if in fact they are men and not rather cattle, are being transported on an empty hope as far as the Waters [Baiae] and Puteoli.

Cicero, *Philippics* 8.9

Among the many accusations that Cicero levels at Antony there is the charge of having made reckless promises of financial gain to his soldiers. The fertile Campanian land is an attractive target, and Cicero singles out two officers of Antony's army, Cafo and Decidius Saxa, as noteworthy examples of greed, encouraged by their criminal leader.

b)   But if the chaste wife should play her part
                         In caring for the home and sweet children
                     Like some Sabine wife or sun-burnt wife   40
                         Of a nimble Apulian,
                     She would heap up the hearth with aged logs
                         Awaiting the arrival of her weary man
                     Shutting the rich flock in wattle pens,
                         She would milk their swollen udders   45
                     And pouring the year's wine from the sweet jar
                       She would make ready the unbought meal.

Horace, *Epodes* 2.39–48

These lines of Horace's Second Epode put forward an idealized picture of the quintessential soldier: the emphasis on his Italic background (note the references to Sabine and Apulia) are very much in keeping with the place that Italy has in Octavian's political discourse – the *Epodes* were published in 30 BC. Stressing this overlap does not of course amount to dismissing an original poet like Horace as a spokesman of the new regime.

c)   Has the soldier of Crassus lived with a barbarian wife   5
                     A shameful wife grown old in the armies
                       – Alas the shame of the Senate and changed ways –
                     Of fathers-in-law our enemies

                     Marsian and Apulian under a Parthian king
                     Sacred shields and name and toga,   10
                       And sacred Vesta forgotten,
                       With Jupiter and city of Rome unharmed?

Horace, *Odes* 3.5.5–12

The war prisoner, caught after the defeat of Crassus at Carrhae in 53 BC, is typically a rural citizen of Marsic or Apulian stock. The first three books of Horace's *Odes* were published in 23 BC. The captured standards and prisoners would be restored in 20 BC.

APPENDIX A

CONSULS 88-31 BC

All dates are BC. This list is essentially derived from A. Cooley, *The Cambridge Manual of Latin Epigraphy* (Cambridge, 2012) 455–457.

88	L. Cornelius Sulla – Q. Pompeius Rufus
87	Cn. Octavius – L. Cornelius Cinna
	[suffect: L. Cornelius Merula, in place of Cornelius Cinna]
86	L. Cornelius Cinna II – C. Marius VII
	[suffect: L. Valerius Flaccus, in place of Marius]
85	L. Cornelius Cinna III – Cn. Papirius Carbo
84	Cn. Papirius Carbo II – L. Cornelius Cinna IV
83	L. Cornelius Scipio Asiagenus – C. Norbanus
82	C. Marius – Cn. Papirius Carbo III
81	M. Tullius Decula – Cn. Cornelius Dolabella
	[dictator: L. Cornelius Sulla Felix]
80	L. Cornelius Sulla Felix II – Q. Caecilius Metellus Pius
79	P. Servilius Vatia Isauricus – Ap. Claudius Pulcher
78	M. Aemilius Lepidus – Q. Lutatius Catulus
77	D. Iunius Brutus – Mam. Aemilius Lepidus Livianus
76	Cn. Octavius – C. Scribonius Curio
75	L. Octavius – C. Aurelius Cotta
74	L. Licinius Lucullus – M. Aurelius Cotta
73	M. Terentius (Licinius) Varro Lucullus – C. Cassius (Longinus ?)
72	L. Gellius Publicola – Cn. Cornelius Lentulus Clodianus
71	P. Cornelius Lentulus Sura – Cn. Aufidius Orestes
70	Cn. Pompeius Magnus – M. Licinius Crassus
69	Q. Hortensius Hortalus – Q. Caecilius Metellus Creticus
68	L. Caecilius Metellus – Q. Marcius Rex
	[suffect: (Servilius ?) Vatia]
67	C. Calpurnius Piso – M'. Acilius Glabrio
66	M. Aemilius Lepidus – L. Volcacius Tullus
65	[P. Cornelius Sulla] – [P. Autronius (? Paetus)]
	L. Aurelius Cotta – L. Manlius Torquatus
64	L. Iulius Caesar – C. Marcius Figulus
63	M. Tullius Cicero – C. Antonius (? Híbrida)
62	D. Iunius Silanus – L. Licinius Murena
61	M. Pupius Piso Frugi Calpurnianus – M. Valerius Messalla Niger
60	Q. Caecilius Metellus Celer – L. Afranius
59	C. Iulius Caesar – M. Calpurnius Bibulus
58	L. Calpurnius Piso Caesoninus – A. Gabinius
57	P. Cornelius Lentulus Spinther – Q. Caecilius Metellus Nepos
56	Cn. Cornelius Lentulus Marcellinus – L. Marcius Philippus
55	Cn. Pompeius Magnus II – M. Licinius Crassus II
54	L. Domitius Ahenobarbus – Ap. Claudius Pulcher
53	Cn. Domitius Calvinus – M. Valerius Messalla Rufus

52	Cn. Pompeius Magnus III – Q. Caecilius Metellus Pius Scipio
51	Ser. Sulpicius Rufus – M. Claudius Marcellus
50	L. Aemilius (Lepidus) Paullus – C. Claudius Marcellus
49	C. Claudius Marcellus – L. Cornelius Lentulus Crus
48	C. Iulius Caesar II – P. Servilius Vatia Isauricus
47	Q. Fufius Calenus – P. Vatinius
46	C. Iulius Caesar III – M. Aemilius Lepidus
45	C. Iulius Caesar IV [abdicated about 1st October]
	Q. Fabius Maximus – C. Trebonius
	[suffect: C. Caninius Rebilus, in place of Q. Fabius Maximus]
44	C. Iulius Caesar V – M. Antonius
	[suffect: P. Cornelius Dolabella, in place of Caesar]
43	C. Vibius Pansa Caetronianus – A. Hirtius
	[suffects: C. Iulius Caesar – Q. Pedius (in place of both consuls, from August; C. Carrinas – P. Ventidius Bassus]
42	M. Aemilius Lepidus II – L. Munatius Plancus
41	L. Antonius Pietas – P. Servilius (Vatia) Isauricus
40	Cn. Domitius Calvinus II – C. Asinius Pollio
	[suffects: L. Cornelius Balbus – P. Canidius Crassus]
39	L. Marcius Censorinus – C. Calvisius Sabinus
	[suffects: C. Cocceius Balbus – P. Alfenus Varus]
38	Ap. Claudius Pulcher – C. Norbanus Flaccus
	[suffects: L. Cornelius – L. Marcius Philippus]
37	M. (Vipsanius) Agrippa – L. Caninius Gallus
	[suffect: T. Statilius Taurus (in place of Caninius Gallus)]
36	L. Gellius Publicola – M. Cocceius Nerva
	[suffects: L. Nonius Asprenas – Q. Marcius [? Philippus]
35	L. Cornificius – Sex. Pompeius
	[suffects: P. Cornelius Dolabella – T. Peducaeus]
34	M. Antonius II – L. Scribonius Libo
	[suffects: L. Sempronius Atratinus (in place of Antonius); Jul.: Paullus Aemilius Lepidus – C. Memmius; Sep.?: M. Herennius]
33	Imp. Caesar II – L. Volcacius Tullus
	[suffects: Jan., L. Autronius Paetus (in place of Caesar); L. Flavius; May, C. Fonteius Capito; Jul., M. Acilius Glabrio; Sep., L. Vinicius; Oct., Q. Laronius]
32	Cn. Domitius Ahenobarbus – C. Sosius
	[suffects: L. Cornelius – M. Valerius Messalla]
31	Imp. Caesar III – M. Valerius Messalla Corvinus
	[suffects: May, M. Titius; Oct., Cn. Pompeius]

APPENDIX B

SENATUS CONSULTUM ULTIMUM

This appendix provides an overview of the evidence for the emergency decrees of the Senate (the *senatus consulta ultima*) that were passed during the late Republican period. It covers a wider time span than that covered in this volume.

1. 121 BC, against Gaius Gracchus and his supporters

The Senate once decreed that the consul L. Opimius should see to it that the *res publica* suffer no harm.

Cicero, *Catilinarians* 1.4

Since the consul L. Opimius spoke about the *res publica*, they resolved that the consul L. Opimius should defend the *res publica*. Thus the Senate acted with words, Opimius with arms.

Cicero, *Philippics* 8.14

2. 100 BC, against L. Appuleius Saturninus and C. Servilius Glaucia

A decree of the Senate was passed that the consuls, C. Marius and L. Valerius, call upon the tribunes of the plebs and the praetors, whom they considered fit, and that they see to it that the empire and majesty of the Roman people be preserved.

Cicero, *Defence of Rabirius Charged with Treason* 20

The consuls were instructed to choose 'praetors whom they consider fit', because Glaucia was actually praetor at the time.

3. 77 BC, against M. Aemilius Lepidus

My proposal, therefore, is this: whereas <M.> Lepidus, contrary to the *auctoritas* of this order, has raised an army on his own private initiative with the worst elements and enemies of the *res publica* and is leading it against the city, that the *interrex* Ap. Claudius with the proconsul Q. Catulus and the others who have legitimate authority (*imperium*), defend the city, and see to it that the *res publica* comes to no harm.

Sallust, *Histories* 1.67.22 McG = 67 R.

This proposal concludes the speech of L. Marcius Philippus in the Senate.

4. 21 October 63 BC, against Catiline and Manlius

We possess a decree of the Senate against you, Catiline, powerful and authoritative; the *res publica* does not lack the counsel and authority of this order.

Cicero, *Catilinarians* 1.3

And so, as regularly happens in a dire crisis, the Senate decreed that the consuls should see to it that the *res publica* suffer no harm.

Sallust, *Catiline's War* 29.2

5. 62 BC, against Metellus Nepos

The senators forthwith assembled in the senate-house, changed their attire, and entrusted to the consuls the protection of the city so that it might suffer no harm.

Cassius Dio, *Roman History* 37.43.3

In 62 BC the tribune Q. Caecilius Metellus Nepos, an ally of Pompey, publicly criticized Cicero's handling of Catiline's conspiracy and urged that Pompey be recalled to Italy and put in charge of the campaign against Catiline. The proposal met with widespread opposition, in which another tribune, Cato the Younger, had a leading role; Nepos was not even allowed to read out his proposal in the Senate. Violence ensued in the city, and the Senate passed a *senatus consultum ultimum*. Nepos fled Rome and joined Pompey; he later went on to have a successful career, holding the consulship in 57 BC. – According to Suetonius, *Divus Julius* 16.1, Julius Caesar (then a praetor) was a vocal supporter of Nepos, and was removed from office along with the tribune by decree of the Senate (*decreto patrum*), only to be reinstated by overwhelming popular pressure.

6. 52 BC, against Milo and anarchy in Rome

And first of all a decree of the Senate was passed that the *interrex* and the tribunes of the plebs and Pompey, who as proconsul was near the city, should see to it that the *res publica* suffer no harm.

Asconius, *Commentary on Cicero's Defence of Milo* p.34C.2–5

There being no curule magistrates in office, owing to violence and disorder, only the *interrex*, tribunes and Pompeius were available. – See above, **L23**

7. January 49 BC, against Julius Caesar

To Tiro. … Our friend Antony and Q. Cassius, driven out by no show of force, set out with Curio for Caesar, after the Senate had given the consuls, the praetors, the tribunes of the plebs and us, who are proconsuls, the task that we take care that the *res publica* suffer no harm.

Outside Rome, 12 January 49 BC.

Cicero, *To his Friends* 16.11.2 (SB 143)

See **B144**.

Recourse was had to that last and final decree of the Senate … that the consuls, praetors, tribunes of the plebs and the proconsuls who were near the city, should see to it that the *res publica* suffer no harm.

Caesar, *Civil War* 1.5

This is the one literary text which uses the phrase 'final decree' [*extremum atque ultimum senatus consultum*], the term most commonly used by modern scholars. The decree was also used in 48 BC against Caelius Rufus, in 47 BC against Cornelius Dolabella and in 43 against M. Antony and Octavian.

8. January 1 43 BC

Wherefore . . . . . I propose that the entire *res publica* be entrusted to the consuls and that they be given leave to defend the *res publica* and to take precautions that the *respublica* suffer no harm.

Cicero, *Philippics* 5.34

This proposal, which Cicero attempted without success in the Senate against Mark Antony, probably gives the fullest version of the decree.

APPENDIX C

TRIBUNICIAN VETOES

This appendix provides a list of occasions, which are recorded in the text of the LACTOR, where tribunes interposed a veto: it is, therefore, not a complete record. Tribunes interposed a veto to block proposals (*rogationes*) or actions of other tribunes or decrees of the Senate (*senatus decreta*), in which case it might be recorded as an authoritative statement of the Senate (*senatus auctoritas*).

1. 67 BC: the tribunes L. Trebellius, L. Roscius Otho and P. Servilius Globulus vetoed the proposal of A. Gabinius to give Pompey a command against the pirates.
2. 67 BC: the tribune P. Servilius Globulus vetoed the proposal of C. Cornelius concerning exemption from the laws.
3. 67 BC: colleagues of C. Cornelius vetoed most of several other proposals of C. Cornelius.
4. 66 BC: tribunes threatened to veto the appointment of A. Gabinius as *legatus* to Pompey in his command against Mithridates.
5. 65 BC: a tribune vetoed a decree of the Senate against L. Catiline and Cn. Piso for their involvement with P. Sulla and Autronius, who had been convicted of *ambitus* in the elections of 66 BC.
6. 64 BC: Q. Mucius Orestinus vetoed a proposed decree of the Senate on *ambitus*.
7. 63 BC: L. Caecilius Rufus promised to veto the land proposal of P. Servilius Rullus; the proposal was never put forward.
8. 63 BC: Q. Metellus Nepos used his veto to block Cicero addressing people upon the termination of his consulship.
9. 62 BC M. Porcius Cato and Q. Minucius Thermus blocked the proposals of their colleague Q. Metellus Nepos that Pompey should be summoned home to command against Catiline and to stand for the consulship. Disorder ensued and take up the the SCU was passed.
10. 61 BC: Q. Fufius Calenus vetoed a senatorial decree concerning the judicial procedure in the matter of P. Clodius and the *Bona Dea*.
11. 58 BC: L. Ninnius Quadratus withdrew his proposed veto against the first proposals of P. Clodius, following agreement with Cicero, and himself was subsequently dishonoured by Clodius.
12. 57 BC: Sex. Atilius Serranus Gavianus opposed the recall of Cicero in the Senate on 1 January 57 BC; fearing to veto, he sought an adjournment and proceeded thereafter to talk the debate out.
13. 57 BC: Sex. Atilius Serranus Gavianus vetoed a senatorial decree in favour of the restoration to Cicero of his house on the Palatine and its rebuilding.
14. 56 BC: C. Porcius Cato used his veto to block the holding of elections, in the interests of Crassus and Pompey.
15. 55 BC: P. Aquillius Gallus and C. Ateius Capito intended to veto the proposal of their colleague C. Trebonius to give provincial commands to the consuls Pompey and Crassus, but were physically prevented from doing so.

16. 52 BC: T. Munatius Plancus Byrsa, with the support of Pompey, blocked, presumably by veto, the convoking of the patricians to hold the election of an *interrex*.

17. 51 BC: tribunes friendly to Caesar blocked with the use of their vetoes the proposal of the consul M. Marcellus that Caesar should be superseded in the Gallic provinces.

18. 51 BC: on 30 September, four tribunes, C. Coelius, L. Vinicius, P. Cornelius, C. Vibius Pansa, used their vetoes to block a number of senatorial resolutions concerning Caesar and the Gallic provinces.

19. 50 BC: from 1 March onwards the tribune C. Scribonius Curio used his veto to block the appointment of successors to Caesar in the Gallic provinces; at the beginning of December Curio opposed the consul C. Marcellus, when the latter first tried to censure him and then proposed that Pompey be given forces to the rumoured invasion of Italy by Caesar, which Curio showed to be false.

20. 49 BC: on 1 January, the tribunes M. Antony and Q. Cassius, vetoed the decree of the Senate that Caesar dismiss his army before a certain date. On 7 January, the *senatus consultum ultimum* was passed and the tribunes, together with Curio, were advised that their safety in the city could no longer be guaranteed. In disguise they made their way to the camp of Caesar.

21. 49 BC: L. Marcius Philippus, tribune, vetoed a proposal to send Faustus Sulla to Mauretania to gain allies there for Pompey.

APPENDIX D

THE ROMAN CALENDAR

the following diagram of the Roman calendar is derived mainly from A. G. Michels, *The Calendar of the Roman Republic* (Princeton, 1967). Other important studies: M. Beard, J. North and S. Price, *Religions of Rome* (Cambridge, 1998); J. Scheid, *An Introduction to Roman Religion* (Edinburgh, 2003); J. Rüpke, *The Roman Calendar from Numa to Constantine: Time, History, and the Fasti* (Oxford, 2011).

The entry for each day gives: 1. day of the month; 2. the sequence of the nundinal days [a-h, which marked the eight-day period between nundinae market days]; 3. the day of the Roman calendar; 4. the character of each day (in **bold type**). On nundinal days Michels, Calendar, pp. 27–28 and 84–89 provide essential details and explanation.

The Roman calendar had twelve months: *Ianuarius, Februarius, Martius, Aprilis, Maius, Iunius, Quinctilis, Sextilis, September, October, November,* and *December*. These are all adjectives to which the Romans added *mensis* (month). The latter sixth months are numerical, and reveal clearly that the year originally began on the Kalends of Martius; the first six months have character names. The intercalated month was *mensis intercalaris. Quinctilis* was renamed *Iulius* in 44 BC, *Sextilis Augustus* in 8 BC.

Four months in the year, March, May, Quinctilis [July, after Julius Caesar] and October had 31 days; the rest, excepting February [28 days], had 29 days, making a total of 355 days. It was therefore necessary regularly to adjust the calendar so as to keep it in sequence with the solar year. This was the task of the college of *pontifices*; the means was to intercalate a month, by which February was shortened either to 23 or 24 days, and then followed by an 'intercalary' month of 27 days, or, as some scholars reckon, the intercalary month commenced on 24 February and was of 27 or 28 days.

The intercalary month is shown after the 12 regular months of the year. In the late Republic, owing to the rather haphazard operation of the *pontifices*, the calendar could get seriously out of sequence. The matter was finally put to right by Julius Caesar in 46 BC. No further changes were made until the reform of Pope Gregory XIII in AD 1582.

The Romans reckoned their calendar backwards from three fixed days each month: **Kalends**, 1st day each month; **Nones**, 5th [short months] or 7th [long months, March, May, Quinctilis, October]; **Ides [EIDUS]**, 13th [short months] or 15th [long months]. The diagram below clarifies this arrangement.

Each day also had a specific character: **C** *dies comitialis* [comitial day], on which voting assemblies [*comitia*] of the Roman people could be held (unless it were a market day, *nundinae*); **F** *dies fasti*, on which court proceedings might be held (they were also possible on *nundinae*); **N** *dies nefasti*, on which neither *comitia* nor court proceedings could be held; **EN** *dies endotercissi* [falling between days], which were *nefasti* morning and evening, but *fasti* in between; **NP**, of which there are 49 in the year, whose precise definition is unclear: they all occur either on named festival days or the Ides, apart from the Kalends, March, in origin the beginning of the Roman year. They were clearly *feriae*, public holidays.

Diagram of the Calendar: January to June

IAN		FEB		MAR		APR		MAI		IUN	
1a **KAL**	F	1f **KAL**	N	1b **KAL**	NP	1a **KAL**	F	1f **KAL**	F	1e **KAL**	N
2b IV	F	2g IV	N	2c VI	F	2b IV	F	2g VI	F	2f IV	F
3c III	C	3h III	N	3d V	C	3c III	C	3h V	C	3g III	C
4d PR	C	4a PR	N	4e IV	C	4d PR	C	4a IV	C	4h PR	C
5e **NON**	F	5b **NON**	N	5f III	C	5e **NON**	N	5b III	C	5a **NON**	N
6f VIII	F	6c VIII	N	6g PR	C	6f VIII	N	6c PR	C	6b VIII	N
7g VII	C	7d VII	N	7h **NON**	F	7g VII	N	7d **NON**	F	7c VII	N
8h VI	C	8e VI	N	8a VIII	F	8h VI	N	8e VIII	F	8d VI	N
9a V	NP	9f V	N	9b VII	C	9a V	N	9f VII	N	9e V	N
10b IV	EN	10g IV	N	10c VI	C	10b IV	N	10g VI	C	10f IV	N
11c III	NP	11h III	N	11d V	C	11c III	N	11h V	N	11g III	N
12d PR	C	12a PR	N	12e IV	C	12d PR	N	12a IV	C	12h PR	N
13e **EID**	NP	13b **EID**	NP	13f III	EN	13e **EID**	NP	13b III	N	13a **EID**	NP
14f XVII	EN	14c XVI	N	14g PR	NP	14f XVII	N	14c PR	C	14b XVII	N
15g XVI	NP	15d XV	NP	15h **EID**	NP	15g XVI	NP	15d **EID**	NP	15c XVI	*F
16h XV	C	16e XIV	EN	16a XVII	F	16h XV	C	16e XVII	F	16d XV	C
17a XIV	C	17f XIII	NP	17b XVI	NP	17a XIV	N	17f XVI	C	17e XIV	C
18b XIII	C	18g XII	C	18c XV	C	18b XIII	N	18g XV	C	18f XIII	C
19c XII	C	19h XI	C	19d XIV	NP	19c XII	NP	19h XIV	C	19g XII	C
20d XI	C	20a X	C	20e XIII	C	20d XI	N	20a XIII	C	20h XI	C
21e X	C	21b IX	F	21f XII	C	21e X	NP	21b XII	NP	21a X	C
22f IX	C	22c VIII	C	22g XI	N	22f IX	N	22c XI	N	22b IX	C
23g VIII	C	23d VII	NP	23h X	F	23g VIII	NP	23d X	NP	23c VIII	C
24h VII	C	24e VI	N	24a IX	*F	24h VII	C	24e IX	*F	24d VII	C
25a VI	C	25f V	C	25b VIII	C	25a VI	NP	25f VIII	C	25e VI	C
26b V	C	26g IV	EN	26c VII	C	26b V	C	26g VII	C	26f V	C
27c IV	C	27h III	NP	27d VI	C	27c IV	C	27h VI	C	27g IV	C
28d III	C	28a PR	C	28e V	C	28d III	C	28a V	C	28h III	C
29e PR	C			29f IV	C	29e PR	C	29b IV	C	29a PR	C
				30g III	C			30c III	C		
				31h PR	C			31d PR	C		

The intercalary month:

INTER	1g **KAL** F	2h IV F	3a III C	4b PR C	5c **NON** F
6d VIII F	7e VII C	8f VI C	9g V C	10h IV C	11a III C
12b PR C	13c **EID** NP	14d XV F	15e XIV C	16f XIII C	17g XII C
18h XI C	19a X C	20b IX C	21c VIII C	22d VII C	23e VI N
24f V C	25g IV EN	26h III NP	27a PR C		

Diagram of the Calendar: Quinctilis [July] to December

QVI	SEX	SEPT	OCT	NOV	DEC
1b **KAL** N	1a **KAL** F	1f **KAL** F	1c **KAL** N	1b **KAL** F	1g **KAL** N
2c VI N	2b IV F	2g IV F	2d VI F	2c IV F	2h IV N
3d V N	3c III C	3h III C	3e V C	3d III C	3a III N
4e IV N	4d PR C	4a PR C	4f IV C	4e PR C	4b PR C
5f III NP	5e **NON** F	5b **NON** F	5g III C	5f **NON** F	5c **NON** F
6g PR N	6f VIII F	6c VIII F	6h PR C	6g VIII F	6d VIII F
7h **NON** N	7g VII C	7d VII C	7a **NON** F	7h VII C	7e VII C
8a VIII N	8h VI C	8e VI C	8b VIII F	8a VI C	8f VI C
9b VII N	9a V C	9f V C	9c VII C	9b V C	9g V C
10c VI C	10b IV C	10g IV C	10d VI C	10c IV C	10h IV C
11d V C	11c III C	11h III C	11e V NP	11d III C	11a III NP
12e IV C	12d PR C	12a PR N	12f IV C	12e PR C	12b PR EN
13f III C	13e **EID** NP	13b **EID** NP	13g III NP	13f **EID** NP	13c **EID** NP
14g PR C	14f XVII F	14c XVII F	14h PR EN	14g XVII F	14d XVII F
15h **EID** NP	15g XVI C	15d XVI N	15a **EID** NP	15h XVI C	15e XVI NP
16a XVII F	16h XV C	16e XV C	16b XVII F	16a XV C	16f XV C
17b XVI C	17a XIV NP	17f XIV C	17c XVI C	17b XIV C	17g XIV NP
18c XV C	18b XIII C	18g XIII C	18d XV C	18c XIII C	18h XIII C
19d XIV NP	19c XII F	19h XII C	19e XIV NP	19d XII C	19a XII NP
20e XIII C	20d XI C	20a XI C	20f XIII C	20e XI C	20b XI C
21f XII NP	21e X NP	21b X C	21g XII C	21f X C	21c X NP
22g XI C	22f IX EN	22c IX C	22h XI C	22g IX C	22d IX C
23h X NP	23g VIII NP	23d VIII C	23a X C	23h VIII C	23e VII NP
24a IX N	24h VII C	24e VII C	24b IX C	24a VII C	24f VII C
25b VIII NP	25a VI NP	25f VI C	25c VIII C	25b VI C	25g VI C
26c VII C	26b V C	26g V C	26d VII C	26c V C	26h V C
27d VI C	27c IV NP	27h IV C	27e VI C	27d IV C	27a IV C
28e V C	28d III C	28a III C	28f V C	28e III C	28b III C
29f IV C	29e PR C	29b PR C	29g IV C	29f PR C	29c PR C
30g III C			30h III C		
31h PR C			31a PR C		

There were 195 *dies comitiales* [C]; 58 *dies nefasti* [N]; 49 days classified as **NP**, whose precise character is unclear, but which were festival days of some sort; 45 *dies fasti* [including 3 *dies fissi*, marked *F in the diagram, which are half *fasti* and half *nefasti*;] 8 *dies endotercissi* [EN], making a total of 355 days in the Roman year.

BIBLIOGRAPHY

This bibliography is weighted towards publications that have appeared over the last thirty years or so, and is restricted to English-speaking scholarship.

Works that are listed in 'General' are not listed subsequently under specific topics. For further reading suggestions see the bibliographies of the ninth and tenth volumes of the second edition of the *Cambridge Ancient History* (Cambridge, 1994 and 1996) and C. Steel, *The End of the Roman Republic* (Edinburgh, 2013).

Commentaries and other books on the main literary sources
Appian: K. Welch, ed., *Appian's Roman History* (Swansea, 2015)

Asconius: R. G. Lewis, *Asconius. Commentaries on Speeches by Cicero* (Oxford, 2006)

Caesar: A. Riggsby, *Caesar in Gaul and Rome. War in Words* (Austin, 2006); J. M. Carter, *Caesar. The Civil War*, 2 vols. (Warminster, 1991–1993); L. Grillo, *The Art of Caesar's* Bellum Civile*: Literature, Ideology, and Community* (Cambridge, 2012).

Cassius Dio: R. Meyer, *From Republic to Principate: an Historical Commentary on Cassius Dio's Roman History, Books 49–52 (36–29 B.C.)* (Atlanta, 1988); J. Rich, *Cassius Dio: The Augustan Settlement (Roman History 53–55.9)* (Warminster, 1988).

Cicero: *Letters*, ed. D. R. Shackleton Bailey (Cambridge Classical Texts and Commentaries): *Cicero's Letters to Atticus* (6 vols); *Cicero, Epistulae ad familiares* (2 vols); *Cicero, Epistulae ad Quintum fratrem et M. Brutum* (1 vol)); A. R. Dyck, *Cicero, Catilinarians* (Cambridge, 2008). General overviews: A. Lintott, *Cicero as Evidence* (Oxford, 2008); J. Murrell, *Cicero and the Roman Republic* (Cambridge, 2008); C. Steel ed., *The Cambridge Companion to Cicero* (Cambridge, 2013).

Plutarch: C. Pelling, *Plutarch, Caesar* (Oxford, 2012), *Plutarch, Life of Antony* (Cambridge, 1988); J. L. Moles, *Plutarch. Life of Cicero* (Warminster, 1989); A. Lintott. *Plutarch: Demosthenes and Cicero* (Oxford, 2013).

Sallust: J. T. Ramsey, *Sallust's Bellum Catilinae* (Oxford and New York 2007); P. McGushin, *Sallust The Histories* (Oxford 1994).

Suetonius: D. Wardle, *Suetonius. Life of Augustus* (Oxford, 2014).

Velleius: A. J. Woodman, *Velleius Paterculus. The Caesarian and Augustan Narrative* (Cambridge, 1983).

General
Cambridge Ancient History, volumes 9 and 10 (Cambridge, 1994² and 1996²).

M. Dillon and L. Garland, *Ancient Rome: From the Early Republic to the Assassination of Julius Caesar* (London and New York, 2015²).

C. Steel, *The End of the Roman Republic 146 to 44 BC: Conquest and Crisis* (Edinburgh, 2013).

H. Scullard, *From the Gracchi to Nero* (London, 1963, 2nd ed.) 71–177.

N. Rosenstein and R. Morstein Marx eds., *A Companion to the Roman Republic* (Oxford, 2006).

H. Flower ed., *The Cambridge Companion to the Roman Republic* (Cambridge, 2004).

P. A. Brunt, *Social Conflicts in the Roman Republic* (London, 1971).

P. A. Brunt, *The Fall of the Roman Republic and Related Essays* (Oxford, 1988).

M. H. Crawford, *The Roman Republic* (London, 1992²).

M. Beard and M.H. Crawford, *Rome in the Late Republic: Problems and Interpretations* (London, 1999²).

F. Millar, *Rome, the Greek World, and the East. Vol. 1: The Roman Republic and the Augustan Revolution* (Chapel Hill, 2002).

PART I: NARRATIVE

A Prologue: Land and Politics in Republican Italy, 133–88 BC

D. Stockton, *The Gracchi* (Oxford, 1979).

L. de Ligt and S.J. Northwood eds., *People, Land, and Politics. Demographic Developments and the Transformation of Roman Italy, 300 BC–AD 14* (Leiden and Boston, 2008).

A. Launaro, *Peasants and Slaves. The Rural Population of Roman Italy (200 BC–AD 100)* (Cambridge, 2011).

H. Mouritsen, *Italian Unification: A Study in Ancient and Modern Historiography* (London, 1998).

F. Santangelo, 'The Social War', in G. Bradley and G. Farney eds., *The Peoples of Italy* (Berlin and New York, 2017) 233–55.

The Eighties

F. Santangelo, *Marius* (London, 2016) 71–94.

E. Badian, 'Waiting for Sulla', *Journal of Roman Studies* 52 (1962) 47–62.

B. Frier, 'Sulla's Propaganda: the Collapse of the Cinnan Republic', *American Journal of Philology* 92 (1971) 585–604

The Civil War and Sulla's Victory

F. Santangelo, *Sulla, the Elites and the Empire. A Study of Roman Policies in Italy and the Greek East* (Leiden and Boston, 2007).

A. Thein, 'Reflecting on Sulla's Clemency', *Historia* 63 (2014) 166–86.

A. Thein, 'Booty in the Sullan Civil War, 83–82 BC', *Historia* 65 (2016) 450–72.

C. Steel, 'The Roman Senate and the Post-Sullan *res publica*', *Historia* 63 (2014) 323–39.

After Sulla, 78–71 BC

E. S. Gruen, *The Last Generation of the Roman Republic* (Berkeley, 1974) 6–46.

F. Santangelo, 'Roman Politics in the Seventies: a Story of Realignments?', *Journal of Roman Studies* 104 (2014) 1–14.

P. O. Spann, *Quintus Sertorius and the Legacy of Sulla* (Fayetteville, 1987).

A. Schiavone, *Spartacus* (Cambridge, Mass. and London, 2013).

A year of changes: 70 BC

R. Seager, *Pompey. A Political Biography* (London, 2002) 30–39.

A. M. Ward, *Marcus Crassus and the Late Roman Republic* (Columbia and London, 1977) 99–112.

Political fronts, home and away: 69–64 BC

E. S. Gruen, *The Last Generation*, 47–82.

K. Tempest, *Cicero. Politics and Persuasion in Ancient Rome* (London, 2011) 59–83.

H. van der Blom, *Oratory and Political Career in the Late Roman Republic* (Cambridge, 2016) 113–247.

63 BC: a fateful year?

R. Seager, 'The First Catilinarian Conspiracy', *Historia* 13 (1964) 338–47.

T. N. Mitchell, *Cicero. The Ascending Years* (New Haven, 1979) 205–219.

J. Murrell, *Cicero and the Roman Republic* (Cambridge, 2008) 56–72.

A new context: Caesar's consulship

C. Meier, *Caesar* (London, 1995) 204–223.

T. Stevenson, *Julius Caesar and the Transformation of the Roman Republic* (London and New York, 2014).

Civic disruption, 58–52 BC

K. Morrell, *Pompey, Cato, and the Governance of the Roman Empire* (Oxford, 2017).

W. J. Tatum, *Clodius. The Patrician Tribune* (Chapel Hill, 1999) 63–78.

The run-up to the Civil War

C. Steel, 'The *Lex Pompeia de Provinciis* of 52 B.C.: a Reconsideration', *Historia* 61 (2012), 83–93.

R. Morstein–Marx, 'Caesar's alleged fear of prosecution and his *ratio absentis*', *Historia* 56 (2007), 159–78.

Beyond the Rubicon: the Civil War

M. Griffin ed., *A Companion to Julius Caesar* (Oxford and Malden, 2009).

L. Grillo, *The Art of Caesar's Bellum Civile: Literature, Ideology, and Community* (Cambridge, 2012).

Caesar's victory

Z. Yavetz, *Julius Caesar and His Public Image* (London, 1983).

S. Weinstock, *Divus Julius* (Oxford, 1971).

J. North, 'Caesar at the Lupercalia', *JRS* 98 (2008), 144–60.

The Ides of March and their Aftermath

R. Syme, *The Roman Revolution* (Oxford, 1939) 97–175.

J. Osgood, *Caesar's Legacy: Civil War and the Emergence of the Roman Empire* (Cambridge, 2006).

The Triumviral period

A. M. Gowing, *The Triumviral Narratives of Appian and Cassius Dio* (Ann Arbor, 1992).

K. A. Raaflaub and M. Toher eds., *Between Republic and Principate. Interpretations of Augustus and His Principate* (Berkeley, 1990).

L. Keppie, *Colonisation and Veteran Settlement in Italy, 47–14 B.C.* (London, 1983).

An Epilogue: the Advent of Monarchy

J. S. Richardson, *Augustan Rome 44 BC to AD 14: the Restoration of the Republic and the Establishment of the Empire* (Edinburgh, 2012).

W. Eck, *The Age of Augustus* (Oxford and Malden, 2007).

F. Millar & E. Segal eds., *Caesar Augustus. Seven Aspects* (Oxford, 1984).

A. E. Cooley ed., *Res Gestae Divi Augusti: Text, Translation, and Commentary* (Cambridge, 2009).

PART II: KEY THEMES

Rome and Italy

A. Cooley ed., *A Companion to Roman Italy* (Oxford and Malden, 2016).

G. Bradley and G. Farney eds., *The Peoples of Ancient Italy* (Berlin and New York, 2017).

G. Bradley, E. Isayev and C. Riva eds., *Ancient Italy. Regions without Boundaries* (Exeter, 2007).

E. Bispham, *From Asculum to Actium: the Municipalization of Italy from the Social War to Augustus* (Oxford, 2007).

Rome and the Empire

W. V. Harris, *War and Imperialism in Republican Rome, 327–70 B.C* (Oxford, 1979) 68–104.

E. Badian, *Roman Imperialism in the Late Republic* (Oxford, 1968).

G. Woolf, *Rome. An Empire's Story* (Oxford, 2012).

J. R. W. Prag ed., Sicilia Nutrix Plebis Romanae: *Rhetoric, Law, and Taxation in Cicero's* Verrines (London, 2007).

R. Kallet-Marx, *Hegemony to Empire. The Development of the Roman Imperium in the East from 148 to 62 B.C.* (Berkeley, Los Angeles and Oxford, 1995).

P. de Souza, *Piracy in the Graeco-Roman World* (Cambridge, 2000) 97–197.

A. Riggsby, *Caesar in Gaul and Rome: War in Words* (Austin, 2006).

A. Erskine, *Roman Imperialism* (Edinburgh, 2010).

The Imperial Economy

P. Kay, *Rome's Economic Revolution* (Oxford, 2014).

J. Tan, *Power and Public Finance at Rome* (Oxford, 2016).

M. H. Crawford, *Coinage and Money under the Roman Republic* (London, 1985).

K. Hopkins, *Conquerors and Slaves* (Cambridge, 1978).

P. A. Brunt, *Italian Manpower* (Oxford, 1971).

M. H. Crawford, 'States Waiting in the Wings: Population Distribution and the End of the Roman Republic', in L. de Ligt and S. J. Northwood (eds.), *People, Land, and Politics. Demographic Developments and the Transformation of Roman Italy, 300 BC–AD 14* (Leiden and Boston, 2008) 631–643.

N. Purcell, 'Romans in the Roman World', in K. Galinsky ed., *The Cambridge Companion to the Age of Augustus* (Cambridge, 2005) 85–105.

Law, Lawyers and Lawcourts

A. Schiavone, *The Invention of Law in the West* (Cambridge, Mass. and London, 2012).

M. C. Alexander, *Trials in the Late Roman Republic, 149 BC to 50 BC* (Toronto, 1990).

E. Lo Cascio, 'The Size of the Roman Population: Beloch and the Meaning of the Augustan Census Figures', *Journal of Roman Studies* 84 (1994) 23–40.

Intellectual Life

E. Rawson, *Intellectual Life in the Late Roman Republic* (London, 1985).

C. Moatti, *The Birth of Critical Thinking in Republican Rome* (Cambridge, 2015).

A. Wallace-Hadrill, *Rome's Cultural Revolution* (Cambridge, 2008).

J. Rüpke, *Religion in Republican Rome: Rationalization and Ritual Change* (Philadelphia, 2012).

Wives and daughters in late Republican society and politics

S. Treggiari, *Terentia, Tullia and Publilia. The Women of Cicero's Family* (London and New York, 2007).

J. Osgood, *Turia. A Roman Woman's Civil War* (Oxford, 2014).

S. Dixon, *Reading Roman Women. Sources, Genres and Real Life* (London, 2001).

Politics in the late Republic

H. Flower, *Roman Republics* (Princeton, 2010).

R. Morstein-Marx, *Mass Oratory and Political Power in the Late Roman Republic* (Cambridge, 2004).

K.-J. Hölkeskamp, *Reconstructing the Roman Republic. An Ancient Political Culture and Modern Research* (Princeton, 2010).

C. Steel and H. van der Blom (eds.), *Community and Communication. Oratory and Politics in Republican Rome* (Oxford, 2013).

F. Millar, *The Crowd in Rome in the Late Republic* (Ann Arbor, 1998).

T. P. Wiseman, *Remembering the Roman People. Essays on Late-Republican Politics* (Oxford, 2009).

V. Arena, *Libertas and the Practice of Politics in the Late Roman Republic* (Cambridge, 2012).

H. Mouritsen, *Plebs and Politics in the Late Roman Republic* (Cambridge, 2001).

H. Mouritsen, *Politics in the Roman Republic* (Cambridge, 2017).

A. Lintott, *Violence in Republican Rome* (Oxford, 1967).

A. Russell, 'Why Did Clodius Shut the Shops? The Rhetoric of Mobilizing a Crowd in the Late Republic', *Historia* 55 (2016) 186–210.

A. Yakobson, *Elections and Electioneering in Rome. A Study of the Political System of the Late Republic* (Stuttgart, 1999).

CONCORDANCE

OF LITERARY SOURCES

Appian
Civil Wars

1.1	B21
1.7	A1
1.21	A2
1.23	A3
1.34–36	A4
1.49	A9
1.49	A10b
1.53	A10c
1.56–7	B5
1.57	L36a
1.71, 1.73	B8
1.84, 1.86	B15
1.96	B23a
1.97	B20
1.119–120	B41
1.121	B43a
2.13	B93c
2.19	B126c
2.20–23	B131b
2.30–31	B139
2.32–33	B143f
2.107	B167c
2.118	B173
3.4	C15a
4.2–3	C1
4.8–10	C2
4.36	C15b
4.47	C3
5.24	C12
5.122	C22

Mithridatic War

17–19	B3
22–23	F3
64–66	E32
96	E29
97	E33a
112–3	E12
114	E9
116	B81b

Asconius
Commentary on Cicero (ed. Clark)

3C.7–12	L30a
3C.20–23	D5
7C.9–26	L10b
8C12–9C2	B101b
17C.4–10	G46a
31C.12–35C.16	B129b
33C.25–36C.5	B131a
36C.5–17	B132
36C.6–13	G46b
39C.5–42C.2	G47
45C.12–17	L31a
53C.19–54C20	G48
57C.7–59C14	B51a
59C.7–11	G4c
60C.10–62C5	G44
82C.4–83C.12	B57
83C.6–9	L14b

[Asconius]
Commentary on Cicero

p.199 Stangl	G13b

Asinius Pollio (FRH 36)

F3	B156b
F7	C4b

Augustine

City of God, 6.5.1	H30

Aulus Gellius
Attic Nights

3.10.13–17	H28
4.12.1–2	G13c
5.19.9	G8
10.1.7	B120
14.7.1–2	B43b
15.11.2	H5
16.13.7	G13c
19.14.1–5	H22

Brutus
Letter (Jones)

21	C9a
30	C9b

Caesar
Civil War

1.1–7	B142
1.12–13	B146
1.22	B145
1.61	E20b
2.18.7	E20c
3.96	B156c

Gallic War

1.1.3	F10b
1.39.1	F17a
1.42–45.1	E37
1.54.3	E17a
2.35.4	B108a
4.16.1	E38
5.1.5	E17b
5.2.1	E17c
6.1.1–4	F18a

7.3.1–2	F17b	9	B101a
7.55.1–8	F17c	50	G9
7.77.12–16	E43	68–71	H17
Cassius Dio		*Against Vatinius*	
Roman History		36	E35
36.20.1–23	E28	14	H21
36.24.5–6, 30, 36a	E30	*Against Verres*	
36.38	L14a	1.13–14	E1
36.42.3	L31b	1.35–47	G42
36.43.4–5	B59	1.40	E2
36.44.1–2	G43a	1.45	B44a
37.9.3–5	G18	1.54	B46c
37.25.3	L28b	2.1.119	G4b
37.25.3–4	B64b	2.1.120	K5
37.37.1–2	B62	2.2.31–34	E15
37.39–40.1	B79	2.2.95	E3
37.42	B77a	2.2.174	B45
37.43.1–4	L17	2.3.213	E26a
37.46.4	G19	2.5.26	B47
37.49–50	B88	2.5.143–4	L4a
38.6.1–4	L18	2.5.161–2	L32
38.15.5–17	B102b	2.5.175	B44b
39.7.2–3	L19c	*Agrarian Law*, 2.10–13	G5a
39.9.2–4	B98	*Brutus*	
39.12.1	B95b	1–6	H1
39.27–30.3	L21	91	H3
39.33.2–36.1	E41	138–144	G36
39.37.1–3	B116	152–153	G29b
39.55–59.1	B117	169	H4
40.45.3–4	G49	183–185	H2
40.51.2–3	B133a	203, 205	G37
40.51.2, 40.56.1–2	B134	233	G38a
42.32–33	L24	261	B50
44.1	B170	290	G33
44.4–7.4	B167b	301–303	G39a
44.47.4	L27b	312, 326	H9
48.4.1	K16	306	H6a
48.13.6	C10	315	H13
48.17	C15c	*Catilinarians*	
48.45.1–7	C21	1.1–5	B68a
49.11–12	C23	2.17–23	B64c
50.4.4–5	C27	3.18–19	B75
50.11.4–12.1	C30	4.4	B71
51.2.1–2	C32	4.7–10	B76a
52.42.6–7	E23	4.20–22	B76b
Cicero		*Defence of Balbus*	
Academica		19	E20a
1.9	H25a	50	L29
2.4	H14	*Defence of Caecina*, 70–75	G12
2.11	H7	*Defence of Caelius*, 30–34	K11
After his Return, to the Senate		*Defence of Cluentius*	
22	L19a	23–25	B29
Against Caecilius, 8	G13a	197–198	D4
Against Piso		*Defence of Flaccus*	
3–7	B78	15–19	L2
8	L10a	67	F7

Defence of Fonteius, 11	F10a	2.3.3–4	B91a
Defence of Marcellus		2.12.1–2	B96
23–24, 25, 27	B164	2.17.1	B97a
Defence of Milo		2.18.1–2	B97b
27–29	B129a	2.19	B97c
72	L33	2.20.2–4	B97d
79–80	B130	2.21	B97e
Defence of Murena		3.15.6	G5b
19–25	G29a	4.1.1–5	B103
24–26	L22	4.1.6–8	B107
42	L38	4.3.4–5	B105
49	B25	4.9.1	G21
48–50	B66	4.15.7–8	B125a
67	L14c	4.17.2–3	L13
81–83	B73	5.21.11 and 13	F1
Defence of Plancius		6.1.14	B136a
19–21	D2	7.4.2	B140a
44–45, 47	L12	7.6.2	B140b
62	B58	7.8.4–5	B140c
64	B32a	7.9	B141
64–65	E16	7.11.1–3	B150
66	L4b	7.21	B152
Defence of Rabirius Postumus		8.13	B153
3	L6	9.4	L34
4	B95a	9.16	B151
Defence of Rabirius on Treason Charge		10.4.2–4	B154
14	G5c	11.6.3–6	B158a
18	B61a	12.4.2	B161
20	Y2	13.18.2	H27
Defence of Roscius of Ameria		13.52	B166
15	B27	14.1.2	B172
25–26	B28	14.11.1	B177b
136	B14	14.12.1–2	B177c
Defence of Sestius		14.14.2–4	B177d
15, 24–26, 34–35	B102a	15.11.1–2	K10b
55	L11	*Letters to his Friends*	
55	G20a	1.1.2	B109a
75	L19b	1.4.2	B109c
75–76	B104	1.7.10	B113
96–105	L7	1.8.2–4	B115
106–109	B106	1.9.8–10	B112a
Defence of Sulla		2.15.3	B137b
62	B24d	3.8.4–5	E18
Letters to Atticus		4.3.3–4	G29c
1.1.1–2	B55a	5.2.7	B77b
1.2	B55b	5.6.2	B80a
1.13.6	B80b	5.7.1–3	B81a
1.13.3	B82	6.15	B177a
1.13.4	B83a	7.2–3	B121
1.14.1–4	B83b	12.21	E22
1.16.1–6	B84a	14.4.1–6	K3c
1.16.6–10	B84b	14.7.1	K3d
1.16.12–13	L15	15.4.10	E13
1.17.8	G45	16.11.2	B144
1.17.9	B86	*Letters to Quintus*	
1.18.3–7	B89	1.1.6–7	H16a
1.19.4	B90	1.1.16	H16b

CONCORDANCE

OF COINS AND INSCRIPTIONS

COINS:

Ghey, Leins & Crawford

2010, 357.1.1	B16
2010, 359.23	B17a
2010, 367.3.7	B17b
2010, 374.1.4	B18
2010, 381.1.1	B19
2010, 401.1.1	B39
2010, 403.1.2	B46d
2010, 433.1.6	B171a
2010, 443.1.12	B147
2010, 447.1.2	B148
2010, 449.4.6	B157
2010, 458.1.13	B163
2010, 461.1.7	B159a
2010, 462.1b	B159b
2010, 470.1.1	B159c
2010, 480.2.1	B165
2010, 488.1.2	C6a
2010, 490.2.1	C6b
2010, 492.1.1	C7a
2010, 492.2.1	C7b
2010, 498.1.1	B171b
2010, 500.2.1	B171c
2010, 508.3.2	B171d
2010, 511.2.4	C16
2010, 529.1.2	C13
2010, 535.1.4	C19
2010, 543.1.3	C28
2010, 553.415.7	A8

INSCRIPTIONS:

Aphrodisias and Rome (ed. Reynolds)

6	C14

Année Épigraphique

1979, 377	E19

Ashmolean Latin Inscriptions

428	C11

Corpus Inscriptionum Latinarum

CIL 6.40897	B67b
CIL 6.40904	B67a
CIL 6.41062	K13
CIL 10.844	B24b
CIL 10.852	B24c
CIL 14.4707	D7

Customs Law of Asia

Lines 74-81	F9

Choix d'Inscriptions de Délos

162	E11b

Ehrenberg & Jones, *Documents illustrating the reigns of Augustus and Tiberius*

EJ page 32	C8a
EJ page 33	C20a
EJ 300	C8c

Inscriptiones Latinae Liberae Rei Publicae

ILLRP 360	F11a
ILLRP 374	F11b
ILLRP 408	F11c
ILLRP 426	C18
ILLRP 508	D6
ILLRP 513	L26
ILLRP 515	L25
ILLRP 1026	F14
ILRRP 1046	L23
ILLRP 1050-1	B133b
ILLRP 1276	C20c

Inscriptiones Latinae Selectae

ILS 871	B22
ILS 9459	E11e
ILS 5915	B24a
ILS 5922c	G22

Inscriptiones Italiae

10.4.21	C20d
13.1.18	C8a

Inscriften von Milet

162	E11c

Res Gestae Divi Augusti

1.4	C8b
7.1	C20b
8.2	G24
25.2	C29
34	C33

Roman Statutes ed. Crawford

1.12	E4
1.19	E6

Supplementum Epigraphicum Graecum

SEG 46.1565	E11d

Sherk, *Roman Documents of the Greek East*

67B	E24b

Sylloge Inscriptionum Graecarum

SIG³ 748	F4
SIG³ 751	E11a

INDEX OF PERSONS

The following usual and ancient abreviations for *praenomina* (first names) are used:

A.	Aulus	M.	Marcus
C.	Gaius	P.	Publius
Cn.	Gnaeus	Q.	Quintus
D.	Decimus	Sex.	Sextus
L.	Lucius	T.	Titus
M'.	Manius		

Other abbreviations
cos = consul (all consular dates are BC)
praet. = praetor
suff. = suffect
tr. pl. = tribune of the plebs

Ancient authors did not follow a set rule in their use of Roman names; Modern usage has anglicized the names of some of the most famous individuals.

References are to source numbers. Y = Appendix B; Z = Appendix C

INDEX OF PLACES

Places are followed by the modern country the town is in (as of 1 June, 2017). Provinces and regions in CAPITALS are listed with the approximate equivalent in terms of modern countries and are indexed to mention of the province in the texts, not to every town mentioned within the province. Information on the ancient sites relies enormously on R.J.A. Talbert (ed.) *The Barrington Atlas of the Greek and Roman World* (Princeton, 2000)

Printed in the United States
by Baker & Taylor Publisher Services